the encyclopedia of
GARDENING

Golden Hands Books

Marshall Cavendish
London and New York

Pictures supplied by:

A.P.H. 307CL
Amateur Gardening 5, 160B, 198
H. R. Allen 345T
B. Alfieri 235CR, 357
H. Angel 273CL, 274BR
Animal Photography 203BC
D. C. Arminson 269BR, 221T, 235TR, 287T, BL,
288CR, BR, 297CL, B, 209BL, 312CL, 315TR,
316B, 338TL
P. Ayres 295TL, 311, 312TC, CC
Barker 131T
Barnaby's 100T, 102, 129B, 160TL, TR, 202,
204B, 307TR
P. Belker 231CC, 254TL, CL, BC, CC
R. B. Benfield 270, 271
C. Bevilacqua 363BC
Boarder 42B
J. Bonks 315TL
P. Booth 36R, 369T
Burras 66C
Chilstone 261, 262CL
Collier 144T, 200R
R. J. Corbin 15R, 23B, 26, 28, 30TR, 30B, 33, 39,
43L, R, 46B, 57, 58, 61, 62, 64, 67, 68R, 69B, 70C,
76, 77, 78, 81, 85, 86, 87T, 91, 92, 93T, 97T,
115CL, CR, 116, 117, 118, 119, 123BR, 126T,
128TR, 134, 135, 138TR, 139, 140, 141, 143T,
145TR, C, B, 148BR, 150TL, 153B, 164, 166, 167,
179, 181TC, TR, 184, 189B, 191, 193, 200CL, CC,
BL, 209, 210, 212, 216, 217BL, 218CR, 220TL,
222TL, 224, 226, 227, 228, 229TC, TR, 243, 246,
249TC, TR, 251BC, 252T, C, 253, 255, 256B, 265,
266, 267, 272, 175, 276, 277, 278, 279, 280, 282C,
BL, BR, 283, 284, 286BC, BR, 287C, 288TL, CL,
BL, 289, 290, 291TL, TC, C, 292TL, 327, 328,
329, 334BR, 337C, 340TR, C, 342BE, 356, 358,
361, 365B, 368B, 370, 371T
J. Cowley 181BL, 186CL, 292TR, 293B, 294,
340TC, 344T
C. J. Dawkins 142TC, 144C, 368T, C
C. Dawson 46T
A. F. Derrick 180T
J. E. Downward 10, 181CL, 185T
Dr. Elkan 40C, 42T
V. Finnis 22T, 31TR, BL, BR. 37B, 41, 47BL,

48BL, 51, 52, 95BR, 98TL, 130T, 133T, 152TL,
155BL, BR, 165BR, 186TL, 198, 208, 217BR,
229B, 244T, 252B, 258BL, 259C, 260T, 319CL,
371C
B. Furner 101T, 103T, 107T, 128CR, 158T,
200BC, 222TR, 286T, C, 306, 307TL, CR, B,
349B, 350, 352TL, 356T, 362TL, TR, 364CC, B,
368C
Fisons 80, 83
G. Ganney 225
P. Genereux 124, 165BL, BR, 188BL
M. Hadfield 338TR, 339TL, 341
I. Hardwick 55, 69T, 163B, 172BR, 178B,
188CL, 219TR, 249B
R. Hatfield 223B, 288TR, CC, 293T
Hovell 79, 149T, 155TR, 156T
P. Hunt 7L, 8B, 9BR, 11T, B, 13BL, TC, BC,
BR, 18B, 19, 21TL, TR, 21BC, BR, 25T, 35,
36BC, 50T, 66R, 70B, 72, 73, 145TL, 146R,
147BL, 158B, 162T, 169TL, 171T, 174T, 180CL,
BL, 186TR, 188CC, 180T, CR, 215, 244B,
262CR, B
R. J. Hunt 181CR
A. J. Huxley 20, 94T, 248B
G. E. Hyde 27L, 50B, 96TR, 127TR, 132T, 149B,
150TR, 151C, 181CC, 230B, 232TL, CR, 238BL,
250, 254TC, CR, 269, 273CR, B, 274TL, CL, BC,
299CR, 307TC, 316CL, 339TR, 343BL
I.C.I. 214, 254TR
B. Johns 182
L. Johns 40B, 47BR, 96BR, 98C, B, 142C,
147BR, 185B, 197, 263CR, 263BR, 333, 335BR
K.N.S. 178T
D. J. Kesby 347TL
J. Markham 142TL, TR, 175B, 181BR, 219TL
Marks 97B
Maxicrop Ltd. 88C, B
E. Megson 297CR, 299TC, 308BR, 317BL,
318T, 319T
Murphy Chemical Co. 27R, 30TL, 63, 65
L. H. Newman 254BR
M. Nummo 181TL, 219CR, 220CL, 231TR, BR,
297T, 339TC, 342BL, 343C, 346TC, TR
Orchid Society 233, 234B
S. Orme 96BL. 313T

K. Paisley 87, 128TL, 129T
Picturepoint 3, 7R, 8C, 22B, 106T, 159B, 199,
230T, 245, 352TR, 359
M. C. Pratt 21CR
N. J. Procter 75B, 126B, 136, 183, 218BL, BR,
295TL, TR, C, 296, 312TL, TR, CR, 318B, 324,
325, 326BL, BR, 338TC, 342C, 364CR, 365T, 366
C. Reynolds 274C
J. Roberts 321, 333, 323
G. Rodway 234T, 235TL, 236, 237, 238TL, C,
239, 240, 241T, C, 242
I. Ruthven 367TR
R. Rutter 207, 262TR, 263B, 332TL, TR, 334T,
BL, 335B
K. Sanecki 219CL
A. Shell 14, 15L, 16, 23T, 34
D. Smith 66L, 75T, 93B, 105, 111, 112, 114,
115B, 120, 121, 123B, 125, 127TL, 128CL, 130BL,
BR, 131B, 138TL, 151T, 152TR, 222C, 268,
274R, 285B, 287BR, 337B
H. Smith 13TR, TL, 25B, 29, 31TL, 44, 45,
47TL, 48TL, 54, 71, 88T, 94B, 95BL, 96TL,
98TR, 106B, 108, 109, 144B, 146T, C, 148TC,
CC, BL, 157, 169TR, 170B, 172B, L, 173, 174B,
176T, 187B, 188BR, 194, 231CL, 241B, 247,
248T, 251BR, 256TL, TR, 257B, 258BR, 259B,
262TL, 298BL, BR, 299BL, BR, 300, 301, 302,
303, 304, 305, 308BL, BR, 309BR, 313B, 314TL,
TR, 316TL, 317TL, 331, 332C, 343BL, 345B,
347TR, C, 349T, 351, 353, 355B, 360, 362C,
363BR, 367TL, 369B
V. Stevens 48R
V. Stevenson 147T, 196B, 249C
G. S. Thomas 59
Tjaden 40T
Tourist Photo Lib. 36TL
A. Turner 9TL, TC, TR, CR, 177
C. Watmough 1, 6
C. Wildridge 316TR, 317TR
C. Williams 217CL
H. G. Wood 18TL
D. Woodland 147TR, 171B, 313TL, 316CR,
317BR, 319CR

Edited by Vivien Bowler and Rose-Marie Hillier

Published by Marshall Cavendish Publications Limited,
58, Old Compton Street,
London W1V 5PA

© Marshall Cavendish Limited 1968, 1969, 1970, 1971, 1975

This material has previously appeared in the
partwork *The Encyclopedia of Gardening*

First printed 1975

ISBN 0 85685 143 4
Printed in Great Britain by the Severn Valley Press Limited

Page 1: *Lilium japonicum requires semi-shade in slightly moist conditions.*
Opposite: *The rewards of a meticulously-planted and well-tended rose garden can be seen here.*

Introduction

Gardening is one of life's most enjoyable pastimes, and to help and guide you, an accurate, informative and easy-to-follow book can be invaluable. Here is the gardening book that will tell you everything you need to know, a complete alphabetical encyclopedia with a comprehensive cross-referenced index which enables you to look up any information quickly and easily. Whether it be the visual delights of a colourful flower border, the well-ordered beauty of a formal garden or the culinary pleasures of a well-stocked fruit and vegetable plot that attracts you, gardening has immense rewards. As a hobby or leisure activity, it can provide hours of enjoyment and satisfaction. This encyclopedia contains information on a myriad of subjects—general techniques and gardening principles, cultivation information, specific planting lists, garden pests and diseases, fruits and vegetables, fertilizer mixes, growing under glass, propagation, pruning, tree and shrub planting.
Beautifully illustrated with colour photographs and easy-to-read charts and drawings, this book will help the would-be gardener begin, the advanced gardener improve.

Note: The charts in this book are written with Imperial measurements. Consult the metric chart for conversion opposite page 376.

Left: *A gathered harvest of fresh vegetables from the garden.*
Right: *This attractive border garden edged with catmint, is planted with achillea, lupins, monarda, delphinium and kniphofia.*
Overleaf: *Primula auricula, a pretty alpine shown in its full beauty.*

A

Acclimatization see Hardening off

Aeration see Lawn construction and maintenance

Aggregate
Ballast, gravel, or shingle, the hard, granulated material which forms the bulk of concrete. Horticulturally, the term is used for the rooting material used in soil-less cultivation, pebbles, gravel or clinker. In the ring culture of tomatoes the aggregate consists of weathered boiler ash or fine clinker or gravel and coarse grade vermiculite.

Alpines and their cultivation
True alpines are classed by botanists as plants which grow only between the permanent snow line and the limit of conifer tree growth. Around the world the equivalent of this area is found at

sea level in arctic regions and above 6000 feet in other parts. Alpines are adapted for survival in extreme conditions. The most difficult to grow are those from the highest altitudes. Our humid atmosphere, winter rainfall and difference of light intensity create an environment in which these plants do not easily thrive.

For many months of the year the plants are protected by a deep layer of crisp snow which keeps them dry and at a constant, low temperature, but not nearly as low as the air temperature above the snow. In the spring these plants receive copious moisture as the snow melts and they make rapid growth. The higher the natural habitat the more quickly plants must grow for the snow may not disappear until late June, and the plant must make new growth, flower and produce seed, before the ground is again covered with snow in September. For this reason the higher one goes the smaller the plants. Again, large plants could not withstand the gales that roar around the high peaks, so many alpine plants are of prostrate habit and grow in crevices in the rock face which affords some protection.

Another point is that although the ground will be saturated in the spring, being mountainous it drains rapidly and even the high meadow land may be only temporarily boggy for the sub-soil is rocky, and at the higher altitudes the scree, which contains only a trace of soil, is cool and moist, but exceptionally well drained. In their mountain homes few plants are in full sun all day, although the many varieties of dianthus enjoy a south-facing cliff and the moun-

1 Phlox subulata, is an easily grown alpine, available in various colours. 2 Gentiana sino-ornata, an alpine for a lime-free soil.

tain avens, *Dryas octopetala*, does well in poor, well-drained soil and full sun where it will spread its low, thick, evergreen mat of attractive foliage over a rock, covered in summer with comparatively large white flowers, followed by pleasing woolly seed heads.

One other important matter to consider before planting is the soil; some plants are lime-haters and will perish where lime is present. For instance, the glorious autumn-flowering *Gentiana sino-ornata* will not produce its brilliant blue trumpets when there is lime in the soil, but otherwise it is quite easy.

Cultivation To ensure that alpine plants will flourish in our gardens it is obvious that we must do the best we can to provide conditions not too far removed from those in their mountain homes. Many plants will present little difficulty as long as they are planted in sun, if they are sun-lovers, and in partial shade, if they normally grow in cool, moist conditions. They are hardy enough as far as frost is concerned but some detest our wet winters and fluctuating temperatures—a foggy, damp day, followed by a frosty night and then a sunny morning is not to their liking, particularly those plants with grey, hairy foliage.

However, such plants can be grown quite well in a porous soil and when the weather is at its worst a cloche or even a sheet of glass placed over these plants will protect them from excessive wet.

Two more colourful alpines. 1 Pulsatilla vulgaris 2 Narcissus cyclamineus both flower in spring.

Alpines for Special Purposes

Full sun and a well-drained soil

Achillea	Cytisus	Hypericum	Phlox
Aethionema	Dianthus	Helichrysum	Potentilla
Alyssum	Draba	Helianthemum	*Saponaria ocymoides*
Antennaria	*Dryas octopetala*	Iberis	Sedum
Armeria	Erysimum	Linum	Sempervivum
Aubrieta	*Gyposphila repens*	Oenothera	Thymus
Campanula garganica	Hebe	Penstemon	Zauschneria

Shade or half-shade

In Scotland and northern England these plants may be grown in almost full sun as long as there is sufficient moisture.

Anemone nemorosa	Epimedium	*Omphalodes*	Shortia
Astilbe	Gaultheria	*cappadocica*	Thalictrum
Cassiope	Hepatica	Primula	Trillium
Cyclamen	Meconopsis	Saxifraga	Trollius
Dodecatheon	Mimulus	(Kabschia Section)	

For a lime-free soil

Andromeda	Calluna	*Gentiana sino-ornata*	Rhodohypoxis
Androsace carnea	Epigaea	Lewisia	Shortia
Arcterica	Erica (most)	*Lithospermum diffusum*	*Trifolium alpinum*
Cassiope	Gaultheria	Rhododendron	*Viola pedata*

Lime-loving or lime-tolerating

Achillea	Cyclamen	*Gentiana dinarica*	*Primula auricula*
Acanthus	*Cypripedium calceolus*	Gyposphila	*Primula marginata*
Aethionema	Dianthus	Hepatica	Saxifraga, (with
Aubrieta	*Dryas octopetala*	Helleborus	a few exceptions)
Carlina	*Gentiana clusii*	Leontopodium	

They can, of course, be grown in pans in a cold greenhouse or planted out in an alpine frame, which is a most pleasing way of growing rare alpines, particularly when the frame is raised about 1m (3ft) from the ground which makes weeding easy and the plants can be admired more readily. With such a raised frame there should be ample rubble beneath the soil to provide first-class drainage and during wet weather the light can easily be placed over the top.

Propagation Many alpines may be raised from seed sown in pans containing a well-drained, sandy compost. March and April are suitable months for sowing and the pans should be plunged in peat or old ashes in a cold frame which should be shaded from hot sun. Some seeds, in particular those of androsace, some campanulas, gentianas, primulas and saxifragas, are best sown as soon as ripe and not later than December. Germination can be erratic and may take 12 months or longer so do not discard the contents of the pans hastily.

Although seed is useful where quantity is required, quicker methods of raising new plants are by division or cuttings. Division is not possible with all plants but those that form clumps, such as achillea, aubrieta, campanula, gentiana, phlox, thyme and the like present no difficulty. Early autumn is the best time to lift and divide such plants, although it may also be done in the early spring if necessary. If the pieces are

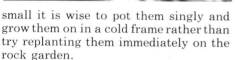

small it is wise to pot them singly and grow them on in a cold frame rather than try replanting them immediately on the rock garden.

Cuttings are, in general, best taken in August and September although those of campanulas and some gentians should be taken in spring. After flowering, that is in June, is the best time to take cuttings of aubrieta. Whenever cuttings are taken they should be rooted in a cold frame and shaded from the hot sun. Cuttings about 2.5cm (1in) long will usually root best when inserted in, say 10cm (4in) pots, containing a very sandy compost. The cuttings should be sprayed over daily with water during warm weather until roots have formed.

Where only a few cuttings are required these will root more readily if a polythene bag is placed over the top of the pot and the open end kept in place with a rubber band around the pot, or minicloches are excellent for this purpose. This will keep the atmosphere moist around the cuttings and daily spraying will not be necessary. Do not attempt this method with hairy or silver foliage plants, such as helichrysums, which will quickly damp off in a moist atmosphere. Such plants should be rooted in an open, shaded frame, or under a tent cloche with the ends open, and in a sandy bed.

Dwarf conifers make a permanent feature among alpine plants and are attractive throughout the year, even in winter when lightly covered with snow. These may be propagated by cuttings which should be about 6-8cm (2-3in) long and taken with a 'heel' of old stem. They are slow to make roots but treat them in the same manner as other alpine plant cuttings. Do not try to root them in heat which will merely shrivel them up. Hormone rooting powder used according to the maker's instructions will encourage cuttings of conifers and other woody plants to root more quickly.

Alpine cultivation indoors

Quite different in purpose from most

A selection of plants for the alpine house: Pulsatilla vernalis 1 Anemone apennina 2 Primula minima 4 and Primula denticulata 6 all flower in spring. Dryas octopetala 3 and Potentilla crantzii 5 are summer-flowering plants.

other types of greenhouse, a proper alpine house is little more than a means of protecting, from the extremes of our weather, plants which are among the hardiest when growing in their natural environment. Though we rarely experience the low temperatures which occur in alpine regions, our comparatively mild winters are not enjoyed by high alpine plants. This is because in their natural habitat, during their winter resting period, they are usually snugly hidden under a layer of snow which acts as insulation against extreme cold and, most important, keeps them comparatively dry. The chief purpose of an alpine house is, therefore, to prevent uncontrolled moisture, an excess of which usually leads to rotting, from reaching the plants during their resting period.

Alpine plants, some delicate in cultivation, can be given individual needs in separate containers in full control of the grower within the alpine house. The first consideration is usually a growing mixture similar to that in which the plants grow in the wild, together with proper drainage, shading, etc. Such conditions are not so easily arranged in the open. There is also the question of plants which flower in the depth of our winter being damaged by wind or heavy rain. Well known among these are the Engleria and Kabschia saxifrages. *Narcissus bulbocodium romieuxii* and early primulas–*P. allionii* and *P. edgeworthii*. The protection of the alpine house allows them to remain unspoiled by rough weather.

The grower has the advantage of being able to study the plants at a convenient level on the staging, no matter what the weather conditions outside. Further, not

9

all the collection need be housed together. Specimens can be kept in special frames attached to the outside, and taken in for viewing when they are at their best.

Shading Though alpine houses are made to allow maximum ventilation, the addition of shading is needed to break the direct rays of the sun while it is at its strongest in late spring and summer. It helps further to keep the house cool and can be applied in a number of ways. Proprietary washes have the serious disadvantage of being semi-permanent and cannot be easily removed during dull spells. Shading in position during prolonged dull periods can irreparably damage alpine plants by causing them to become drawn, due to insufficient light, a condition from which they seldom recover (many are of compact cushion-forming habit).

Shading is best done by means of one of the various kinds of adjustable blinds made either of green plastic material or of laths.

Heating Many purist alpine growers would object to the use of heat in the house, in any form. The fact is, however, that when used with discretion by the amateur it can save losses, in just the same way as other adjustments are made to the plant environment for the same purpose. The house prevents direct rainfall on to the plants but little can be done to control atmospheric humidity which becomes very high during dull, dark and foggy spells. The 'woolly' plants are among the first to suffer in these conditions. A little heat during such times can help to dry the air in the house.

Again, the usual method of plunging the plant containers in a base of chippings can allow severe prolonged cold to penetrate and freeze roots which would, in nature, be too deeply situated for this to happen. In their natural environment the plants would also have the added protection of an insulating layer of snow over them, which they lack in the alpine house. Even where their root systems can stand being frozen, evergreens are liable to perish through being unable to take up moisture continually being lost from the foliage. A little heat can prevent all this.

Plant collection A properly built alpine

A general view through the Alpine House at the Royal Horticultural Society's gardens, Wisley, Surrey in spring. Note how the pots are plunged in gravel.

house is not essential to enable a keen gardener to enjoy growing a few alpine plants, though the conditions described should be provided as nearly as possible for easier kinds to be tried.

Cushion-forming plants are perhaps the most typical grown, and a start could be made with a selection from the wide choice of mossy saxifrages. No collection would be complete without representatives of the many species of bulbous plants which provide lovely miniature blooms, often of the original parents of our much larger garden hybrids–narcissus and tulips for example. Others include species iris, fritillarias, galanthus (snowdrops) and scillas (squills). Most of these are best kept in frames when out of bloom.

Small shrubs provide added interest and often permanent evergreen features. The dwarf conifers are well known and obtainable in all shapes from rounded to spire-like in habit, typified by the popular juniper, *Juniperus communis compressa*.

Alpine lawn

Just as the gardener's rock garden is an attempt at imitating, in miniature, part of a rocky piece of mountain slope, so the alpine lawn provides an opportunity of growing plants best suited to planting together as a lawn, or in grassy patches among rocks. If the rock garden is large enough the alpine lawn can be part of it. Otherwise it can be an unusual though most attractive feature on its own, with a few rocky outcrops tastefully placed here and there to add interest to the setting.

Preparation As with other permanent garden features, a thorough preparation is worth while to avoid setbacks later on from weeds or impeded drainage, two common troubles. Much will depend on the original state of the chosen site. Preferably avoid a depression, which can be bad from the point of view of drainage and the collection of cold frosty air. A site on a piece of sloping ground will allow both excessive moisture and heavy cold air to pass freely to a lower level.

It is obviously important to clear the area of all perennial weeds, taking, if necessary, a further season to allow the regrowth of any pieces left after the first digging through. A suitable weedkiller could be used for the first clearing but thereafter hand weeding of pieces of root is the most efficient. The largest unwanted stones will have to be removed by raking. One way of disposing of them is by burying, either at the side or at a spot which might require improved surface drainage.

1 Here an alpine lawn forms part of a large rock garden. The lawn, in which various alpines grow, slopes gently up to the rocks. 2 Erythronium dens-canis, the dog's tooth violet is one of the bulbs suitable for an alpine lawn.

Paths Unless quite small, it is useful to plan the courses of paths or position of steps well in advance so that planting can be made accordingly. These should be in keeping with the general theme, using flat-topped rocks for steps and widely spaced flat stones for paths, which may be interplanted with plants which do not mind being stepped on occasionally.

A personal choice for this purpose can be made from *Acaena buchananii* and *A. microphylla*, *Arenaria balearica* and *A. caespitosa aurea*, *Campanula pusilla* and *C. p. alba*, *Dianthus deltoides*, *Sedum album* and all forms and varieties of *Thymus serpyllum*.

Soil According to the type and condition of the soil a certain amount of reconsolidation will be required after digging over. This is best done by treading systematically to ensure even coverage. It is quite certain that weed seeds will have been brought to the surface. These must be allowed to germinate and be killed before planting begins. A scorching type of weedkiller, based on paraquat, is ideal because it becomes immediately inactive in the soil. Pockets of a different soil type, if required, can be provided for fussy plants, otherwise there is no need to add further nutriments in a normal situation.

Planting A rough plan on paper is useful in enabling a general picture to be visualised, especially if colour can be included. Graph paper will be helpful in plotting space allocation for the carpeting plants, to prevent undue hacking back as they mature, though some cutting might be necessary from time to time to prevent fast growers from swamping the less vigorous.

While carpeting plants will predominate, room should be allowed for others of tufted habit and, not least, a good selection of dwarf bulbs. The idea is to create a complete coverage of low-growing plants which will prevent the establishment of weeds and require minimum upkeep. Plants already recommended for growing between paving stones can create an equally good effect if used in open planting.

A section devoted to the various thymes, planted together where space allows, can be a beautiful sight when they flower in solid masses of shades of crimson, red and pink, to white. Varieties with variegated or golden foliage complete the picture. Other good carpeters include antennarias, *Cotula reptans* and *C. squalida*, *Dryas octopetala*, *Frankenia laevis*, *Geranium pylzowianum*, *Mentha requienii*, *Mimulus radicans*, *Raoulia glabra*, *Veronica pyroliformis*, *V. repens* and others.

The lowest mat-forming plants can be used effectively over the spots where groups of bulbs are planted for naturalising. From the considerable choice of suitable kinds the miniature daffodils and crocuses will play a leading role.

Although they take time to build up to spectacular drifts of gold or mauve, this can be helped by lifting and dividing the clumps every three years or so in the early years. A selection of dwarf narcissi could be chosen from a specialist's catalogue, but these ought to include *N. cyclamineus*, *N. bulbocodium* and *N. pseudonarcissus* (the Lent Lily).

Of the crocus, *C. tomasinianus* and its varieties should do well, as will *C. vernus* 'Vanguard'. The large-flowered yellow, mauve and white hybrids can also be used for naturalising. Scillas, chionodoxas, and blue-bells should steadily increase. Cyclamen are attractive for most of the year if species are chosen for their flowering sequence. They provide a bonus of marble-patterned foliage. These and anemone species are used to best advantage in shaded areas.

Alum

Best known for its use in producing hydrangea flowers of intense blue. Some other plants including rhododendrons, camellias and most heathers, require an acid soil in which to thrive well. Alum may be used at up to 0.5kg (1lb) per sq m (sq yd) to acidify a soil, raked or lightly forked into the surface. For potting soil add at the rate of about 51kg per (1cwt) 1.25k (2½lb).

As a pest deterrent alum may be used against birds by spraying a solution on to buds of threatened trees, and against slugs by watering on to infested ground. In both cases use at the rate of 112g (4oz), dissolved, per 4.5l (1 gal) of water. Slugs can also be caught by spreading dry alum around vulnerable plants.

Animal repellents

There are now a number of animal and bird repellents on the market. Commercial alum and quassia were often used against birds in the past but were not consistently successful. Now a number of proprietary repellents are available based on various substances such as anthraquinone, thiram, etc. Success, however, depends on a number of factors, such as timing and number of applications made. Seasonal weather and food scarcity may also affect results. The marker's instructions regarding timing and frequency of application should be carefully followed.

Rayon cobwebs can be bought to enmesh the trees and bushes to keep away birds. Since the substance rots away within a few months, it can be used to give protection over a vulnerable period as an improvement on black cotton.

Animal repellents include rabbit smears which are often evil-smelling concoctions used to soak rags which are then placed in burrows or mole-tunnels to disconcert the inhabitants. Another use of the smears is to soak twine which is then fastened to sticks to form a fence

a few inches from the ground round areas to be protected such as flower beds.

There are also aerosol repellents for use on such things as garden furniture and gate posts. These deter dogs from contaminating them. To repel cats and domestic pets from such places as seed beds there are repellents based on commercial pepper and other substances. Repellents of this kind need renewing after rain. There are even mouse repellents available under proprietary names.

Annuals

Hardy annuals are easy to grow and will give a quick and brilliant display provided they are grown in an open, sunny position in any good garden soil. Many annuals are tender and easily killed by frost, so these kinds are sown under glass in the spring and planted out when all danger of frost is over. Some hardy and half-hardy kinds make excellent pot plants for the greenhouse and there are others that need greenhouse cultivation entirely.

Some, such as the nasturtium, flower better if grown on rather poor soil. Most annuals will make too much leaf growth if grown in soil that is too rich or in shady places. Their rapid growth makes them invaluable for the new garden when flowers are wanted the first year, or for filling in gaps in newly-planted herbaceous borders. Some, such as trailing lobelias, dwarf nasturtiums and petunias are useful plants for hanging baskets. Many are useful for providing colour in urns, terrace pots, window boxes, tubs and other plant containers. Certain low-growing annuals find a place in carpet bedding schemes such as are still found in public parks. Although the purist may frown upon their use in this way, a few annuals are suitable for the rock garden.

A number of annuals have very fragrant flowers, as well as rich colour. Some have flowers or seed heads which may be dried for winter decoration indoors.

Some annuals, including a number of those used for carpet bedding, are grown for the sake of their colourful foliage.

Apart from removing faded flowers, keeping them weeded and staking the taller kinds they need little attention.

1 Lychnis githago, the corn-cockle, is one of many easily-grown hardy annuals
2 Linum grandiflorum, a hardy annual flax has flowers in scarlet, red or rose
3 and 4 Two forms of the Californian poppy, Eschscholzia california, a hardy annual now available in a wide colour range with single or semi-double flowers
5 'Yellow pygmy' with double flowers is a useful variety of the tall annual sunflower, Helianthus annuus
6 Papaver somniferum, the opium poppy, a hardy annual with single or fully double flowers in shades of pink and red.

A Selection of Hardy Annuals

Botanical Name	Common Name	Height inches	Colour
Althaea	Annual Hollyhock	48–60	various
Anagallis linifolia	Pimpernel	6	blue, red
Argemone	Prickly Poppy	24	yellow, orange, white
Calendula officinalis	Pot Marigold	24	orange, yellow
Centaurea cyanus	Cornflower	12–30	various
Centaurea moschata	Sweet Sultan	18–24	various
Chrysanthemum carinatum	Tricoloured Chrysanthemum	24	various
Chrysanthemum coronarium	Crown Daisy	12–24	various
Clarkia elegans	Clarkia	18–24	various
Collinsia	—	12–15	various
Convolvulus tricolor	Annual Convolvulus	12–18	various
Delphinium ajacis	Larkspur	24–36	pink, red, blue, white
Dianthus sinensis	Indian Pink	6–9	various
Eschscholzia	Californian Poppy	12	various
Gilia × hybrids	—	3–6	various
Godetia	Godetia	6–30	pink, crimson, white
Gypsophila elegans	Annual Gypsophila	18	white, pink, carmine
Helianthus annuus	Sunflower	36–96	yellow, bronze, brown
Helipterum	Everlasting	12	white, pink, yellow
Lathyrus odoratus	Sweet Pea	cl	various
Laverata trimestris	Mallow	24–36	white, pink
Leptosyne stillmanii	—	18	golden-yellow
Limnanthes douglasii	Butter and Eggs	6	white and yellow
Linaria maroccana	Annual Toadflax	9–15	various
Linum grandiflorum	Annual Flax	15–18	red, blue, pink, white
Lobularia	Sweet Alison	3–12	white, pink, lilac
Lupinus hartwegii	Annual Lupine	12–36	various
Malcolmia maritima	Virginia Stock	6–12	various
Malope grandiflorum	Mallow	24–36	pink, crimson, white
Matthiola bicornis	Night-scented Stock	12	lilac
Mentzelia lindleyi	Blazing Star	18	yellow
Nemophila menziesii	Baby Blue-eyes	tr	blue
Nigella damascena	Love-in-a-mist	18	blue, pink, white
Papaver rhoeas	Shirley Poppy	18–24	various
Papaver somniferum	Opium Poppy	18–36	various

A Selection of Hardy Annuals

Botanical Name	Common Name	Height inches	Colour
Phacelia campanularia	—	9	blue
Reseda odorata	Mignonette	12–18	red, yellow, white
Rhodanthe manglesii	Everlasting	12	rose and white
Salvia horminum	—	18	blue
Saponaria vaccaria	Annual Soapwort	30	pink, white
Scabiosa atropurpurea	Sweet Scabious	18–36	various
Silene pendula	Annual Catchfly	6	various
Thelesperma burridgeanum	—	18	yellow, red-brown
Tropaeolum majus	Nasturtium	6 & tr	oranges, yellow, red
Tropaeolum peregrinum	Canary Creeper	cl	yellow
Viscaria oculata	Catchfly	6–12	various

Hardy Annuals to Sow in the Autumn

Botanical Name	Common Name	Height inches	Colour
Calendula officinalis	Pot Marigold	24	orange yellow
Centaurea cyanus	Cornflower	12–30	various
Cladanthus arabicus	—	30	yellow
Clarkia elegans	Clarkia	18–24	various
Delphinium ajacis	Larkspur	24–36	pink, red, blue, white
Eschscholzia	Californian Poppy	12	various
Godetia	Godetia	6–30	pink, crimson, white
Gypsophila elegans	Annual Gypsophila	18	white, pink, carmine
Iberis	Candytuft	6–15	various
Lathyrus odoratus	Sweet Pea	cl	various
Limnanthes douglasii	Butter and Eggs	6	white and yellow
Lobularia maritima	Sweet Alison	12	white, pink, lilac
Lychnis githago (syn. Agrostemma githago)	Corn-cockle	24–36	pale lilac
Malcolmia maritima	Virginia Stock	6–12	various
Nigella damascena	Love-in-a-mist	18	blue, pink, white
Oenthera biennis	Evening Primrose	30	yellow
Papaver rhoeas	Shirley Poppy	18–24	various
Saponaria vaccaria	Annual Soap-wort	30	pink, white
Scabiosa atropurpurea	Sweet Scabious	18–36	various
Specularia speculum-veneris	Venus's Looking Glass	9	blue
Viscaria	Catchfly	6–12	various

1

2

3

4

5

6

Growing hardy annuals The soil should be broken down to a fine tilth and well firmed before the seeds are sown. Sow in shallow drills or scatter the seed broadcast after previously marking out the position for each group of annuals selected. Cover the seeds in the drills by drawing the soil over them, or rake in the seeds sown broadcast. It may be necessary to protect the seeds and seedlings from birds and cats by placing wire netting or brushwood over the seed bed.

Some hardy annuals may be sown in August or September to flower early the following summer. See Table page 13. As soon as the seedlings are large enough to handle they should be thinned. With autumn-sown annuals leave the final thinning until the following spring. Distances apart vary considerably, depending on the ultimate height of the annual, but as a general guide dwarf-growing annuals should be thinned to 10-16cm (4-6in) apart. Those that grow to 38-46cm (15-18in) tall should be thinned to 23-30cm (9-12in) and taller kinds should be thinned to 30-60cm (1-2ft) apart.

If seed is wanted for sowing again next year it is best to mark a few good plants early in the summer. The seed-heads should not be gathered until they are fully ripe.

Ants

Ants are unwelcome in the garden for various reasons but chiefly on account of their nest-building activities which interfere with the roots of the plants, often causing death.

They may also be a nuisance on lawns. They are often seen running over plants infested with greenfly to which they are attracted by the sweet honeydew. They may help to spread the greenfly to other plants and they may also encourage root aphids underground.

The black ant, colonies of which can be a nuisance in the garden.

Under glass, they may remove newly-sown seeds. They may also attack ripe fruit. Where possible, the nests should be located and insecticidal dust or liquid should be inserted. The majority of insecticides are effective but should only be used in extreme cases. In garden frames or indoors, a proprietary bait poured on to a piece of glass may be used. Infested seed pans may be plunged to the rim in water. The bases of infested plants may be greasebanded to prevent the ants from climbing up.

Aphids

There are many kinds of aphids and they vary greatly in colour and in general appearance, e.g., 'greenfly', 'blackfly', 'woolly aphid', etc.

Often the pest is not noticed until large colonies have built up, which can happen very quickly in warm weather. By the time the damage is noticed, the aphids may have migrated, leaving only their cast skins. Aphids feed by sucking the sap which gives rise to various types of damage. Flowers, shoots and fruits may be deformed; foliage curled, blistered or discoloured and galls are sometimes formed on stems or leaves. Other effects of infestations include the transmission of virus diseases; the attraction of ants to the honeydew excreted by the aphids and the growth of sooty moulds on this sticky deposit, which gives affected plants a dirty and neglected appearance.

Most aphids lay overwintering eggs on trees and shrubs. In spring, these give rise to aphids which produce living young, not eggs. After several generations, winged forms appear and these are able to migrate to herbaceous host-plants where breeding goes on throughout the summer months. In autumn, winged aphids return to the trees and shrubs where the winter eggs are laid.

Tar oil or DNOC-petroleum sprays may be used against the egg stage when trees are completely dormant. Various combination sprays can be used on fruit trees at the bud-burst to green cluster stage in early spring. If BHC is used after petal fall, derris should be added against red spider (see Bud stages), or malathion can be used whenever an infestation is noticed. On ornamentals, aphids may be controlled by malathion, dimethoate, nicotine, BHC or derris. It is necessary to read makers' instructions carefully to ascertain how long should elapse between spraying and harvesting edible crops and whether any plants are liable to damage by the chosen insecticide.

Aphids have many natural enemies, including ladybirds and their larvae, lacewing larvae, syrphid fly larvae and braconid parasites.

Apple aphids: Apple-grass aphid (*Rhopalosiphum insertum*). Sometimes known as oat apple aphid. Attacks apple, pear and quince etc. Light green with darker stripes Feeds among blossom, buds and young leaves, causing some leaf curl. About mid-May, migration takes place to grasses for the summer months. In early autumn, winged

Typical examples on apple of attacks by rosy leaf-curling aphids.

1 Gooseberry aphids on gooseberry shoots.
2 Black bean aphids on broad bean shoots.

forms return to fruit trees where over-wintering eggs are laid.

Green apple aphid (*Aphis pomi*). Attacks apple, pear, quince, rowan, hawthorn, cotoneaster, etc., and can be a severe pest of nursery stock. Young shoots become thickly coated with velvety-green aphids. Leaf-curl is caused and the shoot-tips may be killed. The shiny, black, oval eggs are laid on the shoots in vast numbers in early autumn.

Rosy apple aphid (*Sappaphis mali*). Colonies of aphids varying from pink to blue-grey and slightly 'mealy', infest the shoots, causing severe leaf-curl and small, distorted fruits. In June most of the aphids migrate to plantains. A winged generation returns to apple in September, when overwintering eggs are laid.

Rosy leaf-curling aphid (*Sappaphis devecta*). Easily detected because attacked leaves become bright red and severely curled. The aphids feeding within are mealy bluish grey. They tend to infest the same trees year after year. Eggs are laid in late June and July in cracks in the bark and sites well protected from winter sprays. Therefore, a combination spray

should be applied at the bud burst to green cluster stage in spring, (see Bud Stages), or malathion may be used whenever the pest is noticed.

Woolly aphid (*Eriosoma lanigerum*) also called american blight. Attacks apple, pyrus, cotoneaster, puracantha, etc. Brownish purple in colour but protected by conspicuous tufts of white, waxy cotton wool' especially in the summer months. Feeding causes galling of shoots and splits may develop allowing disease to enter. Fresh infestations are liable to occur annually as the pest migrates freely. Root infestations occur abroad but rarely in Britain, although colonies may be found at the base of the trunk or on exposed roots. The aphid hibernates under loose bark, etc., making control by winter sprays difficult. Small infestations may be painted over with methylated spirits. Otherwise, spraying with BHC and a succinate wetter at the pink bud stage of apple, or with malathion whenever an infestation is noticed, should give control. The woolly aphid parasite, *Aphelinus mali*, has been used commercially against the pest but needs to be kept in cold storage during the winter as wet seasons appear to be unfavourable to its survival. The galls are often pecked out by birds.

Auricula root aphid (*Pemphigus auri-*

culae). Pale greenish aphid covered with white 'wool'. Found on the roots of potted primulas and occasionally out of doors. The foliage of attacked plants becomes yellow and the plant eventually wilts. Dipping in a solution of nicotine or watering with malathion or diazinon should check this pest.

Beech aphid (*Phyllaphis fagi*). An attractive aphid which secretes feathery trails of white 'wool'. Found in colonies on the underside of the leaves of beech trees or infesting beech hedges, causing a sticky deposit of honeydew.

Black bean aphid (*Aphis fabae*). Blackish aphid with lighter coloured legs. Over-wintering eggs are found on spindle and snowball trees, as are those of several very closely related aphids. Leaf-curl is caused by their feeding. In due course, migration takes place to beans and weeds such as goosefoot and thistles. Closely related aphids infest rhubarb, dahlias, nasturtiums, docks etc. In autumn there is a return to the woody hosts to lay overwintering eggs.

Cabbage aphid (*Brevicoryne brassicae*). Waxy, greyish aphids which infest brassica leaves, causing them to become yellow and crumpled. Young plants may become stunted or killed in severe infestations. Overwintering eggs are laid on the stems and leaves but the aphids

15

themselves may also survive a mild winter. It is advisable to destroy old plants before mid-May because in June and July migration takes place to newly planted brassicas and probably also to weed hosts, such as charlock and shepherd's purse.

Cherry blackfly (*Myzus cerasi*). A brownish-black, shiny, aphid which often occurs in great numbers on the shoots of fruiting and ornamental cherries. Severe leaf-curl is caused and often the death of the shoots. In June, migration begins to weeds such as cleavers, bedstraw and speedwell. In autumn, winged aphids return to cherry and overwintering eggs are laid.

Chrysanthemum aphid (*Macrosiphoniella sanborne*). A brownish-black aphid which causes distortion of shoots and buds. It is often accidentally taken into the greenhouse in the autumn with the plants and thus is able to breed on them throughout the year.

Currant and gooseberry aphids: Currant root aphid (*Eriosoma ulmi*). Grey aphids found on the roots protected by 'wool'. The overwintering eggs are laid on elm and the feeding of the aphids in spring galls the elm leaves. In early summer, migration to currant and gooseberry roots takes place.

Currant-sowthistle aphid (*Hyperomyzus lactucae*). A green aphid with black markings in the winged stages. It occurs mostly on currants where stunting of shoots and leaf-curl is caused. The summer host is sowthistle.

Gooseberry aphid (*Aphis grossulariae*). Greyish green aphid which deforms the shoot-tips of currant and gooseberry. Spends the summer on a species of willowherb.

Lettuce aphid (*Nasonovia ribis-nigri*). A shiny green aphid which infests currant and gooseberry. In summer, a severe pest of lettuce on which it may overwinter in a mild season.

Red currant blister aphid (*Cryptomyzus ribis*). A cream-coloured aphid found on the underside of the leaves in spring causing severe red blistering. (On black-

The rose aphid can be a serious pest of roses. Here, greatly enlarged, are both the winged and wingless form.

currants, the blisters may be yellow.) The summer is spent on hedge-woundwort and hemp nettle.

Glasshouse potato aphid (*Aulacorthum solani*). A yellowish-green aphid which causes severe leaf-curl on potatoes and other plants outdoors and under glass. Tomatoes and carnations are among the plants attacked.

Lettuce root aphid (*Pemphigus bursarius*). This pale, mealy aphid has two main host plants. Overwintering eggs are laid on poplar trees and the resulting aphids form 'purse galls', reddish, hollow, pear-shaped swellings on the leaves. In summer, many of the aphids migrate to various plants, including lettuce where colonies covered in 'wool' are formed on the roots. In autumn, there is a return to lay overwintering eggs on poplar, but some aphids may remain on lettuce roots if conditions are favourable. Watering with nicotine, malathion or diazinon, following makers' instructions, should check this pest.

Mottled arum aphid (*Aulacorthum circumflexum*). Shiny, yellow green aphids mottled with black. A pest of many greenhouse plants including arum, chrysanthemum, cyclamen, etc.

Peach-potato aphid (*Myzus persicae*). Ranging in colour from pink to yellowish-green, the pest infests all kinds of plants, from potatoes, lettuce and brassicas to shrubs, peach trees and garden and glasshouse plants, causing curled leaves and distorted blooms. Overwintering eggs are laid on woody hosts, but some aphids survive in protected sites on plants under glass and out of doors.

Pear bedstraw aphid (*Sappaphis pyri*). A pinkish-grey aphid which often builds up enormous populations before winged migrants leave to infest bedstraw. There is a return to pear in early autumn when overwintering eggs are laid.

Plum aphids: Leafcurling plum aphid (*Brachycaudus helichrysi*). Yellowish-green aphids which hatch early in spring and feed on the developing buds and later on the foliage, causing severe leaf-curl. Migration takes place in summer to such plants as asters and chrysanthemums. In autumn, there is a return to plum, where overwintering eggs are laid.

Mealy plums aphid (*Hyalopterus pruni*). Mealy, pale green aphids which hatch late in spring, but which form enormous colonies on the underside of the leaves in summer. Some migrate to reeds and grasses but others continue to breed on plum and damson, where the overwintering eggs are laid in autumn.

Potato aphid (*Macrosiphon euphorbiae*). This varies in colour from pink to green. It damages the growing point and causes leaf-curl in potatoes and a wide range of plants, including lettuce, antirrhinums and annual asters.

Raspberry aphid (*Aphis idaei*). Mealy, grey-green aphids which infest raspberry, loganberry, etc. Overwintering eggs are laid at the base of the buds. The aphids cause leaf-curl and stunting in severe infestations on young growth.

Rubus aphid (*Amphorophora rubi*). Large, pale green aphid, usually in small groups on raspberry and blackberry.

Rose aphid (*Macrosiphon rosae*). A pinkish green aphid with black cornicles, this is the most common of rose-infesting species. They increase rapidly and severe infestations cripple shoots and buds. Some migration to other plants takes place but the pest may remain on the rose throughout the year. Overwintering eggs are laid in autumn but some female aphids may also survive.

Spruce aphid (*Elatobium abietinum*). A green aphid which infests spruce, causing a mottled appearance on the needles, stickiness and often sooty mould, frequently followed by severe defoliation.

Strawberry aphid (*Pentatrichopus fra-gaefoliae*). Small pale aphids with knobbed hairs. They breed continuously on strawberry except in the coldest weather. Winged forms are often responsible for spreading virus to other stocks.

Shallot aphid (*Myzus ascalonicus*). Small, greenish brown aphids which cause twisted leaves and stunted plants. Breeding continues through autumn and winter, but about early June a migration to other host plants takes place.

Tulip bulb aphid (*Sappaphis tulipae*). A yellowish aphid which infests bulbs and corms, continuing to breed in store where conditions are favourable and infesting young shoots when they arise. Infested bulbs may be immersed in a gamma-BHC (20 percent) solution, 0.5l (¼pt) to 45l (10gal) water, for 15 minutes. Fumigation with paradichlorobenzene crystals under hessian in an airtight tin, with the bulbs or corms laid on the hessian is effective. 112g (4oz) of crystals are needed per 0.3 cu m (cu ft) and the tin should be left for five days.

Waterlily aphid (*Rhopalosiphum nyphaeae*). A dark, slightly mealy aphid which builds up large colonies on water plants in summer, causing distortion and discoloration of water-lily leaves and flowers. The winter hosts are prunus species from which the winged migrants return to water plants in June. Control is difficult if fish are present or if there is an outlet to water containing fish, because most insecticides, including derris, are harmful to them. Nicotine is perhaps the least dangerous for this purpose; or a strong jet of water might be used to wash off the aphids.

Apples see Fruit

Apricots see Fruit

Archways

These are often found in the older type of garden where much of the property is enclosed or divided by walls. Entry into the various parts of the garden is through archways built into these walls. Often the feature is enhanced by a wrought-iron gate, or where privacy or shelter from wind is required, a solid door is used. Archways can be formed if hedges are trained and trimmed regularly to form a living arch over a path. Another method is to use a formed metal arch over which plants are trained.

Archways may be used to good purpose in the modern garden. They provide an excellent means of supporting suitable trailing or climbing plants, and several arches may be used in the construction of a covered way or walk along a path.

Most archways are constructed from brick or stonework, but there is no reason why designs should not be made from timber. As its name implies, an archway usually has a semi-circular arch. If timber is used for construction it is easier to design a feature which has either a flat or apexed roof. The actual design should take into consideration the character of the garden and the house itself. The selection of material for construction is particularly important. If bricks are used, these should be old or weathered. Timber produces a natural rustic result especially if oak or cedarwood is selected. Proportions are important too and adequate headroom must allow for the plants which may be trained over the archway. Usually a height of 2m (6ft 6in) is adequate. The width will depend on the path or driveway it is covering. It should not be less than 1m (3ft).

The construction of a brick or pre-cast stone archway requires some skill, not only in the laying of the bricks but in the production of a wooden support or template which supports the arch of bricks or stone until the mortar which binds them has set. The template is made by first sawing two wide lengths of wood to the required shape and span of the required arch. The two shapes are screwed to several strong spacing blocks of wood so that the distance between them is a few inches wider than the width of the brickwork or stonework. A strip of resin-bonded plywood is screwed down on to the top of the two shaped pieces of timber to provide the support for the stonework.

When this template is in position it is supported from the ground by suitable lengths of strong timber. It is possible to purchase specially wedge-shaped bricks for arch construction although ordinary kinds can be used successfully if they are bonded well with mortar.

The archway may be part of a high wall or it may be a feature on its own, supported by strong brick or stone piers. It is very important that foundations for piers are strongly constructed. A hole should be excavated 0.3m (1ft) deep at least, and the bottom 20cm (8in) filled with small rubble rammed in well. The remainder of the hole should be filled with cement, using a mixture of 1 part of cement and 6 parts of mixed ballast. The finished surface of the cement should finish just lower than the level of the surrounding soil.

Wooden archways are much easier to assemble. The best timber to use is either oak or cedar. Both are highly resistant to rot and insect damage. Larch may be used but must be treated with a wood preservative where it is buried below ground. Cuprinol or Solignum are suitable for this purpose if the horticultural grade is used. The main supports for the archway must be selected from strong timber and 8-16cm (3-6in) size will be required according to the proportions of the archway and the width of the path or drive. These should be buried 0.6cm (2ft) below ground level and preferably cemented in position, using a mixture of 1 part of cement and 6 parts of mixed ballast. A flat-topped archway will be the easiest to construct. Cross pieces of 8cm (3in) square timber can be screwed or bolted to the tops of the supporting posts or to long lengths of 8cm (3in) timber which have been previously secured to the tops of the supporting posts and running in the direction of the path or drive. To enhance the design, the cross pieces can overhang the sides by about a foot.

It is possible to purchase commercially-made arches of metal. These are usually of heavy-gauge, galvanized wire or tubular metal. It is necessary to take particular care when these are being erected to see that the feet, or posts which go into the ground, are consolidated with rubble or cement. When covered with plants they are liable to move in strong winds and would be seriously loosened unless inserted carefully. This type of archway has the merit of being practically invisible once the plants are established.

Suitable plants for covering archways
Good though the design of an archway may be, its attractiveness will be considerably enhanced if it is clothed with suitable plants. These will not only add colour and interest but will conceal hard outlines and bring a natural beauty to the garden design.

High on the list of plants are the climbing and rambling roses. The shrub roses should not be forgotten with their display of flowers and berries. There are many climbing shrubs ideally suited for training over archways. These include clematis, forsythia, *Hydrangea petiolaris*, the climbing hydrangea, *Jasminum nudiflorum*, the winter jasmine, *Jasminum officinale*, the summer jessamine, loniceras (honeysuckles) and *Wisteria sinensis* (see also Climbing Plants).

When selected plants are planted, a hole should be taken out a little larger than the maximum spread of the root system. The hole should be positioned so that the plant's main stem is about a foot away from the archway upright or the base of the wall.

Aromatic plants
Certain garden plants are grown more for the aromatic quality of their foliage than for the beauty of their flowers. Their flowers may be insignificant, their leaves may not be particularly handsome, yet the plants are beloved of gardeners because of the scents given off by their leaves, sometimes in hot sunshine, sometimes when the leaves are brushed

with the hand, or crushed between the fingers. The latter kind were described long ago as being 'fast of their scent', meaning that the scent was released only by touching the leaves. Such a plant is the well-known lemon-scented verbena (*Lippia citriodora*, once known as *Aloysia citriodora*). This is usually grown as a greenhouse plant although it is nearly hardy and will succeed outdoors in most winters in the milder parts of the country, given some protection. It should be planted by a warm, sunny wall, preferably by the doorway or near a path so that the leaves can be pressed in passing to yield their piercingly sharp scent of lemons. Spikes of lilac flowers are produced in late summer.

The white, many-stamened flowers of the myrtle (*Myrtus communis*) are by contrast much more showy and it would be worth growing this shrub for its flowers alone. But to beauty of flower it adds fragrance of leaf. Again, it needs a warm sheltered wall or a pot in the cold greenhouse or conservatory. The old-fashioned lad's love (*Artemisia abrotanum*), also familiarly known as southernwood, rarely flowers; it is a hardy shrub grown for the interest and aroma of its finely divided grey-green leaves, so fine as to be almost like hairs. This is another plant which needs to be touched or squeezed to catch the scent which is of lemon, but oilier and not so sharp as that of the lemon-scented verbena. The evergreen leaves of the sweet bay or poet's laurel, *Laurus nobilis* also release their scent when handled.

Rub the shiny evergreen leaves of the Mexican orange (*Choisya ternata*) between your fingers and you can smell varnish; those of *Hebe cupressoides* smell of pencil shavings. The smell of wintergreen is released when the leaves of the *Gaultheria procumbens* are handled and the smell of eucalyptus oil is given off by the leaves of the blue gum (*Eucalyptus globulus*) often grown in the conservatory.

The smell of garlic is not liked by everyone; anyone who dislikes it should be careful when planting the bulbs of the spring starflower (*Ipheion uniflorum*), for if these are by a pathway their lax leaves may be trodden on, when the air will be filled with this unmistakable aroma.

The scented-leaf pelargoniums ('geranuims') constitute a class by themselves. The ordinary bedding pelargoniums have a powerful aroma when handled, which most people find pleasant enough, strong though it is. But there are twenty or more kinds which are grown mainly for their leaf-scents rather than for their far from showy flowers. The catalogues

1 Some pelargoniums with aromatic leaves 2 Aronia arbutifolia 3 Like those of the pelargoniums the leaves of skimmia are aromatic when crushed.

of specialist nurserymen will list perlagoniums with leaves smelling of roses, lemons, oranges, citronella, eucalyptus, peppermint, pine, and other scarcely definable scents or aromas, released when the leaves are pressed.

It is difficult, too, to define the scen given off by the slightly sticky leaves of *Dimorphotheca barberiae*, not only when pressed but also on a hot, still summer's day, when the sun's heat releases it.

A few aromatic plants are worth planting between the cracks in paving for they will bear being trodden upon. One of the mints, *Mentha requienii*, scarcely 1.5cm (½in) high, is one such plant. Trodden upon, it smells distinctly of peppermint. Another useful plant for similar positions is the wild thyme and its varieties. Its relative, *Thymus herba-barona*, smells of carraway seed, a scent disliked by many because of its associations with seed cake, but not too unpleasaant in the open air. This is a shrubby little plant about 16cm (6in) tall which would be damaged by being trodden upon; it is a good dry wall plant. Other thymes, quite apart from the culinary thyme, have leaves with varied scents including orange, lemon and camphor. The leaves of the Carolina allspice (*Calycanthus floridus*) also smell strongly of camphor when handled.

The mints have a surprisingly wide range of scents, too, for there are varieties which when handled give off such scents as Eau de Cologne, apple, pineapple and ginger. By contrast the leaves of *Caryopteris mastacanthus*, a low-growing shrub with lavender blue flowers, smell of mint when bruised.

Another good garden plant, especially for edging a pathway where it is easily touched in passing, is the catmint (*Nepeta faassenii*), grown mainly for its long display of spikes of lavender-blue flowers, but its season of charm is even longer than its flowering period for its grey-green leaves are always aromatic. Lavenders, too, are aromatic in all their parts, flowers, stems and leaves and these make fine internal hedges. So, too, does the old-fashioned rosemary (*Rosmarinus officinalis*), taller than the lavenders, free-flowering in spring but a delightful plant to have at any time, for the sake of its sharply fragrant leaves. Another of these old plants is the rue or herb of grace (*Ruta graveolens*) usually grown in the form 'Jackman's Blue', for its blue-green foliage, although not everyone likes that somewhat odd aroma its leaves give off when handled. This is a dwarf shrub which does well on chalky soils. Yet another shrub which comes into the aromatic group is the skimmia, a beautiful evergreen for shade, bearing in most of its garden forms ample crops of persistent bright red berries. A curiously aromatic shrub is the sweet brier or eglantine (*Rosa eglanteria*) sometimes used to make a low informal hedge. The aroma of its leaves is most apparent on a warm day, after a shower of rain.

Many conifers have a distinctive aroma, often resinous or like that of turpentine. It is usually more noticeable on hot, calm days, though even dead pine needles or the leaves of other conifers smell pleasantly as one walks over them on a winter's day.

Artichokes see Vegetables

Asparagus see Vegetables

Aspect

Many plants will grow only if planted on the south side of a wall, fence or hedge, others will be scorched by the sun on the south side but will thrive in a shady border or bed on the north side.

The warmest aspect is a border protected from cold winds, facing south and preferably on a slight slope. Many tender plants can be grown under these conditions, so reserve any such site in the garden for the choice, tender plants.

A south-west aspect, protected by a wall, fence or hedge is also warm and it has the advantage of being away from the early morning sun in the spring which is so damaging to fruit in particular. If there has been a frost during the night the rapid thawing may cause the fruitlets to split. For this reason a south-west wall is ideal for fruit growing and a south-east the least desirable for this.

A north-facing border by a wall, fence or hedge need never be despised; there are many climbers, shrubs and plants of all kinds that will thrive in the shade.

When considering aspect in the garden a great deal will depend on whether the site is protected from wind, which is so damaging to plant growth.

Aubergines see Vegetables

Autumn colour

By the autumn many of the summer-flowering plants are all but over and, although there are many plants which will provide a display of flowers in September and October, and even into early November, much can be done to make the garden colourful in these months by planting some of the shrubs and trees the leaves of which turn brilliant colours be-

Open, sunny aspects suit many plants. Protection from wind can be provided by trees.

fore they fall. The intensity of colouring and its duration varies annually, as much seems to depend on the weather. A mild, calm, but not too dry, autumn following a hot summer may result in a display of colour lasting for several weeks, the leaves turning gradually from one shade to another and remaining on the plants for a long time. Conversely, in a wet windy autumn following a dull summer, the leaves may turn quickly, the colours will be less brilliant and the gales may quickly strip much of the foliage from the trees.

However, the gardener should always take the long-term view, particularly when planting such permanent specimens as trees and shrubs. It is worth remembering when making a selection of such plants that many of them will give two or even three seasons of beauty; the first when they flower, then when their leaves turn, finally when their colourful fruits hang from the leafless twigs, adding their quota of colour to a dull scene in late autumn and winter.

The most brilliant autumn leaf colours are found among the Japanese maples (acers), but, unfortunately, the flowers are insignificant and the fruits, if they are formed, are but smaller replicas of the winged fruits of the common hedge maple. Even so, there is much beauty in the leaves before they turn colour for they are often much-lobed, divided into as many as eleven narrow segments, giving the small tree or shrub a delicate, airy appearance. Among the best of these Japanese maples is *Acer palmatum septemlobum osakazuki*, the many-lobed leaves of which turn to the most fiery scarlet. Others turn all imaginable shades of crimson, bronze and gold. There is a wide selection, including some which have bronze, crimson or yellow leaves during summer.

Amelanchiers can usually be guaranteed to give good autumn foliage colour and they have more to offer as they produce attractive trails of white flowers in April, followed by maroon fruits. These, alas, are too attractive to birds to remain on the tree long. The deciduous azaleas are very much two-season plants, colourful in spring when they flower and again in autumn when their leaves turn. Others of this kind, beautiful in flower and leaf, include a few of the spring-flowering cherries (*prunus*), the Chinese wych-hazels (*hamamelis*), the buffalo currant (*Ribes aureum*) and certain viburnums. Among those with handsome fruit as well as worthwhile autumn colour are several crabs (*malus*), viburnums, including the native guelder rose, *V. opulus*, and mountain ashes (*sorbus*).

Conifers, on the whole, provide little autumn colour. The exceptions are *Cryptomeria japonica elegans*, a form of the Japanese cedar in which the foliage turns a pleasant reddish-bronze with the approach of winter, resuming its normal green in spring; *Ginkgo biloba*, the

maidenhair tree, the fan-shaped leaves of which turn a good yellow before falling; *Metasequoia glyptostroboides*, the dawn redwood which turns pinkish-brown, and *Taxodium distichum*, the swamp cypress, the foliage of which turns bronze-yellow before falling.

For further details of the cultivation and propagation of the trees and shrubs providing autumn colour, reference should be made to the entries under trees and shrubs.

B

Balcony gardening see Town gardening

Ball

The gardener's name for the mass of roots and the adhering soil which should be as intact as possible when a plant is potted-on to a slightly larger pot. To attain this object the plant pot should be reasonably clean, for unless this care is taken there is a great likelihood of the roots getting such a hold upon the pot wall that the root-ball will not come away intact and undamaged. The roots of certain plants, such as rhododendrons, are balled in sacking or hessian when they are lifted from the nursery for despatch.

Balling

This term well describes the unfortunate condition of the buds of some very double roses, which, in wet weather, decay in a half-open state instead of opening fully. To prevent this balling, to which some roses are prone, it is as well to protect the buds from excessive rain, to feed the plant less generously, and not to thin the buds too severely, although it will also occur even if there is no thinning carried out at all.

Banks

The simplest treatment of that interesting feature in the garden's structure—a bank—is to make a grassy slope of it. This is, however, quite the worst of the many ways in which a bank can be treated, since it lacks interest and will be more difficult to mow than a level lawn.

If the bank is fairly extensive an excel-

1 Nyssa sylvatica and 2 Liquidambar styraciflua are two trees which colour well in autumn 3 Polygonum cuspidatum, a Japanese knotweed, is a herbaceous plant which provides autumn colour 4 The leaves of Ginkgo biloba, the maidenhair tree, turn yellow before falling. Those of 5 Euonymus alatus turn crimson, while those of 6 the climber Vitis coignetiae turn orange and scarlet 7 Autumn at Scotney Castle, Kent.

3

4

5

6

7

lent way to cover the soil is to plant some of the many fine climbing and rambler roses. The long shoots are secured to strong wooden pegs and stride across the ground in a series of low arches. It is surprising how this treatment causes the whole plant to flower most generously.

A treatment suited to a sunny aspect is to plant the bank with a variety of low-growing flowering shrubs to produce a kind of 'maquis'. Suitable shrubs for this purpose would include: rock roses such as *Cistus cyprius* and *C. laurifolius*, the prostrate cotoneasters, lavenders, genistas, halimiums, helianthemums, hypericums, *Phlomis fruticosa*, rosemary, the red-leaved sage (*Salvia officinalis rubrifolia*), *Berberis thunbergii atropurpurea*, rutas, several artemisias and santolinas, and the Scotch brier roses, which are, unlike most roses, completely trouble free. The Scotch briers have been developed from the native burnet rose *Rosa spinosissima*. They have a fair range of colour and they increase slowly and steadily by suckering. Even in winter their close sheafs of branches make an effective note of warm brown colour. The chief disadvantage of these briers is that they are somewhat rare now. The search for these precious shrubs is itself an adventure, but several specialist rose growers offer a small selection.

If there is a path which dips between banks, the feature is, in effect a 'dell' and here, if the soil permits it, there is a splendid opportunity to plant rhododendrons in a way which seems to set them off to the greatest advantage.

On the same banks of acid soil as the rhododendrons enjoy the dell might more modestly be a heather dell, and this could give colour the whole year through, for even in the coldest winter weather there are masses of bright heather blossoms cheerfully glowing. And soil is less important where the winter-flowering heaths are concerned, for *Erica carnea* and its numerous cultivars, which flower from November to April, will succeed on chalky soils.

It is possible, also, to make rough terraces and these may be planted up with the more amenable rock plants. In fact this treatment reaches a stage when it might well be regarded simply as a rock garden (see Rock gardening, Rock garden plants).

Terracing the bank in this way can give it a somewhat exotic look if the top of the bank has one or two of the large noble-looking but perfectly hardy yuccas placed so that they can be seen against the sky. When they bloom the effect is superb. Either *Yucca gloriosa* or *Y. recurva* will give this effect, and the much

1

2

1 On the bank massed plantings of the dwarf narcissus cyclamineus are effective in spring 2 Massed plantings of kurume azaleas on a bank in the Punch Bowl in the Valley Gardens at Windsor.

smaller *Y. flaccida* will give an annual show of its white lily blooms. A list of plants suited to the terraced bank would include: wallflowers, snapdragons, thrift, rock pinks, iberis, aubrieta, alyssum, arabis, *Campanula garganica*, *C. portenschlagiana*, the mossy saxifrages, dianthus, *Genista lydia*, *Phlox subulata*, and many others.

As can be well seen from a railway carriage window, many flowering plants are capable of taking care of even the most difficult conditions provided by the steep banks of raw earth which often border the permanent way. Here may be seen *Hypericum calycinum*, the rose of sharon; the periwinkles, *Vinca minor* and *Vinca major;* and particularly on raw chalk, the red valerian, *Centranthus ruber;* with an occasional taller note provided by that easy-going shrub the bladder senna, *Colutea arborescens.*

Bark-bound
It sometimes happens that through some deficiency in the soil a tree or shrub may grow so slowly that the bark becomes tough and unyielding. This impedes further development and the plant is then described as bark-bound.

A bark-bound tree may, by splitting its bark, effect its own cure, but should this not occur the gardener is advised to take his knife and slit through the bark in a longitudinal cut. This treatment should be followed by generous feeding and watering of the tree. An application of Stockholm tar or hot grafting-wax may well be applied to the slit bark. This should be done in the spring.

Bark-ringing
When an apple tree or pear tree is excessively vigorous it may make much new wood instead of producing fruit. Under such conditions a method of checking root growth is resorted to which is called bark-ringing. This entails removing a narrow strip of bark and cambium right round the trunk and deep enough to reach the hard wood beneath. Some gardeners modify this by removing two semicircles, one on each side of the trunk. Another modified treatment is to remove a spiral strip. The process is completed by the application of some protective paint to the wound.

Another less drastic operation is knife-edge ringing, which consists in drawing a knife blade right round the trunk in such a way as to cut quite deeply to the woody layer, but no bark is removed. If this treatment is applied in late April or early May dormant buds may actually be caused to develop in a few weeks. The above treatment is not recommended for plums and cherries and other stone fruits since it may well cause gumming.

1 Bark ringing: two semi-circles on bark removed from the tree 2 The wounds painted with protective paint.

Basal rot of daffodil bulbs.

Barrows
A barrow is one of the essential pieces of garden equipment. In essence it is a box on two levers which terminate in a wheel. At least, this quite well describes the old heavy oak barrow, weighing between 35-40kg (70-80lb). A modern barrow will generally consist of a chassis of metal tubing with a body of sheet metal or some light but strong plastic material. The body may well be detachable to allow for easy emptying, and the whole thing may run on a pair of wheels instead of the single one so customary in the past. The wheels may also have inflatable tyres, though keeping these pumped and puncture-free does add one more chore, when pros and cons are being weighed up by a prospective purchaser.

It is certainly wise for the person about to buy a barrow to go to a supplier who can show him a good range of the latest types, and he should certainly be able to try the feel of the barrow when it is carrying some fairly weighty object. It is interesting to note what a difference to the ease of working lies in the placing of the wheel, or wheels. With the cumbersome old wooden types one was always half carrying the load. An extension which increases the height of the sides may be purchased which allows for the transport of light but bulky loads such as autumn leaves and lawn mowings.

Basal rot
A general term used to indicate diseases which in their attack on plants cause a rotting of the lower parts. It can only be

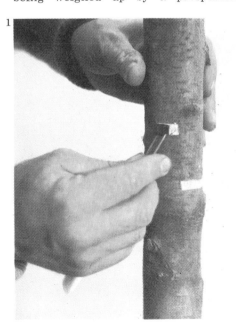

used generally because confusion easily arises with these diseases by using terms such as bottom rot of lettuce, basal stem rot of peas or foot rot of cacti and carnation. Usually the term basal rot is meant to indicate a disease of some bulbous plant, e.g., narcissus basal rot or even a rhizomatous one such as the well-known basal or rhizome rot of bearded irises. Other basal rots occur on lilies, tulips, onion, etc. Bulbs affected by narcissus basal rot should be burned. The parts of iris rhizomes affected by rhizomes rot should be cut away and burned and the cut surfaces dusted with copper-lime dust.

Basic slag

This is a crushed waste product of blast furnaces, and is valuable as it contains phosphoric acid in a form which causes it to be liberated slowly over a long period. The finer the powder obtained the quicker will the phosphoric acid be liberated.

The effect of an application of a phosphate fertilizer is not obvious at once. It is, however, essential to seedlings and is connected with the formation of a root system, and is a useful fertilizer for fruit trees.

Basic slag is useful on acid soils since, in addition to the phosphoric acid, it has calcium in the form of free lime, at an average of 3 percent. In the autumn on heavy soil an application of from 112-224g (4-8oz) per sq m (sq yd) is to be recommended. In judging the quality of the product you are offered it is as well to note that an 80 percent solubility is good but below 40 percent indicates a poor product. Because of its free lime content it should not be mixed with organic manures, inorganic manures containing ammonium salts or super-phosphate of lime.

Beans see Vegetables

Bedding

The description bedding plant is not an exact one and only means that the plant is grown elsewhere in some quantity and then planted out as a temporary occupant of the bed; this being known as 'bedding out'.

The bedding plant in private gardens has, in general, had its day, since this style of gardening entails much expense. In public gardens and for certain formal occasions the bedding plant still has its uses.

Bedding out This term, in use by gardeners, describes a form of gardening in which plants raised elsewhere in a nursery garden or greenhouse are planted out in a previously prepared bed. This style of gardening is seen at its best in some of the many excellent public parks, but because it is comparatively expensive and entails the use of a reserve garden it is not particularly well suited to the needs of the modest suburban gardener. The Victorian garden of the more opulent parvenu was generally devoted to the most elaborate form of bedding out called carpet-bedding, in which numbers of potted plants were sunk in the beds to their pot rims. In really ambitious plantings of this sort even exotics such as palms, bananas, tree ferns, castor oil plants, giant cannas and agaves were sometimes used, though this necessitated a considerable amount of heated glass in the nursery garden and today this style is more likely to be seen in a public garden of one of the larger seaside resorts than in a private garden. Many gardeners will treasure the memory of the period when Thomas Hay was superintendent of the Royal Parks. Then one saw some very rare plants used in bedding schemes of an entirely new and very refreshing kind, a complete change from the hackneyed combination of 'Paul Crampel' pelargoniums, blue lobelias and sweet alyssum.

Though it was crotchety old William Robinson who often in *The Garden* made sharp attacks upon bedding-out and particularly carpet-bedding, it is a strange fact that he was fascinated by another type of bedding-out in which large numbers of plants with showy foliage were used to make an elaborate planting that he called a 'subtropical' garden. This style originated at Battersea Park when it was in the care of a Mr Charles Gibson about a hundred years ago. Today when large exotics with handsome leaves are used it is generally as 'dot' plants, standing aloof though assailed by massed ranks of the usual brightly flowered summer bedding favourites.

Spring bedding Beds planted for spring display rely very heavily upon bulbous plants including: tulips, hyacinths, narcissi, Spanish and Dutch irises, crocuses, scillas, and grape hyacinths and some others less important. Because they are very reliable, tulips and hyacinths are particular favourites for this treatment, for if the bulbs have been purchased from a trustworthy source each will invariably produce its flower or flowers in due season. A scheme in which

Bedding Plants

Botanical Name	Colour	Height Feet	Planting Distance Inches	Remarks
Abutilon	Variegated leaves	2–4	36–48	Dot plants
Ageratum	Mauve, blue, white	¾	6	Edging and small beds
Amaranthus	Purple, dark red	2	12	Dot plants
Antirrhinum	Various	½–1½	6–12	Best when massed
Alternanthera	Coloured foliage	¾	4–6	Edging
Alyssum (sweet)	White, pink, lilac	⅔–1	4–6	Edging
Aster (annual)	Various	½–1½	6–12	Good for cutting
Begonia (fibrous)	Pink, red and white	1	9	Good for small beds
Begonia (tuberous)	Various	¾–1	9	Shady beds
Calceolaria (shrubby)	Yellow-bronze	1	9	Well-drained soil
Canna	Yellow and red	2–3	12–24	Good dot plants
Celosia (cockscomb)	Red and yellow	1	9	Rich soil
Celosia plumosa	Red and yellow	2	9	Rich soil
Centaurea candidissima	Silver leaves	¾	9	Provides a good foil
Cineraria maritima	Silver leaves	½–¾	6–9	Good foliage plants
Dahlia	Various	1–7	12–48	Needs a rich soil
Echeveria	Grey-leaved succulent	1	6	Sunny, dry soil bronze or red foliage
Fuchsia	Pink, red or purple, white	1–4	18–36	Standard dot plants
Gazania	Yellow and orange	tr	9–12	Good for edging
Godetia	Pink, white and crimson	½–2	9–12	Sunny position
Grevillea	Feathery foliage	4	60	Use as dot plants
Heliotrope	Purple, blue, white	¾–3	9–48	Can grow as standard
Iresine	Red or variegated leaves	1	9	Good foil plants
Kochia	Green foliage later red	2	18	Use as dot plants
Leucophyton	Silver leaves	2–3	12–36	Sunny position
Lobelia	Blue, carmine, white	⅓	6	Edging
Marguerite	White, yellow	1½–2	12–18	Sunny position
Marigold (African and French)	Yellow, orange, crimson	½–2	6–12	Hot, dry soil
Mesembryanthemum criniflorum	Various	tr	9	Full sun
Nemesia	Various	¾–1	8–8	Best when massed
Nicotiana	White, crimson	2–3	12	Will grow in shade
Pansies	Various	½	9	Edging or small beds
Pelargonium (Geranium)	Pink, red and white	1½	12	Sun or shade
Pelargonium (ivy leaved)	Pink, red and white	tr	18	Standards or dot plants
Pelargonium (coloured leaves)	Variegated foliage	1½	12	Good foliage effect
Penstemon	Various	1½	12	Sun or shade
Petunias	Various	⅓–1	12	Useful for shade
Phlox drummondii	Various	¾	8–12	Best pegged down
Ricinus	Green and bronze foliage	3–5	36–48	Dot plants
Salvia	Blue	1½–2	12	Sunny position
Salvia	Scarlet	1–2	12	Sunny position
Stocks (10 week)	Various	1–2	12	Good rich soil
Venidium	Various	2–3	18	Full sun
Verbena	Various	tr	9–12	Edging
Viola	Various	½	9	Edging or small beds
Zea mays	Coloured foliage	3–4	36–48	Dot plants
Zinnia	Various	¾–2	9–12	Full sun

tr = trailing

tulips are underplanted with arabis, aubrieta, alyssum, or forget-me-nots is so
well known as to be a gardening cliche.

Various large-flowered polyanthus
primroses are much in favour, as are also
the so-called winter-flowering pansies,
and the fragrant wallflower. It is very
important in this style of gardening to
keep the taller plants to the centre of the
bed. A popular flower for the outermost
edge planting is the old-fashioned double
form of the daisy.

Since there is no winter bedding the
bedding plants and bulbs can, of course,
be put in the beds in September or October, and such plants as the winter-
flowering pansies will give some flowers
right through the winter, though this
will not exactly be an arresting sight. On
the French and Italian Riviera, winter
bedding schemes are important, but our
climate makes it unsuitable here.

Most of the spring bedding plants will
be past their best by June, and those
which it is considered are worthy to be
kept may be heeled-in in a reserve bed of
the nursery garden. It is well to remember, however, that tulips and hyacinths
must not be relied upon to give flowers
for two successive seasons.

Summer bedding Bedding plants for
summer planting must be raised in early
spring under glass. The skill of the operation is proved when a good uniform
crop of plants is ready and hardened-off
in time to replace the spring bulbs and
other plants now well past their decorative best. Most of the bedding plants
may be conveniently grown from seed,
though sometimes cuttings are needed,
and cannas, dahlias, tuberous begonias
and *Salvia patens* are generally grown
from tubers. The latter plants may all be
grown from seed but this is a longer operation and generally the plants are not
capable of giving the uniform result
which is one of the aims in bedding
schemes.

The seeds may be grown in boxes
(fairly deep) or one or more plants may
occupy a pot. The latter method is certainly to be preferred for the more precious and difficult plants, since the root
ball, if intact, gives the plant protection
against the rather drastic operation
which transplanting certainly is. For
some weeks after this operation the
plants must be given a daily watering,
for in high summer there will be a considerable loss of moisture.

In planting out it is necessary to bear
in mind the ultimate spread of the plants,
though should they be planted too closely there will be an opportunity of thin-
ning-out later. A supply of reserve plants
should be kept as it is inevitable that a
few casualties will occur.

1 A wide variety of bulbs may be used for
spring bedding purposes. Here tulips,
narcissi and hyacinths are massed to give
a colourful display 2 Summer bedding
using half-hardy plants.

A point of importance in preparing the bed previously to planting is to mound it up quite considerably. With a flat bed the full effect of the planting scheme will not be appreciated, except, of course, in those rare instances when the beds are planned for those who will view them from above, as, for instance, from a terrace.

Bedding schemes The preparation of bedding schemes involves some elementary knowledge of colour and a feeling for the combination of those hues which enhance each other.

There is not space here to deal with the whole theory of colour, but a few suggestions may be given to aid in making harmonious mixtures.

Since all plants will have leaves the one colour which may not be avoided (except with a very few foliage plants) is green. To produce harmonies which take this foliage green into consideration it is necessary to use the portion of the spectrum which includes the yellows, both cold (lemon) and warm, the range of apricots and orange colours, and the reds of hot vermilion hue. Maroons and tawny brownish colours such as one sees in wallflowers are also most pleasing with the green of spring leaves. Salmon and coral pinks are also included in this harmony. The range of colours above mentioned is particularly well represented in the flowers used for spring bedding, and such combinations represent the essential spirit of spring-time.

Because of the great range of colour obtainable in tulips it would be possible to vary the spring bedding schemes al-

1 Planting out polyanthus for spring bedding. A hole is taken out with a trowel, large enough to accommodate the roots 2 Soil is returned round the roots and firmed with the hands.

most indefinitely. In addition to the colours mentioned the tulips embrace: cold silvery pinks, mauves and violets, scarlets and crimsons, white and cream, and even one or two with a colour so intense as to approach black. A good blue is, however, lacking. When using tulips (or any other flower) of these colours the foliage is used merely as a background and not as part of the total colour scheme.

It is important to avoid certain discordant effects, such as combining scarlet and crimson or orange and the well-named 'shocking' pink. Blues and mauves are unhappy together, and so are magentas and purples. It is true that these discords are resolved when the beds are seen at a distance, but, in fact, the schemes will be judged at quite close range.

A brilliant effect may be obtained by using complementary colours. A mass of blue is set-off by some orange; yellow finds its complement in purple; and the reds are taken care of by the predominant green of foliage.

If the beds are planned to be seen from a more or less fixed view-point the problem is simplified somewhat, and it will be possible to take into consideration the enhancing of the perspective. White, yellow and other pale colours will be used in the foreground, and the distant beds are taken further back (in appear-

ance) by the use of predominating mauves, blues, and colours which, as the Victorian gardeners said, retire.

Having considered general principles it is not necessary to give lists of plant combinations, and it is refreshing to come upon new and original plants used in bedding schemes. The list on page 24 contains many plants from which a choice may be made, but should it be desired to use other plants for this purpose it is most important to use those which will give a long period of blossom, and which do not present a disconcerting green jungle halfway through the summer season (see Beds, marking out).

Beds, marking out

One of the exciting stages of garden construction is the marking out of beds. The sites for the flower displays are marked out in the garden in the form of beds or borders. These may be of various shapes and sizes and much will depend on the character of the garden as to the exact shape which is used. Formal beds are those which have straight, defined edges whereas the informal types have irregular or natural edges. It is a good idea to draw up scale plans on paper before any marking out is begun. This will enable the gardener to design and measure the beds accurately especially where it is necessary to accommodate collections of plants such as shrubs and herbaceous plants.

Marking out formal beds Square or rectangular designs require right-angled corners. A permanent marker can be made up from three pieces of scrap wood if a triangle is made having sides measuring on the outside 1, 1.3 and 1.6m (3, 4 and 5ft) respectively. Placed at each corner of a bed, accurate marking is assured. A circular bed is easily drawn out if a peg is driven into the approximate centre of the bed and a line attached, half the diameter of the required bed. A sharp stick fastened to the other end will mark out an accurate circle if the line is kept taut as the stick is drawn through the soil, using the peg as a pivot.

To mark out an oval bed two pegs are inserted a short distance apart (the closer together the more circular the bed will be drawn out) and a line is measured out three times longer than the measurement between the two pegs. The line is fastened into a loop and placed around the two pegs. A marking stick is used to describe the oval in the soil as it is pulled so that the slack is taken up in the looped cord.

Marking out informal beds The irregular outline is first marked out in the soil with a pointed stick and a semi-permanent outline is achieved if a light trickle of lime or sand is used to cover the original marks afterwards. Another useful method is to use a length of hosepipe to define the edge of the irregular bed. This is easily moved about until a satisfactory result is achieved.

Gentle sweeps and curves should be made especially if a bed is to be alongside a lawn so that the mower can be guided around the edges easily. If beds are to be made in an existing lawn, the outlines can be nicked out with a spade or edging iron.

Beetles and Weevils

There are more than 3,000 species of

Some beetles are friends since they prey on other insects and others, which attack plants, are enemies. The grubs of the cock chafer 1 damage the roots of various plants; those of the asparagus beetle 2 feed on asparagus 'fern'.

beetles and weevils (*Coleoptera*) in the British Isles.

They vary greatly in size, appearance and habits. A number of them are garden or household pests, but others are useful predators on other insects and soil creatures. These include the carabid beetles, the devil's coach horse and tiger beetles. Ladybirds are well-known predators of greenfly.

Beetles have six legs and biting mouth parts. Their forewings are modified to form hard wing-cases and the hindwings, when they are present, are folded beneath them. Most of the weevils can be distinguished from beetles by their long 'snouts'. Among the more obvious adaptations for the life they lead are the fierce jaws and long legs for swift running which distinguished the hunters; the hind legs of fleabeetles adapted for jumping and those of the waterbeetles adapted for swimming.

Beetles are found in every part of the garden. In the vegetable plot fleabeetles perforate the leaves of brassica seed-

lings; the turnip gall weevil (*Ceuthorhynchus pleurostigma*) damages the roots; pea and bean weevils (*Sitona spp.*) notch leaves of broad beans and peas; wireworms (click-beetle larvae) attack root crops and asparagus beetles (*Crioceris asparagi*) feed on the fern.

In the orchard, weevils cause capped blossoms (*Anthonomus pomorum*), sever the young shoots (*Rhynchites spp.*) spoil the fruit of raspberries (*Byturus tomentosus*) and feed on the foliage (*Phyllobius spp.*). Shothole borers invade unhealthy trees.

Ornamental trees and shrubs also suffer from weevil attack and also from cockchafer larvae feeding at the roots.

Under glass, the vine weevil (*Otiorrhynchus sulcatus*) is a well-known pest, the larvae feeding on the roots of pot plants and the adult insects making ragged notches in the foliage.

Many beetle pests are to be found in the flower garden. They include the garden chafer (*Phyllotherpa horticola*) which damages lawns in the larval stage and often spoils rosebuds when adult. The waterlily beetle (*Galerucella nymphaeae*) makes lily pads ragged and unsightly; weevil grubs feed on primula and other plant roots and chafer grubs may flourish in the herbaceous border, to name but a few.

Most beetles are controlled by spraying their host plants with insecticide and repeating the application 14 days later. The larvae may be treated by applying 5 percent insecticidal dust to the soil at the rate of about 28g (1oz) per sq m (sq yd) and potting compost may have it incorporated at the rate of 0.25-0.30kg (8-10oz) per bushel.

Bark Beetles There are several species of these small beetles which attack trees and shrubs, including fruit trees, especially those in poor health through disease, unsuitable conditions at the root or damage such as broken branches, etc.

The female beetles burrow between the bark and the wood and lay eggs in the tunnels. When the legless, white grubs hatch, they extend the galleries, thus making complicated patterns which earn them the name of 'engraver beetles'.

In due course, the larvae pupate and emerge through conspicuous exit holes. Among the most destructive species are the fruit bark beetle (*Scolytus rugulosus*) and the large elm bark beetle (*Scolytus scolytus*).

It is advisable to burn all dead branches and to remove the bark from any larger limbs or felled tree trunks which may harbour the beetles.

Beetroot see Vegetables

Bell-glass
The true cloche or bell-glass, which was developed in France as an important aid in the early production of market garden crops, is seldom seen in the modern garden. Its place is now largely taken by the

A true cloche or bell-glass of a type now superseded by the so-called continuous cloches.

badly named continuous cloche in which sheets of glass are wired together to form a miniature glass case. The true cloche had some advantages to offset its great cost; it was quite air-tight and its considerable stability and weight made it proof against all that the stormiest weather could bring. Where cuttings have to be given summer rooting treatment the bell-glass or cloche is superior to the so-called continuous cloche as a close humid atmosphere is secured with ease.

Bending
A method of encouraging buds to break more evenly along a branch than may occur normally. It is mainly used by fruit growers but may be tried successfully with some flowering shrubs. A weight is attached to the end of a branch or, where possible, the branch can be tied down to a lower branch or to pegs in the ground. It is sometimes used for the long shoots of vigorous roses.

Besom
This useful garden broom consists of a bunch of birch twigs fixed to a pole, and the making and selling of besoms was at one time an important part of the way of life of the gipsy. Nowadays it is still required to remove leaves and stones from the lawn before using the lawn mower, though even for this operation some prefer a springy wire or bamboo-tined rake. Modern besoms are often made of springy whalebone.

Biennials
This is a valuable division of garden plants, for by the biennial habit of storing up in the first season a reserve which is expended wholly in the second season, a much greater quantity of blossom is possible than with either the annual or perennial habit of growth.

It is also notable that many of our important vegetable crops are in this category; though where these are concerned (e.g. cabbage, beet, turnip, etc.) the plant is not permitted to flower and seed but the food stored up for these functions is taken for culinary use.

Where a new garden is being made annual and biennial plants will be of great service, for it generally takes from three to five years to achieve a garden furnished satisfactorily with perennials and shrubs; and even then biennials will still be needed.

The chief drawback to the cultivation of biennials is the space which must be given to them in the reserve garden or frame, since they are not moved into their final stations until they are large healthy plants.

The term biennial is not used too strictly by the gardener and some short-lived perennials, some monocarpic plants and, certain annuals also are sometimes given biennial treatment.

Cultivation Biennials may be sown in spring in a frame or cold greenhouse or outdoors from May onwards in beds of fine weed-free soil.

If seeds are sown in drills instead of broadcast it will be easier to keep them free from weeds by running the hoe between the rows from time to time.

After a severe thinning seedlings should be pushed on with adequate feeding until by October they will be large, leafy plants, which may then be put into their final stations in the flower border. If the weather is dry when the time comes to transplant give the bed a thorough watering. Careful lifting, using a trowel, will minimise root disturbance, and subsequent checks to growth.

If it is intended to treat hardy annuals as biennials (excellent results in mild areas) the only way in which the operation differs from that described above is in the time of the seed sowing, which should be at the end of the summer or even in early autumn, but do not sow too early or the plants will flower in their first year. Given this biennial treatment annuals will make much larger plants than when grown in the normal way and this must be allowed for when they are planted out in their final positions.

Half-hardy biennials will need overwintering in frost-free conditions in a frame or a cold greenhouse. They are not an important section and one may well do without them, devoting precious greenhouse space to other things.

The following are biennials, or are often treated as biennial: adlumia, althaea (hollyhock), antirrhinum (snapdragon), *Campanula medium* (Canterbury bell), cheiranthus (wallflower), cnicus (fishbone thistle), *Dianthus barbatus* (sweet william), *Digitalis purpurea* (foxglove), *Erysimum arkansanum*, *Hedysarum coronarium* (French honeysuckle), *Humea elegans* (half-hardy), hunnemannia, lunaria (honesty), matthiola (Brompton, Nice and intermediate stock), some meconopsis, myosotis, *Oenothera biennis* (evening primrose), onopordon (cotton thistle), *Papaver nudicaule* (Iceland poppy), verbascum (mullein).

Bird damage

Damage by birds appears to be increasing, which is perhaps understandable as more trees are felled and more hedgerows replaced by fences, thus greatly reducing the insect population, seeds, fruit, etc., available to them.

Widespread damage is done every season to the buds of fruit trees and ornamental trees and shrubs, such as prunus and forsythia. Not only orchard fruits are attacked, but also the ornamental berries of shrubs such as pyracantha. Flower petals of crocus and polyanthus are destroyed and the tips of shoots of plants such as chrysanthemum are pecked off for reasons not yet understood.

This damage is very difficult to prevent and, as far as fruit is concerned, the only completely satisfactory answer is netting or a fruit cage. Polythene bags may be used to protect fruits.

A temporary deterrent may be obtained in the form of a rayon mesh which is teased out to form a 'cobweb' to cover the trees or shrubs during the danger months for buds, from late autumn to spring. The mesh rots away in a few months so does not remain to look unsightly during the rest of the year.

There are now a number of repellents on the market which are said to remain effective for periods of up to six months. They are based on substances such as thiram and anthraquinone etc., and provide useful protection for buds and berries if put on in good time and renewed as necessary. Among low-growing plants, a scattering of mothballs is said to have

Dianthus barbatus, the well-known sweet william 1 and Lunaria biennis, the honesty 2 are two of the plants known as biennials, seeds of which are sown one year to flower the following year.

been effective occasionally.

Bird scarers need to be changed frequently so that the birds do not become used to them and lose their fear. Devices which combine movement with noise and glitter seem to be most effective and many gardeners have invented ingenious devices to serve the purpose, suspending such things as slivers of broken glass, electric light bulbs or strips of kitchen foil, among their plants.

More ambitious projects have included lengths of hosepipe intended to represent snakes and life-like effigies of predators such as cats, owls and hawks, (the latter kept hovering with the aid of a balloon).

Blackberries see Fruit

Black currants see Fruit

Black spot

A term which can be used to describe certain plant diseases which reveal themselves as black spots on the leaves. Some are quite startling in the colour contrast with the green of the leaf, for example black or tar spot on sycamore leaves. But the best known of all ornamental plant black spot diseases is that which affects roses, called rose black spot. In this the spots are usually circular and well de-

fined but sometimes they are very diffuse and roughly follow the veins in a branched fashion. In the disease of delphiniums called black spot or black blotch the black spots are of all sizes and very irregular shape. In black spot disease of elm leaves the spots are shiny, coal black, and slightly raised.

In general most black spot diseases may be controlled by picking off and burning the affected leaves where this is practicable, or by spraying with a proprietary copper fungicide or with a modern fungicide containing thiram.

Rose black spot is often more difficult to control and it may be necessary to spray at fairly frequent intervals with one of the fungicides mentioned above, or with Bordeaux mixture. Spraying the bare bushes and the soil beneath them with tar-oil emulsion in winter is sometimes resorted to with success. All prunings and affected leaves should be picked up and burned. An excess of nitrogen in the feed may predispose roses towards an attack of black spot. Where the disease is troublesome it may be advisable to reduce the nitrogen content of the feed. A spring dressing consisting of 2 parts of superphosphate, 1 part of magnesium sulphate, $\frac{1}{2}$ part of iron sulphate applied at 168g (6oz) per sq m (sq yd), is a suitable low nitrogen feed. A rose leaf badly affected by black spot is illustrated on page 30.

Blanching

This is a method of culture by which light is excluded from edible portions of vegetable crops, thereby preventing the formation of chlorophyll (green colouring), rendering the growths crisper, more palatable and more attractive. The method used varies with the vegetable concerned. Celery has the stems either earthed up or encircled with cardboard. Chicory and seakale crowns are lifted, packed close together in boxes, covered with sand and placed in a shed or cold frame. Dandelions (for salad) and endive are both blanched by inverting a pot or box over them. Leeks have the soil drawn up round the base as they grow, gradually extending the length of the white of the leaves. Except for leeks all crops should be fully matured before blanching, otherwise growth may be checked.

Bleeding

The word bleeding, when used in connection with plants, is meant to indicate the loss of sap which occurs when plant tissues are cut or injured in some way. In most plants healing is fairly rapid, especially in the growing season on a healthy specimen, but some trees do not seem to heal quickly and 'bleed' copiously through a wound. Young birch saplings, if cut off in spring, soon produce a great flow of sap but will gradually heal. The walnut is the worst and these trees must not be damaged, and any extensive wound will probably need expert treatment.

Blood

Dried animal blood is a valuable fertiliser containing, on average, about 12 per cent nitrogen. It is obtainable in the form of a powder which is applied dry to vacant land or around growing crops at the rate of 56g (2oz) per sq m (sq yd.) It is a safe fertilizer in that it will not scorch the leaves of plants if it falls on them, but in order to prevent loss of ammonia it should be worked into the soil as quickly as possible after it has been applied. It may also be used to form a useful liquid fertilizer by stirring 28-56g (1-2oz) into 4.5l (1 gal) of water, although it is not completely water-soluble and the liquid must be kept stirred to avoid sedimenta-

tion. However, a more soluble form is available. In this form it is particularly useful for greenhouse pot plants and greenhouse crops in general. Fresh blood may be used, provided it is dug in immediately, but it is seldom available and, in any case, is unpleasant to handle. If there is a choice of available dried bloods, that of a reddish colour should be chosen; black or blackish samples contain an undue proportion of charred material and less nitrogen.

Dried blood may be mixed with most other fertilizers safely and is often used with sulphate of potash and superphosphate to make a balanced fertilizer. It is also available mixed with fishmeal and bonemeal for use on greenhouse crops.

Bog gardens

No water garden is complete without a bog garden as some of the most beautiful and interesting plants thrive in such situations. Many ponds and lakes have a natural perennially damp surround which requires no more attention before introducing plants than to remove unwanted weeds.

If the pond is fed by a natural water supply, it is usually possible to channel the overflow into surrounding land, thus producing an area which is permanently moist without being waterlogged. Alternatively, any low-lying site with a clay subsoil can be periodically flooded over with water to produce a bog garden. During the winter months, rain will supply all the moisture that is required as most bog plants are then dormant.

To make a bog garden on raised ground or where the drainage is very free, creates a different problem which, however, can be overcome with a little effort. Excavate the site to a depth of 38cm (15in) and line the area with poor quality concrete consisting of 12 parts of ballast to 1 part of cement or even weaker, or cover the base with slates, tiles or asbestos sheets slightly overlapping. Another idea is to line the base with a single layer of 500 gauge polythene sheeting perforated in a few places so that it allows water to leak away slowly.

Whatever method is employed, put

1 A rose leaf badly affected by black spot. 2 Chicory crowns placed closely together in boxes for blanching. 3 The chicory crowns produce blanched shoots which are cut off and used in salads.

1

3

2

4

6-8cm (23in) of stones or pebbles over the lining to provide adequate drainage. Cover these with a layer of peat tailings or old turves turned upside down. Replace the soil, incorporating liberal quantities of peat, manure or other fibrous material to hold the moisture during times of drought. When finished, the top soil will look like any other herbaceous border, but the roots of the plants will feel the influence of the water, and such conditions should produce an ideal bog garden. Although it is important to water the area in dry weather, it is equally important never to allow the soil to become waterlogged.

Suitable plants There is a wide range of plants suitable for the bog garden. Some of the more popular and interesting kinds include the aconitums (monkshood). The most commonly grown species is *A. napellus*, with finely cut leaves and purplish-blue flowers, its variety *bicolor*, with blue and white flowers, and 'Newry Blue', flowering June–July on 1-1.3m (3-4ft) stems.

Aruncus sylvester (goat's beard) if space permits, is a wonderful plant for the back of the bog garden, with large plumes of creamy-white flowers in June and foliage very similar to that of the astilbes and growing to 1.3-1.6m (4-5ft). The numerous varieties of astilbe make excellent bog garden plants, but unfortunately they are frequently grown in dry borders with inadequate moisture, where they never acquire their full splendour. Some of the most popular varieties include: 'Deutschland', pure white, 'Fanal', deep red with reddish foliage, 'Koblenz', rose, 'Red Sentinel', very deep red and 'Rhineland', bright pink.

The native marsh marigold (*Caltha palustris*) in both its single and double-flowered forms, is a fine plant for really moist soils. It makes a bold splash of yellow in spring.

Gunnera manicata is probably the most impressive bog plant it is possible to grow in this country, but it is only suitable where there is ample room, as in a large water garden. The foliage resembles enormous rhubarb leaves, often reaching 2.5-3.3m (8-10ft) in diameter, on stems 3.8m (12ft) or more in height. The flowers are brown—borne in heads about 1m (3ft) long and something like a bottle brush in appearance. Gunneras require plenty of moisture during the growing season but must not become waterlogged, especially during the winter months, when it is necessary to give the crowns protection by packing the dead leaves over the roots. Extra protection with straw or leaves should always be added in very severe weather.

No garden is complete without hemerocallis (day lily). The species come from Asian riversides and will grow anywhere in the bog garden, in shallow water, in shade or full sun, in heavy wet soil or dry sandy situations. Many hybrids have been produced, giving a wide variety of colour from pale yellow to deep red and a flowering period from June to September. Given ample room for development, the plants may be left undisturbed for years. A vast range of hybrids include: 'C. P. Raffill,' 0.7m (2½ft) apricot flowers, July–August; 'High Tor,' 2m (6ft) or more in height, yellow flowers, June–July; 'Pink Damask,' rich pink, and 'Hiawatha,' 0.7m (2½ft), copper-red.

Hostas are invaluable semi-shade plants with leaves in various shades of green or green and silver or gold variegations and pale mauve or white flowers. Species include *H. fortunei alba*, yellow leaves edged with green; *H. sieboldiana*, blue-green foliage; *H. undulata*, large oval leaves; *H. minor*, 30–38cm (12–15 in), pale green leaves and white flowers.

Iris kaempferi and its forms are the most notable of the bog iris. Natives of Japan they are grown beside the paddy fields which are flooded during the summer months but drained in the winter, thus producing ideal growing conditions. As they are lime haters, they must have adequate peat or leafmould in the soil. These plants are rarely sold as named varieties, but usually as the 'Higo Strain' of hybrids.

Lysichitum americanum, the skunk cabbage, indigenous to North America, has large bright yellow arum flowers in April, before the leaves, which make a bold show at the pool side during the summer months. *L. camtschatcense* from Japan has white flowers and is less vigorous than its American counterpart.

Bog primulas provide some of our best waterside perennials, especially when grown in semi-shade with a background of moisture-loving ferns. Among the best are *P. florindae*, 0.7m (2½ft) sulphur-yellow flowers, June–July; *P. japonica splendens*, crimson-purple, May–June; *P. japonica* 'Postford White', an outstanding candelabra type with white flowers; *P. pulverulenta* 'Bartley Strain', rose-pink flowers, May–June and *P. viali*, with mauve flowers, which has bright red buds before opening.

Moisture-loving ferns make an excellent background for bog and water gardens with some shade. *Matteuccia struthiopteris*, the ostrich feather fern has symmetrical 1m (3ft) long fronds like a shuttlecock. *Onoclea sensibilis* (the sensitive fern) thrives in shade and moisture and has pale green fronds, 0.3–0.4m (1–1½ft) long; *Osmunda regalis* the royal fern is a noble plant, easily grown if given an adequate water supply. When well established it reaches 1.6–2m (5–6ft) in height and will set off any bog or water garden.

Bolting

An appropriate word used to describe a plant that produces flowers and seeds prematurely. It is an inherited tendency with some plants or strains and plant breeders avoid using such plants when selecting parent stock. Lettuce and beetroot are two crops that are liable to this trouble which may be brought on by drought when the plants are young, or by poor, starved soil.

Bone Meal see Fertilizers

Bonfires

There are several ways in which garden rubbish can be disposed of. Waste material may be incorporated in the compost heap or it may be dug into the ground during the autumn and winter soil preparations. There are, however, many occasions when it is advisable to burn rubbish, and the garden bonfire has an important part to play in the routine management.

One of the most important uses for a bonfire is for the disposal of diseased material. There are occasions, for example, when a particularly bad attack of potato blight, leaf mould, and black spot is experienced. This affected foliage must not be left lying around, nor should it be dug in when preparing the beds and borders. Affected material should be burnt as quickly as possible, and this is not always easy when the foliage is wet and green. It is surprising how much can be done if this material is quickly dried out by placing it carefully on top of a fierce bonfire, supported by netting or other suitable non-combustible material.

A bonfire comes into its own where a new or neglected site is taken over. There is often a good deal of waste material, such as pieces of timber and old or dead foliage which can be got rid of very quickly. Quite often there is a problem with waste disposal in the very small garden where the siting of a compost heap would either take up too much valuable growing room, or would look unsightly wherever it was positioned in the garden. Here, the use of a bonfire has much to commend it.

Bonfires are efficient only if they burn fiercely with a good red fire so that the amount of smoke produced is kept to the minimum. This can only be achieved if a constant draught is provided or plenty of air is allowed to enter the fire. The commercially produced incinerators are specially designed to provide this essential draught by having open sides and base. Most of the cheaper types consist of a wire framework which is so arranged that the bars are wide enough to hold a wide range of waste without dropping through. Unfortunately, some of these incinerators burn out after they have been in use for a few seasons. The more expensive types are moulded in thicker sections, are more substantial and have longer lives.

A bonfire made in an incinerator is easy to start and manage. Dry waste, such as old newspapers should be used to start the fire, and some dry foliage and pieces of old timber should be placed on top. Once a good red fire has been established, the remaining waste should be placed in the incinerator a little at a time. Quite a lot can be packed inside these incinerators without the danger of choking the fire, as the all-round open structure ensures that every part of the fire is constantly supplied with sufficient draught.

A successful bonfire can be made without an incinerator. It is essential to have an open base which can be provided by the selection of the coarsest and driest of the waste. Old branches and twiggy wood are ideal for this purpose. Old newspapers should also be worked in. Once the fire has gained a firm hold, the remainder of the waste should be added a little at a time.

It is of the utmost importance that a bonfire is sited where there is no danger that it can set fire to neighbouring property such as a shed, greenhouse or fence. It should be appreciated that a great deal of heat is created which can badly scorch plants, including trees and their foliage, if the bonfire is made too close to them.

It is a mere matter of good neighbourliness to refrain from lighting a bonfire when the wind is blowing towards neighbouring property, particularly when there is washing hanging on the line or in warm weather when the windows of nearby houses are open. This is of less importance, perhaps, when the bonfire is well made and the waste material burns quickly, without producing much smoke. Unfortunately, a bonfire that is not burning efficiently

1 Laying the bonfire, using dry material. 2 The initial feeding, using drier sticks. 3 The fire is going well and is fed with weeds and other damp material. 4 Quick combustion reduces the smoke.

and on which damp vegetable matter is being burned may burn slowly for hours, producing much evil-smelling smoke.

Where the Clean Air Act is in operation, provided that no undue smoke or nuisance is caused, there is usually no objection to the lighting of bonfires. The best course where there is any doubt, is to clear the matter up with the local town hall.

Borders see Herbaceous borders

Broad beans see Vegetables

Broccoli see Vegetables

Brussels sprouts see Vegetables

Bud stages
Sprays to control pests and diseases of fruit trees must be applied to the trees

according to the condition of their growth and not to calendar dates. Both tree growth and the development of disease depend upon weather conditions not the time of year. It is vital to apply the sprays at the right time. Buds and shoots may be damaged if caustic chemicals are applied too late: pests and diseases may be unaffected by too early applications.

The following are the bud stages for various fruits:

Apple: dormant, swelling, breaking, bursting, mouse-ear, green bud (or cluster), pink bud, petal fall (80 percent), and fruitlet (two to three weeks after petal fall); Pear: dormant, swelling, breaking, bursting, green bud (or cluster), white bud, petal fall (80 percent), and fruitlet (two to three weeks after petal fall); Plum: dormant, swelling, breaking, bursting, white bud, and cot split; Cherry: dormant, swelling, breaking, bursting, and white bud; Blackcurrant: dormant, breaking, bursting, and grape stage; Gooseberry: dormant, breaking, early flower, fruit set, and fruit swelling (approximately three weeks after fruit set); Raspberry: dormant, bursting, green bud, open flower, fruitlet, and pink fruit.

The dormant period is the time to kill pests which overwinter in the form of eggs and to free trees of moss and lichen by applying a winter wash. Caterpillars, aphids and several sap-sucking pests can be killed collectively up to, and during the green-bud stage. Other individual pests are controlled by spraying at the other specific stages.

Budding see Propagation

Bulb cultivation

Botanically, bulbs are buds, commonly subterranean, producing roots from their undersides, and consisting of layers of fleshy rudimentary leaves, called scales, attached to abbreviated stems. There is considerable uncertainty in the minds of many gardeners as to the difference between bulbs, corms, rhizomes and tubers, for their function is the same—to tide the plant over a period of adverse conditions, such as summer droughts and winter cold. All have common factors: food storage; rapid growth under suitable conditions; and the same life-cycle, in that during growth and flowering, next year's flower is formed in miniature, the foliage soon reaching maturity and dying away, as do the roots in most cases when the whole plant enters a period of rest.

A true bulb, such as that of a tulip, hyacinth or narcissus, is a bud surrounded by fleshy or scaly leaves, arising from a flat disc of 'basal plate'. In 'tunicated' bulbs the fleshy leaves are rolled close together, as in the tulip. In 'imbricated' bulbs the bulb leaves are thick and overlapping, as in the lily.

The determination of whether or not a

particular plant is a bulb depends upon the structure of the storage organ. If the botanical definition of the bulb is strictly accepted, many plants that gardeners ordinarily consider bulbs, such as crocuses, calla lilies, cannas and dahlias, must be eliminated. These and many other plants not technically true bulbs have bulb-like organs that function in the same way as bulbs but are not structurally scaly buds. They include rounded or flattish, solid, swollen stem bases called corms as in gladioli, crocuses; elongated thickened stems called rhizomes as in cannas, calla lilies, lily-of-the-valley; thickened terminal portions of stems called tubers as in anemones, begonias, caladiums; and swollen tuber-like roots as in dahlias.

Propagation This book will use the word 'bulb' like the ordinary gardener does and include all organs obviously bulb-like as well as true bulbs. Nearly all bulbs produce offsets sooner or later, and these, except for rarities, give

The flower bud stages of apple: 1 bud burst as growth commences in spring. 2 Mouse-ear (the size of the leaflets). 3 Pink bud. 4 Petal fall. Spray after petal fall to spare pollinating insects.

sufficient stock for the ordinary gardener. All that needs to be done is to dig up the clumps, separate the bulbs, sort out the small ones and replant them, treating them like mature bulbs until they reach the flowering stage. Rhizomes and tuberous roots may be treated in the same way, so each eye will produce another plant if care is taken of it. The exceptions are erythroniums, which rarely produce offsets, and cyclamen, which never do, and therefore can only be increased from seeds.

This leads to a consideration of raising bulbs from seed. Except for the most enthusiastic of amateurs, this should be left to the specialist. Where seed is produced, it is easy to obtain a supply, but the seed of many bulbs does not come true. That is the seedlings raised have characteristics which differ from their parents. There is also the question of cross fertilization to take into account, and, of course, raising bulbs from seed is a lengthy undertaking, often a risky one as well. However, with these provisos it may be said that raising lilies from seed is an interesting process.

Corms replace themselves annually. After having thrown up their leaves and flowers, each corm shrivels away and a new corm, sometimes several, forms while the leaves and flowers of the old one are growing.

Without bulbs all gardens would be the poorer the whole year round, but particularly in autumn, spring and summer. Bulbs are so popular because they yield such big rewards for so little in terms of money and care. Bulbs make it possible to have a continuous succession of colour outdoors and indoors throughout the year. Bulbs will flourish in virtually any kind of well-drained soil. Bulbs will thrive in almost every conceivable position or situation in the garden, in sun or partial shade. Bulbs offer infinite variety in colour, form and texture. When in bloom they vary from an inch or two in height to several feet and the characteristics of their foliage are as diverse as their flowers. The flowers of most bulbs last well when cut and are ideal for flower arrangements. Gardening with bulbs requires a minimum of work. Bulbs are easy to cultivate, giving a high percentage of successful results even for the beginner. Bulbs are not only inexpensive but are easily obtainable.

Planting Always purchase good-size, healthy bulbs from a reputable dealer. Early ordering is vital to ensure the best selection. Plant immediately the bulbs arrive and if this is inconvenient open the bags for ventilation and keep the bulbs in a cool, dry place until you are ready to plant them. Plant in well-drained soil. The vast majority of bulbs will do well in any soil provided it is well drained. It is advisable, however, to treat heavy soils with applications of peat or well-rotted leafmould.

The planting period for bulbs will depend upon their flowering season. The planting period for spring-flowering bulbs extends from September 1 to December 15 in Britain, but daffodils should be planted before the end of

Fritillaria meleagris, another spring-flowering bulbous plant is the chequered lily or snake's head, so called because of the colours of its drooping flowers borne in May.

October. Autumn-flowering bulbs (crocus and colchicum) should be planted in August. Most summer-flowering bulbs should be planted in March and April, although some, such as lilies, should be planted in November and December. Stem-rooting lilies can also be successfully set out in early spring.

Plant bulbs at the right depth. Although there are exceptions, bulbs are generally set with their tops about three times the diameter of the bulb below ground; small bulbs deeper proportionately. Usually it is the pointed end of the bulb which should be uppermost, but some tubers are planted horizontally. Some bulbs, such as anemones, give no indication which end is up, but there are usually signs of previous stem or root sources. Spring-flowering bulbs such as hyacinths, daffodils and tulips are planted 16cm (6in) deep and most spring-flowering small or miscellaneous bulbs are planted 8–10cm (3–4in) deep. Variation in depth depends upon the height of the stem and on the type of soil—the longer the stem and the lighter the soil, the deeper the planting.

No general guidance can be given on spacing of bulbs, for this may range from 2.5cm (1in) to 0.6m (2ft) apart, depending upon the size of the plant, its flower and foliage. Bulbs planted in

1 *Lilium 'Green Dragon' is one of the*
beautiful modern lilies known as olympic
hybrids, bred in Oregon, USA. It is not
a difficult bulb to grow, provided the
soil is well-drained.
2 *Crocuses are favourites for spring*
colour, but though listed by bulb mer-
chants they are not bulbs, but grow from
corms which are thickened stem bases,
renewed annually.
3 *Fritillaria imperialis is a spring-*
flowering bulb, usually known as crown
imperial. It grows from a large, rounded
bulb and sends up a stem about 1m (3ft)
tall. The nodding flowers are borne in
May. There are various colour forms.

groups or clusters produce the best effects, and if flowers are wanted for indoor decoration extra bulbs should be planted in the vegetable garden or special cutting garden.

Bulbs can be grown virtually anywhere in the garden. There is a place in every garden for some kinds of bulbs in beds, borders, edges, shrubberies, rock gardens, orchards, woodlands, lawns, on walls, between paving stones, in tubs or window-boxes. Many bulbs can be naturalised, that is, planted in informal groups or drifts and left to increase naturally. This is often done in rough grass or woodland, The grass should be left uncut until the bulb foliage has died down naturally, usually in June.

Most bulbs do not require full sun but can be planted in partial shade. Indeed, partial shade makes for longer lasting blooms. Flowers should be removed when petals fade and the foliage should not be cut off, but should be allowed to die down naturally, permitting the bulb to replace energy and flower the following season. Most spring-flowering bulbs (the exceptions are lilies, anemones and ranunculuses which require winter protection) should be lifted. Lift bulbs carefully only after the foliage has died down and store them in a cool, frost-free and well-ventilated place until it is time to replant them again. Generally, if bulbs are doing well, natural increase will make lifting of the clumps and separation of the bulbs necessary every few years. Be careful when separating clumps of bulbs not to damage them. Bulbs should always be handled carefully to avoid physical injury.

The most commonly grown bulb flowers in our gardens are narcissi, tulips and hyacinths, with lilies, snowdrops, grape hyacinths and several others also represented in the list.

Daffodil is merely the common name for narcissus, of which there are more than 10,000 named varieties, with some 500 in normal commercial cultivation.

With the exception of one or two kinds, such as tazettas, narcissi are hardy, tolerant and adaptable plants. They will grow in almost any situation except heavy shade or in badly-drained soil. In open ground they flower from February to the end of May. Normally most varieties remain in flower for three to four weeks and if they are picked in bud for cut flowers they will last in water for ten days or more.

Narcissi will flourish in beds and borders, naturalised in meadows, open woodlands, lawns, orchards or under scattered trees, among shrubs, in tubs and window boxes. The smaller kinds do well in rock gardens and many varieties are suitable for forcing.

Out of doors daffodils will flourish in any well-drained soil although *N. bulbocodium* prefers sandy soil and *N. cyclamineus* peaty soil. The best sites are in sun or light shade with shelter from sweeping winds. Plant the bulbs as early in the autumn as they can be obtained. Robust kinds that have large bulbs should be planted 13–16cm (5–6in) deep, less vigorous kinds with smaller bulbs 8–10cm (3–4in) deep, and tiny species 8cm (3in) deep. Space vigorous growers 16–23cm (6–9in) apart, moderately vigorous growers 10–13cm (4–5in) apart, and small species 6–10cm (2–4in) apart. In naturalised plantings these distances are varied considerably and it is best to scatter the bulbs at random, in groups or drifts, planting them exactly where they fall.

For planting bulbs out of doors, especially in turf, special planting tools are available. Some of these are long-handled tools, shod with a circular metal cutter which is forced into the soil. When the tool is lifted a core of turf and soil is removed intact. A bulb is then placed in the hole and the core of turf replaced over it and firmed with the foot. To enable the cutter to be driven easily into hard turf the tool is fitted with a foot bar. There are versions of this tool with short handles, without the foot bar. Otherwise, when planting in soil or in the rock garden it is always advisable to do so with a trowel, never with a dibber. If a dibber is used an air pocket may be left below the bulb, into which the roots will not grow, thus preventing proper development. If the soil is dry, water thoroughly after planting.

Where winters are severe, protect bulbs which are not planted in grass with a covering of leaves or other suitable material. Feed established plantings in early autumn and early spring, using a complete fertilizer in spring and a slower-acting organic fertilizer in the autumn. Water copiously during dry spells when the foliage is above ground. Never remove the foliage until it has died down naturally. When plantings become crowded so that the bloom deteriorates in quantity and quality, lift, separate and replant the bulbs as soon as the foliage has died down.

Tulips are equally numerous, with several thousand named varieties and some 800 in commercial cultivation. They differ more than narcissi and are divided into 23 main groups of classes, of interest mainly to the specialist.

Some tulips flower early (in mid-April, some in mid-season (late April),

Narcissus 'February Gold' is an early-flowering, long-lasting plant with bold trumpets of a fine golden-yellow.

and others bloom late, in May. The colour range is from white to almost black, from softest pink to deepest purple; there are broken colours, self-colours, striped, streaked, shaded and tinged. Some have oval flowers, some are shaped like turbans, and others are square at the base. Some tulips resemble paeonies, others have lily-like flowers. There are tulips with fringed or curled petals and others with pointed petals. A number produce several flowers on a stem. Some have tiny flowers, while others produce blooms up to 38cm (15in) in diameter. Heights range from a few cm to nearly 1m (3ft).

Cultivation Bulbs can be planted out of doors between mid-September and mid-December. Species or botanical tulips should be planted 10cm (4in) deep and about 13cm (5in) apart with the exception of *T. fosteriana*, which should be planted 13–16cm (5–6in) deep and some 16cm (6in) apart, like all divisions of garden tulips. Good drainage is essential; they will thrive in virtually any well-drained soil, but in light sandy soils the bulbs should be planted a little deeper than normal. Tulips can be interplanted with roses or with annuals or with other bulbs flowering at the same time, taking into account the differing heights of other plants when interplanting. Species tulips do best in sunny positions, but garden tulips can be planted in sun or in partial shade. Early-flowering garden tulips planted in sheltered sunny spots will come into flower sooner, or if late-flowering tulips are planted in partial shade, they will last longer.

Apart from *kaufmanniana* tulips which are naturalized, all tulips should be lifted every year when the foliage has turned completely yellow and begun to die off. The old flower stems should be cut off a little above the newly formed bulbs at the end of June or early July. They should, under no circumstances, be left on the bulb in storage trays. If the bulbs must be cleared from the ground before the foliage begins to die, to make way for other bedding plants, they may be lifted and heeled into a shallow trench in a spare corner until the leaves yellow. The lifted bulbs should be kept out of sunlight, cleaned and stored in a cool, airy, frost-free place until planting time comes round again. Indoor cultivation is the same procedure as narcissus, but forced tulip bulbs are not really worth keeping for later outdoor planting.

There are far fewer hyacinths than tulips or daffodils, but because of their beauty and their perfume they continue to be firm favourites for the garden.

Cultivation Bedding hyacinths are best planted in late October about 10cm (4in) deep in well-drained soil and in a sunny position. Space the bulbs about 20cm (8in) apart for maximum colour effect. Bone meal forked into the soil before planting at the rate of 112g (4oz) to the sq m (sq yd) will ensure good heads of flower in April.

Watering, feeding, mulching It is essential for all bulbs to have plenty of moisture when growing actively, but excess water during the dormant period is harmful. Like all plants, bulbs respond to fertile soil, but manures and fertilizers must be used carefully. Well-rotted manure improves soil structure and provides nutrients for all plants and may be used to advantage with bulbs as long as there is a protective layer of soil

A Recommended List of Bulbs

Early Spring (February–March)

Botanical Name	Common Name	Botanical Name	Common Name	Botanical Name	Common Name
Camassia	Quamash	*Iris reticulata*	Iris	Tulipa	Tulip
Chionodoxa	Glory of the Snow	*Iris danfordiae*		(Species tulips)	
Crocus	Crocus	*Leucojum vernum*	Spring Snowflake	*T. kaufmanniana*	
Eranthis	Winter Aconite	*Narcissus*		*T. fosteriana*	
Galanthus	Snowdrop	*cyclamineus*		*T. greigii*	
Ipheion uniflorum		*Scilla sibirica*	Siberian Squill		

Mid-season (March–April)

Hyacinthus	Hyacinths	Narcissus	Daffodil	Tulipa	Tulip
Muscari	Grape Hyacinth	Medium Cupped		Double Early	
Narcissus	Daffodil	Tulipa	Tulip	Triumph	
Trumpet		Single Early		Mendel	

Late (April–May)

Iris (Dutch)	Iris	Tulipa	Tulip	Tulipa	Tulip
Narcissus	Daffodil	Lily-flowered		Darwin Hybrid	
Short Cupped		Double Late		Parrot	
Scilla campanulata	Spanish Squill	Paeony-flowered		Cottage	
				Darwin	

Summer (June–September)

Acidanthera	Abyssinian Wildflower	Galtonia	Spire Lily	*Ornithogalum thyrsoides*	Chincherinchee
Anemone	Windflower	Gladiolus	Gladiolus	Ranunculus	
Begonia	Begonia	Iris	Iris	Sparaxis	African Harlequin Flower
Brodiaea		English Spanish			
Crinum	Cape Lily	Ismene		Tigridia	Shell Flower
Crocosmia		*Leucojum aestivum*	Summer Snowflake	*Vallota speciosa*	Scarborough Lily
Dahlia	Dahlia	Lilium	Lily	Zantedeschia	Arum Lily
Freesia	Freesia	Montbretia	Montbretia		

Autumn (September–November)

Crocus (some)	Crocus	Sternbergia	Winter Daffodil	*Zephyranthes candida*	Flower of the West Wind
Colchicum	Autumn Crocus				

Rock Garden

Chionodoxa	Glory of the Snow	Galanthus	Snowdrop	Narcissus	Daffodil
Crocus	Crocus	*Ipheion uniflorum*		Dwarf Species	
Erythronium dens-canis	Dog's Tooth Violet	Iris	Iris	*Scilla sibirica*	Siberian Squill
Fritillaria Dwarf Species		Dwarf Species		*Sternbergia lutea*	Winter Daffodil
		Muscari	Grape Hyacinth	Tulipa Species	Tulip

Naturalising

Anemone blanda		*Endymion nonscriptus*	Bluebell	Leujocum	Snowflake
Camassia	Quamash	Eranthis	Winter Aconite	Muscari	Grape Hyacinth
Colchicum	Autumn Crocus	*Erythronium dens-canis*	Dog's Tooth Violet	Narcissus	Daffodil
Crocus spring and autumn-flowering	Crocus	*Fritillaria meleagris*	Chequered Lily	*Ornithogalum umbellatum*	Star of Bethlehem
		Galanthus	Snowdrop	*Puschkinia libanotica*	Striped Squill
				Scilla sibirica	Siberian Squill

Cut Flowers

Alstroemeria	Peruvian Lily	Iris	Iris	*Ornithogalum umbellatum arabicum pyramidale*	Star of Bethlehem
Anemone De Caen St. Brigid, etc.	Windflower	Spanish English		Ranunculus	
Convallaria majalis	Lily-of-the Valley	Lilium	Lily	Scilla	Squill
		Montbretia	Montbretia		
Crocus chrysanthus	Crocus	Muscari	Grape Hyacinth	Tulipa Taller Species all tall-stemmed garden tulips	Tulip
Dahlia	Dahlia	*Narcissus triandrus*			
Freesia	Freesia	*N. cyclamineus*			
Gladiolus	Gladiolus	*N. jonquilla*		Tritonia	
Iris Dutch	Iris	Doubles Trumpet Small Cupped *N. poeticus*		Ixia	African Corn Lily

between the bulbs and the manure. Fresh manure should never be used. Slow-acting fertilizers other than manure are particularly recommended for feeding bulbs. Bonemeal is one of the best and 3kg (6lb) to a 11sq m (100 sq ft) is not too heavy an annual application.

Mulches are useful in the summer to help the soil to retain moisture and peat is excellent for this purpose. Mulches intended for protective winter covering should be applied to the surface of the ground after the ground has frozen and should be removed after bulb growth is under way in the spring.

Weeds, pests, diseases Areas planted with bulbs should be kept as free of weeds as possible and the surface soil should be loosened from time to time. Injured or infected foliage should be removed and burned. Diseases can be avoided by buying only healthy, top quality bulbs, and few gardeners who do this are troubled by diseases.

The major pests are slugs and snails and fortunately these can be controlled by modern slug killers. In dealing with any diseases or pests, proper diagnosis is important before resorting to drastic measures. Should a disease appear among a planting, lift the healthy bulbs, disinfect them, and move them to an area not previously used for growing bulbs of the same kind. This will usually save them from infection.

Cabbages see Vegetables

Cactus cultivation
The growing and collecting of cacti has been a popular hobby in this country for many years. Their varied shapes and colours together with the coloured

1 Preparing a pot before sowing cactus seeds. 2 Sowing the seeds. 3 The seedlings have appeared. 4 Crocking a pot for drainage before pricking out the seedlings. 5 Pricking out the tiny seedlings. 6 Potting a larger specimen, using a spoon to place compost round the plant. 7 Firming the soil. 8 Grafting a cactus.

1

2

3

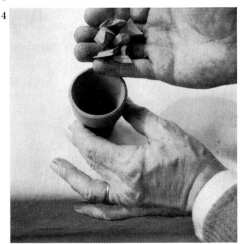

4

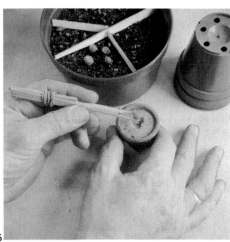

5

6

7

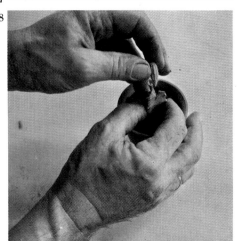

8

spines make them fascinating and their spectacular flowers are an added interest for the grower. Some of the larger types may not flower in this country owing to the lack of intense sunshine, but many hundreds of other species should flower every year.

Flowering cacti Some species flower the year after the seed has been sown, while very many more can produce flowers within two years. As the native habitats of these plants are arid regions it is essential that they be allowed all the sunshine possible to enable them to grow at their best. Most cacti come from Mexico and the southern States of the USA, and also from many countries in South America, including Peru, Paraguay, Uruguay, Chile and Brazil. A few are found in the West Indies but none in Africa, India or anywhere in the east.

Defining cacti All cacti are succulents but not all succulents are cacti. Spines are found on all true cacti and these spines grown from a small tuft of hair or wool. This is known as an areole and no other plant has it. No cacti have leaves except the genus *Pereskia*. This plant has areoles and leaves and also a multiple flower, unlike true cacti which have a simple or single flower. The flowers of cacti have no stem or stalk, the ovary being connected directly with the plant. Exceptions to this rule are the pereskias.

The flowers of most cacti are formed at the areole but a few genera produce flowers away from this point. Plants of the genus *Mammillaria* produce their flowers at the axil, the spot between the tubercles. This genus also makes new plants or offsets at the axil as well, whereas most cacti make offsets at an areole. The flowers of cacti vary considerably in size from 1cm (⅓in) in some mammillarias to 36cm (14in) across in some of the night-flowering types. The larger flowers may not be produced in profusion but some of the cacti with smaller flowers can have rings of flowers all round the top of the plants for months at a time.

Cacti are often described as desert plants but this is not quite true. Many are found in prairie type country where there may be a few small trees and shrubs with coarse grasses intermingled. Some are found in good loam while others are found growing on rocks and the mountain side. Some of the best flowering cacti, the epiphyllums, grow in the forests of Brazil, usually on trees. Such cacti are classed as epiphytes or epiphytic cacti.

1 Echinocactus, Opuntia and Mammillaria form part of a collection of cacti and other succulents 2 Brilliantly colourful when in flower, cacti are not difficult to raise from seed 3 Very tolerant of neglect, cacti are becoming increasingly popular as house plants for sunny-window-ledges.

40

As cacti vary so much in size from perhaps 2.5cm (1in) to 10m (30ft) or more there are many species available to the grower to suit almost any situation or condition. Although the best place to grow a collection of cacti is in a sunny greenhouse, there are many kinds which can be grown quite well in a sunny window.

Although all cacti can go for long periods without water, it is essential that they are provided with an adequate supply during the growing period or they cannot flourish.

To grow cacti well and flower them it is imperative to provide them with a porous soil as the roots soon rot if they are wet for days on end. Many types of potting soils have been used and recommended, even different ones for each genus; it is possible, however, to grow practically all types of cacti in one kind of potting compost. The art of growing cacti is in the watering and the amount given can vary according to the type of compost. Plants can only obtain their nourishment in a liquid form and so if little water is given the plant cannot obtain too much food.

Potting composts A very good potting compost for cacti may be made up from John Innes potting compost No. 1, to which is added a sixth part of coarse sand to make it more porous. Some additions of broken brick or granulated charcoal may be incorporated in the added sand. If it is desired to mix a compost for general use, the following will be found quite reliable. Take 2 parts of loam, 1 part of peat and 1 part of sharp, coarse sand. Mix well and to each bushel add 21g (¾oz) of ground chalk or limestone, 21g (¾oz) sulphate of potash, 42g (1½oz) of superphosphate and 42g (1½oz) of hoof and horn grist. All the globular and columnar types of cacti may be grown in this compost, while for the epiphytes some John Innes potting compost No. 2, may be used, as these plants will benefit from the richer soil. The very spiny types of cacti do not require heavy feeding with fertilizers and as long as they are repotted at least every two years they will grow quite well. If these plants are fed too liberally they will become lush, open in texture, and be very liable to rot off in the winter. Also it will be found that the spines formed when the plant has been fed with fertilizers may not be as stout and well coloured as if the plant had been grown harder. When making up the cactus compost it is very important to find a good loam as a basis for the mixture. An ideal type is the top spit from an old-standing meadow. Unfortunately these meadows are becoming few and far between and the loam is often only the under spit after the top turf has been removed. The peat is not so important but the sand must be very sharp and coarse. Silver sand is useless for cactus compost and the type known as washed

Cacti and other succulents offer the enthusiast remarkable variety not only in flower colour but also in habit of growth.

grit, or river grit is the best.

The potting compost should not be used immediately after it has been mixed and a lapse of a fortnight at least is desirable before potting. The time to repot varies considerably, being determined by many factors. Some cacti are very slow growers and so may be left in their pots for two or three years while others may need a move twice a year. Many cacti never flower because they have been in the same stale, worn-out soil for many years. With fairly frequent watering during the growing period the roots of the plant use up the nourishment in the soil, and clearly there can be little food value left in it after about a year.

Repotting The best time for repotting is during the growing period, which with most cacti will be between March and September. Once new growth is seen on a plant it can be repotted. When dealing with a fairly large collection it will be found better to make a start with the larger pots. These can then be cleaned for use with other plants which may need a bigger pot. It is also a good plan to make a clear place in the greenhouse and place all repotted plants there so that none may be missed. The pots should be clean and well crocked. It is unnecessary to place a large number of crocks in the pot as they will only take up valuable space which would be better occupied by good soil. The best

way to crock a pot for a cactus is to cut as large a piece of broken flower pot as will lie in the bottom of the pot. This large crock will then form a kind of platform when the plant is removed the next time. If a stick is pushed up through the drainage hole the crock will force the whole ball of soil up in the pot, whereas if a number of small pieces of crock are used it is possible to damage the roots when trying to remove the plant another time.

Place some of the coarsest particles of compost over the crock and then a little soil. Remove the plant from the old pot and hold it by the root system. Gently work all the old soil away from the roots. If any appear dead they should be cut-away. Now rest the plant in the pot and gradually work in some fresh compost. Because most of the plants are spiny it may not be possible to work the soil in with the hands as is possible with ordinary plants. A tablespoon can be used to insert the soil and it can be gently firmed in with an old table-knife handle. A wooden stick must not be used as it would catch in the spines and break them. Once a spine is broken it will never grow again. See that the plant is in the same relative position in the soil as it was before. See also that at least 1cm (½in) of space is left at the top of the pot for watering. The plant should look right in the new pot; do not use one too large so that the plant looks lost or yet one so small that there is no room for soil as well as the base and roots of the plant. For the globular kinds of cacti a pot which is 1cm (½in) bigger all round than the plant will do for pots up to 9cm (3½in) in diameter, but for a larger plant a pot at least 2.5cm (1in) larger all round must be provided. This will not be sufficient for many of the taller growing types as the pot must be large enough to form a firm base to stop the plant and pot from falling over.

Plastic pots may be used, especially for small plants; they do not appear to dry out as quickly as clay pots. Once the plant is potted it is important to insert the label, and a good plan is to put the date of repotting on the back. This is a useful guide in a large collection. As it is essential that the soil should be able to discharge all surplus water as soon as possible, the pots should not be stood on a flat surface. Some coarse gravel makes an ideal base on which to stand the pots. If slats are provided in the greenhouse it is better to cover them with corrugated asbestos sheeting on which the gravel may be placed. Any plants stood on shelves must have a saucer containing gravel under them to allow the free removal of surplus water.

Watering cacti Watering the plants presents the most important part of cactus culture. More plants are lost through overwatering than from any other cause. As has been stated before, cacti will not grow without water but if they get too much they can soon die. Newly potted cacti should not need watering for about a week. The potting soil should have been crumbly moist at the time of moving the plant. If it is too wet or too dry it cannot be firmed in the correct manner. The whole secret of watering can be described in one sentence. Never water a plant if the soil is still damp. It is not easy to tell when a cactus needs watering. Ordinary plants soon show by drooping leaves when water is required, but cacti cannot show their needs in this way. The condition of the top of the soil will indicate when water is needed. After a hot day the soil may appear dry, but this may only be the top inch. If pots are inspected in the mornings the soil should be of a uniform dampness throughout.

Rain water is better than tap water but if rain water is not available let some tap water stand in the open for a day or two before it is used. Water may be given from a can with a small spout so that it can be directed into any pot. Do not water by immersion except for the first watering after the winter. If plants are watered this way often, all the nourishing matter will soon be washed out of the pot. Cacti may be sprayed in the evening of a hot day. No water need be given from the end of September to early March. Then water when the soil has dried out, not before. The Christmas cactus, *Zygocactus truncatus*, may be watered during the winter as long as the temperature is not below 50°F (10°C). Other cacti may be left at 40°F (8°C), so that they get a winter's rest.

Taking cuttings Propagation is by cut-

1 Mammillaria geminispina. 2 Aporocactus flagelliformis, the rat-tailed cactus. Both these are easy to grow on a sunny window-sill and should produce flowers regularly each year.

tings, taking offsets or by seed raising. Cuttings taken from opuntias and epiphyllums are removed with a sharp knife and the cut part is allowed to dry in the sun. The cuttings are then rested on a mixture of equal parts of peat and sharp sand (not silver sand). Cactus potting compost may be used to fill three quarters of the pot, with the rooting medium on top. Place in a sunny position and spray occasionally. Too much water must not be given until roots have formed. Tall cuttings will have to be supported by a stick, as they must not be pushed into the medium.

Grafting Grafting may be done to assist the growth of a small, slow-growing type. A tall type is used for the stock, such as *Trichocereus spachianus*. The top is cut from the stock where the growth is new and healthy. The scion is cut at the base so that it is about the size of the top of the stock. It is brought in contact with the freshly cut stock and kept in position with two small weights on a piece of string, pressing the scion down firmly. Keep in the shade for a

week or two and a firm joint will form.
Raising cacti from seed Some cacti never make offsets and these have to be raised from seed. A small propagating frame can easily be made and heated with an electric cable or even an electric lamp. Half-pots of about 10cm (4in) in diameter are very good for sowing small quantities of seed. They can even be divided with celluloid labels if more than one species is to be sown in the pot. Use John Innes seed compost and sieve a small quantity through a perforated zinc sieve.

Place the coarse material over the crock and then top up with ordinary compost, having an inch of the fine soil on top. Small seed must not be buried, but fairly large seeds can be just pushed into the soil. Water the first time by standing in containers of water so that the whole soil can be well moistened. Place in the frame with a piece of glass on top and then cover with dark paper. The best time to sow is in early spring, in a temperature of 70°F (21°C); seeds will germinate at a lower temperature but will take longer to do so. Once seedlings have appeared, the paper must be removed and the glass should be raised slightly. The seedlings must be kept from the direct sun for the first year but they must have plenty of light or they will become drawn. Do not allow the seed pots to dry out while germination is taking place; watering may be done with a fine spray.

Prick out when the cotyledon or food-bag has been absorbed. Before this the root is so tiny that it can be broken very easily, in which case the seedling would die. The seedlings may be placed 2.5cm (1in) apart in the cactus compost as described above. Do not pot up too soon into small pots as these dry out very quickly. Boxes made of concrete or plastic are better for the seedlings until they are ready to go into 5cm (2in) pots.
Summer treatment Cacti may be planted out in beds from June to September. If they are removed from their pots it may be quite impossible to put them back in the same sized pots in the late summer or autumn. They may be left in their pots, but the drainage hole must be freed from soil when they are removed. A few cacti may stand the winter out of doors but a very severe winter would probably kill them. If the grower wishes to experiment, he should make sure that any cacti left out during the winter are those which can be parted with, and not specimen plants.

All the spiny types of cacti can stand plenty of sunshine as long as there is plenty of air available in a greenhouse. The epiphytes benefit from shade during the hotter months of the year, and may be stood outside the greenhouse provided no frosts are forecast. Cacti kept in windows of the house must be where they can get the maximum amount of light and they will not flower well unless they can get a fair amount of sunshine.

Most cacti flower in spring, summer or autumn, and it will be found that many flower on new growth only. If the flowers are pollinated many colourful seed pods can be formed. On the mammillarias these pods can look very attractive.

Miniature cactus gardens Cacti are very suitable for miniature gardens. The bowl need not have drainage holes provided it is not overwatered. Place some crocks in the bottom and only half fill with a porous soil. When the plants are in position the rest of the soil may be added and firmed. If the soil under a flat stone, pressed into the top of the soil, is damp do not water.

Pests If cacti are grown well they suffer little disease but there are a few pests which may attack a sick plant. The most frequent one is mealy bug. This appears in a small tuft of wool or powder. Scale may also attack some cacti and looks like a small scab. Red spider may be a nuisance if the atmosphere is too dry. All these pests can be killed with malathion, used as directed on the bottle.

Choosing cacti Many species of cacti from the following genera grow well on a window ledge. chamaecereus, echinopsis, epiphyllum, gymnocalycium, lobivia, mammillaria, notocactus, opuntia, rebutia and zygocactus. A few of the smaller types of cereus can be grown and *Cleistocactus strausii* will also grow for many years before it gets too large. The dwarf types of opuntias, such as *Opuntia microdasys*, too will be suitable.

For planting in bowl gardens any of the small plants of the above genera will be a good choice but not the epiphyllums unless they are very small. If any of the plants grow too large for the bowl they can be removed and replaced by a smaller specimen. A suitable collection in a bowl can last for many years without it being necessary to change any plant.

Carrots see Vegetables

Catch cropping

The term applied to a short period crop which is planted in vacant ground and matures before the main crop is planted. A crop which can be grown and used before the main crop grows sufficiently to require the total space available. A catch crop such as lettuce, spinach, turnip or radish is frequently grown on the ridges of celery trenches in June and July, before the celery has made much growth or, on rich, good growing soils, dwarf beans may be used for this purpose. In cloche gardening, catch crops are even more popular. So that the maximum use is made of the glass available, plant lettuce on either side of a crop of autumn sown peas. The lettuce matures as the cloches are removed in April. In glasshouses and frames, lettuce, radish or carrots can be grown between the main crop of tomatoes during early summer or, if glass is at a premium, the catch crop can be grown in pots or boxes, e.g. tomatoes for outdoor planting of ornamental plants grown for bedding purposes.

Cauliflower see Vegetables

Ground that will be occupied later in the season can be used, for an early catch crop. 1 Lettuce on the ridges of celery trenches. 2 Lettuce as a catch crop with runner beans.

Celeriac see Vegetables

Celery see Vegetables

Charcoal

Charcoal is charred wood containing a large amount of unburnt carbon. This not only assists in drainage, but also corrects an acid soil and will prevent sourness if a piece the size of a thimble is placed at the bottom of a flower pot. When moist in the soil, charcoal absorbs gases and is said to produce carbonic acid which is so beneficial to plant life. It may be used either crushed or in small pieces. A knob the size of a walnut placed in the bottom of a hyacinth glass will keep the water clear throughout growth. Charcoal is used in bulb and other composts. Powdered charcoal stops the bleeding of stem cuttings in the propagation of plants like ficus and monstera.

Cherries see Fruit

Chicory see Vegetables

Chives see Herbs

Clamp

This is the structure used for storing roots, particularly vegetables in the open during the winter. It consists essentially in covering a pile of roots with a layer of straw and earth to protect them from frost and rain. The natural respiration of the roots within a clamp engenders a little heat, which prevents the temperature within sinking to a dangerous level in the winter. A clamp may be a conical pile of roots or a ridge-like heap. It must be built on

well-drained land, or have a trench dug round the site and the soil dug out and put on to the clamp base to raise it and provide drainage. This is then covered with a good layer of clean straw 30cm (1ft) thick. The roots are then piled on evenly to form a heap or pile. The sides should be kept as steep as possible to prevent the penetration of rain water. Next clean straw is piled over the roots, again 30cm (1ft) thick; this is covered with a layer of soil about 25cm (9in) thick which is well beaten down with the back of a spade. Some ventilation must be provided; this is done by pulling up a little of the straw through a vent hole in the middle of the ridge, or at several places in the ridge if the clamp is large. Suitable sectional dimensions for a ridge clamp are base 1.2-1.5m (4-5ft) wide and height at the ridge 90cm-1.2m (3-4ft).

Garden clamps are mostly used for potatoes, but other vegetables, such as beets, swedes and turnips may be clamped, as may also dahlia tubers. If carrots are clamped stack them so that the top ends are outwards, use no straw and cover with sand or sifted ashes. Do not allow beets to sprout in the spring when in the clamp as they will allow aphids to multiply and spread disease to sugar beet and other crops.

After opening a clamp in winter to extract some of the contents make sure that it is sealed again to protect the contents against frost. Care must be taken, particularly with potatoes, to put only healthy tubers in a clamp. Potatoes infested with blight will spread the disease rapidly through the clamp.

Climbing plants

House walls, garden walls, fences, archways, pergolas, trellises, poles, either single or erected tripod fashion and other vertical or near-vertical features, provide the gardener with another dimension in which to grow plants. There are attractive plants available for this purpose, many of which benefit from the extra shelter provided by a wall or fence.

Types of plant Suitable plants include those which are true climbers, clinging to some form of support, either by tendrils (e.g. clematis), by twining stems (e.g. honeysuckles) and those known as self-clinging climbers, which adhere to their supports by aerial roots (e.g. the ivies) or by sucker-pads (e.g. the Virginian creeper and some of its relations). In addition to these true climbers, there are many woody or semi-woody plants which are not, in fact, climbers but may be trained against walls. Examples of these are the well-known chaenomeles ('japonica'), climbing roses, ceanothus and certain cotoneasters.

Types of support Self-clinging climbers need little in the way of extra support except in their early stages. Once started they cling to walls, fences and the like and need little more attention.

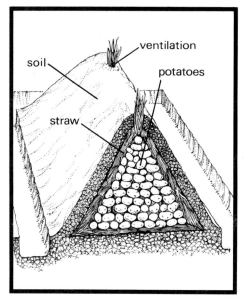

A section of a potato clamp showing construction. Good drainage and the exclusion of frost are vital.

Some gardeners are a little wary of the more vigorous self-clinging climbers such as ivies, but, provided they are not allowed to interfere with drain-pipes, guttering, roof tiles or slates, etc., they are unlikely to harm the wall itself. It can be argued that they help to keep the wall dry and the house warm, by providing a leafy covering which keeps off even the heaviest rain.

Tendril climbers and twining climbers obviously need something to which to cling. In the open, garden poles, driven

vertically into the ground or set tripod fashion, pergola posts and archways will provide support for twiners, but not for tendril climbers. These will need further support such as wire-netting placed loosely round the poles to which the tendrils can cling. The growths of non-climbers will need tying in to the support as they develop.

Against walls and fences there are various ways of providing support for plants. Trellis-work is a well-tried method and panels may be bought in various sizes. Before they are fixed to the wall they should be treated with a copper naphthenate wood preservative to prolong their lives. Suitable trellis may also be made at home, using lathing, which is obtainable cheaply from builders' merchants or timber merchants. It may be made to a square-mesh pattern or to the traditional diamond mesh. So that the growths of the climbing plants can attach themselves properly the trellis should be fixed 3-5cm (1-2in) away from the wall, using wooden distance pieces or spacers. Old cotton-reels are useful because they have a hole through which the fixing screw may pass. All fixing should be done firmly as eventually the mature plant may be quite heavy. Wall fixings such as Rawlplugs are admirable; an electric drill with a masonry bit is useful but not essential as the necessary fixing holes for the plugs can be made with a hammer and jumping bit. Where walls are painted or otherwise treated it is handy to arrange the trellis in such a manner that it can be easily taken down to enable the wall behind it to be painted. One way of doing this is to hinge the bottom of the trellis to a wooden bar of suitable dimensions fixed to the wall. The top of the trellis is fixed to a similar bar in such a way that it can be undone and the trellis and its plants gently lowered, thus minimising the risk of damage to the plants.

Panels of plastic-covered, heavy gauge wire-netting (Gro-Mesh) are obtainable in various sizes, and these provide excellent support for plants. They may be fixed to the wall in much the same way as wooden trellis.

Wires, preferably covered, stretched across the face of a wall or fence, about 2.5cm (1in) away from it, will also provide adequate support for many plants. However, unless the wire is properly strained it may sag in course of time. Vine eyes (drive-in pattern for walls, driven into the perpendicular jointing, screw-in type for wooden posts) are useful devices for fixing wires for climbing plants. Straining bolts, which can be tightened when necessary to take up any

Many climbing honeysuckles are well known for their delightful fragrance. They are not difficult to grow in any ordinary soil if trained over arches or bushes as in the wild state.

slack are also obtainable. Lead-headed wall nails, nails with flexible lead tags, are used for individual ties, when it becomes necessary to tie in long, woody growths such as those of climbing or rambler roses.

An unusual way of growing certain climbers such as clematis, honeysuckles, is to let them clamber over dead trees or even up the trunks and into the branches of living trees. It is better to avoid for living trees the very vigorous climbers such as *Polygonum baldschuanicum*, the Russian vine, although this is perfectly suitable for a dead tree, which it will quickly smother with its long, twining growths.

Some climbers may easily be grown in well-drained tubs or other large containers and this method is useful where there is no soil bed near the wall, or in courtyards, patios or on town balconies. John Innes potting compost is suitable but vigorous plants may need regular feeding when in full growth.

Preparing the site Most climbers and other wall plants will grow in ordinary garden soil, but of course, they will grow better and begin to cover their allotted space more quickly if they are given, a richer diet. The soil should be deeply and widely dug, adequately

drained, and the opportunity should be taken to dig in a good supply of garden compost, well-rotted manure, leafmould, spent hops, and other bulky manures, plus about 110g (4oz) per square metre (yard) of bonemeal, well worked into the top 15cm (6in) or so of soil. Sites by walls present certain problems which are not always appreciated by gardeners. The soil in such places is often poor, full of builders' rubble and other rubbish buried when the house was built. It is often dry, protected from rain by overhanging eaves. To ensure that the plants do well it is necessary to carry out considerable soil improvement. In some instances it may pay to remove the existing poor soil and rubble to a depth of a foot or so and replace it with good soil from elsewhere in the garden, adding quantities of rotted manure, compost, leafmould etc., all of which will not only provide plant foods but will also help the soil to retain moisture. Even so, in periods of drought, it may be necessary to water copiously, soaking the site from time to time.

If the soil is replaced it should be

The garden brought into contact with the house by means of wall plants such as wisteria and clematis, flowering in May.

allowed to settle for some weeks before planting is done. During this time the wall supports can be fixed in position.

Planting The footings of walls usually project beyond the line of the wall itself and to avoid these and the drier soil at the base of the wall, the plant should not be closer to the foot of the wall than 15cm (6in). Where there is enough room, a planting hole about 60cm (2ft) wide and 46-60cm (1½-2ft) deep should be taken out, to allow sufficient room for the roots to be spread out properly. If the soil is heavy clay it is better not to replace it but to use instead some specially made up planting soil. The basis of this might be old potting soil or good loam to which should be added generous quantities of garden compost and leafmould plus a couple of handfuls of bonemeal per barrow-load of the mixture to provide slow-acting food.

The roots of the plants should be well spread out round the hole, not cramped up or doubled over. Many climbers arrive in pots and to avoid damaging the roots it may be necessary to break the pot and gently tease out the drainage crocks and spread out the roots. Some plants arrive with their roots 'balled-up' in sacking. With these the root ball should be preserved; it is necessary only

to cut the ties, after the plant has been placed in position in a planting hole of suitable size, and pull away the sacking. If this is difficult it may be left in place as it will rot away gradually and the roots will, in any case, grow through it into the soil beyond.

Planting should be done firmly, returning a little soil round the roots first and working this in among them and firming it with the hands. More soil is then added and firmed with the boot, provided the roots are adequately covered, until the hole is filled. The soil-mark on the stem gives a guide to the correct depth to plant, although it is usually best to plant clematis a little deeper than is indicated by the soil-mark generally given.

Some temporary support should be provided for the plants until their growths reach the wire, trellis or other support and can begin to cling or twine. Even though this is temporary it should be firmly fixed to prevent the growths blowing about and being damaged. Short canes, twiggy sticks, strings or wires fixed to pegs driven into the ground, are all suitable.

Training and pruning Left to their own devices many climbers quickly become a tangled mass of growths, new shoots clinging to or twining round older ones, instead of neatly covering the supports provided and filling their allotted spaces. Some initial training may be needed to overcome this tendency. Such training consists in starting the new shoots off in the right direction and occasionally during the season ensuring that they are carrying on in the way they are desired to go. This is particularly necessary where it is required to train the shoots horizontally or nearly horizontally, since the natural growth of the plant is upward.

Shrubs trained flat against walls and fences usually need to have their breast-wood removed from time to time. Very young growths developing from forward-pointing buds can often be rubbed out to prevent their development; otherwise the secateurs will have to be used judiciously.

Pruning is often needed to keep plants under control or to ensure the production of new flowering growths.

Mulching An annual mulch round the bases of the plants, but not actually touching the stems, will help to prevent the soil from drying out in hot weather, particularly near walls and fences, will keep down weeds and will supply plant foods and improve the soil texture as the mulch is gradually absorbed into the soil by the action of worms and weather. Such a mulch might consist of garden compost, leafmould, partially rotted leaves, or moist peat. Late spring is a suitable time to apply the mulch which should be fairly deep. The covering may be renewed from time to time during the summer if it shows signs of dispersal.

Providing protection Some slightly tender plants may be grown successfully against walls in many parts of the country although in severe weather some protection may be necessary. Bracken fronds may be sandwiched between two layers of wire-netting to make an excellent protection which can be placed round the plant when necessary. Wire-reinforced plastic material can be used to make a roll, stapled together along the edges. This roll can be used to surround the plant but should be fixed firmly to a stake to prevent wind movement. Hessian sacking may be draped over the plants in bad weather but should not be too close to them. In fact, no form of protection should surround the plant too closely and it should be removed as soon as possible to allow light and air to get at the plants again.

Supports Supports will need some attention from time to time as the plants grow and, for vigorous specimens, it may be necessary to provide further supports in the course of time. Many plants in full leaf present a good deal of wind resistance and inadequate supports, or those which have been weakened through age, may easily be brought down, possibly doing irreparable damage to the plants or at least undoing the work of some years. Any suspect supports should be replaced as quickly as possible.

Feeding In time the plants will exhaust the plant food available in the soil, but before that time arrives some extra feeding will be necessary. Annual mulches will provide a good deal of food in time but spring and summer feeds with sulphate of ammonia, nitrate of soda, Nitro-chalk, all at about 25-50g (1-2oz) per square metre (yard), or proprietary fertilizers at rates recommended by the manufacturers, are quick stimulants. Over-feeding must be avoided; small doses given at regular intervals are much more effective than large doses given infrequently. Feeding should cease by the end of August to avoid the production of soft, frost-tender growth. Bonemeal stirred into the top soil at up to 115g (4oz) per square metre (yard) in the autumn or winter will release plant foods slowly during the following growing season and possibly for longer.

Annual climbers There are a fair number of annual climbers which may be used to form quick screens if grown against appropriate supports. It almost goes without saying that the quickest results are obtained by growing the plants in rich soils and by feeding them with dilute liquid feeds at regular intervals once they are growing well. The exceptions are the climbing nasturtiums which tend to make foliage at the

1 Passiflora caerulea, a beautiful climber for warm walls. 2 Thunbergia alata, black-eyed susan, an annual.

1 *Polygonum baldschuanicum*, the Russian vine, roofs this garden retreat.
2 *Vitis coignetiae* is superb in autumn.
3 *Lonicera sempervirens*, the trumpet honeysuckle.
4 *Jasminum officinale*.

1

1 *Humulus lupulus aureus, the golden hop, is a hardy perennial climber.*
2 *Lonicera periclymenum is beautiful on the roof, and reaches 3-6m (10-20ft).*
3 *Morning glory or Ipomoea (a synonym for Pharbitis tricolor).*

2

3

expense of flowers if grown in too rich a soil. However, even these do better if the soil is not too poor and dry. Dead-heading will do much to keep the plants flowering instead of spending their energies on ripening seed. Some of these climbers may be grown from seed sown out of doors in spring where they are to flower, others give the best results if they are grown from seed sown in heat in the greenhouse.

Some climbing plants growing along a fence appear almost to transform it into a hedge, and there is no doubt that in general terms a growing, living hedge is always more attractive as a garden boundary or division than the plain and somewhat stark surface of a fence or wall. There is a much wider selection of plants suitable for hedging than is generally realized and the gardener will be advised to spread his net wider than to choose the somewhat drab and greedy-rooted privet or the commonplace beech.

Cloche gardening see Growing under glass

Coir screening

This is a woven fabric spun from the fibre between the kernal and outer skin of the coconut. It is a naturally rot-proof material which does not shrink or stretch. It is light and is, therefore, easily portable and can be moved conveniently from one crop to another.

Coir screening is particularly useful horticulturally as a protective material. It will protect or screen crops from cold prevailing winds and, used in thicker grades, is a good form of protection against frost. The material is useful for frame and cloche work when made up into mats or long rolls and placed over them during cold weather.

Used as a portable screen, it is nailed to poles or stakes. These supports are usually spaced 2.5m (8ft) apart and are long enough to allow for 45cm (18in) of stake in the ground and 15cm (6in) above the screen, the latter allows for the fixing of guys where necessary. The screening is best attached to the poles or posts by laths. When it is necessary to remove or move the screening. The poles can be lifted and the screening rolled up, poles and all. To preserve the fibre when stored, it must be dried beforehand.

Coleworts see Vegetables

Colour planning your garden

The colours chosen in the planning of a garden are very much a matter of personal taste but there are particularly pleasing combinations.

Nature seldom, if ever, makes mistakes with colour. Every hue seems to have full value and expression, not only to its own advantage, but also to that of the others surrounding it. Colour clashes seldom occur in nature.

Climbers for Particular Purposes

Annual

Cobaea (P as A)	Maurandya	Rhodochiton
Cucurbita	(P as A)	(P as A)
Humulus (P as A)	Mina	Thunbergia
Ipomoea	Pharbitis	Tropaeolum
Lathyrus		

Tendril

Ampelopsis (D)	Lathyrus (D)	Passiflora (E)
Clematis (D & E)	Mutisia (E)	Smilax (D & E)
Eccremocarpus	Parthenocissus	Vitis (D)
(D)	(D)	

Twining

Actinidia (D)	Jasminum	Pueraria (D)
Akebia (SE)	(D & E)	Schizandra (D)
Araujia (E)	Kadsura (E)	Senecio (D)
Aristolochia (D)	Lardizabala (E)	Solanum (D)
Berberidopsis (E)	Lonicera (D & E)	Sollya (E)
Billardiera (E)	Mandevilla (D)	Stauntonia (E)
Calystegia (D)	Muehlenbeckia	Trachelospermum
Celastrus (D)	(D)	(E)
Holboellia (E)	Periploca (D)	Wistaria (D)
Humulus (D)	Polygonum (D)	

Walls north and east

Berberidopsis	Hydrangea	Pileostegia (E)
(E)	(D & E)	Vitis (D)
Ficus (E)	Jasminum (D & E)	
Hedera (E)	Lonicera (D & E)	

Shrubs, Wall plants (not true climbers)

Abelia (D & E)	Cotoneaster	Indigofera (D)
Abutilon (D)	(D & E)	Itea (D & E)
Adenocarpus	Diplacus (D)	Jasminum (D & E)
(D or SE)	Escallonia	Kerria (D)
Buddleia (D & E)	(D & E)	Magnolia (D & E)
Camellia (E)	Feijoa (E)	Phygelius (E)
Ceanothus (D & E)	Forsythia (D)	Piptanthus (E)
Ceratostigma (D)	Fremontia (D)	Pyracantha (E)
Chaenomeles (D)	Garrya (E)	Ribes (D)
Colletia (D)	Hebe (E)	Rosa (D & E)
Corokia (E)	Hypericum	Rubus (D)
Crinodendron (E)	(D & E)	Schizandra (D)

Key: D Deciduous. E Evergreen. P as A Perennial grown as annual. SE Semi-evergreen.

Foliage has as important a part to play as flowers in garden decoration; colour variation in foliage is wide and of the utmost significance, vital to be borne in mind, especially where all-the-year-round decoration is the aim. Deciduous and evergreen leaves, therefore, should be allowed to play their full part, and not only through choice of plantings, but also by intelligent positioning in order, say, to catch the sun in certain seasons, or to match and contrast with other plantings nearby.

This applies also to the wide and vivid range of ornamental berries and barks, so useful especially during the later and winter months, when blossom is scarce. Let the many winter-flowering plants, trees and shrubs be given their proper role. If planted in the right proportion

they guarantee the complete twelve month colour cycle.

Generally speaking, red can be one of the most difficult colours to handle, and where several shades are to be included in a border or throughout a garden they are best if fairly well distributed, unless differing flowering seasons conveniently prevent clashes. In this way, each retains its full value and in addition may also heighten the effect of yellows, blues and whites.

White is a key colour, which not only stands on its own merits but also acts as an incomparable foil. It softens many an otherwise harsh effect where two bold colours might, perhaps, have come together. It can make a charmingly gentle picture with pink, pale green and pale blue for example, a dramatic splash with reds and strong blues. Quite definitely, here is a colour which in the garden has infinite value and which should be exploited to the full, not regarded as a little dull and empty.

Blue is tremendously useful, and as with white fits practically anywhere. The dark and mid-blues have a cool and telling effect. Paler blues are every bit as significant with immense scope in achieving beautifully soft effects. No matter how much it is used throughout any garden, blue seldom if ever bores; unlike red and pink which can, if present in quantity, tend to become monotonous.

Adroitly handled, pink is vastly interesting, appearing as it does in every mood from riotous to demure. Shades need to be arranged with a little thought for best results, in order to prevent one robbing another of impact. The blue/pinks tend to cancel out the red/pinks and either will make pale pinks more pallid still if allowed to predominate. Allied with carmine, pinks in the paler range are given added warmth; often a good thing where they might otherwise appear washed out.

As a wide selection of dianthus will show, pink goes well with a variety of silver tones; admirably demonstrated by its own foliage. There are many other forms of silver foliage among plants, trees and shrubs and these could be made a good deal more use of to very great advantage.

Almost any other colour goes well with it, for example *Senecio laxifolius*, a charming small shrub whose golden-yellow, summer-borne daisies contrast perfectly with its silvery-green leaves. The same effect can be seen in another small shrub, *Santolina incana*, and in *Potentilla fruticosa* whose blossoms extend through quite a wide range of yellow and gold and also include some whites. The silvery leaves of *Pyrus salicifolia pendula* contrast richly with the plum-purple foliage of *Cotinus coggygria foliis purpureis*, where this tree and shrub (both of fair size when full-grown) have been wisely sited near each other.

Bedding plants, particularly those used in summer schemes, provide scope for brilliant colour weaving. *Senecio maritima* 'Diamond', bright with silver leaves, is outstanding for providing contrast with, say, pink antirrhinums, or the purplish-mauve *Verbena venosa*. A mixture of all three is remarkably striking (see Bedding).

Yellow is one of the loveliest colours of all. And it has the ability to give the utmost life to any border without ever tending to harshness. It can become monotonous if used excessively—especially in its darker tones—though, pale, can be superb as anthemis and annual chrysanthemum in some of its varieties can show. Superb with blue, as *Platystemon californicus* with *Echium* 'Blue Bedder' will demonstrate in any annual border, it is equally so when in company with mauve, as a further example: *Clematis × jackmanii* grown near climbing rose 'Mermaid' will prove.

Any comprehensively stocked border of hemerocallis, or day lily, will make it clear how well yellow tones with orange; together, a rich mixture to be remembered. Orange, though brilliant in itself, can become tedious if used too liberally, though vibrant in the extreme where used in correct contrast. blue and orange and white and orange are superb. Arrange them by growing love-in-a-mist and calendula, and sweet alyssum with *Ursinia anethoides*, for instance; all among the loveliest of annuals.

Green is everywhere, nearly always precisely where it is wanted from a colour point of view and just the right shade. It is so acceptable that it may be taken for granted, though less so during the spring where deciduous trees and shrubs are concerned, for it is then that they are at their brightest.

But green really comes into its own where conifers are concerned, combining with foliage textures and character to yield remarkable beauty. Appearing in an infinite number of shades, it extends in one direction into various golds and bronzes, and in another into shades of blue and silver-blue that are classic. *Cedrus atlantica glauca* and *Picea pungens kosteriana*, for example.

Where space permits, conifers are almost essential for helping to ensure colour-interest throughout the twelve months of the year. Clearly, they come into their own during autumn and winter months, though can make wonderful backgrounds for spring and summer blossoms and foliage if planted thoughtfully.

Evergreens in general, carefully

1 Spring bedding in which tulips, wallflowers and forget-me-nots are happily combined. 2 Lobelia and phlox drummondii in a predominantly blue border are long flowering plants.

selected from the wonderfully wide range, can yield gold, silver, dark green, light green and a host of brilliantly variegated leaves, some almost vying with blossom. Sometimes dismissed as dull and uninteresting, evergreens are anything but, and of course many of them bear some of the loveliest blossom in cultivation (see Evergreens).

Deciduous foliage effects should come high on the list of garden adornments, making as they do a major contribution to the continuity of colour. The Japanese acers could scarcely be more brilliant in this respect, nor could liquidambar, lindera and that charming little shrub or small tree—*Amelanchier canadensis*, foaming with white blossom in May, bright with purple berries in June, and aflame with autumn fire as its leaves make a final flourish before falling as the year draws to its close.

Though deciduous, beech will retain its dead leaves, crisp and richly brown, throughout winter, when clipped as a hedge. Their effect can be greatly enhanced where dark evergreens have been planted close by. *Chamaecyparis lawsoniana* is first rate, here, and if planted in company with a clipped beech will make as handsome a combination of green and brown as anyone could wish to see.

So it can be seen that by a degree of prior thought, hardly a day need see an absence of effective colour of some kind in the garden. And colour planning can be great fun as well as vastly rewarding, with foliage and flower, berry and bark making their own special contribution.

And barks are, perhaps, the most neglected of all the sources of garden decoration. There is little justification for this, and it seems a pity to forego for example the magnificent red of *Cornus alba sibirica*, the green of *Leycesteria formosa* and the orange-gold of *Salix vitellina britzensis* during the dormant season in particular.

The colour year has no beginning and no ending where the shrewd gardener has been at work. He has his traditional spring flowers in masses, allied to spring-flowering shrubs such as chaenomeles, forsythia and ribes (and how magnificent *Ribes sanguineum* looks in company with daffodils and narcissi), not to mention the hosts of ornamental cherries, plums and apples.

Summer is filled with blossom and foliage of every conceivable kind. Autumn has sufficient attraction where late blossoms have been grown and where fruiting trees and shrubs have thoughtfully been provided (the ornamental crab apples really come into

Herbaceous borders composed of perennial plants provide colour and interest. Staking can be reduced by planting self supporting up-to-date cultivars.

51

their own at this season) similarly, trees and shrubs with leaves that flare before they fall.

Winter, though always a little sombre, sees many things in display: the sweetly-scented *Viburnum fragrans, Chimonanthus praecox* and *Daphne mezereum,* as examples of some lovely shrubs. *Helleborus niger,* though sometimes wayward, will offer its sheer white 'Christmas roses,' the cheerful winter aconites will shine, snowdrops need no introduction.

Over all this, the conifers and evergreens in general maintain a perpetual source of attractiveness and interest if selected with a little imagination. And a special word must be said for the whole range of ericas, for here are species, hybrids and varieties to provide blossom of many forms and colours throughout the year with never a break; many of

Borders can be mixed or confined to plants producing flowers in varying shades of one colour. This all yellow border is at its best in early summer when this colour tends to predominate.

them offer foliage in several different hues in addition to their flowers.

Several factors come to bear when selecting planting material for stocking a garden with the intention of providing as much colour as possible. One of these is that of size and it is one of the most important. It should be remembered that sharp colour contrasts are rendered more so in confined areas. Sometimes this is acceptable, but may also produce too bright an effect at close quarters; wiser, perhaps, to reduce the number of violent colours in small gardens unless adequate white is used to soften them.

Larger gardens obviously afford greater scope and even the brightest array of flowers will appear to have less individual impact, even though they retain their proper significance. It is, of course, under these circumstances that large herbaceous borders come into their own where there is ample space to accommodate them. Vivid as the constituent colours may be, the overall picture is one of tasteful blending.

And it is in larger gardens that additional scope arises for self-coloured borders. Not, perhaps, to everyone's taste, they can nevertheless be most attractive, though certain colours are more suitable than others. A completely blue border would, perhaps, be the easiest to look at. Blue is a restful hue and there are a great many shades, sufficient to avoid any suggestion of monotony. Twelve herbaceous plants to form a sound basis would be: *Anchusa azurea*, *Lupinus* Russell Strain 'Gladys Cooper'; *Salvia uliginosa*; campanula in variety; *Polemonium caeruleum*; delphiniums in many blue varieties; *Geranium grandiflorum*; blue flag iris; *Echinops ritro*; *Penstemon heterophyllus*; *Linum perenne* and *Platycodon grandiflorum*. Such a border could be effectively backed by flowering shrubs to include ceanothus in some of its forms; *Hibiscus syriacus coeleste* and *Hydrangea macrophylla* 'Blue Wave', kept adequately blued.

A solely yellow border might well prove too much of a good thing, though perhaps not if kept to reasonable proportions. The same goes for orange, even though there could be a remarkably striking effect with, perhaps, certain kniphofias, alstroemerias, hemerocallis, lilies of various kinds, *Ligularia clivorum* and *Geum* 'Prince of Orange', as a basic half dozen. Better, however, or so it would seem, to blend orange with yellow, with maybe the occasional dash of white; in all producing considerable richness. This would certainly allow the full range of hemerocallis varieties to be brought into play, worthwhile under any circumstances.

Compost see Fertilizers

Conservatories see Growing under glass

Cottage gardens

The cottage garden tradition is one that is peculiarly English in character. The old-world charm of the cottager's plot owed little or nothing to any of the major developments in garden design or landscape architecture. The English cottage garden just 'happened' and its chief attraction lies in the effect of ordered chaos that it produces.

Like the wild gardens and herbaceous borders of William Robinson and Gertrude Jekyll, the cottage garden is, to a great extent 'natural' but, as in the former instances, nature needed a good deal of taming and direction before the desired effect of studied carelessness could be achieved.

The heyday of the cottage garden covered a period that roughly coincided with the Victorian era, give or take a decade or so at either end. Its main characteristics were colour and fragrance coupled with a joyous abandon that suggested nature running riot.

It had few permanent features of real importance—no stone figures or towering conifers, no exotic trees and shrubs, while for hedges, the quickthorn, beech or hornbeam of adjacent fields and farmland could normally be used.

From sheer economic necessity, most cottagers had to be self-supporting in fruit and vegetables. Families were large so that it is not surprising that a major part of the available garden was devoted to these food crops.

But this did not prevent the cottager or his wife from creating the traditional mass of colour with what remained. He would often grow, as well, flowers for picking and herbs for the kitchen in the vegetable plot. Many of our favourite present-day flowers achieved their initial popularity in the cottagers' gardens. Pinks, wallflowers, sweet williams, stocks, pot marigolds, and love-in-a-mist are a few that come first to mind. There are countless others.

Today, the true cottagers are rapidly disappearing. They move out of their cottages as soon as they can into more easily-run flats and houses. Their place is being taken by a new kind of cottage-dweller, the week-end countrymen and country commuters, for whom the peace of the countryside holds great attractions.

We cannot put the clock back, but there is no reason why the contemporary cottage garden should not reflect the old-world charm of its predecessors while making use, at the same time, of the new and improved varieties of older plants as well as some of those plants that have become more recently available.

Simplicity must always be the keynote of the well-designed cottage garden. This can be best achieved by a well-chosen mixture of suitable plants, by unpretentious design and accessories and by the use of old-fashioned climbing plants to cover walls and fences.

Spring Spring is a season of major interest in the cottage garden, beginning with the emergence of the snowdrops and winter aconites. The yellow buttercup-like flowers of the latter, with their attractive green ruffs, start to open during the first mild spells in January. Snowdrops, which come a little later, look best naturalized in grass. A position under old fruit trees—often to be found in the cottage garden—suits them best. Both aconites and snowdrops seed freely if left undisturbed.

These will be closely followed by the early daffodils and many kinds of primula. Although few species of the latter were known to the cottagers by their proper names, surviving specimens of many present-day gems were found growing in cottage gardens by plant-lovers interested in their survival.

'Kinlough Beauty', a bright pink hybrid of *Primula juliana*, is one of these. It was formerly known as 'Irish Polly'. Its polyanthus-type blooms would never win prizes for size, but are attractive and have a central blotch of white surrounding a yellow eye.

'Cottage Maid', with more restrained colouring, is somewhat similar. There are also a number of lavender and pink

Plants for the Cottage Garden

Bulbs and Corms—Spring Flowering

Allium	*Eranthis hyemalis*	Galanthus	Narcissus
Anemone	*Erythronium*	Hyacinthus	Ranunculus
Chionodoxa	*dens-canis*	*Iris danfordiae*	*Scilla sibirica*
Crocus	*Fritillaria imperialis*	*Iris histrioides*	*Scilla tubergeniana*
Cyclamen repandum	*Fritillaria meleagris*	*Iris reticulata*	Tulipa
		Muscari botryoides	

Bulbs and Corms—Summer and Autumn Flowering

Agapanthus	*Cyclamen*	*Galtonia candicans*	Lilium
Amaryllis	*neapolitanum*	Gladiolus	Montbretia

Annuals and Biennials

Alyssum	Cheiranthus	Heliotropium	*Nicotiana affinis*
Amaranthus	Clarkia	Iberis	Nigella
Anchusa	Dianthus	*Impatiens balsamina*	*Reseda odorata*
Calendula	Godetia	*Matthiola bicornis*	Tropaeolum
Centaurea	Helianthus	*Matthiola incana*	Verbena

Herbaceous Perennials

Althaea	Centaurea	Helianthus	*Paeonia lactiflora*
Anchusa	*Chrysanthemum*	Hemerocallis	Papaver
Aquilegia	*maximum*	Lathyrus	Phlox
Armeria	*Dielytra spectabilis*	*Meconopsis cambrica*	Pulmonaria
Asperula	Doronicum	Mimulus	*Pulsatilla vulgaris*
Campanula	Geum	*Monarda didyma*	*Stachys lanata*
		Oenothera	Veronica

Shrubs

Artemisia abrotanum	*Daphne mezereum*	Lonicera	*Taxus baccata*
Artemisia absinthium	Euonymus	Myrtus	*Viburnum fragrans*
Buxus sempervirens	Ilex	Rosa	*Viburnum opulus*
Chaenomeles	*Kerria japonica*	Rosmarinus	*Viburnum tinus*
Clematis	Lavandula	Sambucus	

coloured primroses, formerly widely grown and including 'Reine des Violettes', 'Sweet Lavender' and 'Rosy Morn' that are becoming increasingly rare in cultivation.

Even more typical, perhaps, of the cottage garden are the richly-coloured, gold-faced polyanthus. Fortunately, it is still comparatively easy to obtain seed of these which can be sown in a cool greenhouse in February to produce full-sized flowering plants for putting out in autumn, or sown out of doors in May. The plants from the later sowing will be a good deal smaller and only a proportion will produce flowers the following spring. The true gold-laced polyanthus or primrose is a deep mahogany-red with petals narrowly margined with gold.

One early-flowering spring shrub that was widely grown in cottage gardens was our native mezereon, *Daphne mezereum*. It still retains its former popularity and although sometimes short-lived, provides one of the most welcome sights and scents of winter with its bright carmine flowers, smelling of hyacinths, that cluster the bare twigs and branches in February. Less often seen is the white form, *alba*.

Daphne mezereum is easily raised from seed, if you can rescue the red fruits—which, incidentally are poisonous to humans—from the birds. It is a good idea to have a few seedling plants coming along, to act as replacements when the older plants die off.

There is a whole group of tulips that have earned the suffix 'cottage'. These cottage tulips, which are tall-stemmed with pointed petals, flower in May a little in advance of the Darwins. They have, however, no more special claim to be grown on the cottage plot than any of the others, especially the early-flowering species such as the lady tulip, *Tulipa clusiana*, the brilliant scarlet *T. fosteriana* 'Red Emperor' or the beautifully-formed waterlily tulip, *T. kaufmanniana*.

Crown imperial (*Fritillaria imperialis*) is a spring bulb formerly closely associated with the cottage garden that has been elevated out of its former humble station by its present-day scarcity value. Crown imperials seem to thrive on neglect and some of the finest clumps are found in untidy corners of old gardens in places where the fork and hoe seldom penetrate.

They are certainly neither as common, nor as varied in colour as they were when they formed a major component of almost every seventeenth century flower arrangement, if paintings of the

1

2

1 A cottage garden in Essex made colourful with hollyhocks, dahlias and salvias.
2 Spring in a cottage garden when colour is provided by wallflowers, violas and alpines easily grown on a retaining wall.

period are anything to go by. Today, our choice is restricted to yellow, and orange, although there were once also white, bluish-purple and spotted varieties.

So many of these former cottage garden flowers have won universal esteem that we are apt to overlook their humble origins until their popular names bring them to mind. This is true of the lungworts or pulmonarias, that cottagers grew and delighted in under a variety of titles that included boys and girls, soldiers and sailors, spotted dog and hundreds and thousands.

These are all different names for *Pulmonaria officinalis* whose spotted leaves and pink-and-blue flowers make their appearance towards the middle or end of March. Today, we have the choice of several garden species: *P. angustifolia* with its sky-blue flowers and narrow green leaves; *P. rubra* which, in favoured situations will open its coral blooms as early as January and *P. saccharata* which, with its white-marbled green leaves and rose-pink to blue flowers comes closest to the older species. All the lungworts make first-class ground cover. They thrive equally well in sun or partial shade.

Summer As spring progresses towards summer, the cottage garden provides a continuous succession of colour and fragrance. Wallflowers, often assuming their true perennial character and coming up year after year are followed by the sweet clove-scented dianthus—the cottage pinks and clove carnations.

Here again the present-day gardener has a much wider choice where the latter plants are concerned. Interest in the old laced pinks has revived and forms are now obtainable that flower continuously throughout the summer. 'London Poppet' is white, tinged with pink and laced with ruby-red; 'Laced Hero' has large white flowers laced with purple and a central eye of chocolate-brown.

The old garden pinks have a shorter flowering season, but give a generous display of scented blossom. 'Mrs Sinkins', a favourite white of long standing is still among the most widely-grown of these; there is now a pink 'Mrs Sinkins' as well. Other good whites include 'Iceberg' and 'White Ladies'; 'Inchmery' is a delicate shell pink of outstanding quality while 'Priory Pink' has a distinctive mauve tinge to its flowers.

The name of Allwood Brothers and pinks are practically synonymous and the modern gardener can call upon the great number of hardy hybrid pinks (*allwoodii*) for whose development and

1 A garden at Tarrant Hinton in Dorset in which colour is provided by sweet williams. 2 A thatched roof on a cottage in Selworthy, on the walls of which Clematis montana climbs.

introduction Allwoods were responsible. These combine all the virtues (including fragrance) of the older forms with great vigour and a flowering season that lasts from spring to early autumn.

Herbs Among the major attractions of the cottage garden in summer are the fragrant herbs that provide material for sachets and *pot-pourris*, as well as for use in the kitchen. Lavender, of course, is the most widely-grown of these. *Lavandula spica* is the old English or Mitcham lavender, distinguished for its fresh, strong fragrance. Today, there is a wide choice of cultivars of differing habit and colour but none of these can quite compare with the old-fashioned kind where perfume is concerned. 'Munstead Dwarf' and 'Twickel Purple' are compact in habit with spikes of a really intense blue; *L. s. rosea* is an unusual lilac-pink variety, while the dwarf form 'Hidcote' is the deepest purple-blue of all the lavenders.

Rosemary, as well as being a useful seasoning for roast chicken or veal makes a decorative small garden shrub. Very old plants can still be found growing by cottage doors; planted originally for convenience of picking and now serving in a more ornamental capacity. *Rosmarinus officinalis* is the common culinary kind but for more decorative effects, there are a number of others, including that unusual erect form, 'Miss Jessup's Variety' which makes a slender grey-green column that is studded with pale blue flowers in April and May. 'Benenden Blue', from Corsica with very narrow leaves and deep blue flowers has an interesting, compact, white-flowered form.

Artemisia abrotanum, known variously as lad's love, southernwood and old man, is a herb that must have found a place in almost every cottage garden. Its aromatic foliage has always been enjoyed by country folk and we find it planted in strategic positions, at the junction of paths or by the kitchen door, where a sprig can be plucked in passing and crushed to release its unmistakable aroma. For the modern cottage garden there are several other species of artemisia that now share in the popularity engendered by the current vogue for grey and silver-leaved plants *A. arborescens* is noteworthy for the delicate filigree of its silvered leaves; *A. nutans* is a compact and elegant shrub with finely divided foliage silver-white colour. Good for associating with them are some of the perennial forms, such as the lacy-leaved 'Lambrook Silver' and 'Silver Queen' with its narrow willow-like foliage.

All the culinary and medicinal herbs, including mint, thyme, chervil, borage, sage, bergamot and angelica are very suited to the cottage garden and the plantsman can enjoy them even more by growing decorative garden forms in the beds and borders or, where thyme and some of the mints are concerned, in crevices in paths and paving.

There are several mints deserving of a place in the ornamental garden. The variegated apple mint and the prostrate peppermint-scented *Mentha requienii*, whose dense mat of dark green foliage comes to no harm when trodden underfoot, can both be used in this manner.

Thymes are obtainable in great variety. The soft lavender flowers of the lemon thyme, *Thymus citriodorus* 'Silver Queen' make an attractive contrast to the silver-variegated foliage. For planting in paving the prostrate forms of *T. serpyllum* are useful. One of the most interesting of these is *T. s. lanuginosus*, which quickly forms a dense carpet of grey woolly foliage.

It would seem that almost any plant with the suffix 'sweet' has affiliations with the cottage garden. Sweet peas, sweet williams, sweet sultan and sweet rocket are just a few of the cottage flowers that have earned this name, probably because fragrance plays so important a part in determining the cottager's choice of plants.

Roses It is doubtful whether he would have had much time for many of the modern, practically scentless roses in spite of their great size and exquisite form. Sweet briar, moss and cabbage roses would have been more to his liking and it is not surprising that many of the old roses that are today enjoying such a welcome renaissance, should have been rescued from oblivion by their discovery in these surroundings.

On the walls the cottager's choice might well have been the great maiden's blush, with its grey-green foliage and quilted pink blooms, or another old favourite 'Caroline Testout', with its loose-petalled deep pink cabbage flowers.

Climbers On the walls of a cottage, there is no need for formality. Climbing plants can be permitted to run riot and intertwine one with the other. This will particularly suit clematis such as *Clematis montana rubens* and many of the vigorous *jackmanii* types. The yellow stars of *Jasminum nudiflorum* will brighten the walls in winter and in summer the more rampant and sweetly-scented *J. officinale*, the sweet jessamine, will take over.

Other typical cottage climbers are the sweetly perfumed honeysuckles, whose modern garden forms are in striking contrast to our native woodbine, and *Lathyrus latifolius*, the everlasting pea which lacks the fragrance of the annual varieties, but which puts on a magnificent show each year.

Upkeep of the typical cottage garden should not entail a great deal of work. Normally, the plants are so closely packed together that weeds get little opportunity to take hold. For the contemporary cottage, grass is almost certain to play a more important part than formerly but generally speaking, the lawns will be relatively small and it should be possible to maintain it in first-rate condition at all times.

Courgettes see Vegetables

Crocks and Crocking

Crocks are the pieces of broken flowerpots which are used as drainage material in pots, pans and seed boxes. During the gardening year, it is inevitable that a number of clay flowerpots of various sizes are either broken completely, or so badly cracked that they are unfit for further work. These pots can be broken down still further to provide invaluable drainage material. It is a good policy to have a box set aside so that this material can be stored as it becomes available.

The term 'crocking' is used to describe the process of placing drainage material, in the form of broken pieces of pot, in the pots, pans and seed boxes. It is an important operation in the cultivation of plants in a greenhouse or frame. Without the provision of good drainage, many composts, despite the fact that they are mixed well and are of the highest quality, will become sour after a time. Poor soil conditions will result in unsatisfactory growth.

The usual method of crocking a pot is to place one large crock, convex side upwards, over the drainage hole in the bottom of the pot. This is covered with a layer of smaller pieces of crock and this in turn is covered with some of the coarse material which has been left in the sieve after the soil has been passed through it. This coarse material is often called roughage. To some extent broken crocks are now being replaced with pieces of perforated zinc, a change which will no doubt be accelerated as clay pots give place more and more to the unbreakable plastic pots. Disks of foam rubber may also be used.

Cucumbers see Growing under glass

Cultivation

Cultivation is the practice of working the soil to produce and maintain conditions favourable to healthy plant growth. It has to be carried on continuously, and has short lasting effects and varies according to the soil.

Destruction of weeds Before any land can be cultivated weeds have to be destroyed or got rid of, either by weedkillers or by mechanical means. Perennial weeds are always the most difficult to eradicate and there is no short cut to getting land really clear of them. Much can be learned from the kinds of weeds that a soil supports. Sorrel, spurrey, bracken and foxglove tolerate high acidity in the soil, whereas wild clematis (old man's beard), campion, chicory and toadflax usually abound on the chalky, alkaline soils. Silverweed, plantains, dandelions and horsetails thrive on clay soils.

Once the surface is clear, and the land is fallowed for a few weeks, it is easy to ascertain if it is badly drained because surface water will not drain away. Apart from introducing mechanical drains underground, the improvement of the texture of the soil will often relieve the drainage problem.

When to cultivate Only coarse textured or very sandy soils can be cultivated soon after wet weather, the medium textured soils tend to make clods if worked too soon and the clay or fine textured soils simply turn slimy and their structure is spoiled for many months. It is general, therefore, to carry out deep or main cultivation operations in the autumn or during the winter in open weather, not only because the soils are drier at this time but to harness the help of frost in breaking up the particles to fine tilth and improving the texture of the soil.

Winter operations Digging is the major soil operation carried out with a spade, and designed to aerate, level, and turn the earth. Soils left rough during the winter are broken down in the spring, using the fork or where heavy clods are concerned, the Canterbury hoe.

Forking is carried out in both autumn and spring and on heavier soils a flat-tined fork may be found easier to manage for autumn or winter work.

The object of the operation is to break up and aerate the top 15cm (6in) of the soil, hand clearing weeds as work progresses. Forking is less laborious than digging and can be carried out among established plants in the border, the shrub garden, and among soft fruit bushes. One always works backwards when forking to avoid walking on the lawn already forked.

When a vacant piece of land is to be forked, begin by working right across one end of it. It is useful to put a line across the plot and work over an area about 60cm (2ft) wide before moving the line back another 60cm (2ft). The fork is plunged into the soil at an angle of about 50°, the soil lifted, slightly turned and dropped back. Work progresses across the plot, working strips of 60cm (2ft) at a time until the whole plot has been forked.

Dressings of lime, manure, compost and such slow acting fertilizers as bonemeal are added to the soil in autumn and winter and it is often convenient to spread them at the same time as the forking is being done.

Spring and summer operations Forking is the quickest way of grooming the garden in spring. Annual weeds which make an early appearance, such as groundsel can be cleared at the same time and the winter surface of the soil just pricked over to aerate it and break

down any clods.

Treading Once spring forking is done on ground that is destined for seed sowing or vegetable planting it can be lightly rolled or trodden to prevent it from being too puffy. Treading is especially useful (and easy to do) on sandy soils that might dry out too quickly otherwise. Walk sideways across the land, keeping the feet almost together and shuffle across the soil. The surface is tidied afterwards by raking.

Raking The rake is used not only to collect up the surface rubbish, but to level the surface and break down the top inch of soil into a really fine tilth, like grains of rice, in preparation for seed sowing.

Currants see Fruit

Cutting see Propagation

Cultivations should vary according to requirements. For seed sowing: 1 Any accumulation of rubbish is removed. 2 The soil is lightly forked to break up clods and create a tilth. 3 The seed bed is made firm by treading. 4 Large stones and clods are removed with a wooden rake. 5 A fine tilth is obtained. 6 Borders are forked over to remove perennial weeds in the spring.

D

Damping down

This operation is carried out in the greenhouse when a humid atmosphere is required. It is essential to maintain the correct amount of atmospheric moisture for many plants to survive, especially in high temperatures, and by keeping the surroundings damp this can be achieved. Moisture retaining material such as ash, gravel, peat are used as staging material rather than metal, concrete or wood for this reason and greenhouse floors are often ashed over where high temperatures and high humidity are to be maintained. Damping down is done up to four or five times daily when necessary, either with a watering can with a rose spray, or a syringe or even with a rotary sprinkler attachment to a hose in large greenhouses and staging, walls, floors, pots are all made wet rather than the plants themselves. High atmospheric humidity is not only essential for the survival of many plants but is the best condition to prevent the spread of red spider mite in greenhouses.

DDT

This once common insecticide is no longer available in England. Ask your supplier to suggest an approved alternative.

Dead-head

To dead-head plants means to remove the faded flower heads before seed is produced, not only to enhance the appearance of the plants but to divert the strength into making new flower buds rather than seed. Dead-heading is a common practice with rhododendrons to encourage free flowering. Lilacs require practically no pruning, but benefit from dead-heading. Among border plants the operation is carried out as a routine to preserve the appearance of the plant and general effect of the border. Among bedding plants, pansies, tagetes and petunias are commonly dead-headed to maintain a succession of flowers throughout the season, as also are most other annuals unless it is intended to gather seed.

To 'dead head' is to remove faded flowers and prevent the production of seed.

Deblossoming

This is the removal of either individual flowers or complete flower trusses. In fruit growing the operation is sometimes necessary to prevent fruiting at too early an age: for instance, any blossom produced by top fruits in the first spring after planting should always be removed.

Partial deblossoming is also carried out as a first stage in fruit-thinning to prevent a glut crop in a year of prolific blossom following a resting year when the crop was abnormally light (probably as a result of frost damage). This action may help to prevent a habit of biennial cropping developing. Apples which are notoriously prone to this are: 'Cottenham Seedling', 'D'Arcy Spice', 'Dumelow's Seedling', 'Ellison's Orange', 'Laxton's Superb', 'Melba', 'Miller's Seedling', 'Newton Wonder', 'Ontario' and 'Wagener'.

Strawberries are sometimes deblossomed in their first spring because, although first-year berries are bigger and earlier, the total yield in the first two years is then less than that in the second year alone from deblossomed plants which have had a whole year

and more in which to build up their strength.

Defruiting

The removal of all the immature fruit from a tree, or part of a tree. This may be done when deblossoming was intended but left until the fruit had set.

Dehorning

Cutting main branches hard back. This is sometimes done to re-invigorate old fruit trees but such drastic pruning should be spread over five or six years. Always cut to a side branch so that no 'snag' remains and make a saw cut on the underside first so that the bark is cut through cleanly. Pare smooth any rough patches with a knife.

Derelict gardens and their renovation

At a first glance, a derelict garden seems a most depressing problem and one which would appear to be insurmountable. Certainly its renovation and reclamation will require a great deal of hard work but it is a task which can be made much easier and pleasanter if a plan of campaign is worked out beforehand.

There are, of course, degrees of neglect. Some gardens may have been

1

3

2

4

unoccupied for a few months only, a few will have been neglected for years. Whatever the condition, the work of reclamation should be tackled in easy, logical stages. A garden is as good as its initial soil preparation and any hurried or glossed over soil cultivation will repay in poor growth and even more vigorous weeds later on.

Examining the site The first thing which will have to be done will be to examine the site carefully to see where original beds and borders are and to identify these with long stakes. In extreme instances, it may even be difficult to trace paths, but these must be given priority as, if they are in reasonable condition, they will be most useful when the wheelbarrow is required.

The extent of the site examination must depend on the time of the year the garden is taken over. The work will be difficult at the height of the season when most of the garden's occupants are in full growth, but it will prove to be a most useful time as it will be possible to assess

1 The derelict garden at Rufford Old Hall before renovation. 2 After renovation has been completed. 3 The garden at Wallington with beds and borders demanding labour for maintenance. 4 After renovation with the simplified labour-saving design. The regularly shaped lawn creates an impression of space, is easy to maintain.

the quality of these plants. Those which are obviously weak and of very poor quality should be suitably marked or noted so that they can be removed. It might be possible to salvage some if they are cut back hard at the end of the season to encourage sturdier growth the following year.

If the garden is occupied in the autumn or winter, most of the plants will have died down and may be rather difficult to find and examine. It will, however, be an easier time to tackle the clearance problem, as much of the growth, including that of the weeds will have died down.

Clearance Once main features and plants have been located, the task of clearance or renovation can start. The first part will consist of weed removal. This can be done manually, by chemical means or a combination of both. In a seriously neglected garden where few established plants are worth keeping, the site can be cleared by the application of a powerful weedkiller such as sodium chlorate. This must be used with extreme caution since it is so powerful that ground treated cannot be used for at least six to seven months afterwards. It must be applied away from neighbours' boundaries, too otherwise many of their plants growing close by will be seriously affected and even destroyed.

A safer method is to use weedkillers based on dalapon or paraquat. The former is especially useful for the control of grasses, especially that particularly troublesome weed, couch grass. Paraquat is a most remarkable weedkiller as it kills all plants but is completely inert as soon as it touches the soil. It enables the gardener to control and deal with weeds round established plants such as shrubs, roses and fruit trees. It deals most effectively with annual broad-leaved weeds and the tops of perennial weeds. It is reasonably economical to use as a 115g (4oz) pack makes up 15l (4 gall) of liquid which is sufficient to deal with 30 square metres (yards) of ground.

Another useful chemical aid is found in the form of SBK brushwood killer. Tough weeds such as docks, brambles, briars, nettles and many other common weeds are controlled by applications of the diluted chemical. A 300g (10oz) tin makes up sufficient liquid to cover 600-1200 square metres (yards).

Weeds can be dealt with by the more laborious method of hand weeding. Annual weeds such as chickweed can be killed if they are buried well beneath the soil surface during the cultivation of the soil. Perennial weeds such as dandelions, docks, thistles, plantains, couch grass, ground elder and bindweed must *never* be buried otherwise they will quickly take root again and grow even more vigorously. As many of these perennial weeds are deep rooted, care must be taken to see that they are dug or forked out as carefully as possible. Throw them into a heap as they are collected and allow them to dry out as much as possible. As there will be a lot of general rubbish being burnt during cleaning up operations, the best place for these dried weeds is on the bonfire; they will quickly burn if a good fierce fire is maintained.

The clearance of a neglected garden must never be hurried. It is a good idea to tackle small areas at a time. This will ensure that the work does not become too tiring, and it will also mean that it is carried out more thoroughly. Once most of the weeds and unwanted growth have been cleared, the soil itself will require attention. One of the first things to do is to gather any rubble which may be on the surface. This need not be discarded as it may come in useful for the foundations of new paths.

Cultivation The depth of cultivation must depend on the type of soil. If it is heavy, it will require deep digging in order to improve drainage. Light soils, on the other hand, will not need such thorough treatment. The heavy types should be double dug. That means that the top spit or 25cm (10in) of soil is turned over and the bottom of each trench is broken up to the full depth of the fork. This will provide about 50cm (20in) of well-worked soil.

The sticky types of soil can be opened up still further if sharp sand or well weathered gritty ashes are incorporated as the work proceeds. Small rubble can also be worked into the bottom spit to ensure adequate drainage. Organic matter is essential for neglected soils. It can be supplied in several ways. A neglected garden can always supply quite a lot of its own in the form of grass clippings, annual weeds and other waste vegetation. These can be incorporated fresh or stacked to rot down in a compost heap.

Horticultural peat is an ideal form of humus which can be dug in large quantities. It can be purchased reasonably cheaply in bulk. Moss peat is particularly suitable as it is extremely fibrous and has such a low degree of decomposition that it will last in the soil for several seasons.

Spent hops can sometimes be purchased from local breweries and are very useful for digging into the soil at about 1 barrowload to 6 square metres (yards). Where the gardener is lucky enough to be able to purchase some farmyard manure, this can be applied at the rate of a barrow-load to 8 to 10 square metres (yards).

There are many other products available from sundriesmen which take the form of composted or concentrated preparations for digging into the soil. Most are very useful, but some are rather expensive to use on a large scale and it is important to read the application rate carefully before buying, so that the economics can be assessed. The lighter types of soil require much more organic matter than others. Humus or organic matter is essential, as it acts as a sponge and retains valuable moisture, as well as providing food for the plants.

The heavy soils can be lightened by the application of hydrated lime or gypsum. The former is used at the rate of approximately 230g (8oz) per square metre (yard). The latter is particularly good for neglected, heavy soils. It, too, is applied at the rate of 230g (8oz) per square metre (yard) and is worked into the surface immediately.

Ideally all soil cultivation should be carried out during the winter except for the light soils. During the preparation of the soil, a dressing of bonemeal should be applied and worked in at the rate of 115g (4oz) per square metre (yard). This is a slow acting fertilizer which supplies nitrogen and phosphate.

Establishing plants The busiest time in the newly reclaimed garden is the spring when new seeds and plants are established. It will be a problem time, too, as many seedling weeds will be appearing. The reason for this is that many weed seeds will have fallen to the soil the previous year. Regular use of the hoe is one way of killing most of these, especially if the work can be carried out during dry weather.

The chemical paraquat will be useful at this time of the year for keeping seed beds or rows free from weeds. If it is applied prior to germination, weeds will be killed and the soil will be clear so that the young seedlings can grow without competition from the weeds.

Before the main sowings or plantings are carried out, the soil must be supplied with sufficient foods to ensure sturdy, healthy growth. Neglected soils will be short of basic fertilizers such as potash, nitrogen and phosphates. These can be supplied individually or in a compound form. Sulphate of ammonia at 30g (1oz) per square metre (yard), sulphate of potash at 60g (2oz) per square metre (yard) and super phosphate of lime at 60g (2oz) per square metre (yard) will supply these essentials. A balanced or general fertilizer such as National Growmore at 450g (1lb) per 10 square metres (yards) will supply all three essentials at one application.

There are several proprietary 'all in' feeds or dressings which can be used instead. All have been specially blended, many with extras such as trace elements. Maker's directions should always be carefully followed.

It will be necessary to provide extra feeds at frequent intervals during the growing seasons. Again individual fertilizers can be applied or proprietary ones which have been specially formulated for particular plants. If the weather is dry during the summer it will be necessary to provide plenty of water by means of sprinklers so that the various plants can become established as quickly as possible to transform what was once a neglected garden, into a place of beauty and charm.

Deshooting
The complete removal of young shoots on fruit trees, often performed with the nails of the finger and thumb. This is frequently necessary with wall trained trees to prevent shoots growing directly towards the wall or at right-angles away from it and to concentrate the tree's growth into laterals in the desired position and direction. Fruit-growers now consider that this is a preferable term to 'disbudding' which has been used in the past, particularly in the case of peaches, because 'disbudding' might also refer to the removal of blossom buds.

Digging
The various operations carried out on the soil by the use of a space are all known as digging. The general purpose is to break up the soil to improve its physical nature, rendering it more suitable for supporting plant life.

Digging is generally carried out in the autumn and winter, when a solidly compact soil can be broken up and left rough throughout the winter. The more surface that can be exposed to the weather the better, and the action of frosts, drying winds and rain break up the surface into small crumbs or tilth, generally increase aeration, and render the soil more open in texture. Rain and snow drain from the surface more quickly, leaving the surface dry and, therefore, the soil absorbs warmth from the spring sunshine more easily. Drainage is improved and the air that exists between the soil particles supports the beneficial bacteria.

The term digging means turning over the top soil one spit deep or the depth of the spade's blade, ie 25cm (10in). Surface weeds are buried, the level of the land remains the same and the clods of earth are left unbroken.

It is important that the spade is thrust into the soil to its full depth and in a vertical position. If this is not done, the land is dug quicker but cultivation is not deep enough or thorough enough and the weeds will not be properly buried.

Single digging To dig over a plot of land, a trench a spade's width and a spade's depth is dug out across one end and the soil removed and taken in a wheelbarrow to the other end of the plot and left in a heap so that when the plot has been dug there will be soil ready to put into the last trench. Alongside the first trench mark out with a line another strip and by standing facing the open trench and working along the line soil can be dug out and thrown well forward into the open trench, at the same time making a new trench. The importance of throwing each spadeful of soil well forward cannot be emphasized too much because a slight discrepancy will after several trenches result in there not being sufficient space in which to work properly. Repeat the method of filling the last trench while making a new one and when the last strip is dug at the other end of the plot the soil heaped there from the first trench is ready to fill the last one.

Manure or compost can be put on the land at the same time and is scattered along the trench and the soil is thrown on to it.

Double digging This is a method of breaking up the soil to a greater depth than in single digging but retaining the topsoil in its relative position. As the name suggests the soil is disturbed to the depth of two spits. Alternative names are half trenching or bastard trenching. The method though difficult to describe is quite straightforward to execute and is really an extension of the process described for digging.

A trench 60cm (2ft) wide and a spade's depth is taken out across one end of the plot and the soil carried to the far end of the plot and put in a heap. The bottom of the open trench is then forked as deeply as possible and the surface left level. Mark out another area 60cm (2ft) wide alongside the open trench and dig soil out of this to a full spade's depth and

In double digging the soil is cultivated to the depth of two spades (spits), but the position of the layers of soil remains unchanged. 1 A 60cm (2ft) wide trench is taken out down to the subsoil. 2 The subsoil is forked over and broken up to a fork's depth. See page 62 for 3 and 4.

throw the soil into the open trench and on top of the forked or broken up surface. Thus topsoil remains topsoil but the land is aerated to twice the depth that it is in single digging. If manure is added, and it is a usual practice to do this during double digging, it should be scattered over the forked surface before the topsoil is thrown on thus getting it down a good depth.

Double digging on grassland Where land that has not been cultivated before is being broken up and prepared for crops by hand rather than by mechanical means, double digging is the method recommended. The turf is first skimmed off with a spade over the area of the first strip or trench position, taken to the far end of the plot and left there. Then the topsoil is dug out of the trench to a spade's depth and also taken to the other end of the plot. The bottom of the trench is forked to a spit's depth and then the line moved back 60cm (2ft) to mark out the second trench. Skim off the turf from this second trench area, putting it upside down over the forked area of the first trench so that eventually the bottom of the whole trench is lined with inverted turf. Chop up the turf roughly into 10cm (4in) squares with the spade. No manure is added as the turf itself will rot and provide plant food but a general artificial fertilizer may be scattered at this level if required. Then the top spit of soil from the first trench is thrown over the inverted turf, the bottom spit of the second trench forked and turf taken from the third area inverted over that, and so on until the whole area has been broken up. When the last trench to be opened has been forked, put in the turf taken from the first trench, then cover it with the soil from the same trench.

Trenching This is an extension of the method used in half or bastard trenching and if the principle of half trenching has been mastered it is not difficult. Full trenching is heavy work and is often spread over three or four seasons by dealing with a portion of the land only each winter. It is justified in exceptional circumstances only. It can increase the depth of fertility quite quickly but naturally cannot be carried out on some clay or stony soils where the subsoil would be impenetrable with a spade.

The trenches are cut 90cm (3ft) wide for full trenching, to allow better working space. As for half trenching the topsoil from the first trench is removed to the other end of the plot and left there.

There are two methods of dealing with the soil in this opened trench, equally advantageous to cultivation. In the first method, stretch a line along the middle of the opened trench and remove all the

3 Organic matter, such as compost or well-rotted manure, is incorporated in the soil at this stage. 4 The last trench is filled with soil taken from the first trench.

soil on one side of it and put this soil in a heap at the side of the plot quite distinct from the topsoil already removed. The base of the trench is now in the form of a step, the trench depth at one side being two spits deep, about 50cm (20in), and at the other side one spit deep, 25cm (10in). Get down into the lower part of the trench and fork the subsoil, as in half trenching. Stand then on the upper part of the step and working backwards turn this soil over onto the lower half of the step that has just been forked. The fresh strip of subsoil thus exposed is then forked to the full depth of the fork.

Mark out another strip at ground level alongside the original trench and only 45cm (18in) in width. Dig the top spit out, throwing it right forward on to the raised step of the open trench. Turn the second spit on to the forked surface of subsoil in the first trench, then get down into the narrow trench thus cut out and fork the base to a full fork's depth. The work proceeds in 45cm (18in) strips along the plot and the smaller heap of topsoil is used to fill in the bottom of the last trench and the larger heap of topsoil goes over the last two 45cm (18in) strips.

The second method is a version of full trenching which has exactly the same result but allows more working space and is probably, therefore, quicker. In this method not only the first but every subsequent trench opened is 60cm (2ft) in width. The topsoil and the second spit of soil are carried away from the first trench and kept separately at the far end of the plot. The base or third spit is then forked and broken up. The first spit from the second trench is then taken to the other end of the plot and left apart from the larger heap of soil from the third trench. The second spit of the second trench is thrown on to the forked subsoil and the base of the second trench forked to break it up. The top spit of the third trench is taken right over to the top of the first trench; the second spit of the third trench turned over on to the forked surface at the bottom of the second trench and the base of the third trench broken up. Thus the pattern is repeated until at the far end of the plot the next to last trench has one of the heaps of topsoil put on to it and the last trench has the second spit pile put in on top of the broken up base of the trench and the top spit soil put on the top.

Deep trenching is a variation of full trenching in which the subsoil is brought on top of topsoil but this practice is drastic and could be disastrous.

Ridging As an alternative on heavy land to ordinary digging, where the surface is left level, the soil can be thrown up in ridges and furrows resembling ploughed land in a method known as ridging, in which a greater surface of soil is exposed to the action of the weather.

The plot to be dug is divided into 90cm (3ft) strips running across it, starting at one corner of the plot. At one end of the first strip take out soil to a depth of 25cm (10in) (one spade's depth) and two spade widths and take the soil in a wheelbarrow to the other end of the strip. Then working backwards stand on the soil and dig three spadesful of soil side by side throwing each forward onto the space from which topsoil has been taken. The right-hand spadeful goes forward and slightly towards the centre, the next spadeful to the left and slightly towards the centre and the third spadeful goes on top of these two. Step backwards and repeat the process and a ridge of soil will be made the length of the strip, the hollow at the end being filled in with the soil taken and reserved from the beginning of the strip. Continue digging in this way forming parallel ridges until the whole area has been dug.

Disbudding see Deshooting

Diseases and their control

The word disease in connexion with plants is considered to refer to any disturbance in the normal life processes which results in such things as (a) abnormal growth (b) temporary or permanent check to the development or (c) premature death of part or all of the plant. Plant diseases can be divided into two sorts (i) Parasitic, where the trouble is due to attacks of parasites such as fungi, bacteria or viruses and (ii) Non-parasitic in which the trouble is a result of faults in the environment (soil, temperature, moisture etc). The biggest group of diseases is that caused by fungus parasites (including bacteria) which are spread about by spores produced in the fruiting bodies (equivalent to seeds of higher plants but, of course, microscopic in size). Viruses are incredibly small in size and in nature are carried from infected to healthy plants by insects, mainly aphids, and also by trimming knives and hands (in glasshouses), by knives etc, (in propagating houses) and in a very few instances by seed transmission. It will be noticed that the great difference between parasitic and non-parasitic disease is that the former is infectious while the latter is not.

A chrysanthemum plant attacked by the disease powdery mildew.

Despite this, where a non-parasitic trouble begins, there is likely to be great loss unless the fault in environment is quickly corrected. The symptoms in either kind of trouble can be very similar and even almost identical so that to judge the cause it is often necessary to consult an expert to get microscopic examination and sound advice.

The control of plant disease depends on an accurate estimate of the symptoms shown by the affected plant so as to arrive at the exact cause of the trouble. Even with parasitic diseases the cause is usually microscopic, requiring a careful examination and often laboratory tests on the diseased tissues. Similarly with non-parasitic troubles the environment must be studied as well as the plants and the details of cultivation carefully considered. There may have to be a careful soil analysis as well as a study of the drainage and soil texture and there may also be an analytical test of some of the foliage or fruits which could reveal a shortage of some essential plant food.

Precautionary measures Before considering measures which have to be taken to check diseases in plant crops we may look at some of the things which can be done to guard against disease ever appearing. These can best be termed precautionary measures. They aim at building up the vigour of the plants to help them to resist any possible attack by a parasitic disease and they also include various precautions which can be taken to eliminate the possibility of disease being in the neighbourhood of the crop, more especially in the soil.

It is of the utmost importance to study the special requirements of any particular plant so that the soil can be prepared in order to ensure good drainage and also that it contains sufficient organic matter (humus) and the necessary plant foods. Where some plants are concerned, for instance camellias and rhododendrons it is important to ensure that there is no lime present in the soil. Everything should be done to get vigorous plants with robust stems and foliage. In glasshouses, proper light and ventilation must be arranged and in fruit trees skilful pruning helps to build up strong, healthy shoots and buds with good circulation of air among the branches.

Rotation of crops is intended to avoid growing the same kind of plant on the same spot year after year. If crops are grown on the same site year after year any disease of that crop is encouraged to build up and the soil can become heavily infected, addition to which the same plant foods are taken out of the soil. A different crop takes different amounts of the various chemical elements so that a balance can be easily kept. In glasshouses the same crop is very often grown each year but the disease build-up is checked by suitable methods of soil sterilization. Other precautionary measures are weed eradication (eg wild celery harbours celery leaf spot disease and the common plantain can carry the virus of spotted wilt). Careful spacing is also helpful so that diseases are not provided with the humid and moist conditions between plants which they need to germinate their spores and infect the leaves.

The protection of large wounds is another obvious precaution and one which is very important where large specimen trees or even expensive fruit trees and shrubs are concerned. It is not suggested that small pruning cuts need to be treated but where a large branch is broken down by wind or snow or cracked during severe frosts it is wise to try to protect the broken or cut places. After any branch is removed the cut should be painted over with a suitable protective paint such as Stockholm tar or Arbrex to prevent the entry of fungus parasites. Not only are plum trees likely to be infected by the silver leaf fungus but many fine ornamental trees and shrubs can be lost by neglecting this simple precaution. Even after cutting out a canker from apple trees the wound should be painted.

Resistant plants An important method of avoiding plant disease is to use resistant plants. A plant immune to a particular disease is highly valued by the grower if its quality is as good as those which are susceptible to the disease. Growing immune varieties is the simplest way of avoiding disease and it is a pity that such varieties are so limited in number.

Soil sterilization One of the most important precautions taken to avoid disease in horticultural crops is the practice of soil sterilization. In this the soil in a greenhouse intended for tomatoes, cucumbers, lettuces etc, is treated by passing hot steam through it (a commercial practice) or by watering with chemicals (eg formaldehyde or cresylic acid) before the crop is planted so that any dormant spores of disease are killed. However, at the temperature used, the spores of beneficial bacteria such as the nitrogen fixers are not killed, so that after the process is completed these can begin to enrich the soil without any immediate competition from other organisms. For use in small pots and seed boxes sterilized soil made after the John Innes formulae can be bought by gardeners. Similarly, sterile soilless composts are now available. Small glasshouses can be washed down inside with formalin or other disinfectants and the same sort of treatment can be given to garden frames, pots, boxes, seed trays and tools. Cresylic acid is one substance used for this purpose and in some instances also for sterilizing the surface of the oil, but there are several other good disinfectants available for the gardener.

Preventing the spread of disease When, despite the precautions referred to, a disease makes its appearance it is necessary to act quickly and to take direct action measures. The chief of these is to cover the plant with a protective film of a chemical which will kill the fungus or at least prevent the germination of its spores. Diseased parts can be removed before treatment, but it must be remembered that in most diseases an affected plant is often doomed (except where the disease is superficial or where affected parts can be cut away). The object of the treatment is to protect still healthy tissues, so that it is wise to spray or dust early.

Various chemicals, known as Fungicides, which will deal with all types of disease, are widely obtainable on the market. These are applied as a fine misty spray or as dust (most people hold that spraying is more efficient than dusting). Many types of spraying and dusting machines are in use. There are also smokes which are lit to fumigate glasshouses, which have previously been cleared of all plant life. Seeds, bulbs and corms are also treated by dusting or by immersion in a liquid fungicide to give them protection from soil-borne diseases, etc., after planting.

Fungus diseases These are diseases which are caused through the attack of various parasitic fungi. Sime fungi obtain food by living on the decaying organic matter which we call humus in the soil, but some obtain their food by attacking living plants and injure or kill them in the process—these are called parasites. In general, the harmless saprophytes are large and easily seen but the parasites are very small and need a microscope for their proper identification, although their presence may be detected because of some whitish or greyish mould or furry growth (eg rose mildew). These parasitic fungi grow microscopically inside plants but some have also a smothering effect (mildews) and grow on the outside of leaves and stems etc. They reproduce and spread themselves by means of innumerable spores.

Fungicides Fungicides are chemical substances which are used in the control of those diseases of plants which are caused by fungus parasites (see above). The ideal fungicide is a substance which will kill a fungus or prevent its spores from germinating, without doing any harm to the host plant. These substances are used in various forms and in various ways and many chemicals have been tried in the search for the most effective safe fungicide. Sulphur and copper are two of the oldest elements used for this purpose and in various forms are still used against some diseases. For instance copper sulphate is used to make the well-known Bordeaux mixture which has been in use for a century, while sulphur probably dates from Biblical times.

In recent years many of these fungicides have been replaced by more modern ones as the result of much research and there is now a much greater choice. In general the modern fungicide is more specific, that is to say it will prove very effective against a certain disease but is not so generally useful against many others, whereas the older kinds had an all-round fungicidal effect and exercised a check on many diseases likely to attack the plant.

Fungicides are applied either as sprays or dusts on the foliage or in empty greenhouses as sprays or in the process of fumigation. They may also be applied as a 'smoke' from a special generator or tablet which is lit.

But although fungus diseases are those we most frequently come in contact with in our gardens, the viruses are also important.

Virus diseases A virus is a minute particle, visible only under the electron microscope, which causes disorders or diseases in living cells. The presence of viruses may result in leaves developing yellow or brown spots, streaks or ring patterns. Other symptoms affecting the leaves may include dark green areas along the veins (vein banding), a loss of colour (vein clearing), complete yellowing, distortion and small outgrowths. Streaks and stripes may appear on stems. Other symptoms include witches' brooms (large numbers of side shoots), distortion, colour breaks or white flecks on flowers. A condition where flowers become green and leaf-like is called 'phyllody'. Fruits may be small, misshapen or bumpy. Less distinct symptoms of virus infection are a general stunting and reduction of cropping. Viruses can also change the internal structure and the metabolism of plants; for example, virus-infected tomatoes are said to have a better flavour.

A plant may contain a 'latent' virus without any visible symptoms. There may also be interactions due to the hidden presence of viruses. Indicator plants, which give a quick and characteristic reaction when inoculated with the sap of a virus-infected plant, are widely used in the identification of viruses. Good indicator plants include *Nicotiana* species, beans and *Chenopodium* species.

Non-persistent viruses adhere to the mouth parts of insects feeding on infected plants and are carried to healthy plants. The particle remains infective for up to about two hours.

Powdery mildew of roses, Sphaerotheca pannosa. This fungus disease is detected by the presence of whitish mould on the leaf surface.

Persistent viruses are absorbed into the digestive system of the insect, and from there pass into the salivary glands where the virus multiplies. When feeding the insect injects saliva containing virus particles into plants and remains a disease carrier all its life.

Virus diseases may be mechanically transferred from one plant to another by man. Plants propagated from infected material will contain virus particles. This is important in all vegetatively propagated crops such as potatoes, fruit and bulbs.

Control Heat therapy kills or inactivates the virus, and apical meristem culture is another method of approach. As a general rule avoid the spread of virus diseases by regular spraying against the insect vectors. Clean cultivation prevents weeds acting as carriers of infection. Remains of the previous year's crop are another source of infection. Plants susceptible to the same virus should not be grown close together. Regular inspection and rogueing of obviously diseased plants is often effective. Seed should not be sown near an old infected crop. Barrier crops are sometimes grown by planting immune plants around those liable to a particular virus infection. Early sowings may enable plants to become established before the activity of disease-carrying insects.

Physiological disorders In the study of plant diseases it is usually found that most diseases are due to the attack of some small organism such as a fungus, a bacterium, or one of the microscopic viruses. The work of the plant pathologist when confronted with a disease is to try to identify the parasite which is causing the trouble and then to take steps to combat it. Long ago it was realized that plants sometimes become sick and show symptoms of ill-health although they are not infected by any parasite. This type of trouble in plants is referred to as non-parasitic disease or physiological disorder. It can arise from a multitude of factors such as unsuitable soil, lack of lime, excessive moisture, drought, lack of some essential food element, spray, fume or fumigation damage, and so forth. There is no parasite present so there is no infection to spread but it is obvious that unless something is done all the plants will become affected and weakened.

The identification of a physiological disorder is not easy and, in general, must depend on finding the symptoms as it does with the parasitic diseases which are microscopic. In both groups symptoms from different troubles are so

similar that it requires an expert to recognise them.

Attempts have been made to form a rough classification of symptoms and the most study has so far been given to the effects of shortages of essential food elements which are often referred to as mineral deficiencies. These include shortages of the major elements such as nitrogen, potash, phosphate, magnesium and lime, which plants absorb in fairly large amounts and the lesser known minor or trace elements, such as boron, copper, zinc, manganese and iron, which are needed only in very small amounts. Although some shortages, for example of potash, show as a reddish-brown scorching of the leaf margin, it is usually necessary to obtain an analysis of the soil or of the leaf tissues to identify such deficiencies.

The absence of iron shows as a lack of green colour until the leaves are very pale yellow or even white and this condition often results from excess of lime and is called 'lime-induced chlorosis'. This, however, is easily tested by one of the soil-testing field kits which will give the pH measurement of the soil showing its acidity or alkalinity. A quick remedy for iron shortage is now available by watering with the chelated compound called Sequestrene 138 Fe, which should be applied in January. A modern treatment for deficiencies is to use the spray called Foliar Feed. This is sprayed on to a crop and is said to supply all the necessary food elements through the leaves.

Dormant periods

The dormant period is one of apparent inactivity. Some plants, such as bulbs, corms and tubers, may undergo quite long periods of rest, usually in winter, but few plants are completely dormant in the sense that no development is taking place within them. Some plants, for instance lily-of-the-valley crowns,

trilliums and certain bulbs, can have the dormant period prolonged considerably by refrigeration at a constant low temperature. This is of great value to commercial growers who can bring the plants out of cold store and time the flowering when market prices will be advantageous.

Deciduous trees and shrubs are considered dormant when they have dropped their leaves in autumn, but many of these plants have some dormant buds on the stems throughout the year. Many seeds have a period of dormancy after ripening and nothing will induce them to germinate until they have had this natural period of rest. Other seeds may germinate almost as soon as they fall to the ground.

Buds on fruit trees may belong to one of two classes—either wood or growth buds, or blossom or fruit buds. During the winter these buds usually cease to develop but some wood buds may remain dormant for years.

Drainage

The soil must have adequate drainage otherwise air may be excluded and the more beneficial micro-organisms may be destroyed. Soils which have poor drainage are often sour and acid. It will be necessary to improve this acidity by applications of hydrated lime. Wet soils are cold ones, and this means that plant growth is severely retarded. The situation is even more critical in the northern, colder parts of the country. Waterlogged soils cause roots to rot and a combination of all these problems can produce complete failures in some gardens.

Soils which are well-drained have sufficient natural coarse, gritty material or sand and many soils have a high proportion of small stones also. A high humus or organic content will also ensure good drainage. It is usually the clay soils which are the most difficult with regard to drainage, although a

1 Green petal on strawberry flowers is a symptom of virus disease.
2 The attractive colour breaking of the parrot tulip is due to a virus.
3 A bracket fungus growing where bark has been stripped from a tree trunk.

hard 'pan' or layer beneath the surface of some soils can also present a problem. Such a pan is usually produced by mechanical cultivation which, in some instances, can consolidate the lower soil layers. Setting the plough or cultivators to cultivate to the same depth season after season will also produce this hard, unbroken layer. Varying the cultivating depth occasionally usually overcomes this difficulty.

Clay soils are composed of finer particles and these tend to pack so tightly together that they soon form a solid mass through which excess water cannot pass easily. Improving the drainage here consists in opening up these fine particles. This can be done by liming the soil. The particles of soil cling together in large granules after this treatment. If sharp, gritty material such as coarse sand or well-weathered cinders is worked in, the clay particles will be separated and made more open. Bulky materials such as peat, composted vegetable waste and strawy manure are invaluable as soil conditioners. Gypsum is another preparation which has proved excellent for the breaking up of heavy, waterlogged clay soils.

Where cultural methods are not sufficient to provide a marked improvement in difficult conditions, it will be necessary to improve drainage by a system of drains or drainage trenches. The most efficient method is to use field or pipe drains. These are expensive, especially if drainage on a large scale is necessary. The pipes are sold in several sizes; those 5-7cm (2-3in) in diameter are the best for the amateur.

Trenches are dug out to receive these pipes, at least 40cm (15in) deep. All trenches should slope in one direction and this slope need not exceed 1 in 40. The trenches should be arranged in a herringbone fashion and should lead to one main trench which runs from the highest point in the garden to the lowest. The side or intermediate trenches should meet this main trench at an approximate angle of 45°.

The pipes should be laid, for preference, on a 5cm (2in) layer of coarse gravel or cinders. Each pipe should be kept about 1cm (½in) away from its neighbour and the junction covered with a piece of slate, broken tile or a small piece of tough plastic sheeting. More gravel or cinders should be carefully placed around and on top of the pipes as work proceeds. The gaps between the pipes are essential to allow excess water to enter them and drain away inside the pipes. Frequent checks should be made with a little water from a watering can or hose pipe to see that water flows steadily along the pipes.

The main pipe line must be taken to a suitable outlet such as a ditch or soakaway. The latter can be constructed by digging out a large hole as deeply as possible and filling it in with stones,

Drills are depressions made for sowing seeds, using a line and draw hoe or dibber.

clinker, gravel or ashes. This hole must be at least 60-90cm (2-3ft) square and deep. Under no circumstances must drainage water be allowed to flow on to neighbours' property. Where a stream or ditch is available for the emptying of drainage water, the local Borough Surveyor's Department should be consulted to make quite sure whether it is permissible to discharge the water in this way.

An efficient drainage system can be provided if trenches are lined with rubble and coarse cinders. A similar system of trenches should be taken out and the bottom half filled with rubble. This layer of rubble should be then covered with about 15cm (6in) of coarse cinders. The trench is then filled up with soil. Surplus water will run through the coarser base material and finally into the large drainage sump at the lowest part of the garden.

It is possible to use a third system, although this is not quite so satisfactory as the others. This method employs brushwood which is laid in bundles at the bottom of the trench systems. The brushwood is then covered with soil to the surface of the surrounding ground. The unsatisfactory part of this method is that the brushwood gradually rots away and loses its efficiency. It will be necessary to renew the system every few

years, and unless the layout is small, this will involve a great deal of time and labour.

Where a new site is taken over, it is a very good idea to examine it thoroughly to see whether or not the soil requires attention to drainage. If it does it will provide an excellent opportunity to gather all the usual kinds of rubble which can be found on a new or neglected site. Builders often leave behind them a surprising amount of broken bricks, old paint tins, and lumps of concrete.

All this type of waste should be placed in convenient piles in the garden and used in the bottom of drainage trenches. If insufficient is available from the garden, it is quite likely that the local builder will be only too glad to supply some from his building sites.

During the planning of a drainage system for a waterlogged or poorly drained garden, it is a good plan to look ahead and visualise the positions for structures such as sheds, greenhouses or home extensions. All these buildings shed water and it will certainly aggravate the situation if this water is allowed to flow into the garden.

The position of a convenient drainage trench should be marked with a stake so that, later on, excess water from a gutter or down-spout can be directed into this drainage trench. The emptying of a fish pond is also facilitated if the water is directed on to an area of ground which is drained in this way, or if an outlet pipe is built into one of these drainage trenches.

Drill

This is a shallow furrow made in the soil usually in a straight line, in which seeds are sown. There are various ways in which this may be done. The usual way is to push into the soil a stick to which is attached a length of cord or string. This is drawn taut just above the soil to another stick pushed in the ground at the required distance. Then a hoe, or sometimes the edge of a rake, is drawn parallel to the length of line making a furrow of the required depth.

It is important that the depth of the drill is uniform throughout its length and that the depth is correct for the seeds which are being sown. Obviously such large seeds as those of peas and beans will require a deeper drill than the small seeds of flowering annuals, such as mignonette, polyanthus or clarkia. Where seed is being sown in a frame or small flower bed a cane is often used to mark a straight line in the soil by pressing it lightly on the surface. A furrow may then be carefully drawn along the impression with a dibber.

When the seeds have been sown they are covered with the soil which was displaced by making the drill. This may be done by drawing a rake diagonally across the drill or by using the edge of a

1

2

wooden label for small drills. For most seeds a depth of 1cm (½in) is adequate for the drill, but when sowing large seeds, such as broad beans or peas, it may be necessary to make the drill up to 5cm (2in) in depth, according to the type of soil.

Drought

A term loosely used to describe a period which is comparatively rainless. Officially a drought is any period of 14 days or more without measurable rainfall. During such weather many plants flag and make little growth unless some means of irrigation is available. As plants obtain nourishment from the soil in the form of solutions, it is evident that adequate water is of the utmost importance. A good gardener can help to conserve moisture in the soil by deep digging, which encourages plants to root deeply, and by incorporating plenty of garden compost, peat, or manure. An adequate water supply, particularly for commercial crops, is however the answer to the drought problem. It has been shown that in a normal summer in southern England, the application of 5cm (2in) of water by overhead irrigation will double the carrot crop yield and the same can be said of many other crops. Inadequate amounts of water applied spasmodically can cause trouble in that plants may be encouraged to form surface roots which are liable to be damaged if the soil dries out. A fine spray of water applied over for an extended period is far more beneficial than a flood of water given during a

short period. Watering is one of the most important operations, yet in some establishments it is left to the least experienced, sometimes with disastrous results.

Dutch hoe see Tools

Earthing up

This is an old gardening term referring to the process of banking up soil around plants such as potatoes and celery. Potato plants are usually earthed up as they develop, but with celery this should not be done until the heads are fully developed, as the plants make little or no growth after earthing up. The work is usually done with the aid of a hoe, although in large vegetable gardens a mechanical cultivator fitted with the

1 Earthing up potatoes is an operation carried out to ensure that the tubers are not made green by exposure to light. 2 When earthing up, you should make the sides as upright as possible so that the spores of potato blight will not contaminate the tubers.

necessary attachment will make a neat and quick job with long rows of potatoes and the like. A garden fork with its tines bent at right-angles, is useful for earthing up and for other forms of cultivation. In windy gardens it is sometimes necessary to earth up around the stems of broccoli, the taller varieties of kale and cauliflowers, to keep them firm in the ground.

With celery and leeks the earthing up is done to blanch the stems and a spade is often used to pile up the soil to the required height and to firm the wall of soil, thus made, using the back of the spade to smooth the soil. Care must be taken not to get soil between the stems and into the heart of the celery. When growing for show purposes gardeners often wrap brown paper around the celery stems before earthing up. Where leeks are grown for exhibition planks of wood are placed on each side of the row, about 12cm (5in) away from the plants, and the trough made by the planks is gradually filled with sifted soil as the leeks develop.

Edging plants

These are low-growing plants used for the front of flower beds, either annuals

raised under glass and bedded out in the spring, or sown in the open where they are to flower, or perennials. Although they are seen more often in public parks these days, rather than in private gardens, they can, nevertheless be most colourful. The contrast of colours is a matter of individual taste. Yellow, red and blue are contrasts in all their shades, and the variations formed by the union of any two of these produces a harmonious effect.

A great variety of plants can be used for this purpose. Edging plants raised from seed include candytuft (iberis), convolvulus, such as 'Royal Marine', which carpets the ground, *Dimorphotheca*, 'Glistening White', the cheerful yellow edged white, free-flowering *Limnanthes douglasii*, *Linaria maroccana*, mignonette, the sky-blue *Nemophila insignis*, 'Tom Thumb' nasturtiums, midget sweet williams and Virginian stock. Plants used for bedding out in May include dwarf antirrhinums and dahlias, ageratum, dwarf asters, lobelia, mesembryanthemum, nemesia, dwarf petunias, portulaca, *Phlox drummondii*, tagetes, and verbena. In early spring polyanthus and small primulas, such as the purple 'Wanda' and the cherry-pink 'E. R. Janes' are most attractive and good use should be made of crocuses, scillas, muscari and other miniature bulbous plants. Pansies and violas may be bedded out to give colour throughout the summer months.

For a more permanent edging use can be made of box (buxus), dwarf lavender, and the trailing evergreen *Euonymus radicans*, particularly in its silver and golden variegated forms. A neat form of edging between a lawn and a border is made with paving stones interplanted with various dianthus, thymes, campanulas, aubretias and saxifrages.

For the formal bedding schemes the following are among the many plants used for edging: alternantheras with various-coloured foliage which can be clipped to keep them dwarf, echeverias with their beautifully coloured rosettes, the mat-forming *Cerastium tomentosum*, or snow-in-summer; mesembryanthemums in many brilliant colours, sedums, sempervivums, the creeping *Herniaria glabra*, and *Stellaria graminea aurea*. These and many other bedding plants are still used extensively in formal planting schemes in parks, particularly at seaside resorts.

Edging tools

A lawn is only as neat as its edges so the purchase of an efficient edging tool is an important investment. The choice of tool

1 Violas, used as edging plants, flower over a long period if they are 'dead-headed'. 2 Edging plants, such as alyssum, lobelia, candytuft, dwarf nasturtiums and French marigolds play a useful role in summer bedding schemes.

69

must depend on the amount of lawn which has to be dealt with. For the more extensive ones, a mechanically propelled type will be necessary to reduce time and labour. This does not mean to say that the hand-operated types do not save time—they do, for there are several ingenious designs available.

One interesting tool has a long arm, at one end of which is a trigger-like handle that operates the cutting blades at the other end. These can be rotated so that the vertical and horizontal edges of the lawn can be dealt with. The complete unit is mounted on wheels so that it is pushed along as work proceeds. In operation this design is comfortable to use, but can be a little hard on the hand muscles if used continuously.

Another rapid edge cutter has star-like blades which are rotated by rubber wheels as it is pushed along. A similar tool has cutters operated by a ribbed metal roller. Both designs are very easy to operate. The simplest edger consists of a pair of long handled shears. Several designs are available with such refinements as moulded rubber grips, aluminium shafts or stainless steel, hollow ground blades. Models are available which can turn vertically or horizontally.

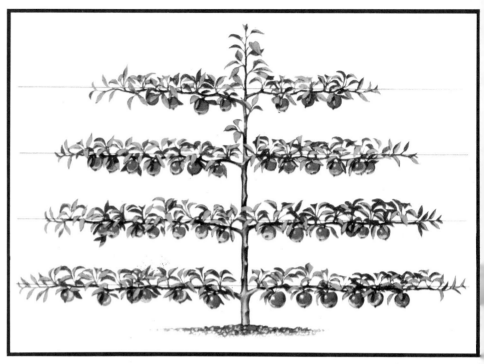

A dessert apple tree trained espalier-fashion, with horizontal branches.

For complete ease of edge trimming there are some motorized tools available which are astoundingly rapid in their work. One is powered by a 2-stroke engine and the complete machine weighs only about 12.5kg (25lb). It is claimed that about eight miles of edges can be cut on one quart of fuel.

Battery power is playing an important part in mechanized garden tools. The battery-operated lawn edger is specially designed for the smaller areas. The capacity of the small battery is quite surprising as it is capable of allowing the trimmer to cut about two miles of lawn edge. The method of cutting is similar to that of the motor-powered model. The weight is a little over 10kg (20lb) and the plug-in battery charger makes the recharging of the battery a very simple matter. One distinct advantage of this particular tool is that it is very quiet in operation. The edging iron or verge-cutter is a useful tool with a straight handle about 90cm (3ft) in length, to which is fitted a half-moon-shaped steel blade. It is used for trimming the edges of lawns and also sometimes for making the vertical cuts when lifting turf with a turfing iron.

Espalier
The literal meaning of this term is a fruit wall, a framework upon which fruit trees are supported. A well-constructed espalier has an upright post every 3m (10ft) securely embedded in the ground and standing about 1.8m (6ft) out of it. Horizontal wires are strained at intervals of about 38cm (15in) along the posts, connecting one post to the next. The end

1 An edging-iron is used once a year with a line to straighten the edges of lawns.
2 Edging shears in use.

posts are supported by diagonal stays to enable the wires to be pulled tight in order that the ultimate weight of fruit shall not overload the erection.

Fruit trees are then planted at intervals along the fence so constructed, and trained in a horizontal fashion to the wires. Trees trained in this way have come to be called, quite erroneously, espaliers, though they may be referred to as espalier-trained trees.

There are two methods of training the young plants. In the first the stem is allowed to grow upright and as laterals develop they are tied in to the wires horizontally on each side of the main stem. On maturity the general effect along the fence is of horizontal ribbons of blossom and later fruit. The second form of training uses the side branches in exactly the same way but after they have been trained for a short distance in the horizontal position, they are turned upwards, thus forming a broad-based letter 'U'.

When fruit is grown on this system, more can be accommodated in a given space, light reaching all branches and air circulating freely, resulting in a heavier crop than would be possible were the trees grown as bushes.

Pears and apples are commonly trained in this way, either in the open or against walls. The method can also look effective for training apricots and soft fruits against walls and even foliage plants such as ivy are sometimes trained in this way on house walls.

Established-spur system
This is a system of winter pruning, sometimes adopted with weak growing

varieties of apples which fruit on short spurs. It is a modification of the old spur-pruning, popular in the early part of this century, but not quite so drastic. The aim is to produce short, permanent ('established') spurs on which fruit will be borne close to the main branches. Some outward-pointing laterals are left unpruned until they have fruited and then are cut back to a fruit bud as near their base as possible. The established spurs are cut back according to vigour—to one bud for the weakest and to five buds for the strongest. Leaders are tipped by about 5cm (2in).

Evergreens

Evergreens have an important role to play in our gardens, particularly during the winter, when their value is so much enhanced by the way in which they brighten otherwise dreary surroundings.

It is not, however, at this season alone that they add their lustre to the garden scene. In spring and summer, as well, their foliage, in many instances a rich dark green in colour and glossy in texture, provides interesting contrasts to the more delicate green of deciduous shrubs and trees. It acts also as an interesting foil to the brilliant colours of the floral displays of spring and high summer, while in autumn, its sombre hues make the leaf colours and bright berries shine more intensely by contrast.

Although some herbaceous plants might be called evergreen, in the sense that their summer foliage does not die down in winter, and there are a few trees, such as the holly and the holm oak, that retain their leaves all the year round, in general, when we talk about evergreens, we are thinking of shrubs.

Evergreens as Hedging Plants A number of evergreen shrubs make useful hedging plants; apart from certain conifers, such as yew, cypress and thuja, nothing makes such a dense, permanent screen that ensures year-long privacy. Furthermore, a hedge made of flowering evergreen shrubs, is valuable for the sake of its colourful blossoms.

The choice of suitable material is wide; it includes many of the barberries, such as *Berberis stenophylla* and *B. darwinii*, escallonias, with their pink or crimson tubular flowers, ideal seaside shrubs, *Pyracantha rogersiana*, a form of the well-known scarlet firethorn, well suited for hedging, and the useful *Viburnum tinus*, or laurustinus, with its pinkish-white flower clusters that appear in such lavish profusion from late January until the end of April.

Given the necessary acid soil, rich in humus, there are a number of rhododen-

Evergreen plants frequently bear showy flowers.
1 The double-flowered form of Rhododendron fastuosum.
2 Siphonosmanthus (Osmanthus) delavayi.

drons that make handsome evergreen hedges, including the common purple-flowered *R. ponticum*, a vigorous shrub that has naturalized itself in many parts of the British Isles, and the early-flowering *R. praecox*, ideal for the milder parts of these islands, where late frosts cannot spoil the beauty of its lilac blossom.

Where beauty of foliage alone is desired, box, laural, holly, aucuba or *Lonicera nitida* would all be good choices for hedging. As a last resource, there is always the much maligned privet, which although not strictly evergreen by nature will retain its leaves throughout the winter if it is kept regularly and closely clipped during its growing season.

Evergreens as Specimen Shrubs Used in the lawn, or at focal points of interest in the garden, evergreens make first-rate specimen shrubs. For the rock or heath garden, too, miniature versions of many larger shrubs are available, scaled down to proportions more in keeping with these lilliputian surroundings.

One of the handsomest evergreens suitable for use either as a lawn or wall specimen is the stately *Magnolia grandiflora*, whose king-sized oval glossy leaves make a wonderful setting for the beauty

1

4

2

5

Many evergreens have additional value in fragrant flowers or showy fruits.
1 The brilliant red young foliage of Pieris forrestii turns pale green as the season advances.
2 Griselinia littoralis variegata, from New Zealand, grows up to 6m (20ft), and has leathery variegated leaves.
3 Although the flowers of Yucca aloifolia are arresting, the long, pointed leaves are distinctive in themselves, and account for the name Spanish bayonet.
4 The shrub Phillyrea decora grows up to 3m (10ft). The smooth leaves droop to display spikes of flower.
5 Rhododendron 'Temple Belle' has large single, bell-like flowers. The foliage is soft in both colour and texture.
6 Santolina neopolitana, the lavender cotton, a sub-shrub, with yellow button flowers in July. The foliage is silver grey and somewhat felted.
7 Aucuba japonica crotonoides has shining leaves spotted with creamy-white. The white flowers in early spring are followed by red berries.
8 Pyracantha rogersiana, the firethorn, is smothered in creamy white flowers in May. They are followed by orange berries which persist most of the winter.
9 Berberis darwinii a thorny plant, has small decorative orange flowers in early summer, followed by purplish fruits. The small leaves are holly-like in appearance and texture.
10 Prunus laurocerasus, the common laurel or cherry laurel, makes a small tree. The white flowers are fragrant and are followed by dark purple fruits.

3

9

10

of the creamy-white scented blossoms, many of which will be 20cm (8in) or more in diameter. This shrub flowers from July to September and the cultivar 'Exmouth', sometimes listed as *lanceolata*, although very similar to the type plant, scores additional points for the attractive cinnamon indumentum, or 'felting' on the underside of its magnificent leaves, and because it flowers when younger than the type.

The arbutus makes a lawn specimen of almost equal beauty and dignity. The strawberry tree, *A. unedo*, which reaches 4.5-12m (15-40ft) or more and has dark green foliage and cream-coloured, heath-like blossoms, is the form most widely grown. Rivalling the beauty of the polished foliage are the scarlet, strawberry-like fruits that ripen as the following season's flowers start to open, so that you have fruit and blossom on the shrub at one and the same time. There is a hybrid, known as *A. x andrachnoides*, which is less vigorous and easily distinguishable by its handsome mahogany-red bark, its grey-green foliage and vivid orange-coloured fruits.

Evergreens in the Shrub Border For the border itself, the choice of species and varieties is even more varied. Many of the shrubs available are members of favourite plant groups that contain also deciduous species. Prominent among them are the cotoneasters and barberries with striking evergreen forms such as the ever-popular *C. lactea*, the prostrate *C. dammeri* and the grey-foliaged *C. franchetii*, together with *Berberis darwinii* with small, holly-like leaves, and *B. gagnepainii*, with crimpled foliage.

We tend sometimes to forget that heathers are shrubs and evergreen ones into the bargain. For the border where space is restricted, they are among the most valuable and few evergreen shrubs would be capable of giving a more striking all-round display. The winter-flowering species. *E. carnea* in particular, put on an amazing show in the garden's 'off' season, but this is not their only virtue, as their foliage remains fresh and attractive even when they are out of flower. Used as carpeting plants among other taller shrubs they will act as highly effective weed smotherers, as also will a number of other prostrate evergreens such as *Gaultheria procumbens* or *Cotoneaster dammeri*.

Variegated Evergreens During the winter months, variegated evergreens, such as the green and gold wood olive, *Elaeagnus pungens aureo-variegata*, the gold and silver-variegated hollies and the golden box, *Buxus sempervirens elegantissima*, will all give an impression of sunshine in the garden, even when winter skies are grey and overcast.

Evergreens in More Formal Surroundings In pots, tubs, urns or other similar containers, evergreens, with their all-the-year-round beauty, are more useful, than any other plants for

73

use on terraces and stretches of paving or as an adjunct to other formal garden features. The sweet bay, *Laurus nobilis*, clipped box, and some of the semi-dwarf rhododendron hybrids such as the scarlet-flowered 'Britannia', are examples of shrubs that can be used in this manner.

Evergreens provide, as well, an attractive permanent covering for house walls, fences and pergolas and are unsurpassed for screening or camouflaging unsightly sheds and outbuildings. Climbing evergreen shrubs include the ivies— the gold and silver-variegated forms are the most attractive—pyracanthas, honeysuckles and others that will soften the sometimes over-severe lines of contemporary architecture or emphasize the mellow charms of older buildings.

A selection of genera containing evergreen shrubs

Adenocarpus	Danae	Halimiocistus	Mahonia	Rhamnus
Andromeda	Daphne	Halimium	Myrtus	Rhododendron
Atriplex	Desfontainea	Hebe	Nandina	Rosmarinus
Aucuba	Elaeagnus	Hedera	Olearia	Ruscus
Azara	Embothrium	Helianthemum	Osmanthus	Santolina
Berberis	Erica	Hypericum	Osmarea	Sarcococca
Buxus	Eriobotrya	Ilex	Pachysandra	Senecio
Calluna	Escallonia	Itea	Pernettya	Skimmia
Camellia	Eucryphia	Kalmia	Philesia	Stranvaesia
Carpenteria	Euonymus	Laurus	Phillyrea	Sycopsis
Cassinia	Fabiana	Lavandula	Pieris	Tricuspidaria
Ceanothus	Fatsia	Leucothoe	Piptanthus	Vaccinium
Cistus	Garrya	Ligustrum	Pittosporum	Viburnum
Cotoneaster	Gaultheria	Lonicera	Prunus	Yucca
Daboecia	Griselinia	Magnolia	Pyracantha	

Fairy rings
This is the name given to the deeper green circles or parts of circles that sometimes appear on lawns or in meadows. Later dead areas may appear. This condition is caused by the growth of certain fungi. The most common one on lawns in this country is *Marasmius oreades* which produces small toadstool type fruiting bodies about 3cm (1½in) high and the same distance across the cap. These are tan coloured at first and then pale, with the centre slightly raised. Under the cap the gills are pale and rather wide apart. There are other toadstools which may form fairy rings but Marasmius is the usual one.

The grass outside the ring of fungi is darker green compared with the brown inner area owing to the outer turf being stimulated in some way. The inner area is either killed directly by the fungus or death is due to the fungus preventing water percolating to the roots. The latter fact also makes it difficult to cure the trouble as fungicides do not easily percolate through the soil to the roots.

It may be necessary to strip the affected part of turf and form in Quintozene (PCNB) or other fungicide before replacing the turf. Another way would be to 'spike' the area with a tined fork and water in a suitable fungicide such as Bordeaux mixture.

Family tree
In the so-called 'family tree' several different varieties are grafted on a single common rootstock. Such grafting can be done with suitable compatible ornamental shrubs or trees but is more commonly carried out with fruit trees. Theoretically the only limit to the number of different varieties which can be grown on one tree is the number of branches which can be made: in America there is supposed to have been an apple tree with more than 60 varieties on it. In practice, the greater the number of varieties, the greater is the difficulty of keeping a proper balance between growth and fruit production.

The value of a family fruit tree lies in its ability to offer you several varieties (with a consequent spread of maturity dates) which can be grown in the same space as one normal tree. Further, as varieties should be chosen which flower at the same time and pollinate each other, it is possible to plant a single

Fairy rings are caused by the fungus Marasmius oreades.

tree with every prospect of a good crop, a boon to the owner of a small garden. And, of course, gardeners with room for several family trees can grow a really wide range of varieties in a comparatively small plot.

A number of nurseries sell family apple and pear trees, three varieties on each. A typical example is one with three famous dessert pears on it— 'Williams' Bon Chrêtien' (September), 'Louise Bonne of Jersey' (September– October) and 'Conference' (October– November).

The management of a family tree follows normal lines but pruning must be directed to prevent any one variety growing away at the expense of the others. Strong vertical shoots, for instance, should be removed entirely as these grow most strongly.

Leaders are treated in the usual way, being cut hard if weak, lightly tipped if strong. If the branches are sturdy, the branch system can be doubled by pruning to a pair of growth buds, one on each side of the branch, which will subsequently grow out in the desired direction.

Fan
This is a form in which fruit trees may be trained, the branches springing from a short leg and spreading out like the ribs of a fan, all on a single flat plane. Thus, a fan is an appropriate shape of tree to grow against a wall but this is not essential: fans can be trained against supporting wires in a similar way to espaliers. The fan is a popular form for peaches and other stone fruits but it is quite possible to grow apples and pears as fans.

Feeding plants
Under natural conditions plants feed themselves. Water makes up 80 to 90% of their weight, and the assimilation of carbon dioxide from the air provides a high proportion of the rest of the tissue material. Three elements only—carbon, hydrogen and oxygen are concerned in this: the other 1 or 2% of the plant

The elements that are not essential just find their way into the plant—for better or for worse. Substances definitely harmful, such as sodium chlorate weed-killers, can also get in because plants have no mechanism for rejecting what is bad for them.

So, plants, like us, have to eat to live. It is the minute root hairs just behind the tip of the root and not the large roots that you see when you dig or pull a plant from the soil, that collectively form the 'mouth' of the plant. But of course, they do not eat, but drink their food which is obtained from the soil solution. This is like a thin soup of soil moisture and dissolved salts that surrounds soil particles and partly fills the spaces between them.

But plants require oxygen to release the energy needed to take in foods which are then used to build cell walls, proteins or storage materials such as starch, sugars and fats. So it is most important to see that soils are kept in a well-aerated condition so as to make this oxygen available; a waterlogged soil is one in which there is no air and the uptake of foods is prevented.

Essential nutrients Of the 16 elements that are essential three, nitrogen, phosphorus and potassium are taken out of the soil in comparatively large amounts and supplies have to be replenished regularly for best results; these are the 'big 3' in your fertilizer needs. Calcium and magnesium are sometimes lacking and have to be added as lime and Epsom salts. Sulphur, boron, copper, iron, manganese, zinc, molybdenum and chlorine are needed only in very small amounts or traces—hence their name trace elements. They are like the tiny bearings in a watch—very small parts, but essential to its working.

You need to consider them only for special crops and soils. Each of these elements has a particular job to do. For example nitrogen is the leaf maker, phosphorus the root maker and potassium the flower and fruit maker. No one element can replace the other; you cannot have normal plants when nitrogen is in short supply even though you have given plenty of phosphates or potash. In fact an excess of one element can easily cause symptoms of deficiency of another element to become apparent: for example, apples and tomatoes often show symptoms of magnesium deficiency when given too much potash.

Nearly all soils have large stores of plant foods, but most of these are held in the form of complex substances in the soil minerals and in the organic matter of the soil. They are released too slowly

however, consists of 60 or more different chemical elements, all of which are taken up from the soil. There are large stores of plant foods in most soils but these are released by the normal soil processes too slowly for high yielding vegetables, fruits and vigorous flower plants that the plant breeder has produced for us. So we have to supplement the natural supplies with fertilizers.

Fortunately you do not have to in-

clude carbon, hydrogen and oxygen in your feeding programme, nor is there any need to add all of the 60 nutrients, since only 16 elements are known, at present, to be essential for healthy growth. Three only of these, nitrogen, phosphorus and potassium—are required in really large amounts and are likely to be deficient in your soil. It is necessary to add magnesium and even elements such as copper in certain conditions.

Growth is limited by the plant food present in the smallest quantity relative to the plants need, as for example at 1 by the amount of phosphate present. It is not enough to increase the phosphate alone, 2 because potassium then becomes the limiting factor. Only when all three foods are supplied in sufficient amounts 3 is the best growth possible.

to sustain a rapid succession of crops or the yield and quality that you would really be proud of. Plant breeders are constantly raising higher yielding and bigger plants which need heavier feeding to do them justice.

So, we have to provide additional supplies of plant foods in the form of fertilizers but first one has to find out whether our plants are well fed, hungry or starving.

Hunger signs How much fertilizer, what kind, when to apply and where to apply are the questions we now have to answer in order to get the best results from our fertilizers. But this is no easy matter to solve; there is no indicator that you can push into the soil or fasten on to the plant that will tell you whether it is hungry or not. If only plants squealed like pigs when they are hungry it would be a much easier task for us.

The feeding of plants is still a matter of intelligent guesswork with the aid of a little science.

The plant reflects the level of nutrition in many ways. The type of growth, the colour of the leaves and yield are obvious indications of soil productivity. Plants develop characteristic symptoms when they are poorly nourished. Many of these deficiency symptoms have been recognized and described for all the essential elements for many plants. Deficiencies are easy to see, but not so simple to identify since several may show the same symptoms. There are many other things that can cause poor plant growth; the weather has a great deal to do with it; if the weather is cold and wet plants will make little progress. Poor drainage can produce symptoms like those of nitrogen deficiency; wind scorch often looks like potash deficiency.

By the time symptoms are shown the plant is suffering from acute hunger and it is often too late to correct the trouble.

Prevention is always better than cure and you should always make sure that deficiencies are corrected before sowing by having your soil tested. Then fertilizers can be used to compensate for the missing nutrients (see Soil testing).

Sometimes, even though a plant may look well, it can still be suffering slightly from a lack of certain nutrients; this is known as 'hidden hunger' and it will respond greatly to a fertilizer dressing that contains the food of which it makes

extensive use. For instance your cabbage may be doing nicely, but they would do much better if nitrogen were added.

Three things must be done should your plants be suffering from the lack of certain nutrients. First, find out what ails the plant, ie diagnose the deficiency. Second, try to find out how serious the deficiency is. Third, determine, as nearly as you can, how much of the missing nutrient is needed to bring the plant back to health.

Chemical soil tests may help to pin

point the trouble. Another way is to diagnose the trouble as closely as possible, then spray the foliage with a foliar feed (see Foliar feeding); if the plants show marked improvement within two weeks you are on the right track. Continue to apply fertilizer every two weeks until the plant resumes vigorous growth. It is possible to let the plants speak for themselves by carrying out a chemical test on the leaf; this is known as tissue testing—a valuable tool in the hands of one who understands soils, fertilizers

ration of food that will last annual plants for quite a long time. But never scatter fertilizers down the seed drill because they will injure most vegetable and flower seeds.

Starter solutions Dilute liquid feeds may be watered on to drills, seed trays of plants or potted plants before planting to give a rapid start.

After planting

Top dressing Putting fertilizer along the rows after the plants have started growing is often done to add some extra nitrogen. You are most likely to need to top dress under these conditions:

1 On sandy soils and thin chalky soils because leaching is common.
2 After heavy rains have washed out nitrates.
3 On soils that are low in organic matter.
4 Where you have not given enough nitrogen when you planted.

This is the best way of feeding perennial plants growing in borders, established lawns, fruit trees, roses and shrubs. The fertilizer should be spread as far as the branches reach to contact the actively absorbing root hairs.

To apply fertilizer in perennial borders, spread a small handful in a wide ring around each plant and mix carefully with soil. Either solid or liquid feeds are suitable for these dressings.

Liquid feeding Liquid feeds which are merely fertilizers in solution, are often more convenient to apply, particularly in crowded borders where it is difficult to spread a solid fertilizer without getting it on the foliage.

The foliage of many potted plants completely covers the surface of the pot and feeding with solid fertilizers can be hazardous. With liquid fertilizers feeding and watering is done in one operation—a distinct advantage when you have large batches of pots to look after.

Liquid feeding is essential if you intend to use drip irrigation in which the water issuing from nozzles gently trickles into the soil and spreads sideways underneath, leaving the surface dry.

Ring culture Ring culture in which plants are grown in bottomless containers or in ring pots filled with compost and stood on an aggregate layer is another variation in feeding technique. After planting, the rings and the aggregate layer, which consists of gravel or a sand-vermiculite mixture, are both watered until the roots penetrate the aggregate. Then the aggregate only is watered daily with a liquid feed to keep it thoroughly damp, so that the nutrients are taken up by capillary action.

Soilless cultivation It is quite easy to grow plants without using soil at all and

and plant growth but one which can lead you to apply fertilizer that is not needed and will not help your crop. A more refined method known as leaf analysis is used for guiding fertilizer programmes in fruit and other perennial plants.

Methods of feeding with fertilizers
Before planting

Broadcasting If new beds or borders are being prepared fertilizers are best scattered evenly all over the ground after digging. Then mix with the top few

inches of soil by raking, lightly forking or with a rotary cultivator.

This is best suited to the crops that you sow in shallow rows or plant closely.

Banding along the row For peas, beans and other vegetables that are sown in widely spaced rows the best place to put the fertilizer is in a band 2.5cm (1-2in) to the side and 2.5-5cm (1-2in) below the depth of the seed by hoeing out a trench. The roots of the young plant contact the fertilizer within two or three days after the seed germinates and get a big enough excellent specimens can be raised in plastic troughs or plastic-lined wood filled with sand, fine gravel, mixtures of peat and vermiculite or several other materials.

Nutrient solutions made with special fertilizers are either applied on the surface or are pumped up from below through the aggregate which in this case must be in waterproof troughs. This is known as soilless culture (hydroponics).

Feeding through the leaf It is not only roots which can absorb plant foods but the foliage also can absorb nutrients very quickly thus short circuiting the long journeys from the root. Although it is unlikely that this method will supersede normal soil applications, it has advantages (see Foliar feeding).

Obviously the above comments are very general; soil conditions and the needs of the individual plants will determine which and how much fertilizer to use (see also Fertilizers).

It must be stressed, however, that fertilizers are not a cure-all for all garden troubles—they merely supplement the soil's store of nutrients. And not only must the plant be well fed, the roots must have a good home to live in, otherwise fertilizers can never produce their best results.

For most species there is a fairly definite relation between root and top growth and so it follows that a well-developed, healthy root system is essential for the production of a vigorous plant. The soil condition needed for normal root development can be described as good depth and friability. Such an ideal soil provides a well-distributed system of water reservoirs, a good ventilation system and plenty of large spaces into which roots can grow and develop freely. Such a condition is brought about by draining waterlogged soils, adding humus-forming manures, avoiding cultivating soils when they are too wet and watering during dry periods.

Fences

Two things are very important in the garden. They are privacy and shelter. The latter is often a problem in gardens which are exposed to cold prevailing winds. Both these points are important not only for the gardener himself, but also for the plants in his garden. Young growth can be severely damaged by cold winds and frequent buffeting will cause a great deal of root disturbance. Although privacy and shelter can be provided by trees and shrubs, fences also have an important part to play.

The choice of fencing must never be undertaken lightly, for serious consideration must be given to its appear-

1

2

1 Top dressing tomatoes to stimulate growth and encourage ripening.
2 Replacing compost at the top of a pot invigorates the plant.

78

ance and construction. Strength is very important, especially in exposed, windy localities. A fence is only as strong as its supports, and particular care must be taken to see that these are not only substantial but inserted securely. Most fences are supplied with strong posts, usually 10-15cm (4-6in) square, depending on the type of fence that has to be supported. Sometimes concrete posts are supplied; these are extremely strong, although a little more cumbersome to install. It is very important to see that concrete posts are inserted deeply and firmly. Strength of timber also depends on the prevention of rot, and unless cedar wood is used (except for posts), all timber should be treated with a suitable preservative. Creosote can be used, although it should be allowed to soak into the timber for several weeks before plants are trained against it. Unless this is done, there is the danger of stem and leaf scorch and its use is not generally recommended where plants are to be grown against or near a fence. A safer treatment consists of the use of copper naphthenate preservatives such as the green, horticultural grades of Cuprinol or Solignum.

Types of fencing The most popular types are purchased as units or panels. Usually they are from 1.5-1.8m (5-6ft) in length with heights varying from about 90cm-1.8m (3-6ft). A solid or close-boarded fence is, as its name implies, a design which consists of upright or horizontal strips of wood, some 15cm (6in) wide and 2-2.5cm (¾-1in) thick. The strips are nailed to two or more supporting rails at the rear of the panel. These provide complete privacy and wind protection, but are rather uninteresting in appearance.

Weatherboard fencing provides a little more interest in its appearance as it consists of wedge-shaped strips of wood, 2cm (¾in) in thickness at one edge, tapering to 1cm (⅛in) at the other. Each strip overlaps the next by about 2cm (¾in). The advantage of this design is that it is virtually peep proof.

Interwoven fencing is very attractive but inclined to open up a little, especially in the cheaper units. Thin strips of wood, approximately 10cm (4in) wide and 1cm (⅛in) thick, are interwoven one with another. It is a strong fence if it is supported well. Trellis fencing is very cheap and more suited as a support for climbing and trailing plants. It is not a strong design but can be used to good effect for covering unsightly walls or as an additional part of a fence design. Sections 45-60cm (18-24in) deep look most attractive if attached to the top of, say, a close-boarded fence. Used in this manner it helps to lighten an otherwise heavy, solid design.

Trellis fencing usually consists of laths of wood 2.5 by 1.5cm (1 by ½in) thick, fastened across each other vertically and horizontally to form 15-20cm

A wooden fence remains neat if repaired and painted regularly.

(6-8in) squares. The laths are attached to a more substantial framing of 2.5 or 3cm (1 or 1½in) square timber.

Two other cheap types of fencing are wattle and cleft chestnut. The former is useful where a rural or rustic effect is desired. The woven, basket-like construction produces a very sturdy fencing panel. The panels are usually attached to lengths of oak stakes driven securely into the ground. The latter fence can be purchased with the individual pieces of cleft chestnut spaced out at different intervals. It is possible to purchase rolls of this fencing with the paling nearly touching. The rolls are usually attached to strong oak posts by galvanized wire. In their construction, individual cleft chestnut palings are wired top and bottom to strong horizontal wires.

One of the latest advances in fence production is the sale of kits which are so accurately machined and complete that even an unskilled person can erect panels without any trouble. With these kits have come new ideas in design, and many can be made up into contemporary designs. This is especially useful where bold effects are required in the construction of patios. Many ultra-modern properties are being built and this advance in fence appearance will be welcomed by their owners.

Fencing can also be provided in the form of chain link or mesh netting. The best quality is heavily galvanized to withstand the rigours of the weather.

A more recent innovation is the plastic coating of chain link over the galvanized wire. Standard colours of dark green, black, white, yellow and light green can be obtained.

Wire netting is another cheaper and useful fencing material. Wire netting is easy and quick to erect as it requires only moderately substantial supporting posts of timber or angle iron spaced approximately every 1.8-2.4m (6-8ft) apart according to the height and length of the fence being erected.

Another type of fencing is known as rustic. This is constructed from larch or pine wood of circular section. The main

uprights are usually quite substantial and are cut from 7-10cm (3-4in) diameter timber while the design work between them is of thinner section, usually about 3-5cm (1½-2in) diameter. The most popular design consists of a diamond pattern approximately 45cm (18in) in area. It is sold by the square foot either with the bark on or removed, stained and varnished. The result is a most natural fence or screen which blends in very well with the surroundings.

Fertilizers

Fertilizers provide plants with nutrients; they are commonly listed in catalogues under: Straight fertilizers, Compound fertilizers, Liquid fertilizers.

Straight fertilizers These are used to supply a specific nutrient. If you wish to make your spring cabbages grow away more quickly in the spring you could top-dress with Nitro-chalk. If your tomatoes are not ripening quickly enough in dull weather sulphate of potash could help. Straight fertilizers are either inorganic 'artificials' or 'organics'.

Artificials, which may be manufactured in factories, or are the purified salts from natural underground deposits, are more correctly known as inorganic fertilizers. They generally dissolve easily in water and when applied to moist soils act quickly. But this does not mean that they will be washed out of your soil. Both phosphates and potash are absorbed by soil constituents and so is nitrogen when applied as ammonium fertilizers. Nitrates, however, may be lost from the soil if applied during the winter or too far away from plant roots. Hence the need for top dressings.

Most inorganic fertilizers are fairly concentrated and we know exactly how much of each nutrient is present in any weight of fertilizer and so you can calculate how much fertilizer to apply to the soil to provide a desired quantity of any particular nutrient. But great care must be taken in handling them because being concentrated, overdoses are often harmful.

'Organics' are of animal or vegetable origin and their nutrients are locked away inside the complex structure of proteins and other materials. They must break down into soluble forms—nitrates or in some instances ammonia—before they can be used by plants. Since bacteria and other living organisms in the soil break these down, their effectiveness largely depends upon the soil conditions being satisfactory for the organisms; they are most effective when used in moist, well-aerated, well-limed soils. Many are fairly concentrated, but their nutrient content often varies.

Fine dusty particles break down much more quickly than the coarse fragments in organic fertilizers. For example a fine grade of hoof-and-horn meal works very nearly as quickly as some inorganic

Straight fertilisers in general use

Fertiliser and main nutrient supplied	Properties	When and how much to use	Fertiliser and main nutrient supplied	Properties	When and how much to use
Basic slag Phosphates 8–16% P₂O₅ (insol)	Slow acting inorganic. Active ingredient is calcium silico-phosphate which is an insoluble material; slow acting and long lasting. Its lime content makes it a useful fertiliser for acid soils that are also low in phosphates	Autumn or winter open ground 8 oz per square yard before sowing or planting. Not to be used with lime	**Magnesium sulphate** 10% Mg	Inorganic Coarsely crystalline soluble material. Tends to cake on storage. Used only where magnesium is lacking	Can be used at 1–2 oz per square yard or applied as a leaf spray ¼ oz per gallon of water
Bone flour Phosphates 27–28% P₂O₅ (insol) 1% N	Concentrated organic. Active ingredient calcium phosphate which is insoluble; being very finely ground it is fairly quick acting Has a very small amount of nitrogen. Useful for keeping home-made mixtures of fertilisers in dry condition	Open ground autumn or winter 4 oz per square yard before sowing or planting. Can be used in potting composts	**Meat and bone meal** Nitrogen and Phosphates 4–6% N 12–14% P₂O₅ (insol)	A good organic fertiliser for general use, which comes from waste meat, offals and condemned carcasses from slaughter houses. The mixture is steamed under pressure to remove fat and then dried at a high temperature to kill disease organisms. The nitrogen and phosphate content varies. The higher the content of bone the more phosphates it contains. These are insoluble in water and only slowly available to plants. The nitrogen portion works quickly in warm moist soils	Autumn or winter. Fork into open ground, 4 oz per square yard before sowing or planting. Safe to use in greenhouse borders and can be used in composts. Should be mixed with sulphate of potash to give a balanced feed.
Bone meal 20–25% P₂O₅ 3–5% N	Concentrated organic. Active ingredient calcium phosphate, insoluble but releases its phosphates slowly over a long period Has a useful content of nitrogen which works quickly	Open ground autumn or winter 4 oz per square yard before sowing or planting. Can be used in potting composts 4 oz per bushel	**Nitrate of soda** Nitrogen 16% N	All the nitrogen is present as a soluble nitrate and is immediately available to plants as soon as it has dissolved in the soil moisture. If watered in its effects will be seen in a few days. It can destroy the crumb structure of some soils if large dressings are given too frequently	Spring and summer as a top dressing for green crops or plants that are growing very slowly after cold wet weather. ½ oz per square yard at intervals of several weeks
Dried blood Nitrogen 7–14% N	Concentrated organic. Quick acting especially in warm, moist soils and it is one of the most rapid of organic fertilisers. There is a fully soluble form that can be dissolved in water and used as a liquid feed	Used as a top-dressing mainly for greenhouse plants throughout season. 2–3 oz per square yard	**Nitro-chalk** Nitrogen 21% N	A mixture of ammonium nitrate and chalk. It has some nitrate for immediate action and the ammonia comes into play somewhat later. The chalk present largely balances any loss of lime from the soil that may be caused by the ammonia part of this fertiliser. Its granular form makes it easy to spread It becomes pasty if left in air for long periods. The chalk content is so small that it does not make the soil alkaline	Spring and summer top dressing for many crops including lawns ½ oz per square yard at intervals of several weeks
Hoof and horn meal Nitrogen 7–13% N	Concentrated organic. Acts fairly quickly in warm moist soils but long lasting. Available in a number of grades: Fine grade ⅛ inch to dust as used in John Innes Base Fertiliser, acts quickly but hoof parings and other coarse grades very slowly	Open ground and greenhouse borders 4–6 oz per square yard John Innes Base Fertiliser for potting composts. Coarse grades are best for perennial borders			

fertilizers, while coarse particles break down slowly and release their nitrogen over a long period of time.

Synthetic organics such as Urea-Form are chemical combinations of urea and formaldehyde and are designed to give a slow release of nitrogen for several months. Their granules are almost insoluble and do not break down in the soil. The outer surface of each granule is gradually worn away in much the same way as you would suck a sweet. The process begins within a few days in warm moist soils and continues to release nutrients as the plants need them for long pre-determined periods. So, a 'one-shot' application may nourish plants throughout the growing season, whereas several applications of quickly available forms may be necessary.

Fruits and vegetables, properly fertilized with quickly available forms of nutrients are as healthful and tasty as those fertilized with slowly available forms; plants obtain their nutrients as

Brassicas suffering from manganese deficiency have stunted blue leaves.

simple chemicals through the roots. And these chemicals are exactly the same whether they come from an 'artificial' or an 'organic' fertilizer.

Compound fertilizers These contain two, or more usually, all three of the major nutrients, nitrogen, phosphorus and potassium. These are the ones that are used by plants in the largest amounts and are, therefore, most likely to be deficient in soils. When you buy a fertilizer, therefore, you generally buy it for its content of these nutrients in order to give a balanced feed before sowing or planting.

You can make your own compounds by simply mixing together two or more straight fertilizers. The following are often made at home:

A fertilizer for general use:
Sulphate of ammonia 5 parts by weight
Superphosphate 5 parts by weight
Sulphate of potash 2 parts by weight

Analysis 8% N, 8% P_2O_5 8% K_2O.

John Innes Base Fertilizer for potted plants:

Hoof and Horn meal 2 parts by weight
Superphosphate 2 parts by weight
Sulphate of potash 1 part by weight

Analysis 5.1% N, 7.2% P_2O_5, 9.6% K_2O

Analysis When you buy a fertilizer you want to know how much of each plant food it contains and this information is given in the analysis provided with the fertilizer. The analysis states the content of nitrogen as N, phosphorus as P_2O_5 (phosphoric acid) and potassium as K_2O (potash). Plants do not absorb their plant foods in these forms, since nitrogen is an inert gas, pure phosphorus and potassium are very active chemically and burn if exposed to the air or water. So these elements can only be absorbed by plants when combined with other elements to form materials suitable for use in fertilizers. So the figures mean that the fertilizer contains the equivalent of the elements.

As an example, nitrate of soda contains 16% of nitrogen; what does the remainder consist of? The chemical name for nitrate of soda is sodium nitrate which is a chemical compound of nitrogen, sodium and oxygen. So there is about 26% of sodium and 58% of oxygen in this compound.

You are advised to read the labels very carefully and look for the analysis very carefully in order to save disappointment and money by avoiding 'miracle' or 'wonder-working' fertilizers bearing no guaranteed analysis.

1

1 Nitrogenous fertilizer is applied here in a ring around each plant.
2 The soil is scraped over with a cultivator to work in the fertilizer.

2

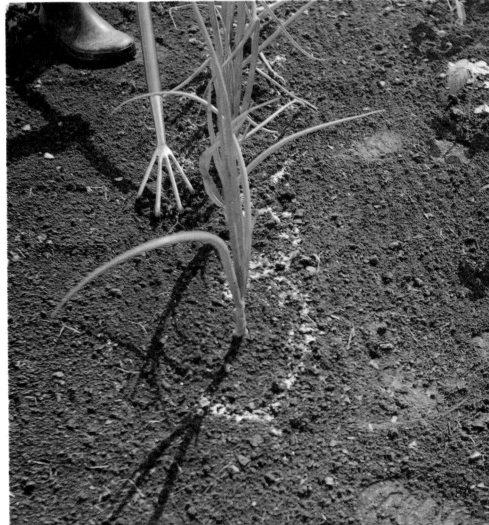

Straight fertilisers in general use

Fertiliser and main nutrient supplied	Properties	When and how much to use	Fertiliser and main nutrient supplied	Properties	When and how much to use
Potash nitrate Nitrogen Potash 15% N 10% K_2O	A mixed nitrate of sodium and potassium. Acts quickly. Useful two-in-one fertiliser for supplying potash as well as nitrogen in early spring crops that would make too much soft growth if nitrogen only was given. Useful for soils that are low in potash as well as nitrogen	Spring and summer, used as a top dressing for many crops. Apply 1–2 oz per square yard direct to the soil or mix 1 teaspoonful to one gallon of water two or three times during the growing period	**Sulphate of iron** Iron	When one part is mixed with three parts of sulphate of ammonia and sand it will kill moss, clover and broad-leaved weeds in lawns and freshen up the colour. Can be used for correcting iron deficiency in acid soils, but is ineffective for this purpose in limey soils. It should be powdered finely	Used in lawn sands
Potassium nitrate Nitrogen Potassium N 12–14% K_2O 44–46%	This is a pure concentrated fertiliser that is used mainly in liquid feeds. It is suitable for all greenhouse plants when dissolved in water	Mix 1 teaspoonful to one gallon of water and apply regularly as a liquid feed	**Urea-form** Nitrogen 38% N	Synthetic organic. A combination of urea and formaldehyde which is sold under a trade name—which in spite of its high analysis, will not burn plants. Although mainly insoluble in water its nitrogen is gradually converted by soil bacteria to a form which is available to plants, and will feed plants continually for several months from one application. It is non-corrosive and will not rust fertiliser spreaders and other equipment	Use at any time of year before sowing or planting in the open or in the greenhouse. The slow release action of this fertiliser encourages durable healthy turf and reduces the danger of burning the lawn 1–2 oz per square yard. Can be used in place of hoof-and-horn in soilless composts 1 part by weight of Urea-form 2 parts by weight of super-phosphate 1 part by weight of sulphate of potash
Sulphate of ammonia Nitrogen 20·6% N	When applied to the soil the ammonia part is held by the clay and organic matter and is preserved from immediate loss during wet weather. When the soil is warm enough the ammonia is quickly turned into nitrate by soil bacteria. But this conversion is very slow when the soil temperature drops below about 42°F (5°C) When mixed with sand is called lawn sand. Repeated heavy dressings may make the soil too acid for good growth but acid forming property is an advantage to chalky soils	Spring and summer direct to soil at ½–1 oz per square yard. Or dissolve 1 teaspoonful in 1 gallon of water and use as liquid feed. Often mixed with superphosphate and sulphate of potash but do not mix with lime			
Superphosphate of lime Phosphate 18–19% P_2O_5	This contains phosphates that are soluble in water and it acts quickly, being particularly suitable for seed beds and root crops. It does not supply lime in spite of its name	Can be used at any time at rate of 1–2 oz per square yard before sowing or planting. Used in John Innes Base Fertiliser to supply phosphates	**Wood ashes** Potash	Freshly made wood ashes contain potassium carbonate, which is soon washed out by rain water unless the ashes are protected. Ashes from prunings and other young plant material are richer in potash than old stumps. Heavy dressings may cake the surface and spoil the tilth of clayey soils. Do not give large dressings to chalky soils because ashes may make them more alkaline	Autumn or winter in open ground. 4–8 oz per square yard well ahead of sowing or planting
Sulphate of potash Potash 50% K_2O	The best form of potash for most garden plants. Acts quickly. It is held by the clay and humus in soils until required by plants. To correct potash deficiency quickly dissolve 1 oz in a gallon of water and wet soil thoroughly. Always use for gooseberries, red currants and other soft fruits in preference to muriate of potash	Generally used in combination with other fertilisers and raked in before sowing or planting at any time of the year ½–1 oz per square yard	**Soot** Nitrogen 1–7% N	Contains nitrogen mainly as ammonium sulphate and therefore acts rapidly. Since fresh soot contains substances harmful to plants it is best left under cover for three months before use. Light and fluffy soot contains more nitrogen than the heavy dense type. Most soots supply useful amounts of trace elements	Spread over soil after digging and then rake in at rate of 4–6 oz per square yard. Can be used as top dressing for brassicas at the same rate

Ready for use compounds Garden supply shops offer for sale a wide variety of materials for feeding garden plants and lawns. Some of these products are much more expensive than others. They vary in price because of:

Nutrient content Fertilisers with a high percentage of plant nutrients cost more per pound than those containing a small percentage of nutrients. So always find out from the supplier what the guaranteed content of nitrogen phosphoric acid and potash is. The plant nutrient content of a compound is often indicated by its grade—a series of three numbers separated by dashes. The numbers show the percentage of nitrogen, phosphoric acid and potash, in that order, contained in the product.

Form Pelleted or granular fertilizers, and soluble fertilizer concentrates cost more than powdered fertilizers. But the granular form may be more convenient for you to use.

Powdered fertilizers often contain a lot of very fine dusty material which may blow away or be objectional to use on a windy day. They may become damp more easily and may cake and fail to spread properly through your fertilizer spreader.

Granular fertilizers are not as dusty as powdered fertilizers and they do not cake so easily; they flow freely through fertilizer spreaders. The granules roll off plant foliage, reducing the danger of fertilizer burn.

Ingredients Nitrogen is the most expensive ingredient in a fertilizer compound. Slowly available forms derived from organic sources and Urea-Form are more expensive than the quickly available forms. So, the more nitrogen a compound contains—especially slowly available forms of nitrogen—the more expensive the product is.

Added materials Products that contain added trace elements, pesticides or herbicides cost more than plain fertilizers. Fertilizer weed killer combinations are generally prepared for use on lawns. These combinations can be quite satisfactory if:

(a) the best time for applying the fertilizers and the best time for applying the weedkiller are the same.

(b) the nutrient content and the weedkiller concentration of the mixture are adjusted so that each is applied at the proper rate.

Package size Fertilizers sold in small containers cost more per pound than the same product in larger packages.

Liquid fertilizers are simply fertilizers in solution; if you mix 28g (1oz) of sulphate of ammonia with 4l (1gall) of water you have a very weak solution containing nitrogen. You can make up feeds to your own prescription, using concentrated chemicals such as potassium nitrate, ammonium phosphate and urea, but this does require a fair amount of technical knowledge and it is usually more convenient to purchase one of the readymade products which are of two main types:

Concentrated liquids that have to be diluted with water according to the maker's instructions. Mixtures of solid chemicals for dissolving in water. These are the cheapest since you do not have to pay for the cost of transporting the water.

Liquid compound fertilizers are much more expensive than solids, as they have to be manufactured from purer materials. But they are popular for the ease and speed with which nutrients can be applied in balanced form to meet the changing needs of plants at different stages of growth and weather conditions. Also feeding and watering is done in one operation—a distinct advantage when there are large batches of plants to be dealt with.

But they are not necessarily better than solid feeds, merely more convenient, and of course liquid feeding is essential when using certain forms of irrigation equipment.

Some facts to remember when using fertilizers

Never guess at amounts; overdoses can be harmful or even fatal to plants; too little may be ineffective. Either weigh on household scales or buy a special graduated gardener's measure.

A match box will do if you have no scales available. When full a standard match box will hold:

15g (½oz) of superphosphate

22g (¾oz) of sulphate of ammonia, bone

Potash deficiency in potatoes is indicated by blueing of the leaves.

How to cure deficiencies with straight fertilisers

Plant food	Plants most susceptible to deficiency	Deficiency may occur in these soils	Fertiliser to use	How to apply fertiliser
Nitrogen	All plants especially brassicas and other leafy plants	Wet, acid, very sandy and thin soils	INORGANIC: Nitrate of soda, nitro-chalk, potash nitrate, sulphate of ammonia. ORGANIC: Hoof and horn meal, dried blood	When plants are growing
Phosphorus (Phosphates)	All plants: fruit, flowers, vegetables and shrubs	Very wet areas strongly acid soils. Some peaty soils	INORGANIC: Basic slag, superphosphate of lime. ORGANIC: Bone meal	At sowing or planting
Potassium (Potash)	All plants especially potato, beans, gooseberry, apple, currants	Light chalky; badly drained; or very sandy soils	INORGANIC: Sulphate of potash, muriate of potash. Potash nitrate	At sowing or planting in top dressing
Calcium (lime)	All plants	Only in very strongly acid soils	Lime (see Lime)	Before planting
Magnesium	All plants: especially potato, cabbage, carrot, apple, gooseberry, tomato, Solanum (winter cherry)	Wet areas and seasons. Very sandy soils. Soils over-manured with potash fertilisers	Magnesium sulphate (Epsom Salts) Magnesian limestone	Broadcast in fertiliser or spray leaves Broadcast
Boron	Brassica crops, celery, beetroot, carnations	Very limey; Very sandy or overlimed soils	Borax (sodium tetraborate)	Mixed in pre-planting fertiliser
Iron	Apple, plum, pear, cherry, raspberry, currants, strawberry	Very limey or overlimed soils	Iron chelate. (Fe-Edta, sold under trade names)	Leaf spray or soil application
Manganese	Potato, brassica crops, peas, dwarf and runner beans, onion, carrot, celery, apple, plum, cherry, raspberry	Very limey; overlimed or on many peaty soils	Manganese sulphate	Leaf spray
Copper	Vegetables and some fruits	Some peaty soils and sandy reclaimed heathland	Copper sulphate (Blue stone) Copper oxychloride fungicide	Broadcast before sowing or planting Leaf spray
Molybdenum	Cauliflowers	Very acid soils	Usually cured by liming. Sodium molybdate may be applied	Before planting

83

meal, many compounds
28g (1oz) of sulphate of potash

Always follow the instructions on the label of the container when using proprietary compounds.

Always scatter them as evenly as possible otherwise patchy growth will result. Distributors can be used for lawns and large beds.

You can buy dilutors for liquid feeds which meter the correct amounts.

Always rake fertilizer into the top 5 or 7cm (2 or 3in) of soil or rotary cultivate, but do not bury deeply. Slow acting ones are best mixed thoroughly with the top 15cm (6in) by raking or rotary cultivation.

Never apply liquid fertilizers to dry soil or composts. Always water first.

Keep fertilizers in a dry place and keep the tops of the containers closed up; always keep bags off the floor.

Do not allow fertilizers to touch leaves or flowers—they may scorch.

NPK These are the chemical symbols for the three plant foods that are needed in the largest amounts by plants, and are the ones most likely to be deficient in soils. When you buy a fertilizer you generally buy it for its content of these plant foods. Hence the value of a fertilizer depends upon its analysis which should be stated on the bag or other container.

N stands for nitrogen which is a gas and cannot be absorbed by plants in this form; it is taken from nitrates which result from the chemical combination of nitrogen with oxygen.

P stands for phosphorus, which is a chemical element that catches fire when exposed to air; so plants cannot take it up in this form. Plants get their phosphorus from soluble phosphates which are a combination of this element and oxygen. Unfortunately an archaic expression is still used to denote the content of phosphorus in a fertilizer—this is P_2O_5—which is commonly called 'phosphoric acid'.

K stands for potassium, the Latin name of which is *Kalium*. Since potassium is a metal that bursts into flame when it comes into contact with water it cannot be used by plants in the raw state. It is taken up from soluble potassium salts in soils.

The word potash, the chemical name of which is potassium oxide—K_2O, arose from the old custom of concentrating the solution of ashes, which contain potassium, in pots. The plant food content of a compound fertilizer may be indicated by its grade—a series of three numbers separated by dashes. The numbers show the percentage of nitrogen, 'phosphoric acid' and potash, in that order, contained in the compound.

Manure Manure may be defined as any substance applied to the soil to make it more fruitful—a term which may also be

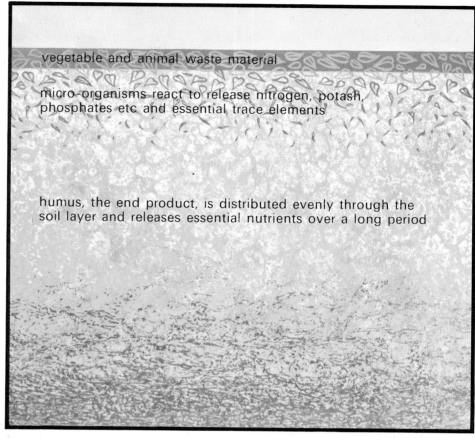

vegetable and animal waste material

micro-organisms react to release nitrogen, potash, phosphates etc and essential trace elements

humus, the end product, is distributed evenly through the soil layer and releases essential nutrients over a long period

applied to fertilizers; so really it is without precise meaning. But we generally think of a manure as a bulky, humus-forming substance that is formed from animal or vegetable origin or in other words, it is a 'natural' manure.

Some bulky manures are inconvenient to handle, usually smelly and expensive to buy. So, will we get better plants, more nutritious vegetables and fruit, and do a better job of conserving soils if we use organic manures instead of relying solely on factory made or 'artificial' fertilizers that supply plant foods alone? The answer is that bulky organic manures add to the content of organic matter, which plays a vital role in building and maintaining soil fertility. Every time you dig, hoe or cultivate a soil you let more air in. Then the soil organisms become more active and these break down organic matter, which is their food, and soils often lose their structure and become more difficult to work and soils on sloping ground often erode.

When first applied, the fibrous material opens up all soils making them more porous, better aerated and drained. Small animals and minute organisms break them down and in so doing produce waste products that bind and cement small particles together to form clusters and in some soils porous crumbs. These have large spaces between them that hold moisture yet allow surplus water to run away. The minute spaces within the crumbs hold moisture and plant foods available for plant use. A soil with a good crumb structure does not fall to paste when rained upon nor

Humus is one of the end products of decay. It absorbs many times its own weight of water thus helping sandy soils to hold moisture better. Substantial amounts of plant foods—nitrogen, phosphates, potash and others including trace elements—are produced in the process of decay. These become available to plants at a slow steady rate over a long period.

does it crush easily when cultivated.

Humus is one of the end products of decay. It absorbs many times its own weight of water and this helps sandy soils to hold moisture better—an effect that is most noticeable in dry periods. Close-grained soils, either silts or clays, which tend to pan or are difficult to work, are much improved. Garden compost, farmyard manure and most other organic manures also supply substantial amounts of plant foods—nitrogen, phosphates and potash and many others including trace elements. But being formed from plant and animal residues they differ from most factory-made fertilizers because their nutrients are not in a form that can be used by plants. For example the nitrogen may be part of a complex protein molecule and as such it cannot be absorbed by a growing plant as it stands. As the material begins to decay the resident nitrogen in its proteins undergoes chemical change and is eventually converted into ammonium and nitrate forms that may be absorbed by plant roots. While these forms of nitrogen are exactly the same, whether they come from an inorganic fertilizer or a manure, they are released at a slow and steady rate over a very much longer period. This long-lasting effect is now being imitated in some of the newer synthetic organic fertilizers.

As 'natural' manures are long lasting in effect they are not exhausted as quickly as inorganic fertilizers, and generally leave useful residues for crops that follow. This is important to remember when planning vegetable rotations; cauliflowers and many other vegetable crops thrive in soils generously manured with organic manures, while others prefer the residues from a previously well-manured crop—a fact that leads to economy in the use of bulky manures.

Apart from the incorporation of manures in the soil before planting or during the life of the plant these materials are of great value when used as surface mulches. Mulches are like a blanket in retaining moisture. Water vapour from the soil surface diffuses very much more slowly through a loose mulch than it does from the bare soil surface. A wet bare soil can easily lose 1.5cm (½in) of rain in a week, whereas a mulched soil will take about six weeks to lose this amount.

Mulches usually allow water to penetrate soils more easily, the raindrops trickle slowly through the fibrous material and do not compact the soil as badly as they do when falling on bare soil. So mulches are of particular value to silty soils that are subject to surface panning through heavy rain. On such soils even a very light mulch will break the force of rain and prevent compaction and, by protecting the surface from exposure to rain, lessen the chance of cracking.

The best-known organic manure is farmyard manure, but rotting plant remains, usually called composts, are manures too, and undecomposed materials like straw may be included. Organic wastes from industrial processes, town refuse and sewage sludges are also offered as organic manures.

All organic manures are not perfect. Some may have a bad effect on plants. For example straw, sawdust and even very strawy farmyard manure. These contain only a very little nitrogen but a lot of carbon and hydrogen, in the form of carbohydrates such as cellulose. But the attacking organisms need supplies of nitrogen while they feed on the carbohydrates and if extra nitrogen is not applied, they will take it from the soil and rob the plants.

This effect can be overcome by adding extra nitrogen to materials of this kind or by allowing them to undergo a partial decay before they are mixed with the soil.

Farmyard manure (FYM) Foldyard manure and dung are names used to describe a mixture of the excreta of farm animals and the straw or other litter used in yards or stalls to absorb the urine and to keep the animals clean.

If you live in a livestock-producing rural area it is easy to get a load of manure delivered to your garden. The average 3-ton lorry usually holds about 5 cubic metres (yards) of manure which is sufficient for about 500 square metres (yards) of soil so that may be too much for your garden and it is necessary to share the load with a neighbour; a cubic yard weighs anything from 10 cwt to 15 cwt according to the amount of straw contained and the age of the manure. The main trouble, of course, is getting the manure into your garden. You need a gate at least 2.1m (7ft) wide for lorry or tractor and trailer access otherwise the manure has to be dumped outside the garden and barrowed in rapidly to prevent it from becoming a nuisance to passers-by.

Town gardeners are hindered by the problems of access and the high cost of transport. Even so, many town gardeners do buy FYM, either directly through manure contractors or through garden centres. Composted farm manures that are sold in bags are an obvious alternative to the fresh bulky material direct from the farm.

Quality Like all organic manures farmyard manure can vary in many ways from load to load, in contrast to inorganic fertilizers that have a fixed and definite composition.

The type of animal producing the dung has a big effect on quality. The dung (the solid excreta) of horses is the richest in all nutrients and it is drier than that of cows or pigs, so that the bacterial changes during rotting are much more rapid and a greater amount of ammonia is produced. Horse manure when stacked soon begins to steam showing that fermentation is going on; so it is called a 'hot' manure, specially suitable for mushrooms and for greenhouse work. Pig dung is the next richest, followed by cow dung; both of these are much wetter than horse dung and in consequence heat up more slowly and are referred to as 'cold' manures.

So far as nutrients are concerned, farmyard manures are weak; for example you need about 25kg (50lb) of horse manure to supply as much nitrogen as there is in .5kg (1lb) of sulphate of ammonia. The average analysis of most farmyard manures is about ½ per cent nitrogen, ¼ per cent phosphates and ½ per cent potash. All animal manures contain in addition useful amounts of magnesium and calcium and are very good suppliers of trace elements, together with other substances which are believed to have growth-promoting properties.

Quality also depends upon the kind of litter used for bedding. The most commonly used litter is straw, which absorbs about three times its own weight of urine and of course provides additional humus-forming matter. Peat moss is an even better absorber of urine and

makes a manure which is easily spread and mixed with the soil. Sawdust and wood shavings are poor absorbers of liquids and are very slow to break down in the soil.

Benefits of manure In view of the foregoing you may well think that in a space age it is an archaic practice to use farmyard manure at all. But the results of experiments with good quality products show that it is the yardstick for comparing all other organic manures. In addition to its content of plant nutrients it is a humus supplier and for every ton you buy you will get about 3 to 5 cwt of organic matter which soon becomes humus in the soil and gives all the benefits associated with humus. It supplies its nutrients in a slowly available form and, therefore, has a long-lasting effect; the benefits of a single dressing can last for 3 or more years.

Using farmyard manure If you have some ground ready when the manure comes in, you will lose less of your manure by digging it in right away; but it is often a question of getting a load when you can and storing it until the ground becomes vacant. If you buy a ton of manure now, you will only have about ½ a ton in six months time because the microbes change parts of the manure into carbon dioxide and ammonia gases which blow away in the wind; nutrients are also washed out of the manure during heavy rain, forming the brown liquid which you often see round the bottom of a dung heap.

While in the heap it is best kept under cover and always kept trodden down tightly to exclude air, and if the drainings can be collected in a bucket or tank a great waste of precious plant nutrients can be avoided.

In very dry weather, moisten the heap periodically. By stacking fresh manure straight from the stable or piggery for a

A mulch of peat around runner beans not only keeps the roots cool and moist, but also provides food.

few months the product is improved; you get a better balance in nutrient content, the nitrogen part becomes slower-acting and is less likely to burn seedlings or the delicate roots of tender plants. The well-rotted manure is much easier to spread and mix in with the topsoil. You can tell if it is well rotted by the absence of unpleasant smell and even texture of the product—the straw part will no longer be recognizable. Fresh manure is much more difficult to spread and mix; if you intend to sow or plant soon after an application you have to bury it deeply otherwise it interferes with plant bed preparations.

Deeply buried manure does not give the best results; ideally it is spread on well-broken soil and then worked in to a depth of 7 or 10cm (3 or 4in) with a cultivator, then turned with a spade or fork. Take care not to turn the soil completely upside down, but rather at an angle wide enough just to cover the surface material. Manure covered with slabs of wet soil merely prevents humus formation. By mixing it with 7 or 10cm (3 or 4in) of topsoil, hard crusts which prevent seedlings from pushing through easily, are obviated. To do any real good to soil that is low in humus it is essential to cover the soil with a layer thick enough to obscure the soil beneath it; this will need at least 5kg (10lb) of well-rotted manure per square yard. For vegetables this is done every 3 years before you plant crops such as brassicas that respond to generous dressings of manure.

Well-rotted farmyard manure can be applied at any time of the year before sowing or planting, but fresh or 'long' manure as it is called, is best dug in during the autumn or early winter so as to allow it to break down and lose its caustic nature in time for spring plantings.

For mulching during the summer the manure is useful for suppressing weeds and retaining moisture; when dug in at the end of the season it adds to the humus content of the soil.

Since large dressings of farmyard manure supply appreciable amounts of plant nutrients you can reduce your fertilizer dressings by half if 5kg (10lb) of well-rotted farmyard manure per square metre (yard) has been added.

Composted manures There are a number of products derived from fresh animal manures that are sold in bags under brand names. Large heaps of the fresh manure are allowed to decay under cover for several months during which time the coarse material is broken down and the heat of decomposition drives off much of the moisture.

The resultant dark brown spongy manure is applied at the rate of 180-240g (6-8oz) per square metre (yard) and is lightly forked in or mixed with the topsoil by means of a rotary cultivator.

These products are clean and convenient to handle.

A cultivator handles manure easily.

Soil composts These are balanced mixtures designed to support healthy and active plant growth throughout all stages of propagation, pot and container culture and other forms of simulated growth conditions. They are also, on occasions, used for mixing into outside planting positions in order to give trees, shrubs and plants a good start.

There were at one time innumerable, highly individual soil composts, especially where potting was concerned, and some years ago the John Innes Horticultural Institution at Bayfordbury in Hertfordshire, decided to seek some standard formulations.

After considerable work and research by Mr. W. J. C. Lawrence, a series of standard potting and propagating composts was developed, making it clear that apart from certain modifications in special cases, such standard mixtures would work efficiently for an extremely wide range of plants. And they came as a very welcome simplification of what had been a highly complex, not to say hit and miss process; satisfactory for the skilled gardener, perhaps, but certainly not for those with little experience.

Five composts were devised, three for the various stages of potting, and one each for seed sowing and propagation by cuttings. The primary ingredients are partially sterilized loam – steamed at 200°F (93°C) for twenty minutes, essential in order to destroy pests, diseases

and weed seeds – granular peat with a minimum of dust, and coarse river sand with nutrient materials in the form of hoof and horn, grist (13 per cent nitrogen), superphosphate of lime (16 per cent phosphoric acid) and sulphate of potash (48 per cent pure potash) and, finally, ground limestone or chalk.

For potting composts Nos. 1, 2 and 3, the basic formula is:

7 parts by loose bulk of medium loam – partially sterilized
3 parts of granulated or moss peat
2 parts of coarse sand

It is important to note that in each instance the measurements are by *loose bulk* and not by weight. The fertilizers and limestone or chalk are measured by weight, not by bulk.

These materials are mixed most efficiently by placing them in three complete layers, one upon another, and then turning this flat, sandwiched heap over, working from one end to the other and shovelling from ground level throughout. The heap should be turned at least twice – out and back – for maximum success.

Fertilizer mixed in the ratio of:
2 parts by weight of hoof and horn
2 parts by weight of superphosphate of lime
1 part by weight of sulphate of potash plus 21g (¾oz) of ground limestone or chalk, making sure to mix all thoroughly throughout.

This complete mixture is suitable for most basic potting in small to medium pots, for delicate and hothouse plants and those which are not to be kept for any length of time.

Plants other than delicate and hothouse, when requiring a shift beyond the 10cm (4in) pot stage, should be potted into John Innes No. 2; made by adding twice the amount of combined fertilizer and chalk to each bushel of loam, peat and sand. John Innes No. 3 comes from adding three times the amount of these materials and is suitable for the more robust and long-standing plants requiring, perhaps, shifts into 20cm (8in) pots and beyond.

Compost made up for plants objecting to lime should obviously have the chalk or limestone omitted; it should be reduced where lime is present to any extent in the loam used in the basic formula. Ideally, this should not be so, with loam with a pH of 6.5, the kind to use if possible.

The John Innes standard seed sowing mixture consists of:
2 parts by bulk of loam – partially sterilized
1 part by bulk of peat
1 part by bulk of sand
to each bushel of which is added only 45g (1½oz) superphosphate of lime and 12g (¾oz) ground limestone or chalk. The loam and peat may have to be rubbed

through a 1cm (½in) sieve to make them sufficiently fine for seedling growth.

Certain plants require special composts; orchids, for instance, are traditionally potted in a basic mixture of osmunda fibre, sphagnum moss and charcoal.

Where many tiny alpines are concerned, extra grit in the compost is often required in order to allow them very adequate drainage, essential to many of them, especially in their early stages.

Sometimes commercial growers handling plants, trees and shrubs in containers for immediate planting, use a 90 per cent peat, 10 per cent soil compost for general expedience, nutrients being supplied in balanced liquid form.

Using the compost Well-made composts from vegetable wastes may contain more nutrients and more organic matter than good farmyard manure.

If you know that your soil is very low in humus, about 5kg (10lb) per square metre (yard) should be mixed with the topsoil for a year or two and in subsequent years give 2.5kg (5lb) per square metre (yard).

Seaweed One of the oldest manures known is seaweed, which is widely used for improving the soils of gardens and farms in coastal districts. The different weeds vary in plant food content; the long broad-leaved species, which is usually found just below the low water mark, is richer than the bladder wrack (*Fucus*) found between low and high tides. It is gathered all the year round but the richest harvest is thrown up by spring tides, or during storms.

About three-quarters of seaweed is water, the remainder being humus-forming material. It contains about ½ per cent nitrogen and up to 1½ per cent phosphates and about 1–1½ per cent potash. Since seaweeds have no roots they obtain all their nutrients from the dissolved substances in the sea, which is constantly being enriched by drainage from the land. So they absorb very large quantities of nutrients and are, therefore, an excellent source of trace elements.

The actual organic matter consists very largely of alginic acid which, unlike the cellulose which you get in farmyard manure, rots readily in the soil

1 Leaves collected in the autumn can be composted to form leafmould.

2 The site is prepared for a compost heap with a layer of old hedge clippings to ensure drainage and aeration. Wire netting surrounds the heap.

3 Pea haulms, cabbage stumps, egg shell and general garden rubbish are added in a thick layer. The sides of the heap must be kept firm.

4 Sulphate of ammonia is lightly spread over the heap at the rate of 15g (½oz) per square metre (yard) to encourage decay and hasten decomposition.

and is an excellent soil conditioner. The other carbohydrates and simple sugars found in seaweed also decompose readily in the soil.

It is best dug into the soil immediately after spreading to prevent it from drying out into a hard, woody mess. The usual rate of application is 5kg (10lb) per square metre (yard). Seaweed is particularly suitable for sandy soils in view of its comparative freedom from fibre, thus allowing rapid humus formation. Freedom from weed seeds and disease organisms is an additional advantage of this manure. Its content of common salt is not usually harmful to plants when the manure is used at the normal rates of application.

Dried seaweed products Whole seaweed dried and ground is now available under brand names. Thus prepared the natural product can be transported inland economically and is four to five times as concentrated as wet seaweed or farmyard manure. The product is dry and pleasant to handle and is sold in small packs. Some manufacturers reinforce their products with fertilizers to give them a higher plant food content and to overcome the tendency of dried seaweed temporarily to tie-up nitrogen in the soil.

The best results are obtained from dried products to which fertilizer has been added when they are applied to the surface of the soil during winter cultivation and left for a few weeks to break down; this time varies according to weather and soil conditions, but about four weeks is sufficient in most instances. A reasonable dressing is 60-120g (2-4oz) per square metre (yard).

Products reinforced with NPK fertilizers are sold by some manufacturers and are intended to overcome the initial 'tie-up' of nitrogen in the soil. These can be used in the spring and summer on growing plants, at the rate of 60-120g (2-4oz) per square metre (yard) for all crops.

Dried seaweeds are also used in soil composts and in topdressings for lawns. The usual rates of application already quoted may seem to be rather low for a bulky organic manure whose main function is to supply humus, but seaweed preparations contain alginates which stimulate the soil organisms to greater activity that results in better tilth formation in heavy soils and greater water-holding properties in sandy soils.

Their trace element content is most valuable and makes this class of manure one of the best and safest means of providing soils with nutrients that are needed in very small amounts.

Spent hops The residue after hops have been extracted with water in the brewery is usually sold to haulage contractors who supply commercial growers with the entire output from many breweries and in consequence the amounts available for gardeners is

somewhat limited. Much of the output is purchased by fertilizer manufacturers who reinforce the spent hops with concentrated fertilizers in order to raise the food content.

In the fresh wet state straight from the brewery, spent hops contain about 75 per cent water, about $\frac{1}{2}$ per cent of nitrogen, $\frac{1}{4}$ per cent phosphates and traces of potash. But since the moisture content varies considerably so does the plant food content. So an analysis based on the dry matter is the best figure. On this basis the nitrogen content ranges

1 Peat is used as a mulch for strawberries, and is forked in after picking.
2 Chrysanthemum cuttings rooted, right, in a seaweed meal compost, and left, without the meal in the compost.
Although it is not usual to grow cuttings in such a compost, there is the advantage that food is available if potting-on has to be delayed.
3 French beans, grown with the addition of a seaweed compost, germinate better and are pest free.

from 2–3 per cent and the phosphate content is about 1 per cent. If you are able to get a good supply of spent hops locally you can improve the plant food content by adding ½ cwt of National Growmore fertilizer to every ton of hops. The fertilizer should be sprinkled over the hops and the heap turned over twice to ensure even mixing.

You can not, as a rule, get small quantities of spent hops; they are usually sold by the lorry-load which may weigh several tons. If you have large areas of shrub borders to mulch or a very large vegetable garden you will need a lorry load to do any real good.

Hop manures are proprietary products prepared from spent hops and reinforced with fertilizers. They are sold in bags together with instructions for use in the garden.

Spent hops are regarded mainly as humus suppliers and are used in the preparation of ground for planting and also for mulching established plants. The best results are obtained when they are incorporated thoroughly with the top 15cm (6in) of soil at the rate of 5kg (10lb) per square metre (yard) during the winter. For mulching purposes spent hops are very effective in keeping down weeds and retaining soil moisture in shrub borders and soft fruit plots, provided the ground is covered really thickly. If you apply a layer 10-15cm (4-6in) thick it will last for two years before rotting noticeably. The material gives off an objectionable odour after application but this usually disappears after 2–3 weeks. Although spent hops are slightly more acid than most soils they are used with great success for practically all trees and shrubs except for some of the outstanding lime-requiring plants. The fire hazard from burning cigarette ends is low since spent hops do not burn readily when used as mulches.

Spent mushroom compost The material left after a mushroom crop has been cleared from the beds in which the spawn was planted usually consists of a mixture of well-rotted horse manure and the soil which was used for covering the beds before planting the mushroom spawn. Peat and chalk is often used in place of soil in which case the compost will have a proportion of lime in it.

So the quality of the product depends very much upon the proportion of casing soil which it contains. The organic matter of spent mushroom compost is generally more decomposed than in strawy farmyard manure and hence it may be less useful for improving heavy soils.

Being fibrous and well-rotted the compost is an ideal material for mixing in with the topsoil of all soils. The nitrogen content of fresh spent horse manure compost including soil is usually lower than farmyard manure and the phosphate and potash content is just slightly lower.

The lime-rich composts are unsuitable for rhododendrons and other lime-haters, and may contain excessive amounts of lime for fruit crops.

Normal rate of application is 2.5-5kg (5-10lb) per square metre (yard).

Fertilizers and manures must, as a general rule, be bought and must therefore add to the overall cost of your gardening. It is possible to a great extent to make your own by using waste products. Well-made, home-produced compost can be most helpful.

Compost heaps

There are several ways in which compost heaps can be made and various theories exist as to the way in which they should be treated. There are two important points which are essential for successful compost making and these are adequate drainage and aeration and sufficient moisture.

A compost heap is a necessary feature in the average garden. It provides a means of collecting the surprising amount of waste material which is gathered together during regular garden maintenance and it supplies the garden, or rather, the soil, with valuable organic matter. This organic matter fulfils several vital functions. It helps to improve the structure of the soil, especially the heavy clay types and the light sandy kinds. It encourages a vigorous root system and also acts as a sponge to retain moisture. Light, sandy soils tend to dry out rather badly and a high humus content is necessary to overcome this problem. Well-rotted composted vegetable waste can be used as a mulch around plants and between rows of vegetables where it will smother small annual weeds and prevent the surface soil from drying out badly.

It is advisable to give some thought to the siting and layout of a compost heap, particularly where the garden is small. A compost heap can look ugly and untidy if neglected, but fortunately there are several ways in which the material can be contained neatly and efficiently. Although the heap should be placed in an unobtrusive position in the garden, it should not be put in a position which is damp, heavily shaded or closed in. In these conditions the waste material can become offensive and will certainly not rot down into the dark friable mass it should.

The size of the area a compost heap will require will depend naturally on the size of the garden and especially on the number and sizes of the lawns, for the biggest proportion of compost heap ingredients consists of lawn mowings. The usual recommendation is that the heap should not be more than 90cm (3ft) wide or 90cm (3ft) in height when first built. There will be considerable shrinkage later on due to the decomposition of the waste vegetation in the heap. One of the neatest ways of making a compost heap is to purchase a specially

constructed bin or container. Some are made from extra stout gauge wire, stove enamelled dark green, others have a rustic appearance with a strong wooden framework. Most types have either a removable side or one which hinges so that the heap can be filled or emptied easily.

It is quite an easy matter to construct a compost bin from the following material: four corner posts 1.2m (4ft) long (30cm (1ft) to be inserted in the ground), and 5-7cm (2-3in) square. The sides or 'filling' in pieces are made from 90cm (3ft) lengths of timber 7cm (3in) wide and at least 2.5cm (1in) thick. Six will be required for each side making a total of 24 pieces. They are spaced approximately 10cm (4in) apart and screwed into the corner posts. To provide for a removable side, one set of side pieces, 3cm (1¼in) less in length than the others, are screwed to two separate corner rails 5-7cm (2-3in) wide and 2.5cm (1in) thick. The complete unit slides into two of the fixed corner posts, in a groove or channel made from two 90cm (3ft) pieces of 2.5×7cm (3×1in) timber spaced from the two fixed corner posts by two thin strips of wood 3cm (1¼in) thick and 2.5cm (1in) wide. All timber must be thoroughly treated against rot and Cuprinol, Rentokil or Solignum are suitable. The ends of the corner posts should be well soaked for several hours before they are inserted in the soil.

Where appearance is not important, or where the compost heap is so sited that it can be hidden from view, old sheets of corrugated iron could well be used in the construction.

The successful decomposition of waste material in a heap depends on the action of bacteria and fungi. The bacteria depend on plenty of nitrogen as food and the rate of decay can be increased by supplying some readily available nitrogen. This can be provided by sprinkling the material with a nitrogenous fertilizer such as sulphate of ammonia or Nitro-chalk. Another method of adding Nitrogen is by placing layers of good quality, fresh animal manure between the layers of garden waste. The heap is, in fact, built up in sandwich fashion with alternate layers of manure and waste.

To get rid of air pockets, each 15-20cm (6-8in) layer of material to be rotted down is trodden fairly firmly. It is customary, though not absolutely essential, to cover each trodden layer with a further layer of soil, about an inch thick. The next layer of waste material is put on this and trodden when it is about 15-20cm (6-8in) thick, sprinkled with fertilizer, then covered with soil, and so on.

There are proprietary preparations on the market which accelerate the decomposition process. Some are specially formulated to deal with tougher ingred-

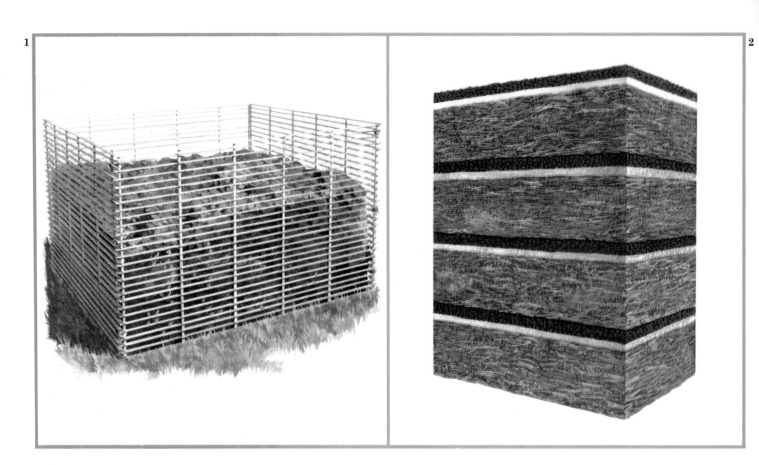

ients of a heap such as herbaceous trimmings, pea and bean haulms, or top growths. Others are particularly suited to the softer materials such as lawn clippings, lettuce leaves, annual weeds and such. Some proprietary formulae include seaweed which produces a very rapid fermentation of the heap. These accelerators are sprinkled on the layers of waste as the heap is built up, in lieu of the nitrogenous fertilizers mentioned.

Where the tougher materials are to be rotted down without the use of a proprietary compost maker, it is a good idea to bruise or chop the stems to aid rotting. Plenty of water must be provided also as this type of harder waste is built into a heap. Some gardeners can obtain quantities of straw and this is very useful as an addition to the compost heap. As a successful heap requires plenty of aeration and drainage, it is wise to start a heap with some of this coarser material at the bottom. Some gardeners like to drive in one or two stakes into a heap so that, when they are withdrawn, air holes or passages are provided which pass right into the material.

Although a well-made compost heap should rot down satisfactory by itself, the contents can be turned after a period of three to four weeks. This is done by transferring the heap to a position close by its original one. Forkfuls of rotting waste placed in the same area, but as the work is carried out, the outer portions of the heap are placed towards the centre of the new one. It may be necessary to add a little

1 Leaves are a valuable source of organic material and unless diseased should never be burnt. In autumn the leaves should be raked up and collected into a wire enclosure.
2 Waste organic matter is rotted down in heaps to make compost but the process must ensure the destruction of weed seeds.

water to areas which may be a little dry.

It is necessary to appreciate the fact that acids are produced as byproducts of even the most favourable decay and that too much acid will spoil compost. This problem can be overcome if some lime is included in the heap. This can be done if some powdered chalk or limestone is sprinkled on alternate layers of waste vegetation. A fertilizer or a dressing containing lime such as Nitrochalk can be used instead. It is important to note that lime and chalk must not be allowed to come into contact with sulphate of ammonia which might be used as an accelerator. If this is done, ammonia will be liberated and nitrogen lost as ammonia gas.

Decay is also hastened in a fairly warm temperature and in a damp atmosphere. The spring and autumn periods, therefore, will be times when rotting down will be at its peak. One would assume that the summer months would be ideal also. This is true to a certain extent, but if a heap is situated where it receives the direct rays of the sun, considerable drying out of the material will result and decay will not be as rapid.

Much of the value of the compost can

be lost if the heap is exposed for long to rain. The nutrients will be lost by being washed away. Where compost has to be stored for any length of time, it is wise to provide some form of shelter for it. An open-sided shed is suitable or a temporary roof can be made. To do this, four strong posts are required about 5cm (2in) square. Two of these should be about 15-25cm (6-10in) longer than the others. Their total length should be such that they clear the top of the compost heap by 60cm (2ft).

The longest posts are inserted at the front of the compost heap, close by the existing posts or bin sides. The other two posts are placed at the use of the heap. Across each pair of posts a rail should be fastened on which the roofing material will rest. The two rails should be cut from timber approximately 5×3 cm (2×1½in) in section.

Various types of material can be used for the roof. Corrugated metal sheets or cheap PVC sheets are ideal. The sheets are nailed or screwed down on to the cross rails. Where necessary, an overlap of 5-7cm (2-3in) on the sheets should be provided. The finished roof will have sufficient pitch or slope to shed rainfall. The sheets must be purchased large enough so that they overhang all four sides of the compost heap by at least 10cm (4in).

There are different opinions as to the length of time compost should be kept before it is ready for use. It must be kept until it has decayed to such an extent that the individual ingredients of which it is composed can no longer be distinguished. Usually the material is in an ideal condition when it has become a dark, friable or crumbly mass. A slimy state is not satisfactory and shows that the heap has been made up incorrectly.

In warm weather, soft refuse will take about four to six weeks to decay but in winter the period will be much longer, and anything up to three or four months will be necessary before thorough decomposition has taken place Where the refuse is harder or tougher, the period necessary for decomposition will be longer.

But the best of soils in both content and texture is useless unless it is moist. Plants need water to sustain themselves and because all plant foods are absorbed in the form of liquid chemical compounds. The source of nearly all the water that a garden needs is natural rain, and only in comparatively rare periods of drought is artificial watering necessary. This is a relatively simple matter today with the many watering aids available to us, some of them automatic. The main rule when watering is to do it thoroughly, for if only the soil surface is moist the roots of plants will tend to turn upwards in the soil towards this area and expose themselves to drought or to burning by the sun. It is almost impossible, except in low-lying areas or poorly drained soils, to over-water artificially. Overwatering occurs with repeated heavy rains.

Figs see Fruit under glass

Flame guns

One of the most time-consuming tasks around the garden is weed control. They must be checked to keep gardens tidy. They must not be allowed to compete with the other plants for food, light and air. Although the hoe is an ideal tool to use for checking weed growth, flame guns can play a useful part and are much more versatile than many people imagine.

Not only does a flame gun kill weeds by fierce heat, it will also destroy seeds which are dormant in the soil. Many pests and diseases are harboured in weedy corners which are often difficult to reach with other tools. The flames and intense heat from these guns will effectively clean out those positions.

Weeds can be particularly troublesome in pathways, especially when they grow between cracks and close up to the house walls. A flame gun is invaluable for dealing with this problem, and also with moss.

In spring there is a considerable

1 The flame gun provides a quick and controlled method of clearing weeds and weed seeds, on neglected land.

2 To start the gun, pump to the required pressure and ignite the fuel. Only paraffin should be used as fuel.

the form of prunings and dead material not required for the compost heap. All these can be burnt quickly. Those with very small gardens where it is not convenient to make a compost heap will find the problem of waste disposal much reduced by the flame gun. Soil can be sterilized by the heat from a flame gun if it is spread out to a depth of an inch or so and the gun passed to and fro over it several times without actually burning it. During the summer most of the work will be directed to weed control and the destruction of insect pests. This work will be carried through into the autumn also, when dying vegetation, especially diseased growth, can be destroyed. Old tomato and cucumber growths, decaying or diseased fruits of all description are obvious flame gun material. The winter brings its own problems such as frozen pipes and soil. A flame gun will deal efficiently with these.

For the maximum benefit from a flame gun, the rows of plants should be planned to accommodate the size of gun used. The average size of the hoods of most flame guns is 30cm (12in) wide and about 45cm (18in) long.

How a flame gun works
A flame gun is very similar to a blow-lamp. The fuel, which is paraffin (*never* petrol) is contained in an air-tight tank and fed to a burner via a control valve by pressurized air. The latter is provided

by a built-in pump. The burner is a vaporizing type in which the fuel is pre-heated and vaporized by passing through a coil which is heated by the flame.

The gun is started by pre-heating the burner to a temperature which will vaporize the fuel as soon as the control valve is opened. A core temperature of about 2000°F (about 1090°C), is produced in some models, with the most economical use of fuel in the ratio of about 6% fuel vapour and 94% air.

The tank of the apparatus is filled with paraffin and the valve closed. The pump is used until the required pressure is registered on the built-in gauge. The valve is opened a small amount so that a little fuel flows to the special asbestos wick in the burner. This wick is then lighted. After approximately 3 minutes the burner is warmed up and the valve can then be opened slowly until the most suitable flame is produced.

Types available
There are several different models, depending on the type and amount of work required. The simplest, and one very suitable for the lady gardener, is merely a long tube with a priming plunger at one end. All controls are kept to the minimum and a thin fierce flame is emitted. There are larger models which can be carried easily in one hand and which have a bigger flame capacity.

Some models can be fixed to a special

2-wheeled chassis fitted with a metal hood which covers the flame head. This concentrates the heat to a small area and enables the operator to work close up to plants, fences and even glass cloches without any danger of damage. The carefully designed cranked handle also ensures greater manoeuvrability.

Foliar feeding
This is the application of nutrients to the aerial parts of plants. It can be used for the treatment of all deficiencies for all types of growing plants. But you can only spray very small amounts of nutrients on to the leaves at a time, otherwise leaf scorch or even defoliation may follow. If foliar spraying is to be successful there must be sufficient foliage to hold the applied nutrients, and plants cannot develop to a stage of growth when foliar treatment would be effective unless the soil has been prepared properly before sowing or planting. So, although foliar feeding cannot take the place of the traditional method of applying fertilizers and manures to the soil, it is a useful supplement, for the following purposes:

1 To give a quick boost to growth which has been checked by water-logged soils, cold nights, biting winds and frosts.

2 To provide nutrients quickly when roots are unable to absorb sufficient nutrients from the soil, due to an infertile soil, lack of soil moisture, low soil temperatures or a restricted, injured or diseased root system.

3 To correct a deficiency of a particular nutrient, which is applied to the soil could be locked up in an unavailable form eg manganese.

4 To supplement the usual soil fertilizer treatment during flower production when there is a big increase in nutrient uptake by the roots.

Foliar applications of potassium nitrate to roses have often produced more richly coloured blooms and dark green glossy foliage.

Methods of application Nutrients can be applied as dusts or sprays. Finely ground fertilizers may be dusted on to damp foliage but these are not as efficient as sprays because more of the fertilizer falls off the leaves and about twice as much fertilizer is required to give as good an effect as a spray.

So it is best to use sprays, especially when applying trace element fertilizers, which are required in very small amounts. The fertilizers listed in the table below are applied at the rate suggested, using an ordinary garden sprayer or a watering can with a fine rose.

Time of application If deficiency symptoms have occured at an early stage

Plant nutrient	Fertiliser	Ounces per gallon
Nitrogen	Urea	$\frac{3}{4}$–1$\frac{1}{2}$
	Potassium nitrate	$\frac{1}{2}$
Phosphates	Triple-superphosphate (powdered)	$\frac{1}{2}$–1
Potash	Sulphate of potash	1$\frac{1}{2}$
Magnesium	Magnesium sulphate, Epsom Salts	3
Iron	Iron chelate, proprietary products	According to directions
Manganese	Manganese sulphate	$\frac{1}{2}$–1
Copper	Copper sulphate	$\frac{1}{2}$
Boron	Borax	1/12th
Mixed foliar feeds	Proprietary products according to directions	

spraying should be done immediately there is enough leaf to spray, followed by a further application in 2–3 weeks, since most of the first application will have fallen on bare ground.

Where a deficiency occurs every year it is best to apply the foliar spray before symptoms appear.

Special hints Always spray both upper and lower surfaces of the leaves, because absorption is greater through the under

Rhubarb is forced, under a forcing pot, to encourage etiolated growth.

surfaces of the leaves.

Use a fine mist sprayer and add a leaf wetting agent (not a soap type) to the spray. This will help to reduce the risk of leaf scorch. Spray in late afternoon or on a dull day, since best results follow applications made under slow drying conditions.

Don't spray if weather is hot and sunny, or scorching will be severe. Avoid showery weather, or most of the nutrient will be washed off.

Always get an expert to diagnose a deficiency before you start treatment.

Forcing

This is the practice of encouraging plants to flower or fruit early. The simplest form of forcing is done by inverting a tub over rhubarb crowns to encourage etiolated growth. Similarly rhubarb, sea-kale, dandelion and chicory can be forced under the greenhouse staging in mild heat and darkness, which also blanches these crops, rendering them more palatable.

Another very simple method of forcing is to cut sprays of winter or spring-

A foliar feed is applied in small amounts to all leaf surfaces.

flowering shrubs such as *Jasminum nudiflorum* and forsythia in bud and place them in a warm room to bring out the flowers before those out of doors bloom. The sudden change from very cold to warm encourages quick growth and is employed in the forcing of flower bulbs. It has been found that some bulbs make better and speedier growth under conditions of forcing if they are pre-treated by cold storage. Daffodils, in particular, respond to this treatment, and are put in cold storage for several weeks during August and September before being forced. Pre-treated bulbs such as 'Golden Harvest' and 'Carlton' are available to amateurs. Hyacinths, too, are offered as pre-treated bulbs, such varieties as 'Ostra', 'Pink Pearl' and 'Jan Bos' responding well. They should be planted as soon as they are received, otherwise normal temperatures will nullify the cooling treatment.

The importance of keeping newly planted bulbs for forcing in really cool conditions initially, cannot be over-emphasized. A good root system has to be developed before quick growth can be

expected, and it is in very cool conditions that root formation takes place. Whether pre-cooled or not, bulbs can be forced by artificial light, where natural light can be excluded completely and the usual temperatures for bulb forcing be maintained 65–75°F (18–24°C). Light is given for any consecutive twelve hours of the twenty-four and one 100-watt lamp is sufficient for 1 square metre (yard) of bulbs when mounted 90cm (3ft) above the bowls or boxes. Commercially the use of such growing rooms is increasing, and artificial light is used in the cultivation of chrysanthemums to provide flowers all the year round, by a system of forcing and delaying. Considerable progress is also being made in the use of carbon dioxide to enrich the atmosphere of both growing rooms and greenhouses, to encourage speedier growth, once leaves are formed, of such crops as lettuce, cucumber, tomato and chrysanthemum.

Many shrubs can be brought into flower early for greenhouse display (or once they are flowering they can be transferred to the house for room decoration) in late winter or early spring. Young plants can be lifted from the ground or, bought specially, potted up and brought into the greenhouse about New Year. Keep a buoyant atmosphere and cool conditions for two or three weeks then increase the temperature gradually, watering and feeding as required. Such plants as *Deutzia gracilis, Prunus triloba,* Indian azalea, forsythia, philadelphus, syringa, hydrangea and spiraea, respond well to this type of cultivation but it is wise not to force the same plants year after year.

Forks see Tools

Formal gardens

In the early days of gardening in the British Isles, garden designs were based on geometric patterns, always emphasizing regularity of form. During Elizabethan times topiary and terraces with heraldic beasts as ornaments, and quiet lawns were the order of the day; trees were always planted in a row or regular pattern. Later, avenues became longer, 'walks', square fish ponds, and mazes or labyrinths were constructed and parterres of the most intricate design represented the height of garden beauty and decoration. These parterres were intricately designed, the outline traced in clipped hedges, often very low and usually of box, the interstices filled, either with plants or coloured stones and other minerals, one colour to a space, to form a pattern in the parterre garden as a whole. There were frequent

1 Clipped trees are a feature of the formal garden at Blickling Hall, Norfolk, a National Trust property.
2 Knot beds, at Vannes, using box edging, coloured earth and plants.

variations on this theme, height being added by clipped trees, often cut into formal shapes, but always the gardener's handiwork imposed formal arrangement upon nature. Frequently great vistas were treated in this way, always executed on level ground and matching the design of the house. Terraces and vantage points were usually constructed so that these large designs could be looked down upon and enjoyed as a whole. Examples still exist at Cliveden, in Buckinghamshire, and at Oxburgh Hall, Norfolk, where from the high gatehouse one can look down upon the formal garden.

Thus, up to the eighteenth century, every garden was formal, regularly designed and ornamented with topiary, statues, arbours and fountains. Pope and Addison had in their writings loudly criticized formality and when Lancelot ('Capability') Brown some years later advocated the great sweeping aside of the closely designed plots in favour of landscape effects, such great parks as Longleat, Harewood House and Blenheim were created. Humphry Repton, working in the late eighteenth and early nineteenth centuries, followed in Brown's footsteps, although his schemes were not on as large a scale and he made the transition between house and garden more gradual by introducing terraces and balustraded walks. But the great sweep towards the natural, spacious style, where plants were used to emulate nature in woodland, water

gardens and stonework continued; except for a sudden retrogression during Victorian days. Then intricate and elaborate bedding schemes became fashionable. Carpet bedding was used for effect and drawing-board design returned to the flower garden. Since then, chiefly through the work and writing of William Robinson and his followers, natural planting schemes have been very widely used, exploiting plant colour, form and texture in many ways. But formality still had its adherents in such men as Sir Reginald Blomfield, Harold Peto and Sir Edwin Lutyens, all architects. Modern examples of formal gardens are those of several private houses designed by Lutyens, the gardens perfectly integrated into the design by his partner Miss Gertrude Jekyll. Such places as Orchards, Godalming (1896), The Deanery at Sonning, on the Thames (1899) and Tyringham, Buckinghamshire (1924) were designed by this remarkable partnership. Around the turn of the century Major Lawrence Johnston, architect and artist, started to make his famous garden at Hidcote Bartrim, Gloucestershire, one of the finest examples of a formal garden, although it is informally planted. It consists, in fact, of a number of gardens, separated by fine

1 Philadelphus lemoinei is one of the strongly fragrant mock oranges.
2 The late Dutch honeysuckle is fragrant, particularly in the evening.

hedges, each one a perfect garden on its own.

Examples of formal gardens open to the public are Belton House, Lincolnshire; Castle Ashby, Northamptonshire; Cliveden, Buckinghamshire; Compton Wynyates, Warwickshire; Easton Neston, Northamptonshire; Hampton Court, Middlesex; Haseley Court, Oxfordshire; Hidcote, Gloucestershire; Holkham Hall, Norfolk; Lanhydrock (rose garden), Cornwall; Oxburgh Hall, Norfolk; Packwood House, Warwickshire; Shrubland Park, Suffolk; Wightwick Manor, Staffordshire.

Fragrant flowers
Fragrance in flowers is such a desirable attribute that it is a perennial complaint of many gardeners that modern varieties of various plants, particularly roses, lack all or most of the fragrance of the older varieties. This is demonstrably untrue of many varieties, of course, yet there is a good deal of truth in the generalization. Some varieties are certainly much less fragrant than the 'old-fashioned' roses and a few seem to lack detectable fragrance, but, on the whole, a good modern variety will number fragrance among its qualities. Much depends, of course, upon the individual sense of smell, coupled with the 'scent memory' which all of us possess to some degree. It is, in fact, usually well developed and most of us are readily and instantaneously reminded by present

scents of past incidents, places, and persons, and although the actual vocabulary of scent is limited, it is usually possible for us to describe a scent fairly accurately by comparing it with another. Thus it is quite usual for us to say that a flower has a lily-like fragrance, or that it smells like new-mown hay.

In general, it is true to say that, although the modern roses may be fragrant, the fragrance is lighter than that associated with the 'old-fashioned' varieties, which have returned to popularity in recent years, partly because of the rich, heavy fragrance of their blooms, Few gardens are too small to accommodate one or two of these; they may not have the perfectly-shaped blooms associated with the present-day hybrid tea varieties, but around midsummer, and with some kinds, until late in the season, they will fill the garden with the true rose scent which, like all scents, is difficult to describe precisely, but is unmistakable when it is found.

Just as distinctive is the true 'clove' fragrance of carnations. It is not, alas, found in every variety and sometimes those with the most shapely blooms lack fragrance entirely. The gardener in search of the clove scent will ignore these in favour of such varieties as 'Dusky', 'Ice Queen' and 'Oakfield Clove' which possess it very strongly. It is also found in the 'Sweetness' hybrids, often treated as annuals, grown from seed sown in the spring, and producing single flowers in a good colour range.

It is usually possible to find a corner in which to plant a clump of lilies. But, again, it pays to be careful about the choice of species and varieties, for not all are fragrant, and some, such as the Turk's cap lily, *Lilium martragon*, have a decidedly unpleasant scent. Even among fragrant types there is a great range of intensity of scent. Among those with the strongest and sweetest fragrance are the regal lily (*Lilium regale*), the madonna lily (*Lilium candidum*), the golden-rayed lily of Japan (*Lilium auratum*), usually obtainable in its hardier form, *platyphyllum*, *L. henryi*, and such hybrids as 'Crow's Hybrids' and *L. × testaceum*.

Because they are more permanent than other plants, and need considerably less attention, flowering shrubs are becoming more and more popular. Where space is

1 *Hesperis matronalis, sweet rocket, in both the mauve and white forms.*
2 *Sweet peas, strongly scented annuals, are in a wide colour range.*
3 *Nicotiana, the tobacco plant, is particularly fragrant at dusk.*
4 *The tree lupin, a quick growing shrubby plant, is delicately perfumed.*
5 *Salvia sclarea, clary, has a pungent smell, which increases in sunshine.*
6 *The wych hazel flowers scent the February air, before the leaves appear.*

fairly limited it is worth while choosing some of those with fragrant flowers. There are plenty of them, blooming at various times of the year. Among those flowering in winter are such fine shrubs as *Hamamelis mollis*, the wych hazel, with its yellow, cowslip-scented flowers. *Mahonia japonica*, its yellow flowers strongly fragrant, reminiscent of lily-of-the-valley, the sweetly fragrant white *Viburnum fragrans* and *V. tinus*, the old-fashioned but still excellent laurustinus. These are followed in spring by the native *Daphne mezereum*, the lilac-purple flowers of which are thickly clustered along the leafless twigs, the honey-scented, yellow azalea, *Rhododendron luteum*, the double gorse, *Ulex europaeus plenus*, its golden flowers filling the air with the scent of vanilla, other viburnums including *V. × burkwoodii* and *V. carlesii* and the wisterias. Late spring brings the white flowers of *Choisya ternata*, the Mexican orange blossom and the lilacs with their refreshing, unmistakable fragrance. These are soon followed by the mock oranges or philadelphus, their fresh, sweet scent of orange blossom, bringing in early summer, more powerful than that of the choisya. It pays to choose these with care for not all are fragrant and the intensity of fragrance varies. Among those with the strongest scent are the common *P. coronarius*, *P. delavayi*, the hybrid *P. × lemoinei* and the double-flowered 'Virginal'.

Summer is the time for roses and these have already been discussed. But there are several other fine fragrant shrubs flowering at this time. The sweet jessamine, *Jasminum officinale*, trained against a wall will bring its delicious fragrance through open windows, lavenders seem to give off their fragrance best on hot summer days, the spikes of buddleias attract the butterflies. Their fragrance is not to everyone's liking, but can scarcely be classed as objectionable. The white or yellow flowers of the tree lupin, *Lupinus arboreus* are borne for most of the summer, as are the rich yellow peablooms of the Spanish broom, *Spartium junceum*.

The climbing honeysuckles come into flower in summer but carry the season on well into the autumn. Again, not all are fragrant but those that are include, the late Dutch honeysuckle, *Lonicera periclymenum serotina*, which is usually still producing its reddish-purple flowers in October. Late flowers will still be found on the buddleias, on *Spartium junceum* and, of course, on the roses. Both *Choisya ternata* and the double gorse will often produce a second crop of flowers at this time of year and it is not unusual to find early flowers on the laurustinus, the first of the many clusters which will be produced between late October and April.

There is not the same wide range of fragrance among hardy herbaceous perennials, nor is it spread over so long a period. But it is worth remembering that among the tall bearded or flag irises are a good many fragrant varieties, some with a lily-like scent, others defying identification but delicious, nevertheless. A good catalogue should be consulted as new kinds are constantly being introduced. Other perennials which have flowers more or less fragrant include the sweet rocket, *Hesperis matronalis, Paeonia,* especially the old cottage garden paeonias, varieties of *P. officinalis,* border phloxes, *Astrantia carinthiaca* fragrant, of all things, of marzipan, the perennial wallflower, *Cheiranthus* 'Harpur Crewe', the herbaceous clematis, *C. recta,* the border pinks and carnations, not all with the 'clove' scent described earlier, nepetas or catmints, perhaps more accurately described as aromatic rather than fragrant, some evening primroses (oenotheras), *Petasites fragrans,* the winter heliotrope, its purple or white flowers borne in February, smelling attractively of vanilla, but a plant to be used with caution as it can spread so rapidly and, for this reason, to be confined to banks and rough places, where it can do little damage. Among the primulas there are a number which qualify, including the alpine auriculas, the dwarf *P. involucrata,* the somewhat taller *P. alpicola, P. chionantha* and *P. nutans. Salvia sclarea,* the clary, is pleasantly aromatic, especially on hot, sunny days, *Saponaria officinalis roseo-plena,* a double form of a native plant, sometimes known as Bouncing Bet, has fragrant pink flowers and, of course, many varieties of *Viola odorata,* the florist's violets, are exceptionally sweetly scented.

Those in search of fragrance are more likely to find it among the annuals and biennials and perennials treated as such, than among the hardy perennials for it is a quality possessed by many of the plants that are raised from seed sown in the spring, either under glass or in the open ground (see Annuals). Of these undoubtedly the most popular are the delightfully fragrant sweet peas, varieties of *Lathyrus odoratus.* As with other plants the fragrance varies a good deal but a good seedsman's list will make a point of describing those which possess it more strongly than others. Among other annuals and biennials which have it are sweet alyssum (*Lobularia maritima*), wallflowers (cheiranthus). snapdragons (antirrhinums), ten-week Brompton and East Lothian stocks (*Matthiola incana*), night-scented stock

1 *Jasminum officinale, has heavily scented flowers in late summer.*
2 *The flowers of this Lilium auratum hybrid are strongly scented.*
3 *The evening primrose opens its fragrant flowers in the evening.*
4 *Another type of lily.*

(*Matthiola bicornis*), marigolds (calendulas), nasturtiums (tropaeolums), mignonette (*Reseda odorata*), sweet sultan (*Centaurea moschata*), the sweet-scented tobacco plant (nicotiana), sweet scabious (*Scabiosa atropurpurea*), annual lupins and the biennial evening primrose (*Oenothera odorata*). All these are popular with most gardeners, but less well known, perhaps, is the Marvel of Peru (*Mirabilis jalapa*), a half-hardy annual with small trumpet-shaped flowers in various colours, their fragrance identical with that of the sweet-scented tobacco plant. *Cleome spinosa,* the spider flower is another less common annual, 1m (3ft) or so tall, with spidery-petalled pink or white flowers which add fragrance to their other attractions. Unusual, too, is *Calonyction aculeatum,* the moon flower, its great white trumpets opening at night. In warm places it is possible to grow this out of doors against a protected south or west wall, otherwise it needs conservatory or greenhouse treatment.

Taking them as a group, the bulbous plants include a good many fragrant plants, most of them fairly well known. Among the narcissus the scent range is very wide, from the pleasing fresh fragrance of many of the trumpet narcissus, to the heavy, sickly, almost overpowering scent of the jonquils. Few gardeners would consider tulips to be among the fragrant bulbs, although such varieties as 'Bellona', 'Prince Carnival' and 'Yellow Prince', all early singles and 'Orange Favourite', a parrot tulip, have a certain amount of fragrance. The strong but pleasing fragrance of hyacinths is one of the qualities which make them so popular for early forcing in bowls; a few spikes can fill the room when in flower. Lilies have been dealt with earlier in this article; but mention should be made of the plant which used to be called *Lilium giganteum,* but which is now correctly known as *Cardiocrinum giganteum,* which may reach 2.5-3m (8-10ft) and bears large trumpet-shaped flowers, heavily and almost intoxicatingly fragrant, although one almost needs a ladder to appreciate it properly unless the spikes are cut and brought indoors, when they will last a fair time in water.

There are also some fragrant greenhouse bulbs and it is certainly easier to appreciate their fragrance in such close confines than it is in the open air. Freesias, for instance, grown in pots, as they usually are, distil an indescribably sweet fragrance. Tuberoses (*Polianthes tuberosa*) are not grown as often as they were years ago, but the bulbs, or rather tubers, are obtainable from specialist suppliers and are well worth growing for the sake of the wonderful scent of the flowers in autumn and winter.

There are other greenhouse plants notable for their fragrance. Here, perhaps, is the place to bring in the lily-of-the-valley (*Convallaria majalis*) because it is so easily forced in boxes, or grown in pots, either for greenhouse use or for bringing into the living room when the plants are in flower. They can, of course, equally well be grown out of doors, particularly in a shady moist spot just as various other hardy fragrant plants such as Brompton stocks, lilacs, narcissus and lilies of various kinds, may either be grown outside or in pots in the greenhouse, usually flowering a little earlier, even when very little heat is available. Where more heat is available in winter it is possible to grow such fragrant flowers as stephanotis, acacias (usually mis-called mimosa), carnations, bouvardias, the little annual *Exacum affine,* gardenias, *Hoya carnosa, Jasminum polyanthum* and other tender jasmines, the jasmine-scented *Trachelospermum jasminoides,* the lily-scented *Datura arborea* as well as many others.

Frames see Growing under glass

French beans see Vegetables

French gardening
A system of cultivating vegetables and salad crops all the year round with the full utilization of frames, cloches, belljars and hot beds. Frames can now be heated by soil warming cables and insulated if necessary, but hot beds can also be made up on level ground and covered with frame lights or cloches.

Intense intercropping and catch cropping is practised to utilize the soil and, by a highly organized schedule, just as much as is possible is produced from a given area of land.

Similarly, fruit trees are trained to crop intensively for a given available space by training them into somewhat unconventional forms. Arcure, double espalier, oeschberg and pillar are systems employed.

Fruit
Where there is space in the garden most people like to grow fruit and vegetables, better flavoured, fresher and less expensive than those from the shops. If the are to be grown at all it is worth growing them really well. So before planting make sure that your soil is deep, well dug, clean of weeds, moist, open to sun and air and as free as possible from frosts. Choose your plants with care from a reputable supplier and seek advice about the most suitable varieties for the soil and space available.

Many fruits require fertilization from another tree or bush if they are to give generously of their produce, so wherever possible plant more than one of a type, choosing another that flowers at the same time. Tables of flowering times follow where necessary.

Probably the most popular of all home grown fruits is the apple, a comparatively easy fruit to grow in this country and giving the bonus of beautiful blossom in the spring.

Apples
Some varieties set no fruit at all when self pollinated, while others under favourable conditions set a fair crop. Yields are better when there are enough varieties for cross-pollination. There are a number of popular varieties which are poor pollinators (triploid varieties) but most are diploid, which pollinate each other very well. It is important to have at least two diploid varieties in a collection, unless the pollinator chosen is sufficiently self-fertile alone. When choosing varieties select those which will flower about the same time or overlap by a few days with others. There is some variation in the flowering periods of varieties but on the whole the times are very consistent. Winter temperatures and district can affect flowering periods.

In the following tables varieties are in seven flowering groups. Select if possible varieties within the same group for pollination. The old very late variety 'Crawley Beauty' is sufficiently self-fertile to set a crop.

Most varieties bear their fruit mainly on spurs formed on the older branches. The tip bearers do so on the tips of one-year-old shoots. Some sorts fruit on both kinds of wood.

Named varieties are propagated by vegetative means, as they do not come true from seed—by budding in July or August or by grafting in March or April (see Grafting) on to clonal rootstocks appropriate to the size of tree desired. The following rootstocks are commonly used: Malling IX (very dwarfing), Malling 26 (dwarfing), Malling VII (semi-dwarfing), Merton-Malling 106 (semi-dwarfing), Malling II or Malling I, the latter for wet soils (moderately vigorous), Merton-Malling III, Malling XXV and Crab C (vigorous).

Dwarf trees permit spraying, pruning and harvesting to be done without the need for step-ladders; they are also more easily protected from bird damage.

A number of small trees in a range of varieties covering a long season is preferable to a few large trees each giving an excessive quantity of fruit at one season and with one flavour. On average, a cordon tree gives 1.5-2.5kg (3-5lb) of apples, pyramids 3-4kg (6-8lb), bush trees on Malling IX rootstock 12.5-15kg (25-30lb), bush trees on Malling II 40-50kg (80-100lb), and larger trees according to size.

Alternatively, a 'family' tree having several varieties grafted on the one trunk can be grown or additional varieties be grafted on to an established tree which is yielding glut crops.

Apple trees have a long expectation of life and may remain fruitful and healthy for 50 years or more.

Cultivation Apples prefer deep loams but can be grown on sandy soils and heavy clays, if care is taken to drain wet soils and irrigate dry ones.

Apple 'Granny Smith' a firm green eating apple.

Cordons [planted 75cm (2½ft) by 1.8m (6ft)] espaliers [3-5m (10-18ft) apart], and arcure trained trees [90 × 180cm (3 × 6ft)], are grown against walls, fences or on post and wire supports; dwarf pyramids [105 × 210cm (3½ × 7ft)], spindle bushes [180 × 390cm (6 × 13ft)], pillars [180 × 300cm (6 × 10ft)], bush [360 × 360cm (12 × 12ft)], and half-standards [480 × 480cm (16 × 16ft)], on an open, but sheltered, site. Provide wind-breaks if natural shelter is not present.

Plant in November, if possible, or up to the end of March whenever the soil is sufficiently friable. It is best not to incorporate farmyard manure before planting into any except the poorest of soils. Plant as firmly as possible, ramming the soil round the roots with the square end of a stout post, and tie the tree to a substantial stake. Mulch the root area to conserve moisture in the soil during the first season, thereby minimizing the transplanting check to growth.

Subsequently, control the vigour balance by applying farmyard manure annually as a mulch in the spring and fertilizers according to the tree's needs.

Trained trees respond to being summer pruned in July or August, the side shoots being shortened to five leaves, the leaders remaining unpruned. Winter pruning consists of shortening summer-pruned shoots to two buds and reducing the lengths of the leaders by a third. Bush and half-standard trees are not summer pruned: in winter, the dead and crossing shoots are cut out and also sufficient branches to keep the head of the tree to an open habit. The leaders are shortened by a third for the first four

Flowering times for apples

Very early
Aromatic Russet (B)
Gravenstein (T)
Keswick Codlin (B)

Early
Adam's Pearmain (B)
Beauty of Bath
Ben's Red (B)
Bismark (B)
Cheddar Cross
Christmas Pearmain (B)
Discovery
Egremont Russet
George Cave
George Neal
Golden Spire
Irish Peach
Laxton's Early Crimson
Lord Lambourne
Lord Suffield
McIntosh Red
Melba (B)
Michaelmas Red
Norfolk Beauty
Patricia (B)
Rev W. Wilkes (B)
Ribston Pippin (T)
St Edmund's Pippin
Scarlet Pimpernal
Striped Beefing
Warner's King (T)
Washington (T)
White Transparent

Early mid season
Arthur Turner
Belle de Boskoop (T)
Blenheim Orange (TB)
Bowden's Seedling

Early mid season cont.
Bramley's Seedling (T)
Brownlee's Russet
Charles Ross
Claygate Pearmain
Cox's Orange Pippin
D'Arcy Spice
Devonshire Quarrenden (B)
Early Victoria (Emneth Early) (B)
Emperor Alexander
Epicure
Exeter Cross
Fortune (B)
Granny Smith
Grenadier
Howgate Wonder
James Grieve
John Standish
Jonathan
King's Acre Pippin
Kidd's Orange Red
Lord Grosvenor
Merton Pippin
Merton Prolific
Merton Russet
Merton Worcester
Miller's Seedling (B)
Ontario
Peasgood's Nonsuch
Red Victoria (B)
Reinette du Canada (T)
Rival (B)
Rosemary Russet
Sturmer Pippin
Sunset
Tydeman's Early Worcester
Tydeman's Late Orange
Wagener (B)
Wealthy
Winter Quarrenden (B)
Worcester Pearmain

Mid season
Allington Pippin (B)
Annie Elizabeth
Chelmsford Wonder (B)
Cox's Pomona
Delicious
Duke of Devonshire
Ellison's Orange
Golden Delicious
Golden Noble
Herring's Pippin
Lady Henniker
Lady Sudeley
Lane's Prince Albert
Laxton's Superb (B)
Monarch (B)
Orleans Reinette
Sir John Thornycroft

Late mid season
American Mother
Coronation (B)
Gascoyne's Scarlet
King of the Pippins (B)
Lord Derby
Merton Beauty
Newton Wonder
Northern Spy (B)
Royal Jubilee
William Crump
Winston
Woolbrook Pippin (B)

Late
Court Pendu Plat
Edward VII
Heusgen's Golden Reinette

Very late
Crawley Beauty

B=biennial or irregular flowering varieties. T=triploid varieties with poor pollen. Those not marked T are diploid varieties. Coloured sports eg Red Millar's Seedling usually flower at the same time as the parent.

'Lord Lambourne', a sweet dessert apple.

years only—leaving them unpruned from then onwards induces the branches to droop and become more fruitful.

Putting the soil down to a mixture of fine grass and clover, which is kept cut short, retards tree growth and induces fruitfulness. In addition, dessert apples take on a better colour when grown in grass than under clean cultivation and have a longer storage life.

Many varieties set an excessive number of fruitlets and hand thinning is necessary if the apples are to grow to a worthwhile size. Many fruitlets fall naturally to the ground during the 'June Drop' but additional thinning is necessary in June and July. Each cluster of dessert fruit must be reduced to two fruitlets, always removing the largest one—the 'king' fruit—first, and the clusters reduced to at least 7cm (3in) apart. Thin cookers to single fruits 16-20cm (6-8in) apart.

Apples are ready for harvesting when well coloured, with the seeds becoming brown in colour, and when they part readily from the fruit spurs. Test for fitness for picking by raising each apple to a horizontal position, giving a slight twist—if the stalk separates readily from the spur, without tearing, the apple is fit to pick.

Eat early maturing varieties direct from the tree or within a few weeks after

Forms of apple trees: 1 maiden 2 fan-trained 3 dwarf pyramid 4 espalier 5 cordons 6 bush.

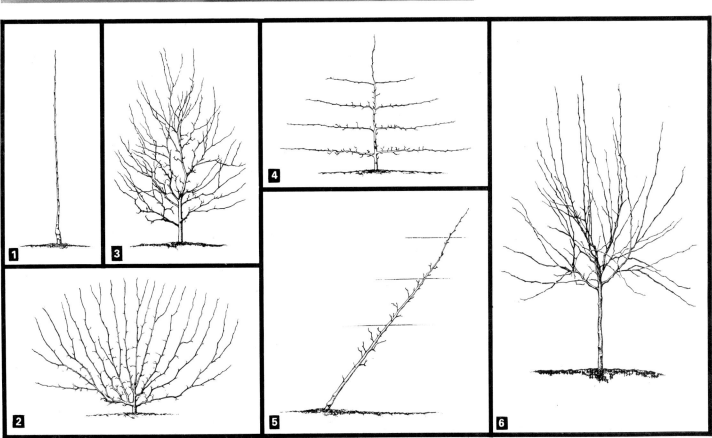

Apples for the garden—dessert

Variety	Pick	Eat	Flavour	Texture	Crop
*American Mother	Late Sept.	Oct.–Nov.	Very good,	Crisp, juicy	Irregular
*Ashmead's Kernel	Oct.	Nov.–March	Excellent, very aromatic	Firm	Light, occasionally heavy
*Beauty of Bath	July	Aug.	Good for season	Very soft	Sometimes irregular
Brownlees' Russet	Mid.–Oct.	Jan.–April	Good	Tender	Irregular
Claygate Pearmain	Mid.–Oct.	Dec.–March	Choice, aromatic	Crisp	Abundant
Court Pendu Plat	Early Nov.	Dec.–May	Acidly sweet	Firm	Very good
*Cox's Orange Pippin	Late Sept.	Oct.–Feb.	Excellent	Tender	Good to fair, depending on soil
*Crimson Cox	Mid.–Oct.	Nov.–Feb.	Not as good as Cox's Orange	Firm	Very good
D'Arcy Spice	End Oct.	Nov.–April	Aromatic	Firm	Medium, sometimes biennial
Discovery	End July	Aug.	Good for an early, pleasant aroma	Firm	Regular, precocious
Duke of Devonshire	Oct.	Feb.–March	Very good	Crisp	Good
*Egremont Russet	Late Sept.	Oct.–Dec.	Choice, nutty	Firm	Very good and regular
Ellison's Orange	Late Sept.	Sept.–Oct.	Good	Crisp	Very good, sometimes biennial
Epicure	End Aug.	Sept.	Very good	Firm	Prolific
*Fortune	Early Sept.	Sept.–L. Nov.	Sweet, aromatic	Crisp, tender	Good, sometimes biennial
George Cave	Mid.–July	early Aug.–Sept.	Pleasant for early sort	Firm at first	Regular and heavy
Granny Smith	Leave until first frost	Dec.–May	Moderate	Crisp	Free, tending to be biennial
Gravenstein	Late Sept.	Oct.–Nov.	Rich, aromatic	Soft	Good
Ingrid Marie	End Oct.	Dec.–April	Moderate	Firm	Good
Irish Peach	July	Aug.	Good straight from tree	Soft	Irregular
*James Grieve	Early Sept.	Sept.–Oct.	Very good, refreshing	Soft	Very good, regular
*King of the Pippins	Mid.–Oct.	Oct.–Nov.	Medium	Crisp	Good, regular
Lady Sudeley	Early Aug.	Aug.–Sept.	Good straight from tree	Soft	Good
*Laxton's Superb	Mid.–Oct.	Nov.–Feb.	Very good, aromatic	Soft	Good, sometimes biennial
*Lord Lambourne	Late Sept.	Oct.–Nov.	Excellent	Soft	Very good
*May Queen	Oct.	Jan.–May	Dry, nutty	Crisp	Very good
Melba	Early Aug.	Mid.–Aug.–Sept.	Distinctive aroma	Soft	Heavy, tending to be biennial
*Merton Beauty	Early Sept.	Sept.–Oct.	Rich, slight aniseed	Tender	Moderate
*Merton Charm	Mid.–Sept.	Sept.–Oct.	Excellent	Soft	Regular, good
Merton Prolific	Mid.–Oct.	Nov.–Feb	Acceptable	Firm	Exceedingly fertile
*Merton Russet	End Oct.	Dec.–March	Acid	Crisp	Good
*Merton Worcester	Mid.–Sept.	Sept.–Oct.	Sweet, aromatic	Firm	Excellent, liable become biennial
Orleans Reinette	Mid.–Oct.	Nov.–Feb.	Excellent, aromatic	Crisp	Fair
*Red Ellison	Mid.–Sept.	Sept.–Dec.	Aniseed	Crisp	Heavy and regular
*Ribston Pippin	Mid.–Oct.	Nov.–Jan.	Excellent, aromatic	Firm	Moderate
Scarlet Pimpernel	End July	End July–Sept.	Sweetly acid	Soft	Heavy
Spartan	Mid.–Oct.	Nov.–Feb.	Acceptable	Firm	Heavy
*St Cecilia	Early Oct.	Dec.–March	Excellent	Solid	Good
St Edmund's Russet	Sept.	Sept.–Oct.	Excellent from tree	Tender	Heavy, regular

(continued from first column)

Variety	Pick	Eat	Flavour	Texture	Crop
St Everard	Late Aug.	Sept.	Very good	Crisp	Irregular
*Sturmer Pippin	Leave until first frosts	Jan.–June	Very good	Firm	Good
*Sunset	Oct.	Oct.–Feb.	Very good	Medium firm	Heavy
Tydeman's Late Orange	End Oct.	Feb.–April	Excellent	Firm	Heavy
Winston	End Oct.	Jan.–April	Good	Very firm	Good
Worcester Pearmain	Early Sept.	Sept.–Oct.	Very good	Firm	Very good and regular

Apples for the garden—culinary

Variety	Pick	Eat	Flavour	Texture	Crop
Annie Elizabeth	Mid.–Oct.	Nov.–June	Good, acid	Cooks to froth	Good when settled down
Arther Turner	July–Sept.	July–Nov.	Good, acid	Firm	Regular and abundant
Bramley's Seedling	Late Sept.	Oct.–April	Excellent, acid	Firm	Very good
Crawley Beauty	Mid.–Oct.	Dec.–April	Good	Firm	Prolific and consistent
Edward VII	Mid.–Oct.	Dec.–April	Exceptionally good	Firm	Moderate
Emperor Alexander	Mid.–Sept.	Sept.–Nov.	Good	Tender	Fair
*George Neal	Sept.	Sept.–Oct.	Rich, slightly acid	Frothy cooked	Very free and regular
Golden Noble	Sept.	Sept.–Jan.	Excellent, acidly sweet	Tender	Good and regular
Grenadier	Mid.–Aug.	Aug.–Sept.	Good, acid	Frothy cooker	Very good and reliable
Howgate Wonder	Sept.–Oct.	Oct.–Feb.	Slightly acid	Cooks to froth	Heavy
*Lane's Prince Albert	Early Oct.	Nov.–March	Very good, acid	Soft	Very good
Lord Derby	Late Sept.	Oct.–Jan.	Excellent, sharp	Soft	Very free
*Monarch	Sept.	Oct.–March	Good, acid	Soft	Very good
Newton Wonder	Mid.–Oct.	Dec.–May	Very good, medium acid	Crisp	Irregular
Rev. W. Wilks	Early Oct.	Oct.–Nov.	Good	Cooks frothily	Very fertile
Warner's King	Late Sept.	Nov.–Feb.	Good	Tender	Moderate
Wellington	Mid.–Oct.	Nov.–March	Briskly acid	Solid	Moderate

Apples for the garden—dual purpose

Variety	Pick	Eat	Flavour	Texture	Crop
Allington Pippin	End Oct.	Oct.–Jan.	Good, acid	Firm	Very good
Barnack Beauty	Mid.–Oct.	Dec.–March	Good	Crisp	Fair to heavy
Belle de Boskoop	Mid.–Oct.	Dec.–April	Good, acid, aromatic	Firm	Moderate to heavy
Blenheim Orange	Mid.–Oct.	Nov.–Jan.	Excellent, nutty, acid	Crisp, cooks to pulp	Good and regular when settled down
*Charles Ross	Sept.	Oct.–Nov.	Moderate, sweet	Tender	Good and regular
Cheddar Cross	Mid.–Aug.	Late Aug.–early Sept.	Refreshing, slightly acid	Soft	Good
Cornish Gilliflower	Oct.	Dec.–April	Rich, sweet	Firm	Light
Herring's Pippin	Early Oct.	Oct.–Nov.	Good, spicy	Soft	Very good and regular
Mutsu	Early Oct.	Oct.–early April	Mildly sub-acid	Crisp	Heavy and regular
*Peasgood's Nonsuch	Early Sept.	Sept.–Nov.	Good	Soft	Irregular
*Rival	Early Oct.	Oct.–Dec.	Moderate	Firm	Fair
Wagener	Early Nov.	Dec.–	Fair	Firm	Very regular

Particularly good as cordons.

'Moor Park' is one of the best apricots for outdoor cultivation in the small garden. Fruits ripen in August.

being harvested. Store keeping varieties in a cool, dark, moist and frost-proof place.

Apricots

Of Mediterranean origin and flowering in late February and March, outdoor apricots demand a frost-free sunny site. Bush trees can be grown only in south-west and south-east England; elsewhere, as fan-trained trees on walls facing east, south, or south-west, or in greenhouses.

Apricots prefer a moisture retentive, friable and well-drained soil: they object to stiff clay and heavy loam. A pH of 6·5 —tending to alkalinity—is desirable.

Bush trees are spreading in habit. The leaves are broad and heart shaped, the flowers white or pale pink, borne singly or in pairs. Apricots are self-fertile and may be planted singly.

Forced apricots are ripe from mid-July, outdoor fruits to the end of September. Use them for dessert, bottling, preserving and jam making.

Propagation is by budding on to plum root-stocks—Brompton or Common Mussel (medium to large trees), St Julien (small to medium trees)—or on seedling peach or apricot.

Cultivation Plant preferably between late September and November, particularly under glass, or up to mid-March, at 4.5m (15ft) apart. Sprinkle two handfuls of bonemeal in the planting hole, give a spring mulch of 51kg (1cwt) of well-rotted manure per 10sq m (10 sq yd), plus 28g(1oz) of sulphate of potash per sq m (sq yd). Give 140g (5oz) per sq m (sq yd) of basic slag every third year. Water the trees regularly the first season and subsequently in dry spells—mature trees may wilt badly. Saturate greenhouse soils in February and mulch with spent hops or peat.

Force with gentle heat in February to a maximum temperature of 55°F (13°C), rising to 65°F (18°C) in summer with free ventilation. Syringe the foliage with water daily. Give full ventilation at leaf fall to induce complete dormancy.

Protect outdoor blossom from frost by draping hessian over the trees at night, removing this by day to allow pollinating insects to work. Assist pollination under glass by hand. Remove the blossom the first season.

Fruit forms both on young wood and old spurs. Maintain a proportion of each. Shorten the leaders by half to two-thirds after planting, laterals to a few inches. Subsequently, shorten the leaders annually by one-third. Tie in one healthy shoot per 25cm (10in) of main branch, remove ill-placed and upright growing shoots and pinch back the rest to four leaves from mid-June onwards.

Thin the crop when the set is heavy, first at pea size to one fruitlet per cluster then again after stoning, and when the natural drop is over, to 8-13cm (3-5in) apart. Test for stoning by pressing a pin into a few fruitlets.

Defer picking until the apricots are well coloured, ripe and part readily from the spurs without tearing.

Apricots are subject to silver leaf, bacterial canker and brown rot diseases, but are unaffected by peach leaf curl. Aphids, wasps and flies are the main pests.

The following are the best varieties:

'New Large Early'	early July
'Early Moor Park'	early August
'Hemskerk'	August
'Breda'	mid-August
'Moor Park'	August-September

Blackberries

Blackberries are vigorous and exceptionally spiny, hardy perennial cane fruits belonging to the genus *Rubus*. The species and hybrids listed below are grown for dessert, bottling, tarts, jam and wine.

Blackberries prefer deep, moist and rich loam but are adaptable to light sands and stiff clays, given free drainage and freedom from perennial weeds. Incorporate bulky organics such as farmyard manure, compost, shoddy, and feed with fish- or meat-meal and sulphate of potash. Correct iron deficiency on soils containing free lime by dressings of chelated iron.

Planting sites subject to frost are suitable as flowering is late, in early July. Provide shelter from strong winds for the brittle laterals and tie them into training-wires.

Cultivation Plant first-year plants, shortened to 23cm (9in) in the autumn at up to 3.6cm (12ft) apart, against walls or fences or posts and wires. Train the young replacement shoots of established plants to one side of, or above, the fruiting canes to prevent contamination with fungus diseases. Cut out fruited shoots after harvest.

Propagate by tip layering in June or July, by leaf bud cuttings in August, or by rooted suckers in the autumn.

Control greenfly, capsid bug, raspberry beetle and cane spot and destroy plants infected with crown gall.

Variety	Pedigree	Fruiting season
Ashton Cross	Hybrid	Late July-Aug.
Bedford Giant	Hybrid	Late July-Aug.
Cut or Parsley-leaved	*R. laciniatus*	Aug.-Sept.
Evergreen	*R. ulmifolius*	
Thornless	*inermis*	Aug.-Sept.
Himalaya Giant	*R. procerus*	Aug.-Sept.
John Innes	Hybrid	Sept.-Oct.
Merton Early	*R. nitidiodes*	Aug.
Merton Thornless	Hybrid	Aug.-Sept.

Cherries

Two main groups of cherries are cultivated for the merit of their fruit, the 'sweet', dessert (*Prunus avium*) and the 'sour', culinary (*Prunus cerasus*); a third group, the 'Duke' cherries, form an intermediate class. The sweets are subdivided into the 'black' and 'white' varieties. All fruiting cherries are hardy in the British Isles, though the blossom may be damaged by spring frosts.

Named varieties are propagated on to rootstocks by budding in July and August, or by grafting in March, which would be rather unusual. Seedling Gean Mazzard and the clonal Malling F 12/1 rootstocks are used. Unfortunately, as yet, a dwarfing rootstock is not available and a mature sweet cherry tree may be up to 10m (30ft) tall with a corresponding spread—too large for the average modern garden. Bush Morello (sour) trees rarely exceed a height of 5m (15ft).

Sour cherries do well in almost any situation and are particularly valuable for training as fan trees against a north-facing wall unsuited to other fruits. Although sweet cherries can also be grown as fans, they dislike hard pruning and are happiest as standards or half standards given minimum pruning. Plant standards 10m (30ft) apart, half standards 8m (25ft), bush and fan trees 5m (15ft). Cherries as a class dislike poorly drained, heavy soils. The sweet varieties do well on deep, light to medium loams while the sour ones will tolerate poor soils, provided they are not waterlogged. Lime in the soil is not an essential as is commonly supposed.

Morello cherries are self fertile and will pollinate any sweet cherry flowering concurrently. Most sweet cherries are infertile with their own pollen and often with certain other varieties also. The John Innes Institute has classified the sweets into a number of groups but not with their companions (see table above). It is important to select varieties for interplanting whose blossom period coincides or overlaps. A few varieties called universal donors are compatible with all groups flowering at the same time. The dessert cherry season extends from mid-June to mid-August; culinary kinds are used throughout the year for cooking, bottling and making into jam or cherry ale.

Cultivation Young trees, not exceeding five years old, transplant best. Planting can be carried out at any time from mid-October to mid-March, whenever the soil is sufficiently friable to be worked between the roots.

Excavate a wide hole just deep enough to allow the roots to be covered with 10-13cm (4-5in) of soil. Plant firmly and stake securely. Shorten the previous season's growth on the leading branches by half, and side shoots to 8cm (3in). In the spring, mulch the soil surface over the root area with composted vegetable refuse or decayed straw. Do not let

weeds encroach for the first few years.

Sweet cherries fruit chiefly on the spurs formed freely on the older wood. Pruning consists in maintaining the tree to an open habit with an evenly balanced head, together with the removal of dead, crossing and rubbing branches. This minimal pruning should be confined to the spring and early summer when infection from silver leaf disease is least likely.

Sour cherries fruit on shoots formed the previous season. After the basic fan of branches has been built up by shortening the leaders annually as for sweet cherries, annually replaced side-growths are tied in parallel to the permanent branches. The replacement shoots are selected during May to August—one near the base of a fruiting shoot and another at its tip to draw sap to the fruit; all others are pinched out when quite small. The tip of the terminal shoot itself is pinched out when 8-10cm (3-4in) of growth has been made.

After the cherries have been gathered, the fruited shoots are pruned back at their junction with the selected replacement shoots. The latter are then tied in neatly as before.

Cherries appreciate a spring mulch of farmyard manure at the rate of 51kg (1cwt) to 10 sq m (10 sq yd), or 56-84g (2-3oz) per sq m (sq yd) of Nitro-chalk if manure is unobtainable, plus an autumn application of 28-56g (1-2oz) per sq m (sq yd) of sulphate of potash. Trees on walls respond to being fed with liquid manure.

Protecting the fruit from bird damage is necessary, using fish nets or rayon spider's web material on trees of a suitable size, or by bird scaring where trees are too large to net.

Sweet cherry pollination groups

Group 1. 'Early Rivers' (e), 'Bedford Prolific' (e), 'Knight's Early Black' (e), 'Roundel Heart' (m).

Group 2. 'Bigarreau de Schrecken' (e), 'Waterloo' (e), 'Merton Favourite' (e), 'Frogmore Early' (m), 'Merton Bigarreau' (m), 'Merton Bounty' (m).

Group 3. 'Bigarreau Napoleon' (m), 'Emperor Francis' (m).

Group 4. 'Merton Premier' (m), 'Amber Heart' (m).

Group 5. 'Merton Heart' (e), 'Governor Wood' (m).

Group 6. 'Bradbourne Black' (l), 'Gèante de Hedelfingen' (l).

Universal Donors: 'Noir de Guben' (e), 'Merton Glory' (m), 'Bigarreau Gaucher' (l).

Flowering period: (e) early; (m) mid-season; (l) late.

Currants

Of the three kinds of currants, black currants derived from *Ribes nigrum* are grown more commonly than red currants (derived from the intercrossing of three *Ribes* species) or white currants (derived from red currants). All three are self-fertile, fruit prolifically and take up only a relatively small area.

Red and white currants withstand drought better than black currents and are less greedy for nitrogen. Otherwise, their requirements are very similar.

Choice Cherries for the Garden

Variety	Class	Flavour	Colour	Crop	Flowers	Fruits
Amber Heart (Kentish Bigarreau)	D	Rich	Yellow and red	Prolific	Mid	Mid July
Archduke	D & C	Sweet	Dark red	Good	Late	July
Bigarreau Gaucher	D	Rich	Almost black	Good	Mid	Late July
Bigarreau Napoleon	D	V. Fine	Yellow and red	Good and Regular	Late	Late July
Bigarreau de Schrecken	D	Good	Black	Good	Mid	Late June
Bradbourne Black	D	Rich	Black	Heavy	Late	Late July
Early Rivers	D	Delicious	Black	Good	Mid	Mid June
Emperor Francis	D	Richly Aromatic	Dark red over yellow	Productive	Mid	Late July
Frogmore Early	D	Good	Yellow and red	Heavy and Regular	Late	Early July
Gèante de Hedelfingen	D	Rich	Black	Good	Late	Late July
Governor Wood	D	Good	Yellow and red	Good	Late	July
Kentish Red	C	Acid	Red	Good	Late	Early July
Late Duke	D & C	Fair	Deep Red	Good	Late	August
May Duke	D & C	Fair	Black	Good	Late	June
Merton Bigarreau	D	Winey	Purplish-black	Heavy and Regular	Mid	Late July
Merton Bounty	D	Sweet	Dark crimson	Good	Mid	Early July
Merton Favourite	D	Rich	Black	Good	Early	Early July
Merton Glory	D	Good	Cream and crimson	Good	Mid	Mid July
Merton Heart	D	Rich	Dark crimson to black	Heavy	Early	Early July
Morello	C	Acid	Dark red to black	Prolific	Late	August to September
Noir de Guben	D	V. good	Black	Fair	Early	July
Roundel Heart	D	Sweet	Deep crimson	Heavy	Mid	Early July
Waterloo	D	Rich	Black and red	Slightly biennial	Early	Late July

D Dessert   C Culinary   V Very

104

Red and white currants blossom early and so must not be planted in low-lying frost pockets. Black currants tolerate being partially shaded by trees or buildings though this delays ripening.

Black currants are in season from July to early September, fruiting on the previous season's shoots. Red and white currants ripen from late June to late July and fruit on spurs formed on the old wood.

Cultivation The modern method of planting black currants is to insert three cuttings 10cm (4in) deep at each planting position and allow them to fruit *in situ*. Plant at 2×1m (6×3ft) intervals. Cuttings 30cm (12in) long, are taken in the autumn from well-ripened shoots of the current season's growth—it is unnecessary to make the cuts directly below the nodes as the cuttings root readily wherever the cuts are made.

Alternatively, plant one to two-year old bushes between October and mid-March, the earlier the better. The soil should be dug deeply prior to planting and have 51kg (1cwt) of well-rotted farm-yard manure dug in every 10 sq m (10 sq yd). Do not allow the fibrous roots to become dry while awaiting planting;

1 Red currant 'Red Lake' produces heavy crops of large fruits. 2 Black currant 'Mendip Cross'. 3 White currant 'Transparent' fruits on permanent spurs.

heel them in until planting can be carried out. The roots should not have more than 5cm (2in) of soil above them when planted in their permanent positions.

Cuttings rooted *in situ* can be allowed to fruit the first season but transplanted one-year-old bushes should be pruned to help them recover from the transplanting check and induce strong growth, by shortening the shoots to four buds.

Prune established black currant bushes as soon as their crop is harvested. Remove about a third of the older branches to maintain vigour and to induce sucker shoots to form below ground. Retain a good supply of last year's shoots, spaced evenly over the bush. Mulch the bushes in April with hop manure, matured deep litter poultry manure or decayed farmyard manure.

Feed black currants in the spring with 56g (2oz) per sq m (sq yd) of sulphate of ammonia or Nitro-chalk and in the autumn with 28g (1oz) per sq m (sq

yd) of sulphate of potash. Red and white currants manage with 28g (1oz) of sulphate of ammonia per sq m (sq yd) in the spring and the same amount of potash in the autumn.

Generally, red and white currant bushes are grown with a short leg, 10-13cm (4-5in) in length, sucker growths being removed; on dry gravel soils, die back may be severe and a multi-stemmed bush may be more practical. Bushes with a leg are obtained by first removing the buds from the bottom half of each cutting before insertion.

Single or double cordon red or white currants, planted against a wall, give extra-large berries and are easily netted against birds. Plant bushes 1.5×1.5m (5×5ft), single cordons 0.3m (1ft) apart in the row, double cordons, 0.5m (1½ft) apart in the row; rows 1.3m (4ft) apart.

Prune red currants in the winter by shortening the leading shoots by a third and the sideshoots to two or three buds. Summer pruning in July promotes fruit bud formation. Shorten the sideshoots to five leaves; leave the leading shoots unpruned.

Gooseberries

The gooseberry, *Ribes grossularia*, is

Gooseberry varieties

Variety	Colour	Season	Habit	Flavour	Notes
Careless	white	mid	drooping	good	not under trees
Cousen's Seedling	yellow	very late	drooping and spreading	sweet	rather prickly
Crown Bob	red	mid	drooping	good	prone to bullfinch attack
Early Sulphur	yellow	early	upright	good	one of the best earlies
Golden Drop	yellow	mid	upright	strong	needs mildew control
Green Gem	green	late	upright	fair	heavy cropper, prone to mildew attack
Keepsake	green	early (cooking) late (dessert)	drooping	excellent	heavy and certain cropper
Lancashire Lad	red	mid	upright	fair	excellent all-rounder, resists mildew
Lancer	green	mid	upright—spreading	superb	heavy crops
Leveller	yellow	mid	drooping	very good	immense fertility plus quality
Whinham's Industry	red	mid	spreading	very good	does well under trees
Whitesmith	white	mid	upright—spreading	good	excellent all-rounder

native to Britain where it has been cultivated since the thirteenth century at least. Being self-fertile and productive, it is ideal for the small garden. Gooseberries excel in the cooler areas of the Midlands and North.

They are tolerant of most soils but not of waterlogging. Growth may be weak on poor gravel soils or soft and disease-susceptible on heavy clays. Both these extremes benefit from enrichment with garden compost, peat or leafmould. Gooseberries are very sensitive to potash deficiency.

A position in full sun is best for early ripening; bushes can be planted against north or east walls to give extra-late crops. As gooseberries flower early in the spring it is important not to plant them in low-lying, frosty areas. For economy of space, they may be planted between plum trees as both appreciate generous manuring.

Besides the more usual bush forms, single, double, or triple cordons can be grown for special dessert or exhibition berries. Standard gooseberries are easier for elderly people to grow and pick.

Cultivation Gooseberries are propagated from hardwood cuttings in mid-October, choosing well-ripened shoots 20-23cm (8-9in) long. The lower buds are removed to prevent suckers from forming. The prepared cuttings are planted 10cm (4in) deep in a slit trench with sand or grit in the bottom. Standard gooseberries are formed by grafting scions on to *Ribes aureum* rootstocks with stems of the required height.

Planting is carried out from November to February on ground previously enriched with farmyard manure. Bushes should be set out 1.2-2m (4-6ft) apart each way; single, double and triple cordons at 0.3, 0.5 and 0.7m (1, 1½ and 2ft) respectively; standards at 1.2-2m (4-6ft) apart.

Bushes and cordons should have a 16cm (6in) stem devoid of roots and shoots to prevent suckering. Cut off the topmost roots if need be.

Plant firmly, covering the roots with 8-10cm (3-4in) of soil. Shorten the leading shoots by a half and side-shoots to two buds. Give a generous mulch in the spring and thorough waterings in dry spells during the first summer. Keep the soil weed free by hoeing shallowly—deep cultivation damages the surface roots.

Gooseberries demand an ample supply of potash, particularly on light soils; potash deficiency induces poor growth and premature defoliation. Feed annually in the spring with 28-56g (1-2 oz) per sq m (sq ft) of sulphate of potash, not muriate of potash which causes leaf

1 Gooseberry 'Rote Preisbeere' at the green stage in early June, when the berries are hard and bitter, before they are ready for picking.
2 Gooseberry 'Careless' when fully ripe is rather transparent.

Bunches of white grapes grown on the cordon system, are harvested.

scorching. Scatter bonfire ash round the bushes to give extra potash. Avoid promoting lush growth susceptible to American gooseberry mildew disease by excessive use of nitrogenous fertilizers.

Summer prune the sideshoots to six leaves in July to promote blossom bud formation and to remove mildew-infected tips. Tear out suckers—cutting only induces more to develop.

Thinning the crop produces larger berries. Defer thinning until the small berries are worth being picked for cooking (about Whitsuntide). Late varieties mature about the end of August. Harvest the berries when they are under-ripe for cooking or when fully coloured and soft for dessert use.

Winter prune the bushes in November or defer pruning until the spring where bird damage to the buds is known to be severe. Shorten leading shoots by one third. Spur prune sideshoots to 4cm (1½in) for heavy crops or to two buds for large dessert berries. Prune upright bushes to outward-pointing buds, weeping bushes to upward-pointing buds. Keep the centres of the bushes open.

Grapes

Grapes can be grown quite successfully out of doors in the southern part of the country, preferably given the protection of a warm wall. Plant between October and February in a rich, deep soil.

Plant firmly and immediately after planting, prune the young plant to within 30cm (12in) from its base to encourage a strong shoot to grow.

Plants out of doors can be grown as cordons, espaliers, fans or bushes.

The bush method is the simplest and consists mainly in cutting the branches of the plant back each year to within 2.5cm (1in) of the main stem. The straggly habit of the bush form makes it a nuisance in the garden and the berries may be spoilt by trailing on the ground.

The cordon is the most common form. It consists of a rod trained to a wire framework about 1.2m (4ft) high. The rod is encouraged to grow in the same way as an indoor plant.

The laterals from the rod are trained 30-38cm (12-15in) apart and cut back each winter to one bud. Horizontal cordons can also be grown and these have the advantage that they can be covered with tall cloches in late summer to help to ripen the berries.

Espaliers are grown by developing pairs of branches 30cm (12in) apart from the main stem. Two- or three-tier espaliers are quite sufficient.

Fan shapes can be grown quite easily by training 5-8 shoots from the main stem to grow on a wire framework. The general pruning treatment is the same as for indoor plants, but of course, much less growth will be made during the summer months. In August, cut away as many of the side shoots as possible, so that light and air will get to the berries and ripen them properly.

Planting distances for the various types are: Cordons' 1m (3ft) apart; Espaliers' 2m (6ft); Fans, 2.5m (8ft); Horizontal cordons' 2.3m (4ft).

Each winter give the soil round the plant a dressing of good general fertilizer, together with a mulch of farmyard manure. Once again prune in November.

Propagation Vines can be propagated by eyes or cuttings. Cuttings should be 30cm (12in) long and inserted to half their length in good soil in November or December. Vine eyes can be propagated in a greenhouse or warm place.

Vines are self fertile and there is no problem with pollination.

There are a number of lesser known fruits which can also be grown, such as medlars, quinces, figs, mulberries and others. They are not included here because they are of specialist interest only and full information concerning their culture can be obtained from the supplier of stock.

Varieties of grape

For the open border

Gamay Hâtif des Vosges	Black, small, early
Madeleine Royale	White, medium, early
Perle de Czaba	White, small, very early, muscat
Noir Hâtif de Marseilles	Black, small, early, muscat
Seyve-Villard 5–276	White, very prolific, late

For walls

Golden Chasselas	White, medium, late, prolific
Chasselas Rose	Red, medium, fairly late

Under cloches

Any of the above, also:	
Muscat Hamburgh	Black, exquisite flavour, muscat
Madeleine Noir	Black, early
Reine Olga	Good
Millenium of Hungary	Good
Ascot Citronelle	Good but uncertain cropper

Loganberry

The loganberry is, perhaps, the supreme bramble type of berry, as it is ideal for stewing, jam- and jelly-making, bottling, canning, juice extraction and wine-making. The berries can also be eaten as dessert when fully ripe, but may be too tart for some palates.

Opinions are divided as to whether the loganberry is a red-fruiting form of the common Californian blackberry, *Rubus ursinus vitifolius,* or a seedling from a cross between the 'Red Antwerp' raspberry and the American blackberry 'Aughinburgh'. The plant appeared in 1881 in the garden of Judge J. H. Logan of Santa Cruz, California, from whom it takes its name. It has been cultivated in England since 1897.

The loganberry produces vigorous, prickly canes carrying 3- to 5-lobed leaves. As flowering is late, the plants may be grown in low-lying situations; spring frosts rarely damage the blossom, though severe winters may affect the canes. Loganberries are self-compatible and yield heavy crops of blunt, firm, very juicy, deep red berries of a rich flavour, from August to September. The yield may be sustained for 15 years or more. The berries do not plug, so are picked complete with core. Picking is best done when the berries are quite dry.

Heavy, rather than chalky and light and dry, soils are preferred—chalky soils induce iron and manganese deficiencies. Well-drained loams and brick earths are ideal. Loganberries love rich soil and respond to generous manuring. Nitrogen is the most important plant food requirement. Mulch annually with farmyard manure in late autumn or feed with 56g (2oz) of fish manure and 28g (1oz) of sulphate of potash per sq m (sq ft).

A sunny and open but sheltered site is best with protection from north-east winds. The rows should run north-south.

Propagation is usually by tip-layering between June and mid-August. The tips of young canes are pegged down 6-8cm (2-3in) deep (or weighted with a flat stone), into small pots filled with a rooting compost and sunk in the ground. The young plants are severed from the parent canes when well-rooted in the following February. Alternatively, leaf bud cuttings are rooted 6cm (2in) apart in a bed of sandy soil in a closed and shaded garden frame in July or August. Each cutting consists of a leaf and bud with a 2.5cm (1in) length of cane bark devoid of pith. Roots are produced in three to four weeks; the young plants are hardened off a month later and transplanted the following spring.

Rooted tips or cuttings are planted 2-3m (6-10ft) apart in February or March against fences, north or east walls, and up arches. Post and wire supports with wires at 0.6, 1.2 and 2m (2, 4 and 6ft) from soil level are used on open sites. Shorten the young plants to 23cm (9in) after planting, to encourage the production of strong new shoots on which fruit will be borne the following year. To reduce disease infection from the older canes, the young canes are trained fan-wise on the opposite side from the old canes. The two ages of cane occupy alternate sides annually. Ten to 12 fruiting canes are retained per plant. Fruiting is on one-year-old canes which are cut down to ground level in October after fruit harvest.

Pests and diseases are the same as those which attack raspberries.

Two good varieties are the following: 'LY 59', which is a virus-free clone available since the late 1950s. It is free from the debilitating viruses which reduce the crop of infected loganberries. It is the heaviest cropper—it may yield 8.5kg (17½lb) of fruit per bush. 'American Thornless', a prickle-free mutation was found in 1933. It is a pleasure to prune. Slightly less vigorous than the common loganberry, it is an ideal variety for the smaller garden and may yield up to 7.5kg (15lb) of fruit per bush.

Peaches and Nectarines

The peach, *Prunus persica,* is closely related to apricots, cherries and plums. It was introduced into England in the early sixteenth century via Europe and Persia from China. The nectarine is a natural sport of the peach with smaller, more delicately flavoured fruits, which are smooth-skinned, whereas peaches have a rough skin.

Bush peaches are hardy in southern England; the protection of a south or south-west wall is needed further north. Nectarines invariably are grown on walls. Both fruits need abundant sunshine and crop to perfection under glass. A well-drained, deep, medium loam soil gives the best results. Soils with a high lime content are disliked; but acid soils should be dressed with mortar rubble. An application of 0.25kg (2½lb) per sq m (sq yd) of coarse bonemeal should be given at planting time and an annual summer feed of a balanced fertilizer at the rate of 112kg (4oz) per sq m (sq yd) should be applied. Give the trees a spring mulch of decayed dung if the material is available. Plant one to three-year-old trees between mid-October and mid-March, preferably in October or November. Trim any damaged roots,

The loganberry is a vigorous plant, producing long whippy runners and big juicy berries with a distinctive flavour.

Peach 'Dr Hogg' is a variety producing large velvety fruits with a rich apricot-coloured flesh.

cover them with no more than 10-16cm (4-6in) of soil, tread firm and ensure that the graft union is above ground. Keep the trunks of wall trees 10cm (4in) away from the walls. Fan trees should be tied temporarily until the soil has settled, bush trees should be staked, putting the stake in the planting hole before the tree. Planting distances are: for fan trees 5m (15ft) apart, and for bush trees 5-7m (15-20ft). Mulch either with compost or strawy manure in March, and rub off the first season's blossom buds.

Frosty sites are unsuitable as the trees flower in February or early March, and wall trees should be protected with hessian or tiffany at night, though this should be removed by day to allow pollinating insects access to the flowers. Although both fruits are self-fertile, hand pollination ensures a full set. Fan trees, however, often set an excessive crop, and the fruitlets should be thinned progressively so as to leave peaches at one per 10 sq dc (1 sq ft) and nectarines at one per 23cm (9in) square. Give copious waterings while the fruits are swelling. Leave the crop to ripen fully on the tree, and check daily for ripe fruits by palming off—finger pressure causes bruises. They should be used promptly, for dessert, bottling, canning or jam making.

When pruning it should be remembered that peaches and nectarines fruit on the previous season's shoots, so prune them hard enough to induce plenty of new growth, at least 30cm (12in) in length annually. However, do not go to the other extreme as excessive pruning induces lush growth and diminished cropping. Cut out any dead wood, crossing branches and a third of the old growth of bush trees in May, cutting always at a strong sideshoot. Disbud the fruiting shoots of fan-trained trees during April, May and June, retaining one new shoot at the base, tip and middle. Pinch out the growing tips of the last two at five leaves, but allow the basal shoots to grow to their full length. Cut out the fruited shoots after harvest and tie in the replacements in fan formation at 8cm (3in) apart. Over-vigorous trees should be root pruned.

Trees are easily raised from seed but do not come true. Named varieties are budded on to seedling peach or plum rootstocks in July or early August (see Propagation). Plum rootstocks are best for heavy soils—'St Julien' gives medium-sized trees; 'Common Mussel' the smallest, coupled with early fruiting, and 'Brompton' the largest. Seedling peach rootstocks sucker less than plum rootstocks.

Peaches and nectarines are prone to

Peaches for the greenhouse or outdoors

Variety	Flavour	Colour	Size	Fruit
Bellegarde	Rich, very juicy	Yellow and crimson, white flesh	Large	Early September
Duke of York	Very sweet	Crimson, white flesh	Very large	Mid-July
Erly Redfre	Rich	Creamy-yellow with crimson flush white	Large	Early August
Hales Early	Sweet, aromatic	Yellow with red flush	Medium to large	Late July
Peregrine	Juicy delicious flavour	Bright crimson	Large	Early August
Rochester	Rich, sweet juicy	Yellow, mottled red	Good size	Mid-August
Nectarines				
Early Rivers	Tender, juicy	Bright scarlet	Large	Mid-July
Lord Napier	Brisk, rich and delicious	Yellow and crimson	Large	Early August
Pineapple	Delicious and melting	Orange and red	Fairly large	Early September

being infected by many diseases.

Pears

The pear grown in Britain is the European Pear which derives from *Pyrus communis,* native of the temperate parts of Europe and the western part of southern Asia as far as the Himalayas. In America some varieties are grown which are hybrids between the European Pear (as represented by 'William's Bon Chrétien', known in America as 'Bartlett') and *Pyrus serotina,* the Japanese sand pear.

Pears have been cultivated since very early times (Pliny, the Roman writer, knew of 39 distinct varieties) and they may have been introduced to Britain during the Roman occupation. They were certainly grown in monastic gardens and were popular in Tudor times. The nineteenth century saw the introduction of hundreds of new varieties, many originating in France and Belgium. Today, the number of varieties favoured by market growers can be numbered on one's fingers.

In the opinion of most people dessert pears have a flavour superior to that of apples; it is more pronounced and the pears themselves are frequently much juicier. The best dessert pears have a melting consistency like butter (and hence the French word *beurre* applied to many varieties), although, for texture, many people prefer a crisp apple.

Although pear trees are longer-lived than apples, they tend to spur more freely forming too many clusters of buds. They are less prone to pest and disease attack, they flower earlier and therefore are more vulnerable to spring frosts. A few varieties only are suitable for growing in the open in most parts of Britain. Others need the protection of a wall, and some not only require such shelter but will thrive only in our warmer districts.

Although all dessert pears can be cooked if they are picked while still slightly unripe, particular varieties are usually grown for this purpose. Special varieties, too, are grown for the making of perry, a fermented drink made from the juice in much the same way as cider is from apple juice.

A slightly acid soil suits pears best and a very alkaline soil should be avoided as, in such conditions, pears suffer badly from iron deficiency.

Compared with apples, pears are more likely to withstand poor drainage, but are less able to tolerate dryness. A very light sandy soil, therefore, must be liberally enriched with humus-forming and moisture-holding materials. The ideal soil is a deep, rich loam somewhere between light and heavy.

Standard or half-standard trees take many years to come into bearing and eventually become too large for the average garden. Bush-type trees, pyramids, cordons, fans or espaliers are, therefore, more appropriate for small gardens, and these are usually grown on 'Malling Quince A' rootstocks.

The form of tree to be grown depends rather on the space available. For the open garden, bushes, pyramids or cordons are the usual choice. Bushes take up most room but their maintenance takes least time. Pyramids come into

Pears which suit the garden (Dessert varieties unless otherwise stated)

Variety	Season	Fruit quality	Crop	Special remarks
Baronne de Mello	Oct–Nov	Excellent, very juicy	Heavy	
Beurré d'Amanlis	Aug–Sept	Melting, sweet, very juicy	Heavy	Succeeds almost anywhere
Beurré Clairgeau	Nov–Dec	Faint musk flavour, firm flesh	Very heavy	Cooker
Beurré Diel	Oct–Dec	Delicious when quite ripe	Heavy	
Beurré Hardy	Oct	Good, flesh tinged with pink	Very heavy	Very hardy, succeeds almost anywhere
Beurré Superfin	Oct	Sweet, very melting, delicately perfumed	Moderate	Dessert variety but good for bottling and canning
Bristol Cross	Oct	Quite good, juicy and melting	Very heavy	
Catillac	Dec–Apr	Firm white flesh cooks red	Very heavy	Best of cookers
Clapp's Favourite	Sept	Fair sweet, juicy but gritty	Heavy	
Conference	Oct–Nov	Melting, juicy and sweet	Heavy	Succeeds almost anywhere. Dessert but good for bottling and canning
Doyenné d'Ete	July–Aug	Melting, sweet and very juicy	Heavy	Regular cropper
Doyenné du Comice	Nov	Tender and juicy delicious	Fair	One of the best dessert varieties but good for bottling and canning
Dr Jules Guyot	Aug–Sept	Melting, very juicy, slight musk flavour	Heavy	
Durondeau	Oct–Nov	Sweet, juicy, good flavour	Heavy	Succeeds almost anywhere
Easter Beurré	Feb–Apr	Sweet, melting with rich musk flavour	Moderate	
Emile d'Heyst	Oct–Nov	Juicy and very sweet	Heavy	Succeeds almost anywhere
Fertility	Oct	Little flavour, juicy and crisp	Heavy	Succeeds almost anywhere
Glou Morceau	Dec–Jan	Delicious flavour, melting and very sweet	Regular	Needs a warm wall
Gorham	Sept	Sweet, juicy, with musk flavour	Moderate to heavy	
Hessle	Oct	Slightly sweet	Very heavy	Cooker, succeeds almost anywhere
Improved Fertility	Sept–Oct	Fruit larger and better quality than 'Fertility'	Heavy	Self-compatible
Jargonelle	Aug	Sweet, juicy, slightly musky	Good	Tip-bearer, does well in north
Joséphine de Malines	Dec–Feb	Good flavour, pinkish-white, juicy flesh	Heavy	Tip-bearer
Louise Bonne of Jersey	Oct	Excellent flavour, melting and sweet	Heavy	Regular cropper but very vulnerable to spring frosts
Marguerite Marillat	Sept–Oct	Juicy but flavour only moderate	Good	
Marie Louise	Oct–Nov	Sweet, juicy, good flavour	Moderate	
Merton Pride	Sept–Oct	Sweet, juicy, excellent flavour	Good	
Packham's Triumph	Nov	Sweet, very juicy, good flavour	Good	Tip-bearer, also good for bottling and canning
Passe Crasanne	Mar–Apr	Sweet, very juicy, good flavour	Fair	Needs wall protection
Pitmaston Duchess	Oct–Nov	Pale yellow flesh, melting, very juicy but flavour only fair	Good	Dual-purpose
Santa Claus	Dec–Jan	Moderate, sweet but gritty	Good	
Seckle	Oct–Nov	Very sweet, rich flavour	Moderate	
Souvenir de Congrès	Sept	Sweet and very juicy, musky flavour	Heavy	
Thompson's	Oct–Nov	Very melting, delicious, rich flavour	Moderate	
Triomphe de Vienne	Sept	Juicy, good flavour but inclined to be gritty	Good	
Vicar of Winkfield	Nov–Jan	Firm flesh, sweet	Good	Cooker
William's Bon Chrétien	Sept	Very juicy, excellent flavour, musky	Good	Popular dessert variety but good for bottling and canning
Winter Nelis	Dec–Jan	Sweet and very juicy, good flavour	Good	Should be eaten while still yellowish-green

1 Pear 'Conference', a reliable variety.
2 'Uvedale's St Germain' is a dessert pear.

bearing more quickly and their small size makes spraying, picking and protection from birds easier. Their pruning, however, takes rather more attention. Cordons require posts and wires for support but have the merit of taking up little room individually so that a single row can comprise a collection of varieties providing a succession of fruit. A row of cordons, too, can sometimes be planted on the southern side of a wall or close-boarded fence, so that full advantage is taken of the wind shelter thus provided.

Fans (trained specimens) can be grown in the open, with suitable posts and wires for support, but this is the best type of tree to grow against walls. Espalier-training may also be used against walls and espalier pears may be planted as a decorative yet useful edging to vegetable plots. The latter idea used to be more popular than it is today; the drawback is that fruit planted on the edge of the vegetable plot is liable to receive too much nitrogen so that growth is encouraged rather than fruiting, and suitable spraying is sometimes difficult where the drift may be harmful to other crops.

Planting should be done between leaf-fall and March—the sooner the better, and provided the soil is friable, following normal lines of procedure. It is particularly important that the union between scion and rootstock should be well above soil level (10cm [4in]). If this point is not observed and roots are formed by the scion, the dwarfing effect of the rootstock will be obviated and the tree will not only grow too large but will be many years coming into bearing. It should be noted, too, that where trees have been double-worked (because of incompatibility between quince and the chosen variety), there will be two unions and it is the lower one which must be quite clear of the soil.

After planting, staking and making firm, it is advisable to put down a 5cm (2in) deep mulch of garden compost, well-rotted stable manure, peat or leafmould which will help to keep the soil moist in the event of a dry spring. Newly-planted pears should be inspected regularly in dry weather and watered liberally if there is any tendency to dry out.

For quality fruit the following planting distances should be regarded as the minimum: cordons (1 x 2m [3 x 6ft]), fan-trained and espalier on 'Quince C' (4m [12ft] apart) on 'Quince A' (5m [15ft] apart) dwarf pyramids (1.3 x 2.3m [4 x 7ft]) on 'Quince A' (5m [15ft] each way), standard and half-standard (11m [35ft] each way).

The subsequent manuring of pear trees should be adjusted according to performance.

In many cases pears will be maintained in good health by an annual (spring) application of rotted dung—a dressing on the surface about 5cm (2in) deep—this mulch then being gently pricked into the soil surface with the fork in autumn. As an alternative or where no dung is available, a mixture of chemical fertilizers should be given early in February; 56g (2oz) of superphosphate of lime, 28g (1oz) of sulphate of ammonia and 14g (½oz) of sulphate of potash per sq m (sq yd) sprinkled as far as the roots extend (approximately the same as the spread of the branches or the height of the tree, whichever is greater) and raked into the surface.

In general the pruning of pears follows similar lines to that of apples (see Fruit pruning), and so does the spraying to control pests and diseases.

In harvesting pears it is particularly important to pick at the right moment. With early varieties it is preferable to pick a little too soon than to wait too long, but with mid-season and late-keeping sorts the pears should be picked only when they separate easily from the spur on being lifted just above the horizontal in the palm of the hand and then given a very slight twist.

In choosing pear varieties to plant it is necessary to consider not only the purpose (dessert, cooking, bottling) and personal taste, but also the provision of

Flowering of pears		
Early	**Mid season**	**Late**
Beurré Anjou	Belle-Julie	Beurré
Beurré	Beurré	Bedford (MS)
Clairgeau	d'Amanlis	Beurré Bosc
Beurré Diel (T)	Beurré Six	Beurré Hardy
Comtesse de	Beurré Superfin	Bristol
Paris	Conference	Cross (MS)
Doyenné d'Eté	Dr Jules Guyot	Catillac (T)
Duchesse	Duchesse de	Clapp's
d'Angoulême	Bordeaux	Favourite
Easter Beurré	Durondeau	Doyenné du
Emile d'Heyst	Fertility	Comice
Louise Bonne	Fondante	Glou Morceau
of Jersey	d'Automne	Gorham
Marguerite	Jargonelle	Hessle
Marillat (MS)	Joséphine de	Laxton's Victor
Passe Crasanne	Malines	Marie Louise
Précoce de	Merton Pride	Nouveau Poiteau
Trévoux	Packham's	Pitmaston
Princess	Triumph	Duchess (T)
Seckle	Souvenir du	Santa Claus
Uvedale's St	Congrès	Winter Nelis
Germain (T)	Thompson's	
Vicar of	Triomphe de	
Winkfield	Vienne	
Winter Orange	Williams' Bon	
	Chrétien	

T = Triploid   MS = Male Sterile

suitable pollinators which must flower at the same time as the variety to be pollinated.

The varieties 'Jargonelle', 'Joséphine de Malines' and 'Packham's Triumph'

are tip-bearers and on that account should be avoided for pyramids, cordons, fans, or other forms of trained tree.

Plums

Plums are popular for cooking, jam-making and bottling or canning, but the sweeter varieties are among our most delicious dessert fruits. Damsons ripen a little later than most plums. The fruits are small, oval and richly flavoured, but not really sweet enough for the general taste for eating raw. They are, however, excellent for cooking, preserves and bottling. Bullaces are small round fruits which ripen even later and are useful on that account to lengthen the season. Bullaces can be eaten raw but are excellent for cooking. Gages are simply a class of plum with a characteristic, and particularly delicious, flavour. Gages, bullaces and damsons are all grown in the same way as plums.

Plums will grow in most parts of the country but as they flower early they are very vulnerable to spring frosts. The

1 The damson 'Merryweather' has purple skin and yellow flesh, and ripens in late September and October.
2 Plum 'Denniston's Superb' crops well in mid-August and has a golden skin and flesh, being one of the hardiest and most reliable of gages.

choicer kinds deserve the protection of a wall where protection from frost (and birds) can more easily be given. They do best in districts where the annual rainfall is between 50 and 90cm (20 and 35in). Damsons will succeed in areas having higher rainfall, and less sunshine, than plums will tolerate.

Plums need a well-drained soil and one containing plenty of humus to hold moisture during the growing season. A very acid soil should be limed, but an alkaline soil should not be planted with plums. Plums (and other stone fruits) do need calcium but they will not prosper in an alkaline soil. Plum trees planted in thin soils overlaying chalk often suffer

seriously from lime-induced iron deficiency.

No really satisfactory dwarfing rootstock has yet been found for plums. The two least vigorous are common plum and St Julien 'A'; the former, however, is only compatible with certain varieties. Trees grown on these rootstocks are sometimes described as 'semi-dwarf' but, even so, a standard or half-standard would be too large for the average garden, and even a bush-type tree requires a spacing of 4-5m (12-15ft) (on Brompton or Myrobalan 'B' rootstock, 6-7m [18-20ft]).

Because plums do not produce fruiting spurs as apples and pears do, they are not so amenable to training, and are seldom satisfactory as cordons or espaliers. They may, however, be grown as fans, for wall-training or with the support of posts and horizontal wires, but root-pruning will probably be necessary every five years or so to restrain growth and maintain fruiting. A fan tree on St Julien 'A' rootstock should be allotted at least 5m (15ft) of wall space.

Plums may also be grown as semi-dwarf pyramids on St Julien 'A' rootstock and this is a form which is best for the small garden. Such a tree requires a spacing of 3.3m (10ft) and, as it will never be allowed to grow much over 3m (9ft) in height, it is possible to arrange some kind of cage or netting over the top of the tree to keep off birds, which will otherwise damage the fruit. An additional advantage is that the branches of a pyramid seldom break and there is thus less likelihood of infection by disease.

For training as a pyramid a maiden should be planted in the usual way and the following March it should be headed back to 1.6m (5ft). Any laterals above 45cm (18in) from soil level should be shortened by half and any arising lower down the stem should be cut off entirely. Towards the end of July or early in August, when new growth has finished, cut back branch leaders to 20cm (8in), making the cut to a bud pointing downwards or outwards. Cut laterals back to 16cm (6in). Repeat this procedure annually. Leave the central leader untouched in summer but in April of the second year cut it back to one-third of its length. Repeat this annually, cutting the new growth back by two-thirds until a height of 3m (9ft) is attained. After that shorten the new growth on the central leader to 2.5cm (1in) or less each May.

Plant plums in the usual way between November and March, the sooner the better, always provided the soil is friable. Stake securely and put down a mulch to preserve soil moisture.

An established plum needs plenty of nitrogen but, until good crops are being carried, on most soils it will be sufficient to give a light mulch of rotted farmyard manure or garden compost in spring, and prick this lightly into the surface the subsequent autumn. When good crops are being borne, the yearly mulch may be supplemented with 28g (1oz) per dressing of Nitro-chalk and 14g ($\frac{1}{2}$oz) per sq m (sq yd) of sulphate of potash, given in February. Every third year, add 28g (1oz) per sq m (sq ft) of superphosphate. Where no manure or garden compost is available, peat may be used as a mulch and the dose of Nitro-chalk doubled.

The wood of plum trees naturally tends to be brittle and branches often break in late summer gales when the crop is heavy. Thinning of the fruit will help to prevent this form of breakage, and it is also advisable to arrange some kind of support for extra-heavily laden branches on bush-type trees. Wooden props may be fixed beneath branches (well padding the point of support) or a tall, strong central pole can be erected

Plums for the garden

Variety	Season	Fruit quality	Crop	Special remarks
Belle de Louvain, red to purple skin, yellow flesh	Late Aug	Fair flavour when cooked	Good	Cooker. Slow to start bearing
Black Prince, blue-black	Early Aug	Slight damson flavour	Heavy	Cooker. Very early flowering and therefore vulnerable to frost
Blaisdon Red, dark red skin, yellow green flesh	Late Aug	Acid. Good for jam	Reliable	Cooker. Picking may continue over three weeks
Bountiful, plum-purple skin, yellow flesh	Mid-Aug	Resembles 'Victoria' but lacks its quality	Heavy	Cooker. Resistant to silver leaf
Bryanston, greenish-yellow skin and flesh	Mid-Sept	Gage flavour but less pronounced than greengage	Good	Dessert. Large fruits
Cambridge Gage, green to yellow skin and flesh	Late Aug	True gage flavour	Fair but regular	Dessert, cooking or preserving. Fruits small
Coe's Golden Drop, yellow skin and flesh	Late Sept–Oct	Sweet, rich flavour	Moderate	Does best on a wall. Will cook well but generally held to be the finest dessert plum
Count Althann's Gage, dark crimson skin, yellow flesh	Mid-Sept	Excellent. Sweet and juicy	Good	Dessert. Good on walls
Czar, dull red skin, yellow flesh	Early Aug	Poor quality. Cooks with red juice	Heavy, regular	Cooker. Very hardy and reliable
Delicious (Laxton's Delicious) Bright red skin, golden yellow flesh	Mid-Aug	Sweet and very juicy. Good flavour	Good, regular	Dessert. Keeps well after picking
Denniston's Superb, greenish-yellow skin	Mid-Aug	Fair gage flavour	Good	Dessert. Hardiest and most reliable of gages
Diamond, blue-black skin, yellow flesh	Early–mid-Sept	Prune flavour	Irregular	Cooker. Very good for bottling
Early Laxton, yellow skin with red flesh	Late July	Sweet and juicy, first-class cooked	Moderate	Dual-purpose. Earliest of all for dessert
Early Orleans, reddish-blue skin, yellow flesh	Late July–August	Sweet. Cooks with deep red juice	Heavy	Cooker
Early Transparent, orange-yellow skin, yellow flesh	Mid-Aug	Very sweet, rich gage flavour	Heavy	Dessert. Repays thinning. Excellent on walls.
Farleigh Damson, purple skin, yellow flesh	Mid-Sept	Good flavour	Very heavy	Cooker
Giant Prune, deep red skin, golden flesh	Mid-Sept	Little flavour	Good, regular	Cooker
Golden Transparent, golden yellow flesh and skin	Early Oct	Very sweet, rich gage flavour	Prolific	Dessert. Best grown as fan on a wall
Goldfinch, golden flesh and skin	Late Aug	Sweet and juicy. Fair flavour	Good	Dessert
Jefferson, golden skin and flesh	Early Sept	Very good gage flavour	Good	Dessert
Kirke's Blue, dark reddish-purple, greenish and yellow skin	Mid-Sept	Choice flavour	Irregular	Dessert. Sometimes known simply as 'Kirke's'
Langley Bullace, black skin, greenish-yellow flesh	Early Nov	Really more a damson than a bullace	Prolific	Cooker. Self-compatible

Flowering of plums

Compatibility		
Group A	Group B	Group C
Early		
Black Prince	Utility	Golden Transparent*
Jefferson		
Early mid season		
Black Diamond	Farleigh	Denniston's Superb
Coe's Golden	Damson	Monarch*
Drop		Ontario*
Late Orleans		Warwickshire
President		Drooper*
Mid season		
Bryanston Gage	Early Laxton	Bountiful
Kirke's Late	River's	Brandy Gage
Orange	Early	Czar*
Washington	Prolific	Laxton's Cropper
	Goldfinch	Laxton's Gage
		Merryweather
		Damson*
		Pershore
		Purple Pershore
		Severn Cross
		Victoria*
Late mid season		
Count Althann's	Cambridge	Blaisdon Red*
Gage	Gage	Early Transparent
Delicious	Early	Giant Prune
Pond's Seedling	Orleans	Oullins' Golden
Wyedale		Gage
Late season		
Late Transparent		Belle de Louvain*
Old Greengage		Belle de Septembre
Red Magnum Bonum		Marjorie's Seedling*
		Shropshire Damson

and branches supported from this by ropes, maypole fashion.

Dessert plums should be left on the tree until quite ripe and then picked by taking hold of the stalk so that the 'bloom' is not spoiled. The season of the best dessert varieties can be extended slightly by storing a few fruits, wrapped individually in paper, in a cool, airy place. They will keep for a couple of weeks or so.

Raspberries

Most raspberries bear red fruit but a few have white or yellow berries. Most ripen in July, some in September or October, and some in either season according to when they are pruned. For varieties fruiting in summer, pruning is carried out immediately picking has finished, the old canes being cut out completely and replaced by the new canes from the perennial rootstock which will then fruit the next year. With autumn-fruiting varieties the fruited canes are cut back during the dormant season (usually in February) and the new canes which appear in spring will fruit in the autumn of the same year (for individual varieties see table: 'A selection of raspberries').

Raspberries are very subject to virus diseases but the health of commercial stocks has been greatly improved in recent years by the scheme of inspection and certification carried out by the Ministry of Agriculture, Fisheries and Food. For this reason it is particularly important to start by planting only canes obtained from a completely reliable source.

Raspberries do best in full sun but this condition is not always easily provided in a small surburban garden and, if necessary, the fruit will tolerate some slight shade. The most important requirements are that the soil should be free of lime and not subject to waterlogging. All fruits need slightly acid conditions but raspberries will stand a more acid soil than most. In an alkaline soil, raspberries are seriously affected by iron and manganese deficiency.

Preparing the bed Although a well-drained soil is essential for success, a sandy soil will need to have plenty of organic matter incorporated in preparation. Raspberries need a plentiful supply of moisture throughout the growing season.

It is sound practice to dig over the prospective raspberry bed during the summer prior to planting, taking particular care to pick out the roots of all perennial weeds which may be encountered. Bindweed and couch grass are often a cause of much trouble and, because raspberries are shallow rooters, deep cultivation after planting is inadvisable.

A generous amount of rotted garden compost or farmyard or stable manure should be worked in as digging proceeds —up to 5kg (10lb) per sq m (sq yd), more on sandy soils. Provided the soil is definitely acid, matured mushroom bed compost may be used with advantage but this material is slightly alkaline and should, therefore, be avoided if the soil is already neutral or nearly so. To insure against any possible shortage of phosphates, also dig in a dressing of 28g (1oz) per sq m (sq yd) of superphosphate.

Feeding the bed After planting the supply of organic matter and plant foods in the soil will be maintained by an

1

annual mulch of farmyard or stable manure at a rate of about 2.5kg (5lb) per sq m (sq yd). Where natural manure is unobtainable peat or straw may be used instead to supply organic matter plus a spring dressing of 28g (1oz) of sulphate of ammonia, 28g (1oz) of superphosphate and 14g (½oz) of sulphate of potash, per sq m (sq yd), to provide necessary nutriment. An excess of nitrogen will stimulate the growth of the canes but without any corresponding increase in the crop. A deficiency of potash, on the other hand, will soon show itself in reduced yield. Incidentally, the site, soil and manurial requirements of the raspberry apply equally to all other cane fruits.

Planting Raspberries may be planted either in the open or against a fence or wall. In the latter case, the canes can be secured simply by lengths of strong string tied to staples at the ends of the row and at intervals of 46cm (18in) or so. A free-standing row, however, will require substantial posts at each end of the row and these should be put in before planting. Concrete or angle-iron posts make a good permanent job and should be embedded in concrete. Struts should be arranged on the inner sides of the posts to take the strain. Two lengths of gauge 12 or 14 galvanized wire will be required at 0.6m (2ft) and at 1.3m (4ft) from the ground (or 1.6m [5ft] where very vigorous varieties are planted). The canes should be planted 06.m (2ft) apart in the row and, if more than one row is wanted, rows should be 2m (6ft) apart.

Early autumn is the best time to plant but planting is permissible at any time between autumn and spring, always provided the soil is dry enough to be friable and is not frozen. Should the soil be too wet when the canes arrive from the nursery, heel them in temporarily, in as dry a spare spot as may be available.

If they arrive when frost prohibits planting, keep them wrapped up, and store in a cool shed where the roots will not dry out. Plant them or heel them in out of doors as soon as conditions permit. If the roots appear at all dry when planting, soak them in a bucket of water for an hour or so.

Too deep planting is a common error with raspberries: the roots should be covered by no more than 8cm (3in) of soil. If the canes have just arrived from the nursery, it is usually possible to see the old soil mark on the stem, indicating the correct depth.

1 Raspberry 'Malling Exploit' has fairly large fruits and crops heavily.
2 The method most commonly adopted in gardens for tying raspberry canes to support wires is to fasten each cane individually with raffia or twine.
3 An alternative method is to let them grow to their full height, tie them in to the wires, and loop back the extremities forming an arch.
4 Raspberry 'Malling Landmark'.

A selection of raspberries

Variety	Season	Colour of berry	Description
Malling Exploit	Summer Early to mid-season	Red	Fair flavour. Larger fruits, heavier cropper than Malling Promise, to which otherwise very similar
Malling Jewel	Summer Early to mid-season	Red	Vigorous. Heavy cropper. Good flavour
Malling Promise	Summer Early to mid-season	Red	Very vigorous. Large fruits of good flavour
Lloyd George	Summer Mid-season, or autumn if cut down in spring	Red	Outstanding flavour. Specify 'New Zealand' strain
Yellow Antwerp	Summer Mid-season	Yellow	Moderately vigorous. Fairly large berries of good flavour
Malling Enterprise	Summer Mid-season to late	Red	Vigorous. Large fruit, good flavour
Newburgh	Summer Mid-season to late	Red	Fairly vigorous. Very fair flavour. Some berries large. Good variety for heavy land
Norfolk Giant	Summer Late	Red	Very vigorous. Heavy cropper. Fruit firm with acid flavour. Good for preserving
Hailsham	Autumn	Red	Vigorous. Large berries
September	Autumn	Red	Vigorous. Good cropper. Pleasant flavour. Bright red berries of medium size

2

3

4

The quickest way to plant a row of raspberries is to take out a shallow trench the width of your spade. As you set the canes in position, spread out the roots evenly and trim off any damaged parts. Replace the soil in the trench, holding each cane erect in turn as the soil is placed over its roots and made firm. When planting as shallowly as this, however, it is unsafe to use one's heel as a rammer—gentle pressure with the sole of the boot will be sufficient. Immediately after planting cut back the canes to a height of 0.6m (2ft) and finally lightly rake the soil to break up the surface.

In February, mulch the bed with a good layer of rotted garden compost, rotted dung or mature mushroom bed compost (again, provided the soil is already definitely acid).

Subsequent pruning In spring, as soon as the growth buds on the raspberry canes may be seen to be swelling, cut back the canes still further—to a visibly live bud about 25cm (10in) above soil level. The idea of this is to leave just sufficient top growth to keep the roots active. No cropping must be permitted the first season and, after this cutting back, new suckers will spring up from the roots and these shoots are the ones which will fruit in the second season. Once these new shoots are growing well, the old 25cm (10in) high pieces should be cut down to soil level.

In the second summer, when the fruit has been picked, cut down all the fruited canes right to soil level. These should be replaced by new canes now springing up. If there are more than five or six, select the best of even size, removing any odd extra-vigorous canes and any growing up between the rows at a distance from the main rootstocks. All prunings should at once be burned to prevent the spread of disease or pests.

The new canes should be tied in to the horizontal wires individually as they grow.

In the following February the canes should be tipped, making the cuts to growth buds some 16cm (6in) above the upper wire. This will stimulate better growth lower down where the berries are less liable to suffer wind damage.

Autumn-fruiting varieties should have fruited canes cut out in February and the new growths will then fruit the same year.

Strawberries

Stocks Strawberries are subject to several serious virus diseases, and at one time these threatened to make commercial cultivation quite uneconomic and garden culture most disappointing. However, there has been considerable improvement in the general health of strawberry stocks since the introduction of a government scheme of inspection.

It is of the utmost importance to start with disease-free stock and one should purchase from a grower with a good reputation to maintain. Where possible one should buy from a grower who has been given a Ministry of Agriculture 'A' Certificate for his stock and will quote the number. Unfortunately not all varieties are eligible for the ministry scheme and in such instances one can only patronize growers who have gained 'A' Certificates for their eligible varieties in the hope that they may be equally careful with their non-eligible stocks.

Site Although the strawberry is of woodland origin, the modern fruit requires all the sun it can get. On the other hand, the site for the strawberry bed needs to be sheltered, for cold spring winds can very seriously check growth. The garden sloping gently towards the south, unshaded but sheltered, will yield the earliest crops.

Although strawberries may be grown in most parts of Britain, late spring frosts may be a limiting factor. This can be quite a local problem and if your garden lies in a frost-pocket there is not much you can do about it except to be ready to give some kind of protection with cloches or plastic to plants in flower or to sidestep the difficulty by growing only the so-called perpetual-fruiting types, removing the first trusses of blossom and concentrating on late summer or autumn fruits.

Soil Strawberries do best in a rich medium loam with a high humus content. Well-rotted leafmould is an excellent material to incorporate in soils deficient in organic matter, but any other decayed vegetable matter can be used. The site needs to be well drained.

Heavy clay, peaty and very light, sandy soils should be prepared well in advance of planting time.

Soils with a very high lime content are unsuitable for strawberries.

Preparation Early preparation will not only assist soil improvement but will also ensure freedom from perennial weeds, which can be a considerable nuisance. When digging, rotted farmyard or stable manure should be worked in, 5kg (10lb) per sq m (sq yd) being regarded as a normal 'dose' and twice this rate is recommended for poor, sandy soil. Follow with a surface dressing of 28g (1oz) per sq m (sq yd) of sulphate of potash.

Where no natural manure or garden compost is available 28g (1oz) per sq m (sq yd) each of superphosphate, sulphate of ammonia and sulphate of potash should be sprinkled over the bed after digging and lightly raked in. If the soil is not already rich in humus, add up to half a bushel of peat per sq m (sq yd).

Planting Strawberries are usually planted in beds, the rows being 0.7 to 1m (2½ to 3ft) apart, the plants 38 to 46cm (15 to 18in) apart in the rows, according to the richness of soil. One reason for early soil preparation is that the soil should be firm.

Summer-fruiting strawberries may be planted either in the late summer to early autumn or even in the spring, provided that in the latter instance all blossom is removed the first summer. The earlier plants can go out, the bigger and stronger plants they will make their first year—so, if you can obtain plants so early, plant in July, August, or even September, but October is late.

The perpetual-fruiting varieties can also be planted in autumn but rooted runners are not available so early. However, as they have time to catch up in spring, October planting is quite satisfactory, provided the soil is properly workable and will break down to a friable tilth. On cold, heavy soils the planting of perpetual strawberries is probably better deferred until spring.

When ordering, for preference stipulate plants which have been rooted in pots. These will be slightly more expensive but they will transplant more readily, with less root damage, and they will have better root development.

Use a trowel for planting and take a hole out for each plant deep enough to accommodate the roots without bending them. Then return a little soil at the centre of the hole to make a mound on which the strawberry plant can 'sit' with its roots spread evenly around it.

The base of the crown should be just at soil level: if it is too high, roots are exposed and dry out, resulting in eventual death of the plant; while if the crown is half buried, it will either produce unwanted weak secondary growths or rot away entirely.

Plant firmly, using the handle of the trowel as a rammer. As you proceed, see that the roots of plants awaiting their turn are not exposed to the wind. Finally, rake the bed smooth and give a good watering to settle the soil.

Follow up Keep an eye on the weather and the state of the soil because many strawberry plants are lost or seriously retarded by the effect of drought during the weeks immediately after planting. Also inspect the bed after hard weather, and refirm with your boot any plants which have been lifted by frost action.

In the early spring scatter fertilizer dressing down the rows at the rate of 56g (2oz) per sq m (sq yd). This is made up of 1 part of sulphate of potash, 1 part

1 The blossom is removed from a strawberry runner to encourage it to make a
better root system.
2 When the berries have formed it is
necessary to put some protective material
beneath them.
3 Clean dry straw can be spread around
the plants, and the fruit lifted above it,
to ripen.
4 'Cambridge Vigour' grown on straw.

of sulphate of ammonia and 2 parts of
superphosphate (all parts by weight). Be
careful that these fertilizers do not go
on the leaves, and gently rake them into
the surface soil. Then apply a light
mulch of well-rotted farmyard manure,
garden compost or peat to help to preserve soil moisture in the event of a
spring drought but be prepared to water
as well when necessary.

Timing the fruit When, in the spring
following planting, the first blossom
buds appear, you have to make a major
policy decision. First-year flowers on
maiden plants will give the earliest
crop and the largest individual berries,
but if you remove this first year's
blossom and wait until the second crop,
the yield will then probably be greater
than the total of two years' crops on
plants fruiting in their first season.

If you are very anxious to secure early
fruit and if you are going to protect
them with cloches or polythene tunnels,
then first-year blossom should be left on.
Indeed, where earliness is considered
all-important, the strawberries may be
treated as an annual crop and a fresh
batch of earlies planted every year, to
be dug up and burned immediately after
harvesting. In such instances, strawberries may take their place in the
regular annual rotation of the vegetable
garden.

Where size of crop is considered more
important than earliness, and the plants
are deblossomed in their first year, there
is every prospect of the strawberries
continuing to yield well for three years,
possibly for four.

The perpetual-fruiting varieties, in
fact, bear at least two distinct crops. In
the first year after planting, the first
batch of blossom should be removed to
give the plants a chance to gain size and
strength. Blossom appearing after the
end of June is allowed to develop and
the fruit will be ripe from late summer
onwards. In subsequent years, you have
the choice between two crops, one in
June and one in autumn, and one,
larger crop, earlier in autumn or in late
summer.

Not long after the berries begin to
develop, runners will appear. Unless
these are required for propagation
they should be cut off at once with
scissors so as not to waste the plant's
energies. With early-rooted plants set
out early, runners may even be produced in the first autumn and these
should certainly be removed. Perpetual-
fruiting varieties tend not to produce
runners so freely as the summer-fruiting
kinds, but nevertheless these, too,
should usually be removed unless required for increase.

Protection Before the first ripening
strawberries are heavy enough to weigh
the trusses down to the soil, some kind
of protection is necessary to prevent the
berries being splashed by mud. The
traditional method is to lay straw on
the soil, barley straw being more easily
tucked close to the plants than the
stiffer wheat straw and less liable to be
a carrier of pests than oat straw. Before
putting down the straw, weed by gentle
hoeing, handweeding, or spot application of weedkiller.

You should not be in too much of a
hurry to put down the straw because,
as it is light in colour, it loses heat
rapidly and increases the risk of
radiation frost damage to open blossom
or tiny fruitlets.

Straw, however, is not always easy to
obtain, and you can buy patented strawberry mats or specially made wire
supports which hold the berries clear of
the soil. Even a scattering of peat is
better than nothing.

Slugs can do much damage in a strawberry bed and slug bait pellets should be
scattered freely among the plants and
kept renewed as necessary during the
fruiting season.

Picking Out of doors the first berries are
likely to ripen between four and six
weeks from when the blossom opened.
The fruit should be picked by taking the
stem about 1cm (½in.) behind the berry
between finger and thumb. In this way
the berry can be broken off without
being touched.

Fruit pruning

The purpose of pruning is to encourage cropping in an orderly fashion on fruit plants. Some fruit trees or bushes may require no pruning while others respond to some degree of control.

The branches of most fruit plants can, if they are left unpruned, become so tangled that there is utter chaos. The fruits become small, cropping is irregular and pest and disease control becomes increasingly difficult. Drastic measures will have to be taken to put matters right while yields are lost for some years until order is restored.

Pruning is not a magic art, understood and practised by a few green-fingered experts. The principles are simple and, when considered sensibly, amount very much to commonsense. Pruning is the technique of dealing with the way the branches of a fruit plant can be arranged round the main stem or trunk so that each has a fair share of space.

In an unpruned tree only those shoots on the outside get enough light for the leaves which, with the roots, feed the whole tree. If the leaves are poor in size and colour, the buds and fruits which they feed will also be poor. Extra soil feeding will simply make matters worse.

Pruning varies according to the plant.
1 Remove the two-year-old wood after black currants have fruited.
2 Dead, broken or crossing branches are taken from a plum tree in summer, to admit more light and air.

The solution is at least some pruning to let in light. Many gardeners get the impression that pruning is essential for good fruiting. This is not so. The less a tree or plant is cut about, the more fruitful it will be. To some extent nature itself may take a hand as winds and storms may remove a number of branches. However, this unselected removal of shoots may not be completely beneficial, particularly since the main branches may be broken at the crotch where they meet the main stem. Sometimes, too, a temporary attack by a pest or disease reduces growth, but this also may be of uncertain value. Pruning is man's way of improving on nature to get earlier and more regular yields.

All fruit plants are perennial and if kept healthy will crop for many years. Even strawberries will grow and crop longer than their normal garden span of 3–4 years. Soft fruits will come into good cropping a year or two after planting but tree fruits take longer. By using dwarfing rootstocks this interval can be shortened, while vigorous rootstocks delay cropping though yields per tree are greater. Some tree fruits, eg sweet cherries may not give worthwhile crops until ten years after planting.

In the garden, fruit plants are valuable assets and we should look after them to avoid disappointment and even despair. If the simple elements of pruning are understood and applied the results are worthwhile.

One of the biggest snags in growing fruit is that the bushes are often planted too close together and suffer from competition. Drastic pruning would in many instances be wrong. Complete removal of some of the plants, and the containment by pruning of those that remain, would be the best proposition. Again, choice of rootstock can play an important part. Pruning aims to use the characteristics of the varieties and the rootstock, together with soil management, to produce a fruiting plant with adequately spaced branches and shoots, to achieve a sensible balance between growth and cropping and to remove old and sometimes diseased shoots and replace them with new growth.

While the basic principles of pruning are the same for all fruits, their interpretation and application may vary, depending on a number of factors. The effects of soil and situation on the plants must be taken into account and in one garden or orchard there are differences between varieties of one kind of fruit as well as between each kind. We do not prune a black currant bush as we would a sweet cherry or a bush apple as we would a cordon. Each type and variety needs a slightly different approach to achieve good results.

To understand what happens when a fruit plant is pruned, it is worth understanding a little about how it grows.

Plants are made up of a collection of cells. Some of these cells do special things. The tough outer skin or bark is for protection. Underneath are the bast cells to transfer food to all parts, the active living or cambium cells, and the wood cells to transport water, and the inner scaffolding cells for support. All these work together and are interconnected so that the plants develop properly.

Raw food materials including water are taken up from the soil by the roots and root hairs into the branches where the leaves, with the help of light and air, transform them into sugar, starches, proteins and oils needed by the plant for sturdy growth. This emphasizes the importance of good leaves and, within reason, the more there are the better for fruiting.

In many gardens and orchards one of the first acts of pruning may be to let in light and air by removing some unwanted branches eg those that are dead or badly diseased, crossing the centre of the tree, or even too near the ground. This action may seem to be obvious and if not overdone in one season can work wonders.

The majority of the best fruits are to be found on the younger branches, with most of the smaller and low quality fruits on older wood. This younger wood is generally to be found towards the outside of the plant and will have larger and better green leaves, which will feed the fruit buds. These in turn give better flowers and more certain crops or larger fruits. On older branches the leaves tend to be small and of poorer colour, also fewer in number. Thus the renewal or replacement of old or ageing branches tend to keep up the production of high-quality fruit.

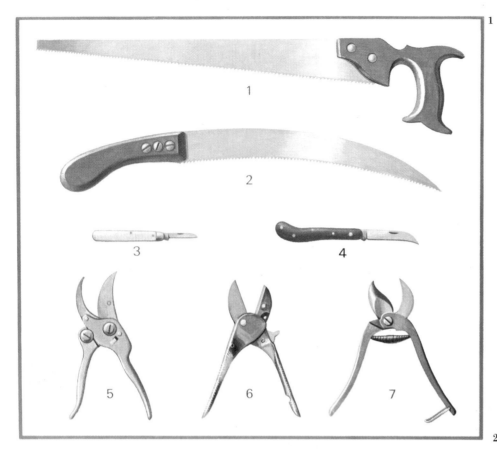

1 Pruning tools: 1 saw, 2 parrot-nosed saw, 3 budding knife, 4 pruning knife, 5 6 and 7 types of secateur.
2 A maiden apple tree, staked to prevent rocking in the wind.

When considering the pruning of any fruit tree the following points are worth noting:

(a) Cut out dead or diseased wood, also broken and overcrowding branches.

(b) Encourage a moderate amount of young growth and stimulate this in stunted and backward plants.

(c) Where the number of fruit buds is excessive reduce them.

Pruning of apples Most apple trees are purchased when they are 1–4 years old. Trees older than this will need special care to help them over the shock of transplanting. A good nurseryman ensures that the trees he sends out have healthy strong shoots, properly spaced for the type of tree which is to be grown —bush, cordon, pyramid or any other shape.

The gardener who wishes to train his own trees will plant maidens. These are one-year-old trees with a single stem, possibly with a few sideshoots, called feathers. This is the cheapest way of buying a tree. There is no reason why the first pruning should not be done in the winter of planting and this is a time to decide what type of tree should be grown. A selection can be made from the following.

A standard tree is one with a 2m (6ft) long stem. These are not suitable for gardens as they make large trees which

are difficult to manage. They can, however, make pleasant shade trees. The early treatment of the standard tree consists in pruning the maiden after planting, removing half to one third of its length to encourage a further upright shoot to form a main stem at 2m (6ft).

The tree should, at one year after planting, be tall enough to prune this main stem so that the lowest branch is at the right height from ground level.

Pruning thereafter may consist simply of the removal of overcrowding branches with the occasional pruning of the ends of the leading shoots to help to form new growth.

Spurs, which are shoots with a number of fruit buds, can be reduced in size, since too many fruit buds can be as embarrassing as too few. In spite of very light pruning some varieties on vigorous rootstocks may take 10–12 years before giving a decent crop. Suitable rootstocks for standard trees are M.XVI and M.XXV.

The half-standard tree has a main stem of 1.5-1.8m (4½-5ft). It is more manageable than a standard tree in the early years, but varieties on a vigorous stock still make big heads with delayed cropping. Half standard trees on medium vigorous stocks eg M.II or MM.111 could be very useful in gardens where other plants are grown underneath and not too big a tree is useful. Pruning is similar to that for a standard tree. The maiden can be pruned at 1.8-1.9m (5-5½ft) from ground level in the year of planting and the shoots which grow the following summer form the basis of the branch

system. Most varieties will grow and crop happily with the minimum of pruning even on medium vigorous rootstocks which usually encourage earlier cropping—6-8 years from planting.

Large bush trees growing about 5-6m (15-18ft) high, are popular in large gardens. The main stem is 0.8-1m (2½-3ft) long. The lowest branches make cropping underneath difficult except for grass. Varieties growing on medium vigorous rootstocks M.II, M.VII, M.IV, MM.104, MM.106 and MM.101 do very well. The trees can be managed fairly easily from ground level. Pruning starts with the maiden which is pruned at a point 1-1.2m (3-3½ft) from ground level. As a result of this pruning a number of shoots, possibly three to five, will grow from the buds below the pruning cut in the following summer. The shoot from the topmost bud (the leader) should be fairly upright, while the remainder become less upright the lower down the stem they are.

If a feathered maiden is planted (and these may be a little dearer than a plain maiden), many of the shoots that will form from the first branches are already there.

Pruning of the main stem in this instance is simply to add a few more shoots as spares and possibly to balance the tree, so that there is even distribution of branches. It is possible at this stage to distribute the main branches over 0.6-1m (2-3ft) of stem above the lowest branch by continuing to prune the central lead for two years after planting.

This will form a delayed open centre

tree which is less subject to loss of main branches than the open centre tree where all branches come off at one level. During this period the side branches (laterals) may receive some treatment. If growth is vigorous it would be wise not to prune those that are well positioned round the main stem. If there are too many, and five to seven should be ample, cut out the remainder close to the main stem. The unpruned shoots will make further extension growth and possibly, depending on variety and continued vigour, a number of useful sideshoots. These unpruned shoots should flower and fruit well three to five years after planting and, other factors being favourable, the tree should be cropping fully four to five years later. This is termed the regulated system of pruning and can be applied to many varieties.

Where the amount of new extension growth falls below 30-40cm (12-15in), pruning and possibly soil feeding will be needed to encourage growth. On any branch or tree which is not making the necessary amount of growth, prune the leaders, removing a half to one third of their length. The same treatment is advised for varieties which tend to form fruit buds on the ends of the young shoots (tip bearers). There will come a time, even with the regulated tree, when one or two branches may have to be cut out and some provision can be made to renew older branches, possibly from nearer the middle of the tree.

Another system is to provide for the replacement of older branches by building up a system of renewal shoots, which can take over cropping when needed. In this way there can always be a supply of young growth in the tree for maximum quality cropping.

Over a period of twenty years much of the tree may have been renewed two to three times. A renewal branch should be carefully selected from shoots growing directly from an existing branch, and should be some five to six years younger than the branch it will replace. There will be occasions when it is necessary to replace an oldish branch by a renewal shoot from a neighbouring branch.

A notable characteristic of unpruned or lightly pruned apple trees is that the branches tend to grow outwards instead of upwards. Where the trees are pruned hard the branches tend to be very upright and difficult to control.

This is important, since near-horizontal branches are more fruitful than upright growing shoots. The weight of crop and leaves will also bring branches down and it is not unusual to find branches of trees weighted or tied down.

Within the tree itself, any unwanted branches or shoots are best cut out completely. Strong growths, known as

A clean cut cannot be achieved unless the branch is cut from underneath. A tear admits fungus diseases.

water shoots, appearing mainly on the crotch area, should be taken out at any time of the year. Similarly, branches that are growing too upright can be cut down to lower and more horizontal branches. If too many young shoots form on fruiting branches a number, eg one third, can be removed completely, a further third left full length, and the remainder shortened to 16-23cm (6-9in). These last will help to form spurs with fruit buds or a further supply of new shoots. While these proportions will vary from tree to tree the method is a means of keeping up a succession of young fruiting wood. The formation of fruit buds on spurs—natural from existing fruit buds or artificial by pruning—can

account for 70% of the fruiting area on an apple tree. Good quality varieties which spur naturally have an advantage over those which need encouragement by pruning. This quality of free spurring can, if carried too far, as in a neglected tree, bring trouble — not enough new growth, too many small fruits.

Unless a large bush tree has been sadly neglected or is suffering from lack of feeding it should manage very well with a moderate amount of winter pruning. If for some reason too much growth is being made, summer pruning in July or tying down of upright branches should help.

Dwarfing bushes are very popular in the

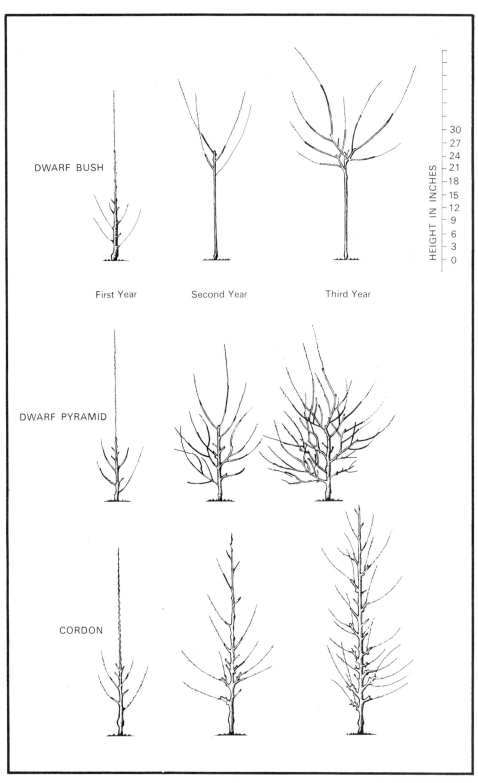

			HEIGHT IN INCHES
DWARF BUSH			— 30
			— 27
			— 24
			— 21
			— 18
			— 15
			— 12
			— 9
			— 6
			— 3
			— 0

First Year   Second Year   Third Year

DWARF PYRAMID

CORDON

Patterns of pruning to build a dwarf bush tree, dwarf pyramid and cordon from a one-year old tree, or maiden.

garden. Varieties grafted or budded on semi-dwarfing rootstocks need not exceed 2.3m (7ft) in height. A number of varieties on these stocks can be even smaller. At their heights the trees are easy to manage and can be planted fairly close together. Suitable rootstocks are dwarfing M.IX and M.IXA, semi-dwarfing M.26.

One feature of rootstock influence on such bushes is the encouragement to produce early fruit bud formation. Pruning is not necessary to bring this about. It often happens that because there are too many fruit buds, hard pruning is necessary to keep the plants growing and a number of the buds may have to be taken off. Unless this is done, too many fruits are formed.

The maiden tree is pruned at 0.6-0.8m (2-2½ft) from ground level after planting. The three to five branches which grow during the following summer are pruned again in the following winter removing about one half to one third of the length, depending on vigour, but in such a way

that there is an even spread of vigour and branches round each plant. At this stage there are probably enough branches to see the tree through its whole life. In the following years more and more fruit buds and spurs appear and good cropping takes place 4-5 years after planting. Not many surplus shoots will appear on the branches and those can be shortened to 2-3 buds from the branches.

When cropping really starts some fruit bud reduction can be made. It is worth noting that each fruit bud can produce 4–5 fruitlets and gross over-crowding can result. This happens especially with free spurring varieties. It is a simple matter to remove surplus buds in winter by hand. With finger and thumb pinch out the upper leaf of some buds and push others out completely.

Allow 10-16cm (4-6in) between fruit buds or spurs. If there are a number of fruit buds together or on spurs leave one untouched, pinch out two and rub out the remainder. Pinching will remove the flower but still allow leaves to form and probably one or two young shoots. Leaf numbers and quality are important if good sized fruits are to form on the buds that remain untouched. The proportion should be about one fruit to thirty leaves.

It will be necessary during the cropping life of these small bushes to prune the ends of the leaders to encourage a little new extension growth each year. If new growth is less than 16cm (6in), cut half the length of the shoot. Tip-bearing varieties eg 'Worcester Pearmain' and free budding varieties eg 'Lane's Prince Albert' will need pruning, in the one instance to form a yearly supply of new shoots and to avoid bare stems, and in the other to reduce the number of buds and encourage some growth. These treatments may seem drastic but it is known that only about 5% of all the flowers on a tree need be pollinated to set a full crop.

When the spurs become rather large they can be reduced in size to a few buds only or if there is overcrowding a few can be removed completely.

Pyramid shaped trees are also small bushes on dwarfing or semi-dwarfing stocks. They are very useful in small gardens as they can be kept compact. The maiden tree is pruned to within 46cm (18in) from ground level after planting.

In the following winter each new leader is pruned to 25cm (10in), depending on vigour, above the cut made in the previous winter.

The direction of the top bud at each cut should be varied so that an upright main stem is made. When this reaches about 2.3m (7ft) high—and this may take many years, if ever—the top can be removed in mid summer to restrict new growth.

While the main stem is growing, sideshoots have grown round it. Space these branches about 16-20cm (6-8in) apart round the stem and cut out the remainder. Those left should not, if possible, overlap each other. They are encouraged to form a few more branches by pruning, removing a third to one half of the length in the first winter after planting. Any branch which is rather upright should be tied to a near horizontal position. This should have the effect of restricting growth and encouraging fruit buds to form. Pruning of shoots (laterals) in the following years should be as light as possible, the aim being to restrict the spread of branches to about 46-60cm (18-24in) from the main stem. If too much extension growth is made, carry out summer pruning of offending shoots in June or July, when they are about 16-23cm (6-9in) long—simply pinch out the end of each shoot. Again, if there are too many branch laterals in any year these should also be rubbed out in summer, allowing 23-30cm (9-12in) between those that remain. With little or no winter pruning for growth and summer pruning to restrict growth, fruit buds and spurs should form freely on most varieties. It will be necessary to remove a number of these in a similar fashion as for bush trees to avoid overcropping and crowding of branches.

The pillar shape of small tree is in some respects similar to the pyramid. The central stem is formed in the same way and the height restricted to 2.1-2.3cm (6½-7ft). The main difference is in the treatment of the side branches, none of which last more than three seasons. The pruning of these is based on the way the fruit buds usually form. A young shoot grows one summer and forms pointed wood or growth buds. The second summer the shoots form plump fruit buds,

which in the following, or third, summer flower and bear fruits. If the shoot is not pruned, some buds will form in the first summer to flower and fruit the next year. If a shoot is not pruned during this three-year period it should carry most of its best fruits in the third summer. The system works as follows: all the three to four sideshoots formed round the main stem when the maiden is pruned 46cm (18in) from ground level after planting are allowed to grow unpruned for three years. These shoots bear fruits in the third summer, and in the winter following are cut back to about 2.5cm (1in) from the main stem. On this stump there are a number of dormant wood buds which in the following summer grow to form new shoots. The number arising from each stump should be restricted to two and the remainder rubbed out in summer.

The two shoots left in are allowed to grow for three seasons and then pruned back to 2.5cm (1in) as before. This sequence of pruning is carried out farther up the tree as new branches develop, until all the branches are being replaced on a three-year basis, resulting in young wood and good crops. As the trees are planted close in the rows, it pays to prune each fruit bud bearing shoot in the second winter at the last fruit bud. This reduces overcrowding, thus letting light and air into the young shoots. It may even be necessary to cut out completely any surplus two-year shoots. In time the 2.5cm (1in) stumps to which the fruit branches are cut back, become rather large and are cut back after 3–4

1 A fine crop of red currants grown on the double cordon system.
2 The cordon system provides an intensive, yet decorative way of growing fruit.

years to 2.5cm (1in) from the main stem to form a fresh supply of new shoots.

Pillar trees in full growth and cropping may look rather untidy but they crop well. Use a dwarfing or semi-dwarfing rootstock to help control the vigorous growth resulting from rather hard pruning.

The spindle bush is another type of tree with a central leader and controlled to about 2.3m (7ft) in height. The main stem is formed in the same way as for pyramid and pillar.

The side branches are left unpruned. To encourage early cropping, these shoots are looped round and tied to the main stem or even suitable neighbouring branches. These branches can be left unpruned for 3–4 years and be replaced completely, as in the pillar tree, or reduced in length to be replaced by young shoots over a period of two years. The basis of this tree form is the continuing replacement of wood which has cropped well for at least one year—but possibly three—by younger potential wood and the bending of these shoots from the first year to bear early heavy crops. The loops should not be too tight and the trees may have to be reviewed each year. It is an untidy but profitable tree shape. Dwarfing and semi-dwarfing rootstocks are used.

Cordon forms of tree have been tried very successfully for many years and each takes up very little space. They can be grown against a wall or wire framework in the open. Using this method a fair number of varieties can be grown in a small area and the trees are easily managed. Single cordons, consisting of one main stem are the most common form. The cordons can either be upright or at an angle, when they are known as oblique cordons. The latter is preferred.

The maiden is planted against its support at an angle of 45°. Pruning of the leading shoot may or may not be necessary and depends on variety, rootstock and soil.

With a semi-vigorous rootstock on good soil the main stem will grow happily without pruning and form enough sideshoots. With a dwarfing or semi-dwarfing root-stock, even on a good soil, very light leader pruning is advised to encourage new extension growth and enough sideshoots. At the most, cut off the top 8cm (3in) of the leader, or none at all if growth is good. In the course of a few years the main stem will reach the top of the support, some 2.1-2.3m (6½-7ft). At this stage it can be cut away from the support and lowered to 30° so that further extension growth is possible. During this time sideshoots have grown and their growth should be controlled quite strictly, as each cordon is only 0.6-1m (2-3ft) from its neighbour. It is possible to contain the growth by summer pruning in June or July, when the shoots are pencil thickness, and about 30cm (12in) long. On plants growing in the open these shoots, about twelve for each year of growth are distributed round the stem. With trees trained against a wall, shoots growing towards the wall are removed. Each shoot left on the tree is summer pruned to 15cm (6in). A number of buds below the cut should form fruit buds, but some will grow in late summer; this is known as secondary growth. In the following winter the spurs so made can be shortened to three or four fruit buds from the base, or left alone if space allows. At the same time any other shoots can be left full length or cut back if more than 30cm (12in) long.

Each year during the life of the tree this system of summer and winter pruning is used. If natural or artificial spurs become too big they can be reduced in size and number of fruit buds to avoid overcropping and shading of younger buds. Two good fruit buds to each spur will give ample flowers.

A modification of the cordon is to encourage young shoots, not spurs, to develop, and to loop these to encourage fruit buds to form, and when these are cropped to replace them with a fresh set. *The espalier shape* of tree is one with a central stem 2.1-2.3m (6½-7ft) high and with a number of equally spread branches coming away from it in pairs. The maiden tree is pruned to within 46cm (18in) of ground level after planting. The following year a pair of opposite branches is selected and tied horizontally.

The upright leader is pruned again at 46cm (18in) and a further pair of side

1 When cordons are summer pruned the leader is not removed. The young laterals (left) are cut back to leave a clear outline (right).
2 A triple cordon apple grown against a wall to utilize a small space.

branches selected the following winter, approximately 40cm (15in) above the first pair and in the same plane. In the following two winters the treatment is repeated so that there are four pairs of horizontal branches five years after planting. The leader on the main stem is suppressed in the sixth summer by summer pruning. During this shaping period the older side branches have been growing horizontally.

Leader growth will be moderate only and leader pruning not necessary unless extension and lateral growth is backward.

Fruit bud formation should take place easily and the general scheme of pruning on each side branch will follow the same pattern as for cordons. Spur pruning and removal of surplus fruit buds will be routine.

In a modification of this shape, the centre leader is stopped at 40cm (15in) from ground level and the branches trained in an upright position to form 'U' and double 'U' espaliers. This type of tree shape is very compact and fruitful. Semi-dwarfing or semi-vigorous rootstocks should be used.

The palmette tree shape is a modified espalier. The basis of this system is still a central leader trained against a support. From this main stem there are numbers of branches in the same plane. These branches, which need not be in pairs, are spaced about 30cm (12in) apart and looped on to the supports. Any of the branches can be replaced partly or wholly and retrained on to the supports. In this way a succession of young fruiting wood is maintained in the tree.

Crop yields can be very good from this system. Use semi-dwarfing or semi-vigorous rootstocks.

Arcure is a system in which the tree is trained on a trellis in a succession of arcs. The maiden tree is bent over and one strong shoot from it is allowed to grow from the centre of the arc and is in turn bent over in the opposite direction. The process is repeated each year until the top of the support is reached and further upward growth is suppressed by summer pruning. As the branches age they can be replaced or retained and a system of spurs developed and treated as any other spurs.

Choose dwarfing or semi-dwarfing rootstocks.

Pruning of pears Pears are pruned in very much the same fashion as apples but most varieties grow rather vigorously as young plants. Quince A or B rootstocks, on which most trees are grafted, have only limited control over growth. It is usually difficult to control the strong upright growth of the trees and weighting or tying is used to bring the branches down to a horizontal position. When cropping does begin, however,

The arcure system of training apple trees is a series of arches. One strong shoot is left to develop at the apex of each arch, to form the arch above. The new growth is arched over in July.

growth slows down and fruit buds and spurs appear in abundance. At this stage the problem is often to encourage young growth in the tree.

During the first two winters after planting a maiden tree, the leaders, the main extension shoots, are pruned, removing a half to two thirds of their length each winter. This will encourage sideshoots to develop as well as form the main branches. After the second winter enough branches should have formed these should be weighted or tied towards the horizontal. With certain trained types of shapes—cordons, espaliers and palmettes this is straightforward.

As pear varieties tend to develop buds which either remain small, dormant or undeveloped blind buds, some pruning of laterals should be carried out. It may be sufficient to remove only the end third of a lateral growth. Unpruned shoots in a tree seldom remain productive for long.

The great majority of pear varieties respond to spur pruning as for apples. Sideshoots are cut back to three to four buds. Two varieties 'Jargonelle' and 'Josephine de Malines' are tip bearers, with the fruit buds forming on the ends

of shoots, and pruning is needed to keep up a supply.

As the trees grow and fill the space given to them there can be a gradual replacing of old branches with younger ones. Very upright branches can be cut back to lower and more horizontal branches. Spur size numbers on a branch can be reduced to let in light, otherwise blind buds occur.

Most of the popular varieties of pears can be grown in the same tree shapes as apples but standards or half-standards are not recommended.

Plums, gages and damsons In many gardens these are planted as maidens and grown as half-standard trees with 1.3-1.6m (4-5ft) stems. Growth is rapid in the first few years. Nurserymen can supply trees already pruned with 3–5 branches. March is the best time to prune these fruits, when growth is beginning.

During the succeeding years the trees should grow quite happily with the minimum of pruning, apart from cutting out—again in spring or after fruit picking—broken, dead or diseased branches and any that have over-reached themselves.

With drooping varieties e.g. 'Early Laxton' or 'Victoria', prune to upward growing buds or shoots. Upright varieties should be pruned to outward pointing buds or shoots.

Fan-trained trees are popular but their formation is a skilled job. Many gardeners prefer to plant trees already shaped. The maiden tree is pruned to 46-60cm (18-24in) from ground level in the winter of planting. Two or more shoots grow the following summer. Select two growths opposite each other and about 30-40cm (12-15in) from ground level. These are trained outwards at an angle of 45°.

In the following March each of the shoots is pruned to 40-46cm (15-18in) from the main stem. In the summer there is a further supply of shoots and three or four are chosen to train outwards and upwards to make a fan. In the third spring after planting, each selected shoot is pruned to about 0.6m (2ft) from its point of growth. The amount of growth made the following summer should suffice to cover a reasonable framework.

Fruit production on the older part of the fan has been started on one-year-old unpruned shoots distributed about 16cm (6in) apart in the line of the branches. Any surplus is cut out completely. Only if the selected shoots exceed 46cm (18in) length are they pruned, to avoid excessive shading. This is done in summer

1 Plum 'Czar', an old favourite variety with drooping fruit, should be pruned to an upward growing bud.
2 A newly planted fan-trained plum. The branches will be tied to canes which are fixed to the horizontal wires.

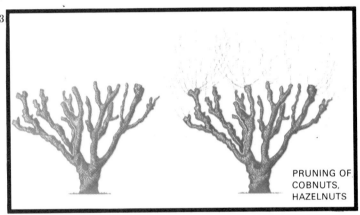

PRUNING OF COBNUTS, HAZELNUTS

when disbudding, pinching and tying are the principal tasks.

As growth begins in early summer, select the best place near the base of an existing shoot and which it will replace. Remove any other near by when quite small. A space of 16cm (6in) between each fruiting shoot may seem a lot in winter but in summer it looks very close. After fruit picking remove the fruited shoot and tie in the new one.

Peaches, nectarines and apricots. These stone fruits can be grown as large bushes or as trained trees in the open. However they are grown, pruning is done either in spring or late summer. The pruning of bush trees is very similar to that given to plums.

Maidens are pruned at 0.6m (2ft) from soil level and 3–5 branches are selected to form the basic shape of the bush and the surplus removed completely. Any further pruning need consist only of removing dead tips and dead and over-crowding branches. This pruning can be done in August or September. Half-standard trees on 1.2-1.3m (3½-4ft) stems are pruned in a similar fashion. If too much summer growth is made, cut out surplus shoots leaving the remainder apart. These fruits are also commonly fan-trained (see Plums above).

Sweet Cherries These are grown as standards or half-standards and grafted or budded on to a vigorous rootstock. Standards have a 1.6-2m (5-6ft) stem and half-standards 1.2-1.3m (3½-4ft). The maiden is pruned at the selected height in the spring after planting.

The result will be 3-4 strong branches and unless growth is hampered by other factors, this should suffice for some years. If crossing, overhanging or dead branches appear these should be cut out in spring or late summer.

Duke cherries are less vigorous than sweet varieties and with similar pruning are more useful in gardens.

Acid (sour) cherries make useful standards. Pruning after the early maiden treatment consists of keeping a supply of one-year shoots on which fruiting takes place the following year. Prune to replace about one-third of the growth in the tree each August after picking as well as dead, diseased and overcrowding shoots.

Quinces Though grafted trees of selected varieties are grown it is usual to plant Quince A, the rootstock for pears.

Quinces make medium-sized bush trees and apart from the first pruning after

1 The ripening fruits of the medlar.
2 Walnuts are grown as standards, but often attain full tree proportions.
3 Large nuts are formed if hazels are cut hard back each year.

planting to make branches, little else need be done other than the removal of unwanted branches.

Any more pruning than this will delay cropping.

Medlars Young plants are trained as standards, with 1.6-2m (5-6ft) stems, or half-standards, with 1.2-1.3m (3½-4ft) stems after planting. Thereafter they need little pruning except the cutting out of surplus shoots.

Figs After planting, fig trees should grow away very happily and often become very untidy. Since full sunlight is essential if the fruits are to mature, drastic removal of unwanted growths is done in the period June to August. The plants will stand up to this hard pruning, provided a number of fruiting spurs are left in. Long sappy growths are cut back hard each autumn.

Hazelnuts and filberts (cobs) Young, 2-3 year old plants are pruned after planting. Each of the leaders is pruned by half for a year or two to form a branch

system. After this the laterals are pruned in early winter to form spurs, about 30cm (12in) from the main stem. As the spurs become too large they can be reduced in size. They are grown as dwarf bushes with about 10-12 main branches and about 1.6m (5 ft) high.

Walnuts These are grown as standard trees with 1.6-2m (5-6ft) stems. Leader pruning during the first year or two helps to shape the tree but in following years little more need be done. Walnuts take years to crop and beating the trees with a long pole to bring down the nuts is a form of summer pruning.

Strawberries The removal of surplus runners is a form of pruning, as is the removal of surplus plants in a bed. Runners form very freely in late summer and may have to be cut off from the parent plant two or three times. Young plants set out from July to September may be starved if runners from them are allowed to develop. Cutting the tops off the plants after cropping is also a form of pruning, carried out not only as a hygiene measure but also to en-courage new growth and better fruit buds in the crowns.

Raspberries Fruit is formed on canes which grew the year before. During the

1 Removing a runner from a strawberry.
2 Raspberries in late March, tied in to supporting wires.
3 Loganberries are rampant plants.
4 Loganberries supported by a wire mesh fence, to make picking easy.

summer the canes make branchlets on which flowers and fruits form. After picking, the canes and leaves turn brown. These canes are cut close to ground level and burnt. Young canes from the ground will take over next season. Young plants are cut to 3-4 buds from ground level after planting. In the following summer a few fruiting laterals will grow from these buds but new canes will grow from the ground to start cropping the year after.

A healthy established plant will produce up to twelve new canes each year. If all are kept in there would be overcrowding, so only the best 4-6 are kept and the rest cut to ground level with the old canes. The new canes are tied to a support and any that are too long, bent over and if necessary pruned to the height of the support the follow-ing spring. At this time also any tips which have been killed by frost are cut to a healthy bud. Though most varieties

fruit in June and July, autumn fruiting can be encouraged by pruning all shoots to ground level in February.

Gooseberries Most gooseberry bushes are already 2-3 years old from cuttings when planted and have already formed branches spaced round the short main stem, known as the leg. Shoots not needed for extension are pruned in February to 2.5cm (1in) to make spurs.

Future pruning aims to keep the bushes reasonably open and replacing old branches with new. Leading or replacement shoots are pruned by half each year to keep up a supply of side-shoots which are cut to 2.5cm (1in). If the plants are really growing well, even leader pruning can be dispensed with, but weak-growing plants may need more drastic treatment and feeding.

Cut out old, weak or dead shoots and with drooping varieties prune to upward pointing shoots or buds. Bushes growing in exposed areas should have more shoots left in them than those growing in shelter.

Gooseberries can be grown as cordons, restricting the number of main growths to one, two or three. The selected leading shoots are pruned hard each winter until they reach the top of the support. Sideshoots are pruned to 2.5cm (1in) to form spurs. Pruning of plants grown as stools without a leg simply consists in cutting out surplus shoots from all types to keep the plants open. As birds can damage buds, a repellent spray should be used as a precaution from mid January onwards.

Blackberries and loganberries Fruiting takes place mainly on young shoots which grew in the previous year. A few varieties, e.g. 'John Innes Berry' form fruits on two-year-old shoots.

Young plants are pruned to 3–4 buds after planting, and the strong shoots which grow are tied to suitable supports to fruit the year after. In the following years new shoots will grow on old wood and also come from ground level. After fruiting, cut out as much of the old wood as possible and train in the new shoots. If there are too many, remove the surplus completely. With the weaker growing loganberries, 6–8 new canes each year should cover the framework. Shoots growing above the framework can be arched over and if need be, pruned in spring.

These fruits can be trained as fans, spread over the framework. New canes are looped along the lowest wire as they grow and then in autumn take the place of the old.

Black currants These are grown as stools after planting. Young plants raised from cuttings are cut to 2–3 buds from ground level after planting. The shoots which grow in the first summer will fruit the year after. In succeeding years pruning, which can be hard or light depending on growth, aims to keep up a supply of new shoots. This will mean the cutting out of a proportion of old, unfruitful wood (and some young shoots). Prune the older shoots as close to ground level as possible. It is possible to grow plants against a framework and the techniques are the same as for bushes but the branches are tied to suitable supports. Pruning should be done as soon as the fruit is picked or in winter.

Red and white currants Young plants from the nursery are usually 2–3 years old and the main branches are already formed on a short leg. After planting the leading shoots are pruned by half to two-thirds depending on vigour. The laterals, or side branches, are pruned in winter to 2.5cm (1in) from the main stem. From time to time old branches can be replaced by new growth lower down. Resist the temptation to keep too many shoots in the mature plants, 8–12 should be ample.

These currants can also be trained as cordons with one, two or three branches. The shoots from the young plants are trained to a suitable framework. The leader is pruned hard, removing half

Red currant 'Laxton's No. 1' is an early fruiting variety.

to two-thirds of the length until the required height is reached. Laterals in the meantime are pruned to 2.5cm (1in) from the main stem to form spurs which are thinned out from time to time.

Fan-shaped bushes are also useful. The five or six branches from young shoots are spread on a suitable support and trained as cordons.

Standard red currants and gooseberries One-year-old plants from the cutting rows can be trained to make standard bushes with a main stem of 0.8-1m (2½-3ft). One shoot, usually the topmost, is retained and encouraged to grow upright to form the main stem. At the desired height it is pruned above a good bud to begin the branch system the following year. It may take three to four years before a main stem framework branches are made, especially with weak varieties. The pruning of the head of the standard thereafter follows the same lines as a bush. Greater care should be taken to avoid overcrowding of branches especially with vigorous varieties. Staking should be done early, as the plants may in time become top-heavy. It may be possible to purchase standards grafted on the sturdier *Ribes aureum* as the rootstock.

Fruit thinning

By avoiding abnormally heavy crops, fruit may grow larger and the resources of the tree are conserved so that there is plant-food to spare for fruit bud formation for the next year's crop.

A newly planted black currant is pruned immediately after planting. The leading shoots are cut by half to two-thirds, depending on vigour.

Without judicious thinning some trees may fall into a biennial habit of bearing, yielding good crops only every other year. With plums, thinning is sometimes necessary to prevent such a weight of fruit developing that branches are broken. In the case of stone fruits, thinning is usually done in two stages— a preliminary thinning when the fruitlets are still only the size of peas and a final thinning when the stones have been formed (this being determined without picking, by inserting a pin into the side of the fruit).

Fruit under glass

While bananas, pineapples and the various members of the genus *Citrus* require so much heat that they are mostly outside the range of the ordinary amateur gardener, a number of hardier fruits can be obtained earlier with the aid of glass protection.

Some heat is necessary. The blossom and newly-set fruitlets of all our so-called hardy fruits are vulnerable to frost. In an unheated greenhouse sun-heat is stored up during the daytime so that the average temperature is well above that prevailing outside. Further, the occupants of such a house are not exposed to chilling, growth-inhibiting winds, and these two factors result in earlier blossoming. This, of course, increases the risk of frost coinciding with flowering. Just sufficient heating, therefore, must be available to keep the temperature above 32°F (0°C) during the coldest weather.

Greater heat than this is not really necessary but if you aspire to eating ripe strawberries in April and early May some regular heating will be required.

Any hardy fruits can be grown under glass but those generally considered the most rewarding are peaches and nectarines, figs and grapes. Strawberries are accommodating because they occupy the house for three or four months only, leaving the space available for other purposes during the remainder of the year. Further, you can force strawberries one year, if you wish, and not the next, but once a tree fruit or a vine is planted, it is 'there for good'. Melons are another possibility for the greenhouse-owner and these are in a category on their own.

Where space is at a premium, fruit trees may also be grown under glass in pots. This restricts root action so that the trees remain small. Pot-grown specimens of apples, cherries, figs, peaches and nectarines, pears, plums and gages may be obtained for this purpose from specialist nurseries.

Peaches and nectarines Both these fruits are treated in the same way, the latter simply being a smooth-skinned form of peach. They are usually grown as fans and are most easily accommodated against the back wall of a lean-to-house, but they may also be trained on wires fixed 0.6m (2ft) away from the glass or on a trellis arranged across the house.

Although plenty of water will be required in the growing season, drainage must be impeccable. If necessary, therefore, the border should be excavated to a depth of about 1m (3ft) and either field-

If heat is available many fruits, otherwise not suited to our climate, can be grown and ripened under glass.
1 An established vinery with a good crop of grape 'Muscat of Alexandra'.
2 Citrus fruits grown under glass.
3 Bananas fruiting under glass.

130

drain pipes laid or a foot depth of rubble put in. A layer of turves, laid grass-side down, will prevent the soil above from clogging the drainage. The peach tree will need a depth of 46-60cm (18-24in) for its roots but this soil should not be too rich or excessive growth will be encouraged in the early years at the expense of fruiting.

For a path, wooden duck-boarding is preferable to concrete so that moisture can penetrate and the roots be free to extend.

Trees should be planted in the usual way and the young growths tied to canes which in their turn, are tied to wires. Training and pruning follow similar lines as for outdoor trees but remember that in the greenhouse the trees will receive only the water you give them. The border will need to be flooded in January to start growth and frequent watering will be necessary when growth becomes active. Syringeing is also necessary, once or twice daily, from bud break until the fruit begins to colour. This syringeing may be quite forceful, to discourage pests. While the flowers are open, the syringeing should be reduced to once a day, around midday, to encourage pollination.

In January the house ventilators should be closed early in the afternoon to trap the sun's warmth, the temperature being maintained as near to 40°F (4°C) as manipulation of the ventilators can secure. In February the temperature may be allowed to rise to around 50°F (10°C) but, should very cold weather prevail during the blossom period, and immediately after, some heating will be necessary to keep the temperature at least above freezing point.

Pollination is the difficulty with fruits under glass because the insects which usually perform the service for us are not present. A hive of bees may be stood in the greenhouse but for most gardeners this is impossible and resort should be made to hand-fertilization of the blossom, transferring the pollen about midday with a rabbit's tail (if you can get one), a camel's hair brush or a small piece of cotton wool tied to the end of a stick. Do this before syringeing as an additional aid.

In March the temperature may rise to 55–60°F (13–16°C), but when outside temperatures begin to exceed this try to keep the atmosphere in the house buoyant by adequate damping down and ample ventilation. From May on some light shading should be provided—with blinds or strips of plastic netting shading material or by spraying or painting the roof glass with a proprietary shading preparation.

Thinning of the fruit should be carried out, as with the outdoor crop, in easy stages. If large fruits are wanted, the final allowance of space should be a 30cm (1ft) square per peach and 23cm (9in) square for each nectarine, but for average size, thinning may be less drastic, allowing from 16-23cm (6-9in) square per fruit.

As ripening begins, all syringeing must stop and more air should be given. Foliage which shades the fruit should be tied back temporarily.

Once the peach crop has been gathered, spray as forcefully as you can and ventilate as freely as possible to assist the ripening of the new wood. Continue to water the border regularly. Ventilators should be left open, night and day, until January when growth is to be restarted. Untying and pruning may be done early in the autumn.

If spraying with tar-oil is considered necessary to control aphis and scale insects, this may be done as soon as it is certain that the tree concerned is quite dormant.

Feeding is seldom necessary in the first year or two as it may result in growth rather than fruit. Some food, however, will be needed once heavy

1 Fan-trained peaches flowering under glass in February.
2 Nectarine 'Early Rivers' protected in a lean-to type greenhouse.

crops are being carried. A mixture of 2 parts of sulphate of ammonia, 2 parts of superphosphate and 1 part of sulphate of potash, all parts by weight, should be scattered over the border at the rate of 140g (5oz) per 2 sq m (2 sq yd), and lightly raked in and then watered. In March put down a mulch of rotted stable manure or garden compost. If the burden of fruit bearing appears to be too great and fresh growth is being made only slowly, an extra fillip can be given after stoning, in the form of liquid manure or dried blood applied at the rate of 112g (4oz) per sq m (sq yd) of border.

Peaches under glass are liable to the same pests and diseases as those in the open, although peach leaf curl is usually less troublesome and red spider mite very much more so. The following varieties, given in order of ripening, are suitable for greenhouse culture, those marked with an asterisk being the most reliable:

Peaches: 'Duke of York*', 'Waterloo', 'Peregrine*', 'Royal George', 'Dymond*', 'Bellegarde'.

Nectarines: 'Early Rivers', 'Lord Napier*', 'Pineapple'.

Figs Whereas figs in the open will only ripen one crop of fruit a year, those in a heated greenhouse can ripen two. With sufficient heat it is even possible to secure three crops a year, but this is a heavy drain on the strength of the tree and expensive in fuel consumption as it is necessary to start growth in December with a temperature of 65–70°F (18–21°C), gradually rising to 80°F (27°C).

The fig is most conveniently trained as a fan against the wall of a lean-to house. The soil in the border should not be rich as this would encourage growth at the expense of fruit—a very average loam will serve. Indeed, to keep growth within the confines of even a fair-sized greenhouse it is advisable to restrict the roots, doing this by making up the border inside a concrete 'box'. Wooden shuttering should be used to make a bottomless box, 1.3m (4ft) long by 0.6m (2ft) wide and 0.6m (2ft) deep. When the concrete has set hard, dig out a little soil from the bottom and replace with a layer of broken brick or stone, well rammed in place, so that free drainage is possible but the formation of tap-roots discouraged.

Fill this box with light soil, adding sand or brick or mortar rubble if the natural soil in the garden is not sandy or gravelly. Do not add manure.

Turn on the heat to start growth in February with a temperature around 55–60°F (13–16°C). The border will need flooding at the start of the season and plenty of water will be required when the tree is in full growth. It helps growth (and deters red spider mites) to damp down the path and syringe the foliage regularly from bud break until the autumn, withholding the spray while the fruit is ripening.

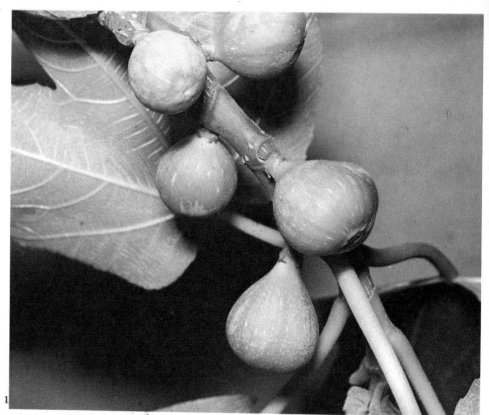

1 The ripening fruits of greenhouse-grown figs.
2 A fan-trained fig, the main branches reduced in number.

When the second crop has been picked, probably in September, gradually cut down the water supply and, when all the leaves have dropped, let the tree rest, with free ventilation, no heat and the minimum amount of moisture. Close the house during frost and give a little warmth only when conditions are severe and the temperature inside the house is likely to fall below freezing point.

Pruning and disbudding follow similar lines as for outdoors figs but it should be remembered that the second (autumn) crop is borne on the new wood made that spring and summer. Embryo figs on the tips of the new growths will give the next season's spring crop. Therefore, there must be no summer pinching of new shoots.

As with peaches, red spider mites may be a nuisance on figs under glass,

Early strawberries grown in the heated greenhouse in a light position.

particularly if conditions have been too dry. Scale insects can also give trouble but remember that it is not safe to deal with these by applying tar-oil winter wash during the dormant period as the tender, embryo figs would be harmed. In bad cases a summer petroleum wash may be used but it is generally better to attempt hand control using a stiff brush to remove the offending brown scale-like insects.

Any of the fig varieties normally recommended for the open may be grown under glass—'Brown Turkey', 'Brunswick' and 'White Marseilles', for instance—but with heat available the choice is widened. 'Bourjassotte Grise', 'Negro Largo' and 'Violette Sepor' are all good.

Strawberries Extra-early strawberries can be obtained quite easily by growing in pots in a heated greenhouse. Fruiting time is governed by when the pots are housed and the night temperature which can be maintained. A minimum temperature of 55°F (13°C) is desirable for ripening and, obviously, much more fuel is necessary to maintain this early in the year than in spring.

The old variety 'Royal Sovereign' is still pre-eminent for this purpose and the first essential is to secure really early-rooted runners. Pot-grown runners should be obtained in July if possible.

Plant them in 16cm (6in) pots using John Innes potting compost No. 3 and stand them outdoors, on a bed of ashes. The latter prevents worms entering the drainage holes and helps to prevent drying out. The pots should be in full sun and watered daily.

If the ash bed is deep enough for the pots to be plunged up to their rims, this will protect them from frost and they may stay there until it is time for them to go into the greenhouse. If the pots are exposed, however, it would be better to remove them in November, when growth has ceased, to some sheltered spot such as on the south side of a wall. Lay the pots on their sides and cover with straw to protect them from frost.

Given sufficient heat, plants housed in mid-December may ripen their fruit at the beginning of April and those brought in at the end of January should have ripe berries during the latter half of May.

The strawberry pots should be stood in the lightest position available in the greenhouse. At first no artificial heat should be given and the temperature should be kept down during the daytime, if necessary by free ventilation. No water should be given but on sunny days the plants should be lightly syringed and the greenhouse atmosphere should be moist rather than dry.

After about two weeks, signs of growth should be observed and a first watering should be given. From now onwards keep the compost in the pots just nicely moist, judging needs by tapping the pots daily—a ringing sound indicating that the compost is dry, a dull sound that it is wet.

Once the plants are growing freely, the temperature may be permitted to rise very gradually. Aim at a minimum of 45°F (7°C) by night. On sunny days it may still be necessary to give extra ventilation to prevent an undue rise of temperature—liable to encourage the leaves rather than the blossom.

When the blossom opens, a slightly higher temperature is wanted—up to 50°F (10°C) at night—and syringeing should stop. A buoyant atmosphere will help pollination but nevertheless, as insects are scarce inside a greenhouse at this time of the year, recourse should be had to hand fertilization of the flowers. Around midday, using a camel's hair brush or a small wad of cotton wool, dab the centre of each flower in turn, thus transferring the pollen.

When the fruit has set and the blossom petals have fallen, night temperature may go up to a minimum of 55°F (13°C), a moister atmosphere may again be

be burned to prevent the spread of red spider mites.

Melons Belonging to the same genus (*Cucumis*) as the cucumber, the melon requires similar conditions but provides us with one of the most refreshing fruits that can grace our table. Certain varieties of melon may be grown under cloches, in cold frames or in an unheated greenhouse, but in each case a high temperature is necessary for germination and early growth. Where this is unavailable, young plants must be purchased from a specialist grower. The owner of a heated greenhouse, however, can grow a wide range of varieties, secure earlier fruits and, if he chooses, raise plants for fruiting in frames or beneath cloches.

It is possible in the sunny south of England to get ripe melons in April by sowing in November but as a minimum temperature of 60°F (16°C) is required, this calls for the expenditure of much fuel in the midwinter months. Few gardeners can contemplate this and most will be content to defer sowing until the end of February or March and have melons in summer rather than spring.

Use 7cm (3in) pots and fill with John Innes potting compost or no-soil potting compost, sowing one seed in each and only just covering. A minimum temperature of 70°F (21°C) is necessary for reasonably quick germination—up to 80°F (27°C) if it can be secured—and as bottom heat is best, use, inside the greenhouse, a propagating frame with soil heating if you possess such a thing. Otherwise, try to arrange the seedpots above a hot pipe or heating tube.

Once germination has taken place the temperature may be allowed to fall to 60°F (16°C) during the night. Four weeks after sowing the roots should be ranging round the edge of the pots, and the young plants ready for transference to their fruiting quarters. These may consist of a box of soil on the staging or, in a glass-to-ground house or one with a very low supporting wall, a bed made up on the border.

Melons require rich soil and good drainage. As they are susceptible to collar rot, it is a good plan to make up the bed in the form of a ridge 45cm (18in) wide at the base and some 38cm (15in) deep. Do not plant deeply; set the plants 60cm (24in) apart.

Strings must be provided to take the melon growth up to the roof wires, as with cucumbers. Stop the shoots, by pinching out the growing points, when 16cm (6in) of growth have been made. This will result in the development of laterals: select two and train them up

permitted and syringeing resumed. This will help, too, to keep the red spider mites at bay. These are often a trouble with forced strawberries and fumigation with azobenzene smoke is the answer when the infestation is severe.

While the fruits are swelling, a little gentle feeding will be beneficial—weak liquid manure once every 10 days or a proprietary liquid fertilizer used according to the maker's instructions.

Once colour shows in the fruit, all feeding must cease, and drier conditions must prevail or botrytis disease will be encouraged: stop syringeing, keep the path drier and give more air. Never,

however, allow the pots to dry out. In sunny spring weather, watering may be necessary twice a day.

To obtain fruit of top size, such as those which win gold medals at Chelsea Show, thinning is essential. Remove the smallest berries at an early stage and be content with nine berries per pot. Once you have your nine, remove all further blossom. Use little forked pieces of twig or bent galvanized wire as props to hold the trusses up and keep the berries in the light and away from the soil or pot side.

Once the berries have been picked the plants are of no further use and should

strings to a height of 2m (6ft) and then stop again.

The embryo melons can be seen as little swellings behind the female flowers. If one is pollinated ahead of the others, it will grow away and later fruit will fail. A good plant should give four good fruits—provided they all start level. To achieve this, remove female blossom until eight open on the same day and then pollinate these by hand about midday, transferring the pollen from the male flowers to the female with a camel's hair brush or piece of cotton-wool.

When the little melons have started swelling, select four of the same size and remove the others. The laterals carrying the chosen fruit should be stopped one joint further on. Also stop the laterals from which any unwanted fruit have been removed.

Aim at keeping the temperature around 65–70°F (18–21°C) during the day, falling no lower than 60°F (16°C) by night. As the spring sunshine warms up, daytime temperatures may rise over 100°F (38°C) but ventilation should always be given when it reaches 80°F (27°C).

Keep the bed uniformly moist and the atmosphere damp be syringeing overhead and damping down the path. The air, however, should be kept somewhat drier when the fruit begins to ripen.

Good varieties for hothouse conditions are 'Best of All' (green flesh), 'Blenheim Orange' (scarlet flesh), 'Emerald Gem' (green flesh), 'King George' (scarlet flesh) and 'Watermelon Florida Favourite' (pink flesh).

Where the higher temperature cannot be guaranteed, 'Dutch Net' (orange flesh) and 'Hero of Lockinge' (white flesh) may be relied upon.

Where no artificial heat is available, plants of one or more of the following varieties should be purchased: 'Burpee's Crenshaw' (salmon-pink flesh), 'Charentais' (deep orange flesh), 'Dutch Net' (orange flesh), 'No Name' (Cantaloupe type with amber-yellow flesh), 'Sweetie' (Cantaloupe type, green flesh, the most likely to prosper in spite of unfavourable weather), and 'Tiger' (orange flesh).

Fruit in pots Fruit trees may also be grown in the unheated greenhouse in pots, tubs or boxes. The restriction of the roots induces early fruiting and keeps the trees small, while the glass catches the sun's warmth, thus forwarding growth slightly, protects the blossom and fruitlets from spring frosts

1 A hole is made in the base of a pot.
2 The young plant is repotted firmly.
3 It needs watering immediately.
4 When the flowers appear the pots are ready to plant on the bench.
5 The pot is sunk in a mound of soil.
6 Water only the mound of soil to reduce the risk of neck rot.
7 Stop growth one leaf beyond a fruit.
8 Fruit setting on a well-grown plant.

and renders protection from birds as the fruit ripens easier. No artificial heating is necessary; in fact it is inadvisable for apples or pears. Cherries, figs, peaches and plums can be brought along earlier, if desired, by a little additional warmth.

Pot-grown trees raised for this purpose should be bought—apples, sweet cherries, figs, peaches and nectarines, pears, plums and gages are all available. Start with pots of 25 or 27cm (10 or 11in) diameter or boxes of similar dimensions. Crock well to ensure perfect drainage and then cover the crocks with a first layer of compost, rammed firmly down and deep enough for the tree to 'stand' on this with its roots properly spread out and with the top roots just covered. The surface of the soil should be at least 2.5cm (1in) below the pot's rim to allow for watering. Work the compost round the roots, little by little, and firm it down as you proceed with a blunt-ended stick.

For potting compost the following formula is recommended by a nursery where they have grown pot trees for over a century: three parts of good fibrous loam; one part of well-rotted manure and to this mixture add one litre (quart) jar of walnut-sized lumps of chalk per barrow-load of compost.

The usual system is to sink the pots in a bed of ashes in the open garden during the winter. Thus treated, the pots will be safe from frost and the ashes will discourage the entry of worms. Outdoors, the wood will ripen better and the cold weather will ensure that the trees have a proper resting period.

At the end of January the pots may be taken into the unheated greenhouse. Ventilate freely during the day in mild weather but shut up early to conserve the sun-heat. Little water will be needed at first—perhaps once in the first week or two and once more in February will be sufficient. In March syringeing will help the buds to break and this should be continued until the fruit begins to colour. Daily syringeing should be resumed after picking, until leaf-fall.

By March more water will be required and this should be given daily attention, testing the pots by tapping. Allow free ventilation when the blossom is open, but avoid draughts. Hand pollination is advisable.

A top-dressing of well-rotted manure should be given when the fruit has all set. Pot trees do not bear very large crops and the fruit will have to be thinned, particularly in the first year or two, to prevent over-cropping. Ventilators should be covered with netting to prevent the entry of birds when the fruit begins to ripen.

Each year the pot trees should be repotted in October or November. A

1

2

little soil is scraped away from the surface and then the pot laid on its side and the tree removed. More soil is then scraped away from the roots and the longest of these are shortened by a third of their length. The tree is then repotted using the same compost formula as before. A larger size pot should only be provided when absolutely essential: probably the original pots will suffice for two or three seasons and then one size larger, only, should be provided. New trees can be purchased to make use of the first set of pots.

Fumigation

In general this is a process used for eliminating pests and diseases from greenhouses although it can, of course, be used in other closed structures such as fruit stores, frames, etc. There are methods of fumigating out of doors but these are only suitable for large areas and not practical for small gardens. It is done by pulling a large sheet over several rows of field plants, such as strawberries, during which a machine is also blowing a gas underneath the sheet. As the latter is drawn along slowly there is time for pests to be destroyed.

We are more concerned with fumigation of plants in greenhouses and the important factors are the condition of the structure and the kind of crop and pest involved. In the first place it is essential that the greenhouse is not leaking and that any gaps or cracks are sealed, besides which ventilators and doors must fit well. The greenhouse is closed up during the process which takes several hours and it is, therefore, usually done in the evening and then locked for the night. A notice warning that fumigation is taking place ought to be put up. Afterwards the greenhouse is aired by opening ventilators and doors.

There are plenty of chemicals now available for eliminating all kinds of insect pests on living crops and they are marketed as the now well-known smokes sold in sizes to suit the capacity of any greenhouse. The small canisters need only be placed in the greenhouse and lit with a match—the operator then leaves and closes the door. The smoke settles as a fine film on the foliage of the plants and this protective covering is finer than can be obtained in any other way, besides which all insects are killed.

Fungus diseases see Diseases and their control

Fungicides see Diseases and their control

Fusarium patch

This is a name often used to describe a disease of grass which is more correctly called snow mould. It shows on the turf of bowling and golf greens and on lawns, occurring as a brown patch which may vary from 2.5cm (1in) up to 30cm (1ft) in diameter. In this area the grass is brown and dead and often seems to have a whitish mould on its surface. Treat with mercurized turf sand at about 112g (4oz) to the sq m (sq yd).

Gooseberries see Fruit

Grafting

The need for grafting arises from the fact that very many plants will not propagate reliably from cuttings.

Nurserymen also find that they can raise more plants more quickly by using standard rootstocks.

Grafting of plants appeals to many gardeners and it can be a rewarding and exciting way of raising young trees and bushes and, especially where fruit trees and their ornamental relatives are concerned, converting old but healthy trees to better varieties.

The aim of grafting is to unite two or more stem parts of a selected variety—the scions, and a suitable rooted shoot—the rootstock. In some respects it is a matter of carpentry, clean sharp cuts and good joints. The rootstock which forms the root system and part of the main stem is a selected seedling. The Malling and Malling-Merton rootstocks for fruit trees are well-known, highly developed forms. These rootstocks are propagated vegetatively and are one year old in the nursery before being grafted. The scions are young and usually one-year-old shoots or buds from selected varieties, which it is intended to grow.

The principles behind grafting and budding are (a) the rootstock and scion must be closely related to each other, they are thus compatible, (b) there must be continuous close contact between exposed living cells, the cambium layer between the bark and the wood.

Grafting can be done at any time of the year but for hardy fruits the work is carried out in the spring and early summer, March to May. It is at this time that cell sap in the rootstock is flowing steadily and union between cut surfaces takes place readily. This is important for a firm permanent union. A simple test of the condition of tissue is the ease with which the thin rind or bark peels off.

The all-important cambium cells are underneath the rind and are seen as a thin white or cream line, quite visible under a low-powered lens. The skill of the operation is to bring as much of the cambium as possible on the scion (or bud) into contact with that of the rootstock.

Grafting young trees There are several ways of grafting young trees but the most common is the whip and tongue method, though there are a number of modifications of this. Scion wood is taken from selected plants and in the main is one year old. For outdoor grafting take enough shoots from dormant plants, tie and label them securely and store them in moist peat in a cool shady spot. Each shoot generally provides two or three scions, each with about four buds. To carry out the operation in spring, have a sharp pruning knife, a small, fine-grained carborundum stone and a pair of sharp secateurs. To hold the graft area securely use wetted raffia or plastic strips and seal the wounds with a cold bitumen wax.

The stocks to be grafted should, in general, be little more than pencil thickness and have been established in the ground at least one season (stem building trees to make family trees may be 3-4 seasons old). The rootstock to be grafted is cut off at a reasonable height above ground level, certainly no lower than 16cm (6in). With the pruning knife make a clean sloping cut 4cm (1½in) long on one side of the stock. About 1cm (½in) down from the top of this sloping cut, a cut is made to form a tongue 0.5cm (¼in) long. From the selected scion wood cut off a four-bud scion.

On one side of this make an even sloping cut 4cm (1½in) long to match that on the rootstock. About 1cm (½in) from the top of this sloping cut make a 0.5cm (¼in) tongue to match the one on the rootstock.

The scion is then edged on to the stock so that the edges of the cuts correspond and the tongues interlock into each other. To aid union, the scion and the rootstock are bound together with wetted raffia or plastic and the whole wound area painted with a cold bitumen wax or enclosed with polythene.

In this way the parts are held securely and rain is prevented from getting into the graft.

With some varieties of pears, direct union with quince rootstock is uncertain and double working with mutually compatible intermediate varieties is carried out. The mechanics of the business are similar to the foregoing. The two pear scions are grafted together first, with the intermediate in the bottom position. Immediately this is done the final link up with the quince rootstock is done. It is also possible to bud or graft the intermediate in one season and in the following add the variety.

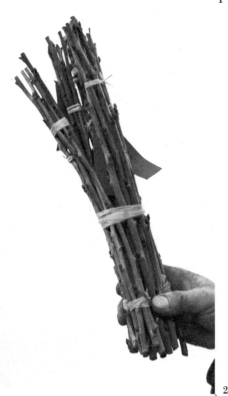

1

2

1 Suitable small branches prepared as scions, each labelled with their name.
2 The first cut is made with sharp secateurs and must be a clean cut.
3 An oblique cut is made, then the knife is pushed back into the wood.
4 The tongue is thus made, not too thin, and not too thick.
5 The scion is cut to a similar pattern, the tongue made slightly thinner than that on the stock.
6 The cut surfaces are matched.
7 The union is bound firmly in place with raffia.
8 Tar or oil is painted over the union to prevent the entry of disease. It is put over the raffia binding.

Williams' Bon Chrétien is double worked and for this variety Beurré Hardy is a good intermediate.

There are a number of trees and shrub plants which can be grafted easily indoors in a warm greenhouse or frame and for these the simple whip graft techniques are sufficient.

The rootstock and scion are tied together and put into moist peat in a heated frame. In this moist warm atmosphere the parts heal together quickly and in a week or two, depending on genus and species, are ready to be potted up and grown on in the cooler atmosphere of the greenhouse bench.

After care When buds begin to grow from newly grafted plants in early summer there should be no rush to take off surplus buds.

So often buds show activity and then dry up, a sure sign that union has failed. If the buds really get away and form shoots, union is satisfactory. At this stage remove rootstock shoots completely as they appear, and also any on intermediate scions. If it is the intention to produce single-stem maiden plants the best shoot is allowed to grow and the remainder cut out completely. To avoid accidents tie this shoot to a nearby cane as it grows. When, however, as with many ornamental plants—syringas (lilac), cytisus (broom) a leg or stem is not needed, the rootstock buds only are removed and the graft shoots grow unhindered.

With indoor grafting, wait until the scion has made 3-5cm (1-2in) of steady growth before potting the plants for growing on.

At all times in the nursery or green-house keep a lookout for insect pests and diseases which can cause loss.

With fruit, the family tree has become popular. For this a rootstock is pruned at a selected height to form 4-5 branches. On to each of these branches a different scion variety is grafted. In this way, in a small garden, several varieties of different fruits can be grown as trees. The method is used especially with apples, pears and sometimes plums. The varieties are chosen to give a succession of ripening and help each other with pollination.

A similar method called stem building is used with plums and sweet cherries. A rootstock or main stem resistant to silver leaf disease or bacterial canker forms the early branches and subsequently the crotch where these troubles often start.

Root grafting This method of grafting clematis hybrids is an indoor operation.

Seedlings of *Clematis vitalba* (old man's beard) are used and scions are cut from clematis plants put in a warm greenhouse in January. Grafting is done from February to March. The seedling stocks are cut back to the root portion and the scion prepared by cutting off a portion of stem with 2·5cm (1in) of wood above and below the leaves. Two wedge cuts 2-2.5cm (¾-1in) long are made in the stock and the scion stem is split with a sharp knife.

Each portion is placed saddle-wise over the prepared stock, secured with raffia and planted in a propagating case to grow on.

Varieties of gypsophila can be raised in a similar fashion using seedling roots, though simple matching cuts on scion and stock are sufficient.

Budding This form of grafting can be used for raising a range of fruit and ornamental plants. The bud is the scion from a selected variety. All varieties of tree fruits and other ornamental relatives can be raised by budding. The operation is done in summer when the cell sap is flowing easily.

Rootstocks to be budded should have been planted one year.

But sticks consisting of one-year-old, half-ripened shoots with several buds are taken from chosen plants in July. About 23cm (9in) above ground level make a vertical cut 4cm (1½in) long in the bark of the rootstock. At the top of this make another shorter cut at right angles, thus forming a 'T'. With the end of the knife partly raise the edges of the cuts. To prepare the buds hold a bud stick firmly and with the knife make a cut 1cm (½in) above a bud. Carry the cut just underneath the bud and surface about 2.5cm (1in) below. The best buds are found in the middle of the shoots. With the knife edge ease the 'tail' of the bud under the long cut on the stock so that the bud will fit snugly on the exposed cambium cells. At the top of the 'T' cut off any spare end and bind the parts with plastic tape or raffia and cover the wound area with petroleum jelly. The bud, if well fitted, will remain dormant until the following spring and then begin to grow and make a shoot. As soon as this is growing well, cut off the rootstock just above the budding area. Tie the young shoot to a cane as it grows.

Bridge grafting This is used to repair damage done to the main stem or branches, eg when they have been stripped of bark by animals. Scions long enough to stretch across the damaged area are prepared with a wedge cut at each end and pressed into bark cuts made into healthy tissue. This method is also used as support bracing between main branches when these are likely to break away.

Grafting established trees In many gardens there are trees which are old but quite healthy or undesirable varieties. These can be converted to new varieties by grafting. There are two

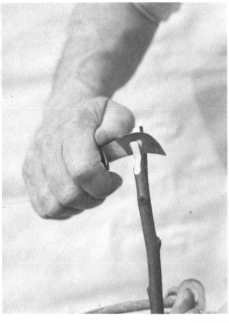

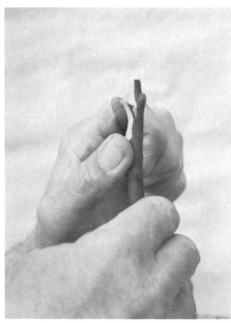

3

4

5

6

7

8

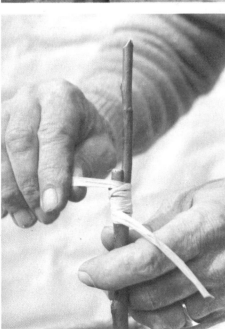

main ways of doing this—top working or frameworking in spring.

The former consists of shortening all the main branches to within 0.6-1m (2-3ft) of the crotch or crown. To avoid having large wounds (those with a greater diameter than 10cm [4in] heal slowly) it is advisable to cut the main branches higher so that this diameter is not exceeded. A few small branches, known as sap drawers, can be left in position below where the cuts are made. The branches can be cut back any time during the winter months. The sap drawers will help to feed the roots and keep the branches healthy, but can be removed as soon as the grafts or scions have taken. It is usual to put more than one scion on 7-10cm (3-4in) cuts and one scion only on small cuts.

Cleft or oblique cleft This method is also known as crown grafting. Cuts are made across the flat surface with a sharp chopper or special tool. Scions are prepared and pushed into the cleft which is kept open, and when they are in position the scions are held firmly by the wood. With oblique cleft grafting the cut is made a short way only into the limb. Remember to cover all cut surfaces with bitumen to shed off surplus water and keep out disease spores.

Rind, bark or veneer grafting This is another method of doing the same job. Here a vertical slit is made in the limb and a pointed scion pushed into the wood and the bark. This scion is held in position by tying the graft round with string, raffia or adhesive tape which must be cut as soon as the scion begins to grow two or three months after the job has been done.

It will be necessary to give some support to the young branches and this can be done by tying them loosely to canes bound tightly to the branches of the tree. The trees which have been top worked may take 5-6 years to crop once again, and a new framework or branch system has to be developed by pruning.

Frameworking This is a means of bringing the trees into cropping earlier, but many more scions are needed than for top working. Again, in the winter season, dead, diseased or badly placed branches are removed completely, but much of the remaining branch system left untouched, except for the removal of overcrowding shoots.

Stub grafting is the most common method of putting shoots into a framework. To do this successfully leave as many young shoots as possible in the tree, those from 1-2.5cm ($\frac{1}{2}$-1in) in diameter. Stubs are inserted into the branches by making a cut about 1cm ($\frac{1}{2}$in) along the side shoots from the main branch, and bending this back so that the prepared stub can be pushed into position. The main shoot is released and grips the stub firmly.

The remainder of the lateral which is to be replaced is cut about 1cm ($\frac{1}{2}$in) from

139

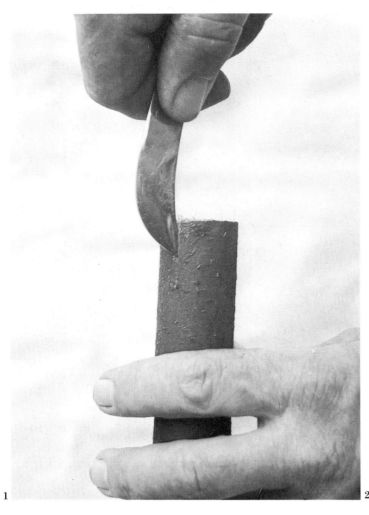

the stub position. Again, cover all wounds with sealing material. Avoid placing stubs or scions on the top or underside of a branch, but put them mainly on the side of the branch in herring-bone fashion and approximately 30-37cm (12-15in) apart. Stub grafting can be started as early as February and continued into May. On branches thicker than 2.5cm (1in) cuts are made into the bark, the branch bent back to open the cut and the stub pushed into position. This is called side grafting.

Side grafting Scions for top working should have 3-4 wood buds, while those for frame working can be longer, about 7-8 buds and never less than six.

Frameworked trees will come into cropping within 2-3 years after treatment.

There are many other forms of grafting, including approach, bottle, inarch, inlay, kerf, peg, ring, saddle and strap. Some are for special purposes and the others are of general use when circumstances allow.

It is not always understood that ornamental trees can be top worked and frameworked in the same way as fruiting plants.

Pruning of grafted trees The first thing to remember about grafted trees is that the original branches will make every endeavour to produce new shoots and these should be removed as soon as they appear and certainly not be left on longer than 7-10cm (3-4in). This will mean going over the trees two or three times during the summer and for several years after the job has been done, otherwise there may be a mix up in the tree and the undesirable variety used as the stock could, in time, take over from the new one. It is sometimes possible to detect the branches of the original tree during the winter months, when they can be pruned out completely. Water shoots, ie strong growths growing from the crotch of the tree, will also grow quite strongly and these should be removed at the same time.

Top worked trees can often be distinguished among others growing in a natural fashion by the fact that most of the branches grow very upright. This is due to the fact that sap in the young branches produces strong growth and it may be 6-8 years before these trees really begin to produce crops of fruit. To assist the tree, however, pruning of these strong shoots should be carried out each winter after grafting. Do not prune the leading shoot too hard; simply remove about 20-30cm (8-12in) of the end. This will encourage side shoots to grow and it is on these that fruit buds and fruit will appear. Strong growing, hard pruned shoots take a long time to form fruit buds. If you have put in more grafts than necessary, cut out the surplus, again in the first winter after grafting, and leave in those which are strongest and best placed. Many gardeners find it advisable to keep the cane support for each branch for a year or two so that this does not blow out after a gale. After a year or two grafted branches become as firm as any others.

When dealing with frameworked trees the general treatment is the same but the grafts do not make such vigorous growths and are, in fact, simply new laterals taking the place of the old.

Because they are less vigorous they will form fruit buds and fruits probably in the first year and certainly in the second. Pruning of these can be done in the ordinary way eg for apples and pears they can be spur pruned to 7-10cm (3-4in) or left full length as is done with plums and sweet cherries.

Remember that grafting is a skilled operation, use a sharp knife, make clean cuts, bind firmly where necessary and cover all wounds so that disease germs do not get in.

Grapes see Fruit

Grass seed for lawns

Of the 150-160 grass species found in Great Britain only about six are used for lawns. Proprietary lawn seed mixtures consist of the merchant's special mixes of some or all of these seeds and are

3

4

1 *Rind grafting. The sawn edge of the* 5
limb or stock is pared and then nicked or
cleft round the bark with a sharp pruning
knife.
2 *The scion has been prepared by making*
five sloping cuts on the point of a bud to
form a wedge. It is pushed into the cleft
on the stock.
3 *Another scion is pushed into the*
opposite side of the stock.
4 *The union is bound with raffia to hold*
the scions in position.
5 *The binding is greased to keep out air*
and prevent disease from attacking.

sold according to the type of lawn required and, of course, price. In purchasing proprietary seed mixtures it is important to buy from a fair and knowledgeable firm. It is advantageous if the supplier states the constitution of his mixtures. Under the Seeds Regulations Act it is not compulsory for suppliers of lawn grasses to disclose the constituents of their mixtures, but many do.

A very important factor in judging a given species or variety of grass is the tolerance of cutting at any given height. This factor must be clearly understood (eg perennial ryegrass will not thrive if cut closer than 2.5cm [1in]) and disappointing results are obtained if over-severe mowing is imposed on a mixture.

The chief species of grass used in lawn mixtures are as follows:

1 Perennial ryegrass, some strains of
which make good lawn grasses.
2 Crested dogstail has hard wearing
qualities as a lawn grass.
3 Long-stalked meadow grass tolerates
drought, but does not like close mowing.
4 Nothing sets off a garden better than
a well-kept lawn.

Perennial ryegrass (*Lolium perenne*)
Some varieties of perennial ryegrass
have little tolerance for regular mowing
at all. The varieties most suited to turf
formation are those selected as late
flowering, leafy, persistent type of which
the Aberystwyth strain 'S.23' was the
first reliable example. This variety
maintains a high standard so that it
continues to be popular although new
Continental varieties are now available
which compare very well. These include
the varieties 'Heraf', 'Pelo', 'Sceempter'
and 'Melle'.

Sown alone, even the best ryegrasses
seldom form a sufficiently dense sward to
suppress weed invasion and none will
persist when mown at 1cm (½in) or less.
Perennial ryegrass is best suited to
conditions of reasonably high fertility
and provided that this facility is maintained, the height of cut kept at about
2.5cm (1in) and mowing is frequent
throughout the growing season, ryegrass
will prove suitable for a second or third
quality lawn, ie the drying ground type
of lawn.
Timothy (*Phleum*) There are new leafy
varieties of this valuable agricultural
grass, the special characteristics of
which are good winter colour and ability
to recover after wear. Unfortunately
establishment from seed is rather slow,
so that the grass does not compete very
successfully with other grasses in a
mixture, especially perennial ryegrass.

The British variety, 'S.50', the Swedish
variety, 'Evergreen', and the Dutch
variety, 'King', are very good but are all
rather expensive and since Timothy is
suitable only for second-class lawns (or
first-quality playing fields) this is not an
attractive lawn grass at the present
time.
Rough-stalked meadow grass (*Poa
trivialis*) A fairly dwarf grass, this is
sometimes employed in the cheaper,
second-class lawn mixtures. There are no
good new varieties of this.
Smooth-stalked meadow grass (*Poa
pratensis*) This is receiving the attention
of the breeders and there are some very
good varieties, particularly the Dutch
one known as 'Prato' which is likely to
appear in quite good lawn seed mixtures.
Slow in establishing, smooth-stalked

meadow grass ultimately forms a very
dense, durable, drought-resistant sward
if not mown too closely and the vigorous
rhizome development allows good recovery after wear. Unfortunately,
smooth-stalked meadow grass does not
thrive under close mowing and in fact is
best kept at 2-2.5cm (¾-1in) in height so
that its use for fine lawns is rather
limited.
Annual meadow grass (*Pao annua*) An
annual, or short lived perennial, this is
seldom sown but often found, since it
invades strongly into lawns. It is a grass
which is not very resistant to either
drought or severe winter weather and is
prone to disease, but because of its prolific seeding habits it continues to form
a considerable proportion of most lawns.
Crested dogstail (*Cynosurus cristatus*)

Phalaris arundinacea picta, ribbon grass, has leaves striped with white.

It is quite a good bottom grass for second-class quality lawn mixtures but again there are no new selected varieties available as yet. This grass is tolerant of low fertility and has good winter colour and hard-wearing qualities. Selected varieties might, therefore, prove extremely useful.

Creeping red fescue *(Festuca rubra var. rubra)* This is suitable for inclusion in good lawn mixtures but does not stand very close mowing and so is not suitable for really high class lawns. There are selected varieties of this grass available, including 'S.59', a fine-leaved winter green selection, which forms an excellent turf either alone or in mixtures. There are also new Continental varieties of creeping red fescue which are good, eg 'Oasis' and 'Brabantia'.

Chewings' fescue *(Festuca rubra sub. spp. commutata)* is the fescue which (usually mixed with browntop bent) is used to form best quality fine turf in Britain and which is also included in less fine mixtures because of its excellent turf-forming characteristics. Very good quality seed is on the market these days from America (no longer from New Zealand) and there are new selected varieties from Holland, namely 'Highlight' and 'Brabantia', which are very good indeed. One of the main disadvantages of all Chewings' fescue is, of course, that their winter colour is poor.

Bent grass *(Agrostis species)* The fine bent grass used for forming fine turf (usually mixed with Chewings' fescue) is normally *Agrostis tenuis* (browntop bent) and the main source of supply is America since New Zealand has more or less gone out of this market. The browntop forms a very fine, dense turf, tolerant of close mowing, while as a constituent of all turf mixtures it is a very valuable bottom grass.

It is, perhaps, interesting that in the parts of the United States where weather conditions are comparable with those in Britain, browntop bent *(Agrostis tenuis)* is not as popular as creeping bent *(Agrostis stolonifera)* of which there are many named varieties, almost all established vegetatively rather than from seed. There is, however, at least one reasonably satisfactory variety of creeping bent which in America is established from seed, this being known as 'Penncross'.

Other grasses From time to time other fine-leaved grasses such as hard fescue *(Festuca longifolia)* are used in lawn seed mixtures but their value is believed to be rather limited except possibly in relation to price.

A demand for grass seed mixtures suitable for shade conditions continues to exist despite the fact that there are really no suitable grasses for growing fine lawns under shade conditions.

Generally speaking the grasses growing on the non-shaded area of a lawn are fairly suitable for growing under the shade if the height of cut is increased. There are no grasses which both tolerate mowing and really thrive under shade conditions.

Grasses for the garden
Apart from the various utilitarian species of grasses used for lawns (see Grass seed for lawns), there are quite a number of grasses grown purely for ornament. Some are annuals, others are perennials and some, the bamboos, are woody-stemmed. Not all are hardy; some need greenhouse treatment or, at best, may be grown outdoors as half-hardy annuals during the summer months. The height range is wide; some bamboos reach nearly 6m (20ft), while one or two dwarf grasses seldom exceed 16cm (6in). Few are grown purely for their flowers, although the pampas grass, *Cortaderia selloana,* is grown as much for its feathery plumes of flowers in late summer as for its foliage effect. In the main the ornamental grasses are foliage plants, often variegated, sometimes bluish-green in colour.

They are, in general, easy plants, not at all fussy about soil. A few are inclined to ramp and should be planted with care, but if the right place can be found for them, where they can be allowed to spread at will, they will make handsome features for much of the year. Otherwise, they are reasonably easy to control with the spade. One such vigorous plant, *Phalaris arundinacea picta,* is known familiarly to gardeners as ribbon grass, lady's garters or gardener's garters. Its leaves, prettily striped with white, are about 1m (3ft) long and a few plants set out about 30cm (1ft) apart will quickly make a large clump.

Another grass which grows even more rapidly is *Glyceria aquatica variegata.* Fortunately this needs a very moist soil and it is often in boggy places that something is needed with precisely this habit, to cover the ground rapidly. It will, in fact, do best in shallow water by the side of a pond or where a pond overflows to keep the soil continually moist. Provided the space is not wanted for other decorative bog plants, the glyceria can be left to its own devices. But it is unwise to plant it near less robust plants as they will be overwhelmed in time. The main attraction, again, lies in the sword-like leaves which are striped with white, but in spring and again in autumn, this variegation is partially concealed beneath the delicate pink or pinkish-bronze flush. The typically grassy flower-heads which rise on spikes above the leaves in summer are brown.

Another white-striped grass is *Miscanthus sinensis,* a plant which older gardeners will recall as *Eulalia japonica.* This is an impressive plant for an isolated bed in a lawn or as a background to a border as its graceful blue-green leaves are 1.6m (5ft) or so long, with whitish midribs. The variety *variegatus* is less tall and the midrib stripe is whiter. Other good forms of this Asiatic grass are *gracillimus,* in which the leaves are more slender and arching in habit and lack the central stripe, and, perhaps the most attractive, *zebrinus,* in which the 1.5-2m (5-6ft) long, 1 cm (½in) wide leaves are transversely banded with yellow. Even taller than these is *M. sacchariflorus,* from Japan, in which the leaves may, in good soil and sheltered position, reach 2.5-3m (7-8ft). There is an attractive form of this, *aureus,* in which the leaves have a central gold stripe.

There may not always be room in the garden for a clump of such a tall grass as this, but such considerations of space hardly arise with the pretty form of the native meadow foxtail grass, dignified with the long name, *Alopecurus pratensis foliis variegatis.* This is a tuft-forming grass, its narrow leaves, little more than a foot tall, striped with yellow. This grass is sometimes used for bedding purposes and two more which may be used in the same way are *Molinia coerulea variegata,* about 37cm (15in) tall, with very narrow, white-striped leaves, and the even dwarfer *Holcus mollis variegatus,* another tufted grass, its leaves variegated with silver.

In complete contrast with these dwarf grasses, is *Arundo donax,* the Provence reed, which, when well grown, may tower to 3-4m (10-12ft) or more. The best forms of this are *macrophylla,* with larger leaves, nearly 5cm (2in) wide, blue-green in colour, and *variegata,* in

which the leaves are variegated with silvery-white stripes, although the latter form is not as hardy as *A. donax* itself which, in any case, should be given some form of winter protection. The less tall *A. conspicua,* from New Zealand, which bears 0.6m (2ft) long panicles of silky flowers, which open pinkish, then turn white, late in summer, also needs a little protection in winter. This is a plant which should be given a fair amount of room, and for this reason it is often grown as a lawn specimen.

There are a number of hardy annual grasses, all easily raised from seed sown in spring outdoors, in the same way as other hardy annuals. Some are more decorative than others, and some are of more interest to the flower arranger who needs material of this habit and texture, than to the gardener at large. They include such grasses as *Avena sterilis,* known as animated oats, about 1m (3ft) tall, and *Agrostis pulchella,* one or two *Bromus* species, the little quaking grass, *Briza minor, Hordeum jubatum,* the squirrel-tailed grass, *Lagurus ovatus,* the hare's tail grass, and *Panicum capillare,* all in the height range of 30-46cm (1-1½ft).

Another hardy annual, often grown for the sake of its large hard, grey seed receptacles, is the 0.6-1m (2-3ft) tall *Coix lacryma-jobi,* known as Job's tears. The receptacles are hard enough to be used as beads.

Less hardy are *Pennisetum caudatum* and *P. longistylum,* both about 0.6-1m (2-3ft) tall and both graceful grasses with large feathery flower-heads. *P. ruppellii* is somewhat taller and equally graceful. All should be treated as half-hardy annuals and sown under glass in March or April or outdoors in May.

But the most ornamental of these tender grasses are the maize or Indian corn varieties, all forms of *Zea mays. Z. m. japonica quadricolor* is the most spectacular of these as it reaches 1.6m (5ft) and its leaves are prettily striped with white, yellow and rose on the normal green. Other handsome varieties are *Z. m. gracillima variegata,* about 1m (3ft), and *Z. m. japonica,* about 1.3m (4ft) both striped with white and both useful as pot plants for the cold greenhouse or conservatory, or outdoors in summer bedding schemes to give height and sub-tropical effect.

The woody-stemmed grasses, the bamboos, possibly because they were overplanted years ago, have to some extent been neglected in recent years. Some, such as *Arundinaria anceps,* which may reach 4m (12ft) or more and *Semiarundinaria fastuosa,* which frequently

1 *Miscanthus sinensis variegata, or Eulalia, has green and white leaves.*
2 *Lagurus ovatus, hare's tail grass, a native, is about 30cm (1ft) high.*
3 *Cortaderia or pampas grass is a large grass with decorative plumes.*

reaches 6m (20ft), are both too tall and too vigorous for small gardens, although they are excellent in the right places, in moist soils and positions sheltered from wind, where there is ample space for them to spread as they will do by underground stems. But the bamboos, on the whole, are graceful plants and a clump of the right kind makes a pleasant feature in the smaller garden. Two such species are *Sasa chrysantha,* about 2m (6ft) tall, its leaves yellow striped, and *Semiarundinaria (Arundinaria) nitida,* sometimes a little taller than this, with slender purplish canes. These are excellent for limited areas by the water-side or in moist but not water-logged woodland soil.

Gravel

The name given to rounded, water-worn stones produced by rock attrition by moving water. Extensive beds have formed on many parts of our coastline, notably Norfolk and the English Channel. River gravels generally form in the upper reaches and in the middle of the stream. Both kinds consist of hard types of stone, flint, granite and sandstone, the colour of the gravel being governed by the rocks from which it is formed.

The sizes of the individual stones vary and from gravel beds the stones are graded and can be purchased as such. Frequently sold as ballast, the best size is a grading from 19-5mm ($\frac{3}{4}$–$\frac{3}{16}$ in). When gravel alone is used to surface paths it is loose and unstable, noisy and sticks to the shoes in wet weather. For this purpose it should be mixed with enough sand to allow it to bind together to form a firm, smooth surface (see also Paths in the garden).

The main use to which the gardener puts gravel is to cover the surfaces of greenhouse staging, and to fill gravel trays in which to stand pot plants. The advantages of using such an aggregate are the provision of non-absorbent material, dust free, weed free and of good appearance. It can be sprayed over in the process of damping down and the water evaporates from such a surface.

The gardener uses slightly coarser gravel as an aggregate in the ring culture of tomatoes, for growing such plants as water cress in suitable troughs and for stabilizing plants during soilless culture or hydroponics. Similarly bulbs can be forced indoors supported only by gravel as a medium and the water level maintained so that the stones are just covered. Narcissus 'Paper White' succeeds happily in this way indoors.

Greasebanding

This operation is used against wingless insects particularly the wingless females of the winter moths, the mottled umber and the March moths.

The moths emerge from the chrysalis in the soil and have to climb up the tree trunks to lay eggs on the spurs. Ornamental trees such as crabs and cherries are attacked, as well as fruit trees.

A sticky substance is applied in a

1 Gravel is used to surface the greenhouse staging.
2 A paper band is tied firmly to the trunk of the tree in autumn.
3 Grease is smeared on the paper to provide a sticky surface to trap insects.
4 The band may need to be replaced in January or February.

band about 10cm (4in) wide and not less than 46cm (8in) above the ground (to avoid blown leaves and mud splashes forming a bridge over the trap).

The grease can be applied direct to the tree trunk if it is a vegetable grease. If preferred, it can be smeared on a paper band which is then tied on the tree, or bands can be bought ready-made. The grease is applied in September and renewed if necessary in February.

Greasebanding is effective only against species in which the female is wingless, so this process alone is not sufficient to control all caterpillar pests.

Greenhouse gardening see Growing under glass

Ground cover plants

Gardening has been described as 'interfering with nature', because in our gardens we try to make plants grow where they do not normally thrive and remove all those plants which distribute themselves naturally. In the wild state each plant grows in positions best adapted to it, and there, together with its neighbours, it covers the ground with a mantle of greenery; this prevents the evaporation of moisture from the soil, ensures a constant deposit of decaying leaves which acts as a mulch and restores goodness to the soil, carried down by the worms and by rain.

Many of our most highly selected strains of flowers and vegetables grow best in isolated groups or rows, in soil that is cultivated. Even here a mulch of decaying matter will help greatly to foster health and prevent weeds. In a garden devoted to shrubs, perennial plants and bulbs, something more closely approaching nature can be attempted with a consequent quiet and gentle appearance and a lessening of cultivation; in fact digging and hoeing can be forgotten. In attempting this type of gardening, by which the largest area can be tended with the least labour, everything depends on cleaning the ground thoroughly first, and on the choice of plants. It is essential that all perennial creeping weeds be eradicated; it is wise in the first year to plant only the shrubs (and trees) so that the ground can be watched for a recurrence of weeds. Thereafter the ground-covering plants can be put in. Until they have grown and made a dense cover we can resort to covering the intervening spaces with a mulch of decaying vegetable matter—lawn mowings, garden compost, dead leaves, soft clippings, peat, wood or bark shavings, etc. (Fresh sawdust wood or bark shavings when placed on the ground are apt to absorb nitrogen from the soil during decomposition; this must be restored by applying sulphate of ammonia or Nitro-chalk.) Modern weed-killers can also be used temporarily.

The most economical use of garden space is by gardening in several layers: at the top are the scattered trees, lower in height are the shrubs, and covering the ground in sun or shade the prostrate shrubs and perennials, with bulbs spearing through them. Trees in gardens do not act as ground cover, but shrubs and plants wisely chosen will do so, permanently and effectively.

When selecting shrubs to act as their own ground cover the choice lies between several categories: (a) those which in maturity make wide, dome-shaped plants, retaining their branches down to the ground and doing their own ground cover; (b) suckering shrubs which create a thicket of stems; (c) rampant creepers; and (d) low spreading bushes. (The branches of most of these, where they touch the ground will root as they grow, thus ever-increasing their potential value.) Examples under these headings are:
(a) *Viburnum tomentosum mariesii; Choisya ternata; Siphonosmanthus dela vayi; Camellia japonica* 'Lady Clare'; *Hydrangea macrophylla* 'Blue Wave'; *Garrya elliptica.*
(b) *Gaultheria shallon; Rosa rugosa alba; Rubus odoratus, R. nutkanus (R. parviflorus); Xanthorriza apiifolia.*
(c) *Hydrangea petiolaris; Hedera helix hibernica; Euonymus radicans carrieri; Rosa wichuraiana* (the species); *R.* 'Max Graf'; *R. paulii; Vitis vitacea.*
(d) *Cotoneaster dammeri, C. conspicua decora; Potentilla arbuscula* 'Charles Musgrave'; *Erica carnea* 'Springwood'; *Juniperus,* various prostrate species and varieties; *Stephanandra incisa prostrata; Hebe subalpina.*

For large areas in public parks and similar places some rampant plants may be needed to plant under established trees or to cover areas while other shrubs and trees are growing; some examples are the hedera and the gaultheria mentioned in (b) above, neither of which are to be trusted in the average garden of today; others are *Hypericum calycinum, Vinca major* varieties, *Luzula maxima, Trachystemon orientale.* In wet ground *Lysichitum americanum* is ideal.

In designing a border to be almost self-supporting it is necessary to know the eventual shape and size of all the shrubs and plants to be included; the spaces between shrubs can be planted with quick-colonizing, low plants over which the shrubs will gradually grow

1 Euonymus radicans variegatus a trailer with prettily variegated leaves.
2 Epimediums are sub-shrubby plants suitable for ground cover purposes.
3 In front is the blue-flowered native bugle used with Geranium grandiflorum.
4 Here the golden leaves of Lysimachia nummularia aurea quickly spread over the surrounding paving stones.
5 Erica carnea, springwood pink.
6 In the front of this bed Ajuga reptans multicolor used as ground cover.

146

4

5

6

and suppress. But ground-covering plants bring not only the suppression of weeds and the conserving of moisture and fertility: they also are flowering plants in their own right, and contribute to the garden scene through the year, providing the lowly and diverse greenery that is needed to make effective contrast and texture to that of the shrubs. Even so, while they are mostly flowering plants, few of them flower for more than a few weeks and their foliage is, therefore, particularly valuable.

The perennials, evergreen (marked *) or deciduous fall into three categories: (a) those which spread freely by underground roots, (b) those which run freely on the surface, and (c) those which are clump forming, relying upon division for their increase. Examples:
(a) Convallaria majalis, Asperula odorata, Cerastium tomentosum;
(b) Vinca minor*, Stachys lanata, Tiarella cordifolia, Waldsteinia ternata*, Asarum europaeum*, Polygonum affine;
(c) Brunnera macrophylla, epimedium, Geranium macrorrhizum, G. renardii, G. ibericum platyphyllum, G. endressii, pulmonaria, tellima*, Stachys macrantha, Alchemilla mollis, Phlomis russelliana.

Yet another category is that of the tall but clump-forming perennials which cover a large area when established, e.g. Aruncus sylvester, Cynara cardunculus, hemerocallis, Verbascum vernale, paeonia and hosta.

Ferns are extremely useful in the shade; Dryopteris felix mas and various polystichums for dry shade, clump forming; thriving in moist ground and of strong colonizing habit are Onoclea sensibilis and Matteuccoa struthiopteris; for moisture and forming large clumps, Osmunda regalis; smaller ground cover is found in Polypodium vulgare for drier positions. Varieties of Hedera helix, the common ivy, are also good for shady banks, but take some years to create an impenetrable carpet. Luzula maxima is an ideal substitute for shady banks where grass mowing is difficult, and thrives best in cool, moist districts. The most difficult positions to cover are found under big trees such as elms, beeches and cedars. Few plants will grow under the first two; but Hedera helix hibernica usually succeeds if the tree branches are high. Under cedars and other trees Cyclamen neapolitanum will establish itself, particularly on on limey soils; an annual which will thrive in the same conditions is Oxalis rosea. For almost any position in sun or shade, on chalk or light or heavy soils, Hypericaum calycinum will be successful, while for really small borders many of

1 Lamium galeobdolon variegatum spreads rapidly, even in shade.
2 The pink-flowered Polygonum vaccinifolium makes large mats.
3 The greater periwinkle, Vinca major.
4 Rose of Sharon, Hypericum calycinum.

the mat-forming rock plants are without peer, such as *Dryas sundermannii*, antennaria, acaena, cotula, ajuga, 'mossy' saxifrages, *Hypericum rhodopaeum*, and many of these are suitable as anti-splash plants for small bulbs.

Growing under glass
Greenhouse gardening

Few gardeners do not at some time or another have an urge to grow plants in a greenhouse. It extends the range of plants that can be grown so that those too tender for our winter climate can be cultivated and it is a branch of gardening that can be enjoyed whatever the weather.

Before purchasing a greenhouse you should decide what plants you wish to grow and choose a design which is suitable for them. For instance, if you wish to grow mainly tomatoes in the summer and lettuce in the winter you could well choose a greenhouse glazed almost to the ground as both these crops need maximum light and they benefit from the extra glazing. If you are mainly interested in growing pot plants the greenhouse could have partly glazed side walls, the lower half being of wood or brick with staging for the plants level with the side walls. It is also possible to have a greenhouse glazed to the ground on one side and with a low wall on the other side to enable plants to be grown in a border on the glazed side and pot plants on the staging on the other side.

Heating Before a heating system is installed you should give careful thought not only to its initial cost but also to how much it will cost each year to maintain the desired minimum winter temperature. As a rough guide, to heat a greenhouse to a minimum temperature of 50°F (10°C) will cost twice as much as one heated to 45°F (7°C); three times as much for a temperature of 55°F (13°C) and four times as much for a temperature of 60°F (16°C).

Management In a greenhouse you are able to control the 'climate' to a great extent and provide the most desirable conditions for the type of plants being grown. You do this by providing a suitable temperature, ventilation, moisture and shade as and when required.

Without a heating system a greenhouse can be difficult to manage, particularly in the winter. Damp, stuffy conditions must be avoided when temperatures are low and the roof ventilators should be opened whenever possible. Watering should be done very sparingly and it is better to keep the soil slightly dry rather than wet.

A heating system is of value not only in maintaining the desired temperatures

1 A well-stocked greenhouse using various electrical aids.
2 One of the many forms of Camellia japonica.

but also in preventing excessively damp conditions from developing, particularly when the weather is very damp. For instance, in early autumn, when the air is often very damp at night, a little heat with some roof ventilation will help to overcome the dampness.

In hot weather in the summer the situation is reversed. To prevent temperatures rising too high inside the greenhouse the ventilators should be opened fully and some shade given with blinds or a special distemper applied to the outside of the greenhouse. In addition, water is sprayed on the floors and stagings to create a humid atmosphere around the plants—hot and dry conditions encourage red spider mites and plants lose moisture too rapidly. Watering should be done freely, particularly with plants that have well filled their pots with roots.

Soil composts To grow plants well they need good soil. This is not simply ordinary soil from the garden; it should consist of a mixture of fibrous soil—preferably obtained from decaying turves—moist granulated peat and coarse sand with fertilizers added. The John Innes Seed and Potting Composts have been scientifically devized for the cultivation of plants under glass and, made up strictly according to the formulae, they give very good results. Soilless composts are being used more extensively these days since they do away with the need for sterilizing the loam and their value does not depend upon the quality of the loam as does the value of soil composts.

Hygiene Pests and diseases spread very rapidly in the warmth of a greenhouse and a careful watch should be kept for the first signs of their presence. Fortu-

1 Melons are among the fruits that may be grown in a greenhouse even without artificial heat. 2 Tomatoes ripening in an unheated greenhouse.

nately many can be controlled effectively by using · insecticidal or fungicidal smokes and sprays.

Growing plants in the same border of soil year after year brings problems, and root diseases can set in. Sterilizing the soil with steam is effective in combating these disorders but, in a small greenhouse, steaming a large quantity of soil is hardly practical. One way out of the problem is to grow tomatoes, for example, on the ring culture system. The plants are grown in bottomless pots stood on a base of coarse weathered ashes.

Seedlings are very vulnerable to soilborne diseases and for seed and potting composts it is well worthwhile sterilizing the soil before mixing the other ingredients of the compost. Should diseases, such as damping-off, appear among seedlings, Cheshunt Compound will help to arrest the disease. Having done all one can to provide 'clean' potting soil, pots and boxes should also be washed whenever possible and dipped in a good disinfectant. This also applies to the interior of the greenhouse. Once a year all the wood and glass should be scrubbed down with disinfectant. The outside of the greenhouse should also be washed, particularly in industrial areas, as soot and grime can exclude light.

Unheated greenhouses What can be grown in a greenhouse depends on the minimum temperature that can be maintained in the winter. A great deal of interest can, however, be had from a greenhouse with no heating equipment

and if you are working to a small budget an arrangement of this sort is a good beginning; heating equipment can be installed later on as you become more experienced and wish to experiment with a wider range of plants.

An attractive display can be had in an unheated greenhouse by growing mainly hardy plants in pots. These will flower a little earlier than those in the open but the flowers will not be spoilt by inclement weather. Other plants that are usually started into growth early in warmth for summer flowering, can also be grown by starting them later when outside temperatures are higher.

Shrubs The camellia is often thought to be tender, possibly because the flowers, which appear early in the year, are sometimes damaged by frost. For this reason the protection of a greenhouse is valuable. All the varieties of *Camellia japonica* will grow happily in pots of lime-free soil, but they should not be cossetted as if they were hot house plants. *Prunus triloba flore pleno* has double pink flowers and is another fine flowering shrub for the cold greenhouse. The yellow-flowered forsythia and rosy-purple *Rhododendron praecox*, lilacs as well as winter-flowering heathers (*Erica carnea*) will all give a bright display. For flowering in the summer *Hydrangea paniculata grandiflora* produces enormous white flower trusses. It is easily grown in pots and the stems should be cut back severely each spring. The 'hortensia' hydrangeas will flower earlier than the species mentioned above and really good blue flowers can be had if the soil is treated with a blueing powder.

Bulbs These can provide a wonderful display in the year. The earliest to flower are 'prepared' daffodils in January followed by 'Paper White' narcissi, the dark blue *Iris reticulata* and named varieties of snowdrop. Other small bulbs well worth growing are miniature daffodils, such as *Narcissus cyclamineus, N. bulbocodium* and *N. triandrus albus,* winter-flowering crocuses and *Eranthis hyemalis,* the winter aconite with buttercup-yellow flowers.

For flowering in the summer, lilies such as *L. auratum* and *L. speciosum* look superb grown in pots. Gloxinias and tuberous-rooted begonias are popular plants and the tubers of these can be started into growth in early April.

Other flowers for a spring display, which can be purchased or lifted from the open garden in the autumn and potted up for the cold greenhouse, are wallflowers, dicentras, astilbes, forget-me-nots, polyanthus, lily-of-the-valley and Christmas roses (*Helleborus niger*).
Fruit and vegetables Even in a cold greenhouse, grapes will succeed but it is important to choose suitable varieties such as 'Black Hamburgh' or 'Foster's Seedling'. The vines can be grown in large pots or tubs with the stems trained up a supporting framework, or they can be planted permanently in a border of good soil.

To have tomatoes fruiting under glass in June the seed has to be sown soon after Christmas in a hot house. They can also be grown in an unheated greenhouse but fruit will not be ripe until late summer. Young plants can be purchased for setting out in a border at the end of April.

There is no reason why melons and cucumbers should not be grown in a greenhouse without artificial heat. As with tomatoes, early fruits cannot be expected but all the same they taste much better when picked fresh from one's own garden.

Peach trees can be grown in the open garden but they flower early in the year and their blossoms are likely to be damaged by spring frosts. Given the protection of a greenhouse this hazard can be avoided. Peaches make luxuriant growth and they can easily 'swamp' a greenhouse. For this reason they should be grown as fan-trained trees with all the stems neatly trained out up the roof or against one end of the greenhouse. Good varieties for a cold greenhouse are 'Peregrine' and 'Duke of York'.

Where there is a vacant border of soil in an unheated greenhouse during the winter, lettuce can be grown. Seed may be sown in October, and will produce seedlings ready for planting in November or December, and they should be fit for cutting in April and May.

It must not be thought that all these flowers, fruits and vegetables can be grown together in a small greenhouse. If you prefer flowers it is best to grow little else although a vine or a peach tree could be grown with them. Tomatoes do not like heavy shade and so it would

1 *'Bellegarde' is one of a number of varieties of peach which do well in a greenhouse with slight heat.*
2 *Grape 'Black Hamburgh' is a popular variety for the greenhouse.*

be unwise to have a vine, which produces a heavy coverage of foliage in the summer, with them. Cucumbers and tomatoes should also be kept separate for the best results. Tomatoes like plenty of light and air in hot weather, whereas cucumbers like tropical conditions—heavy shade, high temperatures and high humidity.
Cool greenhouses Although great interest can be had from an unheated greenhouse a wider range of plants can be grown and earlier fruit and vegetables can be had if the greenhouse has a minimum winter temperature of 50°F (10°C). With the aid of artificial heat it is also easier to maintain a good growing atmosphere or climate for the plants.
Shrubs As in the cold greenhouse, hardy shrubs such as forsythia and *Prunus triloba* can be brought into the greenhouse in winter for flowering much earlier than those in the open. Camellias will thrive, provided the temperature is not allowed to shoot up too high in the day—this causes the flower buds to drop—and hydrangeas in pots can be made to flower early. Indian azaleas are popular florists' pot plants. These can be kept from year to year in a heated greenhouse, provided they are fed regularly. They flower in winter and early spring and can be put outside for the summer. *Acacia dealbata,* or mimosa, with yellow fluffy flowers and a heady scent can be enjoyed in early spring. There are also a great many ornamental

climbers that will enjoy the warmth. The passion flowers, the brightly coloured bougainvilleas, the soft blue *Plumbago capensis* and *Lapageria rosea* with rose pink, waxy bells, all flower in summer.
Bulbs All the popular bulbs such as daffodils, hyacinths and tulips, can be made to flower in the dark days of winter in a heated greenhouse, but after the pots and bowls they should be given cool conditions at first and gradually acclimatized to warmer conditions.

Hippeastrums, often mistakenly called amaryllis, have large, handsome flowers and the bulbs may be started into growth in February for spring flowering. Freesia corms, started into growth in

August, produce their colourful and scented flowers in February and March; they will grow well in a minimum temperature of 40°F (4°C).

Arum lilies are not true bulbs—they have tuberous roots—but in a heated greenhouse they will flower in the spring. An easily grown and handsome bulb is the Scarborough Lily, *Vallota speciosa*. It can be stood outside for the summer and in August it will produce its vermilion trumpet flowers on stout stems. Flowering a little later, rerines have delightful, glistening flowers in pink, red and white; they differ from many bulbs in that they need to be rested and kept dry in the summer.

Begonia and gloxinia tubers may be started into growth in March for flowering in the summer. Achimenes can be treated similarly, grown in pots or in hanging baskets.

Other flowers that will flourish in a greenhouse with a temperature of 50°F (10°C) in winter are perpetual-flowering carnations—they like light and airy conditions and will flower for most of the year; chrysanthemums for autumn and winter flowering; and fuchsias for the summer.

Pot plants that can be raised from seed in spring and early summer for a display in winter and spring are: *Primula obconica, P. malacoides* and calceolarias. Some gardeners, unfortunately, are allergic to *P. obconica* and if they handle plants it sets up an unpleasant skin irritation.

Cyclamen can be grown successfully from seed sown in August, to provide

1 Tapping a pot to see whether it requires watering.
2 Hot air is blown through plastic tubes to warm the greenhouse.

plants for flowering 16 months later. The poor man's orchid, schizanthus, is also easily raised from seed in August for flowering the following spring.

Regal pelargoniums are becoming more popular and they are useful for their handsome flowers borne from June onwards; these are best propagated from cuttings taken in late summer.

Fruit and vegetables Cucumbers and melons need a temperature no lower than 60°F (16°C) to grow well and it is not wise to make sowings before April. Tomatoes also need a temperature of 60°F (16°C) for a germination and seed should not be sown before early April in the cool greenhouse.

Peaches and nectarines can be started into growth early with a little artificial heat but it is important to remember that the trees are given a rest in cool conditions in the winter. Suitable varieties are: peaches—'Early Rivers', 'Royal George' and 'Hales's Early'; nectarines—'River's Orange' and 'Early Rivers'.

In a moderately heated greenhouse grape vines can be started into growth early and a little heat in early autumn helps to complete the ripening of the grapes. Suitable varieties are 'Black Hamburgh', 'Foster's Seedling' and 'Madresfield Court'.

Given good light, lettuce is a useful

winter crop in a moderately heated greenhouse. From a sowing in mid-October the seedlings are pricked out in boxes and planted in prepared beds in November; the lettuce should be ready for cutting in February. A suitable variety is 'Cheshunt Early Giant'.

In addition to those already mentioned, other vegetables and salad crops well worth growing in a cool greenhouse are mustard and cress, radishes and aubergines. Rhubarb and seakale can also be forced under the greenhouse staging in complete darkness.

Warm greenhouses To be able to heat a greenhouse to a minimum temperature of 55°F (13°C) on the coldest night in winter is an expensive undertaking but it is also rewarding. A great many fascinating tropical or 'stove' plants can be cultivated in addition to those already mentioned.

Shrubs Among the shrubby plants with handsome foliage for a warm greenhouse, most of which are rarely seen, codiaeums (crotons) are outstanding. They have leaves of various shades, brightly marked with green, red, yellow and orange. Dracaenas also have attractively coloured leaves and they include *D. godseffiana* with green, white-spotted leaves and *D. fragrans victoriae* with long green and yellow striped leaves.

The poinsettia, *Euphorbia pulcherrima*, a popular plant at Christmas time with red rosettes of bracts, needs a warm greenhouse to grow well and so does its close relative *E. fulgens*, which has small orange-red flowers on arching stems in winter.

Gardenias, which are prized for their pure white fragrant flowers, do best in a warm greenhouse. Less commonly seen is *Brunfelsia calycina,* an evergreen shrub with purple flowers.

For training up the greenhouse roof there are numerous exotic climbers. The Madagascar jasmine, *Stephanotis floribunda,* has thick leathery leaves and clusters of white scented flowers. There are also several clerodendrums with colourful flowers; *C. thompsoniae* has crimson and white flowers and *C. splendens* produces clusters of red flowers.

Bulbs Begonias, gloxinias, hippeastrums and smithianthas can all be started into growth in January or early February; seed of begonias and gloxinias can also be sown in January. Apart from these popular types, *Eucharis grandiflora* with beautiful, white and fragrant flowers will revel in a warm greenhouse. The tuberose, *Polianthus tuberosa,* is another bulbous plant well worth cultivating for its white, fragrant flowers. Caladiums have tuberous roots and they are grown for their handsome foliage. The tubers can be started into growth after resting in the winter.

Other plants that enjoy a warm greenhouse include coleus and *Begonia rex,* both of which have highly ornamental foliage. Winter-flowering begonias, provide a wonderful display of colour in white, pink and red. Saintpaulias, so popular as room plants, do best in a well-heated greenhouse.

Fruit and vegetables Most of the kinds already mentioned can be grown in a warm greenhouse. Cucumbers and melons enjoy high temperatures and a humid atmosphere. Peaches and nectarines do not require high temperatures and the same applies to vines, although that very fine grape, 'Muscat of Alexandra', a tricky variety to grow, enjoys warmer conditions, particularly at flowering time and when the berries are ripening. Strawberries, put in pots in late summer will produce early fruit if they are gradually introduced into warmer conditions in February. 'Royal Sovereign' is a good variety for forcing. Figs are not often grown under glass but they can be cultivated in pots and, gradually given warmth in January and February, will produce ripe figs in late spring.

Heating methods

With so many different forms of heating appliance available, it is often a little difficult for the amateur to make an easy selection or decision. The three main types of heating are electricity, solid fuel and oil. Each has its own particular merits and drawbacks. The final decision as to the best type to use can be simplified if certain points are

carefully considered. The first must be the amount of money which is available, not only for the initial purchase but the running of the apparatus afterwards.

Oil The cheapest to purchase and maintain is the paraffin oil burner. Many different types are available, from the very small model which could be used for heating a frame, to the large types which are quite capable of keeping the temperature inside big greenhouses (6m by 3m [20ft by 10ft]) well above freezing point. Whilst there are some very good models available, there are some which are very cheap and poorly made. It is very important that the purchase of an oil heater is made only from a specialist firm who use good quality metal and provide a suitable burner or wick. The best type of heater incorporates a blue-flame burner which, if properly trimmed and used with a high grade oil, should burn without causing fume damage to plants inside the greenhouse. There is a range of excellent heaters manufactured from solid, hand-rolled copper. These should provide many years of faithful service and will not corrode.

The correct burning of an oil heater depends on the amount of oxygen it receives. If a greenhouse is completely shut down it is quite possible that the burners will not receive sufficient air and consequently may produce fumes. A very small amount of air can be supplied if a ventilator is opened not more than 1cm ($\frac{1}{2}$in) on the sheltered side of the greenhouse. It is also necessary to keep the wick trimmed regularly and a high-grade oil used.

The positioning of the heater is important if the greatest benefit is to be gained. In a small house the heater can be placed at the far gable end, away from the door and on the central path. It is essential that the heater is placed

on a level foundation so that the wick receives a regular amount of oil and also that the fuel gauge indicates accurately.

In a larger house it will be necessary to place the heater in the centre of the greenhouse and on the pathway. To maintain higher temperatures in the larger houses two heaters may have to be used, placing one a little way away from the plain gable end and the second one about halfway along the path. Avoid at all costs a direct draught to a heater as this could cause the flames to flare and set the apparatus on fire.

Oil heaters demand regular attention to filling, wick trimming and adjusting. A heater should be checked about 20 minutes after it has been lit, as it is quite possible that the flames will have increased a little from the first setting and it will be necessary to readjust their height.

Oil heaters are invaluable in the garden shed where they will give frost protection to tubers (eg dahlias or potatoes), which have been placed there for winter storage. They also add considerably to your comfort when you are busy in the potting shed during the cold, early part of the season.

It is now possible to provide a measure of automation to oil heaters by feeding fuel from a large drum by gravity to the heater's supply tank via a length of pipe. The large drum can be placed outside the greenhouse and the feed pipe taken inside.

Solid fuel This is a very popular system of heating a greenhouse: it provides the maximum amount of heat for a low consumption of fuel. Like the paraffin heater, however, it is necessary to attend to it regularly. Great advances have been made with designs and many labour-saving gadgets have been introduced.

A Camplex thermostatically controlled glasshouse fan heater

Although solid fuel boilers require stoking and cleaning, some of the latest are designed to burn unattended for 14 hours or more. Their fuel consumption, too, is surprisingly economical for the amount of heat generated. For a temperature of about 50°F (10°C) in an 3m by 2m (8ft by 6ft) greenhouse only 25kg (½cwt) of fuel is required weekly. Built-in thermostats considerably improve the performance of solid fuel boilers.

Smokeless zone restrictions do not affect the modern greenhouse solid fuel boilers as they can burn most of the recognized smokeless fuels. One problem that arises with these boilers is that of fuel storage. In large gardens it may be possible to allocate an area conveniently close to the boiler for a fuel dump. This enables you to buy in all the fuel you require for the winter period, often at reduced summer prices. The problem of room in the smaller gardens might be troublesome and you may have to have a standing order for fuel so that you receive small amounts regularly.

The maintenance of solid fuel equipment is very easy as there are few parts which are liable to cause trouble or wear out. Everything about these systems is robust and the thermostatic controls are very strongly constructed and extremely simple. Pipes are made from steel or high duty aluminium. The pipe joints are easy to connect by means of special expansion joints which are simply bolted tight when in position. Pipes are usually fastened to the walls or sides of the greenhouse by means of special holders. In this way they occupy the minimum amount of room.

Electricity Electrical heating scores heavily over other systems if complete automation is required. It is, however, one of the most expensive methods to install and run.

Before any form of electric heating can be installed it is necessary to bring the supply of electricity to the greenhouse site. This can be costly if the greenhouse is situated some way away from the source of supply. When siting a new greenhouse it is important to bear this point in mind. There are two ways in which the supply can be brought to the greenhouse; by underground cable or overhead. The former is the best method as the cable is unobtrusive and safely out of harm's way. Underground cable is specially protected against mechanical and chemical damage. It is expensive and should be installed where it cannot be damaged by garden tools. Usually the cable is buried beneath the lawn or close by a path. In certain districts it is permissible to take the mains cable overhead or against a wall, but you must seek the advice of the local electricity authority beforehand.

Where maximum internal working room is important, tubular electrical heaters are ideal as they are fastened to the sides of the greenhouse. Banks of tubes can be quickly installed to maintain any desired temperature. Usually a hand-operated or preferably a rod-type thermostat should be wired to these heaters to ensure automatic and economic running.

Fan heaters can be moved around and are extremely efficient in that they blow warmed air to all parts of the greenhouse. This system ensures that there are no cold corners in the greenhouse. During the summer months the heating elements can be switched off and the fan used for air circulation only. Most fan heaters have a thermostat built in and although not as sensitive as the rod type they ensure reasonable running costs. A fan heater should be placed near the door and at least 0·6m (2ft) away from the side or other obstructions. If there is the possibility of drips of water from the staging, the heater must be placed away from it. In a small greenhouse this type of heater may take up valuable working room, although it could be placed to one side while work is carried out. It is also necessary to make quite sure that there are no plants in the direct line of the hot air.

Convector heaters draw air in at the base, warm it and send it out hot at the top. They take a little longer to heat up the greenhouse as their warmth is concentrated just round the unit. This heater should be situated at one end of the house if it is a small one, or towards the centre of the larger ones.

A great deal of expense can be saved if small areas of the greenhouse can be heated. This can be accomplished in several ways, one of which is to partition part of the greenhouse and install heating in it. This section can be used as an intensive propagation section. If a small cabinet is made, air heating cables can be installed. These are specially designed and can be connected to a thermostat to provide automatic running.

Electric propagators are available in many sizes and these, too, are an ideal form of confined heating. Usually these propagators are made from easily cleaned fibreglass and the heating is supplied by a length of heating cable which in turn is connected to a control box and thermostat. High temperatures of 65–80°F (18–27°C) can be maintained easily and economically.

References have been made in this article to thermostats. The inexpensive types are suitable for loads from 1200 to 2000 watts. They can be regulated to control temperatures between 35 and 75°F (2–24°C). These are hand operated models and are usually accurate to within 4–6°F. The rod types are more expensive but very much more accurate. Usually there is only a differential of 1°F. These models are capable of controlling loads up to 4000 watts. The temperature range is usually wider, 30–90°F. A thermostat must be used with any form of electric heating so that the equipment can be left unattended and running costs kept to a minimum.

With the advent of central heating it is possible for the gardener to make use of the domestic supply if a lean-to greenhouse is purchased. The greenhouse can be placed against a warm sunny wall of the house and a radiator or two can be taken into the greenhouse from the domestic supply. It will be necessary to damp down the greenhouse floor frequently if the floor of the greenhouse is concrete. Central heating is a dry type of heat and a humid atmosphere must be provided to ensure a good growing condition for the contents. The garden frame is less effective than the greenhouse, but it can still be most useful and occupies less space and is considerably less expensive both to buy in the first place and to run.

Frames

The protection which frames afford seeds and plants can be put to good use in several ways. A frame can be a safe harbour for tender plants during the wetter and colder winter months. Such shelter encourages quicker and earlier growth enabling the gardener to force certain crops out of season. Plants raised in the warmth of a greenhouse and intended for outdoor planting need to be inured gradually to more robust conditions and must, therefore, spend a little time in a frame where, by gradually admitting more air, cooler conditions obtain. This process is known as hardening off.

Heating frames Frames are usually unheated but with the advent of safe electric warming cables it is quite easy to convert an unheated frame. The use of warmth in this way extends the versatility of the frame considerably and converts it into a miniature greenhouse.

Propagating frames Another type of frame is the propagating model which is much smaller than the outdoor ones and is intended for use in the greenhouse on the staging. Most of the modern ones are manufactured from fibreglass and are compact in shape and attractive in appearance. To provide the essential germinating temperature, heat is supplied in the form of bottom heat. Special electric cables are used which are placed in a sand base. The more expensive models are equipped with sensitive rod thermostats which can be set to a wide range of temperatures. This ensures accurate, labour-saving use. Two or three sheets of glass are provided so that the top of the propagator can be covered. When necessary, the glass sheets can be opened to provide ventilation.

The site for the frame It is very important to place the frame in the best possible position for good plant growth. Ideally, a frame should face south, but if this is not

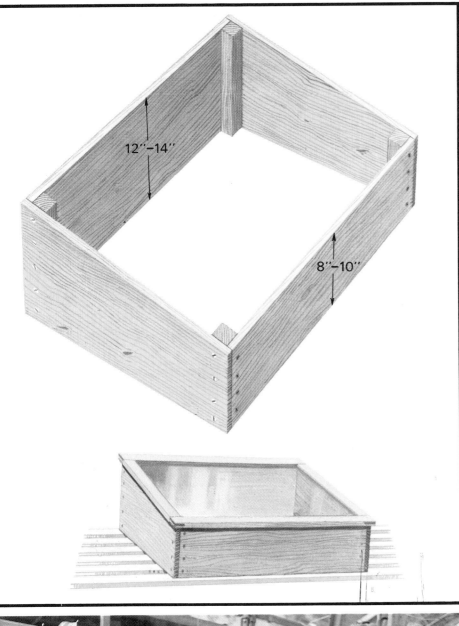

1 A wooden garden frame is a simple structure for the amateur carpenter to make. A single sheet of glass allows the maximum light to get to the plants.
2 A Humex electrically controlled propagating frame, inside a greenhouse.
3 After pricking out, seedlings are protected by a frame.
4 Cuttings of several varieties of erica being rooted in a metal frame.

12″–14″

8″–10″

3

4

155

A frame of galvanized steel affords maximum light. It can be portable.

possible it must be situated where it is sheltered from cold prevailing winds and where it will receive the maximum amount of sunlight. A frame is an important adjunct to the greenhouse where it is used as a place to harden off plants which have been raised under glass. Used in this way, the frame should be placed as close as possible to the greenhouse so that the plants need not be carried far.

The frame should be positioned on well-drained ground, never where water tends to lie. If it is to be used without a greenhouse and is to be heated, it is advisable to site it close to the electricity supply to minimize installation costs. Many of the modern frame designs are attractive and do not look unsightly placed close to the dwelling house.

The soil and site for the frame need careful preparation. The area should be excavated to about 30–40cm (12–16in) deep and a 7–10cm (3–4in) layer of small rubble and weathered cinders incorporated. If the sub-soil is heavy, it should be broken up well beforehand with a fork. The remainder of the site should be re-filled with a specially prepared compost. The various John Innes formulae are the best and can be made up at home or purchased ready mixed. The formula to be used will depend on whether the frame is required for seed raising or for the cultivation of plants to maturity. In a small frame it is a good idea to use seed boxes, pots or pans for the seed raising and to grow plants to maturity directly in the prepared frame.

Frame gardening It is surprising what can be done in a frame with a little preliminary planning. It is excellent as a propagator for a large number of seedlings and cuttings. Seeds can be sown thinly broadcast in the frame soil, in neat rows, or in pots or boxes placed inside the frame. The time to start must depend on whether the frame is heated or not. If the frame is heated work can

begin as early as mid-February; in an unheated frame it is better to delay until about mid to late March.

The hardy and particularly the half-hardy annuals are ideal for frame sowings, to produce sturdy plants for planting out in the late spring and early summer. The following are worth a trial: salvias, nemesias, China aster, antirrhinums, stocks, lobelias, petunias and *Phlox drummondii*. Late spring sowings may be made of perennials; polyanthus and delphiniums are especially good for this purpose. Polyanthus sown in March and delphiniums sown in May, potted on into 7–10cm (3–4in) pots make fine, sturdy plants for planting out into their flowering quarters in the autumn.

Cuttings can be raised in a frame to provide a wide variety of flowers. Good examples are chrysanthemums and dahlias. Chrysanthemum cuttings will be available from February until late April, depending on whether the frame is heated or not. Dahlia tubers boxed up in late March will also produce abundant cuttings. Protection from frost is necessary and a heated frame is better for this type of work.

The simplest possible way to aid and protect plants is to use cloches, in effect a kind of movable, unheated frame which is available in various shapes and materials, but is normally tent-like and made of glass or clear plastic.

Cloche gardening
Cloches are designed to give protection and this feature can be made use of in several ways. During wet or cold weather the soil can be covered with cloches and kept dry and warm. This enables the gardener to sow or plant much earlier than usual. Protection from cold winds and low temperatures encourages earlier and quicker growth and many plants can be started several weeks earlier than normally. In the colder northern counties and elsewhere many valuable winter crops can be brought through severe conditions successfully. Cloches stood securely on edge or wrapped around tender, larger plants, afford protection from cold prevailing winds and will promote healthier growth.

Two or three cloches placed together with their ends sealed with glass, make ideal propagators or miniature frames. If the larger type of cloche is used a number of seedlings can be raised in a comparatively small area.

Cloches protect plants from bird damage. Many seedlings are attacked by birds, especially pigeons, in town gardens. Seedlings raised under cloches are given complete protection. Strawberries are not only forced earlier but are also kept in good condition by the glass. Plants grown to maturity under cloches, particularly flowers, are protected from weather damage, and the keen exhibitor will quickly appreciate this fact.

Planning and preparation Cloche cultivation is an intensive form of gardening and from a small piece of ground a wide variety of produce can be gathered. Cloches are used in continuous rows or strips, which must be sealed at the ends by a sheet of glass, retained in position by a piece of cane or strong wire. The number of rows or strips which are used will depend on the amount of ground available.

One of the best ways to use cloches is to lay down a double row on a 2m (6ft) wide strip of ground with a 10-16cm (4-6in) gap between the two cloche rows. This 2m (6ft) wide strip will also include a 0·6m (2ft) wide path. The rest of the cloche garden is marked out into several of these 2m (6ft) wide strips. If the plot is laid out in this way, the cloches will not have to be moved far when they are transferred from one crop to another.

The basic system of cropping is as follows: a double row is planted or sown and covered with cloches. Later on the vacant double strip near them and separated by the 0·6m (2ft) wide path is sown or planted. The cloches from the first double strip are moved over to cover this newly cropped strip, leaving the de-cloched crop to mature in the open. As soon as this crop has been cleared, the ground is prepared and another crop sown or planted. In due course, the cloches on the second strip are moved back on to the first strip and the crop just de-cloched is either gathered or allowed to mature in the open. This to and fro movement keeps the cloches continually in use. It is possible to devise more ambitious cropping schemes which require more strips and rows of cloches.

The intensiveness of cropping can be increased still further if inter-cropping is practised. This means the cultivation of a quick maturing crop in the same strip as a slower growing main crop. The former is gathered several weeks before the latter is ready. An example of this is the cultivation of a centre row of sweet peas under a row of cloches, with a row of lettuce on either side of the peas. The lettuces grow rapidly and will be cleared before the sweet peas become tall.

Crop selection Intensive gardening such as this cannot be successful unless the crops and their varieties are selected with some care. Most of the cloche crops can be divided into these three sections:
(a) Hardy plants which crop in early spring. Sowings are made under cloches in late autumn and winter and are kept covered until early April.
(b) Half-hardy plants which are covered during April and May.
(c) Tender plants which require cloche coverage during the summer.

Soil preparation Soil moisture must be conserved under cloches as the ground is covered for long periods and protection from rain and the higher temperatures produced under the cloches can cause rapid drying out. To combat this, as much humus material as possible is worked into the ground to act as a sponge which retains moisture for long periods.

The humus can take the form of well-rotted manure worked in at the rate of a barrowload to 8m (8yd) of strip; horticultural peat at a barrowload to 5m (5yd) a strip or composted vegetable waste at a barrowload to 6m (6yd) of strip. The strips are marked out with a line and dug over as deeply as possible to ensure good drainage. As the strip is prepared the humus material is worked into the bottom of each short trench. Where soils are light, some additional peat should be worked into the top 7–10cm (3–4in). This is also done when a small cloche seed bed is prepared.

Each year, at a convenient time in the planning of a new rotation system, the 0·6m (2ft) wide path should be dug over and used as part of a growing strip. In this way, over the years, a very rich area of cloche ground is maintained.

Growing vegetables A week before sowing or planting takes place a well-balanced or general fertilizer is given at 85g (3oz) per sq m (sq yd). This is raked in thoroughly and the raking action will also break the soil down ready for sowing or planting. If cloches are placed over the prepared strips a week before sowing or planting takes place, the ground will be warmed slightly and will be maintained in a suitable condition despite bad weather.

Beetroot For early supplies, a late February sowing is made in the south. For general sowings March is a suitable month. Small or large cloches are used depending on the number of rows required. Sow a single row under small cloches, three rows under larger ones, spacing these 16cm (6in) apart. All seed is sown as thinly as possible, about 2.5cm (1in) deep. Early thinning is necessary when seedlings can be handled easily. A later thinning is advised when roots the size of a golf ball are lifted. These are excellent for salads. Plants left in the rows are allowed to mature. 'Detroit Selected' and 'Crimson Ball' are suitable.

Broad beans Seed is sown in mid November in the north and late January in the south. Tall cloches or additional height provided by special adaptors is necessary in late spring for frost protection to tall plants. Sow a double row in a 7cm (3in) deep, flat bottom drill which is 20cm (8in) wide. Space the seeds 20cm (8in) apart in staggered fashion. Two suitable varieties are 'Aquadulce' and 'Early Long Pod'.

Dwarf beans Three sowings can be made: mid March in the south, early April in the north and, for a late crop to be picked approximately in October a July sowing can be made. For all sowings the variety 'Lightning' is ideal. Seed is sown under the larger cloches in a double row in a flat 16cm (6in) wide trench, 5cm (2in) deep. Stagger seeds 20cm (8in) apart. If drying beans are

required, haricots should be sown in mid April in all districts as above. A good variety to use is 'Comtesse du Chambourd'.

Runner beans In the south seed is sown in mid March and in late April in the north. Large barn cloches are used making a double row sowing with the rows 23cm (9in) apart. Seeds are placed 5cm (2in) deep and 20-25cm (8-10in) apart. As the plants are staked individually later on, the seeds are not staggered, but placed opposite each other.

1 Diagram of a barn cloche illustrating how rain water moves laterally from the sides into the root zone of the crops.
2 Two rows of lettuce under barn cloches with strawed paths.

'Streamline' and 'Kelvedon Wonder' are very reliable.
Brussel sprouts Cloches are used solely as seed raisers to give plants a long growing period after an early start. Seed is sown thinly in shallow drills under one or more cloches. Young plants

are pricked out later into another seed bed and finally planted 1m (2½ft) apart each way in their permanent quarters. In the south a sowing can be made in late January using varieties such as 'Cambridge No. 1' for early pickings and 'Cambridge No. 5' for late crops. As soon as conditions allow in the north a sowing can be made in February using 'Cambridge No. 1' or 'The Wroxton'.

Carrots Five sowings are made according to district. In the south early January will provide the first pickings if the variety 'Primo' is used. The earliest possible sowing date in the north is mid to late February with a variety such as 'Early Nantes'. Gardeners in the south can make another sowing in February for a prolonged supply of the early 'Primo'. For a late November supply of carrots in the north, an August sowing of 'Primo' is advised. The seedlings must be cloched in September before first frosts threaten. Late crops for southern gardeners are obtained if a September to October sowing is made using the varieties 'Early Nantes' or 'Primo'. Large cloches should be used, and four or five rows can be accommodated. Thin sowing is necessary in 1cm (¼in) deep drills space 10-13cm (4-5in) apart.

Cauliflowers Three sowings can be made, using a cloche or two as a seed raiser. Early September for the north and late September for the south are the first sowing dates for early crops. Large cloches should be used so that three drills can be made. Sow thinly and thin later to 5cm (2in) apart. Plant out finally in March and April 2 feet apart each way. If very large cloches are available, some plants can be covered to maturity. A suitable variety for these sowings is 'All The Year Round'. In the south a further sowing can be made in January and late in February for northern districts. In both instances plants are raised under a few cloches and finally planted out in outdoor beds. The same variety can be used.

Cucumbers Frame and ridge types can be used. The former is hardier and cloche protection is necessary during early stages of growth only. Plants can be purchased and set out under cloches in late April or seed can be raised under a cloche in early April in the south and late April or early May in the north. Whichever method is adopted, plants are finally planted out 1m (3ft) apart in a single row. For each plant a special site should be prepared, taking out a hole 0.3m (1ft) square and half filling it with old manure or composted vegetable waste. The remainder of the hole should be filled up with good soil, mixed with a little horticultural peat.

Plants are trained in a special way. When the fourth true leaf has formed, the growing point of the plant is removed. Several lateral growths should form and the two strongest are selected; the others removed. These two are trained to run along the direction of the cloche row, one on either side of the plant. When these growths have produced six leaves, they are stopped. Side growths should form on the laterals and it is on these that the fruit is carried. All side growths are stopped at the third leaf beyond a fruit. Growths not bearing fruit are stopped at the sixth leaf.

All male flowers must be removed regularly from plants, otherwise fruits will be bitter and malformed. This applies only to the frame type of cucumber. Plenty of water is necessary and as soon as the first fruits have formed, weak liquid feeds or dry fertilizer should be given. Some light shading of the glass may be advisable in very warm, bright weather. Suitable varieties to use

1 The clear, rigid almost unbreakable plastic type cloche for which the manufacturers claim a life-span of about 10 years. 2 A Poly-Tunnel cloche being used experimentally for strawberries.

are 'Conqueror', 'Improved Telegraph', and 'Butcher's Disease Resisting' which are frame types, and 'Best of All Ridge', 'Greenline' and 'Long Green' which are ridge cucumbers.

Endive This is a useful crop which replaces lettuce in districts where lettuce cultivation is not very successful. In the south an early June sowing is ideal and later that month in northern gardens. Two rows are sown thinly under large barn cloches, spacing the rows 0.3m (1ft) apart and sowing the seed 1cm (½in) deep. Seedlings are thinned eventually to 0.3m (1ft) apart. The crop is covered in early September to protect from early frosts. The plants must be blanched or whitened. This is easily done if a flat object such as an inverted plate or saucer is placed over the centre of each plant. In about six weeks the leaves will have blanched sufficiently. The best variety is 'Round-leaved Batavian'.

Lettuce Late September is the sowing time in all districts for lettuce which will be ready for cutting from approximately March to May. Large barn cloches are used to accommodate three rows of seeds. Sow thinly and thin in November to 25cm (10in) apart. Cloches remain over until April or late May in colder districts. Suitable varieties are 'Attraction' and 'May King'.

In late January a further sowing can be made in southern counties. These lettuce should be ready for cutting in June. Similar growing techniques are required except that the original sowing must be even thinner to minimize thinning or transplanting checks. 'May King' and 'Perpetual' are good varieties.

Northern gardeners should make a sowing in late March. When large enough to handle thin plants to 0.3m (1ft) apart. Cloches can be removed in early June when frost danger has passed. 'Trocadero Improved', 'Wonderful' and 'Buttercrunch' are ideal varieties.

For a late November supply of lettuce in the north, a sowing can be made in late July. Thin plants to at least 0.3m (1ft) apart to allow plenty of air to circulate round plants in the dull months. Put cloches over the plants in early September' 'May King', 'Market Favourite' and 'Attraction' can be recommended.

The most suitable time to sow cos lettuce in all districts is March. Cover immediately with cloches which are removed in early June. Two rows can be sown under a large barn cloche. Seedlings must be thinned to 0.3m (1ft). A good variety to sow is 'Giant White'.

Marrow Sow in late April in the north and late March in the south. Culture is similar to that required for cucumbers except that the compact bush types are the best to grow. These require no stopping or training. To ensure a good set of fruit, hand pollination is advisable. The cloches are kept over the plants until early June. Suitable varieties are

'Tender and True', 'Green or White Bush' and 'Courgette'.

Peas For first sowings in the north, early October is the best month and southern sowings are carried out in November. The next sowing in the south is January and both north and south can sow again in March.

Sow in 20cm (8in) wide flat drills, 5cm (2in) deep. The seed is scattered in staggered formation 5-7cm (2-3 in) apart each way in three rows. The cloches remain over the plants from early sowings until the foliage is practically touching the roof glass. The peas can be decloched in early April when seed is sown in March. Early training with small twigs or brushwood is essential for good growth. Plenty of water is required once the plants are well established from the spring onwards. Suitable varieties are 'Meteor' for the October or November sowings, 'Kelvedon Wonder' for January sowings and 'Laxton's Superb' for the March sowings.

Radish This crop (like the lettuce and

early carrots), is an ideal catch crop or intercrop. Out of season sowings are more valuable for cloche work and in the south sowings are made in late September and frequently from then onwards until late March. For northern gardeners, September and October are suitable months for late work and the end of February until late April for the early spring. Seed is sown thinly in shallow drills when used as a catch crop or broadcast under one or two cloches. The smaller cloches are particularly suitable for the latter purpose. Suitable varieties are 'French Breakfast' and 'Scarlet Globe'.

Sweet Corn This is one crop in particular which is grown more easily in this country with the aid of cloches. In the north a sowing can be made in early

A well shaped truss of tomatoes ripening in early summer. The plants were given cloche protection after planting out. Bush varieties are particularly suitable for cloche protection.

1 *Radish, the quick maturing 'French Breakfast'. 2 Marrows can be encouraged to set fruit early with cloche protection. 3 Cloches in pairs stood on end to protect young tomato plants.*

May, and in the south in the second or third week in April. Seed is sown *in situ* or where the plants are to grow to maturity. Sow seed 25cm (10in) apart in double rows spaced 0.3m (1ft) apart. Two seeds per station are sown, removing the weakest seedling later on. This crop should not be transplanted. When the foliage reaches the roof the crop can be decloched. Plenty of water is essential during hot, dry weather. There is no need to remove sidegrowths. A little soil should be drawn up on either side of the rows when the plants are about 1m (3ft) high. This helps to anchor them and is an essential part of their culture in exposed districts. The cobs are ripe when the grain inside the cobs exudes a milky fluid as they are squeezed with the finger nails. Suitable varieties are 'Fogwill's Extra Early', 'Golden Bantam' and 'Canada Crop'.

Tomatoes Outdoor tomatoes are usually a rather chancy crop in this country as a long spell of good weather is needed to get the bulk of the fruit ripened before frosts cut the plants down. Cloches have an invaluable part to play in the successful culture of this plant. They can either give the plants vital early protection so that they become established quickly or they can provide continuous protection which will produce crops nearly as early as glasshouse ones. Northern gardeners will welcome this type of protection in districts which are much colder.

The site for the crop should be prepared thoroughly by deep cultivation.

Separate positions can be prepared for each plant as for cucumbers and marrows. A general fertilizer is applied a few days before planting at 84g (3oz) per sq m (sq yd). The plants are best purchased from a reliable source. Good plants are short jointed and deep green in colour. The plants should be set out 0.6m (2ft) apart in the row, with 1m (3ft) between each row.

Two shapes of tomato plant can be grown, the cordon and the bush. Where it is intended to grow entirely under cloches, the bush type is ideal. As soon as the plants have been set out they should be staked and tied securely. All sideshoots must be removed from cordon plants as soon as they are noticed. In early June, it will be safe enough in all districts to remove the cloches entirely except where it is intended to grow to maturity under them. Plenty of water must be given, especially when the first flower trusses have set. Dry or weak liquid feeds will be required to encourage heavy trusses of fruit.

When cordon plants have produced four trusses, they should be stopped. This is done by removing the centre or growing point of the plants. Bush tomatoes require no stopping or side-shooting. Several varieties can be grown out of doors. Of the cordons, 'Outdoor Girl' and 'Essex Wonder' are excellent. There are several very good bush varieties. These include 'Amateur Improved', 'Atom' and 'Dwarf Cloche'. The latter two varieties are exceptionally useful as they grow to a height and spread of only 37cm (15in).

Flowers There are certain flowers which are particularly suited to cloche cultivation. These can be brought into bloom several weeks earlier and the quality of the flower is often much better. Hardy annuals, in particular, are ideal plants for cloche protection during the early stages of their growth. The most important of these are sweet peas.

Sweet peas Sowing time for sweet peas in the north and south is late September. Seed can also be sown in March. The strip of ground should be deeply worked and plenty of organic matter incorporated in the form of peat, old manure or composted vegetable waste. Seed is sown one row per small cloche and two under the larger types. Space the seeds 16cm (6in) apart in the rows. Cloches must be placed over the rows as soon as the seed is sown in the north. Southern sowings need not be covered until early October.

As soon as the plants are 10-13cm (3-4in) high, they should be provided with pieces of brushwood, through which they will grow. If large flowers are required, plants should be grown in the cordon system. Only the strongest side-growth is allowed to grow on after the initial stopping, and this growth should be trained up a strong cane. Plenty of water is required during the summer.

There are so many beautiful, reliable varieties that a selection should be made from a specialist's catalogue.

Other hardy annuals Those suitable for cloche work and autumn sowing include calendula, candytuft, cornflower, scabious, viscaria, sweet sultan and nigella. For spring sowing the following are recommended godetia, mignonette and clarkia. Seed is sown in groups as thinly as possible or in single rows. Large cloches can accommodate two rows.

Half-hardy annuals These benefit considerably from early covering after they have been sown in early April. Seed is sown thinly in single or double rows according to the size of the cloche. Final thinning is from 20-30cm (8-12in) apart. Suitable varieties include zinnias, schizanthus, nemesia, nicotiana, petunia, and dimorphotheca.

Fruit There are two outstanding cloche crops, strawberries and melons. Strawberries can be harvested several weeks before outdoor fruits are ready; cloches provide sufficient protection for melons to produce delicious fruits as good as those grown in greenhouses.

Strawberries The site should be dug over thoroughly to ensure good drainage and organic matter incorporated at the same time at approximately a barrow-load to 8 sq m (8 sq yd). A few days before planting apply a balanced or general fertilizer at 84g (3oz) per sq m (sq yd).

A bed is started by the purchase of one year old plants of virus free stock, which are planted in two rows 0.3m (1ft) apart with 0.3m (1ft) between plants. Early August is a suitable planting time and cloches are placed over the plants in late October in the north and late November in the south. Cloches are kept over the plants until picking is over. This protection will keep fruits in perfect condition and will prevent bird damage. During warmer weather in March and April, a little ventilation, will be necessary. In the second year the second row of plants should be scrapped as two year old plants grow quite large under cloches. If new plants are required, they can be propagated by runners from a healthy parent plant. Varieties to use are 'Cambridge Vigour' and 'Cambridge Favourite'.

Melons Although this crop can be attempted in the north, it is more suited to the warmer southern regions. Melons are gross feeders and should have plenty of well-rotted manure or composted vegetable waste worked in at a barrowload to 6 sq m (6 sq yd). Horticultural peat at 0.25kg (½lb) per sq m (sq yd) should be forked into the top 7-10cm (3-4in) of soil. To conserve manure or compost, individual positions 46m (58in) square can be prepared. These are spaced 1m (3ft) apart in a single row.

Plants can be raised from seed if a greenhouse or propagator is available where a temperature of 60°F (16°C) can

be maintained. Failing this, plants can be purchased from a reliable source. Planting is done in mid May in pre-warmed ground. Plants should be covered with large barn type cloches.

A special training system is necessary as follows: stop plants after they have developed five true leaves. Select two of the strongest laterals which will be produced and remove all others. Train these laterals on either side of the plant in the direction of the cloche run. When they are about 0.6m (2ft) long, stop them. Sub-laterals will form and it is on these that the fruits will be carried. Hand pollination of female flowers is essential and a small paint brush is ideal for this work. As fertilized fruits swell, give plenty of water and weak liquid feeds. Allow two or three fruits per plant and place these on sheets of glass or blocks of wood to prevent damage. As the fruit ripens reduce water. Glass should be shaded and a very light spray with Summer Cloud will be ideal.

Suitable varieties are 'Large Rock Prescott', 'Tiger', 'Best of All' and 'Cantaloup Charantais'.

A cropping plan The following is a cropping plan for one row of barn cloches used on the two strip system. The crops are easy to grow and will provide a wide range of vegetables.

Strip 1		Strip 2	
October-April		**April-May**	
Lettuce	1 row	Dwarf Beans	
Radish	1 row		
Peas	centre row	**October-April**	
		Lettuce	1 row
June-September		Radish	1 row
Cucumber		Peas	centre row

Conservatories

Conservatories really include lean-to greenhouses, glass corridors and perhaps glass-covered courtyards. They are joined to the house and can contain a variety of pot and climbing plants for all-the-year-round decoration.

Conservatories of reasonable size are not expensive to build. They are easy to look after, and give remarkable scope for the gardener to grow a variety of hardy and not so hardy plants.

Near-greenhouse conditions, ideal for growing and rejuvenation, can easily be arranged by installing simple heating systems. Sometimes, in the warmer, more southerly parts of the country or where the conservatory has a warm aspect in a sheltered position, the heat circulating from the house is sufficient.

A solid floor makes it possible to keep a thriving, humid atmosphere by the simple means of damping down. Heat without humidity can be fatal to plants;

moist, warm conditions help to keep most of them at the peak of condition.

Where there is staging to stand the pots on, it should be strong enough to carry a layer of shingle.

Strictly speaking, conservatories are display houses for plants which have been raised and grown elsewhere, though there is not the slightest reason why the conservatory should not be pressed into service for simple propagation and other jobs for which an ordinary greenhouse might be used. The only trouble is that used in this way, clutter can spoil the effect.

Conservatory plants Greenhouse plants which enjoy temperate conditions thrive in conservatories. These include cinerarias, coleus various primulas such as *P. obconica* and *P. malacoides*, the very showy greenhouse calceolarias such as the 'Albert Kent Hybrids', *C. multiflora nana* and 'Victoria Prize'.

Cyclamen, many begonias, certainly many of the highly ornamental, scented-leaved pelargoniums can be grown as well as a wide range of cacti and other succulents. In fact by careful selection

Plants are remarkably adaptable and some can be persuaded to tolerate even quite dark corners in badly heated rooms. Given the garden room, now being built onto so many modern houses, the selection of plants that can be grown with little trouble is surprisingly extensive. Anyone in search of ideas for garden room or conservatory plants should visit one of the national botanic gardens such as that at Cambridge at which this picture was taken. Sinningias (gloxinias), campanulas, marantas, aphelandras and chlorophytums are a few of the pot plants that can be seen. Others, deciduous and evergreen, can be trained up the walls.

and sensible control of heating and other conditions, there need seldom be a time when there is nothing of colour or interest to see. Annuals in pots should not be overlooked; delightful annuals such as schizanthus, mignonette, salpiglossis, clarkia and calendula.

Hanging baskets, which might otherwise be buffeted about can find true expression in a conservatory where

there is room to avoid collision. Ordinary hanging basket plants, lobelia, tagetes, nasturtiums, geraniums and fuchsias and so on, will thrive to perfection, provided extra attention is paid to watering. Fuchsias and pelargoniums, of course, can be used as individual displays throughout the staging.

Hoya bella and *Hoya carnosa* are two plants which will permanently occupy a hanging basket with great success. And if a little extra care is taken, a warm corner might well see *Columnea gloriosa* doing quite well, though strictly speaking this does prefer rather warmer conditions than a conservatory can usually provide. The two hoyas, despite their somewhat exotic appearance, are really quite hard-wearing and will even endure ordinary living room conditions if they have to; though every living room is not always quite right.

A place will have to be found for various ferns. A shady spot, perhaps, beneath the staging.

There is considerable scope for climbing plants. Where there is sufficient room, the passion flower—*Passiflora caerulea*—can hardly be left out. *Cobaea scandens* has great attraction, and with just that extra warmth and protection that the conservatory can provide, here is a fine chance to grow the deliciously fragrant *Jasminum polyanthum* with its large trusses of dainty white blossom.

So many of the plants suitable for these under-cover conditions (both annual and perennial) grow well enough outside in the garden, as will have been recognized, but afforded just that extra welcome offered by the conservatory they can realize a potential that, subjected to the weather, especially in a bad season, they could possibly never know.

And many pot plants traditionally suited to the rough justice handed out by the ordinary living room, will nevertheless make an even better showing in more controlled conditions.

A wide range of bulbs come into the reckoning, not least some of the hardy kinds to be brought on early. Given warmth and light after the statutory period of cool and dark elsewhere (and it is very useful all round if a conservatory can be run in conjunction with cold frames) varieties of daffodils and narcissi, for example, will achieve early perfection not always resulting from ordinary room culture.

The garden room or modern conservatory is a place for relaxation and leisure pursuits. Sir Cecil Beaton's conservatory at his home at Broadchalke, Wiltshire.

Site the conservatory south, if possible, though this is not essential. Allow adequate means for ventilation—efficiency here is vital—and provide watering facilities *in situ* if this can reasonably be arranged.

Hanging baskets

The use of hanging baskets is a simple but very attractive way of decorating a porch or terrace during the summer—and indeed most of the year. They can be bought in sizes from 23-45cm (10-18in) in diameter and 15-25cm (6-9in) deep.

Baskets are made of stout galvanized wire in an open mesh or a weave design or of green, plastic-coated, rustproof wire, in the same patterns. Polythene baskets are also available in green, red, white, yellow and blue and baskets made entirely of alkathene can be purchased with a special drainage device. In greenhouses, square wooden containers made of slats are often used, particularly for orchids of trailing habit, such as *Stanhopea*.

For safety's sake baskets should be hung from strong hooks, well above eye level where they cannot obscure the light or a view or be knocked about as people pass under them.

Planting up the basket For outdoor use plant up during the latter half of May or very early June, wedging the basket in the top of a large bucket, bowl or box to hold it firm while the planting is done. Line it with damp sphagnum moss; about 2l (4pt) of this will be required to make a good lining. Alternatively thickish polythene can be used to line the basket, when holes will need to be punched in the base for drainage although it is possible to purchase perforated polythene which is quite suitable. Polythene does not look as decorative as sphagnum moss but holds the moisture better and if the basket cannot be given daily attention it is probably better to use this material, although a thin layer of peat packed within the sphagnum moss lining will help considerably with water retention.

If sphagnum moss is not available,

hay packed tightly round the interior of the basket, is an adequate substitute.

Some gardeners like to put a small plastic saucer in the base to catch and retain some of the water, and to reduce drip to some extent.

A reasonably rich compost is best because the small amount that can be accommodated has to provide sustenance for a fairly extensive root system. John Innes potting compost No. 2 is suitable, especially if a little leafmould is incorporated. Do not attempt to get too many plants into one basket. A 30cm (12in) diameter basket will hold three plants from 12cm (5in) pots, plus several smaller or trailing plants between them and around the edge.

Choose plants that are just coming into flower, turn them out of their pots and fill the well of the basket with compost, firming it with the fingers. Place the larger plants in position, angling them slightly towards the edge. At this stage small plants such as lobelia and alyssum can be tucked between the mesh of the basket so that eventually the flowers will clothe the sides. Continue to pack in the soil round the root balls and make it firm, leaving a slight depression or well on the surface of the soil, another trick to conserve moisture and to prevent water from overflowing when the basket is watered. The surface should be about 5cm (2in) below the rim of the basket. Seeds of nasturtiums can be pushed into strategic positions at this stage. Immerse the basket in water, then allow it to drain before hanging it up.

Maintenance Avoid positions in full sun or deep shade; the former dries out the arrangement too quickly and the latter discourages showy flowering, although such positions are suitable for baskets planted up with ferns for foliage effect. Water three or four times a week, daily or even twice daily during very hot weather, adding a flower fertilizer to the water at the recommended rate once a week, after flowering has started. Water from above, allow the basket to drain if possible to avoid leaching out the plant food; otherwise immerse it for a few minutes in a tub of water and allow surplus water to drain away before hanging it up again.

Watering a hanging basket from above can be difficult unless one stands on steps. It can, of course, be lifted off its hook but a large basket full of earth and plants can be quite heavy and awkward. Two methods of dealing with this problem are worth mentioning. One is to fix a small pulley in place of the hook. Strong cord, or preferably strong pliable wire or chain, is fixed to the suspension ring of the basket and passed over the pulley. The other end is attached to a roller blind hook fixed on the nearest wall. The basket may then be lowered for watering and easily raised again. The other method is to use a device, obtainable commercially,

1

3

5

2

4

6

1 The basket is balanced on the rim of a bucket to keep it firm while planting is done. The first lining of sphagnum moss is packed into place.

2 An interlining of polythene is put in place, and holes punched half way up to draw off the surplus water, each time watering is done.

3 Compost is put into the basket, so that the finished level will be just above the polythene lining.

4 Small plants are knocked out of pots and planted at an angle in the centre.

5 Smaller plants are put around the sides and positioned horizontally.

6 The plants are watered in once the basket is complete, and either hung up to drain, or left over the bucket.

known as a 'Tommy Longarm'. Basically this is a small watering can mounted on a swivel on the end of a long pole. A length of string fixed to the can runs through a hook and down the pole. Pulling on the string tips the can thus enabling the basket to be watered easily from below. Wash the leaves occasionally and snip off dead flower heads to keep a well-groomed appearance.

Suggested plants. The following plants are highly recommended for growing in hanging baskets.

Flowering plants for summer display: achimenes; ageratum; begonia 'Gloire de Lorraine' and pendulous kinds such as 'Mrs Bilkey', 'Fleur de Chrysantheme',

'Golden Shower', 'Lena', 'Meteor'; Begonia semperflorens for mild localities; calceolaria; Campanula isophylla and C. isophylla alba; Chrysanthemum frutescens (marguerite); Columnea banksii (G); fuchsia, drooping varieties such as 'Cascade', 'Golden Marinka', 'La Bianco', 'Marinka', 'Thunderbird'; heliotrope; Hoya bella (G); Lantana camara for mild localities; Lobelia pendula and L. tenuior; Lobularia maritima (sweet alyssum); pelargonium, upright zonal kinds for top of basket, ivy-leafed varieties for draping the sides, such as 'Abel Carriere', 'Edward VII', 'Galilee', 'L'Elegance', 'Madame Crousse', 'Madame Morrier'; petunia especially 'Balcony Blended' strain; tropaeolum

(nasturtiums), especially climbers or trailers; verbena, dwarf and trailing.
Perennials: aubrietia; *Campanula portenschlagiana; Cerastium tomentosum; Cymbalaria muralis; Glechoma hederaefolia; Lysimachia nummularia; Vinca minor.*
Foliage plants: hedera (ivy) in variety; *Saxifraga stolonifera* (syn. *S. sarmentosa*).
Bulbs: (for late winter and spring display) crocus, *Narcissus* (daffodil), *Galanthus* (snowdrop), tulip (double).

Hardening off
The process of accustoming plants gradually to more rigorous growing conditions than those which they have previously been used to. Considerable skill and experience is necessary to harden off well, and if the process is hurried at all, growth will be checked or the leaves will turn blue or become streaked or blotched with brown.

Considering, as an example, seedlings raised or cuttings started under glass and destined to be grown out of doors, the first stage in hardening off is to lower the greenhouse temperature; this is followed by increasing the ventilation. Subsequently the pots can be moved to a frame where greater control is possible, and conditions can be altered immediately, according to the weather. The frame light can be removed, first during the day and later at night as well, until the plants have become accustomed to outdoor conditions without checking their growth. Cloches of the barn or Ganwick type are very useful in this process for if heavy rainfall or frost is forecast, they can be placed over a block of pots standing in the open, when no frame space is available.

Hardy annuals see Annuals

Haricot beans see Vegetables

Heading back
The operation of cutting back drastically the growth of trees or shrubs, beyond the limit of pruning. Pleaching and pollarding are both forms of heading back, and lopping and de-horning are both mild forms of heading back. When young fruit stocks are cut back to prepare them for grafts in the spring the process is referred to as heading back. This operation generally results in strong growth being quickly produced, and it can be used to advantage when a strong framework of branches is to be built up.

Hedges, screens and shelterbelts
Screens and shelterbelts are usually essential in coastal areas; also to farmers and fruit growers. In gardens, private and public, hedges can do much to prevent the intrusion of animals and human beings and to act as windbreaks.

Before planting it must be decided what purpose is to be served. If the hedge is simply to make a break between flower garden and vegetable or fruit plot, then a flowering or fruiting hedge can be chosen, eg *Berberis stenophylla*, or *B. darwinii*, escallonia or forsythia. For a dwarf hedge, lavender, *Mahonia aquifolium, Santolina chamaecyparissus* or *Senecio laxifolius* are suitable.

Where a boundary hedge is planned merely to provide privacy during the summer months, then a deciduous hedge will be suitable: flowering currant (ribes), forsythia, hawthorn or beech are among the possibilities.

If a permanent peep-proof hedge is required, any evergreen, such as holly, yew or one of the many other conifers or even privet is suitable, though the last can sometimes drop its leaves, especially in very hard winters.

Screens or shelterbelts must also be considered from the point of view of their ultimate use. If it is desirable to block out some eyesore such as a factory, a railway line, or to give shelter in the garden so that other plants can be grown successfully, then screening is more than ever necessary, particularly in coastal gardens. If, however, the

1 Browallia, a greenhouse flowering annual makes a decorative trailing plant for a hanging basket. This makes an attractive display hung to a pergola beam, or hung over a balcony.
2 A floriferous begonia in a basket.
3 A small hanging basket, planted with fuchsias and pelargoniums.

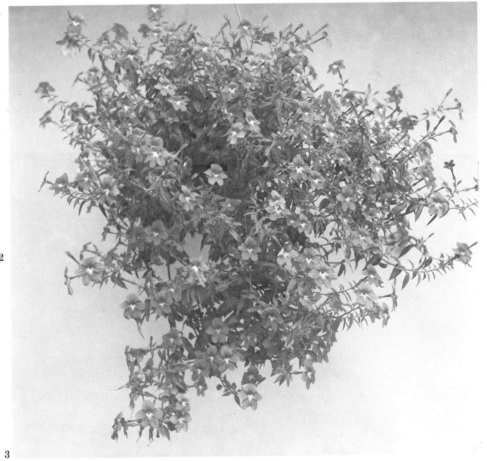

screen is to add interest to the skyline, then a mixture of deciduous and evergreen trees, and conifers is the answer. Farm hedges, screens and shelterbelts are usually designed to break the prevailing wind or to keep in animals and shelter them from wind and rain.

Preparation of site Preparation of the ground for a hedge, screen or shelterbelt must be thorough. Once the shrubs or trees are planted they will remain there for a long time; therefore, see that they get off to a good start.

In light soil, humus must be added: a heavy soil will need to be lightened by digging in peat, leafsoil, rotted farmyard manure or garden compost. In heavy clay soils drainage is important, and path or road sweepings or weathered ashes will help to improve it. When marking out the site, dig a strip 1.2m (4ft) wide; this will leave 46cm (18in) on either side of the hedge. Bastard trench the ground, ie double dig it. This entails digging out a trench 60cm (2ft) wide, removing the top spit of soil and thoroughly breaking up the second spit, ie the sub-soil. Then place the top spit of the next trench on top of the broken up sub-soil; continuing this process until the strip of ground is completely dug. If humus is available this can be incorporated in the top spit at the time of digging. And, of course, if well-rotted farmyard manure can be obtained so much the better. When leaf-soil or garden compost is used, the addition of National Growmore or bonemeal at a rate of 120g (4oz) per square yard will be beneficial. Prepare the ground some weeks before planting time, to allow the soil to settle. Never dig out the trench for the hedge before the day of planting arrives.

If a lot of ground is to be planted, do not attempt to do it all in one day. Therefore, when the plants arrive from the nursery, lay them in or heel them in on a spare piece of ground. By laying the plants in, their roots will be kept plump and moist and they will make new root action more quickly when they are finally planted. If the roots are dry on delivery, give them a thorough soaking before they are laid in.

When all is ready for planting dig out a trench 30-45cm (1-1½ft) wide and about 30cm (1ft) deep. Throw the soil each side of the trench. If you are planting beside a lawn lay down some old sacks or plastic sheeting to protect the grass. As planting proceeds, cover the roots of each plant, first with fine soil, followed by the coarser soil, firming the ground by treading, until normal soil level is reached. If the day is frosty or sunny or there is a drying wind, see that the roots of the plants are covered until each plant is actually placed in the trench.

Times to plant Deciduous hedges are planted from October or November (according to season) until March. Evergreen hedges are planted from September to October or March to April.

Staking It is not usually necessary to stake hedges, but where large bushes are planted, such as yews or hollies, then posts and one or two strands of strong string or plastic-covered wire will prevent movement at the base of the stem at soil level. Trees planted as screens or shelterbelts are best staked until they are sufficiently established and rigid to stand up to gales.

Pleached screens These are useful for adding height to a wall or fence where privacy is required. A pleached screen entails planting young trees, with good straight stems, 2.5-3.5cm (8-10ft) apart. All shoots below the top of the wall or fence are removed, while those above are trained out horizontally to long bamboo canes or poles, such as runner bean poles, and wires to which the shoots are tied. Any shoots which grow out at right angles to the wall or fence, back or front, are removed. The result is a living trellis.

Watering This must not be overlooked either at the time of planting or afterwards. If the roots are at all dry at planting time, soak them in a bath or bucket of water. After they have been set out, the hedging plants must have sufficient moisture at the roots. See that they are given several gallons of water if the soil is very dry. The foliage of evergreens should be kept moist by spraying the foliage after sunset.

Trimming hedges The time to clip or trim a hedge depends on the type, deciduous or evergreen, whether it is newly planted or established and whether it is to be clipped to form a formal hedge or an informal one. Newly planted deciduous hedges are best cut hard back to within 20-30cm (9-12in) of ground level in March or April. Some evergreens such as privet and *Lonicera nitida* may be treated in the same way. On the other hand Lawson's cypress, yew, holly, etc, are best not trimmed, except for a few of the tips of shoots being nipped back. Beech and hornbeam should not be pruned for two years after planting.

To encourage good bushy growth, train the hedge in a wedge shape, wider at the base than at the top. With big-leaved evergreens, such as laurel or holly it is better to trim with secateurs rather than shears, as then there is less likelihood of the larger leaves being cut in half. With established hedges this is not quite so serious. Allow hedges to reach their required height before they are stopped, ie before their leading shoots are cut off.

Overgrown deciduous hedges such as blackthorn, hornbeam, myrobalan plum and quickthorn can usually be rejuvenated by hard pruning during the winter months. Evergreens such as box, laurel, privet and yew are hard pruned in late March or early April.

Farm hedges are frequently rejuvenated by laying them. To do this all

1 Young plants of Thuja occidentalis are planted along a narrow trench.
2 Soil is filled in around the roots.
3 Soil is replaced around the collar.
4 The soil is firmed with the foot.

unwanted growths are cut out to ground level, while the rest, except thick growths, are partly severed near the base. These growths are then bent over at an angle of 45° to the ground and intertwined with dead stakes driven into the ground, 15-20cm (6-8in) from the centre and behind the cut down growths. Suitable stakes can be made of hazel, thorn, beech or sweet chestnut.

General cultivation Once a hedge is planted continual cultivation is necessary. The soil on either side of the hedge should be kept free of weeds and lightly forked over from time to time. An annual mulch given in late spring will help to keep the soil moist and will also feed the hedge. If well-rotted farmyard manure can be obtained, so much the better. If not, leaf-mould or well-rotted garden compost can be used.

Hedging and screening plants described

Shrubs, deciduous and evergreen

Acer (maple) *A. campestre* (common or field maple), makes an attractive deci-

duous hedge or screen tree which thrives in sun or shade, on clay or chalk soils. Plant 30cm (1ft) apart, from October to March. Trim in late summer or winter. Height 1.5-3m (5-10ft). Screens 12-15m (40-50ft).

Alder see **Alnus**

Alnus (alder) *A. glutinosa* (common alder) is a hardy, deciduous tree with attractive catkins. It thrives best in a rich soil, dislikes acid, peaty soils. Plant 1.8-2.4m (6-8ft) 15m (50ft) apart for screens from October to March. Height up to 15m (50ft).

Arbor vitae see **Thuja** (under **Conifers** below)

Arundinaria see **Bamboo**

Atriplex *A. halimus* (tree purslane) is a semi-evergreen with silver-grey foliage, which makes a first-class seaside hedge. Plant 45-50cm (18-21in) apart, from October to April. Trim in early spring. Height 1.2-1.8m (4-6ft).

Aucuba *A. japonica* and *A. j. variegata* are evergreens which bear scarlet berries where male and female bushes are planted. Plant 60-90cm (2-3ft) apart during October and November or March and April. Trim in April. Height 1.8-2.7cm (6-9ft).

Bamboo The following genera and species are suitable: *Arundinaria japonica* and *A. nitida*, *Phyllostachys nigra* and *P. viridi-glaucescens* are useful where

Hedges

Name	Deciduous	Evergreen	Flowering	Fruiting	Chalk Soils	Damp Soils	Dry and Sand Soils	Fragrant	Seaside	Autumn Colour	Remarks
Acer campestre (field maple)	X			X	X	X	X			X	
Atriplex halimus		sX			X		X		X		silver-grey foliage
Aucuba japonica		X		X	X						must plant male and female forms for fruit. Good for industrial areas
Aucuba japonica variegata		X		X	X						
Bamboo	X	X				X					soil must not be water-logged, in a frost pocket
Berberis (barberry)											
B. darwinii		X	X	X	X		X				
B. stenophylla		X	X	X	X		X	X			*B. stenophylla* is quick growing.
B. thunbergii	X		X	X	X						All make decorative garden hedges
B. thunbergii atropurpurea	X		X	X	X		X			X	
B. verruculosa		X	X	X	X		X				
Buxus (box)											
B. sempervirens		X	X		X		X			X	
B. suffruticosa		X			X					X	used as edging to paths and borders
Calluna vulgaris (ling) and its varieties		X	X								best on peat or acid soils
Carpinus betulus (hornbeam)	X					X		X			foliage retained well into the winter
Chaenomeles (Japanese Quince)	X		X	X	X	X					fruit makes good jelly
Corylus avellana (hazel)	X					X				X	for farm or garden
Cotoneaster											
C. simonsii		sX	X	X	X		X				
C. watereri		X	X	X	X		X				
Erica (heather)											
E. carnea		X	X								both will grow in soils containing chalk or lime
E. mediterranea		X	X		X						
Escallonia (many varieties)		X	X		X	X			X		
Euonymus japonicus		X		X					X		good for industrial areas
Fagus sylvatica (beech)	X				X					X	foliage retained well into the winter
Fagus sylvatica purpurea (copper beech)	X				X					X	
Fuchsia magellanica	X		X						X		plant base of shoots 4 inches below soil
Griselinia littoralis		X		X					X		will grow in towns
Hebe speciosa		X	X		X				X		*H. speciosa* subject to frost damage
H. brachysiphon (syn. *H. traversii*)		X	X		X				X		
Hippophae rhamnoides (sea buckthorn)	X			X	X	X	X		X		must plant male and female forms for fruit
Ilex aquifolium (holly) and varieties		X		X	X						thrives in towns and industrial areas
Lavandula (lavender)		X	X		X		X	X			
Ligustrum (privet)		X			X		X				good in towns and industrial areas. Quick growing

sX = semi-evergreen

Hedges

Name	Deciduous	Evergreen	Flowering	Fruiting	Chalk Soils	Damp Soils	Dry and Sand Soils	Fragrant	Seaside	Autumn Colour	Remarks
Lonicera nitida (Chinese honeysuckle)		X			X		X		X		grows well in towns
Mahonia aquifolium (Oregon grape)		X	X	X	X		X	X		X	good in towns and industrial areas
Olearia (daisy bush)		X	X		X				X		does well in towns
Osmarea burkwoodii		X	X		X			X			good in industrial areas
Pittosporum		X			X		X		X		subject to frost damage
Prunus											
P. cerasifera (myrobalan plum)	X				X				X		
P. × cistena	X		X							X	
P. laurocerasus (cherry laurel)		X					X				good in industrial areas
P. lusitanica (Portugal laurel)		X					X				
Pyracantha (firethorn)		X	X	X	X		X				good for industrial areas
Rhododendron ponticum		X	X			X			X		needs an acid or neutral soil
Ribes sanguineum (flowering currant)	X		X		X	X	X				Quick growing
Rosa (rose)											
'Zephirine Drouhin'	X		X					X			thornless
'Kathleen Harrop'	X		X					X			thornless
'Cecile Brunner'	X		X					X			ideal for a dwarf hedge
'Nathalie Nypels'	X		X					X			
'Old Blush'	X		X					X			
R. eglanteria (sweet briar or eglantine)	X		X					X			
'Penzance Hybrids'	X		X					X			
Hybrid musk, several varieties	X		X	X				X			
R. rugosa, several varieties	X		X	X				X			
Floribunda roses	X		X								
Rosmarinus officinalis (rosemary)		X	X		X		X	X			has fragrant foliage
Ruta graveolens 'Jackman's Blue' (rue)		X	X		X		X				glaucous-grey aromatic foliage
Santolina chamaecyparissus (lavender cotton or cotton lavender)		X	X		X		X				grey, aromatic foliage makes a good dwarf hedge or edging plant
Senecio laxifolius		X	X		X		X		X		attractive silver-grey foliage
Spiraea, several species and varieties	X		X		X	X	X				*S. thunbergii* has coloured foliage in autumn
Syringa vulgaris (lilac) many varieties and species	X		X		X			X	X		
Tamarix (tamarisk) several species	X		X		X		X		X		
Viburnum lantana (wayfaring tree)	X		X	X	X					X	
V. opulus (guelder rose)	X		X	X	X	X				X	
V. tinus (laurustinus)		X	X		X		X		X		
Weigela florida variegata	X		X								
W. hybrida and its varieties	X		X								

a screen or wind shelterbelt is needed. Give them good cultivation and avoid water-logged ground. An annual mulch of leaf mould or rotted manure should be given in the spring, plus 30g (1oz) of sulphate of ammonia per square metre (yard) Plant 90cm-1.20m (3-4ft) apart in May. Trim when required from April to mid-May.

Barberry see **Berberis**

Beech see **Fagus**

Berberis (barberry) Suitable evergreen species and varieties are B. darwinii, with orange-yellow flowers followed by plum-coloured berries, height 1.8-2.4m (6-8ft); B. stenophylla, golden yellow flowers, height 2.4-3m (8-10ft). Plant both at 45-60cm (1½-2ft) apart. Trim after the flowers have faded. B. verruculosa, golden-yellow flowers, height 1m-1.20m (3-4ft). Plant 40-47cm (15-18in) apart from October to March. Trim after flowering. Deciduous species: B. thunbergii, B. t. atropurpurea, height 1-1.4m (3-4ft). Plant 40-47cm (15-18in) apart from October to March. Trim in February. B. t. erecta, height 75-105cm (2½-3½ft), makes an excellent dwarf and compact hedge. Plant 30-40cm (12-15in) apart from October to March. No trimming is needed.

Betula (birch) B. alba (silver birch) makes a useful deciduous screen or shelter tree. Plant 2.4–3m (8–10ft) apart from November to March. Birches can also be planted as hedge shrubs, spaced at 45–60cm (1½–2ft) apart. Height as a hedge 2.4–3m (8–10ft) as a screen 12–15m (40–50ft).

Birch see **Betula**

Box see **Buxus**
Buckthorn see **Hippophae**
Buxus (box) *B. sempervirens* (common box) makes a superb evergreen hedge with a pleasant musky fragrance. It does well in any soil, likes chalk soils and succeeds by the sea. Plant 45–60cm (1½–2ft) apart during March and April or September and October. Trim in summer or, where hard cutting back is necessary, in April. Height up to 2.7m (9ft) for hed-

A curving hedge of Lonicora nitida is a feature of this Kentish garden.

ges, screens 4.5–5.4m (15–18ft). *B. suffruticosa* (edging box). One nursery yard will plant 2–3m (2–3yd) of edging. Plant during March and April or September and October. Trim two or three times during the summer. Height not usually more than 1m (1yd).
Calluna (ling) *C. vulgaris* makes a good low hedge on acid soils. Plant 30–45cm (1-1½ft) apart during April and May or September and October. Trim in spring Height 45–60cm (1½–2ft). There are many varieties and cultivars in a good colour range.
Carpinus (hornbeam) *C. betulus* is a hardy, deciduous shrub or tree. Its beech-like leaves have a rougher texture than those of beech. It is excellent for exposed places and it mixes well with hawthorn or quickthorn. One hornbeam should be planted to six quickthorn. Plant either in double rows, 40cm (15in)

between the plants and 20cm (8in) between the rows or in single rows 30cm (12in) apart, from October to March. Trim in July. Height 3–6m (10–20ft).
Castanea (chestnut) *C. sativa* (sweet or Spanish chestnut) is a hardy, deciduous shelterbelt tree for inland planting. It does best on sandy loam. Plant 1m–1.8m (3–6ft) apart from October to March. Trim in winter. Height 18–24m (60–80ft).
Chaenomeles *C. japonica* (Japanese quince) is a deciduous, flowering and fruiting hedge shrub. There are many varieties in varying shades of pink and red. Plant 30–45cm (1–1½ft) apart from October to March. Trim at the end of April or early May. Height 60cm–3m (2-10ft).
Cherry laurel see **Prunus laurocerasus**
Chestnut see **Castanea**
Conifers see separate list below
Corylus (hazel) *C. avellana* (common hazel), a deciduous shrub which thrives in any soil. It is good for a mixed hedge of hawthorn, holly, hornbeam and elm. Plant 30–60cm (1–2ft) apart, from October to March. Trim in late February or March. Height 3–6m (10–20ft).
Cotoneaster There are many suitable evergreen and deciduous species and varieties, including *C. frigida, C. rotundifolia, C. simonsii, C. wardii* and *C. watereri,* all with white and pinkish flowers or orange-red berries. Plant 45–60cm (1½–2ft) apart from October to March. Trim between the end of February and the end of March. Height 1.8–2.7m (6–9ft).
Cotton lavender see **Santolina**
Crataegus (may or quickthorn) *C. oxyacantha,* the common hawthorn, is a hardy, deciduous small tree, a most popular hedge plant for garden and farm. It mixes well with holly, beech or hornbeam and will thrive in any soil and grow in sun or shade. Plant in single or double rows 30–38cm (12–15in) apart, 20cm (8in) between the rows, from October to March. Cut back newly planted hedges in March or April to within 15–25cm (6–9in) of ground level. Trim from June onwards. For formal hedges several clippings can be given during the summer. Farm hedges are usually trimmed in the winter months. Height 1.5–6m (5–20ft).
Cypress see **Chamaecyparis** (under **Conifers** below)
Erica (heather) Several species and many varieties are ideal for dwarf hedges. Plant 25–45cm (9–18in) apart, according to variety, during April or May or September and October. Trim in early spring. Height 30cm–1.2m (1–4ft). Most ericas need an acid soil, though *E. carnea, E. mediterranea* and *E. × darleyensis* will grow in chalky soils.
Escallonia These are hardy and half-

1 Erica vulgaris makes a low hedge.
2 A hedge of Fuchsia magellanica.

hardy evergreen and deciduous flowering shrubs bearing pink or red flowers. They make ideal hedge shrubs for coastal areas, the best being *E. macrantha* or one of its varieties such as 'Crimson Spire' or 'Red Hedger'. Plant 30–45cm (1–1½ft) apart, in September or during March or April. Trim after the blooms have faded, in late summer. Height 1.2–3m (4–10ft).

Eucalyptus *E. gunnii* the hardiest species makes a good screen in milder counties. It has attractive evergreen glaucous grey-green foliage and thrives in well-drained soils. Plant 1.8m (6ft) apart in spring. Trim in April when necessary. Height up to 12m (30ft).

Euonymus (spindle tree) *E. japonicus* is an evergreen, ideal for coastal planting as it does well in wind-swept areas. It makes a good town hedge and it will thrive on any soil. Plant 45cm (1½ft) apart in September or April. Trim once or twice in the summer; any hard pruning should be done in April when necessary. Height 2.4–3.6m (8–12ft).

Fagus (beech) *F. sylvatica* (common beech) is a hardy, deciduous tree, its leaves richly coloured in autumn, and hanging on well into the winter or spring. Little is to be gained by planting bushes more than 1m (3ft) high. The ideal size is 45–60cm (1½–2ft). For single rows space them 38cm (15in) apart in the rows and 20cm (8in) between the rows. Plant from October to March. Height: hedges 1.5–3m (5–10ft), screens 3–5.4m (10–18ft). *F. s. purpurea*, the purple beech, has attractively copper-coloured foliage which mixes well with green beech.

Forsythia These deciduous shrubs which will thrive in any soil, make good flowering hedges. Plant 45–60cm (1½–2ft) apart from October to March. If trimmed annually as soon as the flowers have faded, a neat flowering hedge will be maintained. Height 1.2–2.1m (4–7ft).

Fuchsia Some fuchsias make fine deciduous flowering hedges, best suited in Britain to the south coast and the west country. As they are liable to early frost damage they are best planted with the base of the shoots 10cm (4in) below ground level. Plant at 45–60cm (1½–2ft) apart in May. Trim in spring by cutting back lightly or severely, depending on frost damage during the winter. After severe winters cut back the hedge to ground level. Height 1–2.2m (3–8ft). *F. magellanica* and its varieties are chiefly used for hedge purposes, though some of the larger flowered, so called florists' varieties, can be used. Most fuchsia hedges are treated fairly informally.

Griselinia *G. littoralis* is an evergreen which does well in London and also as far north as the Yorkshire coast. It is an excellent shrub for a wind-break or for providing shelter. It thrives in any soil. Plant 45cm (1½ft) apart in March or April. Trim between May and July. Height: hedges 1.5–2.1m (5–7ft), screens 2.1–3m (7–10ft).

Hawthorn see **Crataegus**
Hazel see **Corylus**
Heather see **Erica**
Hebe (syn. Veronica) Hardy and slightly tender evergreen shrubs. There are many species and cultivars, some of the most colourful being varieties of the somewhat tender *H. speciosa*. Hebes are good for coastal areas. *H. bracyhsiphon*

(syn. *traversii*) is hardy anywhere. Plant 45cm (1½ft) apart in September or April. Trim in April. Heights vary from 60cm–1.5m (2–5ft).

Hippophae (sea buckthorn) *H. rhamnoides* is a deciduous, hardy and dioecious (ie male and female flowers on separate plants) shrub and only when both sexes are planted will berries be produced; one male to five or six female bushes is most satisfactory. It is an excellent seaside hedge or wind shelter shrub. Plant 60–90 cm (2–3ft) apart from October to March. Trim in late March or early April. Height 3–4.5m (10–15ft).

Holly see **Ilex**
Holm Oak see **Quercus ilex**
Honeysuckle see **Lonicera**
Hornbeam see **Carpinus**

Ilex (holly) *I. aquifolium* (common holly). This is one of our oldest evergreens, hardy and dioecious, and like *Hippophae,* there must be a male bush planted if berries are to be obtained. There are many fine varieties, including golden and silver variegated forms. Holly is very wind-hardy, but resents severe exposure. Plant 45–60cm (1½–2ft) apart in September, April or early May. Trim during August or September. When overgrown or neglected hedges require to be cut back, do this in April. Height 1.5–6m (5–20ft). Worthwhile varieties are: *I. a. polycarpa laevigata,* a very free berrying form, 'Golden King' (a berrying form), 'Silver Queen', a male form which, therefore, does not berry. One of the most vigorous is *I. a. altaclarensis,* a male form.

Japanese Quince see **Chaenomeles**
Larch see **Larix** (under **Conifers** below)
Laurel see **Prunus**

Lavandula (lavender) These evergreen shrubs, which produce sweetly scented flowers are suitable for low hedges. *L. spica*, English lavender, 90cm–1.2m (3–4ft) high, *L. s.* 'Twickel Purple', rich purple 60–90cm (2–3ft), *L. s. nana atropurpurea* (syn. 'Hidcote Variety'), deep purple-blue flowers, 12–18cm (1–1½ft) high, are among the best of several species and varieties. Plant 60–75cm (2–2½ft) apart for the tall varieties and 30cm (12in) apart for the dwarf varieties, in March to early April.

Lavender see **Lavandula**
Lavender cotton see **Santolina**
Ligustrum (privet) This is the most freely-planted of any evergreen. *Ligustrum ovalifolium* (oval-leaved privet) should be planted in single rows, 30cm (12in) apart, or in double, staggered rows 38–46cm (15–18in) apart, with 20cm (8in) between the rows, from October to March. Trim at least twice a year, in May and September. Overgrown hedges can be cut hard back in April. Height 60cm–3m (2–10ft). The golden-leaved form is *L. o. aureum,* height 1.2–1.8m (4–6ft).

Berberis darwinii, from Chile, provides a splendid flowering hedge.

The variegated holly is a good evergreen to use for a permanent hedge.

Lilac see **Syringa**

Ling see **Calluna**

Lonicera *L. nitida* (Chinese honey-suckle) is an evergreen, with small, box-like leaves. It is not as hardy as privet, but is neater and denser in habit. Plant 30cm (12in) apart, from October to April. Cut back hedges, after planting, to within 23–30cm (9–12in) of ground level. Trim two or three times during the summer. Height 1.2–1.3m (4–4½ft).

Mahonia *M. aquifolium* (Oregon grape) is a hardy evergreen of the berberis family, with holly-like leaves, dark, glossy green, turning in autumn to a purplish-crimson. It does well in shade and in draughty places, such as, between houses and is also useful for covering banks. Plant 45–60cm (1½–2ft) apart from October to April. Trim as and when required in April. Height 90cm–1.2m (3–4ft).

Maple see **Acer**

Metasequoia see **Conifers** below

Monterey Cypress see **Cupressus macrocarpa** (under **Conifers** below)

Myrobalan Plum see **Prunus cerasifera**

Norway Spruce see **Picea** (under **Conifers** below)

Olearia The daisy bushes are evergreen shrubs, wind-hardy and excellent in coastal areas. *O. haastii* has small, grey, box-like foliage. Plant 30–45cm (1–1½ft) apart in September or October or April or May. Height 90cm–1.2m (3–4ft) *O. macrodonta*, holly-like leaves, dark

No plant is more striking for a low flowering hedge than lavender.

glossy grey-green above, with silvery white felt underneath. Space 60–75cm (2–2½ft) apart. Height 3–4.5m (10–15ft). Both have white daisy flowers.

Oregon Grape see **Mahonia**

Osmarea *O.* × *burkwoodii* is an evergreen with dark green, box-like foliage, and white, sweetly scented flowers. Plant 38–52cm (15–21in) apart from October to March. Trim in April. Height 2.7–3.6m (9–12ft).

Phyllostachys see **Bamboo**

Pine see **Pinus** (under **Conifers** below)

Pittosporum *P. tenuifolium*, is an evergreen, for hedges or screens, especially useful for coastal areas. It grows best in a rich loamy soil, but will grow in sand or chalk soils. Plant 60cm (2ft) apart in September or April. Trim in April. Height 3–6m (10–20ft).

Poplar see **Populus**

Populus (poplar) *P. alba* (white poplar) is a very hardy, deciduous screen tree, resistant to salt winds and suitable for wind-swept cliffs. Plant young trees 1.5–4.5m (5–15ft) apart from November to March. Height 24–30m (80–100ft). *P. nigra italica* (Lombardy poplar) is a hardy deciduous tree with a fastigiate or pyramidal habit. Plant 1.5–3m (5–10ft) apart from November to March. Height up to 30m (100ft).

Portugal Laurel see **Prunus lusitanica**

Privet see **Ligustrum**

Prunus This genus includes the ornamental plums such as the deciduous *P. cerasifera* (myrobalan or cherry plum)

and its varieties, the common laurel, *P. laurocerasus*, and the Portugal laurel, *P. lusitanica*. *P. cerasifera* is often grown as a farm hedge, planted 45–60cm (1½–2ft) apart from October to March. Trim in July or August. When severe cutting back is needed do this in December. Height up to 6m (20ft). *P. c. pissardii* and *P. c. p. nigra* are two good purple and very dark purple-leaved shrubs or small trees. Plant as for *P. cerasifera*. Height up to 6m (20ft) .*P.* × *cistena*. This fairly dwarf growing hybrid with *P. cerasifera pissardii* as one of its parents, has been known since 1910, but it was not put on the market as a hedge shrub before about 1960. It has purple foliage and large single, white flowers with purple centres. Plant 30cm (12in) apart from October to March. Trim immediately after flowering. Height 1.5–2.1m (5–7ft). *P. laurocerasus* (common or cherry laurel). Plants of this large-leaved evergreen should be set out at 45–60cm (1½–2ft) apart during September and October or March and April. Trim with secateurs in April or July. Height 1.5–6m (5–20ft). *P. lusitanica* (Portugal laurel). This is an evergreen with handsome rich, dark green, glossy leaves. Height 3–6m (10–20ft). Other remarks as for the common laurel.

Pyracantha (firethorn) An evergreen shrub, usually grown against a wall or fence for its berrying qualities. However, it makes a first-class evergreen hedge. There are several species. One of the

best is *P. atalantioides,* very hardy, a vigorous grower, with crimson-scarlet berries. Plant 45–60cm (1½–2ft) apart in September, October or April. Trim in April, where possible with secateurs. Another good kind is the hybrid *P.* × *watereri,* with red berries, and a very twiggy habit. It will reach 2.4–3m (8–10ft) though a hedge 1.5–1.8m (5–6ft) tall is preferable. It makes an excellent town hedge. Other remarks as for *P. atalantioides.*

Quercus (oak) *Q. ilex* (evergreen or holm oak). This is an evergreen, with dark green, holly-like but not prickly leaves. It excels on poor sandy soils, is very hardy and does well in coastal areas. It is good as a hedge or screen. Plant 30–60cm (1–2ft) apart for hedges, screens, 3–4.5m (10–15ft) apart, in September, April or early May. Trim in April. Height as a hedge 4.5m (15ft), as a screen 6m (20ft). *Q. robur* (common oak). A hardy, deciduous tree. Useful for planting in mixed screens. Plant 1.5–3m (5–10ft) apart, from October to March. Height up to 9m (30ft) (considerably taller in maturity).

Rhododendron *R. ponticum* (common rhododendron) makes a first-class evergreen flowering hedge. It is very wind hardy, good in coastal areas, and in London and industrial areas. It does well in acid, peaty soils, and equally well in clay soils, although it will not succeed in chalky or limey soils. In June its purplish-pink flowers are carried above dark glossy leaves. Plant 45–60cm (1½–2ft) apart or where larger plants are used 90cm–1.2m (3–4ft) apart, during September and October or March and April.

Trim in April or directly after the flowers have faded. Height 2.4–4.5m (8–15ft).

Ribes (currant) *R. aureum* (buffalo currant) is a hardy deciduous flowering shrub, fine for an informal hedge, its golden-yellow flowers spicily fragrant. Plant at 30–45cm (1–1½ft) apart from October to March. Trim after flowering. Height 1.5–2.4m (5–8ft). *R. sanguineum* (flowering currant). The variety 'Pulborough Scarlet' is the best: it makes a fine hedge. Plant at 45cm (1½ft) apart from October to March. Trim after flowering. Height 2.4–3m (8–10ft).

Rosa (rose) When considering the planting of a rose hedge one must first decide whether it is to be kept moderately formal or be allowed to grow naturally with the minimum of attention. In the latter instance the wealth of flower or hips, where this applies, will of course, be much greater. The most popular roses are the *Rosa rugosa* types and the hybrid musk roses, which are especially fragrant. Many of the floribundas are vigorous growers and very free flowering. Many of the shrub roses have very fragrant flowers and shapely hips.

Preparation of the ground for all rose hedges should be thorough. It should be well-dug and enriched with well-rotted farmyard manure or well-rotted garden compost. When actually planting the hedge, cover the bare roots with a mixture of peat and bonemeal—2 good handfuls of the latter to 13l (3gal) of peat—which should be thoroughly moist before it is mixed and used. Having spinkled the roots with a good covering, place some fine soil

over this followed by coarser soil, afterwards firming it well with the feet. Plant at any time from November to March at the following distances apart.

Low and medium-sized rose bushes, 60–90cm (2–3ft) apart, more vigorous kinds 1.2–1.5m (4–5ft) apart. Pruning of the species roses and the floribundas should be carried out in February and March. The following species and varieties are a few of the many suitable for rose hedges.

'Great Maiden's Blush' (*Rosa alba* hybrid), a strong grower, warm blush-pink, fading to cream, fragrant, 1.8–2.4m (6–8ft). 'Commandant Beaurepaire' (a Bourbon rose). Strong grower, crimson, striped and splashed with pink and purple, flowering June to July, 1.5m (5ft). 'Zephirine Drouhin' (Bourbon). Thornless, cerise-pink, from early June onwards. Very fragrant, 2.4–3.6m (8–12ft). 'Kathleen Harrop' (Bourbon). Clear pink and crimson, thornless, 2.4–3m (8–10ft). 'Cecile Brunner' (China rose). Dainty salmon-coloured flowers, shaded rose. Tea-scented, 90cm–1.2m (3–4ft). 'Nathalie Nypels' (China rose). Double shell-pink, sweetly scented free flowering, 90cm–1.2m (3–4ft). 'Old Blush' (common monthly rose) (China rose). Silvery-pink, flushed crimson. June to October, 1.5m (5ft). *R. eglanteria* (syn. *R. rubiginosa*) sweet briar or eglantine), single pink flowers, 1.5–2.5m (5–8ft).

'Penzance Hybrids' (sweet briars).

1 *Potentilla fruticosa used as a hedge.*
2 *Rhododendrons give a permanent flowering hedge at Lynch, Allerford.*

Vigorous, single to semi-double pink flowers, attractive hips, 1.5–2.4m (5–8ft). 'Georges Vibert' (*R. gallica* hybrid). Carmine-pink with white stripes, 60–90cm (2–3ft). *R. officinalis* (*R. gallica maxima*) (red damask, apothecary's rose, red rose of Lancaster). Bushy habit, bright crimson, sweetly scented, June, 90cm–1.2m (3–4ft). *R. gallica versicolor* (*Rosa mundi*). Bushy habit, light crimson, striped and splashed pink, 90cm–1.2m (3–4ft).

Hybrid musk roses 'Cornelia', double coppery-apricot, flushed pink, delicious scent, June to October, 1.8–2.7m (6–9ft). 'Felicia', silvery-pink, richly scented, June to September, 1.8–2.7m (6–9ft). 'Penelope', semi-double, large, shell-pink blooms, richly fragrant, June to September, 1.8–2.4m (6–8ft). 'Prosperity', bushy habit, semi-double, creamy-pink, richly fragrant, June to September, 1.8–2.4m (6–8ft). 'Vanity', single, rosy-carmine, sweetly scented, June to September, 1.8–2.4m (6–8ft). 'Wilhelm', vigorous habit, rich crimson, June to October, 1.5–1.8m (5–6ft). *R. rugosa*. Single pink flowers in July, with pleasing fragrance, large red hips and yellow and orange foliage, in autumn. Suckers freely, 1.5–2.1m (5–7ft). 'Roseraie de L'Hay' (*R. rugosa* hybrid). Crimson-purple, June to

The rose is a good hedging plant. Rose 'Penelope' forms a flowering boundary.

September, 1.5–2.7m (5–9ft). 'Sarah Van Fleet' (*R. rugosa* hybrid). Semi-double, light pink, fragrant, 1.5–1.8m (5–6ft). 'Schneezwerg' (*R. rugosa* hybrid). Compact, upright habit, with rosette blooms. May to October, 90cm–1.2m (3–4ft). 'Stanwell Perpetual' (*R. rugosa* hybrid). Double flesh-pink, fading to white. June to October, 60–90cm (2–3ft).

Floribunda roses Since World War II the floribunda rose has become extremely popular. Many varieties are very vigorous and exceptionally free-flowering, which makes them ideal for hedges. One variety is better than a mixture, but where the latter is wanted the variety 'Masquerade' can be planted, as its flowers are a mixture of yellow, pink and red. Usually a single row is sufficient, planted at about 40cm (15in) apart, from November to March. In their first year prune the bushes back to within 15–25cm (6–9in) of soil level to encourage plenty of growth from the base. In subsequent years prune sufficiently to keep the hedge neat and the plants in good condition.

The following dozen is a good representative selection of floribundas in-

cluding the 'Grandiflora', 'The Queen Elizabeth', 'Chinatown', deep golden-yellow, edged cherry, scented, 1.2–1.5m (4–5ft). 'Dainty Maid', large single blooms, shaded warm rose and gold, 1.2–1.5m (4–5ft). 'Florence Mary Morse', large rich scarlet flowers which make a continuous show, 1.2–1.5m (4–5ft). 'Iceberg', the greenish-white blooms are produced right into the early winter, 1.2–1.5m (4–5ft). 'Korona', beautiful semi-double, flame-scarlet flowers of great size, 1.2–1.5m (4–5ft). 'Masquerade', this harlequin-like variety has buds which are at first yellow but the open flowers gradually change and deepen to shades of salmon pink and flame red. Height 90cm–1.2m (3–4ft). 'Orange Triumph', though the rich reddish-orange dusky coloured flowers of this 1937 variety are smaller than those of present-day floribundas, they are quite outstanding. Height 1.2–1.3m (4–4½ft). 'Rosemary Rose', attractive flat rosette, currant-red to crimson blooms quartered and sweetly scented, 1–1.3m (3–4ft). 'Shepherd's Delight', large clusters of semi-double orange-scarlet blooms touched with gold at the base. Slightly fragrant, 1.3–1.5m (4–5ft). 'Silberlachs', with its large clusters of warm pink flowers, replaces 'Else Poulsen'. Height 1.3–1.5m (4–5ft). 'The

Queen Elizabeth', very upright, tall-growing variety with rose-pink flowers on very long stems. Height a good 1.5m (5ft) or more.

Rose see **Rosa**

Rosemary see **Rosmarinus**

Rosmarinus (rosemary) This evergreen with aromatic leaves is useful where a small informal hedge is needed. *R. angusti folius* 'Corsican Blue', is an upright bushy shrub, with porcelain-blue flowers from April to June. Height 1.2–1.5m (3½–4½ft). *R. officinalis* (rosemary) has bluish-mauve flowers. Plant at 30–40cm (12–15in) apart, from mid to late April; trim after flowering. Any hard cutting back needed should be done in April. Height 2–2.3m (6–7ft), though 1–1.3m (3–4ft) is usually tall enough.

Rue see **Ruta**

Ruta (rue) Where an alternative to lavender is wanted, rue is ideal. *R. graveolens* 'Jackman's Blue', makes an attractive low evergreen hedge with glaucous-blue foliage. Plant 30–40cm (12–15in) apart in March. Trim in April. Height 60–90cm (2–3ft).

Santolina (lavender cotton or cotton lavender) *S. chamaecyparissus* is a hardy, dwarf evergreen, with silver-grey foliage and yellow button-like flowers. Plant 30cm (1ft) apart from September to April. Trim off old flower heads, when faded, with shears. To keep hedge neat clip in April. Height 45–60cm (1½–2ft).

Senecio *S. laxifolius* is an evergreen, with silver-grey leathery leaves and yellow daisy-like flowers. It makes an informal hedge. It does well in coastal areas, also in industrial cities. Plant 40–45cm (15–18in) apart in October or March. Trim in April. Height 1–1.3m (3–4ft).

Sorbus *S. intermedia* (Swedish white-beam). This is a hardy, deciduous tree, useful for hedging or screening. It has dull white flowers followed by red fruit in autumn. Plant from October to March, as a hedge 60–90cm (2–3ft) apart, for screening purposes 2.5–3m (8–9ft) or 5–6m (16–20ft) apart. Trim in late winter or early spring. Height 6–13m (20–40ft).

Spiraea These are hardy deciduous flowering shrubs. Plant 30–60cm (1–2ft) apart from October to March. Trim spring-flowering kinds after blooms have faded, summer and autumn flowering ones in February or March, at the same time hard pruning can be carried out on either group. *S. arguta* has white flowers in April and early May. Plant 40–60cm (1½–2ft) apart. Height 1.3–1.6m (4–5ft). *S. japonica* 'Anthony Waterer' has deep carmine flowers from July to September. Plant 50cm (1½ft) apart. Height 1–1.3m (3–4ft). *S. menziessii triumphans* has purple-rose bottle-brush like blooms from June to end of September. Plant 60–90cm (2–3ft) apart. Trim in winter or spring. Height 1.3–2m (4–6ft). *S. thunbergii* has bright green foliage, and sprays of white flowers from mid-March to mid-April. Plant 40–60cm

(1½–2ft) apart. Height 1.3–1.6m (4–5ft).

Syringa (lilac) *S. vulgaris* (the common lilac) is a deciduous shrub usually planted for its colourful, scented flowers. It does, however, make a very useful spring and summer hedge, its foliage changing from green to yellow in the autumn. If trimmed formally it will not flower, but if left to grow informally it will. Plant 50–60cm (2½–3ft) apart, October to March. Trim after flowering or in early April. Height 2–3m (5–10ft). Other species which can also be planted as hedges are: *S. chinensis* (Rouen lilac), with graceful foliage and lilac-coloured, fragrant flowers. Height 2–3m (6–10ft). *S. c. rubra,* purplish-red, fragrant flowers. Height 3–4m (9–12ft). *S. persica,* lilac-

1 Rosemary is a plant that can be used for an informal hedge. It is fragrant and likes the sunshine.
2 Climbing roses need the support of a fence or trellis to provide a screen.

1

2

coloured, scented flowers. Height 1–2m (4–6ft). *S. p. alba*, white, scented flowers. Height 1.2m (4–6ft). All bloom in May.

Tamarisk see **Tamarix**

Tamarix (tamarisk) These are deciduous shrubs, much used in coastal areas, as they stand up to salt spray. They will grow in poor sandy soil and also in limey soils. All have attractive feathery foliage and long slender spikes of white or pinkish flowers. Plant 50cm (1½ft) apart from October to March. Trim in late February or March. Species available are *T. anglica*, white-tinged, pink flowers, in late summer, and early autumn. Height up to 3m (10ft). *T. gallica* (common tamarisk), pink flowers in late summer and early autumn. Height up to 3m (10ft), *T. pentandra*, rosy-pink flowers in late July and August, height 4–6m (12–18ft). *T. tetrandra*, reddish-pink flowers in May, produced on the previous year's growth. Trim after flowering. Height 3–5m (10–15ft).

Viburnum *V. lantana* (wayfaring tree) is a deciduous shrub with white flowers in May and June, followed by red fruit in late summer and autumn which eventually turn black; the foliage often colours well in autumn. Plant 60–90cm (2–3ft) apart from October to March. Trim in the winter. It does well on chalky soils. Height up to 2m (8ft), sometimes more. *V. opulus* (guelder rose) is a deciduous shrub with flat bract-like white flowers in early June, followed by bright red berries and colourful foliage in autumn. Plant 60–90cm (2–3ft) apart from October to March. Trim in winter. Height 2.5–3m (8–10ft). *V. tinus* (laurustinus) is a most popular evergreen hedging shrub, especially in south coast areas. It thrives equally well on chalk or non-chalk soils. Its white flowers with pink stamens are produced throughout

Tamarix is a first class plant for a hedge or screen in a seaside garden.

the winter and often throughout the spring. Plant 50cm (1½ft) apart in early autumn or even in spring. Trim in April. Height 2.3m (6–10ft).

Weigela *W. florida variegata,* makes an attractive deciduous hedge with silver variegated foliage and strawberry-ice-pink flowers in May and June. Height 2–3m (6–8ft). *W. × hybrida* and its many varieties are all equally suitable. Plant 60–90cm (2–3ft) apart from October to March. Trim all species and varieties, after flowering. Height 2–3m (6–9ft).

Whitebeam, Swedish see **Sorbus intermedia**

Conifers All the conifers recommended are evergreen except *Larix* (larch) and *Metasequoia* which are deciduous. Conifers, like other evergreens, have the advantage that they provide a permanent screen for twelve months of the year. Many also have attractive colour forms which include varying shades of green, gold and silver through the glaucous blues. The genus with the greatest variety of forms is *Chamaecyparis*, especially *C. lawsoniana*, Lawson's cypress. The two most recent conifers planted as hedges are × *Cupressocyparis leylandii* and *Metasequoia glyptostroboides*.

Chamaecyparis *C. lawsoniana* (Lawson's cypress). The foliage of this conifer ranges through the palest to the darkest greens to glaucous green and blue. Plant at 50–60cm (1½–2ft) apart in late September to October, or March to April. Trim in May or June. When severe pruning is necessary this is done in April. Height 3–5m (10–18ft). *C. l. allumii* has glaucous blue foliage. Height 3–4m (10–12ft). *C. l. erecta* 'Jackman's Variety' has green foliage and is conical in habit. Height 2–2.5m (5–8ft). *C. l. fletcheri* has bluish-grey, feathery foliage. Height 1–3m (4–10ft). *C. l.* 'Green Hedger' is a very rich green. Height 1.5–5m (5–15ft). *C. l. lutea* has golden foliage. Height 2–2.5m (5–8ft). *C. l. pisifera plumosa aurea* (syn. *Retinospora pisifera plumosa aurea*) has soft, golden feathery foliage. Height 2–4m (5–12ft). *C. l.* 'Triomphe de Boskoop', has glaucous blue foliage.

Cryptomeria *C. japonica elegans* has feathery juvenile foliage, which is permanently retained; it is a glaucous green in summer, changing from rich bronze to rosy red in autumn and winter. Plant 50cm (1½ft) apart in September or October, or March or April. Trim in April and again in August. Height 2.5–3m (5–6ft).

Cupressocyparis × *C. leylandii*. This bi-generic hybrid has, since the end of World War II, become very popular, and has in fact superseded *Cupressus macrocarpa* which is one of its parents, the other being *Chamaecyparis nootkatensis*. This tree has the speed of growth of *C. macrocarpa* with the hardiness of *C. nootkatensis*, which is a native of western North America from Alaska or Oregon. It makes a fine hedge or first-rate screen tree. Plant 50–60cm (1½–2ft) apart, in September or October or March or April. Trim in July and August. Height for hedges 2–2.5m (5–8ft), for screens 20–25m (50–60ft).

Cupressus *C. macrocarpa* (Monterey cypress) is a fast growing conifer which is a bright green when young, later turning darker and less bright. It was introduced in 1838 and for 100 years was, apart from *Thuja occidentalis, T. plicata* and *Chamaecyparis lawsoniana,* the most popular conifer planted for hedges, particularly in coastal areas in the south. However, in recent years its popularity has waned because of its tender habit and unreliability in frost, coupled with its dislike of regular clipping. Ten to fifteen years is a good average life span for a macrocarpa hedge. Plant 50–60cm (1½–2ft) apart in late March or April. Trim during the middle of April. Height 3–5m (8–15ft).

Larix (larch) *L. decidua* (syn. *L. europaea*) (common larch) is a deciduous conifer with fresh green foliage. It is useful as a screen tree in a mixed planting. It thrives best on chalk or sandy soils. Plant 1m (4ft) apart, eventually thinning the trees to 2.5m (8ft). A double row makes an effective windbreak. Plant from October to March. Height up to 20m (50ft).

Metasequoia *M. glyptostroboides* (the dawn cypress) is an ancient, deciduous conifer introduced to this country in 1948. Its habit of growth and foliage is remarkably like that of *Taxodium distichum,* swamp cypress. The dawn cypress makes an upright tree with soft-green, feathery foliage in spring which changes to a rich pinky-brown in autumn. It makes a beautiful hedge or an excellent screen tree. Plant 60cm (2ft) apart in September or October or March or April. Trim three or four times a year between spring and late summer. Height for hedges could be anything from 2–3m (5–10ft). The eventual height for screening purposes is at present unknown, but is likely to be at least 15–20m (50–60ft).

Picea (spruce) *P. abies* (common or Norway spruce) is a hardy conifer with deep glossy green needles or leaves, the tree usually grown as the Christmas tree. It is a useful conifer to plant among deciduous trees. Plant 1.3–2.3m (4–8ft) apart in September or October, or March or April. Height up to 30m (100ft).

Pinus (pine) *P. laricio* (Corsican pine) is a very hardy tree, with dark green foliage. It is a good wind resister, but does not transplant well, and it is best to plant 30cm (1ft) high specimens. Plant 1m (3ft) apart in September or April, thinning them later. Height 25–30m (80–100ft). *P. l. nigricans* (Austrian pine) has dark green foliage, is very wind-hardy, and thrives on chalky or poor soils. Plant at 30cm (1ft) high, 1m (3ft) apart in September or April, thinning later. Height 25–30m (80–100ft). *P. radi-*

The various forms of chamaecyparis are useful for an evergreen screen. Here a golden form adds decorative interest.

ata (syn. *P. insignis*) (Monterey pine) has beautiful grassy-green foliage, is very fast growing, does best in maritime areas and is wind-hardy. It prefers deep, rich well-drained soils. Plant 1–1.5m (4–5ft) apart in September or April. Height 25–30m (80–100ft). *P. sylvestris* (Scots pine) is one of the most beautiful and stately conifers when mature. It has a rugged reddish-brown trunk, grey-green needles and small brown cones. Plant at 1m (3ft) apart in September or April, thinning as and when needed. Height 25–30m (80–100ft).

Taxus *T. baccata* (common yew). This is without a doubt the oldest and most revered conifer which we plant for hedging purposes. It makes a wonderful wall-like hedge, is excellent for topiary and can be grown in any soil, lime, clay or sand; and for full measure it flourishes in coastal areas, and is equally accommodating in industrial areas. Yew is not slow growing as it is so often thought to be and a well established hedge will make as much as 30–45cm (1–1½ft) of growth a year. However, you have to be patient with a yew hedge; young bushes transplant better than older ones and they usually make quicker growth. Yews must have good drainage, they also require ample humus in the soil. Before planting, bastard trench or double dig the ground. When preparing the soil, add rotted farmyard manure, or good garden compost, plus bonemeal at the rate of 160g (6oz) per sq m (sq yd). Bushes

1 Formal hedges at Hidcote Manor, Gloucestershire.
2 An archway has been formed in this mixed beech hedge.

Screens and Windbreak trees

Name	Deciduous	Evergreen	Chalk Soils	Damp Soils	Dry and Sand Soils	Seaside	Autumn Colour	Remarks
Acer platanoides (Norway maple)	X		X	X	X	X	X	ideal for exposed sites
A. platanoides 'Crimson King'	X		X	X	X	X	X	purple on under surfaces of leaves
A. pseudoplatanus (sycamore)	X		X	X	X	X	X	ideal for exposed sites
A. pseudoplatanus purpureum	X		X	X	X	X	X	purple on under surfaces of the leaves
Alnus glutinosa (alder)	X		X	X				fast growing—attractive catkins in autumn and spring
Betula pendula (silver birch)	X		X		X	X	X	fast growing—attractive white bark
Carpinus betulus (hornbeam)	X			X	X		X	attractive catkins
Castanea sativa (sweet or Spanish chestnut)	X		X					fairly fast growing
Crataegus (hawthorn, quickthorn or May)								
C. oxyacantha	X		X	X	X	X	X	very wind hardy, often holds its red berries right through the winter
C. prunifolia	X		X	X	X	X	X	large red fruits and crimson foliage
Cupressus macrocarpa (Monterey cypress)		X	X		X	X		ideal as separate screen trees, fast growing
C. macrocarpa lutea		X	X		X	X		golden-yellow foliage, not so fast growing as the species
Chamaecyparis lawsoniana (Lawson's Cypress)	X	X	X					fairly fast growing, requires protection against winds when young
C. lawsoniana allumii		X	X	X				glaucous-blue foliage
C. lawsoniana fraseri		X	X	X				grey-green foliage
C. lawsoniana lutea		X	X	X				golden-yellow foliage
C. lawsoniana stewartii		X	X	X				golden-yellow foliage
× *Cupressocyparis leylandii*		X	X			X		fast growing, reaches 30–40 ft.
Eucalyptus gunnii		X	X		X	X		fast growing, hardiest of the eucalyptus, requires firm staking when young
Fagus sylvatica (common beech)	X		X				X	brown foliage in autumn
F. sylvatica purpurea (copper beech)	X		X				X	copper coloured foliage in autumn
Ilex aquifolium (holly)		X	X		X			slow growing, very tough
Larix decidua (larch)	X		X		X		X	
Metasequoia glyptostroboides	X			X			X	fast growing, prefers moist soil
Olearia macrodonta		X	X		X	X		dark, glossy green holly-like foliage
Picea abies (Norway spruce)		X	X					fine for planting mixed screens
P. omorika (Serbian spruce)		X	X					
P. sitchensis (Sitka spruce)		X	X					both are excellent as screen trees well spaced out
Pinus laricio (Corsican pine)		X			X			bad transplanter, therefore plant very small plants
P. laricio nigricans (Austrian pine)		X	X					very wind hardy
P. radiata (Monterey pine)		X	X			X		fast growing, needs a mild maritime area
P. sylvestris (Scots pine)		X	X		X			very wind-hardy
Populus (Poplar)								
P. alba (white poplar)	X		X			X		fast growing, very hardy and resistant to salt winds
P. nigra italica (Lombardy poplar)	X		X					upright habit, very hardy also fast growing
Quercus ilex (evergreen oak)		X	X		X	X		very hardy and flourishes in coastal districts
Q. robur (common oak)	X							does best on stiff loams, but will tolerate light-sandy soils
Rhododendron ponticum		X				X		dislikes chalk soils, fairly fast growing
Sorbus intermedia (Swedish whitebeam)	X							good for street planting and industrial areas
Thuja occidentalis (American *arbor-vitae*)		X	X	X			X	useful where a colourful permanent conifer screen is needed
T. plicata		X	X					attractive dark green foliage
Tsuga albertiana		X	X		X			fast growing

1

2

1 At Waddesdon Manor, Bucks. Yew hedges emphasise the terrace and stairway. 2 at Ammerdown Park, Somerset, the tall yew hedges are clipped formally.

should be 30–90cm (1–3ft) high. Plant them 30–60cm (1–2ft) apart, in September or early October or late March or April. Trim in August or September. When hard pruning is needed do this in April. Height for hedging 3–5m (10–15ft); for screens up to 7–10m (20–30ft).

Thuja *T. occidentalis* (American arborvitae) is a useful, pleasantly scented conifer, greenish leaved during the summer, turning a brownish-green colour in autumn and winter. Plant at 45–60cm (1½–2ft) apart in late September or October or March or April. Trim in late summer. Young hedges need trimming in early life, though the top is best left until it reaches the required height. Height for hedging 2–4m (5–12ft), as a screen 10–13m (30–40ft). *T. plicata* (giant thuja). For a time between the two world

wars this thuja was not much planted because of a fungus disease to which it was prone, but fortunately this trouble became less evident in the 1960s. Its dark, glossy green foliage makes it a most handsome hedge. Plant 45–60cm (1½–2ft) apart in late September or October or March or April. Trim in late summer. Height as a hedge 2–4m (5–12ft), for a screen 15–17m (50–60ft). *T. p. zebrina*, a golden variegated form requires the same treatment as *T. plicata*. Height for hedging 2–3m (6–12ft), screens 10–13m (30–40ft).

Heeling in

A form of temporary planting which enables plants to remain in good condition until they can be put in their permanent positions. When plants arrive and it is for any reason inconvenient to plant them, they can be heeled in.

A small 'V'-shaped trench is opened, the plants laid up one side of it, close together, and the soil pushed back and firmed with the foot.

Shoots that are to be prepared for grafting are usually heeled in to retard their development so that they will be less advanced in growth than the stock on to which they are to be grafted.

The operation can be undertaken at any time of the year, with herbaceous plants, shrubs and saplings. It is always a good plan, if possible, to arrange them so that the growth lies behind the roots in the direction of the prevailing wind. Bulbs when lifted from spring bedding can be heeled in in a reserve part of the garden until required for planting again later in the season.

Herb gardens

The form and size of a herb garden is determined by the interest these plants hold for the individual. It can be a tiny border of commonly used culinary herbs such as mint, parsley, sage and thyme or an elaborate garden designed to house a wide collection of herbs. Many plants could legitimately be included in one of these large gardens, so that the decorative effect can be the primary consideration when drawing up the plan. For success, a sheltered part of the garden should be chosen. Herbs are always at their best in warm still air and a hedge can be planted to provide both seclusion and decorative completeness to the garden. Choose rosemary, lavender, sage or roses for this hedge. A good temporary shelter can be provided quickly for a season or two by annual sunflowers, until the newly-planted hedge attains a useful size. A gently sloping site often affords the best position as drainage is essential unless a bog garden proper is to be a feature of the herb garden.

Borders Small herb borders, as part of the vegetable garden, to provide flavourings for culinary use, are best treated like vegetable borders. The plants should be set in rows so that the hoe can

run between them as regularly as it is in the remaining part of the kitchen garden. In its widest sense the herb border can be virtually a herbaceous border and include verbascum, chicory, catmint, delphinium, artemisia, tansy and foxglove; then it needs to be planned just as carefully as a perennial border is planned. The herb borders near the alpine house at the Royal Horticultural Society's garden at Wisley, Surrey, provide good examples of the medium-sized border and are confined to sage, balms, thymes, alliums, rue, mints, salvias, borage, marjorams and angelica. It is obvious that the decorative value is less than when the choice of plants is extended to include many flowering plants. The decision as to what to include, or exclude, is determined by personal choice as well as available space.

Natural orders The natural order garden is a favourite way of assembling herbs and examples can be seen at many botanic gardens, including Kew and Oxford. The principle is to arrange plants of one natural order in each bed, making a representative collection as a whole. The idea can be extended according to the selection of plants and each bed can be designed as a small island border, though naturally this is difficult for the *Umbelliferae* and labiates, which all seem to have such strong family resemblances.

Collections The collection may be limited to medicinal herbs, such as belladonna, digitalis, aconitum, betony, comfrey, or may be a cook's corner, or merely include the sweetly-scented and aromatic plants beloved of bees and preserved as pot-pourri. Similarly one may build up a Bible garden, growing only plants mentioned in the Bible, or a Shakespeare garden including only those plants the poet mentioned.

Designs for herb gardens Individual beds lend themselves to a checkerboard effect where small square beds are formed in staggered rows, the alternate spaces between being paved or set with chamomile to form carpets. This draughtboard design makes a good foundation for many kinds of herb garden and is effective when each bed contains a single kind of plant. This sort of herb garden is to be seen at Lullingstone Castle near Eynsford in Kent and was planned by the late Miss Eleanor Sinclair Rohde. Larger gardens can be planned on a more ambitious scale. A favourite approach is to have a central feature such as a sundial or bird bath, bee hive or even a circular chamomile or

1 A narrow trench is taken out and the plants put in to lean against one side of the trench, and away from wind.
2 Soil is replaced around the roots.
3 The soil is firmed with the foot.
4 Once the operation is complete, the plants can remain for some months.

Some plants to include in the herb garden

Alkanet (Anchusa)
Angelica *(Angelica archangelica)*
Aniseed *(Pimpinella anisum)*
Artemisias.
Balm *(Melissa officinalis)*
Basil, bush *(Ocimum minimum)*
Basil, sweet *(Ocimum basilicum)*
Bay *(Laurus nobilis)*
Belladonna *(Atropa belladonna)*
Bergamot *(Monarda didyma)*
Bistort *(Polygonum bistorta)*
Borage *(Borago officinalis)*
Broom (Cytisus spp.)
Caraway *(Carum carvi)*
Catmint (Nepeta)
Celandine *(Ranunculus ficaria)*
Chamomile *(Anthemis nobilis)*
Chervil *(Anthriscus cerefolium)*
Chicory *(Cichorium intybus)*
Chives *(Allum schoenoprasum)*
Comfrey *(Symphytum officinale)*
Coriander *(Coriandrum sativum)*
Corn salad *(Valerianella locusta)*
Costmary *(Chrysanthemum balsamita)*
Cumin *(Cuminum cyminum)*

Curry plant *(Helichrysum angustifolium)*
Dandelion *(Taraxacum officinale)*
Dill *(Anethum graveolens)*
Elder *(Sambucus nigra)*
Elecampane *(Inula helenium)*
Fennel *(Foeniculum officinale and F. vulgare)*
Feverfew *(Chrysanthemum parthenium)*
Figwort *(Scrophularia nodosa)*
Foxglove *(Digitalis purpurea)*
Fumitory *(Fumaria officinalis)*
Garlic *(Allium sativum)*
Germander *(Teucrium spp)*
Good King Henry *(Chenopodium bonus-Henricus)*
Ground Ivy *(Glechoma hederacea)*
Hellebore *(Helleborus niger)*
Henbane *(Hyoscyamus niger)*
Horehound *(Marrubium vulgare)*
Horseradish *(Armoracia rusticana)*
Hyssop *(Hyssopus officinalis)*
Juniper *(Juniperus communis)*
Lady's Mantle *(Alchemilla vulgaris)*
Lavender *(Lavandula officinalis)*

Lavender Cotton (Santolina)
Lime *(Tilia europaea)*
Lovage *(Ligusticum officinale)*
Mace *(Achillea decolorans)*
Mallow (Malva spp)
Marigold *(Calendula officinalis)*
Mignonette *(Reseda odorata)*
Mints (Mentha spp)
Monkshood *(Aconitum anglicum)*
Mulberry *(Morus nigra)*
Mullein *(Verbascum thapsus)*
Musk (Mimulus)
Nasturtium *(Tropaeolum majus)*
Nettle *(Urtica dioica)*
Orache *(Atriplex hortensis)*
Orris Root *(Iris florentina)*
Parsley *(Carum petroselinum)*
Pennyroyal (see Mint)
Peppermint (see Mint)
Periwinkle *(Vinca major and V. minor)*
Purslane (Portulaca spp)
Raspberry *(Rubus idaeus)*
Rhubarb *(Rheum rhaponticum)*
Rose (Rosa spp)
Rosemary *(Rosmarinus officinalis)*

Rue *(Ruta graveolens)*
Saffron *(Crocus sativus)*
Sages *(Salvia officinalis)*
Salad Burnet *(Sanguisorba minor)*
St John's Wort (Hypericum)
Savory *(Satureja hortensis)*
Senna (Cassia)
Sorrel (Rumex spp)
Southernwood *(Artemisia abrotanum)*
Spearmint *(Mentha spicata)*
Sunflower *(Helianthus annuus)*
Sweet Bergamot (Monarda)
Sweet Cicely *(Myrrhis odorata)*
Tansy *(Tanacetum vulgare)*
Tarragon *(Artemisia dracunculus)*
Thymes (Thymus spp)
Valerian *(Valeriana officinalis)*
Verbena *(Verbena officinalis)*
Vervain *(Verbena officinalis)*
Violet *(Viola odorata)*
Woad *(Isatis tinctoria)*
Woodruff *(Asperula odorata)*
Yarrow *(Achillea millefolium)*

1 The herb garden at Sissinghurst, Kent is bordered by a hedge to provide a shelter from wind and weather.
2 Mint, one of the commonest of herbs.
3 Comfrey, or the old fashioned knit-bone, is a decorative perennial.

thyme lawn forming the hub of a wheel and long narrow beds of individual plants forming the spokes. In a plan such as this, the juxtaposition of various plants requires a little forethought, otherwise ill-assorted neighbours can mar the general charm of the idea.

Harvesting and drying The art of harvesting and drying herbs to retain the flavour and aroma is one that can be acquired only by practice. The essentials are to harvest at the right time and in the right condition that part of the plant to be used, say seed, leaf or root, and to dry the material at the correct rate. Our climate is too humid to allow for drying in the open without deterioration. The object in drying is to dehydrate the plant by good ventilation. The process is, therefore, best undertaken in a well-ventilated, shaded or dark place where a temperature of not less than 70°F (21°C) can be maintained.

The part of the plant required should be collected when it is ready, handling a small portion only at a time. Put the material into flat boxes or garden trugs when it is cut in the garden and never collect more than there is time to spread out for drying immediately. Material left about in heaps starts to deteriorate immediately because the essential oils escape. Many umbelliferous plants, notably sweet Cicely, flag at once and cannot really be dried. In general the best time to harvest leaves is usually

just before the flowers are fully open and a sufficient number of leaves must be left on the plant for it to continue to function. Flowers such as lavender and bergamot are at their best when they are fully open, but to catch the essential oils, gather them just before maturity, and select unblemished ones. Seed is ready when it is mature and needs merely to be cleaned of seed pods and husks when dry. Roots, naturally, are lifted at the end of the season. By gathering on a dry

1 Bay leaves come from the evergreen shrub Laurus nobilis, which is a useful addition to the herb garden.
2 Caraway and woad at Sissinghurst.
3 The common sage can be had in this attractive variegated form, Salvia officinalis aureo-variegata.
4 The broad-leaved garlic is native to Britain, a plant as much at home in the herb border as in the kitchen garden proper.
5 A good plant of balm, Melissa officinalis, which has soft aromatic leaves.
6 Bistort, or esterledges, a native plant with pungent bitter leaves.
7 Rue, Ruta graveolens 'Jackman's Blue', is a glaucous-leaved form.
8 Chives, the leaves of which are used in cooking to impart a delicate onion flavour to food.
9 Lovage, Ligusticum officinale, a plant with many old world associations, is not much grown these days.

day, as soon as the dew has gone, the least amount of moisture adheres to the plant material. One kind of material should always be kept separate from another and a minimum amount of handling is important to avoid bruising.

Some plants such as sage can be hung in small bunches in an outhouse or porch to dry, but it is far better to treat all material to a quicker drying method. Domestically the most suitable places are airing cupboards, darkened greenhouses, the plate-warming compartment of a cooker, a slow oven (with the door left ajar), a clothes drying cabinet or a spare room provided with electric heater and ventilator fan. All these places need to be dust free. Flat cardboard boxes without lids, sheets of brown paper, hessian, muslin or nylon tacked to wooden frames to make a tray, may be used to hold the herbs during the process. Wire netting is not suitable, unless it is covered with muslin, because the metal can damage the plant material. The ideal temperature is between 70 and 90°F (21 and 32°C) and ought not to

181

exceed 100°F. An air thermometer is a help and indeed a necessity where any quantity of herbs are to be treated. The ideal is not to have the temperature so high that the plants blacken (parsley does not seem to lose its colour in this way).

A minimum of handling should be the rule during the drying process; a daily turning should be enough because the amount of material being treated should be small in relation to the drying accommodation available. Maintain a temperature around 90°F (32°C) for the first twenty-four hours then reduce it to around 70°F (21°C) until the process is complete. There should be only a faint aroma; if the scent becomes strong this is a certain indication that the temperature is too high. Fresh material ought not to be introduced into the drying chamber before one operation is complete because this increases the humidity, although sometimes this cannot be avoided. The exact time taken over the process is difficult to estimate and will vary according to the space, ventilation and amount of material being treated. Leaves and stems should

be brittle and rattle slightly when touched but they should not be so dry as to shatter to powder when handled. Should the stems bend and not break under the fingers then they are not quite dry. Roots need to be brittle right through and not have a fibrous or spongey core. The amount of water in a growing plant is as high as 80 or 90 per cent. So to obtain an appreciable amount of dried material for winter use a comparatively large amount of the fresh plant needs to be harvested over a period.

Storing The essential requisite is that the dried herbs are stored in such a way that reabsorption of atmospheric moisture is impossible. This can present quite a problem in our climate. First allow the herbs to cool after drying, then chop, rub or sieve them as required discarding stems and other chaff. Pack them away at once to prevent dust from being collected. Glass jars with screw tops are suitable only for small quantities of material destined for immediate use. Otherwise, metal containers or foil lined boxes are suitable, but wooden jars with either tight-fitting lids or screw

caps are ideal. Plastic bags firmly closed with a sealer can be stored in boxes, but it is always a good plan to keep each kind of herb absolutely separate from another.

Freezing Several culinary herbs, particularly the soft-leaved ones such as mint and balm can be successfully stored in the deep freeze. Treat them separately, and store in plastic bags after blanching. Chives, mint, balm, fennel, parsley and sorrel can all be kept in this way. Wash the plants well under running water, plunge them for about thirty seconds into boiling water, cool them under the cold water tap, put them into plastic bags, seal and store until required in the deep freeze. They require very gentle thawing before use.

Herbaceous borders

The herbaceous border, which is a comparative newcomer to the garden scene, is still one of its most popular features. Introduced at the turn of the century by Gertrude Jekyll as a protest against the monotonous formality of Victorian garden design, its popularity has steadily increased until today there are few gardens without some kind of perennial border to enhance their beauty throughout the months of summer and autumn.

Restricted originally to plants of purely perennial habit—in the main, those whose growth begins afresh from ground level each year—the terms of reference have gradually been extended so that today we find included not only spring and summer bulbs and corms but also small shrubby plants and those curious in-betweens whose woody top growth persists throughout the winter, but which otherwise display most of the characteristics of true perennials. These are the sub-shrubs, of which plants such as the plumbago-flowered *Ceratostigma willmottianum, Caryopteris clandonensis,* and the Russian sage, *Perovskia atriplicifolia* are typical examples.

Preparing the site Preliminary preparation of the site for an herbaceous border is of paramount importance. Much of its subsequent success or failure will depend on the thoroughness with which it is carried out. Some soils, of course are a good deal more difficult to prepare than others but whether you garden on heavy, back-breaking clay or easily managed well-drained sandy loam there must be sufficient supplies of humus in the soil if the plants are to give of their best.

Deep digging and thorough cultivation are two further essentials. Most of the occupants of the border will remain in the same positions for at least three years, while other more permanent specimens such as paeonies, helebores,

An established and carefully planned herbaceous border adds an air of permanence to a garden.

romneyas and hemerocallis can stay put almost indefinitely, without the necessity for division or replanting.

To make sure that such conditions are fulfilled it may be necessary to double dig the whole of the projected plot. This will result in a thorough breaking up of both the surface and second spits of soil. As far as medium to light well-drained loams are concerned, bastard trenching, which leaves the lower spit *in situ* but broken up with a fork, is probably just as effective, but it is better to give wet, heavy soils the full treatment.

Humus Thorough digging, however, is not sufficient to create the soil conditions in which perennials thrive best. To provide them, plentiful supplies of humus or humus-forming material must be present in the soil, enough, in fact, to satisfy much of the plants' needs for several seasons, as normally the border will be due for a complete overhaul only once in every three to four years.

Humus can be provided by a variety of materials, the best of which, of course, is the almost impossible to obtain stable or farmyard manure. Most of us, however, will have to settle for alternatives. Compost, properly made and well rotted down, heads the list of these but supplies of this are quickly exhausted unless we supplement our garden and domestic waste with straw, sawdust, or other similar materials brought in from outside.

Leafmould is excellent, but expensive unless you are lucky enough to have access to natural sources of supply. Oak and beech leaves are the richest in plant foods, while bracken rots down to a material of peat-like consistency, good for stepping up the humus content of the soil but otherwise lacking in plant foods. Young bracken shoots, on the other hand, are rich in plant foods and minerals and make a valuable contribution to the compost heap.

For the town gardener and for those who cannot readily obtain the materials mentioned above, peat is the best soil conditioner. It is clean both to store and handle, and can hold many times its own bulk of moisture.

Spent hops are another first-rate humus forming material. If you can obtain supplies in bulk from a local brewery, they will be relatively cheap. The so-called hop manures with added organic fertilizers are a convenient but expensive method of supplying humus to the border.

These, or any other similar materials, are best worked into the upper spit as digging progresses. Alternatively they can be forked into the soil a few weeks before the plants are put in.

Fortunately, the vast majority of the more widely-grown herbaceous perennials are very accommodating. They will thrive in most types of soil although characteristics such as height, vigour and rate of increase will vary consider-

ably between, for example, light, sandy loams and heavy, sticky clays. It is a good rule never to coddle temperamental plants. There is neither time nor room for them in the herbaceous border, where plants are grown more for their effect in the mass than as individuals.

Weeds The best time of the year to prepare the site for planting is late summer or early autumn. This will give the winter frosts a chance to break up heavy clods to a fine planting tilth. This, of course, is not so important with light sandy soils which can be cultivated at almost any season of the year. As digging progresses, it is imperative to remove every possible vestige of perennial weeds; the aim should be to start with a site that is completely weed-free, although when fresh ground is being taken over this can be no more than a counsel of perfection.

Watch particularly for the roots of bindweed, ground elder and couch grass. Any of these can soon stage a rapid comeback even if only a few pieces remain in the soil.

Couch grass, or 'twitch' as it is sometimes called, is easily recognizable; the narrow leaf blades are coarse, with serrated edges; leaves and underground runners are sectional, like miniature bamboo shoots, with nodules at the joints. Ground elder has leaves similar

A hedge provides an ideal background for an herbaceous border.

to those of its shrub namesake and quite attractive flowers. It is easily identified by the pungent aroma of its bruised leaves and stems. Bindweed, also known as bellbind in some parts of the country, has attractive white trumpet-shaped flowers and a twining habit that can strangle any plant that is the object of its attentions.

Any of these weeds are anathema in the border and once established will prove well-nigh impossible to eradicate without a complete overhaul. Other perennial weeds—not quite as difficult but still a nuisance—include docks, thistles, clover and creeping buttercup. In acid soils sorrel, too, can be troublesome.

If annual weeds multiply alarmingly, and they will, in very wet summers, there is no need for undue despondency. Regular sessions with a hand fork or a lady's border fork will keep them in check. Vigorous low-growing perennials will act as their own ground cover.

In autumn, and in early spring if possible, the border should have a thorough forking over, removing and burning all perennial weeds. Any clumps of plants that show signs of weed infestation should be dug up. After

shaking or washing their roots free of soil, offending weed roots or runners that have penetrated the plants should be carefully teased out and removed. The clumps can then be replanted *in situ,* or if their size warrants it, be split up and re-grouped. If the replanting is carried out without delay the plants will not suffer any check. In fact, very vigorous growers such as Michaelmas daisies, *Campanula lactiflora* and *Chrysanthemum maximum* will benefit from this procedure.

It follows from the foregoing that new stocks received from the nursery or from generous fellow-gardeners should have their roots carefully examined for invading weeds before they are put in. We may not be able to suppress entirely the weeds that are present in the soil, but there is no point in deliberately planting trouble.

Supplementary dressings Unless farmyard manure has been available in generous quantities it will be advisable to give a booster of some kind of fertilizer a few weeks before the border is planted up. Bonemeal and fish manure, which are both organic and slow acting, will give good results, applied at a rate of 60–80g (2–3oz) to the sq m (sq yd). As an alternative, a good general fertilizer, such as 'Growmore' can be used at the rate recommended by the makers.

A good way of distributing this supplementary plant food is to rake it into the soil when the final preparations for planting are being made. Alternatively, it can be pricked lightly into the surface with a fork. An established border will benefit from a similar dressing when growth starts in spring.

Siting Most of the more widely-grown perennials are sun-lovers, so that a position facing south or west will be the most suitable for the border. But since this feature is seen at its best when viewed lengthwise, it may be necessary, if we plan to enjoy its beauty from some fixed vantage point such as a terrace or the living room windows, to effect some sort of compromise where aspect is concerned.

Generally speaking, any position except a sunless north-facing one, or one where the plants suffer shade and drip from overhanging trees, will be quite satisfactory.

Background Just as a fine picture deserves an appropriate frame, so the herbaceous border needs a proper setting for its beauty. In the past this has usually been supplied by a background wall or hedge, but nowadays double-

1 Herbaceous plants are divided by levering them apart with two forks plunged back to back through the clump.
2 The small divisions can be replanted.
3 Twiggy stakes are pushed in around each plant to provide support.
4 Taller plants need to be tied around individually to stouter stakes.

1

2

1 and 2 Well planned borders where varying height, colour and texture all play a part in the successful effect.

sided and island borders are becoming popular, where the only background is provided by the adjacent grass or paving. Nothing, however, makes a more suitable backcloth than a well-kept evergreen hedge—yew, holly, cypress, beech, or hornbeam. Mellowed brick or stone wall, too, can act as a pleasing accompaniment, and even wattle hurdles or a wooden fence, when discreetly covered by climbing plants, can provide an attractive setting.

Plants grown against walls or fences will require additional attention where staking and tying are concerned. In rough weather strong gusts and eddies develop at their base which can have disastrous results unless the plants are strongly secured.

Hedges, beautiful though they may be as backgrounds, also have their disadvantages. Most, if not all, hedging plants are notorious soil robbers. Some, such as privet, are much worse than others and should be avoided if a new planting is to be made. The roots of an established hedge can be kept in check by taking out a trench a foot or so away from the base of the plants and chopping back all the fibrous roots with

a sharp spade. This operation, which should be carried out while the hedge is dormant, could very well coincide with the periodic overhaul and replanting of the border.

If space permits, it is a good plan to leave a gap of 60–90cm (2–3ft) between the foot of the hedge and the rear rank border plants. This, incidentally, will also provide useful access to the back of the border for maintenance work.

Yew, of course, is the best plant for a background hedge. Slow and compact in growth, it requires a minimum of attention—one 'short back and sides' trim annually will suffice, and its foliage of sombre green is the perfect foil for the bright colours of the border plants.

Planning Planning the border can be fun. With squared paper and a sheaf of nursery catalogues there could be few pleasanter ways of spending a winter's evening by the fire. Ready-made collections complete with planting plans are useful for the complete novice and can form the nucleus of a wider collection, but it is a good deal more interesting to work out your own colour schemes and to see the plans coming to fruition in the garden.

There is such a wide choice of herbaceous plants that the permutations and combinations of colour, form and texture are infinite in number. Indi-

vidual tastes vary and so do fashions in flower colours. The pastel shades, popular for so many years, are giving place to the stronger reds, yellows and blues of the Victorian era.

A border composed entirely of any one of these primary colours would be striking in its effect, but the planning would need very careful handling and a thorough knowledge of plant characteristics. If you lack experience, you would be well advised to use a mixture of colours, grouped according to your individual taste.

As a general rule, in a border of mixed colours the paler shades should be at each end, with the brighter, more vivid ones grouped mainly at the centre. For example, the pure whites of *Phlox paniculata alba*, *Achillea ptarmica* 'The Pearl', and *Gypsophila* 'Bristol Fairy' could melt almost imperceptibly into the cool primrose yellows of *Achillea taygetea* and *Verbascum bombyciferum* (syn. *broussa*), flanked by the deeper yellows of *Hemerocallis* 'Hyperion', one of the best of the free-flowering day lilies, and *Lysimachia punctata*, the yellow loosestrife.

The middle of the border could explode into brilliant colour with scarlet *Lychnis chalcedonica*, *Lobelia fulgens*, *Potentilla* 'Gibson's Scarlet', and the garnet-red *Astilbe* 'Fanal'. Once past its climax, the border could progress to

1 Campanula glomerata has clustered heads of deep violet flowers in June.
2 The silver-grey foliage of Artemisia gnaphalodes gives a light effect.
3 The papery silver-lilac bracts of Salvia × superba are attractive.

white once more through the blues of delphiniums, sea holly, (*Eryngium maritimum*) whose leaves, as well as the flowers are metallic blue, and the stately *Echinops ritro*, with thistle-like dark green foliage and drumstick flower heads of steely blue. Other suitable blue perennials include the attractive indigo-blue monkshood, *Aconitum* 'Bressingham Spire' and the curious balloon flower, *Platycodon grandiflorum*.

These could be followed by the soft pinks of *Geranium endressii*, *Sidalcea* 'Sussex Beauty', the long flowering *Veronica spicata*—'Pavane' and 'Minuet' are both good varieties—and the later-blooming ice plant, *Sedum spectabile* 'Brilliant'.

And so back to white again, this time represented by Japanese anemones, *Anemone hupehensis* 'Honorine Jobert', *Lysimachia clethroides*, *Potentilla alba* and a good garden form of the sweetly scented meadow sweet, *Filipendula ulmaria plena*.

This, of course, would not constitute a complete planting plan, but is merely a suggestion that could form the framework of an attractive herbaceous border. Colour, though it may take pride of place in the overall display, is not everything where the successful herbaceous border is concerned. The form and leaf texture of the plants, as well as the manner in which they are grouped, all play a part that is vitally important to the ultimate effect.

It is important to plant in relatively large groups, each restricted to one kind or variety, the size depending on the overall dimensions of the border. Blocks of three plants should, as a general rule, be the minimum, while, for smaller edging and carpeting plants, six would be a reasonable number if spottiness is to be avoided.

Although the general trend should be towards 'shortest in the front, tallest in the rear', this is a rule that should not be too rigidly adhered to. Some of the taller plants should be allowed to wander to the middle or even, at certain points, to the front of the border while the lower marginal plants can be permitted to flow unobtrusively inwards to make small pools and rivulets of contrasting height and colour among their taller neighbours.

A number of perennials are grown as much for the beauty of their foliage as for the decorative quality of their flowers. Outstanding among these are the hostas, or plantain lilies with their outsize ribbed leaves, acanthus, whose sculptured foliage formed the classic model for the Corinthian capitals of Ancient Greek architecture, hemerocallis, *Iris sibirica* and kniphofias for the contrasting effect of their sword-like leaves, the variety of rue known as *Ruta graveolens* 'Jackman's Blue' and others whose names have been indicated in the list below.

Other plants are cultivated for their attractive seed heads. These include the fascinating but invasive Chinese lanterns (*physalis*), the silvery tasselled *Pulsatilla vulgaris* or Pasque flower, *Baptista australis* with its soot-black seed pods and the magnificent *Heracleum mantegazzianum*, a garden plant resembling a giant cow parsley whose outsize flat seed heads are borne on stems 3m (10ft) or more tall.

Planting The great majority of perennial border plants can be planted with safety between the end of September and the last week of March. In fact, the planting of late-flowering specimens such as Michaelmas daisies and border chrysanthemums could very well be delayed until April.

Planting holes should be of sufficient depth and breadth to accommodate the roots of the plants without bunching or overcrowding. Small plants can be firmed in by hand, but for large clumps

Monarda didyma, the Oswego tea plant, has aromatic leaves with a slightly pungent scent when crushed.

the heel of the boot will be required. Although firm planting is desirable, this should not entail embedding the roots in a pocket of sticky 'goo'. In heavy clay soils, planting will have to be delayed until the soil condition improves or, better still, the holes can be filled with sifted compost or a mixture of dry soil and peat that has been kept under cover for this purpose.

With the more vigorous perennials such as golden rod, shasta daisies, achilleas and campanulas, it is not necessary, if time presses, to be too fussy over planting procedure, provided that the soil has been properly prepared and is in good heart. Others, however, such as paeonies, alstroemerias and hellebores will need more careful attention. Paeonies, for example, should never be planted with their dormant growth buds more than approximately 5cm (2in) below the surface; planting too deeply is one of the commonest causes of failure to bloom satisfactorily. The

planting or division of catmint is better delayed until spring. Autumn-planted specimens frequently fail to survive. This is a rule that might well be applied to all grey-leaved border plants. Once established they can tolerate severe weather conditions but in their first winter they often succumb to severe frosts if they are planted in autumn.

For the newcomer to gardening, the importance of dealing only with reputable nurseries cannot be overstressed. Their catalogues, in addition to lists and descriptions of plants, will often contain a wealth of information regarding their likes and dislikes. Plants, too, will be delivered at the most appropriate time of year for planting out.

Choice of plants Anyone starting an herbaceous border from scratch would be well advised to take advantage of the many new plants and modern varieties of older favourites that require little or no staking and tying. By this means, one of the major summer chores in the border can be considerably reduced.

Many of these new-style border plants are entirely self-supporting; others need only a few twiggy sticks pushed in among them to keep them in order.

Plants such as tall delphiniums will, of course, have to have each individual flower secured to a stake or stout cane. If space permits, it is better to segregate these and other similar top-heavy plants; they do better where they are more easy to get at for maintenance.

Not all the taller border plants suffer from this shortcoming; *Artemisia lactiflora,* for example, is a plant whose 2m (6ft) stems of feathery milk-white flowers, smelling like meadowsweet, will stand up to a howling gale without turning a hair, while others, for example the moon daisies and taller perennial asters, will collapse and sprawl at the first hint of rough weather, if they are not securely staked.

Careful and judicious selection at the planning stage, therefore, can make

the border practically trouble-free where staking and tying are concerned.

Double-sided or 'island' borders achieve similar results in a different way. Plants grown in an open situation are sturdier and more compact than those grown against a wall or hedge which tends to cause them to be drawn both upwards and outwards. This sturdier habit makes them less liable to damage by heavy winds and rough weather, and, in addition, access at both sides of the border makes routine maintenance a good deal easier. The idea of a double-sided border is not new. Formerly, in large gardens, they were commonly used as a decorative edging in the kitchen garden where they served the dual purpose of screening the vegetable crops and providing flowers for cutting.

Island borders, however, are a more recent innovation, for whose introduction we have largely to thank Mr Alan Bloom, whose borders at Bressingham, Norfolk attract a host of

admirers. One of their attractions, in addition to ease of maintenance, lies in the fact that they can be viewed from above as well as along their length and from the front. For this reason, the height of the plants should not exceed 1–1.3m (3–4ft) in order that the kaleidoscopic colour effects of the plant groupings can be seen to their best advantage.

Prolonging the display One of the main disadvantages of the herbaceous border as a garden feature is the comparatively short period during which it makes a major contribution to the garden display. Normally, it is only in early or mid-June that it really starts to make its colour impact, with lupins, oriental poppies, irises, anchusa, aquilegias and other June-flowering perennials.

Reaching its peak in July and August it continues to delight in early autumn and retires in a blaze of Michaelmas daisies, red hot pokers, perennial sunflowers and border chrysanthemums, which carry it through, in most districts, until mid October.

For the other seven months of the year, however, the border can lack colour and interest, unless steps are taken to extend its scope by supplementing the orthodox planting materials with others that flower both early and late.

Spring bulbs, such as daffodils, tulips, hyacinths, chionodoxas, scillas and grape hyacinths, all make first-class curtain raisers and will fill the spaces between perennials with bright spring colour. A little later wallflowers, polyanthus, forget-me-nots and other spring bedding plants can be used as gap-fillers.

There are quite a few herbaceous plants proper, beginning in January with the hellebores, that will considerably extend the border's period of interest and relieve the monotony of bare brown earth and dead stems. *Helleborus niger,* the Christmas rose, seldom fulfils the promise of its name, unless it has the protection of cloches or a cold greenhouse, but it can be relied on to open its pure white chalices by the middle or end of January, although even then it will still appreciate a little protection to save its immaculate petals from damage by wind and rain.

Following close on its heels comes the Lenten rose, *Helleborus orientalis* and other delightful species that include the stately *H. argutifolius* (syn. *H. corsicus*) and our native *H. foetidus,* whose green flower clusters are a good deal smaller than those of the Corsican species.

1 Geranium pratense, a floriferous plant which quickly makes good clumps.
2 Papaver orientale, the oriental poppy, with stout stems but frail flowers, has cultivars in various colours.
3 The thick woolly foliage of verbascum has earned it the name of blanketweed.
4 The purple spikes of lythrum 'Robert'.

In February and March, too, there will be the pink and carmine flower trusses of the bergenias, among the finest of flowering perennials. These useful plants, that used to be called megaseas, are outsize members of the saxifrage family and most species are evergreen so that their handsome fleshy leaves, bronze or reddish in winter, as well as their striking flowers, make a valuable contribution to the winter border. 'Ballawley Hybrid', a relatively new introduction from Ireland, is one of the most outstanding examples of the group. Other good forms and species include *B. cordifolia* with rounded crinkly leaves, *B. crassifolia,* probably the most commonly-seen, whose leaves are more spoon-shaped than round and *B. schmidtii,* an unusual species the leaves of which have hairy margins and whose loose sprays of clear pink flowers are the earliest to appear.

Blue flowers are always attractive and there are several perennials to provide them once winter is over. The so-called giant forget-me-not, *Brunnera macrophylla* (syn. *Anchusa myosotidiflora*) is one of these, as are the lungworts or pulmonarias. Both of these have foliage that stays attractive throughout the remainder of the season.

There are several species of pulmonaria, the most striking of which is *P. angustifolia azurea,* with clear gentian-blue flowers. It looks superb in conjunction with the yellow daisy flowers of the leopard's bane, *Doronicum* 'Harpur Crewe'. *P. angustifolia rubra* has coral-red blossoms, those of *P. saccharata* are pinkish-purple turning to blue; the multi-coloured appearance is responsible for its nickname of soldiers and sailors, while its strikingly-mottled leaves have earned it the popular title of spotted dog. Incidentally, the foliage of all the lungworts, which remains tidy throughout the summer, acts as an excellent weed-cover.

In the shadier parts of the border *Hepatica triloba* with its leathery, ivy-like leaves and true-blue flowers, together with primulas and polyanthus will all make pools of colour in April and May. The golden flowers of *Alyssum saxatile flore pleno* will shine even more brightly in association with the white flowers of the perennial candytuft *Iberis sempervirens* 'Snowflake', in the sunny spots at the edge of the border.

Heucheras and heucherellas will enliven the early summer scene with their spikes of brilliant coral and clear pink miniature bells. The latter is an interesting hybrid between heuchera and tiarella, the foam flower, which is useful both for its decorative value at this time and as an evergreen carpeting plant later in the season. All these will do well in partial shade.

A complete contrast both in flowers and its ferny foliage is *Dicentra spectabilis,* the lyre flower, better known to cottagers as bleeding heart, lady's locket or Dutchman's breeches. This plant prefers partial shade and blooms in late spring, at the same time as the graceful Solomon's seal, *Polygonatum multiflorum,* with its hanging bells of greenish white.

To provide colour continuity from late summer onwards there are, in addition to the indispensable Michaelmas daisies, various other perennial and bulbous plants. The grey-leaved *Anaphalis triplinervis* is one of these. Its papery 'everlasting' white star-like flowers, which appear first in July, will still be immaculate in October. The Japanese anemone, *Anemone hupehensis,* of which there are now many lovely named varieties, will start to throw up clusters of chalice-like blossoms from early August until the first heavy frosts arrive. The single forms, both pink and white are still firm favourites, but if you are looking for something out-of-the-ordinary you might like to try 'Margarete', a double pink, with

1 Pyrethrum 'Eileen May Robinson', a good herbaceous plant, flowers in May.
2 For a moist spot, or the back of the border, ligularia is a dramatic plant, with large rather floppy leaves.
3 Island borders, an up-to-date idea, can be looked at from all sides.

189

rows of ruff-like petals. 'Prince Henry', sometimes listed as 'Profusion', is one of the most striking singles, its colour much richer than those of the other pinks.

In sheltered bays in the border from August onwards, two closely-allied South African bulbous plants will make a welcome splash of colour. The blue African lily, agapanthus—the species *A. campanulatus* is perfectly hardy in the south of England—has drumstick heads of powder-blue flowers, while those of *Nerine bowdenii* are similar, but less tightly packed with pink florets. 'Fenwick's Variety', an attractive pink, is the best form for out-of-doors.

And so the year goes by in the herbaceous border, with the first Christmas roses plumping up their buds as the last lingering flowers of the border chrysanthemums shrivel and fade. In the well-planned perennial border there need never be a dull moment.

Winter work Apart from the periodic division, replanting and occasional re-planning of the border, winter maintenance will consist mainly of tidying-up and light forking between the plants. There are two schools of thought where the former operation is concerned. Some gardeners prefer to leave the tidying of the border until spring—the dead leaves and stems, they claim, protect the crowns of the plants in really severe weather. Others, who cannot stand the sight of so much dead untidy vegetation cut down the dead stems at the earliest opportunity.

There is a lot to be said for the former point of view, but a lot will depend on how the border is sited. If it is in full view of the house windows, the sooner it is made ship-shape the better. Only a very small number of popular herbaceous perennials are delicate enough to suffer irreparable damage, even in the severest winter. Plants, such as eremurus and *Lobelia fulgens*, which may be damaged by frosts, can be protected by covering their crowns with weathered ashes or bracken.

Where the border is more remotely situated, clearing up operations can take their place in the queue of urgent garden tasks that make their heaviest demands on us during the winter months.

Other uses of herbaceous plants Perennials have become so closely associated in our minds with the herbaceous border that we tend to overlook their many other uses in the garden. For example, bedding schemes employing perennials can be just as attractive as those in which the more orthodox hardy and half-hardy annuals are used. What is more important, management and upkeep will be simplified and costs will be less where these versatile plants are utilized.

Perennials as bedding plants For bedding purposes, it will be necessary to

A selection of herbaceous plants

Name	Height in feet	Colour	Season
Acanthus	4–5	lilac-pink	July–Aug
Achillea spp & vars	1–4	white, yellow	June–Aug
Alchemilla	1–1½	yellow-green	June–July
Anaphalis	1–2	white	July–Sept
Aquilegia hybs	1–3	various	May–June
Armeria	1	pinks	June–July
Artemisia	3–5	grey foliage	Aug–Sept
Aster spp & vars	1–5	various	Aug–Oct
Astrantia	2–3	green-pink	June
Bergenia	1–1½	pinks, white	March–April
Campanula	1–4	blues, white	June–Aug
Centaurea	2–5	blues, yellow	June–Oct
Cimicifuga	2–4	creamy-white	July–Sept
Coreopsis	2–3	golden-yellow	June–Sept
Corydalis	1	yellow	May–Oct
Delphinium	3–8	blues, mauves	June–July
Dianthus	½–1½	various	May–June
Dicentra	1–2	pink	April–May
Doronicum	1–2½	yellow	March–April
Echinacea	2–3	purple-red	Aug–Sept
Echinops	2–5	steely blue	July–Aug
Erigeron hybs	1–2	blue, pink	June–Sept
Eryngium	2–4	glaucous blue	July–Aug
Euphorbia	1–3	yellow	April–June
Gaillardia hybs	2	yellow, orange	July–Aug
Galega	2–4	mauve	June–July
Gentiana	1–2	blues	July–Aug
Geranium	1–2½	pinks, mauves	June–Aug
Helenium	3–5	yellows, copper	July–Sept
Hemerocallis	2–3	yellow, orange	July–Sept
Heuchera hybs	1–2½	pinks, reds	May–Aug
Iris	1–5	various	May–June
Kniphofia	1½–4	yellow, orange	July–Sept
Lupin hybs	2–4	various	June
Lythrum	2–4	purple-red	June–Sept
Lysimachia	2–4	yellow, white	July–Sept
Macleaya	5–8	apricot pink	July–Sept
Malva	2–4	mauves, pinks	July
Monarda	2–4	various	June–Aug
Nepeta	1–2	blue	May–Sept
Paeonia spp & hybs	2–4	pink, red, white	May–June
Phlox	2–4	various	July–Sept
Pyrethrum	1–3	various	May–June
Salvia spp	2–5	mauves	June–Sept
Sidalcea hybs	2½–5	pinks	June–Aug
Verbascum	3–8	yellow, pink	July–Oct
Veronica spp & vars	1–3	blues, mauves	July–Oct

Perennials for cutting

Name	Height in feet	Colour	Season
Acanthus mollis	4–5	lilac-pink	July–Aug
Achillea 'Moonshine'	2	sulphur-yellow	June–July
Alchemilla mollis	1–1½	yellowish-green	June–July
Anaphalis triplinervis	¾	white 'everlasting'	July–Aug
Aquilegia hybrids	up to 3	various	May–June
Aster (perennial)	up to 5	white, pinks, purples	Aug–Oct
Astrantia	2–3	greenish-white, pink	June
Coreopsis grandiflora	2–3	golden-yellow	June–Sep
Dianthus	½–1	various	May–June
Heuchera spp & varieties	2	pinks, reds	June–July
Iris germanica	up to 3	various	May–June
Phlox decussata	up to 3	various	July–Sep
Pyrethrum varieties	2	various	May–June
Trollius	2	yellow, gold	May–June

choose perennials with a relatively long flowering season and/or attractive foliage, plus a solid and compact habit of growth. Among those fulfilling such requirements are *Brunnera macrophylla* (syn. *Anchusa myosotidiflora*), the so-called giant forget-me-not, *Anemone hupehensis*, the Japanese anemone, *Armeria maritima,* thrift, the medium and dwarf Michaelmas daisies and dwarf delphiniums, for example *D. ruysii* or *D. chinensis*. The two last-named, in common with a number of other perennials, have the added advantage of being easy to grow from seed.

Segregation of groups and species
Another good way of making the best use of certain groups and species is to grow them in beds restricted to the one type of perennial. By growing them in this way, it is easy to make satisfactory provision for their special requirements in the way of feeding, staking, tying and general cultivation.

This works well for herbaceous plants such as lupins, flag irises, paeonies, oriental poppies and the taller delphiniums. A further point in favour of this method is that it avoids the bare patches that tend to appear in the border when such early-flowering perennials form part of the general scheme.

Other herbaceous perennials that will benefit from this method of culture are the Michaelmas daisies. Where sufficient space is available, a representative collection, grown in a bed or border devoted to them alone, will make a far greater impact than they would dotted about in groups in the mixed border.

Waterside planting Although the great majority of perennials will thrive in a wide range of garden soils and situations, there are some that prefer shade and moisture, conditions that cannot always be easily provided in the herbaceous border. These make excellent plants for the waterside—by the banks of streams or artificial watercourses or at the edge of the garden pool.

Primulas, astilbes, *Iris sibirica* and *Iris kaempferi*, kingcups (*Caltha palustris*) and the globe flower (*Trollius* species) are just a few that will grow better in damp, shady positions.

Cut flowers Satisfying the demands for flowers for the house in summer, when they fade so quickly, sometimes results in the display in the border being spoiled by too lavish cutting. A satisfactory way of avoiding this is to grow perennials specially for the purpose, either in rows in the kitchen garden, or bordering the vegetable plot. For this, it is only commonsense to choose those that will not only cut and last well, but will also need minimum attention where staking and tying are concerned. A representative, but not exhaustive list of these appears below.

It should be obvious, from the foregoing, that the uses of perennials are many and varied.

Herbicides see Weeds and weed control

Hessian
This is a useful material to have in the garden. It is ideal as a windbreak, and for this purpose it can be fixed to strong wooden posts which are driven into the ground. A long, continuous run can be erected parallel to a bed of plants and small beds or specimen plants can be enclosed by the hessian tacked on to four posts.

The material is also useful for placing over frames or cloches to provide protection against frost in the winter. The hessian must be removed as soon as possible during the day to prevent plants underneath from becoming drawn through lack of light.

Hessian can be used for forcing crops in a greenhouse under the staging. Tacked across the front of the staging and placed over the top, it will exclude sufficient light to encourage the forcing of crops such as seakale and rhubarb.

Small lengths of hessian are useful for placing on the soil or lawn to keep ripening crops such as onions and shallots clean as they dry off. Similar lengths can be placed under the hedge to catch the clippings as it is trimmed. It also makes a useful receptacle for leaves as they are swept off the lawn.

Hoes see Tools

Hot bed
This is a construction of decomposing organic material which, in the process of rotting, creates heat which is used to warm a frame in which plants are raised. Once widely used as a source of heat from natural materials, the old hotbed system has been mainly replaced by electric soil-warming cables, though it is still perfectly sound when quantities of horse manure and leaves or straw are available.

Horse manure should contain plenty of straw and preferably be used straight from the stable. After it has been built into a conical mound, ensuring that it is well wetted, heat will be generated. The heap should be turned within a week and rebuilt so that the outside layers are in the centre. After another few days the process should be repeated. The heap should be left again for a few days and then turned for a third time and left for a further few days.

By this time the manure and straw should be in a fit state for making the hotbed. Construction consists simply in building a flat-topped heap, treading each layer firmly. A 60cm (2ft) depth of manure should be the aim, on to which a final 16cm (6in) layer of good top soil is placed. A deeper hotbed will retain its heat proportionately longer. The surface area will depend upon the size of frame

Mature and strawy manure is packed into a frame to make a hot bed.

which is to be placed on the heap, allowing a margin of about 30cm (1ft) beyond all sides of the frame or frames.

At this stage a soil thermometer plunged into the centre of the heap will be needed to show when the first fierce heat has subsided. When the temperature has fallen to about 75°F (24°C) seeds can be sown, plants set out or pots plunged as required. Useful heat should continue to be generated for two months or more. The use of a hotbed in early spring should be timed so that the sun is sufficiently strong to continue to warm the frame as the heat output from the hotbed declines.

Milder heat, maintained for a longer period, will be had by mixing dead leaves with the manure. The procedure for making a hotbed from straw or chaff is much the same.

Hot water treatment

A number of pests, which are difficult to control by chemicals because they live within the tissues of the plants or between young leaves in the buds, can be destroyed by hot water. The treatment is applied to material used for propagation and to narcissus bulbs. The temperature must be carefully regulated to kill the pest without damaging the plants. It is important to ensure that the stipulated temperature and the period of immersion are carefully observed, otherwise the plants or bulbs may be seriously damaged.

Thermostatically controlled electric immersion heaters are the safest and most satisfactory means of ensuring that the water is maintained within half a degree of the required temperature and, where large quantities are being dealt with, an electric pump can be fitted to keep the water moving. For small quantities, a bath can be made up from a galvanized dustbin lagged with three thicknesses of carpet. The plants or bulbs are held in sieves, slightly smaller in diameter than the bath, and fitted with metal legs to keep them separate. The bath should be used in a draught-proof shed, never in the open air, where it is impossible to regulate the temperature satisfactorily. The water is heated to two or three degrees above the required temperature before the sieves are lowered into it and a gas ring or oil heater underneath is regulated to keep the temperature constant. A thermometer fitted to a cork is pushed down among the plants and it must be watched.

Chrysanthemum stools are given 20 to 30 minutes at 110°F (43°C) to destroy eelworm. They are washed thoroughly to remove all soil and after treatment are plunged immediately into cold water. They should be dealt with as soon as they are dormant. If new growth has started, they may suffer damage. The treated stools are boxed up in sterilized soil and the boxes or frames should also be sterilized, or re-infection may quickly occur. They are kept in a temperature

around 50°F (10°C), and given a minimum of water, until the cuttings appear.

Strawberry runners are treated against aphids, strawberry mite, red spider mite and stem and bulb eelworm (*Ditylenchus dipsaci*). They are given 115°F (46°C) for 7 minutes and are then plunged into cold water. They should be planted out as soon as possible and well firmed in.

Mint runners can be completely cured of rust by immersion in the bath at 112°F (44°C). The heater is then removed and the runners left for 10 minutes. If the plants show signs of stunting and leaf drop, leaf and bud eelworm (*Aphelenchoides fragariae*) is probably present and the runners will need 10 minutes at 115°F (46°C). Plunge in cold water immediately after treatment and plant wider apart than normal because growth will be vigorous.

Phlox stools can be given 20 to 30 minutes at 110°F (43°C) to destroy stem and bulb eelworm and boxed up in sterilized soil in the same way as chrysanthemums.

Narcissus (daffodil) bulbs are treated against stem and bulb eelworm, narcissus fly grubs and bulb scale mite. They require 3 hours at 110°F (43°C) if eelworm is present; otherwise 1 hour. The bulbs which must be fully dormant at the time of treatment, are allowed to cool slowly in trays and should be dry before planting. Treatment is best given in August and early September.

Research is constantly going on into the use of hot water for various dormant plants and it is best to seek advice on the exact treatment required by any particular plant.

House plants

There are two kinds of plant that we bring into our houses. The more spectacular are the flowering plants, cyclamen, azaleas or African violets. Unfortunately their season of attractiveness is limited. All too soon the flowers will fade and the plants then have little attraction. If you have a greenhouse, you can keep the plant going and prepare it for another season, but we usually do not feel inclined to keep it in the house; certainly not in a conspicuous position. The other kind of plant is less spectacular: its beauty is centred in its foliage rather than in its flowers, but it has the advantage that, provided you treat it properly, it will grow permanently in your rooms and increase in size and effect from year to year. These plants, grown for permanent effect, are commonly known as house plants.

Most of us do not live in glass houses; therefore the plants we can grow in our rooms are limited in number. Even a room that appears well lit to us, will seem shady to a plant and, as a result, the majority of houseplants are those that can tolerate shade. If a plant is to

be permanently attractive, it should be evergreen. We can visualize exceptions, such as the bonsai dwarf trees, where the outline of the tree is attractive even when no leaves are visible, but there are not many of these exceptions to the demand for evergreen plants. Again most of us live in rooms of only moderate size and we require plants of moderate dimensions. We also do not want them to grow too quickly. Re-potting is a tedious operation for those who live in flats or in houses without gardens and we do not want to have to undertake it more than once a year at the most. Although plain green leaves are attractive enough, particularly if they have interesting shapes, leaves that contain some colour are usually regarded as more attractive. Colour in leaves occurs in two forms. Some leaves are naturally coloured; for instance those of rex begonias and *Cordyline terminalis,* but there are other plants which produce coloured forms of their normally green leaves. These are described as variegated and the variegation may be due to a number of varied causes, from a virus infection to a periclinal chimaera. Whatever the cause, the result is that some part of the leaf lacks chlorophyll, the substance that makes leaves green. If the chlorophyll is completely lacking, the area appears white, while, if there is very little present, the area appears golden or yellow. Although some plants appear naturally variegated, nearly any plant can occasionally produce a variegated form. Variegation is an exceptional occurrence and the plant can be perpetuated only by vegetative propagation, normally by rooting cuttings or layers. Seeds are very unlikely to transmit the variegation. By no means all people find variegated leaves attractive, but very many do and, as a result, many plants are popular because of their variegated leaves that would otherwise be little regarded. The popular variegated forms of *Tradescantia fluviatilis* and *Chlorophytum capense* may be cited as examples. With half or more of the chlorophyll lacking, the leaves of variegated plants can only do half the work of normal green leaves and so variegated plants tend to grow more slowly than the unvariegated forms. This is not unexpected; a more surprising result of variegation, though it is not always the case, is that the plants are often more tender than the normal forms. There seems to be no very obvious explanation for this.

We can now summarize the qualities that we require for a house plant. It must be compact in habit of growth, tolerant of shade and evergreen. The leaves should be attractive, either by reason of their shape or their colour: if we can have attractive flowers as well, so much the better, but with the emphasis to be laid on the permanence of the attraction, agreeable flowers are

Hot water treatment of chrysanthemums.
1 Remove the green top growth with a
sharp knife and 2 wash the roots entirely
free of soil.
3 The stool is fully immersed in hot water
and left for 20 or 30 minutes.
4 Plunge into cold water afterwards.

obviously a bonus. In fact the combination of handsome flowers and handsome leaves is somewhat rare in any branch of gardening. Among the house plants many of the bromeliads provide an exception to this rule, but even with these plants the showiest part of the inflorescence is due to the coloured bracts that surround the flowers, and these are really modified leaves.

Temperate climates produce few plants with the characteristics that we require. The various ivies form an important exception to this statement, but, even so, the great majority of house plants come from the tropics. Plants are infinitely adaptable, as a general rule (there are, of course, exceptions and these are generally regarded as 'difficult' plants) and most tropical plants will adapt themselves to temperate conditions and even to the fluctuating

lengths of daylight, which, even more than the alteration in temperature, mark the chief difference between tropical and temperate climates.

There are certain temperatures, varying from plant to plant, below which plant growth ceases. The plant may survive perfectly well, but it will neither produce fresh roots nor fresh leaves, until the temperature is raised. It is, obviously, more difficult to produce high temperatures when the outside temperature is very low and so it is most convenient to make our winter the equivalent of the tropical plant's dry season. The dry season in the tropics is generally very hot, but, owing to the lack of water, the plant makes no growth and stays in a dormant condition. This is one of the reasons why all house plant growers are recommended to keep their plants as dry as possible during the winter. How dry you can keep them, will depend on the type of plant you are growing and on how warm you keep your rooms.

The type of heating that you use and the temperatures you maintain in your various rooms during the winter will affect the types of plant you can grow. Some plants, notably begonias, are very intolerant of gas fumes, so that if your rooms are heated by gas, you will not be able to grow begonias satisfactorily. If you have really warm rooms, maintaining, perhaps, an average temperature of 70°F (21°C), they will be far too warm for such plants as ivy or × Fatshedera lizei. With high temperatures such as these, the plants will continue growing during the winter and more water will be required. The winter growth may not be very ornamental, as the lack of light will prevent the formation of good sized leaves.

Many house plants are 'stopped' in the spring: that is to say that the tips of the various shoots are nipped out, so as to induce the formation of secondary shoots that will give the plant a nice bushy appearance, and where this is done the weak winter growth can be removed. However, there are plants, such as most of the ficus, that are not stopped and, where these are concerned, it might be better to move them to cooler positions in the winter. However most of us, alas, cannot afford these high temperatures and it is more a question of keeping the room warm enough for our plants and ourselves. In any natural climate the highest temperatures are around midday, but many sitting rooms are kept cold during the day, when people are out at work, warm in the evening, when everyone is at

A collection of house plants which includes (Back left to right) Hedera canariensis, Ficus elastica, sansevieria, (Front left to right) croton, dieffenbachia, Begonia masoniana, maranta, peperomia and aphelandra.

home, but cool off during the late evening and the early morning after people have gone to bed.

Such a contradiction of natural rhythm is sufficient to disturb any plant and it is easy to see that keeping plants in good condition in the winter is less simple in the house than in a greenhouse. If you have some system of regular central heating, the problem is comparatively simple, but for rooms with only sporadic warmth, the matter is less straightforward. However, there are house plants to suit all conditions. It is as well to know what the average temperature of your room is during the winter, otherwise the problem can be resolved only by a system of trial and error, during which you might well lose the plants that you most prize. It is fairly safe to say that no plant will tolerate the conditions that are to be found on a mantelpiece above a coal fire. The atmosphere is far too dry and the alternations of cold and roasting heat are too much for all plants, except the toughest succulents. Even if the temperature is equable, plants that are put too near the window risk being chilled, or even frosted, when the weather is very cold and they should be moved further into the room during these periods.

Even when the temperature is satisfactory, the dry atmosphere that we like in our rooms is not beneficial to plants. This, however, can easily be overcome, by placing the pots in a larger container and filling this container with some moisture-retentive material. Peat is most frequently used, but moss or mica powder does equally well. Some people get perfectly satisfactory results with damp newspaper, which is topped with moss to look more elegant. By these means we can maintain a moist atmosphere in the immediate surroundings of the plant without either affecting the atmosphere of our rooms or the correct state of moisture of the soil ball. With this we come to the most crucial matter in the successful cultivation of house plants.

More house plants are killed by over watering than by other cause. Like human beings, plants cannot live without water, but, again like human beings, they can be drowned. However, this analogy cannot be pressed too far. Human beings need water at regular intervals, but plants need water most when they are making growth. This is usually during the spring and summer. There is a correlation between the growth of the aerial portion of the plant, the portion we can see, and the growth of the roots which we can't see. If the plant is making new leaves and stems, we can be fairly sure that it is also making new roots. Unfortunately, the root growth is liable to precede the production of new leaves and so these latter may be prevented from developing if the soil is too dry at the appropriate

period. On the other hand, if the soil is too wet, the roots cannot breathe and, far from developing, are liable to rot and, unless this process can be stopped immediately, the plant itself will succumb. We can guard against this to some extent by purely physical means. If we have an open soil mixture that drains rapidly and well, the risk of the soil becoming sodden and sour is reduced, although not, of course, obviated altogether. When to give water is only satisfactory learned by experience, but the following hard and fast rules are generally acceptable.

1 When water is applied, it should be in sufficient quantity to moisten the whole of the soil ball. The water should be at room temperature. Rain water is preferable but not essential.

2 The soil should be allowed to dry out between waterings. This is not too easy to interpret. We do not want the soil to become dust dry, but on the other hand, we want to avoid saturation. A useful rule of thumb with clay pots and soil mixtures, is to strike the side of the pot with your knuckle. If the resultant sound is dull, watering is not needed, but if it is a ringing sound, water should be applied. With peat mixtures the weight of the pot is a more reliable indication. If it feels light, water is wanted, but not if it feels heavy. The same applies, but to a lesser extent, with soil mixtures in plastic pots. These are much the most difficult to gauge.

3 During cold weather plants make little or no growth and so require little water. Growth is also slowed down when there is little light. It is safe, therefore, during the winter to keep all watering down to a minimum, even though the room may be kept at quite a high temperature. Naturally plants in warm rooms will require more than those in cool surroundings.

4 From about mid-April it is probable that growth will start and so more water may be required. Be cautious, nevertheless, until you see new leaves appearing. It is possible to knock the plant out of its pot to see if new roots (characterized by their white tips) are forming and to replace the soil ball without disturbance. When growth is vigorous water will be needed more frequently. 'Stopping' checks growth temporarily and watering should be on a reduced scale until a resumption of growth is seen.

5 By the end of August it is advisable to discourage much further growth and encourage the plant to ripen its new growth. This is done by keeping the plant as dry as possible.

6 The type of leaf will give some indication of the plant's requirements. Plants with thick leaves or with succulent leaves (such as the large-leaved ficus and sansevieria) can tolerate longer periods without water than thin-leaved plants. These latter will probably wilt when they become too dry and they should be

watered at once. The thicker-leaved plants will not wilt and so should be inspected frequently. Drought, unless acute, will not kill them but may cause subsequent leaf drop.

If leaves turn yellow and fall off, it usually indicates over-watering. However some plants, such as *Ficus benjamina,* will naturally shed their year-old leaves in the autumn and most plants shed a few leaves in the course of the year. Excessive defoliation is almost certainly due to incorrect watering; although it can be caused by under-watering as well as by over-watering. If the plant becomes unsteady in the pot, this is generally due to root-rot caused by excessive water and is very difficult to arrest. Some leaves will wilt in the summer if they are in direct hot sunlight. If the soil appears to be satisfactorily moist, a syringeing of the leaves with water will generally restore them to their normal turgidity, and in any case, they will resume their normal appearance as soon as the sunlight goes.

Once the question of watering has been mastered, there are few other problems. Rooms are very dusty which spoils the appearance of the leaves of house plants and also prevents them from functioning properly. It is advisable, therefore, to clean the leaves every two or four weeks. This is best done with cotton wool and tepid water and the leaves should be sponged on both sides. New leaves are soft and easily damaged and should be left until they are older. Some people use milk, or oil, or flat beer to give the leaves a more glossy appearance, but these mixtures do not do the leaves any good.

During the summer, when growth is most vigorous, the plants may be fed. A liquid feed is most easily applied and should be given according to the instructions on the bottle. Little and often is invariably better than doses in excess of those recommended. Unless the plant is really well-rooted, feeding should not be applied and is not necessary for plants that have been repotted. Repotting is done in the early summer. For the majority of house plants the John Innes potting compost No 2 is the best. Plants are usually potted on into a pot one size larger. Plants from 13cm (5in) pots are put into 16cm (6in) pots and so on. The only exception is that the 10cm (4in) pot is very rarely used and plants are moved from 7cm (3in) to 13cm (5in) pots. Plants with very thin roots such as begonias and peperomias do better in a mixture of 2 parts of leafmould to 1 part of sharp sand, while epiphytes, such as the bromeliads, are usually given a mixture of peat, leafmould and sharp sand. However, it is only rarely that epiphytes require any potting on, as they use the soil as an anchorage only. After being potted on the plants should be kept on the dry side until the roots have penetrated the new soil. It is best to move plants from 5cm (2in) pots to 13cm (5in) pots after a year, as the 7cm (3in) pots dry out so quickly, but after that most house plants will need repotting only every other year. The second year the plant will need feeding.

The epiphytic bromeliads (aechmea, neoregelia, nidularium, guzmania, tillandsia and vriesia) need rather different treatment from most house plants. They have a rosette of strap-shaped leaves which form the so-called 'vase'. This must be kept full of water, preferably rain water. The mixture in which they are potted may be kept moist, but this is of minor importance, as the roots serve little purpose except anchorage and it is from the leaves that nutriment is absorbed. During the summer the merest trace of liquid feed may be added to the water in the vase, but this must be done with great discretion.

Most house plants are easily propagated if you have a greenhouse, although some, such as the large-leaved ficus, cordylines and dracaenas, need a good deal of heat to get them to root. There are a few that can easily be propagated in the home. The various tradescantias and zebrinas will root easily in water and so will *Cissus antarctica* and *Rhoicissus rhomboidea.* Shoots of succulents, such as *Sedum sieboldii* and aichryson will root easily, either in ordinary soil or in a mixture of equal parts of peat and sharp sand, which is an ideal mixture for most cuttings. Shoots of the various ivies, taken when they are half ripe, that is neither too young nor too woody, will root easily although rather slowly. The peperomias, with single leaves rising from the base, can be rooted from leaf stem cuttings. The leaf with its stem is pulled off and inserted in the peat and sand mixture, when a new plant will form at the base of the leaf stalk. Sansevierias will produce new leaves on rhizomes, but they do not root until a year has elapsed and should not, therefore, be severed from the main plant before this time. If, however, you

A group of flowering house plants all of which add colour indoors in winter.

1

2

can find the new rhizome without
disturbing the plant and cut half-way
through it, it will hasten the formation
of roots at the base of the new leaf.
Many of the climbing aroids produce
aerial roots and these can be induced to
develop in soil. These climbing aroids
(philodendron, syngonium and scindap-
sus), will grow more luxuriantly if they
are given a cylinder of wire stuffed with
moss up which they can grow. However,
the moss must be kept damp and this is
not easy in the home. They can also be
trained on blocks of cork bark.

Humidity

This term is used to express the amount
of moisture in the atmosphere, as
determined by a hygrometer, or by
calculation from the temperatures of a
wet and dry bulb thermometer.
Obviously little can be done out-of-doors
to deal with problems of humidity other
than to choose plants to suit conditions
in a particular area. But in the greenhouse humidity is of very great importance and modern commercial houses are
fitted with automatic humidity controls,
linked with temperature and ventilation.

Plants vary in their reactions to
different degrees of humidity, some
thriving in a dry atmosphere and others
doing best in air almost at saturation
point. Diseases and pests are equally
varied in their response. Red spider
mites and thrips, for example, thrive in
a dry atmosphere and are checked by a
damp one. Fungus diseases are encouraged by damp conditions. The main
point to remember is that the total
amount of water that can be held in the
air varies according to its temperature.
Thus 100 percent humidity at a low
temperature means a lower water content than the same figure at a high
temperature. This is one of the reasons
why greenhouse plants, such as orchids,
or a crop which requires a high level of
humidity, for example the cucumber,
must also have a high temperature.

For all greenhouse crops, it is useful
to know their needs in this respect and
the humidity level can then be regulated
by increasing the temperature so as to
allow the air to absorb more moisture,
by opening or closing ventilators, by
spraying the plants, walls and paths or
by placing pans of water in the greenhouse to increase the water content of
the air by evaporation.

A good many plants grown as house
plants do better if they can be given a
more humid atmosphere. Although this
is not as easy to achieve in a living room
as it is in a greenhouse, much can be
done by placing the pots in which the
plants are grown inside larger pots or
other containers and filling the space
between the two with moist peat,
sphagnum moss or other moisture-
retaining material.

Humus

Humus is the term used to describe the
organic matter in the soil. Its presence
in adequate quantities is a vital factor
in building up and maintaining soil
fertility. Humus may consist of decayed
vegetable or animal refuse, still showing traces of leaves, stems, stubble,
bones, and so on, or it may have been
completely broken down into a blackish,
powdery substance.

Garden soil which has been regularly
treated with humus, whether from the
compost heap or from organic manures,
has a rich dark colour. This factor is of
benefit in itself, for dark soils, rich in
humus, tend to warm up more quickly in
spring, so promoting early seed germination and earlier cropping.

Humus aids fertility in two main ways.
First, the organic matter stores nitrogen,
which is converted into ammonia by the
micro-organisms in the soil and released
to the plants in the form of nitrate.
Second, humus can hold and store
considerable quantities of moisture.
This moisture-holding capacity helps to
break the soil down into crumbs, giving
sufficient space for the retention of
moisture, but allowing excess water to
drain away. The good soil structure and
aeration, obtained in this way, assist
root development and, together with the
water holding capacity, enable plants to

stand up better to drought conditions. A humus-rich soil also produces the fine tilth necessary for seed sowing.

All cultivated soils lose organic matter and this loss is increased when the ground is limed. Some humus is left in the soil by plant residues, but this is not enough and the losses must be made good. The more rapid and thorough the cultivation, the more rapid the loss of humus. Where farmyard manure is available, it is still the easiest and most practical way of maintaining the organic content of the soil. It should be spread and dug into the ground as soon as possible, for some of the nutrients will be lost if it is allowed to stand in heaps exposed to the rain. In clay soils it should be dug in during the autumn.

The old-time gardeners dug manure into the second spit, but it is far better to incorporate it in the top spit within easy reach of the growing plants. Other manures (from pigs, rabbits, poultry, etc) and spent mushroom compost can all be used to add humus. All gardens should have a compost heap where most of the garden refuse can be broken down (the roots of diseased plants and roots of persistent weeds such as bindweed and couch grass should be burned).

Humus can also be added in the form of peat, leafmould, spent hops, seaweed, shoddy, straw, fish waste, or in prepared fertilizers made up from hoof and horn and bone meal. Blood and offal from a slaughter house can be an equally valuable source. The presence of adequate humus in the soil does not necessarily mean that fertilizers can be dispensed with.

While most crops benefit from high quantities of organic matter in the soil, some flowers, for instance nasturtiums, do better on poorer soils.

I

Insecticides
The term insecticide is used loosely to cover substances intended for the control of pests, though chemicals specifically intended for use against creatures other than insects eg eelworms, mites, slugs etc may be called nematicides, acaricides, molluscicides etc.

Insecticides are marketed in various forms, eg as emulsions, wettable powders, aerosols, dusts, granules, smoke generators, etc.

They act in various ways, eg as a stomach poison when the insect eats contaminated plant tissue or, in the case of sucking insects, imbibes sap carrying a systemic insecticide; as a contact poison when insects are killed by walking over a chemical deposit; as fumigants etc.

In selecting an insecticide, consideration must be given to a number of factors, including the life-cycle and habits of the pest; its manner of feeding (whether biting or sucking); the advisability of changing the type of insecticide used from time to time to avoid building up resistant strains of pests; the possible effects of the chemical on the plant etc.

The range of insecticides available to the amateur is limited by regulations which restrict the use of some of the more poisonous substances to commercial growers. In general, the amateur would do best to choose insecticides of short persistence and to apply them only when strictly necessary. Derris, pyrethrum, trichlorphon, malathion and nicotine are all of short persistence.

There are many other insecticides available to the amateur. Some of them are extremely poisonous in concentration and care must be taken to keep insecticide safely out of the reach of children and animals, and to make sure that they do not come in contact with sprayed plants within the period specified by the manufacturer.

Chemicals which have received Ministry of Agriculture approval for the purposes specified on the label, bear approval mark, a crowned capital 'A' with the words Agricultural Chemicals Approval Scheme written below.

Intensive cultivation
There is very little space for food crops in the small gardens on many new housing estates. What space is available must be put to good use by intensive

A small vegetable garden which has been developed to its fullest.

cultivation. Instead of producing one crop each season, each square yard of soil must be encouraged to produce two, three or even four crops. The method is only practicable where drainage is good, the site unshaded by walls, tall fences, trees and shrubs, the soil extremely fertile and water always to hand during the summer.

Pipe drainage is necessary on very stiff clay. On other soils, drainage is improved by initially digging deeply and adding bulky manure, compost, wool shoddy, peat etc. into the second or third spit. A light, sandy soil also requires similarly heavy dressings of organic matter to assist its capacity to hold moisture. Heavy dressings of very well rotted farmyard manure or garden compost are spread on the surface of the garden each season. After several years, the structure of the topsoil resembles the rich terreau of the French system of gardening. A sprinkler system is an' advantage and windbreaks set up in exposed areas. A cold frame and a set of barn type cloches are also needed. Liming must be regular where large quantities of animal manure are used. Many of the crops benefit, too, from liquid manure feeds in summer.

The season starts in late February or early March in the south—two to three weeks later in most northern areas—when seeds of early maturing varieties of lettuce, radish and cabbage are sown in the cold frame. The cloches will be set over a row of early peas at the same time. In late March or early April, seeds of autumn and winter cabbage, Brussels sprouts, cauliflower and lettuce will be sown in the cold frame or in the open. In the south, seeds of Outdoor Girl tomato may be sown in the frame in early April. The southern gardener may also raise plants of frame and outdoor cucumbers, melons, sweet corn and vegetable marrows by sowing in peat pots in the frame around mid April. In other parts of the country, the frame may be used for a sowing of hardy cucumbers, sweet corn and vegetable marrows in early May. Plants of dwarf and runner beans may also be raised in pots or boxes in the cold frame.

Plants from the earliest sowing are set out in the open in May; those from later sowings in June. The cloches are moved from the pea row in late May to protect tomatoes or melons. During the autumn, the cloches may help to ripen off the tomato crop and from then until the spring, they protect strawberry plants or August-sown lettuce, cabbage, cauliflower and onions. The frame is used for a cucumber or melon crop during the summer and for protecting August-sown plants during the winter.

Successional, catch cropping and intercropping must be practised and some form of rotation of crops devized. Provided quick-growing, short or compact varieties are chosen, traditional sowing and planting distances may often be disregarded. Mulching will prevent most annual weeds by smothering the weed seedlings. Particular care must be taken to prevent outbreaks of green or black aphids among the thick stand of plants.

Intercrop

This is the practice of growing one quickly-maturing crop between rows of another which is slower to mature, for example, a permanent planting of apples, interplanted with gooseberries or black currants until a regular crop of apples is obtained; lettuce between rows of peas or celery or, as found in the Fen district, rows of pyrethrum between young fruit (see also Intensive cultivation).

Cabbage plants have been planted in between rows of lettuces; the lettuces will be harvested soon leaving the ground for the cabbages to develop.

Irrigation

This is a term which describes the method by which water is applied to crops. As watering is one of the most important garden operations, it is essential that the most efficient system be used. Such has been the progress with modern equipment that there is a large number of different types of water appliances on the market.

The selection must depend on the area of ground which has to be dealt with and the type of crop grown and its water requirement. One of the simplest forms of irrigation is practised in China where a large number of channels are dug out of fields so that water from a nearby river can be directed to water crops growing in the fields. This is not done in England but there are several simple methods which can be used.

One of these is by trickle irrigation. This takes the form of a length of thin plastic or rubber tubing which has nozzles fitted at regular intervals. When this tubing is connected to the water supply, the water percolates slowly through these nozzles and soaks the soil around them. If the tubing is arranged so that the nozzles coincide with individual plants, water requirement can be concentrated just where it is needed.

Gardeners will find this system one answer to the holiday watering problem especially as it can be used in the greenhouse or frames equally well. As watering or irrigation is particularly troublesome in the greenhouse, a special irrigation bench has been developed. This works on the capillary system where water is allowed to seep into a bed of sand on the staging. The sand is maintained in a moist condition all the time. Pot plants placed on the sand take up the moisture, aided in the case of clay pots by the use of a small piece of glass fibre wick which is inserted through the drainage hole on the pot's base. Plastic pots do not require this as they are in closer contact to the sand owing to their thin section. One big advantage with this system is that plants can take up just sufficient water for their own individual needs.

For large areas of garden or growing crops, metal spray lines are ideal as these throw a large volume of water through holes or nozzles in the metal pipes. Pipes can be purchased in various lengths and can be quickly connected together so that very long rows of crops can be dealt with at one time. The more expensive systems are oscillating types which turn left and right by a water pressure operated unit at one end of the pipe line. The pipes are laid on low metal legs or supports above the crops. This system of irrigation is particularly suited to the commercial grower.

The amateur gardener can water quite large areas if he uses the oscillating type of sprinkler which can be set or 'dialled' to water pre-set areas. The water pressure drives a system of nylon gear wheels which turn the spray unit. Many models will work successfully on water pressure as low as 10–15kg (20–30lb) per 6 sq cm (sq in). Smaller areas can be watered in the same way if smaller models are used.

Irrigation can be employed in the form of revolving sprinklers which eject a fine spray of water over a circular area. In the more elaborate types the arc of working can be set or adjusted so that difficult areas (a wedge shaped area, for example) can be irrigated.

Successful irrigation also depends on having a good supply of water at convenient parts of the garden, especially if it is a large one. Although hose pipes are necessary for connection purposes to the various pieces of equipment used, convenient points in the garden will considerably facilitate irrigation plans. For this purpose alkathene tubing can be buried underground to connect to a series of stand pipes of the same material. To these can be fitted Hozelock hose pipe connectors and on/off switches.

Irrigation is important for plants grown under cloches and frames. Trickle irrigation lines under them laid on the soil by the plants will ensure that plenty of water will reach the roots quickly. There are some cloche and frame designs which have built-in irrigation in the apex of the roof. This usually takes the form of perforated pipe which, when connected to the hose pipe waters plants underneath by a fine spray of water.

There is no doubt that with a little ingenuity and with the aid of the modern equipment available, the average gardener can install an irrigation system in his own garden.

1 An irrigation spray line which can be used on a lawn or in the kitchen garden.
2 The Hozelock Green Queen spray line.
3 An oscillating head which can be used to swing the pipe from side to side, and thus water a good area.
4 The perforated sprinkler type of hose in use where lawn seed has been sown.
5 A spray of the sprinkler type is useful.

Kale see Vegetables

Kitchen garden
It is far easier to plan a kitchen garden where the garden is a new one. The gardener who takes over a garden used by previous occupiers may first have to remove shrubs and trees. Not only do trees, shrubs and hedges rob the veget-

able garden of plant foods, but they cast shade over the growing plants. Few of the vegetables we grow tolerate shade and the site for the kitchen garden must, therefore, be quite open and unshaded. Brick walls and wood fences cast shade, too, but a wall or fence at the north side is often advantageous in protecting plants from cold north winds. In the past, many kitchen gardens on large estates were laid out in front of a south facing wall and many sites may be made more suitable for vegetable cultivation if windbreaks are set up to break the force of strong westerly or easterly winds. This is particularly true of gardens in coastal areas and although chestnut or wire mesh fences are worth consideration, living windbreaks such as blackberries are more decorative and useful if trained to a strong trellis.

Provision must be made for paths, a garden shed, the cold frame, a site for compost heaps and possibly for a greenhouse. Even in the large kitchen garden, the number of permanent paths should be the minimum necessary, but sufficiently wide for the barrow to be wheeled comfortably without damage to plants nearby. During the season, temporary

200

Season of use of most vegetables

Month	Fresh from the garden	Fresh from under glass	From store	Blanched	Dried
January and February	Brussels sprouts cabbage, celery coleworts Hamburgh parsley kale, leeks parsnips salsify spinach, tree onions	mustard cress	potatoes artichokes carrots garlic onions pumpkin shallots winter radish	chicory endive seakale	peas haricot beans
March	Brussels tops cabbage, kale leeks, spinach turnip tops tree onions Welsh onions for salads, leeks	lettuce mustard cress	potatoes carrots garlic onions	chicory	peas haricot beans
April	cauliflower-broccoli, leeks kale, spinach sprouting broccoli turnip tops Welsh onions	lettuce mustard cress radish rhubarb	potatoes garlic onions	chicory	peas haricot beans
May	asparagus cauliflower-broccoli, kale spinach, rhubarb spring greens spring cabbages sprouting broccoli turnip tops Welsh onions	lettuce radish rhubarb	potatoes garlic		
June	asparagus potatoes, peas broad beans, lettuce cabbage, rhubarb spring onions	lettuce	potatoes		
July	beetroot, cabbage broad beans, peas carrots, dwarf beans courgettes globe artichokes kohlrabi, potatoes spinach, spring onions radish, turnips vegetable marrow	tomatoes			
August	as for July plus: cucumbers, calabrese self blanching celery runner beans, melons sweet corn, tomatoes	tomatoes cucumbers melons aubergines sweet peppers	garlic		
September	as for August except: dwarf beans, broad beans, globe artichokes but with cauliflowers	as for August	garlic		
October	beetroot, cabbage, cauliflower, cauliflower-broccoli, celery celeriac, kohlrabi turnips, swedes, winter radish	tomatoes lettuce	potatoes, onions carrots garlic tomatoes	endive chicory	
November and December	cabbage cauliflower-broccoli celery, celeriac parsnips, salsify Brussels sprouts spinach artichokes Hamburgh parsley	lettuce mustard and cress corn salad	artichokes garlic pumpkin potatoes swedes onions carrots shallots	endive chicory seakale	peas haricot beans

Note: Savoys are included as cabbages during the winter months

paths covered with straw, bracken or peat, allow all crops to be reached with ease. The garden shed may be erected in any out-of-the-way corner provided it is linked to a permanent path so that the gardener does not get wet feet when visiting the shed in winter. The site for the compost heap may be somewhat shaded, but not beneath large, spreading trees. Sufficient room must be left for two heaps because when one is fermenting, another will be built alongside it. There must also be sufficient space left for turning and sifting compost. The gardener who uses animal manure will also leave a few square yards where dung may be stacked. Here shade may be of value in preventing the manure from drying out in summer. Both the cold frame and the greenhouse need a south-facing, open site.

Although most vegetable crops are temporary, rhubarb is generally considered as a permanent kitchen garden crop because the clumps remain in the same soil for around ten years. When allocating a plot for rhubarb, the gardener should bear in mind that although the plants tolerate some shade, crops are better from plants grown at some distance from walls, fences and trees or hedges.

Good cultivation is essential if the best results are to be obtained. The plot should be dug over with great thoroughness and weeds, both annual and perennial, must be kept down.

Vegetables of one plant species do not extract the same quantities of soil chemicals in the ground as do plants of a different species, but the manuring plan and the cropping plan take this into account. After the soil has been well dug and all weeds and weed roots removed, the garden should be divided (on paper or, at any rate mentally) into three plots. These divisions are made so that what is known as crop rotation may be practised. This practice is also aimed at preventing a build up of soil pests in any one part of the garden. It is understandable that if cabbages and their close relatives, for example, are grown for several years in the same piece of ground, the soil will be impoverished (unless the manuring programme is a very generous one) and that pests, which thrive on the roots of the brassica group of plants, are likely to increase. A three-year rotation is generally advised and the following plan suggests how this may be carried out.

The kitchen garden is divided into three plots of approximately equal size—A, B and C.

Until recently the vegetable garden was regularly dressed with animal manures. Those gardeners who are able to obtain farmyard or stable manure (at reasonable prices) are well advised to use them. For all other gardeners, home-made garden compost adequately replaces large quantities of animal manures. Other organic manures such

A general view of the kitchen garden in the Royal Horticultural Society's Gardens, Wisley, Surrey.

Too much shade of this nature is liable to lead to troubles with pests and diseases. Here is an example of inter-cropping. Rows of peas, which make 1m (3ft) high bine, are sown 1m (3ft) apart, leaving 1m (3ft) between which may be used for radish, spinach or lettuce.

Successional cropping is somewhat similar to inter-cropping because many crops, grown for successional crops, may be cultivated between or alongside vegetables needing more time to reach maturity. The aim of successional cropping is to prevent gluts and shortages. The gardener must be able to assess how many lettuces, peas, summer turnips, radishes etc, the family will require from a single sowing. He sows or sets out plants accordingly and he continues to sow every few weeks, providing he has the space for the sowings. He may start with radish, for example, by sowing three short, close rows under cloches in March. A short, double row is sown outdoors in early April, followed by a sowing between the pea rows in mid-April. Further small sowings are made in May, June and July. By sowing in this manner, there will be a supply of fresh, young radishes from mid-May until October. Lettuce seeds should be sown in small batches between March and August. For successional crops of peas, the gardener should bear in mind that there are early, mid-season and late varieties. All three kinds may be sown at around the same time and the plants will come into bearing successionally. There are also varieties of heading broccoli (cauliflower-broccoli) for cutting during the autumn, late winter, spring and early summer. With potatoes, there are kinds which bulk up for lifting in June and July; others mature more slowly for late summer use. Main-crop potatoes are not dug and stored until the autumn.

Catch-cropping, like inter-cropping, is aimed at using every available square inch of the garden. It means no more than making use of any vacant plot for a quick-growing vegetable. Radishes may be sown in April on the site reserved for outdoor tomatoes. The radish crop will have been pulled for use before the tomatoes are set out. The soil banked on either side of leek or celery trenches may be cropped with radish or lettuce.

Even the most experienced gardeners quite often fail to regulate the supply of vegetables throughout the year. In most cases, the weather is to blame. A warm June, for instance, may hasten the summer and autumn cabbage crops but lead to disaster among the lettuces which bolt at once after forming hearts. A severe winter may cripple broccoli and spring cabbages. So very often, too, due

Cropping plan

First season
Plot A cabbages, brussels sprouts, cauliflower broccoli, turnips
Plot B beans, peas, miscellaneous, small crops
Plot C potatoes, carrots, beetroot, lettuce, onions
Second season The crops shown in Plot C above will be grown on Plot A, crops in Plot A on Plot B and those in Plot B on Plot C
Plot A potatoes etc
Plot B cabbages etc
Plot C beans etc
Third season The position of the crops will be as follows:
Plot A beans etc
Plot B potatoes etc
Plot C cabbages etc
Fourth season In the fourth season, the rotation starts off as in the first year

there is generally sufficient food left from a previous manuring.

The following plan suggests how manure, compost or other bulky organics should be applied over three years.

Manuring plan

Plot A cabbages, cauliflowers, brussels sprouts broccoli, kale, savoys, turnips. Possibly inter-cropped with radish and lettuce.
Limed in late autumn, if necessary. Manured or composted during winter digging
Plot B potatoes, followed by broccoli, spring cabbage or leeks.
Not limed. Manured or composted during winter digging
Plot C carrots, parsnips, beetroot, peas, beans summer spinach, onions.
No manure or compost except for pea and bean trenches and for onions. Wood ashes (if available) forked in and a complete fertiliser, such as Growmore, may be applied just before sowings are made

Inter-cropping is referred to in the manuring plan. This practice allows two plants to grow in the place of one. Inter-cropping is of great importance in the small kitchen garden. For good results the soil must be very fertile so that neither of the two crops is starved of food. It is also essential that the rows should run from north to south so that shade does not fall throughout the day from the taller on to the shorter plants.

as municipal compost, seaweed, wool shoddy and spent hops are also of great value in maintaining soil fertility and in improving the actual structure of the soil. Manure, compost or other bulky organic materials should not be applied in an unplanned fashion. This is not only because the gardener may have to purchase organic manures but their addition to parts of the garden may lead to poor crops. In the case of parsnips, for instance, the roots are 'fanged' instead of being single, straight and plump, if the crop is grown in soil which had been recently manured. With other crops, to the vagaries of the weather, there are many fine lettuces and radishes for use when the family is away on holiday. Arrangements should be made for these crops to be harvested and shared by neighbours while the family is away. Unless friends, relations or neighbours help in this way, the gardener is likely to return from holiday to find his bean plants covered with a useless crop of old, stringy pods.

Planning starts in January when the seed catalogues are studied and orders placed for seeds and seed potatoes. Variety is of great importance and the good gardener is always able to harvest something fresh at any time of the year. During the winter, home-grown produce generally consists of cabbage and allied greens together with fresh or stored roots. The owner of a large kitchen garden should consider buying a deep freeze cabinet in which surplus summer vegetables and soft fruits may be stored for winter use so that the diet is more varied. The forcing of such crops as seakale, chicory and endive prevents monotony in winter fare.

1 Dogs and cats are regarded as friends of mankind until proved otherwise. If you wish to exclude them it is up to you to fence them out.
2 To prevent a right of way arising you should put up a notice like this.

Law and the gardener

Your garden is ruled not only by the laws of nature. The laws of the land play a very large part. Here is an outline of the main ways in which the gardener, whether he knows it or not, can fall foul of the law. If the encounter is to be a happy one, the basic rules should be understood.

Traps and trespassers An Englishman's home is his castle. So is his garden. The occupier of a garden is entitled to decide who may and who may not be there. Subject (as we shall see) to rights of way, you are entitled to give people permission to be on your land and to order those who do not have your permission to leave it.

Visitors may have your express authority to be there. You may have invited them to come. Alternatively, they may have your implied consent. They may have used your property as a short cut or have wandered in to admire your flowers without your raising any objection. But whether the permission was express or implied, you can revoke it at any time. Once the visitor ceases to have your permission, he becomes a trespasser and must leave.

If a trespasser is asked to leave your property and refuses, you are entitled to use 'reasonable force' to eject him. The amount of force which is 'reasonable' depends upon all the circumstances of the case. You must use no force at all until you have asked the visitor to leave and he has refused. At this stage, a firm hand on the shoulder or a determined frog-march should meet the situation. If that fails, you should call the police. You are not entitled to use any dangerous weapon except in self-defence. Even then, the methods used must bear reasonable proportion to the violence offered to you.

If someone trespasses on your land, you are not responsible if he suffers injury, unless you have actually laid a trap for him. Setting spring guns or

PRIVATE ROAD
NO PUBLIC RIGHT OF WAY
TO VEHICLES

man traps even for trespassers is definitely unlawful. But note that (except in exceptional circumstances, such as those involving railway property) trespassers cannot be prosecuted. They do not offend against the criminal law. But if you are bothered by persistent trespassers, you can bring a civil action against them. In such cases, a court may grant an injunction restraining the trespassers from repeating their wrongful behaviour in the future. You may also get damages, if you can show that you suffered any financial loss as a result of the trespass.

Trespass by animals In general, the owners of animals are bound to fence them in. If an animal strays and causes damage on neighbouring property, the owner of the animal will be liable to pay compensation. But a special exception is made for dogs and cats. These are regarded as friends of mankind until the contrary is proved against them. If you wish to keep dogs and cats out of your garden, it is up to you to fence them out.

But if it is proved that a particular dog or cat has caused damage, he is then known to have a 'mischievous propensity'. At this stage, his privilege ceases. His owner keeps him at his peril, in the same way as if he were any other sort of animal. A dog is not actually allowed one bite, but until he has once bitten, his owner is unlikely to know that he is liable to bite. Once a dog has misbehaved, his owner is at risk.

If animals stray on to your garden from the highway, however, you will generally have no remedy against their owner. Provided that the owner has not been negligent and that the highway is being used for the ordinary, proper purposes of 'passing and repassing', the owner will not be liable in law.

Rights of way Other people may have a right to cross your land. This right is known as an 'easement'. It is generally called a 'right of way'.

People may acquire a right of way over your garden because you expressly grant it to them. You may allow them to cross your land in return for payment. In that case, you are bound by your agreement to let them pass. But equally, if people use your land openly, freely and as of right for a period of twenty years or more, a right is said to arise by 'prescription'. If, then, you are willing to allow people to cross your garden but you do not wish a right of way to

1 Large trees may block out light from your garden or house, or block the view. Unfortunately, you have no remedy in law.

2 Children visiting your garden may be less careful than adults. So you should take extra care for the safety of child visitors, or children who come to play with your children in your garden.

arise, you should make this clear. Put up a notice to that effect. Close off the garden at least one day a year. And then it can never be said that anyone used the path 'as of right'.

Squatters' titles It is essential, if you wish to preserve a legal right, that you should exercise it. So called 'squatters' titles' arise because people do not exercise their rights over their own land.

Suppose that you have a patch of land at the bottom of your garden which is derelict. You wish to use it for yourself. First you should attempt to trace the owner. Try the Town Hall. Ask the neighbours. But if all else fails, fence the land off so as to form part of your garden; alternatively, put a fence around it and put in a gate to which you alone have the key. If the owner fails to take any step whatsoever to indicate his intention to retain his ownership and inaction continues for twelve years or more, he will lose his rights; you will acquire a squatter's title; and you should register your title at once.

Neighbours' rights If your neighbour builds in his garden so as to rob your windows of their light, your plants of their sunshine and your house of its view, what can you do about it?

If windows of a house have enjoyed uninterrupted light for twenty years or more, an easement is said to arise known as 'ancient lights'. This is a right to have as much light as is reasonably necessary for the enjoyment of life in the room in question. But in fact, very little light is regarded as 'reasonably necessary'. Very few legal actions founded on 'ancient lights' actually succeed.

As for gardens and plants, they have no right to light or to sunshine. There is no such easement known to the law. Even if a flower-bed has been drenched in sun for centuries, you cannot prevent your neighbour from interfering with the sunlight. Nor can he prevent you from doing so, if you wish.

Equally, there is no 'right to a view'. If your neighbour blocks your view or you block his, the sufferer acquires no legal remedy.

Weeds Conscientious gardeners often complain about the unsightliness of an unkempt garden next door. Unfortunately, just as you cannot complain about a view which is taken from you, so the law gives you no remedy if the view is unpleasant. If weeds spread from next door, you might be able to establish that a 'nuisance' has been created (see below). Alternatively, you might be able to get your local council to take action under the Weeds Act (if the weeds are particularly noxious and the council particularly active). But the odds are, in practice, that you can do precious little about it.

Nuisance Each of us must use our property in such a way as not to cause unreasonable disturbance to our neighbour's enjoyment of his property. In other words, you are not allowed by law to do anything in your garden which would unreasonably disturb your neighbour's enjoyment of his garden. Each one of us has to put up with a certain amount of disturbance as 'part of the give and take of neighbourly life'. But if the disturbance goes beyond reasonable bounds, the law will intervene and force the offender to stop his unneighbourly behaviour.

Smoke and fires You may burn bonfires, incinerate your rubbish and create smoke at any time of the day or night. There is no law which places any restriction on garden fires, provided that they are safe. Neighbours have to put up with a reasonable amount of smoke. But if smoke is unreasonable in volume, or fires are habitually lit in such a place and at such times that the next door house is made well-nigh uninhabitable, there is a 'nuisance' in law, as well as in fact.

Noises and smells Voices from the next door garden can be a real aggravation to the gardener, particularly if he is resting. But noise must be expected, especially from children. Only if the reasonable, healthy, normal person would regard the noise as thoroughly unreasonable would the law say that

there has been a 'nuisance'.

Similarly, we all have to put up with a certain amount of smell. Fertilizers in gardens may produce unpleasant odours. So may compost heaps. But if the smells are unreasonably severe, those who suffer from them will have a legal remedy. But note that whether or not a particular unpleasantness constitutes a nuisance will depend, among other factors, upon the situation of the garden in question. That which is a 'nuisance' in a high class, residential district may be part of the ordinary hazards of living in a heavily populated, industrial neighbourhood or, for that matter, in farming country.

Children–and occupier's liability Under the Occupier's Liability Act, 1957, occupiers owe a 'common duty of care' to all lawful visitors. This is a duty 'to take such care as in all the circumstances of the case is reasonable to see that the visitors will be reasonably safe in using the premises for purposes for which he is invited or permitted by the occupier to be there'. So you owe exactly the same duty to the visitor who

1 A fence usually belongs to the person on whose side the posts are. A finer point arises when the posts are centred.
2 Roots and branches of trees may trespass on your neighbour's soil or air space.

is welcome as you do to the visitors (other than trespassers) who are unwelcome.

If someone is hurt in your garden, the court would have to look at all the circumstances of the case to see if you were liable. 'The circumstances relevant for this purpose', says the Act, 'include the degree of care and want of care which would ordinarily be looked for in such a visitor'. It follows that 'an occupier must be prepared for children to be less careful than adults; and an occupier may expect that a person, in the exercise of his calling, will appreciate and guard against any special risks ordinarily incident to it, so far as the occupier leaves him free to do so'.

So you must take extra care for the safety of children who visit you—or who play with your children in your garden. But if you employ a gardener, you may reasonably expect him to guard against such risks as he ought to realise existed.

Garden buildings What you do in your own garden is, to a large extent, your own affair. Subject to the laws on nuisance, your garden is for your own enjoyment. But before you build a garden shed, a greenhouse or any other substantial building, there are a few points to check.

First, if you are a leaseholder, make

certain that you are entitled to build. Many leases (particularly long leases at low rents) lay down that nothing shall be built without the landlord's consent. If you need his consent, get it. Fail to get it and you may be forced to pull down the building you have just spent money putting up. Next, check that there are no local by-laws or regulations which you are about to contravene. A phone call to your town hall should put you in the picture. Finally, if the building is of any size, check with your local planning authority that planning permission is not necessary. If there is any 'material change' in the use of the land, there is said to be a 'development'. And, with certain rather complicated exceptions, when you 'develop', you need planning permission.

Boundary lines Provided that you keep it on your own soil, you can put up any sort of fence, hedge or wall that you see fit. If your neighbour does not like the look of it, that is his misfortune. If he objects to the fence posts being on his side of the fence, he can build another fence on his own soil to improve his own view. If you wish a high fence, to preserve your privacy, that is your business. You are master on your own land.

But what if the fence, wall or hedge is on the boundary? To whom does it belong?

The general rule is that the law runs a notional line along the full length of a boundary, wall, fence or hedge. That portion of it which is on your side is yours. The portion on your neighbour's side is his. Neither can force the other to rebuild it or replace it or even to contribute half the cost of doing so. Wise neighbours share costs. But the law cannot possibly force them to do so.

If the buttresses of a wall or the posts of a fence are on one side only, the wall or fence will usually belong to the person on whose side the buttresses or posts come. But even then, he cannot be forced to keep it in good condition. Nor can he force his neighbour to contribute towards its upkeep.

Boundary disputes. If you and your neighbour cannot agree on where the boundary line comes between your gardens, you will be wise to call in a surveyor, give him the plans of your property, and let him measure up. Boundary disputes not only cause trouble between neighbouring countries —they are a constant source of discord between neighbours.

Trees that trespass Just as you must keep your buildings on your own soil, so if your trees thrust their roots into your neighbour's soil or their branches into his air space, you commit a 'nuisance' and probably a trespass as well. The neighbour is entitled to cut off the roots or the branches at the point where they enter his soil. They do not

belong to him and he must throw them over the fence into your garden. He may not even keep the fruit or the flowers off the branches. But he is fully within his rights in demanding that you keep your plant life in, under and above your own property. Moreover, if the roots thrust themselves far into your neighbour's property (as is common with poplar roots) and damage is done to your neighbour's paths or, worse, to the foundations of his home, you will be liable for damages.

If your trees overhang the highway, you are, technically at least, just as much at fault as if they were overhanging your neighbour's garden. But most important, if an overhanging tree should fall and cause injury, loss or damage, you can be held responsible if it can be shown that you knew or ought to have known that the tree was defective and you did not take steps to cut it back or chop it down.

That which adheres to the freehold Trees, plants and flowers 'adhere to the soil'. They form part of the freehold. And they belong to the freeholder. So if you are a tenant and you have created a glorious garden, do not think that you can take it away with you at the end of your tenancy. In the absence of some special agreement to the contrary, everything growing in the garden belongs to the landlord.

The same rule applies if you are selling your home and garden. You may remove your favourite plants, if you obtain the purchaser's permission (this, in practice, is often given if asked for), or if in the contract certain plants are expressly excluded from the deal (which is very rare). But otherwise you have no right to remove garden produce. You have sold it. But, of course, the converse applies. If you buy a garden, you are just as entitled to insist that the trees, shrubs and plants be left, as you are to prevent the seller from tearing out radiators, fireplaces or fitted cupboards from the house itself.

Buying When you purchase garden produce or garden equipment, whether you know it or not, you are entering into a contract. In consideration of your paying the agreed price, the supplier is providing for you the agreed items.

Section 14 of the Sale of Goods Act, 1893, lays down that, in the absence of agreement to the contrary, you are normally entitled to goods which are 'of merchantable quality' and, usually, reasonably suitable for the purpose supplied. If it turns out that the goods are faulty or that they do not do the job for which they were sold, you are entitled to your money back or, if you

1 Overhanging branches may fall and cause injury, loss or damage and the owner of the tree may be held responsible. 2 Paths may be damaged by tree roots.

wish, to keep the goods and to have them put into proper order at the seller's expense.

It follows that when you buy trees, plants or shrubs, there is an implied term in the agreement that they will be healthy when they are supplied to you. If as a result of faulty planting or careless siting they die or fail to flower or fruit, that is not the fault of the seller. He has kept to his bargain by providing the goods. But if, on the other hand, you can show that the goods were faulty in the first place, you are entitled to your money back. And most reputable suppliers will give it to you (or at least give you credit) without demur.

Similarly, if you buy garden equipment, then, whether the purchase is by mail order or in person, you are entitled to goods which are in good order. If your new garden shed leaks, your greenhouse subsides, your lawnmower proves useless or your hammock collapses, the odds are that you have a good claim against the seller—even though he has given you no 'guarantee'.

Guarantees and warranties the gar-

Trees, plants and flowers 'adhere to the soil' and are part of the freehold.
Therefore, everything growing in the garden belongs to the landlord.

dener who buys any type of equipment is protected by an Act of Parliament. He has a right to expect the equipment he buys to perform the job it is designed to do and be without defect. The buyer is further protected by the Supply of Goods (Implied Terms) Act of April 1973. Under this Act no 'guarantee' or 'warranty' can take away the buyer's normal legal rights. Guarantees are thus only of any real value if they offer rights over and above normal legal rights.

On the other hand, if you choose to buy a 'bargain' on the basis that you are getting the items cheaply and the seller specifically tells you that he cannot accept responsibility if they are defective, that is a matter for you. You have made your bargain and you will be bound by it.

Repair costs Garden equipment and garden building need repair and maintenance. Gardeners who employ contrac-

tors to do repair or maintenance work often complain of the prices they are charged and of the poor standard of workmanship.

The law says that you must pay the agreed price for a job. If, for instance, a firm of landscape gardeners agree to do a particular job in your garden for a set price and you accept that price, you cannot cry off simply because you find another firm who could do the job much cheaper. In the same way, the contractors will have to do the job at the agreed price, even if they find that they have underestimated.

But what if no price has been agreed? What of the extras which always crop up, for example?

Where the parties have not agreed upon a price, the law implies a term into their contract that the contractor will be entitled to make a 'reasonable charge'. As usual, to find out what charge is or is not 'reasonable', all the circumstances of the case have to be considered, including the nature and standard of the work, the amount of time taken, the price of any materials used, the wages of the men concerned and so on.

Faulty workmanship There is another implied term in every contract for work and services that the work will be done in a proper and workmanlike manner and with suitable materials. If the job is bungled or the materials are defective, the contractor has broken his contract. You are entitled to deduct from his bill a reasonable cost of putting his job into proper order.

Stealing and borrowing 'Scrumping' may be a popular pastime amongst the young, but it is quite illegal. A person steals who takes and carries away property capable of being stolen, without the owner's consent or other lawful excuse, intending at the time of taking permanently to deprive the owner thereof.

Growing crops are capable of being stolen. A person who steals your fruit or flowers is a thief.

On the other hand, the man who borrows your gardening equipment, even without your permission, commits no criminal offence whatsoever. He has no intention 'permanently to deprive you thereof': however immoral it may be to help yourself to your neighbour's ladder, mower, sprinkler or drill without his consent, no law is broken. The only exception to this rule is in the case of motor vehicles. It is a crime to take and drive away someone else's motor vehicle without his consent or other lawful excuse.

Lawyers and law suits Litigation is a luxury. Law suits are very expensive. But legal advice is obtainable at a very low fee under the Legal Advice Act and under The Law Society's scheme. If your gardening activities bring you into conflict with neighbours, contractors, visitors or anyone else, consult your solicitor as early as you can. Do not leave it too late.

Lawn construction and maintenance

Most gardeners regard a lawn as an important, if not essential, feature of the garden. The lawn may in fact be the major feature, being a big expanse suitable for garden parties and surrounded by sufficient flower beds to set it off. Alternatively, the lawn may be a minor feature designed to set off flower beds. In either case the requirement is usually a good lawn, ie one which has a uniform cover of good grass and which is free of weeds and blemishes caused by disease, earthworm casts and the like. A lawn which is mainly for children's play or for use as a drying ground does not demand the same high standard as does the real ornamental lawn but should, at any rate, be capable of being regarded without horror!

Layout The general shape and contours required should be decided at an early

A two-year-old lawn, grown from seed.

stage, always bearing in mind that about 16cm (6in) of top-soil should remain overall on completion with gradients designed to allow easy mowing in more than one direction and to allow surface water to escape, without collecting into hollows. The nature of the site— its contours, shape and features such as the levels of the paths, doors, existing trees or rock outcrops determines the form of the new lawn. Generally, simple contours and shapes with no awkward corners or mounds are most satisfactory and these can often be produced with little movement of earth. More ambitious programmes require stripping the top-soil before carrying out the necessary grading in the sub-soil. It is not necessary to think exclusively in terms of a square or oblong patch of lawn surrounded by borders. Some measure of landscaping should be introduced and an irregular shape can be planned with borders of varying width. The site can also be broken up by minor undulations, by terracing, by a shrub break or it can be combined with a crazy path, a rock garden or other features. The effect should nevertheless be bold rather than petty and frivolous.

Clearing the site The first step is to remove as thoroughly as possible any builder's debris or old ironwork, tree roots, etc. There may even be the odd load of gravel which can be used else-

where. Small bushes and long grass can be cut and burnt.

Grading On a great many sites, a new lawn can be made without major alterations in the levels and, in fact, few of us have the energy required to embark on extensive work of this kind. There is no need for the lawn to be absolutely level but it should, of course, be smooth to whatever gradient is accomplished. A gentle slope, say 1 in 80 is, in fact, quite a good thing to help shed surface moisture during rain. Minor adjustments in levels can be achieved by moving top-soil, always subject to the limitation that at least 16cm (6in) (or at any rate a minimum of 10cm (4in) of good top-soil must obtain everywhere on completion. Sometimes it is convenient to buy in a few loads of top-soil to improve levels.

Where considerable grading is required, the really hard work of stripping the top-soil so as to allow grading in the sub-soil is necessary. Such work may have to be accomplished in sections because of space limitations. The top-soil is piled up on one side and the sub-soil gradients altered (usually by cut and fill) before returning the top-soil. There will be few sites where it is necessary to become very technical and use various devices to achieve satisfactory levels; most people will be able to manage satisfactorily by the use of pegs, string and possibly a straight edge.

It is important to remember that soil handled in wet conditions is adversely affected and particularly so where machinery is brought in to help out. Care should be taken to work under dry conditions if at all possible.

Drainage On many sites, particularly where grading has been carried out by machinery, the sub-soil as well as the top-soil is heavily consolidated and, unless this consolidation is removed, the moisture penetration is severely impeded. On relatively small areas, double digging may be needed in order to break up both the sub-soil and the top-soil. On larger areas the sub-soil cultivation can be achieved by means of a tractor-drawn sub-soiler which is usually best used in two directions after replacement of the top-soil.

Whether or not tile drainage or any other form of drainage is required depends on individual site peculiarities. From experience it would seem that most people are able to manage without drainage for their lawns but certainly the possible need for drain-pipes ought to be given some consideration. Clearly, it is not possible to have healthy grass and a good lawn if the soil is waterlogged. On wet land a simple line of clayware land tiles will often suffice provided that some form of outlet can be provided. It is best if the drains can be connected to a main drain somewhere since soakaways, while not without merit, are seldom entirely satisfactory. On large lawns on wet land a proper herring-bone system of drainage may be wanted and whenever land tiles are used it is a good plan to cover them with coarse gravel or clinker ash to within about 16cm (6in) of the final surface of the lawn this being covered finally with 16cm (6in) of top-soil (ie no sub-soil).

Preparing the top-soil All debris such as large stones, big plant roots etc, should be removed and all steps taken to prevent contamination with sub-soil or any deleterious material. Digging is the first operation and any old turf which exists should be buried. If this digging is done in autumn or winter the soil may be allowed to weather during frost. The land can then be worked down by Dutch hoes, rakes etc, in the drier spring weather. During the preparation of the soil it is a good idea to improve it by digging in various materials. Thus, on really heavy soil up to 50kg (1cwt) of gritty lime-free sand per sq m (sq yd) can be worked in with advantage and also on such sites, to keep the soil open after the lawn has been made, up to 3.5kg (7lb) of granulated peat per sq m (sq yd) may be advantageous. Light sandy land benefits from organic materials designed to improve moisture-holding capacity. Well rotted stable manure at say 7-14kg (14–28lb) per sq m (sq yd) is an excellent thing but this is in short supply and may have to be substituted by such things as leafmould or granulated peat (up to 3.5kg (7lb) per sq m (sq yd).

The next thing is to try and ensure that the prepared land is free from roots and seeds of undesirable plants which may establish themselves and compete with the new grass. The best way of accomplishing this is to give a complete summer's fallowing, ie allowing the weeds to germinate and then raking or hoeing them out. To take some exasperation out of all this it is a good plan to grow a potato crop or similar which gives some encouragement and return for the work involved. Chemical cleaners have some merit but

they are not the complete answer to the problem.

Whether the lawn is to be established from seed or turf, the final preparations are fairly similar in that in either case we need a firm, fine soil bed. Repeated cultivations and consolidation are needed. The site may be broken down by means of a Canterbury hoe or mechanically as seems most appropriate and then rough raking follows with the removal of the larger stones. To try to eliminate air pockets in the body of the soil it is wise to 'heel' the surface, an operation which involves close treading with the weight of the body thrown on the heels so that the soil is pressed down into the soft spots. For this operation the soil should be dry enough not to adhere too much to the boots.

Further raking and heeling at right angles to the first set of operations should follow. Final working should aim at achieving a smooth surface from which small bumps and depressions have been entirely eliminated while the soil is sufficiently firm (though not over compacted) to minimize the risks of sinkage later producing an uneven surface. A rather better tilth is required for seeding than for turfing.

Turfing This is popularly accepted as being the best way to produce a satisfactory lawn. This is not strictly true, but undoubtedly the use of turf does simplify matters for the amateur and does make possible the use of less perfect soil conditions. Unfortunately good turf is both rare and expensive so that many people become disappointed with the lawns they have obtained by this method. Frequently the supplier is blamed for the unsatisfactory results despite the original acceptance of the turf as satisfactory, there possibly having been some mistaken idea that the turf would

1 The grass on a newly-sown lawn should be only lightly clipped over.
2 Young perennial weeds which appear in the sward should be removed by hand.

improve after laying. There is now a British Standard Specification for turf so that purchasers buying to the standard have some control over what they receive, though they may in fact require a higher standard than that covered. The major gain from turfing is that of time, since the turf can be laid in the autumn when it is too late for seeding and with good management can appear as a really good lawn, capable of being used, the following summer. Turf laid in spring and summer runs the risk of drying out and not establishing satisfactorily.

Great care should be taken when buying turf, which should preferably be established in soil of a sandy loam nature and free from stones. The delivered turf should be in mown condition, of close texture and good uniform density and colour. There should be sufficient fibre to hold the turf together for handling but excess leads to unsatisfactory results. The quality of grasses in the turf which is bought depends on the requirement but for a first-class lawn there should be little in the turf except fine bent and/or fescue grasses and, even for second-class lawns, weeds and diseases should be absent.

The delivered turf is best in 30cm (1ft) squares (or possibly 60 by 30cm (2 by 1ft) and cut to a uniform thickness of say 3cm (1¼in). If the turf which arrives is uneven in thickness it may be desirable to box the turf, ie to lay the turf, roots up, in a shallow tray of suitable depth and then draw a stout knife across the top edge of the box, thus bringing the turf to the standard thickness.

Before laying the turf the soil should receive such chemical treatment as is required. Acid soils may need lime and this is best decided as the result of a soil test. Usually it is wise, whatever the nature of the soil, to give a fertilizer on the following lines:
3kg (6lb) of fine hoof and horn meal
3kg (6lb) of fine bone meal
3kg (6lb) of powdered superphosphate

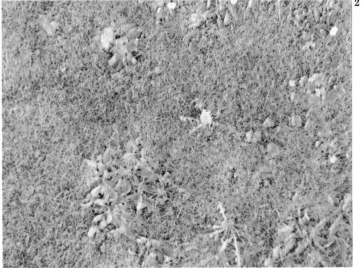

1.5kg (3lb) of sulphate of potash per 100 sq m (100 sq yd).

The fertilizer should be raked in, preferably a few days before laying the turf.

When the actual turfing operation starts it is wise to choose weather conditions when the soil is reasonably dry to avoid damage to the prepared site. On many sites it is convenient to start by laying a single turf round the perimeter of the site. After that, laying turf across the body of the site should be done in a forward direction, working to face the unturfed part which should be maintained in its prepared condition. Traffic should be on planks laid across the turf as required. The turf should be laid with broken joints, rather like bricks in a wall. Each turf should be laid flat and tight up to its neighbours. Where a turf seems to be either high or low adjustment should be made in the soil below rather than by beating down etc. When the whole of the turf has been laid it should be carefully rolled with a light roller and then a sandy compost material applied at 2–3kg (4–5lb) per sq m (sq yd) and carefully brushed in.

Seeding The best time for sowing grass seed on a new lawn is about the end of August. Spring sowing are not ruled out entirely but they do run a greater risk from drought since May is often very dry and in the spring, weed competition tends to be greater than in the late summer. Seeding is the cheapest and probably the best way of getting a good lawn but the best results are only achieved if sufficient skilled work is put into the work of seeding and of looking after the lawn in the first year or so.

In the final stage of preparations and a few days before sowing a suitable complete fertilizer should be given and this might well take the form of:
1.5kg (3lb) of sulphate of ammonia
1.5kg (3lb) of fine hoof and horn meal
1.5kg (3lb) of dried blood
3kg (6lb) of powdered superphosphate
3kg (6lb) of fine bone meal
1.5kg (3lb) of sulphate of potash
per 100 sq m (100 sq yd)

This should be carefully raked into the soil a few days before sowing. Soils of an acid character should have been limed appropriately a week or two earlier.

The kind of grass seed to use depends on the kind of lawn required and on the amount you are prepared to pay. For a first-class lawn a really fine mixture such as 8 parts of Chewings' fescue (preferably a good variety such as 'Highlight') and 2 parts of browntop

1 Putting piles of top dressing on the lawn ready for working it in.
2 Working in the top dressing, using the back of a rake.
3 The lute is another tool which may be used to work top dressing into the lawn by drawing it backwards and forwards.
4 Brushing off surplus top dressing.

bent (American origin) is suitable and the rate of sowing is about 28g (1oz) per sq m (sq yd). Less fine mixtures may be used for hard-wearing, second-quality lawns and, for children's playground type of lawns, even coarser mixtures containing perennial ryegrass may be used. For all these grass seeds a rate of application of 28g (1oz) per sq m (sq yd) is satisfactory. There are, of course, good proprietary mixtures available from reputable lawn seed suppliers and generally speaking one can go on price.

Sowing is best done on a dry, raked surface and it is wise to divide the seed into two lots for sowing in transverse directions. For really careful work it is best to divide the lawn into sections and weigh out the amount of seed for each section and then again split this into two halves for transverse sowing. The seed should be lightly raked in and there has to be emphasis on the lightness of this operation, particularly for the very fine mixtures, since the grass seeds should not be deeply covered. It is not usually necessary or desirable to roll after raking but rolling will be needed when the grass is showing through in order to tighten up the soil round the grass roots preparatory to mowing.

The question of bird damage often arises in suburban areas and certain preparations are sold for treating the grass seed. These are of limited benefit in that frequently most damage is done by birds not so much eating the seed as spoiling the seed bed by having dust

baths! The best protection is usually the very elementary one of having black cotton across the lawn supported by sticks. Some people lay polythene over the newly-sown lawn area but if this expedient is used it is important to get the cover away as soon as the grass shows through or disease attack may well undo all the good work and certainly do more damage than the birds.

After-care Lawns which have been established by turfing need occasional top dressing with bulky material such as sandy compost or of an artificial compost made up from soil sand and peat. The purpose of this dressing is to smooth out the surface and fill in any cracks, so it needs careful working in by a suitable drag brush or other piece of equipment. Occasional rolling may be required but this should not be overdone. During the first year the grass will need mowing regularly but over close mowing should be avoided, particularly if it shows signs of skimming any prominent piece of turf. In the spring following turfing a good general fertilizer should be given as for an existing lawn.

New-sown lawns should not be mown until the grass is about 5cm (2in) high and then it should be carefully topped, preferably using a side-wheel machine which is sharp and in good condition. Before mowing, stones should be picked off the surface and the area carefully rolled. Mowing should then be done when the grass has regained its upright condition. Any coarse grass or weeds which appear in the new sward should be removed by hand at intervals but mowing will dispense of annual weeds satisfactorily. On no account should the grass be allowed to get too long and regular mowing is essential with the height of cut being gradually lowered to the chosen final height. A lawn which has been sown at the end of the summer or early autumn will not need any further fertilizer treatment until the following spring. It should then receive a dressing of general fertilizer such as for an existing lawn.

The surface levels on a seeded lawn are unlikely to be as good as those of a turfed lawn and occasional top dressing with sandy compost at about monthly intervals during the first full year's growth will help to produce the smooth surface which is such an attractive feature of a good lawn. A few weeks after sowing, bare patches which have been missed despite the best endeavours may become visible and at this stage it is useful to have reserved a small quantity of seed so that over-sowing can be carried out straight away with the result that the patches soon catch up.

On new-sown turf the disease called 'damping-off' sometimes attacks, more particularly when heavy rates of seeding have been used or when a normal rate has been washed by heavy rain into concentrated collections in heel marks or similar depressions. Sometimes recovery occurs by natural means but if the disease is serious it is necessary to treat the grass with a suitable fungicide such as Cheshunt compound, which is applied by means of a watering-can, or more conveniently with an inorganic mercury fungicide applied as a dry dust.

Maintenance The essence of a good lawn is that it is uniform in texture, colour and surface smoothness with freedom from patches caused by weeds, disease, earthworms, or bad mowing. The lawn needs to be sufficiently hard-wearing to stand what is required of it and it should maintain a good colour both in summer and in winter. This colour at the various seasons is in part a reflection of the grass variety, in part of the feeding and in part of moisture control. The earth should hold sufficient moisture to keep the grass growing in dry weather but should not be water-logged in winter.

Mowing Regular, not too keen mowing, is essential if the lawn is to be attractive and satisfactory. The first requirement is a good mower in good condition and, of course, buying mowers has much in common with buying cars. Personal choice comes into the matter as well as the engineering performance and the price. For best results the most expensive conventional mower (roller type) of a given size may well be the best and, of course, an important factor as far as grass is concerned is the number of cuts to a linear yard. A motor mower has advantages in reducing muscular effort particularly on large lawns but it is wise to buy as light a machine as possible since regular use of a heavy machine results in considerable compression of the top soil.

A new lawn should not be cut too high at first but gradually worked down to the height of cut that is required. It is a mistake to cut very short since no grass really thrives on such severe defoliation. The really fine grasses of a first-class lawn stand the closest cutting but even they should not be cut closer than 1-2cm ($\frac{1}{4}$-$\frac{1}{2}$in). For medium lawns 2–3cm ($\frac{1}{2}$–1in) is suitable, while for ryegrass lawns 3cm (1in) is more satisfactory since ryegrass (even the best varieties) does not like mowing any shorter. For lawns which are not required to be very fine many people use the so-called rotary mowers. Infrequent mowing damages the grass and during the vigorous growing season a good fine lawn needs mowing as much as three times a week while even a second-class lawn should be mown not less than once a week. It is an advantage if the lawn can be mown in different directions each time it is cut.

Less frequent mowing is necessary when growth is not vigorous but at no time should the grass get very much longer than its accepted height. Even during the winter months careful topping in the right weather conditions may be desirable. At whatever time of the year the lawn is being mown, the best results are produced if the operation is carried out when the grass is dry.

Although allowing the cuttings to fly means the return of plant foods, it is nevertheless considered wise to remove cuttings since they encourage disease, weeds, earthworm castings, coarse grasses and a soft surface.

Edging No matter how good a lawn is produced it looks second rate if the edges are not kept trimmed. Most owners of small lawns use ordinary hand shears for cutting the grass at the edges but long-handled shears or special lawn edge trimmers are more favoured if the lawn is large. Even when given regular attention, edges tend to become uneven and attention with a straight spade or turf cutter is required about once a year. Permanent edges of metal, wood or concrete have decided advantages in keeping clean lines round the lawn.

Top dressing For a really good finish from mowing it is necessary that the surface of the lawn be smooth, otherwise you will find long grass in the hollows and skimmed turf (and later, moss) on any high patches in the lawn. Obviously the smoothness of the surface owes something to the original preparation of the lawn and rolling will help to push down some of the higher areas. Unfortunately rolling accomplishes this smoothing out at the expense of producing consolidation and this is not good for root development or for moisture penetration. Rolling must, therefore, be kept to a minimum.

The best way of achieving a really smooth surface is to follow the practice of professional groundsmen or green-keepers, ie top dressing the surface with bulky material of suitable texture. What is best for most lawns is a sandy compost material which might be made up for example by mixing sand, soil and peat to make a product of a consistency something similar to good potting compost but, of course, without any added fertilizers. This material is spread over the lawn by hand or shovel fairly evenly and then worked into the surface by means of a drag mat or drag brush. On small areas the back of a wooden rake can be used to work the material backwards and forwards so that it disappears into the base of the sward, obviously going preferentially into hollow areas. Care must be taken to avoid smothering. Amazing benefits in the appearance of the lawn can be achieved by this often neglected practice.

Fertilizer treatment Requirements for fertilizer on existing lawns vary considerably: on rich soils fertilizers may not be needed more than once in five or ten years while on poor soils where wear on the lawn is heavy, two good fertilizer dressings a year may be advisable. On average, once a year is at least enough and a reputable brand of lawn fertilizer can be given each spring. If you wish to know what you are putting on, you may care to make up a mixture yourself on the following lines:

1.5kg (3lb) of sulphate of ammonia
0.5kg (1lb) of fine hoof and horn meal
0.5kg (1lb) of dried blood
2kg (4lb) of powdered superphosphate
0.5kg (1 lb) of fine bonemeal
0.5kg (1lb) of sulphate of potash
per 100 sq m (100 sq yd).

Such fertilizers must be well mixed with sandy soil or similar material to the extent of about 12kg (28lb) of this per 100 sq m (100 sq yd) in order to give more bulk to help uniform distribution and also to minimize scorch risk. The addition of 0.5kg (1lb) of calcined sulphate of iron per 100 sq m (100 sq yd) to the above mixture helps to improve grass colour and to check weeds and disease. Careful, even, spreading of fertilizer is best carried out during showery weather but if no rain falls within one or two days of the application, the fertilizer should be watered in to avoid damage to the grasses.

An experienced professional grounds-man obtains the best distribution by hand spreading and the amateur gardener should not despise this method though it needs to be done carefully. Small distributors are available but difficulty is always experienced in matching up adjacent 'breadths' to avoid missing strips or overlapping. while the turns also worry many people.

Liming A good gardener has to use lime occasionally in many parts of the country but he should not transfer this wise practice to the lawn since liming encourages weeds, worms and disease in the lawn. The soil sometimes does, in fact, become too acid and require liming but the disadvantages of liming are such that it pays to try to make sure that liming is really necessary before starting. The soil test, of course, is the ideal way. When liming a lawn a light dressing only, of a material such as ground limestone (ground chalk) is needed at a rate of 50-100g (2-4oz) per sq m (sq yd). Excess of lime encourages worms, weeds etc and reduces the proportion of fine grasses.

Mechanical operations While a great deal of mechanical work is necessary on bowling greens, golf greens, tennis courts etc, it is possible to over-emphasize the amount of work required of this kind on the average lawn.

Nevertheless, regular brushing or light raking of the lawn keeps the grass in good condition, prevents the formation of excess fibre and keeps the grass growing vertically to give the appearance of a nice, new carpet with the pile standing upright. Light raking also brings up the runners of weeds such as clover and thus prevents them from spreading. On old lawns which have become over-fibrous, vigorous scarification with a wire rake to get out some of

the fibre is a good idea. Such vigorous work is best carried out at the end of the summer while there is still sufficient growth to heal up any disfigurement which might be caused, or to a less severe extent in the spring when growth is beginning. If you have a large lawn you may be able to use a mechanical scarifier.

Rolling is useful in the spring to firm up the ground after any upheaval caused by the winter frosts, but after that its use should be kept to a minimum if, in fact, it is done at all following the first spring rolling. This, of course, is because of the consolidation which rolling creates.

To compensate for over-compaction some kind of aeration of the soil is occasionally desirable, but on the average lawn it should not be necessary to do this heavy work annually. Much depends on how much compression is produced by the amount of wear given, by the weight of the mower etc, but probably on the average lawn some kind of forking every three or four years would be sufficient. There are so-called hand forks which can be used. They are pressed into the ground by the foot and make holes which allow water and air to penetrate and also encourage rooting. If there is severe compaction it is wise to use forks which have hollow tines which remove a core of soil, thus allowing the surrounding soil to expand and thus, of course in turn relieving the pressure.

The grass roots very well down these holes and it will be appreciated that a good deep root system helps the resistance of the grass to drought and indeed to wear and tear. Some of the special forks for aerating the lawn have solid tines which may be cylindrical or flat in shape. These do not make such a complete job as the hollow-tine forks, but on the other hand they do not leave holes which are easily invaded by weeds. There is no doubt at all that hollow tine forking can be overdone. Various types of machine, ranging from hand pushed to complex motorized models, are available for carrying out forking work and in view of the labour involved, if you have a large lawn, you will no doubt consider purchasing or hiring such a machine.

Watering Grass cannot grow without sufficient moisture, so that in dry weather a really good lawn needs artificial watering occasionally to keep it at its best. Watering should start early on in the dry weather, ie before the grass starts turning brown and the watering should be done quite copiously when it is done at all, so that the moisture penetrates deeply down to the roots. Light damping of the surface from

1 Aerating a compacted lawn, using a fork and thrusting the tines into the turf. 2 An oscillating sprinkler may be used to water both the lawn and the border.

time to time may do more harm than good by encouraging surface rooting and thus making the grass more liable to damage by drought. Many gardeners apply water to their lawns by means of the hosepipe with some kind of spraying device at the end, but a simple kind of sprinkler, of which there are many now available, is extremely useful and, in fact, may be so used as to water the lawn and the adjacent flower beds at the same time. Where difficulty is experienced in getting the water to penetrate, shallow spiking is useful to start the moisture penetrating the surface.

Artificial watering is not an unmixed blessing in that it tends to encourage annual meadow grass and weeds such as pearlwort, especially if the water is hard.

Weed control If management practices are satisfactory, weed invasion is kept to a minimum but some weeds will always manage to invade even the best kept lawns. The problem is fairly easy to deal with these days since the new selective weedkillers are so effective. Generally speaking, it is best to use one based on a mixture of the chemicals 2, 4-D and CMPP of which there are a number of proprietary compounds available. Repeated applications may sometimes be necessary for resistant weeds. The best conditions for using the weedkillers are when growth is active, when the weather is warm and the soil moist, though there is little prospect of rain, which reduces effectiveness. It is important to ensure that the chemical does not get anywhere but on the lawn since obviously all broad-leaved garden plants and greenhouse plants are susceptible. Any containers used should be carefully and thoroughly washed out before they are used for other purpose. Weedkiller applications are normally best carried out by means of a sprayer but, particularly in small gardens, sprayers are not recommended for lawn use since risk of spray drift on to plants in the flower beds is considerable. It is better to use a watering can fitted with a fine rose or with a dribble bar attachment. Uniform distribution is, of course, essential since missing strips means that some weeds will be untouched, while overlapping or excessively generous treatment to a given weed patch may cause severe damage to the grass.

Moss causes a great deal of anxiety to lawn owners—sometimes out of all proportion to the amount of moss. Usually moss in a lawn is a sign that there is something wrong somewhere in the management; either the lawn is starved, or is mown too severely, or has bad drainage, or is suffering too much from the shade of trees and buildings. Even low shrubs slightly overhanging the lawn can result in moss invading the shaded area and then spreading. The first essential, if moss is to be eliminated, is to find out the cause and to remove it or ameliorate it as far as possible. If this is done, then good results against moss can be obtained by using proprietary preparations containing mercury compounds such as a mercurized turf sand.

Pests The most important pest on a lawn is the earthworm. Generally the earthworm may be the gardener's friend but on the lawn the detrimental effects of the casts are considerable. They make the surface dirty, while their tunnels make the surface soft and the whole effect is that the lawn is wet and muddy. In addition, the casts smother grasses and act as first-class seed beds for weed seeds which may be brought up from below with the casted soil or which may be blown in from elsewhere. The use of lime or excessive amounts of organic fertilizer, or the retention of cuttings on the lawn, all of which encourage earthworms, should be avoided. It is better (and cheaper) if worms can be kept out rather than that they should have to be treated with chemicals. If it becomes necessary to control the earthworms by chemical treatment, mild conditions in autumn (or, rather less satisfactorily, in spring) when the worms are actually working near the surface, provide the best conditions. The two materials most usually used by professionals are lead arsenate and chlordane both of which are poisonous so that many lawn owners would prefer not to use them, especially where there are children and pets. Probably the best material to use in such circumstances would be one of the proprietary derris preparations sold for the purpose. The powder preparation can be applied dry and either watered in or may be left to be watered in during the next rain storm. Most of the earthworms die below ground with this treatment but a few will come to the surface and should be removed. Even derris products cannot be used if there is a fish pond adjacent, since derris is very poisonous to fish.

There are few other pests of lawns (other than the neighbours' pets) but leather-jackets are occasionally troublesome, particularly near the seaside and these can be dealt with by BHC or like powders sold for the purpose.

Diseases The most common disease of lawns is that known as fusarium patch disease (or snow mould) and this is most frequently met on over-fed lawns, particularly in damp, shaded situations. Another fairly common but less damaging disease is corticium which shows as brownish discoloration, generally over quite large areas. This fungus disease is usually associated with insufficient feeding and quite often a dressing of fertilizer is the best remedy, but fungicidal treatment may be necessary to cure bad attacks.

Renovation From time to time patches of lawn become bare as the result of burning with fertilizer or wear and it is necessary to make these good. Sometimes it is convenient to bring a patch of turf from a less important part of the lawn but often it is necessary to prepare the earth and sow a little grass seed, and protect it from the birds. If the edges of the lawn become bare the best procedure is to strip the outside band of turf carefully, say 30cm (1ft) wide, to replace with turf cut from the next 30cm (1ft) of the lawn, and then put the worn turf in place of this. The thin turf can then be overseeded. See also Grass seed for lawns.

Layering see Planting

Leaf scorch see Physiological disorders

Leaf spot see Diseases and their control

Leeks see Vegetables

Lettuce see Vegetables

Levelling see Paths in the garden

Lime and liming

Lime is strictly defined as a white caustic alkaline substance—quicklime; chemically, calcium oxide (CaO); made by heating chalk or limestone. But in gardening, lime means any calcium-containing material which is capable of correcting soil acidity.

Why lime is used The main reason for using lime is to reduce the acidity of a soil that is acid or, in other words, to sweeten the soil. Few plants will grow well in a very acid soil mainly because their intake of plant foods is reduced; phosphates, in particular, get 'locked up' in acid soils. There is often a shortage of calcium in very acid soils.

Aluminium and manganese, on the other hand, are often released in such large amounts that they can poison many plants. Tomatoes, beans and brassicas are particularly sensitive in this respect.

Lime encourages soil life The bacteria that convert ammonium salts to nitrates —one of the steps necessary before nitrogen-bearing foods can be used by the plant—are almost or completely inoperative in very acid soils. The organism which is responsible for fixing nitrogen in the roots of peas, beans and other leguminous plants operates most favourably when the soil is well limed, which is the reason why peas do not thrive in really acid soils. But rhododendrons would be very sickly or even die in a soil limed for peas. Earthworms, too, thrive in well-limed soils; they make channels in soil improving the drainage of clay soils and compacted lawns (we know that wormcasts are unsightly but the good that worms do in improving drainage outweighs their harm).

Lime improves tilth Many clay soils, when limed regularly, become more porous and allow rain to drain away

Club root on brassicas can often be obviated by the addition of lime to the land to reduce acidity.

forms the next layer. The clay content, light and powdery, will dissolve and do little more than colour the water, remaining in suspension for a very long time. Finally the humus will tend to float on the top of the water, or if the shaking has been vigorous, perhaps some will have sunk to form the top layer.

By this simple means you can make a very fair assessment of your soil's capabilities and requirements.

Soil reaction	Dressings of carbonate of lime		
	Sandy soil	Loams	Clay and peaty soil
	lb/sq yd	lb/sq yd	lb/sq yd
Slightly acid *p*H 6·0	½	¾	1¼
Moderately acid *p*H 5·5	1	1½	2½
Acid *p*H 5·0	1½	2¼	3¾
Strongly acid *p*H 4·5	2	3¼	4¾
Very acid *p*H 4·0	2½	4	6

The above figures relate to carbonate of lime (ground chalk or ground limestone); if hydrated lime is used the dressings should be half of the above quantities.

quicker, thus allowing you to get on to the ground earlier in the spring. It is possible to cure a really sticky clay soil by liming, but not all clays will respond since some are naturally limey. Lime has very little effect on the tilth of sandy and loamy soils.

Lime controls some diseases and pests Club root disease of brassicas flourishes in acid soils and can usually be controlled by liming, but it takes two or three years before it works fully. Slugs, leather-jackets or wireworms and several other soil pests are discouraged by liming.

How to tell whether soil needs lime The presence of spurrey, sheep's sorrel, corn marigold and other weeds that thrive in acid soils often indicates the need for lime, but these weeds are not very reliable indicators since they continue to grow for some time in soils that have been limed. If you see rhododendrons and blue hydrangeas growing really well in nearby gardens it is fairly safe to assume that your soil is naturally acid. But the only reliable method of finding out whether a soil is acid or alkaline is to carry out a soil test for lime. An old-fashioned way of telling whether a soil was limey was by pouring some dilute hydrochloric acid on to the soil to see whether it fizzed but this does not help very much; if a soil is rich in calcium carbonate it will react with the

added acid and carbon dioxide gas which causes the fizzing. Lack of fizzing, however, is not a reliable indicator that lime is needed and, of course, this test gives no idea as to the amount of lime required to correct acidity in an acid soil.

How to test for lime The simplest do-it-yourself method is to buy some indicator papers from your garden supply centre and then take a sample of soil (see Soil testing). If the soil is dry, moisten it well with water (distilled water if possible) in a saucer but do not make it runny. After half an hour place a 2cm (½in) strip of test paper so that half of it lies on top of the wet soil and the other half against the side of the saucer. After 5 minutes compare the colour of the paper with the colour panels on the chart, which is sold with the papers.

And while we are talking of old-fashioned but useful techniques, let us have a quick look at a method of determining the texture rather than the acidity or alkalinity of your garden soil. Take a sample of your soil, just a spoonful, and shake this up well in a glass or other clear vessel of water. Then set it aside to settle. If you have reason to believe that your soil differs in different parts of your garden then carry out the same test with more than one sample taken from other places.

After a time you will see that a number of definite layers have appeared. The stones are on the floor or base of the vessel and on top of these is a layer of sand. Loam having a proportion of sand

For peaty soils and those that are naturally rich in humus you will have to increase the amount of lime even more. In fact, it is virtually impossible to correct the acidity of some of them; a few of the fenland soils are so acid that even after enormous quantities of lime have been applied, the soil still shows an acid reaction the following year. So, all you can hope to do is to correct the worst of the acidity. Fortunately such soils are rare.

If you feel that the whole business of determining lime requirement is too complicated and you know that your soil is acid, a good general rule is to apply 0.3kg (½lb) of hydrated lime per sq m (sq yd) on sandy or loamy soils, and 0.8kg (¾lb) per sq m (sq yd) on clay or peaty soils. On the other hand, you may be a precision gardener and will, therefore, want to know more exactly how much lime is required. For you, there is a special lime requirement test kit which gives more accurate guidance, as to the amount of lime needed to correct the acidity of your garden soil or possibly to raise the *p*H value of your potting compost for a particular plant.

Soil test laboratories carry out a special lime requirement test by means of electrically operated *p*H meters and buffer solutions; this is the most reliable method.

Dangers of overliming Too much lime can be as bad as too little. Overliming may reduce the plants' intake of iron, causing yellowing of leaves. Deficiencies or iron and boron are also common in over-limed soils in the garden.

Alkaline conditions produced by liming favour the disease fungus responsible for scab on potatoes.

The danger of overliming is greatest in sandy soils so it is wise to add lime little and often to sandy soils, but there is rather less need to worry with clays and even loams.

Forms of lime Hydrated lime and carbonate of lime are the two forms most commonly listed in garden catalogues.

Hydrated lime comes from quicklime that has been treated (slaked) with water and is known chemically as calcium hydroxide. It is often sold under brand names.

It is a very fine powder which mixes well with soil particles and being slightly soluble in water is a most effective liming material where speedy benefits are wanted. It is an alkaline substance and is caustic and, therefore, likely to burn foliage if it blows on to plants during spreading.

When mixed with soil, hydrated lime combines with carbon dioxide and turns into calcium carbonate; this is the fate of all forms of applied liming materials.

Carbonate of lime or 'garden' lime as it is often called, is limestone or chalk that has been crushed to a gritty powder. Most garden limes are ground to pass through a 3mm ($\frac{1}{8}$in) sieve.

The rate at which carbonate of lime works in the soil depends on how finely ground it is. Even the finest particles produced by grinding are not so fine as those produced chemically during the production of hydrated lime, but nevertheless they work quickly. The coarser particles act as a reserve and are longer lasting. Carbonate of lime does not burn plant foliage and is more pleasant to handle than hydrated lime; it is the best form to use in seed and potting composts.

Although insoluble in pure water, it does dissolve in soil water, forming calcium bicarbonate from which the calcium portion can be taken up by the clay and humus of the soil; some is also absorbed by plant roots, worms and other organisms.

This form of lime is less concentrated than hydrated lime and so you need larger amounts to reduce the acidity of an acid soil; but if you buy it in packs of 25kg ($\frac{1}{2}$cwt) or over, it is cheaper than hydrated lime.

It is important to know that the acid neutralizing value of any form of lime is expressed in terms of its content of calcium oxide (CaO). Carbonate of lime contains about 50 percent CaO, and hydrated lime from 60 to 70 percent CaO.

Other materials used in liming. Marl is a clay rich in lime. This is obtained in many parts of the country from beds that are sufficiently near to the surface to be worked economically as in the new red sandstone formations in the north and west midlands, or the shell marls which occur in Norfolk. It is of particular value in sandy or peaty soils not only for its lime content but also for the clay which gives 'body' to this type of soil. Marling is an ancient practice which is still carried out in areas subject to severe wind erosion; the clay part helps to bind sand grains together and prevent them from blowing away.

Waste materials from the sugar beet, paper, tanning and cement industries often contain calcium carbonate and make useful liming materials. Some may be wet, lumpy and difficult to handle, but if available, nearly all can be a useful source of lime.

Oyster and other sea shells are mostly calcium carbonate. When free from salt and ground finely they make useful liming materials.

Slags, which are waste materials from iron and phosphorus manufacture, contain calcium and magnesium silicates that are capable of reducing soil acidity.

Dolomite lime is a natural form of calcium and magnesium carbonate which supplies two elements important for plant growth, calcium and magnesium, and which also provides the necessary neutralizing effects. It is a useful form of lime to use on acid soils that are low in magnesium and is widely used in soil-less composts for potted and container grown plants.

Spreading lime Lime is not just magic out of a bag. To work properly it must be mixed thoroughly with the top-soil layers. To begin with the lime must be spread over the soil surface by hand from a bucket or a fertilizer distributor if the soil is firm and even. But do not dig it in because digging often shifts the surface lying lime simply into another layer below the soil surface.

It is best spread on a finely broken surface and then stirred about with the soil, using a hand or mechanical cultivator; when the soil is on the dry side, you cannot expect minute particles of lime to mix properly with clods.

When, in the first year after liming, results are disappointing—and this does sometimes occur—the cause is frequently the length of time needed for the dressing to become reasonably mixed into the top soil layer. If the lime fails to penetrate, seeds may be sown in what is locally and temporarily a too alkaline strip of soil. But if it has been dug some way under, seedlings may be trying to grow in a thin layer of very acid soil and plants will grow poorly until the root system reaches the buried lime layer.

When to lime If your soil is very acid, the sooner lime is applied the better—as soon as the ground becomes vacant. Autumn dressing is often recommended so that rain can wash it into the soil.

Loam see Soil types

Loganberries see Fruit

Lopping

A term used to describe a severe pruning operation in which large branches of a tree are removed. The operation should not be undertaken lightly since it usually adversely alters the balance and symmetry of a tree. With conifers, lopping can be disastrous as they do not generally have the ability to produce new growth, which is a property of the broad-leaved trees. The operation known as pollarding and coppicing are really special kinds of lopping. When lopping is essential it should not be undertaken at the time when the sap is rising, and with deciduous trees should be completed while they are leafless. The wounds should be painted with a fungicidal paint, such as Arbrex, to prevent infection and decay.

Lopping is a drastic pruning operation. Here a large branch has been lopped from a pear tree. The cut surface has been painted to prevent decay.

1

2

3

4

5

6

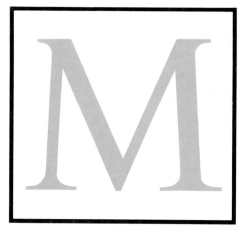

Manure see Fertilizers

Marrows see Vegetables

Melons see Fruit under glass

Miniature gardens

The growing scarcity of building land, particularly in towns and suburbs, with the accompanying shrinkage in the size of plots as prices continue to rise, poses difficult problems. Making a worthwhile garden in such restricted areas requires a good deal of careful forethought. In fact, the proverbial pocket-handkerchief plot has almost become a reality, and this at a time when interest in gardening has never been greater.

A simple indoor miniature garden can be made in a clay seed-pan, using small perennial plants from pots and is a fascinating source of interest.
1 The base of the seed pan is covered with large crocks to ensure sharp drainage, and these are covered with moss and peat to keep the compost open and porous.
2 Compost is added to about half the depth of the pan and levelled.
3 Suitable stones, not too large and not too small, are put in position and firmed in place with a dibber.
4 and 5 Small plants are put into position and planted with a small trowel.
6 The finished garden is permanent.

Where space is really limited, there is only one answer. Design and planting must be scaled down to fit the area available. But gardening on this reduced scale can be just as rewarding. In these pygmy plots, the opportunity for healthy exercise may be lacking, but to many gardeners, especially the elderly and those who prefer to 'potter', this may not necessarily be a great disadvantage.

Miniature gardens can take a number of forms. In the very small plot, you can share the pleasures of those who work on a broader canvas by restricting your planting, not only to single specimens of your favourite plants, but also by growing those that are compact in habit with a slow rate of increase.

The miniature garden proper, however, will not be able to rely on such measures. For its impact, it will have to depend mainly on dwarf plants, some of which may be miniature replicas of their taller counterparts while others will display their own individual characteristics.

A good way of getting horticultural quarts into pint pots is to garden in sinks and troughs. Several of these plant containers, each with its separate planting scheme, can be accommodated in a minimum of space. Many a town forecourt, backyard or balcony could benefit from the inclusion of a feature of this kind.

Unfortunately, genuine stone troughs and sinks are fast becoming collectors' items and, in consequence, increasingly difficult and expensive to come by. The stone sinks of Victorian kitchens and sculleries have long ago been replaced by vitreous enamel and stainless steel, while the larger troughs, formerly used for watering cattle and horses, have given place to galvanized iron tanks.

The occasional specimen still turns up at country sales and in junk yards, but dealers are aware of their value and prices have risen astronomically. As an alternative, concrete or old glazed sinks can be adapted for the purpose. But neither of these will have the charm of the genuine article which, if it has been out-of-doors for any length of time, will be weathered and decorated with mosses and lichens.

Particular attention must be paid to drainage before planting up any of these containers. A piece of perforated zinc should cover the existing drainage hole and the base of the trough or sink should be covered with broken crocks or stone chippings to a depth of 5–8cm (2–3in). On top of this goes a layer of peat moss or chopped turves, the latter grass side down.

The planting mixture should consist of

1 Small succulents have been planted in a small shell to make a really miniature garden.
2 Miniature gardens made up of saxifrages, sedums, campanulas, arenarias, lewisias and miniature conifers.
3 Androsaces, houseleeks, lewisias, dwarf conifers and other alpine plants make an interesting small garden.

2 parts of loam to 1 part of peat and 1 of sharp sand, with a dusting of lime or the addition of mortar rubble. The lime content must be omitted where ericaceous plants, dwarf rhododendrons, or other lime-haters are to be planted.

Among the many plants that can be grown successfully in a sink or trough garden are the hardier small saxifrages, sempervivums (houseleeks), thrift and other alpine plants of tough constitution. In a shady situation, mossy saxifrages, hardy cyclamen and miniature ferns will flourish.

For more permanent effects, use can be made of some of the dwarf shrubs and conifers mentioned below.

Miniature rose gardens Miniature roses have become generally popular in recent years. One of their main attractions lies in the opportunity that they afford of enjoying the beauty of roses where space would not permit the planting of a rose garden of the orthodox kind.

Sometimes known as fairy roses, many of these delightful dwarfs bear a strong resemblance to popular hybrid tea roses and floribundas. Others have equally delightful individual characteristics.

Little interest was shown by gardeners in these pygmy roses until after World War II, when scarcity of garden help and a swing from houses to flats and maisonettes brought their many useful qualities into prominence. These, apart from their compact habit, include permanence and a very long flowering season.

Many of the miniature roses stem from the dainty *Rosa rouletti*, a tiny rose that was discovered in a Swiss cottage garden by a Dr Roulet and named in his honour. From this charming miniature have evolved, directly or indirectly, many of the loveliest miniatures available today, including 'Tom Thumb', 'Pixies' and 'Midget'.

Miniature roses are extremely hardy. They come into flower early—often by the middle of May—and continue to produce their flowers throughout the summer and autumn. They are best planted from pots as they do not like root disturbance. This makes it possible to plant them at almost any time of year although March and April are the best months for this operation. Those planted in summer should be given plenty of water during dry spells in their first season.

The many named forms now available can be used to create a complete rose garden in miniature or can be incorporated as a separate feature of a larger garden. They are also useful for permanent dwarf bedding schemes.

All the features of a full-sized rose garden can be incorporated, scaled down, of course, to suitable dimensions. Pygmy pergolas, trellises and small rustic screens can be used to support climbing varieties, while miniature standards will emphasize focal points and act as central features of miniature bedding schemes.

Miniature roses need only a minimum

of attention where pruning is concerned. This operation is best carried out with a sharp pair of nail scissors. It consists mainly of removing weak growths and cutting back dead or diseased shoots to healthy wood. It is carried out in spring.

These small roses thrive best in similar types of soil to those in which the hybrid tea roses and floribundas do well. They like a fairly heavy, slightly acid loam, rich in humus. Lack of humus can be remedied by forking in well-rotted animal manure or garden compost, a few weeks before planting. If neither of these is available, peat or leafmould, laced with bonemeal, make satisfactory substitutes.

These dwarf roses will also flourish and look well in the old stone troughs already mentioned; the sinks are too shallow and there would be a danger of the roots drying out. They can be used, as well, for another kind of miniature garden, the window box, provided that the latter is at least 23cm (9in) deep.

Among those most widely grown are 'Baby Gold Star' (golden yellow), 'Bit O' Sunshine' (gold), 'Humoreske' (deep pink), 'Little Buckaroo' (scarlet with white centre), 'Sparkle' (single scarlet) and the midget rose that started it all, *Rosa rouletti*.

'Baby Masquerade', a newer introduction, is a perfect replica, in miniature, of the favourite floribunda of the same name, with clusters of flowers that produce the typical kaleidoscope of colour of the latter.

This rose, together with 'Cinderella' (white pale pink-edged), 'Coralin' (coral-pink) and 'Maid Marion' is obtainable in standard form. There are climbing forms of the bright pink 'Perla Rosa', the yellow and orange 'Little Showoff', which is practically perpetual-flowering and 'Baby Crimson', which is also known as 'Perla d'Alcanada'. 'Pink Cameo', too, makes an attractive climber. None of these climbing miniatures exceeds 1.3–1.6m (4–5ft) in height.

A garden of dwarf conifers Another way of making a miniature garden, of interest the whole year through, is to use dwarf conifers. Many of these are replicas of their taller counterparts and can be used to obtain similar effects on a reduced scale.

First and foremost are the various forms of Lawson's cypress, which share the useful characteristics of the larger kinds. *Chamaecyparis lawsoniana minima glauca*, with blue-grey foliage and whorled branchlets makes an interesting focal plant in a garden of dwarf conifers. It reaches an ultimate height of 1–2m (3–6ft), but this only very slowly. Similar

1 Dwarf conifers of many kinds are ideal for miniature gardens.
2 At the RHS Garden, Wisley there is a splendid collection of trough gardens, each one planted up in an individual way with succulents and miniature conifers
3 One of the troughs, which contains a selection of houseleeks.

in habit is *C. l. obtusa coralliformis*, with red twisted branches and close-packed bright green foliage. *C. pisifera* 'Boulevard' is a comparatively new introduction with blue-grey sprays of feathery foliage while *C. p. filifera aurea* is practically a golden counterpart of the former.

There are two charming little cryptomerias that will not exceed 60–75cm (2–2½ft). Both *Cryptomeria japonica pygmaea* and *vilmoriniana* are slow-

growing and make dense globular bushes whose form contrasts well with the pyramidal shape of the dwarf cypresses.

One of the most outstanding of these miniature conifers is the dwarf juniper, *Juniperus communis compressa*. This makes a dense blue-grey column, only 60cm (2ft) tall. There are also two dwarf spruces with a conical habit in the same pygmy category as this juniper. They are *Picea abies pygmaea*, with close-set dark green needles and *P. a. albertiana conica* whose foliage is a softer green. *Pinus sylvestris beauvronensis* is a dwarf Scots pine, only 1.3–1.5m (4–4½ft) at maturity, that can be planted to simulate a large tree in the scaled-down dimensions of a garden which features dwarf conifers.

The remaining space can be filled by the very slow-growing bun-shaped dwarfs such as *Chamaecyparis lawsoniana juniperoides*, a variety that grows only 10–16cm (4–6in) tall, with a spread of similar dimensions or *Picea abies gregoryana*, which makes a 46cm (1½ft) hummock of grey-green foliage and is broader than it is tall.

1 Sphagnum moss is used by the gardener for lining hanging baskets, protecting, air layering, packing material, etc.
2 and 3 Moss can be a nuisance on footpaths and can be removed by hoeing or application of a moss eradicator.
4 Leucobryum glaucum, a moss that forms loose balls which continue to grow when detached.

Moss

The mosses, or musci, form a subdivision of the plant group *Bryophyta*. They are very numerous. While possessing simple stems and leaves, they have no true roots. Mosses are anchored in their growing positions by rhizoids which are hairlike and without colour. The physiological activities of roots are carried out by these. It should be noted that true mosses and the club mosses are different; the latter belong to the family *Lycopodiaceae*.

Mosses are, in the main, terrestrial. They thrive in damp conditions, though some kinds do not necessarily demand constant moisture. Moisture is necessary, however, when fertilization is to occur. But where spore dispersal is

concerned, physiologically dry conditions are essential.

Some of these plants are decorative and a number, sphagnum moss among them, are useful. But in certain circumstances in the garden they are unwelcome, principally in lawns, and on pathways.

Mosses are encouraged by consolidated and poorly-drained soil and they invade shady places, even though they require some light in which to grow. Shade often exerts its influence by

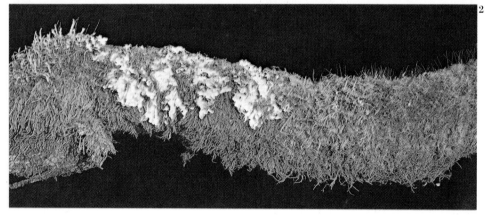

improve the general drainage, autumn spiking using a turf-piercing fork with hollow tines, plunged into the turf at about 16cm (6 in) intervals, immediately aerates and improves a compacted lawn. A mixture of peat and sand brushed into the holes—after the soil cores have been gathered up and disposed about the garden—completes the process. General aeration throughout the year can be done with an ordinary solid-tined fork, if it is desirable to improve the condition still further.

Impoverished lawns, which are highly susceptible to moss invasion, require organic dressings in order to build up humus to encourage the growth of the grass. Autumn is a good time for applying such dressings. Spring is an excellent time to apply complete artificial fertilizers. Supplementary feeds at a lower rate may be applied in summer. A good scarifying with a proper lawn rake provides a good start to any lawn season. It encourages the growth of the grass and also discourages moss.

It is important to remember that feeding must be balanced; indiscriminate use of fertilizers can easily spoil soil conditions, and may easily encourage moss to grow.

Lawnmowers should not be set too low. Extremely close cuts can mow grass out and allow moss to invade. A combination of too low a setting of the blades and an uneven lawn surface, will lead to 'scalping' when bare patches are left and, particularly in shady parts of the lawn such patches will quickly be taken over by mosses.

The surfaces of the soil in flower pots often becomes covered with mosses and liverworts. These are seldom a nuisance where growing plants are concerned and they can easily be removed by hand. But moss growth may prevent the germination of tiny seeds. This can be obviated by keeping the pots in darkness until germination has taken place.

Mowing

Regular mowing is essential to the production and maintenance of a good lawn. Unless this is assured, expense and work on all kinds of recommended treatments are of little value.

A first-class lawn needs cutting two or three times a week during periods of vigorous growth and even a very ordinary type of lawn needs cutting at least once a week. Less frequent mowing is adequate when growth is poor but the grass should never be allowed to exceed the chosen height by very much. Even in the winter months occasional topping may be needed when conditions are suitable. Whenever mowing is carried

retarding the drying-out of the soil.

Permanganate of potash, calomel (a compound of mercury), sulphate of iron, mercurized turf sand, certain proprietary liquid killers, and others, are all easily available as means of moss control. Maintaining soil fertility should, however, come first. Prevention by this means is not only better than cure, it is also more relevant. Antidotes can clear moss, but if general conditions are conducive to its growth and allowed to remain so, it will return.

Moss on paths, depending on the actual surface, is dealt with easily enough by applying chemicals, by raking, or on smooth surfaces by scattering sand and giving the path a good stiff brushing. But it is on lawns that soil fertility and conditions are obviously most relevant.

On lawns it is insufficient merely to apply fertilizer. It is necessary first to deal with the physical state of the soil; the application of fertilizer can then follow. While it may be impossible to out, the best results are obtained if the surface is dry.

The height of cut depends on the quality of the lawn required and the type of grass sown. There is no need to maintain a lawn at the very short length required for bowls or golf. Such close cutting 5mm ($\frac{3}{16}$in) causes great strain on the grass plants and even the very fine grasses thrive best at heights of 8–12mm ($\frac{1}{4}$–$\frac{1}{2}$in). Other grasses do not survive very well at all when cut at this height even, and so a height of 1–2cm ($\frac{1}{2}$–1in) is more suitable. Even the best varieties of perennial ryegrass, however, should not be cut closer than 2.5cm (1in).

Grass cuttings contain a useful amount of mineral matter in their bulk of moist organic material and allowing cuttings to fall back on the lawn decreases the drain on plant foods which arises when cuttings are removed. On the other hand the organic material is known to encourage disease, weeds, earthworm casting and soft surface conditions so that the best rule is undoubtedly to box off the cuttings and use them elsewhere in the garden.

The essence of a good lawn is uniformity and to get a uniform cut it is necessary to have a smooth surface. The best ways of achieving this are care in the original preparation of the lawn (ie obtaining a smooth seed bed which is sufficiently and uniformly firm to reduce the risk of settlement) and top dressing the existing lawn with sandy compost material so as to gradually smooth out the hollows. Rolling helps, of course, but rolling also causes consolidation which restricts root development and impedes moisture penetration so that it is an operation which must not be over-emphasized.

To achieve a really good cut you need a good mower in good condition. Clearly, you cannot achieve a bowling green finish with a second-hand grade C mower. The quality of a mower is generally related to cost, so buy the best you can afford. For really good results you need a good conventional mower giving the maximum number of cuts per yard run. Rotary mowers are undoubtedly very suitable for many purposes but they do not give a first-class finish suitable for the really good lawn. Whatever kind of mower is used, the best results are obtained if it is set correctly, and if regular cleaning, oiling, etc is carried out.

When mowing, start at one edge of the lawn and push the mower continuously, rather than with a 'push-pull' motion, until you reach the end of the lawn. Then turn and mow in the other direction, the cut slightly overlapping the first cut. This produces the alternate light and dark bands which so many people admire.

However, to obtain the best results, you should change the direction of

A well-mown lawn sets off a garden better than any other single feature. Straight lines show the direction in which the grass has been cut backwards and forwards with the machine.

mowing each time you cut the lawn. If you cut from north to south at one mowing, cut from east to west next time, and so on. Continuous mowing in one direction only will produce the so-called 'washboard' effect, a series of alternate ridges and hollows.

An exception to the rule of starting at the edge is when a 'Flymo' mower is used. With this machine the cuttings are not boxed but are left lying in small heaps on the lawn and, to avoid having to spend much time and energy raking them up after mowing, it is better to start by making the first cut down the centre of the lawn and then making alternate cuts, first on one side and then on the other of the first cut, in opposite directions. It will be found that most of the clippings will be pushed gradually to the edges of the lawn and may be raked up much more easily or with the last cut may be blown on to flanking flower beds where they will act as a mulch.

Mulching

A mulch is a cover spread over the surface of the soil. Newly-planted fruit trees and shrubs were traditionally mulched with strawy manure immediately after planting. This practice continues to this day. The mulch protects the newly planted tree or shrub from frost damage in winter and from summer drought. At the same time, the rotting manure supplies the young tree with plant food.

Mulching may be practised successfully in other ways. Most mulches inhibit weed growth; all mulches conserve soil moisture. Thus, a mulched garden needs less time and work to keep it weed-free and watered. During both winter and summer, mulched soils are protected from extremes of temperature. Many plants, notably cucumber, vegetable marrow and tomato, will send adventurous, new feeding roots into the manure or compost. Granulated sedge peat, itself a soil improver, is a neat mulch in the flower garden. A 3cm (1in) thick layer is sufficient for the season. Peat may also be used in the vegetable garden and is recommended for the strawberry bed.

Straw is also a suitable mulch for

1 Paving stones can be used as a mulch around a newly planted young tree, and will serve to maintain moisture and keep the young roots cool in summer.
2 A black plastic mulch on potatoes is useful for keeping weeds down.
3 Strawberries, grown under cloches, can be mulched with peat as an effective way of conserving moisture.

fruit and vegetable gardens but it is not of use around seedlings which it may smother. The rotting straw from summer mulches may be dug into the soil during winter digging. Autumn leaves make an excellent mulch to prevent the growth of annual weeds on temporary paths in the garden. Wood shavings and sawdust serve the same purpose. These materials rot down well and disintegrate within three years of their application. Although the use of leaves, wood shavings and sawdust is not generally recommended for mulching growing plants, autumn leaves may replace straw around established fruit trees and shrubs. Lawn mowings may be used for mulching in all parts of the garden but, if these are obtained from an outside source, you should make sure that no weed-killer or hormone spray has been used on the lawns from which they come. These substances are so persistent that broad-leaved plants mulched with lawn clippings containing minute traces of them, may be seriously damaged or even killed.

A mulch of small stones can be an attractive and useful feature in the flower garden. In the rock garden it is a common practice to mulch the soil surface with pea gravel or stone chippings. This not only helps to retain soil moisture and to keep down weeds, but also does much to prevent alpine plants from rotting off at the collar, the most vulnerable part of the plant. Many plants seed themselves freely in this stone mulch, thus providing a ready means of increasing stock.

Black polythene sheeting does not rot down to add plant foods to the soil and it is not attractive. Its use should be restricted to the fruit and vegetable garden where it has many advantages. Rows of grapevines may be grown in permanent plastic mulches and the soil beneath fruit trees remains weed-free, where square or circular pieces of polythene are laid around each tree. With vegetables, black plastic mulches are temporary and unless cut (as is the practice where potatoes are grown under such mulches), the sheeting should be taken under cover in the autumn and used for several seasons. It is essential that the sheeting be anchored securely to the soil. One way of doing this is to lay house bricks along the edges of the sheets. Pushing the sheeting into slits in the soil is better and very necessary in windy areas. The slits should be made with the spade and, after the sheeting has been unrolled and tucked into them, the soil alongside the slits should be firmed.

Where cabbages, Brussels sprouts, cauliflower, broccoli, sweet corn, tobacco and tomatoes are to be grown in black plastic mulch, the sheets should be set in position before planting. A narrow gap is left between the sheets and the plants are then set out in the gaps. Potato tubers are planted in shallow holes made with the trowel and the sheeting is then drawn over the rows and fixed in position. Small cuts are made in the plastic so that the young shoots of the potato plants may grow through.

All weeds should be removed before a soil is mulched. During the spring and summer the ground must be quite wet before a mulch is laid down. If mulching is done in a drought the soil must be thoroughly soaked with a hose or sprinkler before it is mulched. Except when trees and shrubs are planted in autumn, soil temperatures must be reasonably high when the soil is mulched. Mulching, therefore generally starts in June—the exception being when polythene sheeting is used for potato planting in April.

Mushroom cultivation

From the time of the Greeks and Romans, various fungi have been eaten as a delicacy and the expert can find many varieties growing wild which are equal, if not superior, in flavour to the mushroom (*Psalliotta campestris*). But there are also a number of poisonous fungi, some deadly. The field mushrooms which appear in profusion in meadows in the moist autumn days are perfectly safe, but the inexperienced townsman would be well advised to make sure first that he is actually picking field mushrooms, because some poisonous fungi are very similar. Cultivated mushrooms are absolutely reliable and a valuable food as well as a delicacy.

Since the war, the production of mushrooms on specialized farms has increased rapidly all over the Western world, in answer to a growing demand. There is a very wide gap between the results achieved by the amateur and the commercial growers, but provided attention is paid to a few essential factors, useful crops can be grown in sheds or cellars, in the greenhouse during the winter and in outdoor beds. The amateur has one big advantage; he can enjoy the flavour of ripe mushrooms taken straight from the soil, the very best way to eat them. Most commercial growers pick the mushrooms as buttons or cups with the veils unbroken. If they are picked

A straw mulch round dahlias will discourage weeds and prevent a surface pan from forming during the summer.

fully open, the delicate pink under-surface often becomes brown and dry before they reach shops, and the flavour suffers.

Mushrooms are grown in a prepared compost which enables the spores to produce cotton-like threads called mycelium which, after a few weeks, emerge on the surface to form pin-heads. These develop in a week to 12 days (according to the temperature), into fully grown mushrooms and successive flushes appear for 10 to 12 weeks or even longer. The first and most important task is to prepare the compost making certain that it is the right texture for the development of the mycelium and at the same time provides nutrient and moisture. If the compost is right, there will be no difficulty in getting a crop; if it is incorrectly prepared, the result can be a complete failure.

Fresh horse manure with plenty of straw is the easiest material to use and is generally recommended. But any sort of manure which creates bacterial activity and breaks down organic material will produce good mushroom compost. Horse, pig and cow manure have all been used. One Belgian research station produced excellent results using elephant manure from the local circus.

Compost can also be made by breaking down straw with chemicals. If horse manure cannot be obtained, one of the special activators obtainable from horticultural suppliers should be used to break down straw or chaff.

Manure is stacked in a heap about 1.3m (4ft) wide and 1.6m (5ft) high and watered during stacking so that it is moist but not wet. If an activator is used, this is sprinkled on successive layers of straw and chaff and watered in, until a similar sized heap has been made. The temperature of the heap goes up very quickly because of bacterial activity; a good compost requires the type of bacteria which develop in the presence of oxygen. This means that air must reach all parts of the heap during composting. The process can be helped by a wire frame in the form of an upright triangle along the length of the heap. After seven days, the heap is turned, water being applied sparingly where the material is dry. Four or five more turns are made and at the end, all unpleasant smell should have disappeared. The material should be rich brown and thoroughly damp, but not so wet that it exudes liquid when squeezed.

The compost is then put into boxes or shelves to any depth from 15–40cm

(5–15in). The deeper the compost, the longer the crop will continue; on the other hand, the shallower beds give a larger area and a quicker crop. The beds are then spawned with one of the pure culture spawns available commercially. Manure spawn is inserted into the compost and firmed in. Grain spawn is ruffled in.

After 10–14 days, the tiny white threads will be seen running into the compost and at this point the beds are cased. Commercial growers use a mixture of peat and chalk for casing and this can easily be made up by mixing the peat, after it has been thoroughly wetted with a quarter of its volume of chalk. If soil is used it should be taken from the second spit and heat sterilized. The casing is spread 3cm (1in) deep.

From spring to autumn, mushrooms can be grown without artificial heat. If the temperature falls below about 50°F (10°C) the mycelium will not grow, but this will only delay the crop. Beds can be frozen solid and still produce mushrooms, when the weather gets warmer. Too hot weather will quickly ruin a crop. That is why the greenhouse is suitable only in winter and an insulated building is preferable in summer.

Provided the temperature is satisfactory, the first pinheads will appear about four weeks after casing. For a winter crop, the temperature should be kept at about 65°F (18°C). The beds should be kept fairly dry until the pinheads develop, enough water being given to keep the casing just moist. After that, rather more water is needed and the surroundings should be sprayed to keep up humidity. There should be a free movement of air round the beds. If a puff of cigarette smoke blown over the bed slowly moves away, ventilation is adequate. The ripe mushrooms are pulled out, not cut. and the holes filled with a little peat.

The compost can also be made up into outdoor beds. These should be on a well-drained site and are best built deeper than the indoor beds with a 1m (3ft) wide base and sloping sides. They are spawned and cased as for indoor beds, but are then given a thatch of straw. Extra care must be taken to deal with slugs and woodlice. Mushrooms are subject to a number of insect and other pests, particularly two types of fly, *Phorids* and *Sciarids*, which breed in the manure, and mites, which eat holes in the caps and stems. These can be controlled by modern insecticides, but it is advisable to buy preparations made up specially for the mushroom crop.

Spent mushroom compost is excellent for the garden. Tests at experimental horticulture stations have shown that it is just as valuable as farmyard manure.

Mustard and Cress see Vegetables

1 The compost is put into a suitable box and the surface made firm with the back of a spade. Compost of any kind can be used as long as it creates bacterial activity.
2 Plant the mushroom spawn 15–25cm (6–9in) apart on the surface of the compost. There is nothing to be gained by planting any closer.
3 The first mycelium shows as cotton-like threads after a few weeks.
4 The first button mushrooms.

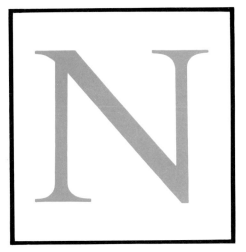

N

Netting

Although netting can be used occasionally for plant training (as, for instance, in the cultivation of runner beans and sweet peas) its main purpose in the garden is for protection against bird damage, especially in the fruit garden. Various sizes of mesh are available but the most useful for the gardener are meshes of 12mm (½in), 18mm (¾in) and 25mm (1in). The smallest mesh is essential against smaller birds such as tits.

Netting is sold in several sizes ranging from about 2×3m (6×9ft) to 25×4m (75×12ft). Pea and bean netting has large mesh which is usually 16cm (6in) square. Net sizes are about 4×2m (12×6ft), 5×2m (18×6ft), and 7×2m (24×6ft). One of the neatest and most efficient methods of providing bird protection is to construct a cage of netting. The netting is supported on a tubular framework of metal rods which have linking cross-pieces which provide the roof supports. Most framework is supplied for heights of 2m (6ft) which allows plenty of headroom inside. Smaller outfits are available for the protection of strawberries. Hanging hooks and ground pegs are available for use in erecting fruit cages, etc.

It is important to remember that, when netting is pulled out ready for use, it is usually not as long as quoted in catalogues. When estimating for requirements, it is advisable to deduct one third off the quoted measurements for lengths. The *width* of the netting is not affected.

There are semi-rigid types of netting

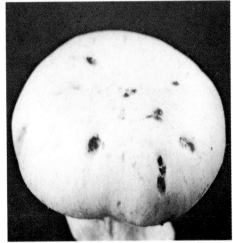

1 The manure for use in the compost for mushroom growing is stacked in a heap and kept reasonably moist by watering when necessary.
2 The first flush of mushrooms grown in a made-up compost bed in a mushroom house. These can be picked and other crops will continue to grow.
3 A distortion of growth in mushrooms, commonly known as 'Rosecomb'.
4 Bacterial pitting causes brown depressions over the cap of the mushroom.

and these are made from special high-density polythene in various colours. These are very useful for the construction of compost bins, fruit cages, plant supports and even ornamental edgings. Very fine mesh versions are used for greenhouse shading purposes. Rolls 1m (3ft) wide and 7m (20ft) long are available in meshes of 6mm ($\frac{1}{4}$in), 18mm ($\frac{3}{4}$in) and 5cm (2in). Rolls 7m (20ft) long by 50cm (18in) with a mesh of 18mm ($\frac{3}{4}$in) are also available.

Galvanized wire netting is invaluable in the garden for a wide range of uses such as protection against birds and rabbits, plant supports and fencing. For protection against rabbits 2.5cm (1in) mesh is most suitable and the bottom should be buried below ground level to prevent rabbits from burrowing underneath. Dig a trench to about 16cm (6in) and insert about 30cm (1ft) of the wire netting below ground, bending it in the shape of the letter 'L', so that the foot of the 'L' faces outwards about 16cm (6in). The rabbits will stop burrowing when they reach the horizontal part of the netting. Wire netting can be used for fencing off parts of the garden but does not look particularly attractive; it is more useful as a boundary fence in conjunction with a hedge. It is usually supplied in 50m (50yd) rolls or in cut lengths by the metre (yard) in meshes of 12mm ($\frac{1}{2}$in), 18mm ($\frac{3}{4}$in), 2.5cm (1in), 4cm (1$\frac{1}{2}$in), 5cm (2in), in widths from 30cm (1ft) to 2m (6ft).

Cold, prevailing winds can cause a lot of damage in the garden but a windbreak can reduce this problem considerably. Netting can be used for this purpose, especially if the smaller meshes are selected, which will provide more of a barrier to the wind currents, without obscuring the view beyond.

It is necessary to provide strong supports for netting which is used in this way and for this purpose tubular steel posts are most suitable.

Another use for netting is for plant training. Large, square mesh netting should be selected and fixed horizontally 30cm (1ft) from ground level on suitable supports such as wooden stakes. The netting must be put in position before the plants have made much growth. The plants will eventually grow through the mesh and will be given adequate support. This system is ideal for many bushy herbaceous plants, especially those of medium growth. For taller plants it will be necessary either to raise the height of the netting or to fix a second, larger area of netting 30cm (1ft) above the first one.

A problem in the water garden can be attacks on fish by cats and birds. This can be prevented if fine mesh netting, especially the nylon type, is fixed across the pool. It should be supported on a metal or light wooden framework placed about 16cm (6in) above the surface of the water. This arrangement will also prevent falling leaves, especially in the autumn, from polluting the water.

Where there is water in the garden, there is always a fascination and danger to small children. To prevent accidents, it is a good idea to make a safety barrier round the perimeter of the pool. This can be done quite easily with galvanized wire netting which is fastened to strong wooden or metal supports. The height of the netting should be at least 1m (3ft) above the ground. If desired, a small gate (which can be securely locked) can be built into the fence barrier.

An alternative solution which con-

3

4

5

ceals the barrier more, but which is just as effective, is to construct a very strong framework which can be laid flat across the surface of the pool. Strong wire netting or plastic netting should be securely fixed to this framework. To prevent breakages or strain on the netting should a child fall on to it, the supports should not be spaced more than 50cm (18in) apart. Make sure also that the edges of the framework are arranged well over the edge of the pool so that there is no danger of it being dislodged.

Netting is a useful training material in the greenhouse for crops such as cucumbers and melons. Supporting bags or nets can be made from netting for the heavy melon fruits.

Another unusual yet very important use for netting is for the protection of tender or newly planted shrubs. The plants are first covered with clean straw which in turn is retained by small mesh netting fixed to the ground. The netting will provide gentle support and prevent the straw from blowing away in the wind. The open mesh also permits adequate air circulation through the

1 When a hare comes up to close mesh wire netting, it is prevented from attacking the plants beyond.
2 Chicken netting attached to a simple wooden fence, makes an animal-proof barrier, and is inexpensive.
3 A high fence constructed of plastic square mesh netting.
4 Coconut fibre netting can be erected as a flexible windbreak around tender plants or young shrubs.
5 Very fine mesh wire netting makes a satisfactory wind break, taking the strength of the storm.

1

straw and prevents a damp condition.

No-digging
A system of organic surface cultivation. In an English method of no-digging heavy dressings of garden compost are spread on top of undug soil. Seeds are sown on the compost and are covered with more of it. To prevent weed growth and to conserve soil moisture the seed rows may be mulched with 2.5cm (1in) or more of sawdust or the seedlings mulched similarly. Neither the spade nor the garden fork are used except where bushes, trees and potato tubers are being planted. No-diggers claim that the system conforms with nature's own practice of not burying seeds and that the results justify the method.

An American variant omits garden compost and uses spoilt hay as a mulch. All growing crops are mulched quite thickly with hay each season. The hay rots down adding organic matter to the soil surface. The hay mulch method has an advantage, it is claimed, for gardeners situated in areas of very low rainfall and where conservation of water supplies is most necessary.

2

4

3

5

228

1 Notching consists of cutting a small half-moon out of the bark above a growth bud to stimulate it.
2 Nicking, on the other hand, is a cut below a bud, and has the effect of arresting growth. Both operations are used to build up a tree framework.

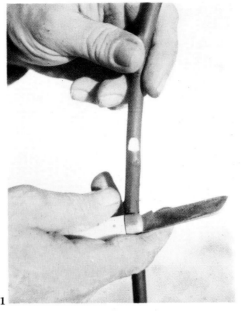
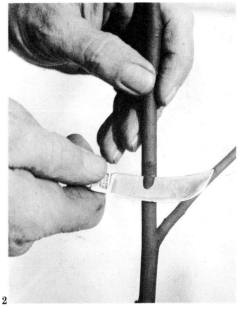

Notching

This consists in cutting with a knife a tiny half-moon of bark immediately above a growth bud to stimulate growth. When the same operation is carried out immediately below a bud it is usually called 'nicking' and has the effect of checking growth.

These operations are frequently used in building up the main framework of fruit trees in their early years. When a maiden tree is cut back, the topmost bud will usually produce a vertical shoot. If this is not desired, however, the top bud may be nicked and then lower buds will develop instead and their shoots will grow away from the main stem. In this way it is possible to get branches with wide crotch angles, such branches being stronger and less likely to break under a heavy crop. The selected buds, below the topmost one, may also be stimulated by notching and any others which are badly placed checked by nicking.

The principle behind this is that the topmost bud secretes a growth-inhibiting hormone which passes downwards and prevents lower buds from competing. A nick beneath the top bud isolates it from those beneath and also from the roots and with diminished food and moisture supply growth is checked. The notch above a bud isolates it from any growth-arresting hormone which may pass down from above.

NPK see Fertilizers

Nursery bed

This is an area of the garden maintained for growing on young plants until they have become large enough to be planted into their final quarters. The majority of plants which spend their early years in a nursery bed are perennials, especially trees and shrubs. Biennials, or plants usually treated as biennials, are also raised in a nursery bed, from seed in their first year. Most annuals are either raised from seed sown under glass and planted out from boxes, or sown in situ. Some hardy annuals can be sown in a nursery bed in autumn and then in spring transplanted to the bed where they are to flower.

In a well-run garden a nursery bed enables you to grow on young plants that will be needed for replacements or for new schemes. These may be new plants to the garden, raised from seed or cuttings, or a particular plant that is being propagated—perhaps by division —in order to have more stock to cover a larger area. It would not be convenient to have quantities of young seedlings, newly-rooted cuttings and small pieces of plants growing in fully stocked borders throughout the garden, because if given enough space to have sufficient light they would create near-empty spaces among the other decorative plants.

Many perennial border plants can, in fact, be conveniently divided and planted back into the flower border during renovations, but trees and shrubs grown from cuttings do require at least a few years growing on before reaching a size suitable for permanent planting. For example, provision of a nursery bed enables dozens of 4cm (1½in) high rooted heather cuttings to be cared for while they are gaining in size.

A nursery bed is an essential part of a vegetable garden. Brassicas which are planted out as young plants, at spacings up to 1m (3ft) apart, are first grown from

Phlox cultivars being grown on in a nursery bed for a season before being put in their permanent positions in the herbaceous border.

seed in rows for obvious economy of space.

Nursery beds should preferably be situated in a warm sheltered site with a finely textured, free-draining soil and be protected from pests such as rabbits and pigeons. A handy water supply is another important advantage when meeting the needs of young plants.

Nut cultivation

The commonest types of nut cultivated in Britain are the hazel and walnut. The two variants of the common hazel, *Corylus avellana*, are the cobnut with short husks and the filbert with long husks. Both are suitable for planting on poor, stony soils unsuitable for fruit trees, where they make medium growth and crop heavily. On rich soils growth is lush but unproductive.

Both tolerate sunny and shaded sites and wide extremes of soil acidity and alkalinity, but detest wet clays. Sandy loams are ideal for them. As the blossom is frost resistant, the bushes may be planted in low-lying, frosty situations. Cobnuts and filberts are grown as open-centred bushes raised from suckers detached in the autumn or from layers from whippy growths positioned near ground level. Seedlings are too variable in fruiting to be worthwhile.

A light dressing of farmyard manure may be dug into the soil prior to planting between mid-October and mid-March at 3–5m (10–15ft) apart. Tread the soil firmly round the roots, and stake and tie the bushes if the site is exposed. Mulch liberally in April with decayed garden compost, shoddy, leafmould, or peat, and feed with 50g (2oz) per sq m (sq yd) of sulphate of ammonia. Repeat this mulching and feeding annually, and each autumn dress with 28g (1oz) per sq m (sq yd) of sulphate of potash and 170g (6oz) per sq m (sq yd) of basic slag. Omit

1

2

1 Young brassica plants in a nursery bed before they are planted in their permanent quarters.
2 The fruit of the Spanish or sweet chestnut, Castanea sativa, is an example of a nut. It is protected in an outer spiky case, which peels off when the nut is ripe.
3 The nuts of the hazel, Corylus avellana, are cultivated in Britain, harvested during dry weather in September, and dried before storing.
4 The young foliage and flowers of the walnut, Juglans regia.
5 The caterpillar of the goat moth sometimes attacks the walnut tree and tunnels along the branches.
6 Filbert nuts are the fruit of the hazel, Corylus avellana, ready for use once they are dried.
7 The holes through which the nut weevil has left the nut. The eggs are laid singly in the setting nut in May and the grub eats its way out of the maturing nut.
8 Walnuts ready for picking at the end of the summer.

231

feeding with fertilizers on rich soils; sow grass around the bushes and mow it regularly if growth is excessive.

For convenience in picking the bushes can be restricted to a height of 2m (6ft). Pull off all suckers. Cut out all inward-growing, dead and weak shoots in February and shorten the leading shoots of young bushes by half. To promote a succession of young fruiting shoots shorten all lateral shoots in February at blossom time to the first male (catkin), or female (small, round, red) flower.

Over-vigorous lateral shoots can be weakened by brutting them in July or August. This consists in partially breaking each in half, leaving the broken pieces hanging. This precludes secondary growth which would appear if the shoots were cut.

Harvest the nuts on a dry day at the end of September or in early October when the husks are yellowing. Allow them to dry thoroughly before storing them with salt in glass or earthenware jars or tins with air-tight lids.

It is best to interplant varieties to get full crops. The two most popular ones are cobnut, 'Cosford'—a good bearer of very sweet, thin-shelled nuts which ripen early, an upright grower and an excellent pollinator—and the filbert, 'Lambert's Filbert', otherwise known as 'Kentish Cob'—a compact bush bearing heavy crops of large nuts with excellent flavour and readily pollinated by 'Cosford'.

If winter moth caterpillars are seen eating the leaves in spring apply an insecticide spray. The nut gall mite feeds on the terminal buds of the fruiting shoots, causing them to swell and preventing normal development. Where this pest is noticed, spray with 3 percent lime sulphur in late March or early April. The chief pest is the nut weevil which lays eggs singly in the nuts during May; the grubs burrow through the nuts. Brown rot fungus then gains entry causing a severe nut drop. Control this weevil by spraying with derris towards the end of May.

The walnut, *Juglans regta*, is a long-lived, imposing and very ornamental tree which makes itself at home in any soil conditions except extreme dryness or wetness. If it has a preference, it is for alkaline soils. As the one-year-old shoots are very susceptible to winter killing, a frost-free site is necessary. An open, sunny position is ideal. Walnuts are sometimes grown in bush form but more usually as a full standard. Allow for an ultimate branch spread of 10m (30ft) diameter. Young trees are propagated by double-tongue grafting under glass in March, or patch-budding in June or July, on seedling rootstocks in both cases. Nurserymen in the British Isles frequently import trees from the Continent where the climate allows grafting to be more certain of success.

The trees should be planted between November and January in well-dug soil, fortified with a general fertilizer. Adding rich organic manure is undesirable as this promotes lush growth susceptible to frost. Ensure firm compaction of the soil round the roots and stake and tie securely. Mulch the soil after it has warmed up in April or May. Subsequently, give an annual dressing of bonemeal at 50g (2oz) per sq m (sq yd).

Young trees require a modicum of pruning in their early years so that they may develop a shapely head. Prune them in July to minimize bleeding of sap, never between November and May. Afterwards, merely remove dead or awkwardly-positioned branches prior to leaf-fall. If wounds do bleed, cauterizing the cut surfaces with a hot iron should stop this.

Walnuts are self-pollinated so they can be planted singly. The French walnut, 'Franquette', is one of the most reliable varieties to grow as its leaves appear late and so avoid damage from May frosts.

Walnuts for pickling should be gathered when their shells are soft enough to be pierced with a needle. It is advisable to wear rubber gloves to avoid getting long-lasting stains on the hands. For storing, gather the walnuts when they start to fall naturally and the husks open easily. Dehusk the nuts, lay them out in a single layer and allow to dry thoroughly before storing them with salt.

The grubs of the wood leopard moth and goat moth sometimes tunnel up the trunk or along a bough, causing structural weakness and inducing invasion of wood-rotting fungi. The grubs may be killed by poking a piece of wire along the tunnel where this is short enough. Otherwise, insert a few crystals of paradichlorbenzene and seal the hole with plasticine or putty.

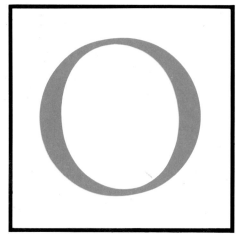

Onions see Vegetables

Orchid cultivation
Orchids seem to do best if a greenhouse is devoted solely to their cultivation, though some types such as *Odontoglossum grande* and *Coelogyne cristata* will succeed very well in a general

collection of plants.

At the outset it is as well to consider the type of orchid collection you desire to grow, or to provide for adding further sections of this large family. A general collection of orchids under one roof containing many species from widely differing habitats is perhaps the most satisfying type of collection. From it you can gain a very broad understanding of the plants. The often wide temperature tolerance of many orchid species makes such a collection possible. Some may wish to establish a collection devoted to perhaps one genus, such as *Cymbidium*.

The ideal method is to divide a small greenhouse into two sections, one for plants requiring cool conditions, ·the other for those needing warm conditions. If an existing house is being taken over for orchids, and it provides cool conditions only, a small area could be enclosed with heavy gauge polythene and a soil-warming cable installed. This would allow the growing of warm types in the enclosure and the cool-growing types could be kept in the main body of the house.

The staging in the house should be of the double type, with a gap of about 16cm (6in) between the upper and lower stages. The upper stage can be of the open wood-slat type for placing the plants on and the under stage should be covered with gravel or ashes. This is referred to as the moisture staging and is frequently sprayed with water to keep up the humidity of the house. A gravel path which can be sprayed is also very useful for this purpose. The type of plant will determine if the staging should be flat or in steps. A wire framework placed on top of the stage, if shaped like a series of step-ladders, will house many more plants if they are hung on the frame. Thin metal rods attached to the main beams of the house just above the path but not over the stage will provide more space, and this system is ideal for the species that prefer more light and many of the smaller orchids.

Ventilators should be preferably under the staging and in the roof. The ventilators found in many greenhouses in the upright glass sides of the house are not advisable for the orchid house, because draughts are produced and excessive drying out will occur.

There are many heating systems available to the orchid grower today. The once much-favoured boiler-heated water pipes of 10cm (4in) diameter have many advantages including a considerable degree of control. Many efficient electrical systems with thermostatic control are much used and the greenhouse fan type of heater is especially suitable. Care should be taken to install a system capable of providing somewhat above the minimum winter temperature decided on for the particular section of the family grown. Paraffin heating is a controversial subject among orchid growers. Many use this form of heating to provide a supplementary source of heat on very cold winter nights and also for emergencies such as power cuts. Double glazing with polythene on the inner side of the glass can reduce heat loss and an increase in temperature of 5 degrees and more has been claimed with the use of double glazing.

A diversity of plants can be managed quite successfully under one roof, because despite attempts to produce uniform conditions in a greenhouse, some parts will inevitably be that much warmer, brighter, or moister, and this with a little experimentation can be turned into a considerable asset. It is well known that with a plant that is reluctant to flower or a slow grower, improved results can be had by moving the plant about the house until it responds to a different environment.

Ventilation The greater number of cultivated orchids require plenty of fresh air which is essential at all times, especially in the cool and intermediate sections of the orchid house. Besides providing an ample flow of air around the plants, ventilation is also used to help to regulate the temperature. In the

warmer orchid houses less air is required as the temperature would be made too low if the house was over-ventilated. Definite rules are difficult to state, but one of the most important is that draughts should be avoided as they can cause more damage than under-ventilating.

The use of top ventilators in the greenhouse roof must depend on the direction of the wind and its force. They should be opened just a little at first and the opening gradually increased if the temperature rises. Considerable amounts of moisture will be lost if these vents are open for too long. In a small greenhouse which heats up very quickly the vents must be opened widely and frequent damping down will be necessary to counteract the moisture loss. Conservation of moisture is most important until the autumn when more air can be admitted to ensure ripening of the plants. The bottom ventilators on the lower sides of the house can be used more frequently, especially if the heating pipes are under the staging. The air

A typical orchid house with double staging is divided into sections for plants requiring different temperatures.

entering from these vents is warmed as it passes over the pipes. In the cool and intermediate sections these vents can be left open at night when it is not too cold, and with the cymbidiums a little ventilation can be used on all but the coldest days. If both top and bottom ventilators are to be open at the same time they should be open on the leeward side, which will reduce direct air currents. Usually it is best to open one set of vents only, the top being open when the bottom is closed and vice versa. If the house has ventilators in the glass sides these should not be used as too much moisture would be removed and draughts would be caused.

In general, air should be admitted whenever possible in both summer and winter provided that excessive moisture and temperature losses are avoided and draughts are not allowed to develop.

Light and shade Orchids, in general, require plenty of light but not the direct rays of the sun, especially during late spring and summer. Some provision for shading will be required. The application of a shading paint such as 'Summer Cloud' can provide the right density of shading and is easy to apply, but it is more or less permanent until it is

removed and it thus provides shade on dull days when it is required less, as well as on bright days. If the permanent shading is to be used it should be in position by the end of March or a little later if conditions are dull. The only really efficient method is to fit movable blinds. These can be of the slatted-wood type or of one of the plastic types such as 'Tygan'. Light canvas can be used but does not give such long service.

An air space between the glass and blinds is essential as this helps to keep a more equable temperature in the house by allowing a free circulation of air over the glass. Blinds other than the wood-slat type, if kept flat on the glass, can cause considerable heating of the glass and hence of the air in the house. Blinds can be usefully lowered in the winter on very cold nights and perhaps even on the very coldest days when an east wind is blowing, as they give some protection.

Blinds have the great advantage of control; early morning and late evening light can be allowed to reach the plants to their great benefit. On days which are expected to be bright they can be lowered before you leave the house and raised again in the evening. On bright days from May onwards, blinds can be down from about 8 am to 6 pm GMT. Spring days demand the most caution in the use of blinds when many tender young growths are present on the plants which can very easily be scorched. As the late summer progresses into autumn more light should be admitted; a gradual increase helps to ripen the bulbs and makes the plants generally firm.

Cattleyas, cymbidiums and especially dendrobiums require abundant light to make them flower, while types such as paphiopedilums and masdevallias are definitely shade-loving. Slat blinds if used for the latter do not provide the correct density of shade, and hence a very light application of shading such as 'Summer Cloud' to the glass will be needed. The blinds can be lowered on the brightest days. This extra shading is also useful as a precaution against damage should the main blinds be overlooked. In large towns heavy fog causes a dark deposit on the glass in winter. This should be washed off, as orchids need all available light at this season.

Feeding The feeding of orchids is a controversial matter and the beginner is advised not to feed orchids at the start. Plants grown in osmunda composts generally have enough nutriment provided as this material breaks down slowly. The various tree bark composts are said to be short of some plant foods, so weak applications of a liquid manure can be given.

Some of the terrestrial types benefit from the addition of old cow manure to the compost. Examples include the deciduous calanthes, thunia, lycaste and phaius. Cymbidiums and paphio-

1 Plants are put on a wooden slatted staging, erected over the moisture staging which is covered with gravel.
2 Tiered staging allows the full display to be effective, and easily available for management.

pedilums, as well as the genera mentioned can take regular applications of weak liquid feeds.

If the plants are to be fed, the weakest solution should always be used and then only during the growing season and on plants with a full rooting system. The more feeding a plant receives the more light is necessary. As the British climate does not always provide sufficient light for the ripening of growths, these frequently become soft when they are fed, and then disease troubles develop and the plants do not produce their usual number of flowers.

Temperatures The temperatures for the various sections must be regarded as being average only. During bright spells temperatures may often rise well above the stated maximum. In winter the day temperatures should not be made higher by forcing the heating system.

Warm section In summer a temperature of about 70°F (21°C) by night and 70–80°F (21–27°C) by day, higher during bright spells. In winter 65°F (18°C) by night and 70°F (21°C) by day.

Intermediate section In summer a temperature of about 65°F (18°C) by night and 65–70°F (18–21°C) by day, higher during bright spells. In winter 55–60°F (13–16°C) by night and 60–65°F (16–18°C) by day.

Cool section In summer as near as possible to a temperature of 60°F (16°C) by night and day. In winter by night down to about a temperature of 50°F (10°C) and 55–60°F (13–16°C) by day. Cymbidiums prefer a winter night temperature minimum of 50°F (10°C); this can drop occasionally in very cold spells to 45°F (7°C). By day 50–55°F (10–13°C). In summer by night a temperature as near 50–55°F (10–13°C) as possible and 55–60°F (13–16°C) by day; this can rise to about 70°F (21°C) on bright days.

Over-wintering and the resting period
An orchid is resting when it exhibits the

1 *Movable blinds provide the ideal method of giving shade in the orchid house, and can be made of slats of either wood or plastic. Orchids need to be protected from the direct rays of bright sunlight.*
2 *A hybrid of Odontioda asca.*
3 *The yellow-brown Cymbidium tracyanum.*

least root and top growth activity, usually in the winter, and the degree of rest varies considerably in this family of widely differing vegetative types. This makes it impossible to lay down hard and fast rules. In one genus, for example, the species vary one from the other in their requirements. The resting period often corresponds to the dry and either hot or cool period of the plant's native climate. The ideal method for resting orchids is to have a resting house or section, but with a small mixed collection grown under one roof. There is always a cooler end to a greenhouse and this can be used to advantage by placing the resting plants at this end.

Plants without pseudobulbs or tubers must not be rested as they are always active to some extent, and they do not have the food and moisture storage facilities provided by these parts of the plant. Examples of this type include the

slipper orchid, paphiopedilum, and the masdevallias. Vandas and aerides and similar types, which have a continuously upward growing stem often have thick fleshy leaves, which in nature are able to resist drought. These plants should receive just enough water to keep fresh the sphagnum moss on the compost surface.

In general, all young unflowered seedlings should be watered at all seasons with due consideration given to the weather. Other orchids with pseudobulbs or tubers require a rest in the winter—generally, the harder the bulb or leaf the longer and drier the rest. Those types that are deciduous or semi-deciduous require a more pronounced rest, for example, in the genus *Dendrobium* the *D. nobile* and *D. wardianum* types will take a longer rest than the evergreen types such as *D. thrysifolium*. Most cattleyas and laelias and their hybrids need several weeks rest after flowering. Always keep a look out for shrivelling of the pseudobulbs; a little can be tolerated but this should never be so extreme as to affect the leading pseudobulb. Odontoglossums need not be rested in the same way as cattleyas, moisture should always be present to some extent, except for very short periods.

A house containing a small mixed collection will normally have a lower winter temperature and this will help to provide the natural conditions for resting. Attention must mainly be given to the frequency of watering. Careful observation of the individual plant will be the only rule. Failure to rest may induce weak, soft, winter growths, which is always a setback for the plant and it subsequently takes a long time to regain its former vigour. While reducing the moisture in the greenhouse as a standard winter practice, extreme conditions should be avoided because an excess of dry heat can produce undue shrivelling of the pseudobulbs.

Propagation The raising of new orchid hybrids from seed is a highly specialized procedure performed under laboratory conditions. The seed is sown on an agar jelly medium containing various mineral salts and sugars. Seed, glassware and implements are sterilized, as aseptic conditions are essential. After germination, which takes a minimum of three weeks and may last many months, the seedlings are usually placed on to a fresh agar jelly, again under sterile conditions. After about six months to a year the seedlings are transferred to community pots of standard potting compost and placed in the open greenhouse.

Propagation by division is the only method of increasing choice varieties. Paphiopedilums can be split at potting time, making sure that each new piece has several growths including a leading growth. Cattleyas are best treated by severing the rhizome behind the fourth or fifth bulb from the front some months before the plant is to be repotted. A bud on the base of the bulb on the older portion may break into growth, eventually forming a new shoot. These pieces can be potted up separately.

Back bulbs of most orchids can be induced to produce new shoots either as single bulbs or in clusters of two or three. Place these in the warmest place, in a pot partly full of crocks and topped with sphagnum moss. Dendrobiums of the nobile section often produce fresh plantlets near the top of old pseudobulbs. These can be taken off with a sharp knife when they have made a few small roots and potted up in the smallest pot available, in pure sphagnum moss. Old back bulbs can be cut up into small pieces of about 5cm (2in) and inserted around the edge of pots filled with moss or sand and peat.

Large plants of many orchids have several leading growths and if these are cut up into pieces with the correct number of bulbs per growth, as many new plants will be formed. Duplication of fine varieties is always advisable against possible loss by accident, but before deciding to break up a large healthy plant the value of such a specimen should be considered. Such

1 A small fan heater and hygrometer control the temperature and humidity.
2 A small section enclosed by polythene, within the greenhouse, provides a place for warm-growing orchids.
3 Orchids with hard bulbs drop their leaves in winter. This swan orchid (Cycnoches) is best kept dry at the roots for long spells during the winter.

plants are very attractive and may receive more attention at shows. A small propagating frame in the greenhouse greatly facilitates the establishment of plants from bulb divisions and at the same time provides a home for small-growing orchids that require extra warmth.

Pests and diseases The main pests of orchids are scale insects, mealy bugs, red spider mites and thrips. Scale insects, as the name implies, appear as small, brownish or greenish scales on the leaves and stems, especially of cattleyas, where in bad infestations they get behind the bulb sheaths. Control is by spongeing or spraying with insecticide. Mealy bugs are small insects covered with a grey meal and can cause considerable damage if allowed to remain unchecked. Like scale insects they also find their way under bracts and leaf sheaths. Small pockets of these insects can be controlled by applying a mixture of nicotine and methylated spirits with a small artist's paintbrush. Red spider mites are small, hardly visible without a hand lens, greenish to red in colour and found on the undersides of the leaves; where they cause, in bad infestations, a

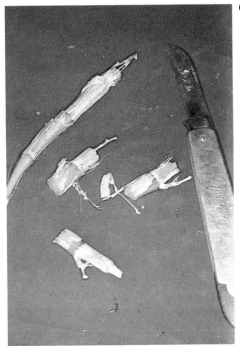

dry silvered appearance on the leaf surface. They are sucking creatures living on the plant sap. They can be considered to be the worst enemy of the orchid grower as they can transmit virus disease in their passage from one plant to another. Alternation of control sprays is very necessary as resistance to a single spray is soon built up and it will have little effect. Malathion, derris and Chlorocide sprays can be used in rotation. Thrip is a minute insect and its presence is detected by small round, punctured discoloured areas on the softer leaves and on flowers. The best approach to orchid pests is regular spraying as a preventive measure. Always follow the maker's instructions as some chemicals can be dangerous if due care is not taken. New plants should

1 Flasks are used for the specialized procedure of orchid seed germination.
2 If back bulbs of old cymbidiums are kept in moist moss, new shoots appear.
3 Some dendrobiums produce plantlets on the cane, which can be used for propagation purposes.
4 If canes of dendrobiums are cut into sections new plants can be obtained.
5 The slipper orchid can be divided.
6 Large orchid plants can be divided as indicated.

always be carefully inspected, especially imported plants. Slugs and snails have a taste for fresh young orchid growths as well as roots and flowers. Good control can be effected with Slugit used either as a spray or as pellets which can be placed on the benches around the pots.

Diseases are in general uncommon in orchids. Good healthy plants which have been grown under well-aired conditions are seldom attacked. An occasional plant may succumb to a black rot disease. Diseased parts can be carefully cut away and powdered sulphur applied to the cut surface. If caught in time these rots can be controlled but very badly infected plants are best destroyed. Virus disease is the one exception. This appears especially in cymbidiums as yellowish streaks or ringed areas which eventually turn blackish. New propagation techniques will ensure that only healthy plants are distributed, while infected plants are best burnt. Control of red spider mites and other sucking insects such as greenfly will reduce the risk of virus spread.

237

already prepared and mixed with sphagnum moss for immediate use. This is often available by the bushel, which will make it possible to pot a large number of plants in 16cm (4in) pots. Larger amounts can be bought in the rough state in bales. The baled fibre should be pulled apart, chopped up and the dust sieved out. Selection of the rough and the finer fibres will provide material for those plants with either coarse fleshy roots or thin delicate roots.

The prepared mixture should be neither wet nor completely dry but just moist. Prior to a potting session the potting compost should be placed in the greenhouse to keep it warm, as the use of cold material can do damage to the roots by chilling them. Many of the cultivated orchids are epiphytes, that is plants which grow on trees, deriving their nourishment from leafmould and other plant debris which accumulates around the roots and also from the air. They are perching plants only, and do not derive food from their host tree as do the parasitic plants. Many of the roots are freely suspended in the air and others cling to the bark or penetrate among the mosses which grow along the branches.

The dividing line between the epiphytes and the other group known as the terrestrials is sometimes rather vague. The terrestrial type grows essentially in the soil or in the humus of forest floors. At one time it was the practice to use these two divisions as a guide for potting materials, using fibre and moss for the epiphytes, adding loam fibre to moss and fibre for the so-called terrestrials, such as the plain-leaved slipper orchids (paphiopedilums), cymbidiums and lycastes. The use of loam fibre is not so frequent nowadays, but if good material is available it does help to keep costs down by reducing the amount of osmunda required in the composts.

With care orchids will grow in a wide variety of materials, provided they are of an open texture. For example, various types of tree bark broken down into small pieces are used extensively in America. Excellent results are produced, but feeding of some sort seems to be necessary, whereas with the standard osmunda compost feeding is not generally necessary. Other substitute or supplementary materials sometimes used are dry bracken fronds, which are said to be rich in potash. Some plastic fibres, which have the same consistency and thickness as osmunda fibre, when mixed with sphagnum moss give good results with feeding. Even pure sphagnum moss as a potting material has been very successfuly used for some orchids.

Bed cultivation of cymbidiums has come into favour and a recently recommended compost consists of equal parts of leafmould, dry bracken stems, coarse sand, sphagnum peat and old cow dung. This compost can also be used for pot cultivation.

Potting composts For many years the standard ingredients of orchid potting composts have been osmunda fibre which is the chopped-up root system of the royal fern (*Osmunda regalis*) and the bog moss known as sphagnum moss. Osmunda fibre is somewhat expensive as it is imported from Italy, and a finer grade from Japan. Though it requires some skill in its use, its long-lasting properties and ability to provide enough food as it breaks down makes it an ideal medium for growing orchids. The beginner would be well advised to gain experience in potting with osmunda fibre and wait until later before experi-

1 and 3 Any repotting that is to be done ought to be started when the roots begin to form, as above left, and not be delayed until the roots have become so long that they will be damaged.
2 The scale insect in its dormant season. Damage is done when the insects get behind the stem scales.

menting with some of the substitute media. A good general mixture would be 3 parts of osmunda fibre and 1 part of sphagnum moss and for the types requiring more moisture the proportions could be 2–1. Osmunda fibre can be obtained from some orchid nurserymen

Potting procedure The best time to repot an orchid is generally in the spring or when root growth begins. The plants then have the summer in which to produce abundant roots and complete their growths. If possible potting should take place when the roots are just showing or at least when they are very short. A plant with long roots is not easy to deal with if damage is to be avoided. The shorter they are the less risk there is of breaking the naturally brittle roots. Potting time must depend on the individual plant, and its growth habits should be studied. Some cattleyas, for example, produce a growth which matures to flowering before roots are formed in abundance, and this is usually in mid summer. Odontoglossums can be potted in spring or in early autumn, at either season avoiding the warmer days when they are making roots. The slipper orchids can be potted after flowering in late winter provided this is done in warm conditions.

In general, orchids need not be potted every year if the compost remains in a wholesome condition, firm and sweet. If the fingers can be readily pushed into the compost attention is needed. Every other year is a good rule for potting. Even then if the plant has enough room and only a small portion of the compost is soft, the bad part can be replaced with fresh compost, or the surface material can be removed if it is sour and broken down and a top dressing of new compost worked in. Orchids do not like decayed compost but they equally dislike too frequent disturbance and this fact should always be in mind when an orchid needs attention; it could be that a drastic treatment such as a complete stripping down of all the compost would prove fatal. Orchids should never be over-potted, rather they should be under-potted if the correct pot size cannot be used. With the exception of cymbidiums, phaius, *Zygopetalum mackayi* and some of the thick fleshy-rooted types which require ample room to grow, the smallest pot should be chosen. Three-quarter pots or pans are preferable for most types. For those with rambling stems or the pendent or ascending varieties, rafts or baskets would be more suitable. Baskets with widely spaced spars are essential for the stanhopeas which send their spikes downwards, the flowers appearing beneath the container.

The plant to be repotted should be lifted out of its old pot by inserting a

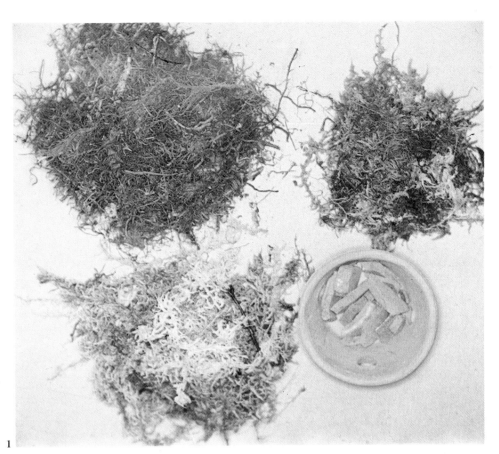

1 The ingredients of the potting compost, osmunda fibre (top left) and sphagnum moss. Numerous crocks are arranged at the base of the pot to ensure open drainage.
2 Orchids, such as stanhopeas, have downward-growing flower spikes, so must be grown in baskets.
3 Small plants look attractive when grown on rafts and suspended.

1 A potting stick is used to lever the plant from the pot for repotting.

2 The old compost is carefully teased away from among the roots.

3 Fresh compost mixture is picked up in small amounts and arranged around the roots.

4 When the roots are covered with new material and inserted into the pot, a potting stick is used to push the compost inward but not downward.

5 The surface of the compost is trimmed with shears.

6 The plant ought to be sufficiently firm in the pot to be held up and gently shaken, without the pot falling.

7 Many orchids grow well in perforated pots, made specially for the purpose.

potting stick at the back of the plant and gently levering the plant upwards. Where the roots are adhering tightly to the outer surface of the pot less damage can be caused by cracking the pot with a sharp blow.

The new pot should be amply crocked from a third to a half of its depth, depending on type, with pieces of broken pot inserted vertically over the drainage hole. Perfect drainage is essential for orchids. The plant should be prepared by holding it firmly in the left hand, and with a potting stick in the right hand carefully remove downwards all the old soft compost, leaving that which is still sound, especially at the front. Old decayed roots should be cut away to the rhizome and any old soft, brown bulb cut off. This will often allow the plant to be replaced in the same-sized pot. In general, about 4 or 5 bulbs and the new growth should form the plant to be potted, again depending on the individual plant and its vigour. The back part of the plant, that is the oldest bulb, should be placed at the rim of the new pot, allowing about 5cm (2in) in front of the leading growth for future development. A small quantity of compost should be placed over the crocks and selected wads of compost carefully placed about the roots of the plant ensuring a good base beneath the rhizome. Insert the plant into its new pot and carefully work in new compost, starting at the back of the plant and keeping the rhizome level with the top of the pot .The fingers of the right hand should work through the heap of compost, selecting wads of fibres and attempting to gather these so that the wad has the fibres running up and down. This wad should be pressed with a potting stick inwards towards the plant and at the same time slightly downwards. This should continue with the lower level and then with the top layer until the compost level is just below the pot rim. Attention should be given to the inward levering of the compost towards the plant, as any excessive downward pressure can make a caked-hard mass, resulting in impeded drainage. A test for the correct firmness of potting is to pick up the potted plant by the leaves or the bulbs which should not part from the pot. The completed surface can be given a trim with shears. As with all practical matters a demonstration by an expert is the ideal way to learn this essentially simple procedure and such a demonstration can be seen at many orchid nurseries.

Stake the freshly potted plant if necessary and keep it in a shadier place than is usual for the type for some weeks. Attention to the cutting of the osmunda fibre when making up the compost makes for easier potting. It is cut finer for small plants and left in larger pieces if large plants are to be potted.

Watering and damping The watering orchids is perhaps the most difficult cultivation procedure for the beginner to understand. Judgement and care must be used. This applies to any pot plant, but orchids do have their special needs. A carefully watered orchid collection can be left for a short time with no ill effect, provided you look after ventilation and shading. Although other plants left for the same time would not be able to withstand the lack of water, this is one of the many advantages in growing orchids.

Rain-water is always preferable to tap

water and a tank to receive this, placed in the house will ensure that the water temperature will be near to that of the house in cold weather. Mains water if it is non-alkaline can be used in some districts. Cold water should never be used. Water well when watering at all; sufficient should be given to wet the whole of the compost. Never water a wet plant. The timing between waterings will depend on many factors such as the type of orchid, the weather and the temperature. Overwatering is without doubt the main cause of unsuccessful cultivation, the waterlogged compost excludes the air that is so important to the orchid roots. Many beginners take this advice to the extreme and let their plants become tinder dry. This can be equally disastrous except when the type requires a hard dry rest to encourage flowering. This rest is given in the winter. If drainage is correctly provided and the compost is not too tightly packed and hence of the right porosity, there is less danger of overwatering. Perhaps the main cause of damage is too frequent watering. This applies especially when the plants are not in full growth, either early or late in the season and in the winter and also in dull weather when drying out of the compost is not so pronounced. Each plant should be treated as an individual. All of one type may not need the same treatment, but it is an advantage to stage their growth, together, when one can be compared to another, thereby gaining experience. A watering-can with a fine spout is ideal as the amount coming out can be easily controlled when watering plants on the benches. Plants in hanging pots tend to dry out and those in baskets even more so, as they are near glass. They should be immersed in a bucket of water to just over the pot rim.

A well-established plant with a healthy active root system and good drainage in its pot will require liberal watering in its growing season. Recently repotted plants require much less water and are best grouped together at the shadier end of the house. Signs of their need for water are difficult to observe, but if there is any doubt it is best not to water the plant until the following day or when the next general watering takes place. Live sphagnum moss on the compost surface becomes yellowish when dry and this can be used as a guide that water is required. Lifting the pots (a wet one is obviously heavier than a dry one) does give some indication, especially if this is coupled with feeling the texture of the compost. Another test sometimes used is to pour a very little water on to the compost and if this soaks in readily the

Orchids vary widely in colour and form.
1 A Phalaenopsis hybrid.
2 Paphiopedilum (Cypripedium) callosum.
3 Odontoglossum 'Florence Sterling'.

plant receives no further water. Tapping of the pots as practised with other plants in loam compost is not recommended, as it is both deceptive and unreliable.

Damping This is the process of spraying the floors, walls and stages of the orchid house to increase the atmospheric humidity which is so necessary for the continued health of the plants. Greenhouses vary considerably, one being naturally dry and another moist, but as a general rule damping should be done two or three times a day according to the weather and time of the year, more damping being needed on hot dry days and none on the coldest days.

Damping is best carried out when the temperature is rising and not when it is falling. Ordinary tap water can be used so as to conserve rain water supplies. Special care is needed in the autumn during dull mild spells when little heating is being used; the atmosphere can become excessively moist at these times. In winter the greenhouse atmosphere will often become dry due to the greater heat in use. Damping should then be increased slightly but only if the temperature is to be maintained, as any marked decrease in temperature would result in over-moist conditions.

Organic gardening

This is a system of gardening in which organic products (derived from organisms which have had life) are used to maintain and increase soil fertility. Until the nineteenth century gardeners relied almost solely on organic wastes for manuring the garden soil. Animal dung was extensively used in Europe. The art of mixing animal and vegetable wastes together and the fermentation of the mixture in heaps developed in various parts of the world—notably in China.

Justus von Liebig, the German chemist and discoverer of chloroform (1803–1873), suggested that plants might feed on chemical compounds and the world-wide application of factory-made chemical plant foods to farm and garden soils has resulted from von Liebig's correct hypothesis. Between 1840 and 1940 the use of chemical fertilizers, known as 'artificials', became an almost unquestioned garden practice. The belief was current that to obtain maximum yields it was necessary but to lime, where lime was needed, and to fertilize the soil with appropriate quantities each season of suitable chemicals containing nitrogen (N), phosphorus (P) and potassium (K).

The German philosopher, Dr Rudolf Steiner ((1861–1925), questioned the wis-

1 The amount of water given can be controlled, if a narrow spouted watering can is used.
2 The condition of the moss in the pots indicates water requirement. The one on the right is dry, the other moist.

1 The products of organic gardening. It is claimed that cleaner root crops can be produced from ground rich in humus and the food value is reputed to be higher in 'clean-grown' vegetables.

2 Seaweed, collected round our coasts makes a good, but rather bulky organic fertilizer, used as a mulch.

dom of the NPK theory and originated the bio-dynamic method of organic gardening. At around the same time Sir Albert Howard (1873–1947) was experimenting in India in an attempt to produce a cheap manure for use by the Indian farmer. It was in India that Sir Albert perfected his Indore (not indoor) way of composting animal and vegetable wastes. Applications of Indore compost not only led to excellent crops but important side-effects were observed. Food plants growing in Indore-composted soil showed unexpected, healthy vigour. Cattle fed on the healthy crops became robust and, like the plants, they showed resistance to some diseases. Sir Albert Howard's book, *An Agricultural Testament*, was hardly noticed by leading horticulturists of the day. The book has since revolutionized the horticultural scene. Knowledgeable gardeners now accept as an axiom that garden compost replaces horse dung and farmyard manure as a source of plant foods and as a soil improver. Not all gardeners reject the NPK theory entirely. Those who do are known as organic gardeners. They seldom, if ever, use 'artificials' claiming that they have no need to buy factory products when by the use of garden compost first-class crops are obtained.

The organic gardener expects his growing plants to have the robust health, noted by Sir Albert Howard during his experimental work, and has no use in his garden for chemical sprays and powders for controlling plant pests and diseases. The practice of organic gardening presupposes that the gardener has some knowledge of horticulture. Exponents of this ancient method, combining a modern approach, rightly insist that no gardening technique, however good, can lead to optimum results unless basic horticultural principles are understood. They also add that it is impossible to state accurately how quickly a garden soil may be renovated and brought to a high state of fertility by organic methods. Much depends on the soil type, on its condition when the experiment begins and also on the amount of suitable organic matter added. During the transition period it may be necessary to buy and use some chemical products; this is the view of an author of a standard work on organic gardening.

In the view of defenders of organic gardening the NPK era was an erroneous, short, but extremely dangerous period in mankind's history.

Organizations based on the work of Dr Steiner and Sir Albert Howard exist in many countries. Their vociferous demand that waste materials should not be dissipated but used to improve and maintain soil fertility is heeded in most parts of the world. The relationship between unadulterated food and good health, prevention of soil and water pollution, prevention of soil erosion and the conservation of many natural resources are among the subjects which concern such organizations. This is in addition to their primary interest in the production of healthy, health-giving food crops from the farm and garden. Cities as far apart as Edinburgh, Tel Aviv, Bangkok and Moscow now make and supply municipal compost from town wastes. The Soil Association, Haughley, Suffolk, publishes books, magazines and leaflets on organic gardening.

Parsley see Vegetables

Parsnips see Vegetables

Paths in the garden

The actual layout of a path should take into consideration the time and amount of money which is available. The garden may be a new one, where paths are to be laid down for the first time, or an existing garden which is to be redesigned. If an old-world, or cottage garden effect is required, it is unlikely that a formal pattern will be suitable.

If the site is very undulating it may

be necessary to match paths with steps and terraces. In the smaller gardens the boldness of a length of path can be reduced or avoided if stepping stones are used, or if the monotony of the path is broken up by means of patterns or by the use of different materials.

Before any planning is contemplated, it is as well to have a good idea what is available in the way of materials.

Concrete The most popular material is concrete. Many gardeners mix this themselves by purchasing the basic ingredients, which are bags of cement, a load of sand and shingle or a load of mixed ballast. Some firms supply bags which contain all the necessary ingredients ready mixed and all you need to do is to tip the contents out, add water carefully and mix thoroughly. This is an expensive way of using concrete for large amounts of work, but ideal for small jobs and for patching.

Crazy paving Another popular paving material is crazy paving. This is available as York stone or broken paving stone. The best type of stone to use for its hard-wearing qualities is the former. There are two thicknesses which are generally available, 3cm (1½in) and 5cm (2in). The irregular outline of crazy paving breaks up the monotony of a plain surface to a path, and it is particularly suitable for the old-world or cottage type of garden.

Precast slabs Paths can be made from precast slabs which are available in a wide range of sizes and colours. This enables you to plan and lay paths of outstanding design and appearance. You do not need a great deal of skill to produce these effects, provided you make quite sure that the foundations are secure. So versatile are these slabs that they can be used for any situation.

Mixtures of materials By mixing materials it is possible to provide endless variations of path design. Old bricks can be used very effectively, especially if they are laid in herringbone fashion or in other unusual patterns. Cobble stones are available as a path-making material and are ideal for mixing with other materials. For example, a square of these pebbles can be framed by old bricks or paving slabs. With a little ingenuity and some artistic skill it is possible to use more than two materials. Various sizes of slab can be patterned or interset with pebbles or old bricks. It is important in this type of design to work it out carefully beforehand, either on paper or on the actual site itself by marking out the pattern with a pointed stick. Careful measurements must be made to make sure that all the designs fit accurately together for a completely professional look.

Cold asphalt compound This provides yet another method of making paths in the garden. The process is extremely simple and as a long-term investment,

compares very favourably in price with other ways of path making. The special material is available in 50kg (1cwt) sacks, together with special granite chippings which are used on the surface for decorative purposes. Two colours of compound are available, black and brown and a bag covers approximately 6m (20ft) square.

Granite chippings Paths can be made from granite chippings but the big drawback with these is that they pick up badly on the feet. They are also liable to drift towards the lower parts of the path if it is on a slope. This type of material is best used for a path or sweep under a bay window, for example, where little treading will be necessary.

Laying the pathway Once the type of material has been decided upon, the preparations for laying should be carried out carefully and thoroughly. The route the path is to take must be marked out with pegs and line. If a curved or winding path is required, make sure that the curves are not acute or that the path weaves unduly. It is best to aim for gentle curves.

The amount of foundation preparation necessary will depend on several factors. The first is the type of soil in the garden. Light sandy ones need much more consolidation than the heavy clay types. Where there is any doubt about the firmness of the soil, plenty of small rubble must be rammed well into the foundation. Usually a depth of at least 15–25cm (6–9in) should be taken out and the bottom 13–20cm (5–8in) filled with rubble and rammed in well. Allowance must be made for the thickness of the paving material itself, also any bedding cement or mortar which may be required. In all calculations the finished level of the paving material should be just above soil level. This will do much to keep the path dry and will prevent the splash back of dirt or soil during periods of very heavy rain.

The width of a path should be considered and should not be under 60cm (2ft) for comfortable walking. It is as well to consider the wheelbase of trucks and wheelbarrows so that sufficient path width is allowed for them. Wider paths should be allocated for main routes to the busy parts of the garden where the wheelbarrow will be required a great deal. Areas around the greenhouse and frames are good examples.

There are several ways in which the paving materials can be laid. One is to place them on a 3cm (1in) layer of sifted soil, sand or ashes. Make sure that the bedding material is as level as possible and as each slab or brick is placed in position it should be tapped firm. It will be necessary to add or take away the bedding material to provide as level a surface as possible. Slight gaps can be left between slabs and filled in with the same material afterwards.

A slightly more secure way of bedding

1 On a gentle gradient a pathway consisting of a series of stepping stones looks attractive.
2 At Sissinghurst Castle, Kent, slabs and random stone are used together.

is to lay paving on the soil, sand or ashes and add under the centre of each a trowel full of mortar which is made up of 1 part of cement to 5 parts of sand. It is a good idea to apply a little more mortar for the larger slabs of paving and this can be done by adding extra amounts of mortar to the four corners.

The best method is to apply about 2cm (¾in) of mortar evenly over the soil, sand or ashes, spreading the mortar over the area one slab will occupy. Work should proceed in this way slab by slab until the site has been completely prepared. Afterwards, a drier mortar mix should be brushed into the joints, taking great care that any excess is removed from the surface of slabs to prevent discoloration.

Particular care is necessary when smaller paving material is laid, such as old bricks or pebbles. The latter can be set in the mortar mix so that approximately ¼ of the base of each pebble is inserted and held in the concrete. The pebbles should be graded for size so that an even pattern is produced. It is advisable to have a 'dummy run' beforehand so that the pebbles can be arranged neatly and to size.

All paving set in mortar should be allowed to set thoroughly for 2 to 3 days before it is used. Work should not be carried out in very cold or frosty weather, but protection can be afforded from wet weather after work has been completed if large sheets of plastic material are placed over the paving.

The use of cold asphalt has revolu-tionised the art of path making for the garden. All that is required is the provision of a solid level foundation over which the preparation is raked to an even depth of about 1cm (½in). A light rolling is given and then the granite chippings which are usually provided, are scattered carefully over the surface and lightly rolled in. The path is ready for immediate use and becomes firmer the more it is walked on. For the first few days after laying it is wise to avoid the use of heavily laden wheelbarrows as their wheels tend to make a slight impression until the path has been made firmer by walking on it.

It is most useful, if not essential, to know how far materials will go when trying to estimate for layouts. The tables in this article provide a guide to the approximate quantities of most of the popular paving materials for given areas or lengths of path. Most materials can be obtained from local horticultural sundries shops, garden centres or builder's merchants. A big advantage with the garden centre is that many materials are on view and in some cases actually laid. This enables you to see the paths as they would be when completed. For making a path 3m (10ft) long see the table 'Making a Path'.

As far as concrete paths are concerned, for the best possible results a suitable mixture of materials would be 1 part of cement, 2 parts of sand, 3 parts of shingle. If mixed ballast is preferred, the proportions should be 1 part of cement, 4 parts of mixed ballast. The aggregate size of the ballast should be graded from 18mm (¾in) to 5mm (³⁄₁₆in). The dry materials should be mixed together thoroughly on a clean, smooth, hard surface before water is added. Water should be added in small amounts as mixing proceeds until the final mix has the consistency of thick, smooth porridge.

It is necessary to be able to calculate material quantities with reasonable accuracy for paths of various lengths, widths, thicknesses and for difficult mixes. Based on the mix formulae already given, the quantities per square yard are shown in the table 'Quantities for Making Paths'. For metric conversion of table see opposite page 376.

The appearance of a plain concrete path can be enhanced considerably if the surface is provided with a design while the material is still 'green' or wet. One simple method is to trace or score the surface lightly with a pointed stick or point of the trowel. The outline or false joins of paving slabs can be represented in this way, or crazy paving can be reproduced. Circles of different sizes can be lightly scored if round, empty tins or lids are pressed into the moist surface. A very pleasing rough cast finish can be provided if a stiff brush, such as an engineer's wire brush or stiff yard broom, is carefully used on

Paving flags used singly run down the centre of a grass path between flower borders making a neat effect in this fine example of an English cottage garden.

Making a path—length 10 feet

Material	Width of Path		
	2 feet	2½ feet	3 feet
Bricks laid flat	71	89	107
Bricks laid on edge	107	134	160
Crazy paving ¾–1½ inches thick	3 cwt	3¾ cwt	4½ cwt
Crazy paving 1½–2½ inches thick	5¼ cwt	6½ cwt	8 cwt
Paving slabs	4 cwt	5 cwt	6 cwt
Gravel 2 inches thick	3¼ cwt	4 cwt	5 cwt

	Amount used	Area covered
Pebbles	2 cwt	1 square yard
Cold Asphalt	1 cwt ½ inch thick	22–25 square feet
Slabs (pre-cast)		
9 inches × 9 inches	16	1 square yard
12 inches × 12 inches	9	1 square yard
18 inches × 9 inches	8	1 square yard
18 inches × 18 inches	4	1 square yard

Quantities for making paths (per square yard)

Path	Using shingle			Using mixed ballast	
Thickness in inches	Cement lb	Damp Sand cu ft	Shingle cu ft	Cement lb	Mixed Ballast cu ft
1½	16.6	0.36	0.55	16.9	0.75
2	24.8	0.54	0.83	25.3	1.12
3	33.2	0.72	1.11	33.7	1.50
4	49.7	1.08	1.66	50.6	2.25

245

the concrete when it is practically dry. A little sharp sand lightly scattered on the surface and worked in with the brush will produce the same effect.

Colouring can play an important part in path construction and special colouring powders can be added to the cement as it is mixed. The only difficulty with this method is where several mixes of cement have to be made up during the work. It is difficult to ensure that every batch is of the same shade. Very thorough mixing is also required so that an even colouring is produced.

Once the concrete work has been completed it should be covered with damp sacking, hessian or plastic sheeting if it has been undertaken during hot weather. This will permit the concrete to dry or mature slowly and set thoroughly hard. Concrete should not be laid during very cold or frosty weather but in late autumn or spring the work can be carried out safely, provided some protection in the way of covering, is handy should there be light frosts.

Levelling All paths in a garden must be made at a gradient which is comfortable and convenient not only for walking unencumbered, but for pushing a wheelbarrow or transporting a mower from one part of the garden to another. Where the garden is on a slope it may be necessary to make steps to change the levels.

There are very few gardens where the operation of levelling is not required in some form or other. Perhaps most of the work is required in new gardens, especially where the ground is very uneven. Old-established ones often require some reorganization in places. There is a limit to the amount of levelling which should be carried out and before any work is started, it is most important that the site is carefully examined. This will enable you to plan your work so that the minimum amount of soil has to be moved during levelling operations.

If the garden has considerable differences in level, you would be wiser to work with the contours. This might involve the construction of sunken gardens, terraces, walling, pools, waterfalls and streams. It is surprising how very effective this type of design looks when incorporated in a difficult site. The most dramatic type of feature would be the construction of a series of waterfalls which finally empty into a pool at the lowest part of the garden.

The actual method of levelling is quite simple and there are several ways in which it can be undertaken. Sites which will need particular attention to levelling are those which are intended for the lawn and patio. To reduce work to the minimum, a place should be selected on the site for the required level which will not entail too much soil removal or addition to bring up the rest of the site level to this mark.

Once this has been decided upon, a

peg should be driven in. From this master level peg, others are then inserted in the site and spaced apart according to the length of the level-board which is being used. This board should be a straight piece of plank, about 2.5cm (1in) thick and 2–3m (6–8ft) long. The level of these other pegs must be the same as that of the master one and this is checked at the start as each is inserted by placing one end of the board on the master peg and the other end on the peg which is being inserted. If a spirit-level is placed at the centre and on the edge of the board, the peg can be driven into the ground until a perfect level is registered on the spirit-level.

Work proceeds by placing one end of the board on this newly inserted peg and a third peg is levelled in the same way. The whole site is dealt with in this fashion peg by peg. The work is completed by either adding to or excavating the soil on the site until the soil is brought to the top of the pegs. In some cases it may be necessary to add a few barrow-loads of soil. A rake should be used to provide a good level finish.

Another method of levelling is by the use of boning rods. These are usually made of wood, 1m (3ft) in length, with a cross piece 38cm (15in) long at one end forming a 'T'. There are three to a set. Boning rods are used in the following manner: insert a peg 3x3x25cm (1x1x9in) into the ground, leaving about 5cm (2in) protruding. This is the master peg, and should be driven in on the high or average high point of the plot. A second peg is knocked in, not more than 60cm (2ft) away, in the general direction to be sighted along. Check the level of these pegs by placing a spirit-level on the top bridging the two. A straight-edge board will be required if a short spirit-level is the only one available. Using the two pegs, place a rod upright on each, and sight across the tops of these to the third one into the distance, held by a second person. By this means you are able to see by how much the third peg requires to be adjusted. Other sight lines may be set out from the master peg, by inserting another peg not more than 60cm (2ft) away, and in the direction of a third in the distance. This method can be used for most levelling purposes, but it is invaluable where the site is very rough and undulating, because sightings can be made over heaps of soil and debris, whereas some difficulty can be experienced using a straight-edge board and spirit level. After all pegs have been inserted it is time to review the whole levelling operation, for 2.5 (1in) taken off the general level all round at this stage will save money in material, soils etc, and of course labour. Whether the

1 To establish a level at the height of the path, a peg is driven in and 2 checked with a spirit level.
3 The level is extended in this way.

pegs are knocked further into the ground or marked with brightly coloured paint, matters not, provided they are firm in the ground.

This type of levelling should be used where the site is very undulating, and will provide a rough first levelling of the soil. To produce a more accurate or even level, it will be necessary to use pegs, level-board and spirit-level as described in the first part of this section.

No matter what type of levelling is used, it is very important that the good top soil should be kept to the top of the site. It is too easy a matter to bury good soil and finish up with a newly levelled site filled with infertile soil. Where necessary therefore, quantities of the good top soil must be carefully removed as deeply as is necessary and placed in convenient positions around the site for re-use later on. Where it is necessary to fill in with quantities of new soil this should be consolidated every 16cm (6in) in depth, by treading, or time should be allowed for it to settle down or consolidate before the site is made use of. Lighter types of soil can be trodden or given a light rolling for this purpose but only when they are in a dry, friable condition.

Patio gardens

The patio, as a feature of our gardens, is a comparative newcomer to Britain although it has, for many years, been popular on the other side of the Atlantic. Its introduction here dates approximately from the end of World War II, when contemporary architects became more greatly concerned with the fusion of house and garden into a unified concept. The word patio, in fact, is something of a misnomer; its original Spanish meaning referred to an *inner* court or enclosed space open to the sky, a feature commonly encountered in Spanish and South American houses.

Today, the description is applied to almost any kind of outdoor paved space adjacent to the house. On a small scale, in similar manner to the terraces of larger houses, the patio has become very popular as a sitting-out place. Even brief spells of fine weather can be enjoyed there when lawns are soggy under foot or cold winds make sitting in the open garden too chilly for comfort.

A patio, too, can provide an effective link between the formality of the house itself and the informality of the garden proper. It should always be in proportion to the actual size of the house and garden of which it forms a feature. The materials of which it is constructed are important, since they must be in harmony with those used for the house as well as with its individual architectural style.

Period cottages seem to demand mellow brick or random paving. Note, however, not 'crazy' paving, which is all too often a mixture of broken concrete slabs and builders' leftovers. What is wanted is natural stone paving broken up into pieces of reasonable size and varying shapes. They should be laid in a random fashion, with or without cemented joints. Where the joints are left uncemented many attractive creeping plants, of the type that are able to recover after being trodden underfoot, may be grown in the crevices between the stones.

Cobbled or gravelled surrounds formed the normal features of Victorian and Edwardian houses. Although these can be made quite attractive by using plants in tubs or terrace pots, they are hardly conducive to relaxation and are better replaced with paving, drier underfoot and a more suitable setting for the garden furniture and other accoutrements of the present-day patio.

Contemporary houses, often with stark lines, call for complementary treatment. Rectangular York paving looks magnificent, but it is not only expensive but also difficult to lay owing to considerable variations in thickness. Synthetic stone slabs, on the other hand, as well as being a good deal cheaper, are of uniform thickness, which makes them easy to lay in a bed of sand or on a concrete foundation. These slabs are obtainable in a variety of shapes, colours and sizes, useful for blending into interesting patterns and designs to suit all tastes and surroundings.

With many new houses, the patio becomes an integral part of the design, having been planned that way by the architect. This is a particularly satisfactory procedure, since it can be correctly sited to take full advantage of sun and shelter. At the planning stage, too, it is possible to arrange for an outdoor hearth with its flue connecting to those of the indoor fireplaces. This would be ideal for those who want to enjoy the evening air without the chill that so often comes at twilight in our climate.

A fireplace of this nature is also useful for al fresco meals. Patios and barbecues go together and, judging by the number of appliances and recipes that one sees nowadays, it would seem that the barbecue, as a form of entertainment, is here to stay. If the patio is to be used for this purpose, it will be necessary to provide some form of lighting. This should always be in keeping with the surroundings and, as with all outdoor electrical work, installation should be carried out by an experienced electrical contractor.

Plants on the patio will consist mainly of climbing and wall shrubs and any other plants suitable for growing in tubs, urns and other containers. Decorative tubs and jardinieres are obtainable in terracotta and natural or artificial stone. Antique pots and figures are costly and increasingly hard to come by, but there are plenty of effective substitutes in artificial stone and other similar materials. Lead urns and cisterns, too, now sell for very high prices. It is possible, however, to obtain reproductions of old ones that are authentic in every detail, down to the grey-green patina that lead acquires with age and exposure to weather. Even these are not exactly cheap, but their cost is only a fraction of that of the genuine article. These fibreglass containers have the

A patio, originally a roofless inner court, has in Britain come to mean an area outside, often covered over.

added advantage of being extremely light and easy to handle. One that, in lead, would take several strong men to lift it, can be easily moved by one person.

Plants grown on the walls adjacent to the patio are best grown in beds. This, however, may not always be practicable because of damp courses, drains or other constructional hazards. But many climbers will do quite well in tubs or boxes. Although their rate of growth may be slowed down considerably, this is not necessarily a disadvantage, as it enables a greater variety of plants to be grown.

Most people require privacy in their gardens. There are various ways of screening a patio to provide this, together with protection from cold winds and draughts. To perform the latter function screens, such as walls or fences, need not be solid or close-boarded. Trellis, wattle, or interlap fencing will filter most of the sting out of any but the fiercest gales, but perhaps the most suitable screen of all for a patio is one constructed of pierced concrete walling blocks. These are obtainable in a number of pleasing openwork designs, and provide a permanent screen that encloses without producing a shut-in feeling. Living screens, too, can be effective and most of the less rampant hedging plants such as box, yew, holly or cypress are suitable.

Where space permits, a small formal pool will greatly add to the amenities of a patio garden. Formality, however, is the operative word and the pool should be square, rectangular or circular in shape. The splashing of a small fountain can be a refreshing sound on sweltering summer days.

Choice of furniture for the patio is important. Chairs and tables of wood or metal, which will stand being left out in all weathers, should be supplemented by folding chairs for longer and more relaxed sessions. In the latter kind, tubular aluminium and synthetic fabrics are rapidly replacing the wooden frames and canvas of the deckchair. Aluminium garden furniture is light to handle and folds compactly for storage. If it should be left out in a summer downpour, it will come to no harm. Metal garden furniture of the permanent kind can take a number of attractive forms, ranging from wrought iron, painted white and preferably rendered rustproof, to reproductions, in cast aluminium, of old Victorian cast-iron seats and tables of pleasing design. Teak and elm furniture, too, stand up well in all weathers, although they do tend to deteriorate after a few years if they are regularly left out through the winter. Storing

1 Round slabs, used in conjunction with in-filling pieces, are used to pave this patio garden.
2 A formal patio where a dripping fountain provides a sense of coolness.

bulky furniture of this kind, however, can create problems where, space is restricted.

A number of creeping and prostrate plants seem to suffer little damage from being trodden underfoot. Crevices left between the stones when the paving is being laid will serve as pockets for this type of plant. Herbs figure largely in this category and all varieties of *Thymus serpyllum*, in particular, stand up well to this harsh treatment. These include 'Annie Hall', with lilac flowers, 'Pink Chintz', *T. s. lanuginosus*, with grey, hairy leaves and *T. S. splendens*, with crimson flowers.

The low-growing mint, *Mentha requienii*, a species that makes dense mats of dark green aromatic foliage, is equally useful, while small alpine plants such as thrift, aubrietas and rock pinks can be used in corners and places that get less wear and tear.

If the patio is of reasonable size, it can also have one or more flower beds. Like the patio pool, these should be geometrical in shape. Circles, rectangles or L-shaped beds will usually be most satisfactory. Such beds are ideal for spring and summer bedding schemes. It is probably a good idea, however, to settle for a major display during summer, bearing in mind that the patio will then get its greatest use. Summer-flowering heaths or floribunda roses provide permanent and trouble-free planting.

Peaches see Fruit

Pears see Fruit

Peas see Vegetables

Peat

Peat is partially decayed, organic matter formed when plant remains collect on waterlogged tracts of land in wet districts or in badly drained hollows where excess water prevents normal decay. Although a tenth of the land surface of Britain is covered with peat, most of it is concentrated into a few areas. If you live in parts of Scotland, Lancashire, Yorkshire, or Somerset, you can buy it locally. Gardeners in most other areas are dependent on supplies purchased in garden shops. The peat you buy in bales or bags may come from home sources, or from Eire, Germany, or Denmark.

Horticultural peat production is a highly technical business involving cutting, stacking and drying, followed by some form of shredding and screening of the natural material. Lower grade materials are used for burning and many other purposes. There are two main kinds of horticultural peat offered by garden sundriesmen. Sphagnum or peat moss, which has been formed from various species of the sphagnum plant, is very spongy and absorbs water very

1 Concrete slabs are used in contrasting colours to provide a formal pattern for this patio.
2 Rectangular tiles make a clean entrance path to the house.
3 A patio in a town garden where colour is provided by plants in a variety of containers.
4 Coloured paving slabs of various shapes, sizes and colours and pierced screen walling.

readily holding up to 15 times its own weight of water. Such peats are often very acid with pH values of between 3.5 and 4.5.

Sedge peats are made up of sedges, reeds, mosses and trees. These hold up to 7 or 8 times their own weight of water and they are often less acid having pH values of 3.5 to 7.0, according to the lime content of the water in which the plant have decayed.

Peat generally is very low in nutrients and while the nitrogen content is often quoted as 1.5 to 3.5 percent, this is

released so slowly as to be of little value to growing crops. If, however, very large amounts of peat are applied every year, then the soil nitrogen content will be raised appreciably. The phosphate and potash content also is low, being in the region of a fraction of 1 percent. Peat may be expected to provide some trace elements such as boron, copper and zinc, but the amounts are never very great, so peat cannot be regarded as a fertilizer. It is a humus supplier.

What peat does Like all humus suppliers it makes soils more porous by giving them a kind of Aertex structure by virtue of the millions of small cells that make up its fibrous structure. As a result heavy soils are opened up and light soils hold more moisture for plant use. Peat is scattered in drills for vegetable crops, the seedlings are able to push their way through the more difficult soils, which form hard crusts during dry periods.

One of the reasons for the popularity of peat is the ease with which it is spread and mixed with the soil; it is also weed free, clean to handle and has a long-lasting effect on the soil.

Using peat When buying a peat for digging in it is best to choose a grade that will benefit your particular soil. If the soil is a clay, or silty, loam, the peat that has a particle size ranging from 1–12mm ($\frac{1}{16}$–$\frac{1}{2}$in) will be the most beneficial. One with a coarse particle size of 12–18mm ($\frac{1}{2}$–$\frac{3}{4}$in) will be best for really sandy soils. If your soil is low in organic matter you will need to give about 5kg (10lb) per sq m (sq yd) to do any real good. In subsequent years you can reduce this to 2.5–3kg (5–6lb) per sq m (sq yd)

To get the best results spread the peat on to a well-broken surface and then mix it in with the top 8–10cm (3–4in) of forking or rotary cultivation. But always thoroughly moisten the peat first; never work it in dry otherwise it will stay dry and fail to give the best results. If peat is to be used in quantity one way of ensuring that it is properly moistened is to break up the bale, and either allow it to be soaked by rain or apply water with a hose and sprinkler, which may take quite a time. Another way is to make a hole in the bale and insert the hose nozzle and allow water to trickle in gently until the bale is thoroughly soaked through. Even then it may be necessary to break up the bale afterwards and use the sprinkler to make sure that there are no dry patches left.

Smaller quantities can be moistened by soaking over-night in a bucket or other container, after breaking up the lumps by hand. The next day the excess water should be squeezed out before the peat is used.

For overcoming the harmful effects of crusting, scatter 85g (3oz) of peat per sq m (sq yd) run when preparing seed drills. To help the roots of trees and

1 Peat occurs naturally in some parts of Britain, and in such districts it can be bought locally. Peat stacks on a southern Yorkshire peat moor.
2 Horticultural peat needs to be moistened before it is ready for use.

shrubs to spread evenly through poorly structured soils, put 1–1.5kg (2–3lb) of peat in under each plant when planting shrubs, roses or fruit bushes; a handful is all that is needed for herbaceous plants. Always mix peat with a little loose soil before positioning the plant.

Mulches of peat help to keep shrub and flower borders free from weeds and the soil moist during the summer after which the material can be worked into the soil. A 1–12mm ($\frac{1}{16}$–$\frac{1}{2}$in) grade product, when applied at the rate of 3–5kg (6–10lb) per sq m (sq yd), is best for this work.

When preparing the soil for sowing lawn seed or laying turves, peat worked into the top 5cm (2in), will give a good start to the germinating seeds or help the turves to knit together. A special grade peat is supplied for autumn dressing of lawns.

Peat pots are being increasingly used for seedlings and bedding plants. The pot is put into the soil thus leaving the roots undisturbed. The roots penetrate the peat and finally it is broken down into the soil. Peat is the main ingredient of bulb fibre, used for growing bulbs indoors (see Bulb Cultivation).

In the greenhouse peat is an important ingredient of mixtures used in raising plants, such as John Innes compost and peat-sand mixtures. Some peats on their own provide an ideal growing medium for a wide range of plants when they are fed regularly with the appropriate fertilizers. Oddly enough, one of the great advantages of peat in greenhouse culture is its low fertility, since you then alan your feeding programme more pccurately from a known low starting point. By contrast animal manures are very much richer in nutrients which also are released in unknown amounts. It is always easier to add nutrients than to take them away. The use of soils with high drainage rates and greater air supply makes modern automatic watering and feeding systems feasible for greenhouse plants.

Although peat is acid it is unlikely to make the soil appreciably more acid unless very large amounts are used regularly or a very acid peat is used.

Horticultural peat is generally sold loose in bags, the weight of which may or may not be declared, or in compressed bales which is the best buy. Since you are buying peat for its organic matter you want to be sure that you are buying organic matter and not water or any other unwanted matter such as earthy materials. All peats contain moisture, however dry they may feel. A tonne (ton) of raw peat straight from the bog may contain 800–900kg (16–18cwt) of water. This is normally reduced by air drying in the field so that the product has 30–50 percent of moisture in it. It is, of course, possible to reduce the moisture content even more but over-drying not only lowers the actual moisture-holding power of peat, but it makes it much more difficult to re-wet the product before use.

Some peats, also, are much more decayed than others; these do not last so long in the soil as the more spongy undecomposed types. You can tell roughly how well decayed they are by soaking a handful and then squeezing it

1 Peat can be used to provide a mulch. Here it is put around Iris stylosa growing at the base of a wall, to conserve as much moisture as possible.
2 The peat garden at Logan, Scotland, contains a wide variety of plants.

through your hand; if the liquid which comes out is almost colourless or just slightly brown, the peat is only slightly decayed, but if the colour is very dark and it squelches through the fingers like porridge it is highly decomposed and much less suitable for most purposes except mulching.

Peat is being increasingly used by commercial horticulturists—not only as an ingredient in potting composts and as a soil conditioner but as a medium in which crops can be grown with no other additions except plant nutrients. So much attention is being paid to these methods of using peat that the International Society for Horticultural Science, at its world congress in 1962, set up a special international working party to study developments. Experiments with crops grown on beds of peat are being carried out in many countries. Tomatoes, cucumbers, carnations, and many other flower crops have been successfully grown in this way. In Britain, the technique has been successfully adopted by some commercial nurseries. The method, however, requires meticulous attention to the ratio in which the plant nutrients are supplied.

Peat beds

It has been discovered that walls composed of peat blocks can be built up from

the ground level to enclose an area which, when filled with acid peaty soil, will provide suitable situations for a number of plants which need just such soil conditions. If the normal soil of the garden is an alkaline one this allows you to grow many fine plants, especially among the *Ericaceae*, *Primulaceae* and *Pinaceae*, which you may otherwise have to forego. The original peat gardens made in this way at Logan in Wigtownshire and in the Royal Botanic Garden, Edinburgh, were on a large scale and both were on a northern slope. Neither of these factors is essential. However, this is not the sort of gardening to be recommended if you have a strictly limited amount of money to expend on your garden. A supply of suitable peat has to be found and cut into block form. The cost of transport will be high unless, of course, your garden is in a part of Britain where peat blocks are used for fuel. The sort of peat sold in bales for garden use is quite unsuited for this purpose but peat blocks may be purchased. These must be thoroughly moistened before use.

A semi-shady site is most suitable, such as below a tree or on the north side of a hedge or fence. If the soil is neutral fork it over first; if it is alkaline it is best to leave it but to lay down a 7–10cm (3–4in) thick layer of rough peat before starting to build the wall.

In constructing the peat wall it must be battered (sloped backwards) somewhat, as a perpendicular or overhanging face is unsuitable. It is an aid to stability to drive iron rods through the peat walls and into the ground beneath, though this is not necessary unless the walls are high. A height of about 30cm (1ft) is, in any case, adequate. The blocks should be bonded, in the same way as bricks, as the wall is built. It helps to work in among the joints, a mixture consisting of 4 parts of leafmould or fine peat, 1 part of lime-free loam and 1 part of coarse sand. A similar mixture is used to fill the bed, which, when it has been filled, preferably in late summer or autumn, is consolidated by treading and allowed to settle properly before it is planted up in the following April, though if the bed is prepared in spring or summer it will be ready for planting up in September. At one time any such provision for lime-hating plants would have been called an American garden, and it is true that many plants native of North America are quite suited to peat beds, but so are many Chinese and Japanese plants.

Among the genera most suited to the peat beds are: andromeda, anemone, arcterica, arctostaphylos, astilbe, calluna, cassiope, clethra, colchicum, corylopsis, cyclamen, cypripedium, daboecia, daphne, dicentra, disporum, enkianthus, epimedium, erica, erythronium, gaultheria, gaylussacia, gentiana (Asiatic spp.), jeffersonia, kalmia, kalmiopsis, ledum, leiophyllum, leucothoe, lewisia,

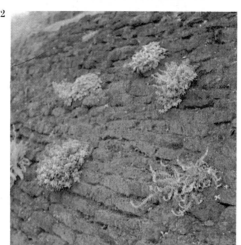

linnaea, magnolia, menziesia, michauxia, mitchella, mitella, omphalogramma, orchis, orphanidesia, ourisia, oxalis, pernettya, phyllodoce, pieris, platycodon, pratia, primula, pyrola, ranunculus, rhododendron, rhodohypoxis, roscoea, sanguinaria, schizocodon, shortia, tanakaea, tiarella, tolmiea, tricyrtis, trillium, uvularia, vaccinium, zenobia.

All species of the above genera are not equally suited to our purpose though none will fail to grow quite well. A complete list of the suitable species of either rhododendron or primula alone would take up more space than can be allocated to this article.

The effect to aim at in planting up the peat beds is a natural wildness. Paths should seem like dry watercourses, and where some shade is needed the most suitable broad-leaved trees would be among the acers and for conifers the *Pinaceae* offer many suitable species.

Perennial

This term is used to describe a plant which does not die after flowering, but

1 Peat blocks are used to build up a peat garden, or American garden, and have to be trimmed to size.
2 A peat wall must be constructed so that it slopes slightly backwards, and if the walls are high it helps stability to drive in iron rods through the peat.
3 A peat wall planted up effectively.

persists for a number of years, in contrast with an annual which flowers once and then dies after setting seed, and a biennial which completes its life-cycle in two years. The term 'perennial' may properly be applied to shrubs and trees but is more often used in conjunction with the term 'hardy herbaceous' to describe the plants which form the mainstay of herbaceous borders, though they are often grown in other parts of the garden. Though the term is applied to plants which live for more than 2 years, many perennials live for many years and such plants as herbaceous paeonias and the oriental poppy (*Papaver orientale*) are particularly long lived. By contrast some perennial plants, for instance lupins, may have a life-span of five or six years only.

Pest

Almost any creature which causes significant damage to plants may be defined as a pest. Most garden pests are insects and they cause many different kinds of damage. These include weakening the plant and spreading virus

1 The paths in a peat garden should be arid or stony for the best effect, and a living mulch at the base of climbers provided by low-growing plants, will help to conserve moisture in the soil.
2 Attractive arrangements can be made, as in this newly constructed peat garden.
3 Lilium regale in raised peat beds.

diseases by sucking the sap. Another form of damage by insects reduces leaf area, impairs the root system and allows the entry of disease, when the plant tissue is eaten away above or below the ground. They also kill shoots by tunnelling along them; and disfigure the plant by the formation of galls, discoloration, distortion, spinning up or mining the leaves, etc.

Pests include mites, which cause galls and chlorosis of the leaves and damage to bulbs; slugs which rasp plant tissue above and below ground; millepedes which damage the underground parts of plants; woodlice which gnaw stems and leaves; springtails which attack seedlings, etc, and microscopic eelworms which attack roots, bulbs and foliage of various plants.

Larger creatures which sometimes become garden pests include mice, voles and squirrels which eat bulbs and corms; rabbits and hares which devour plants and bark fruit trees, especially in severe weather; moles which spoil lawns with their tunnelling; deer and sheep which occasionally break in and create havoc; domestic dogs and cats, which are occasional nuisances; and birds which destroy buds and berries.

Pest Control

Pest control in home gardens is not easy. In general, it is best to use chemicals only when it is strictly necessary, taking into account whether the amount of damage done is sufficient to warrant spraying, or whether it is a small outbreak that can be tolerated without lasting injury to the plant. First, the pest responsible must be identified. The insect found on the plant is not necessarily the culprit. It may be innocent, while the pest causing the damage may be feeding at night or may have completed the feeding stage of its life cycle, or have migrated to another host plant.

A knowledge of the habits and life history of common pests is therefore useful for their correct identification, and for the correct timing of control measures. If necessary, the aid of experts may be called in and most gardening periodicals and some chemical firms run advisory services. The Royal Horticultural Society gives advice to its members and commercial growers can consult the National Agricultural Advisory service.

When choosing chemicals to control the pests, the home gardener is confronted by a huge range of proprietary brands offering a bewildering choice. There are insecticides to kill insects; acaricides to kill mites; nematicides to kill eelworms; molluscicides to kill slugs and snails; vermicides to kill earthworms; ovicides to kill overwintering eggs; repellents to deter birds and mammals, etc. There is also the formulation of the insecticide to be considered. It may be best to use a stomach poison, a systemic insecticide, or a fumigant. The insecticide may be in the form of an emulsion, dust, a wettable powder, an aerosol, smoke, granules or seed dressings. It is necessary to consider what form would be most suitable.

The scientific world moves very swiftly. New formulations of greater efficiency and lesser toxicity are constantly being introduced and older preparations withdrawn or their use discouraged. If in doubt about which material to use to combat which pest or disease, information is always available at the better garden centres and stores, from gardening journals and from the advisory departments of the garden chemical manufacturers themselves.

Some years ago the Ministry of Agriculture introduced the Agricultural Chemicals Approval Scheme. Under this scheme the manufacturers of all types of garden chemicals can provide samples of their products for stringent official tests. If the products pass the tests (which are not only for efficacy but also for safety) they are granted the approval mark, a capital A surmounted by a crown. This sign will be found on the labels of tested and approved products and should be sought by the gardener.

Because a product has been approved does not mean that it can be used carelessly. Instructions must be read carefully and followed meticulously.

It may well be found, for instance where nicotine or malathion are concerned, that an insecticide that is of short persistence on the plant is extremely poisonous in the concentrated state before dilution. Containers should always be kept well out of reach of children and animals and every care taken to ensure that they do not come in contact with sprayed plants or lawns within the period specified. Insecticides should *never* be put in other bottles, such as soft drink bottles, even after they have been diluted for use.

For preference, an insecticide of short persistence should be selected. A double dose of the insecticide will not do twice as much good as that recommended by the manufacturer and may result in damage to the plant. Whatever the chemical, there are almost always a few plants which react unfavourably to it. These will usually be mentioned in the instructions if they are commonly grown plants, but where unusual plants are grown, it is as well to test chemicals on a few of them before spraying them all.

It is often possible to obtain control of more pests at one time by combining two or more compatible chemicals. These may be two insecticides designed to kill biting and sucking pests respectively. An insecticide and an acaricide may be combined or an insecticide and a fungicide, and so on. Many proprietary pest control preparations contain more than one chemical used in this way, or compatible substances can be made up at normal dilutions to form one spray, thus saving two applications. The efficiency of sprays may be increased by the addition of wetting compounds, where these are not already incorporated in the proprietary substance.

Ph values see Soil types

Physiological disorders see Diseases and their control

Planning the garden

Whether you specialize in any particular plant or not, the general design and layout of your garden must be pleasing and practical. There are some hard and fast rules to bear in mind, but in the main gardening is a subject upon which it is very hard to dogmatize, and the

1

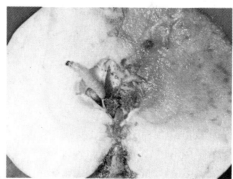

2

4

5

6

7

3

Any creatures that cause damage and unsightliness to plants can be regarded as pests, and should be destroyed.
1 Earwig damage on a chrysanthemum.
2 Loganberry fruits attacked by the raspberry beetle.
3 A sectioned potato showing damage done by the keeled slug.
4 The caterpillar of the codling moth.
5 Cabbage aphid damage on sprouts.
6 Slugs and snails.
7 The female striped hover fly.
8 Ants can cause much damage.

8

thing to remember is that the success or otherwise of your garden depends on the pleasure and satisfaction which you get from it.

If your garden is a new one, just as the builder has left it, the first thing to be done is to make a rough scale plan of the plot. By doing this you will find that you will be able to get everything into proper perspective right from the start. Then make a list of all the features you and your family would like, or think they would like. You may be tempted to include far more items than would be practical—but remember that a garden overcrowded with features is probably less satisfying and more difficult to maintain than one of quiet simplicity. Quite often gardeners clutter their gardens with so many features that the result is a great deal of unnecessary work with nothing really on which the eye can settle. But even if some items have to be crossed off later for reasons of expense and or space available, do try to get down on your list:

Flowering trees, shrubs and herbaceous border
Kitchen garden
Sundial, bird bath, or similar feature
An ornamental pool (formal or informal)
Screened, paved terrace and paths (paths accessible enough for children's tricycles)
As large an expanse of lawn as possible
Rose beds
Screened rubbish corner and compost pit
Perhaps a rock garden, and even a garden shelter or summer house

If you have a family perhaps you would like to include a corner for the children, with their own planting plot, a swing and a sandpit, which may be screened and sheltered by a rose-covered trellis fence, a beech hedge, or a shrub border. Try to get the children interested in the garden and feel that part of it is theirs—at least they can have one corner unhampered by restrictions of where not to walk and what not to pull up. It is important that children where possible are given their own garden corner with its attendant pleasures and responsibilities, so that they can enjoy the pleasures of growing flowers from seed, and sharing in the awakening of spring with the unexpected thrill of finding the first snowdrop flower, as well as learning care and tidiness.

However small your garden, it should have at least one main feature, or focal point. It may be an ornamental pool, a summer house, or perhaps even a specimen standard flowering tree. A paved terrace can also be a focal point for radiating rose beds. When you have decided on these features, position them carefully on your plan. Do not forget the compass direction of the facing aspect, the wind, soil or other factors which

1 Insecticides can be applied as a fine spray from a pressurized container. A fine spray wets the plant evenly.
2 A sprayer of the knapsack design with a long spray gun is useful for roses growing in beds.

must be taken into consideration. Try to set off the features naturally with contrasting elements. For example, the pool should be set off by a lawn, the lawn by a border of shrubs and herbaceous plants, and if the pool is of an informal shape, back it with a bank of carefully-built rock stones. There are infinite variations and possibilities. Let the main features show up as focal points in the garden, and then let the lawns and borders provide a neat, simple foil for them, always remembering that you want to keep maintenance work in the garden to a minimum. Keep the lawn as large as is practicable. Besides being much less work to keep tidy than borders which are perhaps too wide, a large lawn will make your garden appear much larger than it really is. If you wish to have an undulating lawn, give careful attention to the drainage of the depressions, or you may have trouble later.

Let at least one of your features be as far away from the house as possible, so that in attracting the eye to it in the distance you will be making full use of the length of your garden; and do not

forget the value of vistas, or framed views, when designing and planting. A white-painted seat or a bed of scarlet floribunda roses are good distant eye-catchers. If the garden overlooks a particularly attractive view between two trees or with a break in a shrub border try to create a framed view just as the painter might do.

Another principle to remember is that the garden design is governed more by the architecture and shape of the house than the shape of your plot. The terrace and formal parts of your garden should be planned in relation to the lines of your house. All straight lines of paving or beds in these areas should be parallel to, or square with, the main house walls. Designing and planting the terrace can be important in creating the look of the back of your house. The terrace, or patio, is a connecting link between house and garden. Bear this in mind when selecting paving for the terrace, so that it will blend with both the house bricks and the garden. Stone is ideal material, but perhaps rather expensive. Nowadays one can obtain good concrete paving in a variety of quiet colours, and often a careful blending of these can give a very pleasing effect. Sometimes a garden may slope down from front to back. This can be turned into an asset by levelling off the paved terrace area, holding up the raised part of it with a stone or brick retaining wall, and building broad steps down to the lawn (this procedure would

1

2

be reversed should the garden slope down from back to front). Try always to keep your steps, paths and grassed walks wide enough for at least two people to walk abreast. It is also important that steps are always made easily negotiable. Treads should be at least 30cm (1ft) wide and risers (depth of step) never more than 15cm (6in). Let the treads slope very slightly from back to front so that rain-water will easily run off. Under some circumstances a terrace and garden can be made to appear much wider by build-ing the steps to the full width of the paved area. After all, the terrace is part of the garden, and it seems wrong to screen the garden from the terrace with a heavy planting of shrubs and strong-growing floribunda roses, as used to be the custom. For the sake of privacy the terrace may be carefully but effectively screened with walling, fencing or plant-ing.

In shaping the lawn with graceful curves (remembering that the lawn mower will have to get round them), you may like to allow for a grassed path through a shrub border at the end of the lawn leading to your kitchen garden, which will thus be screened from the house. To some gardeners a kitchen garden is more important than to others,

1 In this small garden full advantage has been taken of the ground which rises away from the house. The formal lines of the pool and steps are relieved by the luxuriant plant growth.
2 Ground sloping away from the house can be treated in various ways. Here the bank sloping down the lawn has been planted with shrubs and rock plants.
3 The pergola with its roses is a major feature in this garden. The two levels are connected by steps.

3

so that the proportion of your garden devoted to fruit and vegetables is something which only you can decide. It is essential, however, that provision be made for compost and garden rubbish, perhaps in the furthermost corner screened by a hedge.

It will save much trouble later if, before any work is done on the actual layout of a new garden, the whole area is first of all forked clear of all weeds and rubbish. As far as the planting is concerned, as many shrubs, roses and herbaceous plants should be included as possible. Not only does this provide a more natural and lasting effect but in the long run it saves labour and expense. Additional colour may, if required, be provided by summer-flowering annuals and biennials, but hardy herbaceous perennials, shrubs, and trees should form a permanent backbone to your scheme.

Plant your trees and shrubs singly and your herbaceous plants in groups of 3 or more. If you have any rose beds plant a variety of rose to each bed; you will find that drifts of one colour are always more effective than dotting the colours here and there. Remember that certain combinations of shrubs flowering at approximately the same time look well if planted together; shrubs such as *Cornus mas elegantissima*, a variegated-leaved form of the Cornelian cherry, with yellow and pink leaves, and *Prunus cerasifera atropurpurea* (*Prunus pissardii*), the purple-leaf plum, almond and forsythia; *Potentilla fruticosa* and *Spiraea bumalda* 'Anthony Waterer'; lilac and laburnum.

The plan Before you start any planting, or positioning any features, you should draw a plan of your site. One simple way of doing this is to obtain a fairly stiff piece of cardboard about 40 × 25cm (15 × 10in), and on this affix with drawing pins a sheet of clean drawing paper.

Now draw the shape of your site, beginning with the actual house itself. This is important because in most cases the angles of the corners of the house are right-angles, whereas boundary fence angles may vary considerably. Where such projections as bay windows are concerned the angles may vary, but details of these can be ascertained (see below).

Draw in the house by working round it, putting down details of each wall in succession, remembering, of course, that you are not yet drawing to scale, so that comparisons of such things as length, need not be in accurate detail. Then carry on with the shape of the surrounding fence or hedge, roughly showing any curves or recesses which may occur. If there are any large trees, sheds or any other permanent structures on your site, they should be also drawn in at this stage. While you are sketching, make a note of any view you wish to enhance

Water gardens are always pleasant features. Though this picture was taken in a large garden, there is usually room for a pool, even in the small garden.

and any eyesores you would like to remove, so that these can be taken into account when designing your garden.

Go along each wall of the house, including each recess, bay, or other projection, putting on your sketch the measurements. When this is completed, carry on with the measurements around your boundary fence. If you have a bay window, the angles of which are not 90 degrees, measure along each straight piece of wall, and, by sighting along the front wall of the bay, measure the distance it juts out from the main house wall. With these details you can determine the angles.

In many cases the house and site are not absolutely square with one another, and, therefore, this must be noted on your plan or you will not be able to reproduce a true scale perspective. From each corner of your house draw a dotted line on your sketch until each line (which is really an extension to the line of your house wall) strikes the boundary fence on all sides. These lines are called 'siting lines' and are important to the plan. Now stand along the boundary fence at the point which is directly in

line with the wall of the house (ie on the siting line), and take the measurement from that point to the corner of the building. From the point where the siting line meets the fence take a measurement from there to the corner of your site both to right and left. Repeat the measuring on each siting line, and you will see when you are putting down these measurements that any deviation from the square will be accurately noted on your plan.

If the plot you are surveying is thick with undergrowth and trees which you would like to leave undisturbed until you have completed your plan, and which obscure the siting lines, you can overcome this difficulty by using a few bamboo canes about 1.3m (4ft) long. Walk as far along the siting line as you can until you reach the tree or other obstruction, and place a cane or peg upright in the ground. Then take a measurement along the wall of the house to a point which would clear the obstruction and place a peg opposite this point exactly the same distance from the house as the first peg you placed on the edge of the obstructing trees. This second peg must also be the same distance from the first peg as the measurement along the house wall from the siting line corner. A line can now be sited between the point along the house

wall to which you measured and the second cane which has been placed in position. This siting line will be square with the face and parallel to the side of the house in the same way as the original siting line would have been, and can, therefore, be used as such. You will also find that siting lines can be very useful when showing the position of existing trees, etc. If a boundary fence is irregular or curved in shape, you can place a series of bamboo canes along the siting lines at, say, 3m (10ft) intervals. From each of these bamboo canes you can then take the measurements to the irregularly-shaped side fence, noting the details on your sketch.

You should now have all the details you will need, with the exception of the levels, and any direct variation in these must be noted carefully. The levels are obtained in the following way. First of all shape pegs similar in thickness to bundled fire-lighting wood sold in shops. Let the pegs be long enough to cover the vertical variation in your levels. Now drive into the ground the first peg to the level of the highest point of your garden, and a second peg approximately 2m (6ft) away from the first. Lay a plank of wood approximately 2m × 7cm × 2.5cm (6ft × 3in × 1in) (which must have straight and parallel sides) between the two pegs; and along the top of the plank, known as a

'straight-edge', place an ordinary builder's spirit level. Now the second peg must be adjusted so that the spirit level shows that the top of it is perfectly level with the first peg. This must be repeated over the whole area of the garden so that you can see at a glance the exact variations in levels. These details can be transferred to your sketch by showing the positions of each peg, then taking the first peg as zero, show figures against each of the other pegs in linear measurement so that you have details of variations of levels throughout the site. The measurement shown against each peg will be the actual fall of the ground at that point below the level of the first peg or highest point of your site. To finish off your survey use a simple compass so that you can mark the direction of north on your plan. This will be important because obviously you will want to know which side of your garden will be the warm sunny one, and which the shady side. The design and planting of it will depend largely on these details.

Finally, check the quality of your soil. For this it is possible to obtain expert advice. Your County Agricultural Agent can frequently be asked to advise, and, if he thinks it is necessary, he will take away a sample of your soil to be analyzed. From his report you will know what type of fertilizer and how much humus

1

2

drawing in details of the house, and when you have drawn that to scale, dot along your siting line and mark off the measurements as taken in your survey. Now measure from the ends of the siting lines to complete your boundary fences. If you are using graph paper, you will be able to draw quite easily along the horizontal and perpendicular lines knowing that each one is at right-angles to the other, but if you are using drawing paper you will have to rely on your T-square for the horizontal lines and your set square for the vertical lines. At first, all these details should be put down in pencil and not inked in until the planning has been finally completed. Details of the vertical levels can also be marked on your plan. Mark in any existing features, such as trees, greenhouse and shed, show the compass points and details of any adjoining eyesores you may wish to hide and any attractive views you would like to frame.

General planning On your plan you have now details of your house and boundary fence, and now you should design the area immediately adjoining the house, back and front. This will include paths and terraces, and the first thing to remember is that paving immediately adjoining the house wall must be laid at least two courses below the damp-proof course of the house.

1 From the time this small garden was first planned by the owners, until the time that the photograph was taken, two years only elapsed.
2 Low walls are again a feature of this charming garden, where a small formal pool is set in the lawn. The distant view is framed by trees.
3 Lush planting of herbaceous material, shrubs and trees.
4 The lawn is the main feature in this small but colourful garden.
5 A pathway winding out of sight lends an air of mystery to this garden.

to add to your soil, and it will also give you a guide as to which plants you can or cannot grow.

Obviously the ideal requirements for drawing the plan would be a drawing board, set square, compass and T-square, as well as ruler, pencil, etc. If the former are not available your plan can be drawn quite satisfactorily using pen or pencil and ruler on a piece of graph paper which can be purchased at almost any stationer's. First of all, decide upon a scale to which to work. This can be determined by adding up on your sketch all the measurements which go to make the longest overall length of your site, and the resultant measurement should then be scaled down to fit the size of your paper.

Before you start your plan, write along the bottom whatever scale you have decided to use. Once again start by

Often crazy paving is the cheapest to buy, but to make a good job it should be laid on a foundation of at least 5cm (2in) of 4:2:1: concrete (ie 4 parts of gravel, 2 parts of sand and 1 part of cement, by bulk), over a 10cm (4in) thick layer of rubble and ashes. If crazy paving is only 'spot bedded' (that is, when a trowel of cement mortar is put under each corner of the piece of paving and one in the centre) it has a tendency to work loose gradually and cause trouble later on. Where the area of crazy paving is a large one, pieces of paving could be left out and filled with soil, thus forming planting pockets. In each of these pockets, carpeting alpines and dwarf heathers could be planted, thus creating a softening effect on the paving itself and also providing a colourful relief.

Natural paving stone is by far the best for garden use, but it is expensive. There are many alternatives, however, which are put on the market as reproductions of natural stone paving. As these are usually made accurate in size and evenly thick they are very easy to lay without unnecessary cutting. The basis of their manufacture is usually crushed natural stone which is mixed with sand, cement and, if necessary, a little colouring. These are much less expensive and they can be most attractive if care is taken with their selection. When purchasing these paving slabs, it is usual to ask for 'random paving', slabs of a series of different sizes but all square or rectangular shape.

The type of paving slab you are going

to use should be considered at this stage as it will depend to a great extent upon the type of paths and terrace you would like. If you are moving into a new house, you may wish to lay paving around the house first to prevent soil being carried inside.

A terrace, which should be adjoining a french window or door at the rear of the house, should be large enough to accommodate at least half-a-dozen chairs and a table, and planned in such a way as to ensure as much seclusion as possible. Close-boarded fencing 2m (6ft) high may be erected to give privacy from your immediate neighbours, and trees and shrubs carefully sited to obscure views from other neighbouring houses. Any lawn or border lines immediately adjoining the terrace should be square with or parallel to the lines of that terrace. Thus the borders shaping your lawn for the first few yards at least should be parallel to (but not necessarily in line with) the side of your house. Then you could break into more informal lines as suggested in the illustrated plans. These plans are only suggestions as to principles, from which, you will be able to formulate your own personal ideas.

Whether you design the lawn on formal or informal lines, make any curves gentle ones to render the task of mowing easier. Sharp curves are much more difficult to mow round. For the same reason, any beds in the lawn should be roughly fish-shaped, broad in the centre, tapering to a point at each end, rather than circular, oval or rectangular.

Either consult the children regarding their wants in the garden, or at least include for them in your planning. While they are young you may wish to restrict their playing to an area which is more or less in constant view from the house. This may mean that direct access from the back of the house to the front will need to be restricted by fencing and a gate (with perhaps a temporary sand pit and swing erected within view of the kitchen window) to prevent the children from wandering on to the road. As they get a little older a secluded corner of the garden can be allotted to them. This can be hidden from the house by a hedge or a fence and could include individual garden plots, swing, sand-pit, Wendy house, etc. Garden paths should also be planned with the children in mind. They should be wide enough and accessible enough for a scooter or tricycle to be ridden without danger. When siting the greenhouse and garden shed bear in mind that a greenhouse has to be visited daily whatever the weather, but also that both greenhouse and shed are not the most pleasant of objects upon which to look from your living-room window.

Stepping stones through a large rose bed, shrub, or herbaceous border, are both practical and ornamental, allowing access between two or more points and

making it possible to tend to the plants in large beds or borders, even when the soil is damp. They can also be used to create an additional walk. It is often desirable to be able to take friends around your garden (however small it may be) by one route and return by another. In the suggested plan of the small garden, you will see that you could walk up the lawn, through the trellis arch beyond the bed of 'Korona' roses, across the path between the trellis fence and the kitchen garden and back down the paved garden path. If necessary you could return over the stepping stones from the path to the lawn, all of which must add interest to your garden.

In this small garden the greenhouses are hidden behind a close-panel fence.

When planning pathways bear in mind that paths which are hidden from view from the house can add considerably to the attraction of the garden and even add an air of mystery to it. If you can show friends the whole of your garden without leaving the house, there is no extra inducement (unless they are keen horticulturists) for them to go out and explore it, but if there is a grass or paved path wandering out of sight behind a curved bed or border, there is always the urge to go out and see what is beyond and where it leads.

With regard to your front garden and drive, remember that the function of the drive is purely a practical one and that the front garden should be as neat and as plain as possible solely to provide a suitable setting for the house. Most gardeners, however keen, will prefer to spend their spare time in the privacy of the back garden rather than in the more public and overlooked front of the house. When designing your drive, provision should be made for your car to back out of the garage across the front of your house, and then go forward into the road.

Plant containers

A wide diversity of design is to be found in plant containers, ranging from the humble and familiar flower pot to the sophisticated, automatically watered plant trough. Materials range in age and type from the old stone trough to the very latest plastic. They include asbestos, cement, clay, metal, plastics and fibreglass and wood. They may be adapted for indoor or outdoor use depending on appearance and strength.

Plastics and fibreglass Extruded polystyrene is used by some manufacturers to produce plant containers which are very light and attractive with their troughs. They are ideal containers for the woman gardener as they are light and pleasant to handle. They must be used with care, however, as they are fairly fragile when filled. For example, it is not wise to pull a large trough, when filled, by its rim, as this can break off easily. A long trough must be supported underneath with a piece of timber if it has to be moved when filled. Usually, however, containers should be placed in their correct positions first and then filled and planted.

Some window-box or plant trough designs are manufactured from strong plastic materials which result in lightweight, rot-proof articles. They also have particular appeal to the woman gardener as they are attractively decorated by relief designs. Suitable plastic and fibreglass shallow plant troughs can be obtained for indoor use. These are ideal for placing pot plants in, especially on the window ledge. A few small pebbles in the bottom plus a regular supply of small amounts of water will provide the ideal moist atmosphere for growing many plants. There are several fibreglass plant tubs on the market. These are made from special high-quality fibreglass in various colours, such as red, yellow and green. The material used in their construction is light, so the containers are easy to handle. As their colouring is permanent, there is no need to paint them and they will not rot or warp.

Fibreglass is also used for troughs, window-boxes, urns and other types of plant container. One range consists of facsimile reproductions of antique originals with exquisite motifs accurately copied. Of typical design in the style of these reproductions is a substantial square plant container dating back to an original made about 1550. Its size makes it suitable for a tree or large shrub. Another example is an attractive window-box of narrow proportions with a lead finish from an original of the same period. A King George II period tub, dated 1757, with high reliefs of a ship in full sail, shells, starfish and mermaids and a Queen Anne style urn, dated 1710, with griffon handles and cherubs reliefs, are other examples of originals reproduced in this series. The facsimiles are so good that it

A 'Chilstone' urn, a reproduction of a Regency design.

is virtually impossible to detect that they are made of fibreglass, except that they are very much lighter in weight than the lead originals. An attractive container of this kind can be bought for a reasonable price, some are very fine and the choice is wide enough to cater for most tastes.

Wood Elm, oak, teak and cedarwood are natural materials which are used by the manufacturers of many types of attractive container. They may take the form of square or long troughs, and several have been specially designed for indoor use. Sizes of troughs vary considerably. Some plant troughs can be purchased in 'do-it-yourself' kits, and are very easy to assemble. There are also matching sets of tubs and troughs, especially useful where these containers are to be used on a patio. For indoor use, containers should be as attractive as possible and many manufacturers have paid particular attention to finish. One range of Burma-teak tubs has tapered screw-in legs and a beautiful high gloss, tarnish-proof finish of three coats of a special lacquer.

Cement A particularly useful plant container range is manufactured from a mixture of asbestos and cement. This process results in containers which are extremely durable and not liable to damage by even the severest of frosts. They are a little heavy to handle but their other qualities more than make up for this. Some are made in very unusual shapes. They may have hour-glass-like outlines, others are similar to ice-cream cones. These new shapes add considerably to their attractiveness. They may be particularly useful as water containers for small fountain or waterfall effects. They can be used for plant displays indoors and for outdoor work; it is a simple matter to drill holes in their bases.

There is much to commend the use of concrete containers and there are several attractive designs available. Some specialist stone craftsmen produce quite ornate examples, some of which are very expensive. For the average small garden, the smaller designs should be selected. Tudor or Italian style vases which are about 50cm (20in) high and 40cm (16in) in diameter are quite suitable. For the larger garden and where an informal design is required, pieces such as a large fluted vase, or one in the manner of design developed in the Regency period, about 1m (3ft) high, would blend better with the more spacious surroundings. They can be obtained fairly easily.

Hand-made pots This type of pot for garden decoration is increasing in popularity and some very beautiful designs are available. Shapes and sizes are diverse. Some take the form of 'Ali-Baba' jars, others are quite squat with a diameter of some 45–60cm (18–24in) and a depth of 20–25cm (7–10in). For larger plants such as trees and shrubs there are much deeper designs. Several specialists in this type of wheel-thrown pottery will make pots to customer's special order or design. Among the choices available there are some very charming wall pots which have holes for fixing to walls. All these pots have ample drainage and, provided they are well crocked and filled with a good, well-drained or open compost, they are frost-proof.

Holders or supports For indoor use there are several types of metal pedestals which provide very attractive supports

for plant containers. The use of wrought iron for garden display work seems to be increasing in popularity too, especially for patios, paved areas, etc. These pedestals have a plant container or a platform top for alternative displays. In one or two designs the height is adjustable. Wall units and table pieces are also available, the latter are very useful as they are only about 20cm (8in) high and enable the flower arranger to produce small arrangements most effectively. Various wrought iron bases or stands are made for automatically watered pots and troughs and there is also a special wall support.

The metal stand supporting the plant

1 *An old wine barrel sawn in half makes two large plant containers. Holes must be drilled in the base for drainage purposes and plenty of brick rubble or other similar material put in the tubs to ensure sharp drainage.*
2 *Well-stocked plant tubs on a brick paved terrace.*
3 *A 'Chilstone' reproduction of a Regency basket plant container.*
4 *Old tubs, because of their depth, are ideal for such shrubs as hydrangeas.*
5 *Plant tubs such as this were once used for growing orange trees. They are fitted with lifting rings at the corners to enable them to be moved under cover before the first frosts.*

containers, which may be pots or a trough, sometimes takes the form of scroll-work, or it may consist of short or long legs, perhaps with a magazine or newspaper rack between or an encircling metal 'cage' for pot or trough or a hanging basket. Some of the scroll-work may be covered in white polythene, both to make it more attractive and weather-proof. Some fibreglass plant tubs are provided with a supporting metal tripod as an optional extra.

Hanging baskets An attractive way of displaying plants outdoors is by the use of hanging baskets. These are available in the form of simple wire baskets which, when lines with a piece of perforated plastic sheet or moss, hold soil and plants neatly. More modern wire baskets are coated with plastic. The usual sizes are 25cm (10in), 30cm (12in), 35cm (14in) and 40cm (16in) in diameter. A special half-basket for walls is available in sizes of 35cm (14in) and 40cm (16in).

Inventive ideas If you cannot afford to spend a great deal on ornamental vases

or urns, a wide range of other objects, not originally intended as plant containers, may be pressed into service. Old wine barrels are often obtainable from wine merchants or other sources and the barrels, when sawn in half carefully, make two excellent plant tubs. A number of holes should be drilled in the bottoms for drainage purposes. A poker is possibly the most useful tool for this purpose. It will be easy to drive holes through the wood when the tip is red hot. The tubs should be treated with a copper-based wood preservative before they are used.

Builders' yards can provide many unusual containers, particularly for the imaginative gardener. Old chimney-pots,

1 'Panniers' carried by this old statue are filled with ivies, making unusual containers for a corner of a town garden.
2 A modern container, made from pre-cast concrete, suitable for a large garden or a municipal garden.
3 A low container of classical design forms an excellent focal point here.

plain or decorated may often be picked up quite cheaply. They can easily be provided with concrete bases and allowance may be made for drainage holes by putting in wooden plugs before the concrete has set. These may be knocked out afterwards. Old domestic water tanks of various shapes and sizes make perfectly acceptable containers, particularly if they are painted on the outside and holes are knocked in their bases. Old wash coppers are not difficult to find. Many have rounded bases, which tend to make them a little unstable, but this can be overcome by beating the base more or less flat with a hammer or mallet. Drainage holes are easily provided. The range of sizes is quite considerable; some from old country houses may be 1m (3ft) in diameter and as much in depth. Exposed to the elements they take on a pleasant greenish-bronze patina. Some are made of cast-iron and this is more difficult to drill for drainage purposes, though it can be done. On no account try to knock holes in the base of a cast-iron wash 'copper',

as the material is brittle and you may ruin the container.

From the greengrocer, in spring, it is sometimes possible to obtain tall split-cane baskets in which new potatoes are imported. At best these must be considered as temporary containers, with a life of one or two seasons, although they will last a little longer if they are lined with polythene sheeting before they are filled with drainage material and soil.

Farm sales are worth attending by the gardener in search of less usual containers. It is often possible to pick up quite cheaply such things as feeding troughs, which make suitable long low containers. It does not matter if their bases are corroded; it merely makes it easier to provide the necessary drainage holes. A coat of paint helps to make them more acceptable in the garden. Disused hay-racks may also be found and, when fixed against a wall, as they were originally, make unusual features. Before they are filled with soil they should be lined with fine-mesh wire-netting or perforated plastic sheeting, both of which will retain the soil yet allow surplus water to escape freely.

The day of the heavy wooden wheelbarrow is almost over as modern barrows are made of metal or heavy-duty plastic. If you have an old wooden barrow or can obtain one, do not consign it to the bonfire, for after holes have been drilled in the bottom it makes an unusual and well-adapted container for all sorts of plants. You can either leave it in its natural state and treat it with a wood preservative, or paint it with a good quality lead paint, to give it a new lease of life.

It is occasionally possible to find examples of the large earthenware pots used for forcing rhubarb, when they were inverted over the crowns to exclude most of the light. These already have a hole in the 'base' (actually the top when they are used for forcing) and this will act as a drainage hole when they are used as plant containers.

There is practically no limit to what may be used for growing plants in. Old baths, including hip baths, have been used in town gardens, while it is not at all unusual to see, in country gardens, hollowed-out tree-stumps used as informal plant containers.

A point to remember, particularly as far as deep containers are concerned, is that ample provision should be made for drainage. To prevent the drainage holes from being blocked and to prevent worms and slugs from entering through them, it is wise to stand the containers on bricks or pieces of wood, so that their bases are clear of the ground.

Planting

Of all the operations that contribute to successful gardening, correct planting procedure is one of the most important. Digging a hole, pushing in the plant and hoping is not enough. Any gardener who does just this is doomed to constant disappointments.

Before the actual planting is carried out, careful preparation of the site is necessary, whether the project involved is an extensive border, the planting of a bedding scheme, or the tiniest pocket for an alpine plant. Beds, borders or planting holes should be deeply dug before planting. As far as beds and borders are concerned, full-scale trenching is best although nowadays, most busy gardeners settle for double-digging, or bastard trenching as it is sometimes called.

The surface soil must be broken down to a tilth of a fineness appropriate to the size of the specimens which are to be planted. Obviously, the ground for trees and shrubs will not require such careful preparation as it will for annual bedding plants or alpines.

As well as being thoroughly broken down, the soil should be in good heart. This means that it must contain enough humus and plant foods for the initial requirements of whatever is being planted. This can be achieved by digging in adequate quantities of humus-rich materials such as peat, leafmould, well-rotted garden compost, or animal manures.

These can be supplemented by a dressing of a slow-acting organic fertilizer such as bonemeal or steamed bone flour, forked into the topsoil a week or two in advance of planting or, where individual plantings are concerned, sprinkled into the holes.

Different kinds of plants will obviously need different planting procedures. The smaller they are, the more carefully should the operation be carried out. Appearances, however, can sometimes be deceptive. Nothing could look more delicate and vulnerable than a seedling that has just made its first pair of true leaves. And yet, at this stage—the best stage for planting out most seedlings—they can be surprisingly tough, perhaps because transplanting causes less damage to their rudimentary root system provided that they are transferred, without undue delay, from seed pans into boxes or nursery beds.

Seedlings should be handled gently, yet firmly, easing them carefully out of the seed compost and grasping them firmly by the leaves between thumb and forefinger as you plant them out in their new soil.

After this operation, particular attention should be paid to watering. Little and often is the rule to follow. Over-watering can cause damping-off, but seedlings should never be allowed to dry out completely; this can prove equally disastrous.

Planting alpines Rock plants and alpines seldom thrive in poorly-drained soils. Whether you plant them in a specially constructed rock garden or grow them in raised beds or on the flat, it is essential to take every precaution to ensure that moisture is never allowed to stagnate at the roots of the plants.

In a rock garden proper, alpines will go into pockets of soil between the outcropping rocks. This helps to promote good drainage but if ordinary garden soil has been used in the construction of the rock garden and if that soil happens to be on the heavy side, the actual planting positions will require something richer and more porous in texture. When planting alpines, therefore, the soil should be removed from the holes and replaced with a suitable compost. This could consist of 4 parts of loam, 2 parts of leafmould or peat and 1 part of sharp sand or fairly coarse grit. Sharp is the operative word where the sand is concerned. Yellow builders' sand is useless, sea sand is dangerous, since it contains salt. What is needed is silver sand or any other similar kind with a coarse granular texture. Animal manure is an undesirable ingredient of planting composts for alpines. Its inclusion will result in too much lush growth, will inhibit flower production and increase the risk of winter losses.

Firm planting is essential and in the restricted space of an alpine garden, a narrow-bladed trowel is a great advantage. The soil round the plants should be compressed with the finger-tips or knuckles. After planting alpines should be kept well supplied with water until their roots have secured a firm foothold, taking care, however, that they are not washed out of the ground. It is better to use a watering can with a fine rose.

Planting bulbs and corms An important point, when bulbs or corms are being planted, is a knowledge of the correct planting depths for the different groups and species. As far as the majority of spring bulbs are concerned, a good general rule is to plant with the tips of the bulbs about three times as deep as the bulbs are wide. When in doubt, it is better to plant deeply since most bulbs have a built-in mechanism that eventually raises them to their optimum planting depths.

Small numbers of bulbs are best planted individually, using a trowel or one of the special bulb-planting tools available. The latter are especially useful where daffodils or narcissi are being planted in grass. In the course of its operation the planting tool removes a small circle of turf that is easily replaced when the bulbs are in position.

Where bulbs such as tulips or hyacinths are being used in a bedding display, planting with a trowel or dibber is essential. It is only when you begin to plant in hundreds, or even in thousands, that a more labour-saving method is desirable. The best way is to take off the topsoil to the required depth, set the bulbs in position and then cover them with the topsoil that has been previously removed. To achieve a natural look when

planting in turf or the wild garden, handfuls of bulbs can be scattered at random and be planted where they fall. This is especially effective with daffodils which look completely wrong when they are regimented into straight lines.

Most of the lilies conform to the rule given above where depth of planting is concerned. The Madonna lily, *Lilium candidum*, is one exception. *Cardiocrinum (Lilium) giganteum* is another. The former should be planted with the nose of the bulb about 2.5cm (1in) below soil level, the latter with it just breaking the surface.

Planting annuals and bedding plants
It is important to success when planting annuals, to ensure that they receive as little check as possible; they will then start into active growth again almost immediately. Whether plants come out of boxes, pots or nursery beds, it is always better to wait for a day when the soil is moist (but not soggy) after rain and when the atmosphere is humid. In these conditions, the plants will lose little moisture through transpiration.

If planting out time should coincide with a long dry spell, the only course is to soak both plants and planting holes with water a few hours in advance. The water should be allowed to drain away

Planting a magnolia is a simple job.
1 The hole has been prepared with a good dressing of moist peat. The bush with its root-ball intact is lowered carefully into the hole. The stick laid across the hole is used as a guide to the correct planting depth.
2 Soil and peat are returned round and over the root-ball.
3 Firming the soil round the shrub.
4 Applying a final dressing of peat completes the job.

from the holes before the plants go in.

Bedding plants should never be out of the ground for any length of time. They can suffer a serious check if they are left lying in the sun or in drying winds. The ideal course is to get them straight from box to bed. This is a difficulty that does not arise with plants that are set out from pots.

When planting from seed boxes, the roots of each individual plant should, if possible, be carefully disentangled from those of its neighbours. This will minimize damage and enable the plants to get away again quickly.

Planting perennials With herbaceous plants one of the problems is not so much *how* to plant them as *when*. The vast majority of border plants are pretty

tough and perennials such as Michaelmas or Shasta daisies will quickly take root and establish themselves even if they are left lying on the soil surface. Most border plants, too, can be planted, weather and soil conditions permitting, at any time from September to March. But there is an important minority which, planted in autumn, seem unable to survive their first winter. Catmint (*Nepeta × faasenii*) is one of the classic examples of this characteristic, a characteristic that is shared by other grey and silver-leaved perennials. Reputable nurserymen will automatically defer delivery of this kind of plant until early spring.

The actual operation of planting perennials is simple and straightforward. Planting with the new season's dormant shoots a little way below soil level will be satisfactory for most of the better-known and more widely-grown border plants. Where established clumps are being divided up, it is the younger and more vigorous outside shoots that should be planted.

Herbaceous paeonies require very shallow planting; putting them in too deep is one of the main causes of delay in flowering and poor crops of bloom. The dormant eyes, which are easy to dis-

265

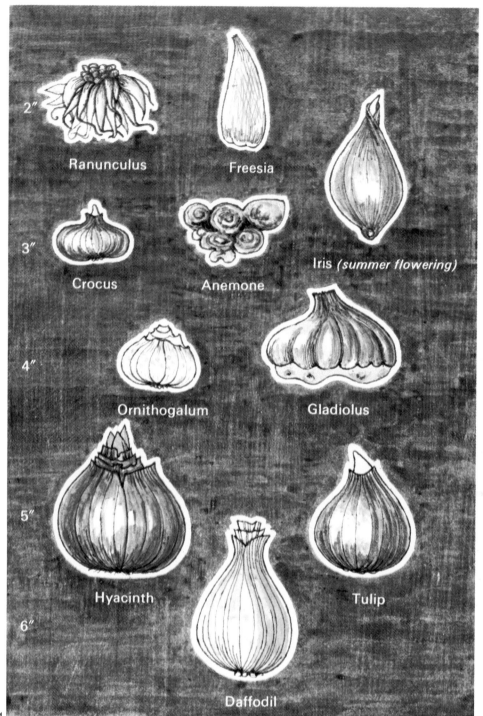

Ranunculus Freesia

Crocus Anemone Iris *(summer flowering)*

Ornithogalum Gladiolus

Hyacinth Daffodil Tulip

2"

3"

4"

5"

6"

1 For planting in restricted spaces, for example between stones in a dry wall, a narrow, two-pronged fork is a most useful tool.
2 For preparing holes for small plants, the best tool is the trowel. The use of a dibber is unwise, as the roots may get hung up in a pocket of air.
3 Firming after planting is important.
4 Bulb-planting chart.

tinguish, since they are crimson in colour, should not be more than 3cm (1in) below soil level.

Bearded irises are another group of border plants that require the shallowest of planting. Ideally the rhizomes should actually be resting on the soil with their upper surfaces above ground level, though on light soils, particularly, they may be planted so that the rhizomes are just covered with soil. This covering will gradually be washed away by rain, by which time their roots will have taken hold. They are rather tricky to plant and are easily disturbed by subsequent weeding or cultivating until the fleshy anchoring roots have had a chance to take hold. It is better to keep the hoe or fork well away from them during their first season and carry out any necessary weeding operations by hand.

Planting trees and shrubs When planting trees and shrubs strict adherence to right procedure becomes a matter of the greatest importance. If an annual plant, or even a perennial, is incorrectly planted, a year's growth only is lost, but trees and shrubs are long-term garden investments and any that get away to a bad start seldom attain full health and vigour. Careless planting, in fact, is probably responsible for more failures than pests, diseases and adverse weather conditions.

Planting holes should be both deep and extensive enough to contain the roots with room to spare. In heavy clay soils, it may be advisable to replace all or part of the earth taken from the planting hole with a mixture similar to the one already advocated for alpines. Alternatively, well-made and well-rotted garden compost can be used as replace-

ment soil. Newly-planted trees and shrubs always seem to get away particularly well when good garden compost is made use of in this manner. They seem to develop an extremely high resistance to disease.

With the exception of dwarf shrubs and small subjects such as heaths and lavender, which are easily planted with a trowel, planting trees and shrubs is essentially a two-man operation—one to hold the plant in position in the hole and jiggle it gently up and down, while the other carefully fills in the soil round its roots and firms it in. The nursery soil mark gives a clear indication of the correct planting depths and if 3–5cm (1–2in) of soil is allowed above this mark for subsequent settling, this will be satisfactory.

When plants arrive, as they often do, during or after periods of unsuitable planting weather, it may be several weeks before the soil returns to a suitable consistency for planting. Heavy clay soils, in fact, often remain in a sticky, unworkable condition for most of the winter.

Although the packing of plants for despatch has been revolutionized, so that they come to little or no harm if they remain in the packing material for several weeks, it is always better to get them into the ground immediately on arrival, unless a really hard frost or a heavy snowfall makes planting impossible. An ordinary winter frost that forms only a thin crust on the soil surface need not prevent the planting of trees or shrubs, unless they happen to be partially tender. It is possible to plant, however sticky the soil may be, if a reserve of good garden soil, fibrous loam or compost, or a mixture of old potting soil, compost and peat, is kept under cover for the purpose. It is only necessary to keep off the worst of the weather; if the reserve supply is slightly moist, so much the better. The wet, sticky soil is removed from the planting holes and the reserve mixture is used in its place.

Normally, newly planted shrubs will not require staking unless they are in very exposed situations where high winds can cause root disturbance. Heavy frosts, however, often lift the plants in their first winter and severe gales may rock them, causing holes round the base of the stems where moisture can stagnate. It is important, therefore, to make the rounds of newly-planted specimens at regular intervals and firm back any that show signs of displacement.

1 Small seedlings are delicate and may easily be damaged. Avoid handling them by the stem; hold them by the seed-leaf instead.
2 Seedlings and small plants may be firmed with the fingers or knuckles.
3 When planting it is important to take out a hole deep enough and wide enough to enable the root to be spread out.

Certain shrubs, such as rhododendrons and azaleas and most conifers come from the nursery with their roots 'balled', ie, surrounded with a ball of soil and tightly wrapped in hessian or polythene. After removing this covering, care must be taken not to disturb this root ball when planting. Rhododendrons and azaleas, incidentally, scarcely need 'planting' as such. They do best resting in holes filled almost to the top with peat or leafmould, and surrounded with more of the same material or with a lime-free compost.

With trees, stakes are essential. They must be stout enough to support the tree during its first few seasons. Ideally, they should be driven into the ground before the trees are planted, so that the fibrous roots can be spread round them. This, however, is not always practicable and the risk of root damage when stakes go in after planting is not great, provided a sharp-pointed stake is used. An alternative method uses two shorter stakes, one driven in vertically 60cm (2ft) away from the main stem, with another meeting it at an angle of 45 degrees. The main stem is secured to the diagonal cross-piece. This is a particularly effective way of staking half-standards, or of staking any tree in a windy situation.

When the tree is being secured to the stake, a tie of sufficient width must be used to avoid cutting into the stem. Narrow ties of string or twine are both useless and dangerous. They invariably get overlooked until it is too late and they have bitten into the cambium layer, with disastrous results. The best things to use are adjustable plastic or rubber ties. Failing these, strips of sacking or hessian make an effective substitute.

Developments in container-grown plants and garden-centre marketing have made it possible to plant trees and shrubs at almost any time of year. Large tins are favourite containers for plants grown in this manner. It will be necessary to slit the tins down on both sides, in order to simplify the removal of the contents without disturbance to the root ball.

Paper pots can be stripped away when the plant is actually in position and the contents of clay pots can usually be removed by up-ending the pot and gently tapping the edge on a wooden surface. If necessary break the pot rather than damage the root ball.

Pleached screens see Hedges

Plums see Fruit

Poisonous plants

More than 700 species of plants have been reported to cause illness or death. However, human deaths from eating poisonous plants recorded in Great Britain amount to only a small number

1 A planting board is a useful device, particularly when trees are being planted. The stem is held at the correct planting depth in the notch in the centre of the board. The board is held in place by the sticks in the end notches, thus enabling planting to be done by one person.
2 Planting a blackberry against a post. The hole has been made and the root-ball is about to be broken up so that the roots can be spread out.

each year. Campers and 'mushroom' collectors and others who eat plants they see growing wild are liable to be poisoned. This problem applies particularly in the United States and on the Continent. Children are particularly vulnerable; the United States public health service reports that 12,000 children every year eat potentially poisonous

plants. Children are the most susceptible group because of the attractiveness of the fruits of many plants; in particular those with red or black ripe berries. The resemblances of certain fruit pods to pea pods may deceive the unwary. If adults become affected, it is normally due to a plant or part of a plant, such as a root, having been eaten in mistake for the plant or part of a plant of an edible variety.

Most of the poisonous elements in plants are either alkaloidal or glycosidal in form; the remainder being volatile oils or resinous substances, all of which will affect the living cell when consumed. Not all these complex principles are harmful, a few are innocuous and many, consumed in a minute amount, are medicinal in action, only becoming toxic in large quantities.

Many factors influence the degree of poisoning that might occur should a plant be eaten. Factors dependent upon the nature of the plant include the quantity of the active principle present and its distribution within the plant—for example, on whether it is the berry or root. The habitat of the plant in question, the climate, the altitude at which it grows and the season during which it is gathered, may affect the proportion of the toxic principle, or principles, present. An acrid or pungent taste may act as a warning. The factors dependent upon the person eating the plant include his general health, age and any particular susceptibility to the poison; the degree of mastication and the rate of absorption of the poison consumed. Heating, drying or cooking may modify the effect.

Symptoms produced vary and there is generally no antidote. In suspected poisoning, medical or veterinary help should be sought immediately. Bearing in mind that prevention is better than cure, infants and small children should be kept away from colourful berries, mushrooms and house plants and taught that what birds and animals eat are not necessarily harmless to man. Parts of plants, such as seeds, bulbs, and corms should be labelled carefully when storing. These factors having been noted you can still enjoy growing these plants for their beauty and colour and it is not necessary to remove them from the garden altogether.

Pools see Water gardens

Potatoes see Vegetables

Potting

There are several important stages in the cultivation of a plant and one of these is the planting of plants in pots. This is known as potting. The move is dictated by the vigour of the plant, especially in its root system. Once it outgrows its original soil area in a pot it is necessary to provide more room for the root development and the plant has to be moved on or potted into a larger pot. If the plant is being raised from seed

Many plants, particularly those that grow wild in Britain can be poisonous to a greater or lesser degree, if eaten. Medical or veterinary help should be sought in the event of suspected poisoning from plants. Children ought to be made aware of the dangers of eating plant material, other than that normally served as food.
1 Seed of the yew, Taxus baccata.
2 Woody nightshade, or bitter sweet, Solanum dulcamara, has red berries.
3 Snowberry, Symphoricarpos albus.
4 The poisonous berries of Arum maculatum, the British native wild arum.
5 The thorn apple, Datura stramonium.
6 The seeds of laburnum are poisonous.

1

4

2

5

3

6

Poisonous Plants

Flowering Garden Plants

Scientific Name	Common Name	Poisonous Part(s)	Poisonous Constituent
Aconitum napellus	Monkshood	All, said by some authorities to be the most dangerous of all British plants	Alkaloids, which persist after drying
Colchicum autumnale	Autumn crocus, meadow saffron	All, particularly corms and seeds	Alkaloids, which withstand boiling, drying and storage
Convallaria majalis	Lily-of-the-valley	All	Cardiac glycosides
Delphinium ajacis and other species	Larkspur	Seeds and foliage	Alkaloids
Digitalis purpurea	Foxglove	All	Cardiac glycosides, not affected by drying and storage
Helleborus niger and other species	Christmas rose, black hellebore	All	Glycosides, not destroyed by drying or storage
Iris versicolor and other species	Iris, blue flag	Possibly all	Glycosides not destroyed by drying and storage
Lupinus species	Lupin	All, particularly seeds	Alkaloids, not destroyed by drying or storage
Narcissus species	Narcissus, daffodil, jonquil	Bulb	Toxic alkaloids, still to be identified
Podophyllum peltatum	American mandrake	All, especially green, unripe berries	Crude, resinous material

Vegetable Garden Plants

Scientific Name	Common Name	Poisonous Part(s)	Poisonous Constituent
Rheum rhaponticum	Rhubarb	Leaves (but not stalks, which are edible)	Soluble oxalates
Solanum tuberosum	Potato	Green sprouting tubers, stems and leaves	Glycoalkaloid

Ornamental Shrubs and Trees

Scientific Name	Common Name	Poisonous Part(s)	Poisonous Constituent
Cytisus (Sarothamnus) scoparius	Broom	Seeds	Alkaloids, but only present in small quantity
Daphne mezereum	Mezereon	All, particularly bark and berries	Resin and coumarin glycoside. Toxicity not destroyed by drying and storage
Laburnum anagyroides	Laburnum, golden rain	All, particularly bark and seeds. This tree causes the most cases of poisoning in Britain at the present time	Alkaloid
Prunus laurocerasus	Cherry laurel	All, particularly leaves and kernels of fruit	Cyanogenetic glycosides
Rhododendron species; Azalea and Kalmia species	Rhododendron, azalea, kalmia, American laurel, calico bush, sheep laurel, mountain laurel	Leaves and flowers	Glycoside
Taxus baccata	Yew	Leaves and seeds, the latter are deadly, the aril (red pulpy covering surrounding the seed) is the least harmful	Alkaloid, not destroyed by drying and storage

1 *Helleborus foetidus, the stinking helle-bore, is poisonous in all parts.*
2 *The seeds of Cytisus scoparius, the native broom, are poisonous.*
3 *The yellow flag, Iris pseudacorus, is frequently found in damp places.*
4 *Aconitum napellus, the monkshood, is poisonous in all its parts and can be dangerous if there are cuts on the hands when working with the plant.*
5 *Daphne laureola, a native plant.*

Poisonous Plants

Weeds and Hedgerow Plants

Scientific Name	Common Name	Poisonous Part(s)	Poisonous Constituent
Atropa belladonna	Deadly nightshade	All	Alkaloids, which withstand drying and boiling
Bryonia dioica	White bryony	Roots and berries	Glycoside
Chelidonium majus	Greater celandine	All, particularly roots	Alkaloids
Datura stramonium	Thorn-apple	Leaves, unripe capsules and especially the seeds	Alkaloids, not destroyed by drying or storage
Euonymus europaeus	Spindle	Bark, leaves and fruit	Still to be identified
Euphorbia species	Spurges	All	Volatile oil
Ligustrum vulgaris	Privet	Berries and possibly leaves	Glycoside
Ranunculus species	Buttercups and crowfoots	Sap	Protoanemonin, unstable to drying and storage
Solanum dulcamara	Woody nightshade, bittersweet	All	Glycoalkaloid
Solanum nigrum	Black nightshade, garden nightshade	All	Glycoalkaloid
Tamus communis	Black bryony	Roots and berries	Still to be identified

Woodland Plants

Scientific Name	Common Name	Poisonous Part(s)	Poisonous Constituent
Amanita muscaria	Fly agaric	All	Alkaloid and others
Amanita pantherina	Panther cap	All	Alkaloid and others
Amanita phalloides	Death cap	All	Deadly cyclopolypeptides
Arum maculatum	Cuckoo pint, lords and ladies, wild arum, etc.	All, particularly berries	Still to be identified but destroyed by drying and heating
Daphne laureola	Spurge laurel	All, particularly bark and berries	Resin and coumarin glycoside
Mercurialis species	Dog's mercury	All	Volatile oil which loses toxicity with age and is destroyed by drying and boiling
Quercus species	Oak	Acorns and leaves	Tannic acid and other constituents
Rhus toxicodendron	Poison ivy	All parts	Resinous

Swamp Plants

Scientific Name	Common Name	Poisonous Part(s)	Poisonous Constituent
Caltha palustris	Marsh marigold, kingcup	Sap	Protoanemonin, unstable to drying and storage
Cicuta virosa	Cowbane	Roots, leaves and flowers	Resinous, not destroyed by drying
Conium maculatum	Hemlock	All, especially young leaves or unripe fruits	Alkaloids, destroyed by drying and heating
Oenanthe crocata	Hemlock, water dropwort	All, especially roots	Resinous, not destroyed by drying

House Plants

Scientific Name	Common Name	Poisonous Part(s)	Poisonous Constituent
Dieffenbachia species	Dumb cane	All parts	Toxic protein and oxalate crystals
Euphorbia pulcherrima	Poinsettia	Juice of stem, leaves, flowers or fruit	Various in milky sap
Hyacinthus species and other bulbs	Hyacinth	Bulb	Still to be identified
Ricinus communis	Castor oil plant	Seeds	Phytotoxin
Viscum album	Mistletoe	Berries	Amines

1 The bright red poisonous berries of black bryony, Tamus communis, are conspicuous in the autumn.
2 The winter aconite, Eranthis hyemalis, is a poisonous plant with yellow flowers.
3 Cowbane, Cicuta virosa.
4 A young death cap fungus emerging from the ground. At this stage it should not be confused with the edible puff ball fungus.
5 The death cap, a poisonous fungus.

Fuchsias may be propagated by cuttings grown in pots.
1 By putting plenty of crocks in the bottom of the pot drainage is ensured and the plant is not waterlogged.
2 A vigorously growing plant should be repotted to make sure the roots have plenty of room to grow.
3 Firming round the edges of the pot is followed by plentiful watering.

or a cutting, it will be necessary to give it more root room eventually and the next move is into a small pot.

Although many plants will eventually be planted out into the ground, some will continue their growth and produce their foliage or flowering displays in pots. These must be large enough to provide adequate root room and feeding facilities. It will be appreciated, therefore, that the potting of plants is a progressive and logical sequence of events.

The time to pot plants must depend on what is being grown. Most of the general potting, however, takes place in the early part of each year—usually from February until late May.

Success with potting depends on the use of a suitable soil mixture. Fortunately one formula is all that is required as this contains all the essential ingredients in the correct proportions. This is the John Innes potting compost and it can be purchased, ready made up, from local garden shops.

Soilless composts are becoming increasingly popular with many gardeners. These are obtainable in various proprietary formulations.

Before potting begins it is important to make sure that all pots are thoroughly clean. Now that plastic pots have practically superseded clay ones, this is no problem. Drainage is important and clay pots will require small broken pieces of crock placed over the drainage holes, or special plastic mesh can be used for the plastic pots.

When the crocks are in place, a little coarse soil (the residue from the sieve is ideal) should be placed on top. This is followed by a small amount of the prepared John Innes potting compost or other mixture. To remove a pot plant for potting on into a pot of larger size, the pot and plant is turned upside down and the rim of the pot rapped smartly on the edge of the staging, bench or other suitable solid surface. If the fingers of one hand are kept over the soil and on either side of the plant's stem, the loosened soil bulk can be guided out of the pot.

The plant should then be placed on top of the soil in the new pot and more soil should be carefully trickled or poured in around the inside of the pot. Gentle firming is needed and this is done with the fingers, pressing evenly all round but a little way away from the plant's stem. A final sharp rap of the pot on the staging or bench will settle the soil even further, and any topping up with extra soil can be done afterwards. Make sure that the level of the soil is a little below the rim of the pot to allow for watering.

Where plants are being potted into pot sizes of 15cm (6in) and over, much firmer potting is required. This can be achieved with a short piece of blunt-ended stick. It is used as a rammer (not *too* hard) to compress the soil between the inside edge of the pot and the plant's soil ball.

Make sure that the potting soil is just moist. Under no circumstances should the mixture be dry when potting is started. It is a good plan to soak the soil several hours before it is required, and then to allow surplus moisture to drain away. If the potting compost is neither too wet nor too dry, a handful when picked up and squeezed firmly in the hand should retain its shape, but should then crumble when thrown back on the heap of prepared soil.

Once the plants have been potted, they should be given shady conditions to prevent drooping or flagging. Blinds or a little shading spray on the glass will help. Keep the plants watered regularly but apply sufficient only to keep the soil moist. As soon as the plants have established themselves and overcome the slight check to growth which is inevitable with potting, they can be placed in full light.

Predators
Garden pests have many enemies apart from gardeners. They must contend with smaller hunters of their own kind, apart from the parasites, fungi and viruses which beset them from time to time.

The predators catch and eat their victims. These hunters range from large creatures such as hedgehogs and birds, to extremely small insects and mites. A few of these creatures have been used in biological control, but it is not always as easy as it might appear to breed predators in sufficient numbers at the right time to control pests before severe damage is done. However, it has been done successfully in a few instances.

Perhaps the most familiar predators in our gardens are the ladybirds and their grey, torpedo-shaped larvae feeding on aphid colonies. The grubs of the yellow and black-striped hover flies feed on them too, as do also the sickle-jawed larvae of the lacewings. Fruit tree red spider mites are attacked by the anthocorids and the black-kneed capsid. The greenhouse red spider mite has a new enemy in the form of a bright orange mite from South America, *Phytosieulus reglei*, which has in recent years been tried as a predator in some commercial

greenhouses.

There are a number of general predators which may devour neutral or beneficial creatures as well as pests in the course of a day's hunting. Probably the best-known general predators are the long-legged carabid beetles and the sinister-looking devil's coach horse beetles. Some of the bigger water beetles are also vicious hunters and may occasionally tackle goldfish. Glow worms, unfortunately not very common these days, eat snails. Centipedes form another common group of predators.

Wasps may be seen carrying off great numbers of insects in the early part of the year and the hunting dragonfly is a familiar sight by the waterside. Spiders lay their traps and less conspicuous predators include the carnivorous testacella slugs, the red velvet mites, the larvae of certain gall midges and many

other small creatures.

Many people are reluctant to use chemicals in the garden for fear of harming predators. The effects may be minimized by using insecticides of short persistence and systemics where possible.

Pricking out
This is an important stage in the cultivation of plants which have been raised from seed. As soon as the young seedlings can be handled easily, they must be moved on into deeper boxes which will provide their roots with more room to develop. If the seedlings are left in their original boxes or seed-pans too long, they will become badly drawn or straggly and they will not grow into sturdy specimens.

The boxes for the pricking-out stage should be a little deeper than those used for the seed sowing. They should be

1

2

3

1 A female spider of species Aranea reaumuri, which feeds on other insects, most of which are plant pests.
2 The black and yellow striped hover fly, the grubs of which feed on colonies of aphids.
3 The carnivorous testacella slug is one of the less conspicuous predators.

Some of the most familiar predators which can be found in the garden.
1 The Southern Aeshna dragonfly.
2 The two-spot ladybird is a common garden species.
3 The male demoiselle dragonfly.
4 The toad is especially active in gardens near water, and helps to keep garden pools clear of insects.
5 The slow-worm.
6 The carabid beetle has long legs and moves quickly to catch its prey.
7 The centipede, a relatively fast-moving and beneficial garden inhabitant.

prepared in the same way by first placing some crocks over the drainage slits or, if plastic ones are used, these will not be necessary, and some of the coarser sievings should be placed over the base instead. The best compost to use is the John Innes seed sowing formula.

All boxes must be thoroughly clean before they are used. As the soil is placed in the boxes, it should be firmed gently with the fingers and, finally pressed flat and even with a piece of board. The finished surface should be about 12mm (½in) below the rim of the box.

The seedlings should be removed carefully from their seed box by levering them up with a light piece of plastic or wood. Roots must be disturbed as little as possible. Seedlings must be held by their seed leaves, never by the delicate stems otherwise they will be damaged. For tiny seedlings a forked piece of plastic or wood will be found to be the best device for handling.

The holes for the seedlings should be made large enough to accommodate their roots comfortably. A round-ended dibber is ideal for this work. Seedlings are best pricked out in rows, spacing each seedling about 5cm (2in) apart each way. As each box is completed, the soil should be given a light watering with a fine rose placed on the end of the can.

Keep the seedlings in a warm damp atmosphere for a day or two after pricking out has been completed. Shade them from strong sunshine otherwise the seedlings will wilt badly. Afterwards the boxes should be given normal conditions.

Propagation

Increasing plants is one of the most interesting and rewarding aspects of of gardening. Nature's usual method is by means of seed, but in many instances cultivated plants do not come true from seed, therefore to perpetuate particularly desirable plants, it may be necessary and quicker, to propagate vegetatively, that is by division, suckers, cuttings, layering (including aerial layering) and budding.

For details of propagation by seed see Seed sowing.

Division This is a simple method of increasing plants, particularly hardy perennials with fibrous roots, such as Michaelmas daisies, solidagos, heleniums, which should be done in autumn, when the plants are dormant, or in spring when just starting into growth. Established clumps are lifted with the aid of a fork and divided into several pieces—an old knife is useful for this purpose, although where the clumps are large and tough it may be necessary to use two border forks, plunging them into the clump back to back and then working them backwards and forwards until the clump falls to pieces. Old pieces of woody root should be discarded

and only vigorous well-rooted pieces retained. The same applies to certain shrubs including some of the berberis, spiraeas, pernettyas and others that produce a number of stems, rather than a single main growth. Rock garden plants, such as aubrietas, alpine phloxes, some of the campanulas and mimulus, may also be carefully divided and replanted.

The rhizomatous roots of the tall bearded, or flag irises should be lifted and divided soon after flowering; July being considered the best month for this work. Replant healthy, strong pieces only, and at the same time cut back the sword-like leaves to within about 15–20cm (6–8in) of the root. When replanting, the rhizome should be on the surface and not buried, making the roots firm in the soil.

Certain orchids, such as cymbidiums, cattleyas and miltonias may also be increased by careful division. This is a major operation in a plant's life and naturally some care and attention is necessary so far as watering and shading are concerned, until they have developed a good new root system to sustain themselves.

Suckers These are shoots of underground origin which may often be removed from the parent plant, with the aid of a sharp knife, complete with roots. This provides a ready means of increase; on the other hand certain plants, such as some poplars, plums, almonds and rhus (sumachs) are liable to send up suckers over quite a wide area which can prove a nuisance. The usual time to remove suckers for propagation purposes is in autumn or spring. Lilacs on their own roots may be increased in this way, also raspberry canes, pernettyas, bamboos, amelanchiers and some rose species, among others.

Cuttings There are various different types of cuttings which are widely used for propagation purposes. The parts of a plant used may consist of young, green stem-growths, semi-ripe wood, hardwood, single leaves, buds and roots. Stem cuttings may be taken about 7–

1 and 2 As soon as seedlings are big enough to handle they are pricked out. The seedlings are dropped into the prepared holes and the compost pressed into place around them, with the dibber. Cheshunt compound will prevent damping off.

10cm (3–4in) in length of half-ripe shoots in July or August of such plants as cistus, hydrangeas, hebes and the like. Some, such as those of camellias, may have a heel of the old wood attached ('heel' cuttings), though most cuttings are prepared by trimming them just below a node or joint ('nodal' cuttings) with a sharp knife or razor blade. The cuttings should be inserted to about a quarter of their depth in pots of moist sandy soil, or John Innes cutting compost, or a mixture of sand and peat, or in a sandy propagating bed in a cold frame. Such cuttings should be shaded from the direct sunlight and be lightly sprayed over with tepid water each morning until roots have formed. Any cuttings that show signs of damping off should be removed.

In the spring young shoots may be taken from the base of such plants as chrysanthemums and dahlias which have been brought into early growth in a warm greenhouse or frame. These are known as soft stem cuttings and after they have been prepared by trimming them cleanly below a node or joint and removing the lower leaves, they should be inserted to a quarter of their depth in moist, sandy soil in a propagating frame with a temperature of about 55°F (13°C). Delphiniums, lupins, heleniums and many other plants, such as the somewhat tender lemon-scented verbena (*Lippia citriodora*), may be treated in this manner. Cuttings of the more tender plants such as dahlias may be rooted more quickly if the propagating frame is supplied with bottom heat and a very moist atmosphere is maintained, by inserting the cuttings in pots of moist sand or other rooting mixture, and plunging the pots in moist peat in the frame, and spraying them

1

2

3

overhead each day. However, as far as the hardier plants, such as lupins and delphiniums are concerned, too much heat and too moist an atmosphere may easily result in the loss of cuttings through damping-off disease or other fungus diseases. Once such soft stem cuttings have rooted they should be potted singly, or in some instances they may be planted out in the open, provided they are not neglected. They should be protected from direct sunlight and drying winds while they are becoming established.

Hard-wood cuttings, sometimes referred to as naked cuttings, are taken in October or November, of pieces of trees, shrubs, gooseberries, currants, hedging plants, such as privet and lonicera, and various other plants. Climbing roses may also be increased in this manner, but the percentage of hybrid tea and floribunda roses that root is so poor that commercially it is not a practicable proposition. The cuttings are made from pieces of the current year's growth, about 25–30cm (9–12in) in length, pencil thick, with a clean cut made just below a bud eye. Remove all the leaves except a few at the top and insert the cuttings in sandy soil to a depth of about 10–15cm (4–5in), making the soil firm around the cuttings. Prepared cuttings of hedging plants, gooseberries, currants and other really hardy plants, may be inserted in sandy soil in the open, choosing a reasonably sheltered place in partial shade—beside a hedge is often a suitable spot for a row of such cuttings. Cuttings of more choice shrubs should be placed in sandy soil in a cold frame, or have cloches placed over them. Most of these hard-wood cuttings will have made roots

by the following spring, when they can be planted out or potted up and grown on for a while before they are planted out in their permanent positions.

Leaf cuttings Healthy, well-developed leaves of numerous plants provide a useful means of propagation. Those that root particularly easily by this means

include various begonias, such as *Begonia rex*, gloxinias, saintpaulias, streptocarpus, and some ferns, both tender and hardy. After removing a leaf from the parent plant make a few light incisions with a sharp knife across the veins on the underside and then lay the leaf on the surface of moist compost,

Division is the simplest method of vegetative propagation, particularly for fibrous-rooted plants like Michaelmas daises and heleniums.

1 After lifting and clearing the soil from around the roots, hardy perennials can be separated by hand.

2 Larger clumps that cannot be handled easily can be pulled apart by placing two forks back to back between the crowns, and levering the handles until the clump is broken up.

3 Removing the offsets of narcissi bulbs, is a method of division. The new bulbs can be grown on as individual plants.

4 The removal of back bulbs on cymbidiums is another form of division. The old soil is teased away from the roots with a stick.

5 The dead roots and fibre are cut away, to complete the cleaning.

6 The back bulbs are potted up separately as individual plants into mossy compost, and protected for a period to overcome the check.

7 The old bulb is also potted up in the same way and will make new growth.

consisting of peat and sharp sand. Peg the leaf down gently; hairpins are useful for this purpose. Leaf cuttings should be shaded from direct sunlight and have a reasonably warm and moist atmosphere. Begonia leaves, among others, will produce roots quite quickly, even when just placed in a saucer of water, but the difficulty is that the roots are so tender that potting on the young plantlets is quite a problem.

Camellias are frequently increased by means of leaf-bud cuttings, which are similar, except that the leaf is taken from the current year's growth, complete with a plump, dormant bud with a small piece of stem wood attached. Such leaves are inserted in sharp, moist sand in pots or in a propagating frame in March in gentle heat. With the aid of mist propagation it is possible to deal with much larger numbers of cuttings over a longer period and the percentage that root is usually greater.

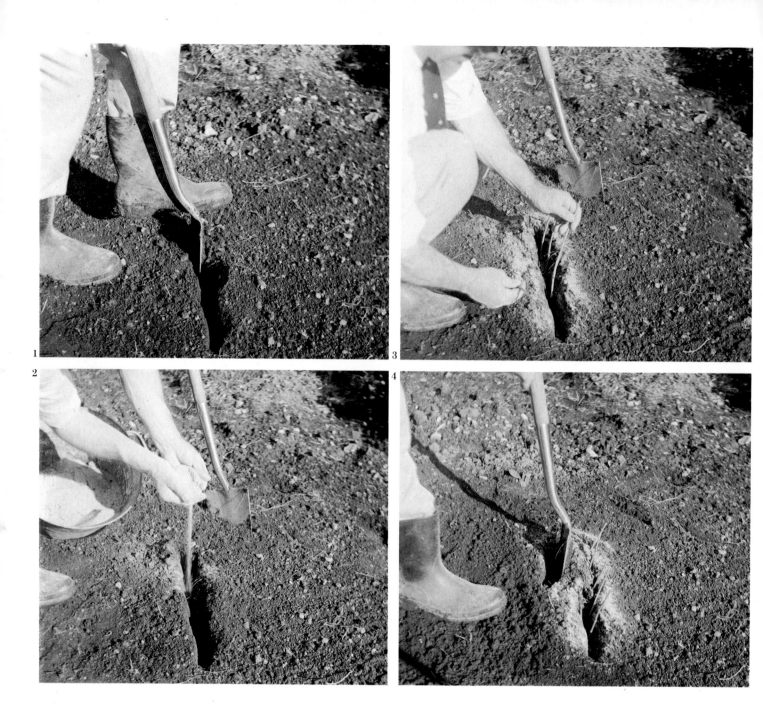

1

2

3

4

Rooting cuttings in polythene film An interesting way of rooting hard-wood or semi-hard-wood cuttings without inserting them in the normal rooting compost, is to use polythene film. The cuttings are prepared in the normal manner and a piece of film about 20–25cm (8–9in) wide and, say 45cm (1½ft) long, is placed on the propagating bench. On one half of this, along the length, is placed a layer of damp sphagnum moss. The cuttings are then placed on this (their bases may first be dipped in hormone rooting powder if desired) about 1–2cm (½–1in) apart, their tops projecting over the edge of the polythene strip. The lower half of the strip of film is then folded up over the moss and the cuttings. Then, starting at one end and working towards the other, the strip of film with the moss and cuttings is rolled up tightly and tied top and bottom with raffia or fillis. Roots should eventually

form and these will be visible through the clear polythene. When all or most of the cuttings have rooted the roll can be untied and the cuttings potted up or planted out, taking care not to break the brittle young roots.

The advantages of this method are that once the roll has been tied up no further watering is needed as moisture will not evaporate through the film (the roll should, however, be kept out of direct sunshine, on the greenhouse shelf or bench, or even on a window-sill), and that a number of cuttings can be rooted in a quite small space.

Hygiene When preparing cuttings, particularly soft stem cuttings which are liable to be attacked by soil-borne diseases or by virus diseases transmitted by insect vectors, it is advisable to take precautions against such attacks. Always use a clean razor blade or knife, if necessary sterilizing the blade in a

1 Hard-wood cuttings are taken during the autumn. A grip, or slit, is made in the cleared and firmed ground.
2 The cuttings are inserted and silver sand is trickled into the grip.
3 The cuttings can easily be started in rows.
4 The grip is closed and the earth firmed hard with the foot.
5 Leaf cuttings can be made of several plants, including streptocarpus. Slits are made in the leaf veins, and the leaf is pegged down onto sandy compost.
6 New plants appear at the incisions.
7 The new plants are seen here complete.
8 The new individual plant.
9 Leaf cuttings from a saintpaulia.
10 Use a small pot and sandy compost.
11 and 12 The cutting and new shoots.
13 and 14 Begonia rex leaves, if cut up and laid flat on sand, will root.
15 and 16 Trimmed sections of sansevieria leaves grow round the edge of a pot.

1   5   9

2   6   10

3   7   11

4   8   12

sterilant or disinfectant such as a weak solution of Jeyes Fluid. When a batch of cuttings of, say, dahlias or chrysanthemums is being prepared for rooting it is essential to ensure that they do not flag while they are waiting to be inserted in the compost. As soon as each cutting has been taken from the chrysanthemum stool or dahlia tuber, drop it in a container of aired water to which a few drops of Jeyes Fluid has been added.

Virus diseases may be transmitted by sucking pests such as aphids. For this reason, when quantities of cuttings are to be rooted, it is advisable to fumigate the greenhouse beforehand and also to spray stools and tubers with a suitable insecticide and to dip cuttings in an insecticidal solution before they are rooted. Trouble with damping-off diseases can be prevented by watering John Innes cutting compost with Cheshunt Compound. This is less necessary with pure sand or sand/peat mixtures as both these should be reasonably sterile.

Root cuttings These consist of pieces of root about 5cm (2in) in length taken from plants with fleshy roots, such as anchusas, oriental poppies, gypsophilas, verbascums, romneyas, seakale and horse-radish. This is an autumn or winter job, the roots being lifted and then cut into pieces of the required length. The cuttings are usually made from roots which are about the thickness of a pencil, though where seakale and horse-radish are concerned they are made from side-roots and may be thicker than this. When making the cuttings make a clean, flat cut across the top and make the base wedge-shaped, then there will be no problem as to which way up the cuttings are to be placed when they are rooted in deep boxes of sandy soil. The top of the cuttings should only be just below the surface and the pieces of root can be placed side-by-side,

Variegated plants are propagated vegetatively to keep their leaf colour.
1 A leaf-bud cutting is made in a variegated form of ficus by making sharp cuts between the nodes, and leaving a bud at the base.
2 A small section of stem is left.
3 Cuttings are potted up singly and a tray of compost is kept in readiness to provide material for firming.
4 Rubber bands hold the leaves together.
5 Taking a leaf and bud at the base to make a leaf-bud cutting of a camellia.
6 A single leaf-bud cutting.
7 The cutting potted up singly.
8 Mist propagation encourages quick rooting for propagating camellias.
9 Placing hard-wood cuttings on sphagnum moss for rooting in polythene.
10 The polythene is folded over.
11 It is then rolled over from one end to the other.
12 Rubber bands are used to make a neat parcel of the cuttings.

horizontally or vertically (wedge-shaped end downwards), and made firm in the soil. The boxes should be stood in a cold frame or cold greenhouse for the winter months, and may be stood in the open in the spring. When top growth is evident, which is usually by the spring, the cuttings should be planted or potted up separately. With plants, such as herbaceous phlox, *Primula denticulata*, or the little alpine *Morisia monantha*, which have much thinner, thread-like roots, these may be treated in the same manner except they are merely placed lying on the soil in boxes, or pots, and then lightly covered with sandy soil. The greenhouse, evergreen, flowering bouvardias may also be increased in this manner, but with these it is best to take the cuttings in spring and bring them along in gentle warmth.

Pipings The rooting of pipings is a method of propagation used primarily for members of the dianthus family, particularly carnations and pinks. Pipings are in effect a type of cutting, but instead of using a knife to make the cutting, the shoot is pulled out from the main stem. The tip of the leading shoot is held gently between the thumb and forefinger, just above the first node, and pulled until it slides out of the node where the first pair of leaves has formed. The main part of the stem should be held with the other hand. There is no need to prepare it in any further way, and the piping can be inserted in a sandy compost to root in the usual way. Pipings are usually taken in early summer from young non-flowering shoots.

Vine 'eyes' Pieces of dormant one-year vine rod, each with a plump bud, are cut into lengths of about 4cm (1½in), which are virtually stem cuttings. With the aid of a sharp knife remove a strip of wood 3mm (⅛in) thick from the wood behind the bud to encourage root formation. The pieces of rod are then pegged down individually into pots containing sandy soil and placed in a propagating frame with a bottom heat of 75°F (24°C) and kept moist. When roots have formed and top growth is evident the pieces should be potted separately and grown on under glass in a temperature of about 60°F (16°C).

Layering Numerous shrubs, such as rhododendrons, magnolias, syringas (lilacs), hardy heathers, as well as figs, loganberries and cultivated forms of blackberries, are readily increased by this means. With these plants the work is done in the autumn or during the dormant season, as with clematis, jasmine and honeysuckle. Border carnations and pinks, however, are layered in July, after they have flowered, and the layers will root in a matter of weeks in the warm soil. The more permanent shrubs may take six months or longer to develop sufficient roots for the layer to be severed from the parent plant. A

layer should consist of a long, healthy shoot that can be bent down to the ground where it is pegged down into moist soil to which peat and sharp sand have been added either in the open ground or into a pot filled with a similar compost. Before the layer is pegged down, or kept in place with a stone or brick, a cut should be made with a sharp knife on the underside of the stem, so that the stem is severed horizontally for about 3–5cm (1–2in), the cut being made so that it passes through a node or joint. This is the part which should be pegged into the soil. The object of making the cut is to check the flow of sap and the cut will then callus and roots develop at this point. The same object may be achieved with many shrubs by merely twisting the shoot, or bending it until it is partially broken, at the point where it is to be pegged into the soil. With such vigorous plants as the blackberry and loganberry all that is necessary is to peg down the tip of a stem and this will quickly make roots in moist soil. This is known as tip layering. With strawberries, the runners are pegged down in June and July. Roots are made quickly and the rooted layers can be severed from the parent plant in August and September and transplanted or potted.

Layers of clematis should not be made from the current year's growth, but from parts of the stem that are 18 months old or more. This also is done in the dormant season and the same method applies to the climbing honeysuckles (loniceras).

Aerial layering or air layering This method is useful with certain plants that cannot readily be layered in the soil because of their erect habit. It may be used with varying success with a wide range of plants, including camellias, prunus, liquidambars, tall rhododendrons which cannot be layered in the ordinary manner, conifers, and so on, as well as certain greenhouse plants, for example, *Ficus elastica*, the India-rubber plant, when it becomes leggy. The basic principles are the same as for ordinary layering, but as the branch cannot be bent to the ground, the ground must be taken to the branch. However, soil is not used, instead damp sphagnum moss is the rooting medium. Another difference is that a complete ring is cut around the shoot with a sharp knife about 23cm (9in) from the apex and then a generous handful of damp sphagnum moss is placed all around the wound, after any leaves on this part of the stem have been removed, but not those at the tip. The moss is kept in place with a piece of polythene; black polythene used in a double layer is best for this purpose. This is then carefully tied top and bottom to form a neat little bundle. Healthy young pencil-thick shoots of ripe wood of the previous year's growth should be chosen for air layering, not old, hard-wood. April is considered the

best month to do this work, but in a late season May or early June may prove satisfactory. When roots are to be seen in the moss, the layer should be severed from the parent and the young plant very carefully potted in an appropriate soil compost. This is tricky, for at this stage the roots are tender and easily broken, also the period during which the plants are making further roots into the soil compost can be a difficult one, so that they will require careful attention and nursing until they have become adjusted to their new conditions. Careful shading from direct sun and daily spraying with tepid water will assist them at this period, either in a cold frame or cold greenhouse. Certain greenhouse plants may be propagated in this way and these will require much warmer conditions when they are being grown on. The time for an air layer to make roots varies considerably with the type of plant, in some instances it may be many months, though the time may often be reduced by the use of a hormone rooting powder sprinkled round the cut on the stem before damp

1 Strawberry runners can sometimes be pushed into the ground.
2 Alternatively, they can be trimmed of excess leaves first.
3 Then pegged down into the soil so that roots will grow behind the bud.
4 Root cuttings are made of horse-radish during the winter, taking side roots and cutting them into short lengths. The pieces are trimmed with a flat cut across the top and a slanting cut at the base.
5 The cuttings are dibbled into open ground, a small distance apart.
6 Pulling the shoot out of a carnation stem to make a piping.

moss is placed round it.

Budding This is a method widely used by commercial growers, in particular of roses and fruit trees. By selecting closely related root stocks on which selected buds are inserted vigorous plants are obtained more quickly than if they are propagated by other means. Budding is done from June to about mid-August and showery weather is the most favourable, hot dry weather being avoided whenever possible. A plump bud

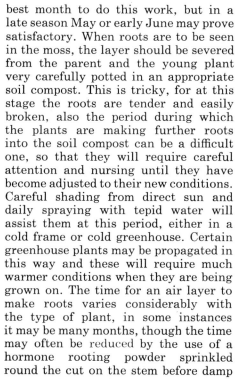

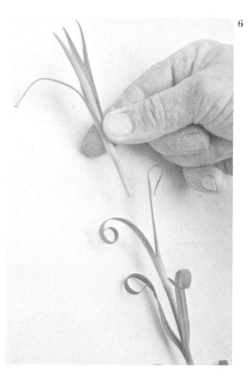

from the current year's growth is selected and carefully cut out with the aid of a sharp budding knife. Start the cut about 2.5cm (1in) above the bud and end it about 2.5cm (1in) below. The bud, complete with a thin sliver of wood beneath it can then be removed, with a piece of leaf-stalk which is helpful when handling the bud. This should be trimmed back later. Next a neat, T-shaped incision is made into the bark of the stock plant and with the aid of the handle of the budding knife the layer of bark is opened so that the bud may be inserted in the T-cut, pushing the bud as far down the vertical cut as possible. It is most important that the bud is not allowed to become dry before it is put in position. Finally bind the bud in position with raffia or adhesive tape. Bush roses are budded as near as possible to ground level, but standard roses and weeping standard prunus, and the like, are budded on stocks 2–2.3m (6–7ft) in height (2.3–2.5m [4–4½ft] for standard roses). If the bud turns brown and shrivels, this is evidence that the bud has not 'taken'; this is usually apparent within three weeks. Where the rose bud has taken it will be necessary the following February to cut off the growing top of the rootstock, above the point at which the bud was inserted, leaving about 2.5cm (1in) of the stem of the stock above the bud for protection.

Scales Plump scales, mainly from lily

Air layering of Ficus elastica.
1 The leaves at the top are tied together to keep them out of the way.
2 The leaves are removed on a section of stem below the growing shoots.
3 Either a slanting cut is made behind a bud, as shown, or a complete ring of bark can be removed around the shoot in preparation.
4 Damp sphagnum moss is the rooting medium used for air layering.
5 Moss is tied around the cut part of the stem.
6 The moss is covered and protected with plastic film.
7 The top leaves are released, and the work is completed.

bulbs, provide a useful means of increasing stock. These are best removed from the parent bulb soon after flowering, or in the autumn, and placed in boxes containing moist peat and sand. Small quantities can be put in polythene bags containing moist sphagnum moss where they will soon start to make roots. The bags should be hung in a cool, shady shed or garage. Careful potting will be necessary as the little roots are brittle and easily broken. Lilies increased in this manner will, of course, be true to colour and will not vary as will plants raised from seed. **Gladiolus cormlets** At the base of gladiolus corms, when they are lifted in the autumn, will be found numerous cormlets, known colloquially as 'spawn'. Where good varieties are concerned it may be worthwhile removing and storing these cormlets, putting them in trays of dry peat and storing them in a frost-free place for the winter. In March or April they should be planted out in well-drained beds to grow to flowering size which is usually reached in three years.

Hyacinth bulb propagation The two methods used by commercial growers to increase hyacinths are known as excavation and notching. Both give the same result, but the first method produces numerous small bulbs, while those on notched bulbs are larger in size but less numerous. With notched bulbs four or

1
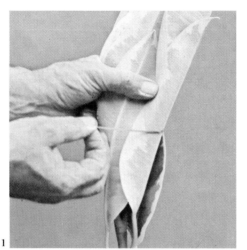

2

4

6
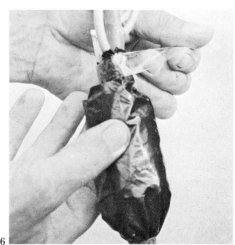

3

5

7

six cuts are made with a sharp knife across the base of the bulb, like the spokes of a wheel, to form a shallow V-shaped channel. The excavation method requires a careful scooping out of the base of the bulb to leave a conical incision. In both instances the base is then dusted with powdered chalk. The bulbs are then placed upside down in an airy room with a constant temperature of 68°F (20°C), and high humidity. This work is usually done in September and in about five weeks time bulbils will start to form on the base of the mother bulb. The temperature should then be raised to 75°F (24°C) and in November the bulbs, complete with bulbils, should be planted in shallow boxes of sharp sand, and protected from frost for the winter. In the spring the bulbils are removed from the mother bulbs and stored in a dry condition until early autumn, when they are planted up and grown on until they reach flowering size.

Mist Modern electrically controlled mist propagation units are fitted with jets that emit a fine mist spray to envelop cuttings with moisture in order to raise the relative humidity. This used to be done with the aid of a hand syringe but it is much more accurately carried out by the 'electronic leaf' which is placed among the cuttings. As soon as the 'leaf' becomes dry the spray is turned on for a predetermined period. Cuttings inserted in a sandy propagating bed heated by electric soil-warming cables will root more quickly than in a cold frame, and with a mist unit installed it is not necessary to shade cuttings, except during very hot, sunny weather.

Soft stem cuttings rooted under mist must be potted at an early stage and grown on in a greenhouse before being hardened off. Semi-hard-wood cuttings can be left in the mist for a longer period as they do not usually make so much top growth, and hard-wood cuttings can remain in the cutting bed until the spring, if necessary. Mist propagation is not the answer to all the problems of rooting cuttings, but it is particularly useful with large-leaved evergreens, such as camellias, and it has also proved successful with acers (maples), large-flowered clematis hybrids, various conifers, dahlias, daphnes,

1 When roses are budded, the T-shaped cut is made in the stock with a sharp budding knife close to the ground.
2 The bud is taken from the scion cutting carefully behind the bud. The pith is then removed from the cut section.
3 The bud is trimmed ready for inserting into the T-shaped cut.
4 The bud is slid into position and should fit closely.
5 The bud is bound with plastic film to hold it in place and exclude air.
6 The finished operation should be firm.

hibiscus, ilex (holly), magnolias, mahonias, pittosporums, pyracanthas, rhododendrons and azaleas, syringas (lilacs) and viburnums.

Rooting compounds Chemical substances, known as rooting hormones, are available both in liquid and powder form, and are useful for accelerating the rooting of cuttings that may otherwise prove difficult. They are not the answer to the rooting of all types of cuttings but when used according to the maker's instructions can prove to be a valuable aid. With the powder the cutting is prepared and then the base is dipped into the powder before being inserted in the rooting compost. When using the liquid formulations the prepared cuttings are stood in a container with 2–5cm (1–2in) of the liquid in the bottom for some hours before being inserted in the rooting compost.

The actual substances are used in minute quantities. For instance, one of them, naphthoxyacetic acid is used at the rates of between 2 parts and 25 parts per million. Three other substances, alpha-naphthalene-acetic acid, indolyl-butric acid and beta-indolyl-acetic acid, are used at rates ranging from 10–200 parts per million, depending on the type of cutting which is being rooted.

Protection

The gardener not only has to protect his garden plants from pests and diseases but also against unsuitable weather conditions. Methods to combat these troubles are suggested here. Many gardeners evolve methods which suit their own requirements.

For centuries the gardener has used glass to protect his less hardy plants and there is a wide choice of design in modern greenhouses, frames and cloches. Although an unheated greenhouse affords some protection against frost, some form of artificial heating is needed if the house is used for over-wintering tender specimens or for an early start with such summer crops as tomatoes and cucumbers. Frames heated by a pile of fermenting manure were once a feature of British gardening. Nowadays, soil-warming equipment is available for the same purpose. Cold frames and continuous cloches play a very important part in the kitchen garden. Both types of protection are used to over-winter young plants of such hardy plants as cabbage, lettuce and onions. During spring, frames and cloches protect seedlings and plants from cold as well as from heavy rain and icy winds. In summer, frame and cloche crops receive protection from the vagaries of the climate which may unexpectedly produce an August frost at night. Clear Polyglaze and other plastics are sub-

stitutes for glass but many modern gardeners continue to prefer the original material.

Protection against excess sunshine During the hotter part of the summer excessive sunshine and heat may lead to scorching of plants under glass. Lime wash or one of the proprietary shading compounds may be used. Alternatively, blinds may be fitted in the greenhouse or green Polyglaze sheeting pinned into position and removed as and when necessary. The cold frame may be covered with a few sheets of newspaper and a piece of old lace curtaining provides adequate temporary shade for cloched crops. Adequate ventilation is also of great importance during the summer months and, unless you are at home all day, it is far better to prop up the frame light and to leave the greenhouse door ajar than to leave both closed on a dull morning and, on your return in the evening, to find the plants suffering from scorch or heat exhaustion.

Protection against cold Seedlings and young plants in the cold frame or under cloches are liable to suffer from late spring frost. When a frost is anticipated,

mats or sacking should be laid over cold frames and cloches at evening and removed in the morning. During late spring all cloches may be in use and none is available for sowings of half-hardy vegetables. Jam jars and preserving jars may be brought into use as miniature cloches. The seeds are sown where the plants are to grow and a jar set over each seed station. The jars not only give protection to the seedlings but may be left over the plants until they need more room. Half-hardy plants, raised in the cold frame or purchased from shops, may have to be set out in their growing positions when there is still risk of late spring frost. Protection against night frost damage may be provided by covering each plant with a paper cap. The caps need be no more than pieces of newspaper twisted to the shape of a dunce's cap. Set the caps in position in the late evening and remove them in the morning. Weigh the edge of the paper down with a few stones to prevent them from being blown away by wind. Some perennials need a little protection against severe winter cold. After cutting off the foliage to soil level in the late autumn, place a piece of

Mist propagation provides the right conditions of humidity and bottom heat, to encourage and hasten rooting.

wire mesh netting, bent to form a low tent, over each plant. Cover the 'tents' with a thick layer of straw or bracken. Retain the straw in position by covering it with another piece of wire netting. The lower piece of netting prevents the straw from being pressed on to the crowns of the plants, which may cause them to rot.

Protection against wind Living windbreaks are suitable in some areas and the blackberry is a good plant for this purpose. Plastic screens, made by nailing polythene sheeting to a light wooden framework, give temporary protection from wind around newly-planted shrubs and trees. Wattle hurdles, hessian sacking nailed to strong posts or even branches of evergreen shrubs afford similar temporary protection.

Lath houses A framework of thin wooden laths can provide protection for plants placed underneath it. The protection it affords can be from strong sunlight, wind and, to a certain extent, frost. Such protection is ideal for producing a cool, airy standing ground for many plants. Usually the framework consists of a span roof supported at the sides by upright posts spaced at not less than 2m (6ft) intervals. A simpler version can be constructed with a single pitch or span. This usually has a slight slope to one side. The laths used should be thoroughly treated with a horticultural grade of preservative or rot-resistant timber can be used, such as cedarwood. The laths are about 3cm (1½in) wide and 1cm (½in) thick. They are spaced about 2.5cm (1in) apart.

Another form of protection is the use of frame lights supported on a simple

1 Crops sometimes need to be protected from being spoiled by birds and animals, and it is better to take precautions than have damage like this—the result of an attack by wood pigeons.
2 Cabbages netted against pigeons.
3 A garden pool covered with netting to protect the goldfish from herons.
4 Netting will prevent rabbit attack.

wooden framework. The height of this framework will depend on the crop which it is to protect. It can be as high as 1.3–1.6m (4–5ft) if plants such as chrysanthemums are being covered. A span roof or a single sloping span should be provided. The main supporting rails should be selected from a minimum timber thickness of 5 × 5cm (2 × 2in). If planks are available, 16 × 2cm (16 × ¾in) will be ideal. The main rails should be nailed or screwed to uprights spaced not more than 2m (6ft) apart along the rows. The timber for these must be at least 5 × 7cm (2 × 3in) with 46cm (18in) in the ground.

Additional protection can be afforded with the frame light technique if the sides are covered in with hessian which can be tacked to the supporting rails and the uprights. A miniature greenhouse can be made in this way.

Pruning ornamentals

Ornamental shrubs and trees by no means all require pruning; certainly not regularly. A number profit from it, however, even though they may survive without it. Pruning ornamentals is simply a matter of assisting them to appear at their best.

Whether to prune or not to prune depends to a great extent on the nature, performance and growth characteristics of individual species and specimens. The subject is not difficult to understand.

Pruning before flowering Many shrubs flower during the second half of summer and after. These should be pruned early to allow time enough for the production of the maximum amount of new growth which should bear flowers of the best

1 Dry straw packed round a tender plant, and a light to prevent rain from soaking into the crown, will generally ensure that the plant survives.
2 The old leaves of Gunnera manicata are laid over plants during the winter to protect the crowns.
3 Cherry trees can be protected in a 'cage' to prevent haphazard pollination.
4 By protecting narcissi with cloches a clean crop is grown for cut flowers.

quality. However, not all shrubs which flower late need pruning—hibiscus, for example.

Among those shrubs that flower in late summer are *Buddleia davidii*, hypericums, deciduous ceanothus, *Spiraea × bumalda*, perovskias, *Ceratostigma willmottianum*, *Leycesteria formosa*, *Hydrangea paniculata grandiflora*, hardy fuchsias, and *Potentilla fruticosa* in its many varieties.

The buddleia, perovskia and ceratostigma should be cut hard back in spring, to encourage as much new growth as possible (in any case, buddleias will become large and ungainly if left alone, even though they will survive). Treat deciduous ceanothus and the taller hypericums in this way, too, if necessary though they do not demand it. Leycesteria may be required to grow very tall; if it is cut back in spring, it will do so. *Hydrangea paniculata grandiflora* will grow particularly vigorously and flower profusely if cut hard back in spring.

Spiraea × bumalda will soon make a probably undesirable thicket if it is not relieved of some of its older wood and its young growths shortened in March.

1

4

2

5

6

3

7

1 *Fibre mats are rolled over frame lights to keep out frost.*

2 *The outer leaves of cauliflowers are folded over to protect the curd.*

3 *Alpines and some herbaceous perennials need to be protected from rain in winter, and frequently a pane of glass is sufficient to divert the rain from the crown of the plant.*

4 *Tender climbers can be protected with a 'cage' of polythene.*

5 *A temporary cover is used to protect opuntia, the prickly pear, in winter.*

6 *Matting needs to be held down against the wind, over a small frame.*

7 *Straw placed between two layers of wire netting gives winter protection for tender plants grown against a wall.*

And, while *Potentilla fruticosa* rarely requires much attention, March is also the time for any pruning that may be needed. Hardy fuchsias—*F. magellanica riccartonii*, for example—when cut back in spring, thrust up strong new growth to bear fine flowers in late summer. The old stems, tied together at their tops, as the year wanes, will give some protection to the crowns against winter weather. Left unpruned, fuchsias flower a little sooner, but in time can attain somewhat unmanageable proportions.

Pruning after flowering Early-flowering shrubs on the whole require to be pruned after they have flowered. This allows new flowering wood a chance to arise and mature in readiness for another year's display. It also allows existing unflowered wood scope for full development, so that it may also flower, probably the following year. The point is that many shrubs flower on one-year-old and older wood. Sufficient of this must be promoted and encouraged to ensure regular and worthwhile crops of flowers.

The growths to cut away are, conveniently enough, those that have just flowered. This, basically, makes much of the pruning of this kind of shrub self-explanatory.

Forsythia is a good example of an early-flowering shrub calling for pruning after it has bloomed. If the job is done before the leaves have fully developed, flowered wood is more easily seen and removed and the risk of severing the growths that will flower the following year is reduced. Forsythia is a shrub which is better for minimal pruning, otherwise it may well throw up much non-flowering, leafy growth. Removal of spent growth, only, therefore suits it very well as a general rule.

Kerria japonica flowers on the early side and the flowered growth is best cut away when the blooms have faded. *Spiraea arguta* and *S. thunbergii* repay similar attention. Philadelphus, or mock orange, flowers in early summer, so does weigela or diervilla. These shrubs also need pruning after they have finished flowering. They soon make unproductive thickets if the older growths are not cut away. Kept clear of spent wood, they will remain in good form, producing ample new growth which will flower when it ripens.

Syringas (lilacs) require the removal of spent flowerheads when at last the petals have all browned and shrivelled. The buds below the flowerheads should not be damaged; new flowering growth will be produced from these. Thin, twiggy growth, can be cut away at the same time. Brooms (cytisus), too, respond by producing new growth if they have their old shoots with developing seedpods removed. This pruning helps to ensure that there need be little or no cutting back into old wood as the plants mature, because brooms respond poorly to this.

It should also be remembered that there are plenty of shrubs which do not require any pruning at all, even though they flower in the spring and summer period. The viburnums, which flower in spring and summer are examples. The winter-flowering species and hybrids also need little attention.

A number of evergreens flower during the first half of the year. *Berberis stenophylla* is one, well-known for its sprays of golden-orange flowers and as an excellent hedging shrub. *Berberis darwinii*, with miniature holly-like leaves, produces its orange flowers in April and May. This, too, makes a good specimen shrub and hedging plant. Both these evergreens may be pruned after they have flowered, though when they are grown as individual specimens, such attention is not essential. Indeed, left unpruned, full pleasure can be taken from their annual crop of handsome dark fruits. When they are used for hedging purposes, however, the need for control does arise.

No pruning needed *Mahonia aquifolium* and *Mahonia japonica* are two very showy, early-flowering evergreens which need no pruning at all. Nor does the evergreen *Garrya elliptica*, whose silver catkins are so handsome during February, although it is better for removal of its dead catkins. If necessary, light trimming is permissible in May. However, those familiar with garrya's excellence for indoor decoration may have trimmed away some of the growth while its catkins were at their best.

Deciduous, winter-flowering shrubs such as daphne, chimonanthus and hamamelis, call for no pruning, though chimonanthus when grown against a wall will. Laterals will require to be shortened after flowering is over.

Evergreen escallonias, flowering in summer, need no regular pruning; any which may become necessary should be done when flowering is over. Evergreen ceanothus, with the exception of those that flower late, come in the same category, particularly when they are grown on walls.

Magnolias, in general, evergreen or deciduous, need no pruning. As far as *Hydrangea macrophylla* varieties (the mophead hydrangeas) are concerned, congested old wood and spindly shoots should be cut away in spring, though regular pruning is unnecessary. Faded flowerheads should be allowed to remain on the plants during the winter in order to afford some protection to the young growth buds. Cut the dead heads away in spring.

The general run of relatively non-

1 Perovskia atriplicifolia is one of the shrubby plants that benefit from being cut hard back before flowering.
2 Perovskia atriplicifolia 'Blue Spire' having been pruned will throw up good flowering shoots in the summer.

flowering evergreens, including conifers, grow away very satisfactorily without the need for pruning, but should it become necessary to reduce their height, this should be done in early May. Where such evergreens are used as hedges, light clipping from early to late summer may be done; conifers, however, should be trimmed in early May or August. Rhododendrons need not be pruned unless in time they become straggly. The fairly hard cutting back likely to be necessary under such circumstances should be done in April or May. This will result in the loss of blossom for a season or two, but recovery will follow. If it is practicable the seed pods of rhododendrons should be removed after the flowers have fallen, breaking them away carefully in order not to damage the buds behind them.

Trimming and pinching Lavender, santolina and the evergreen greyish-leaved senecios, do not require pruning so much as being kept in good shape. To this end lavender and santolina should have spent flower-stems removed after the flowers have faded and then receive a mere trim over in spring in order to keep them compact. If this is not done, lavenders in particular will straggle, making it difficult to restore the bushes to good condition. Avoid cutting back into old wood.

The removal of awkwardly placed branches in spring, will assist *Senecio laxifolius*, for example, to maintain a good shape. Mere pinching of soft growth tips during summer is an easy means of eliminating wayward shoots and encouraging bushiness. Hebes respond well to April pruning, should they need to be brought back under control. Pruning at this time is often necessary, in any case, to remove frost-damaged shoots. Summer trimming keeps these shrubs compact.

Heathers (ericas and callunas) will thrive very well, left quite naturally, unpruned. On the other hand, those that flower in summer can be trimmed over in spring; the winter and spring-flowering kinds may be attended to after the flowers have faded. It must be emphasized that such pruning is not essential, even though it tends to improve appearances and may be convenient in individual cases.

Pruning for bark effects A number of shrubs and trees bear particularly

1 Forsythia is an example of an early-flowering shrub that is pruned after it has flowered in early spring.
2 The stems that have flowered of Forsythia suspensa are cut hard back.
3 The branches of the shrub after the pruning has been completed.
4 Ribes sanguineum, the flowering currant, is pruned after flowering.
5 Old flowered wood is cut hard back.
6 The shrub, when pruning has been completed, looks like this.

1 The gracefully arching Berberis ×
stenophylla needs no pruning.
2 The deciduous Daphne × burkwoodii
also does not need pruning.
3 Some plants do not require pruning at
all, notably evergreens. With shrubs such
as rhododendrons the old flowerheads
need to be removed.
4 The old flowerheads of ericas are cut
back with shears.

brilliant bark if they are encouraged to
throw up plenty of new wood. Examples
are certain dogwoods such as *Cornus
alba sibirica*—vividly red—and willows
such as *Salix vitellina britzensis*—glowing orange. Hard spring pruning is
necessary to induce these to produce the
maximum amount of young wood with
the brightest bark. *Rubus giraldianus* is
one of the showiest of the brambles with
'whitewashed' stems. The strongest and
most spectacular canes arise from
healthy plants which have been cut back
annually after flowering.

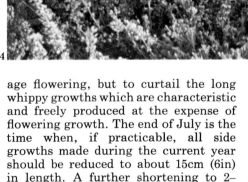

Wall shrubs and climbers Many shrubs
lend themselves to being trained against
walls, as well as making good free-
standing specimens. Examples include
Cotoneaster lactea and pyracanthas, both
evergreen, grown for their colourful
autumn and winter fruits. Prune these
lightly during summer, in order to
encourage them to grow as required.

Chaenomeles (cydonia, japonica or
flowering quince) is a deciduous shrub
which responds well to wall culture. It
needs to be spurred back when grown
in this way. Cut away laterals after
flowering, and then pinch out the tips of
resultant young growths during summer. Alternatively, leave the plant unpruned until early autumn, then shorten
the lateral shoots well back. Keep
forward-pointing growths (breastwood)
cut back or pinched back as they
develop.

Wisteria is a climber which requires
to be spurred back, not only to encour-

age flowering, but to curtail the long
whippy growths which are characteristic
and freely produced at the expense of
flowering growth. The end of July is the
time when, if practicable, all side
growths made during the current year
should be reduced to about 15cm (6in)
in length. A further shortening to 2–
5cm (1–2in) may take place in November.

Hydrangea petiolaris, an excellent
climber for north walls, conveniently
requires no pruning at all. The hederas,
or ivies, also self-clinging, can strictly
speaking, be left alone too. But clipping
them over in spring will keep them tidy
and encourage the production of fresh
young growth. The summer-flowering
fragrant white *Jasminum officinale*,
needs no pruning either, though it may
be thinned in spring, if necessary. Old,
neglected plants may need more drastic
treatment. Thin the growths of winter
jasmine after flowering, if necessary.
Honeysuckle can be left alone, but thin

in spring, if necessary, too.

Clematis pruning is straightforward
enough if given a little thought and if
basic facts about the genus are noted.

The small-flowered species can be left
alone, though if the late flowering kinds
among them grow too vigorously, hard
pruning in February will correct
matters. After flowering is the time to
attend to the early flowering kinds,
should they become a little out of hand.

Splitting the large-flowered varieties
into their groups: varieties belonging to
the *jackmanii* and *viticella* groups
require hard cutting back to the lowest
pair of healthy buds on each stem, every
February, just as the buds begin to show
green. Flowers are prolific on their new
growth of the current year. Clematis in
the *florida*, *lanuginosa* and *patens*
groups need no pruning at all to all
intents and purposes, after the initial
cutting back in February after planting.
The may, however, need a little pruning

in February, where growth definitely appears dead. And should growth ever become beyond control, then they should be cut back hard in February.

Ornamental trees For all practical purposes, ornamental trees call for no regular pruning at all. Dead, diseased or unwanted wood may arise from time to time, however, and this will have to be removed as with shrubs. Deciduous trees, in the main, should be pruned during the dormant season, avoiding periods of hard frost. But flowering cherries and plums should, wherever possible, receive any necessary pruning after flowering, in order to avoid any problems with gumming and possible infection from silver leaf disease.

Flowering, ornamental trees may at times produce too much growth and leaf at the expense of blossom. This may be due to incorrect feeding, but if the problem is not solved by a change of feed then root-pruning may provide the answer. This involves digging a trench in winter halfway round the tree—about 1m (3ft) from the trunk—severing the main roots, and refilling the trench. The circle should be completed the following winter. It is not often necessary to resort to this method in as far as ornamentals are concerned.

Conifers grown as specimens do not need pruning, but any remedial treatment or absolutely necessary cutting back should be done in early May.

1 Wisteria is a climber which must be spurred back to encourage the production of flowering shoots.
2 After pruning, shrubs grown against a wall are tied in to supports.

General winter pruning This pruning, in general, should aim at keeping shrubs and trees in reasonable shape, keeping branch systems simple and open, and where appropriate, aiming at producing an adequate supply of young healthy wood. During the dormant period, however, most deciduous specimens may need major overhaul, particularly if they have been neglected. Some shrubs are best pruned in winter, when pruning becomes necessary, deciduous berberis, for example. Deciduous cotoneasters can also be brought back under control, where such action is called for, in wintertime, preferably in February.

Pruning principles Cuts should be clean and made back to a joint or growing point, or flush to a main stem, so as to leave no snags and stumps. Failure to do this will almost certainly lead to dead snags. With no developing bud to draw up sap, the wood dries and dies. Shrubs to be cut down should be cut right down.

Before making cuts, particularly those that are a little awkward, it pays to decide sensibly the best direction for saw or secateurs, for example. Snags and stumps are very much more likely to arise where there has been crude and

hasty cutting. Neither is necessary. Undercut large branches before making main cuts. They will fall cleanly, without stripping the bark.

Pruning must always be purposeful, directed towards maintaining uncluttered and healthy specimens; bearing in mind, of course, that some specimens are twiggy by nature. Pruning should not be mere snipping. It should be borne in mind that many shrubs and trees (as indicated above) thrive well enough if they are left entirely alone. Pruning just for the sake of it is a very unsound practice.

You should never attempt to reduce a specimen to a convenient shape, unless it is a hedging plant. Proper balance and natural appearance are paramount. And, while by skilful pruning larger-growing specimens may be kept within bounds in confined spaces, it is nearly always better to have chosen, in the first place, shrubs or trees of suitable proportions.

All pruning is a matter of doing what is obviously best for individual shrubs and trees, according to their natural habit.

Tools for the job Light to medium pruning may be done easily enough with secateurs. There are many different makes. It may be wise to have two pairs, one for lighter work and the other for heavier tasks. It is important to choose a pair which you can use comfortably. There are different styles, sizes and

weights, and if work is to be done skilfully and easily, secateurs must fit the hand properly and be used without tedium and strain.

Cuts should always be made in the same plane as the secateur blades. Twisting will result in mangling cuts and straining the tool. Making sloping cuts for the purpose of shedding rain is wise, but cuts must still be made in the same plane as the secateur blades. Cuts should not, of course, be so sloping as to slice wood away from behind a bud or growing point, thus allowing it to dry out.

Secateurs as opposed to shears, should be used for pruning or shaping certain hedges, where practicable. Examples include the larger-foliaged chamaecyparis varieties and the thujas. Cherry laurels and other large-leaved evergreens should be pruned rather than clipped, otherwise the cut leaves will turn brown and die, and look unsightly.

There are several powered trimmers, driven from the electric mains, portable generators, petrol engines, batteries, by flexible drive, and by power take-off units from motor mowers or cultivators.

Loppers, both short-arm and long, are useful. Short-arm loppers or pruners enable tougher cuts to be made with efficiency and speed where it is impracticable to use secateurs. Both anvil-cut and scissor-action kinds are available. Blades are short and very strong. Long-arm loppers, their blades operated by long arms, a form of remote control, enable distant and more inaccessible cuts to be made.

There is a fair range of pruning saws, both single-sided and double-sided. Especially useful is the Grecian pruning saw, short-handled or long. It is curved and pointed and cuts on the back-stroke, making awkward cuts very easy.

Pruning knives were once widely used, but have largely been superseded by secateurs for general pruning. Some craftsmen, however, still use them, particularly in nurseries. They are still useful to have on hand for general purposes, and are still the best instrument for the all-important job of paring smooth the edges of large pruning cuts, especially those made by the saw. They should be used carefully; cuts are best made away from the user.

For the sake of efficiency and safety all pruning tools should be kept in good working order, sharp, clean and well-oiled.

White lead paint, bitumastic paint and proprietary tree-healing compounds should be used for sealing large cuts, to ensure that they heal rapidly.

1 One of the main aims of pruning is to control the shape of the branches. An ornamental vine spurred back for training over an archway.
2 Golden elder, Sambucus nigra aurea, is cut hard back to ensure good leaves.

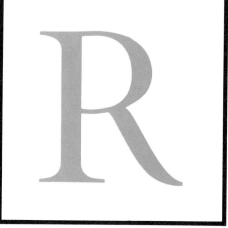

1 Treat large pruning cuts with a lead-based paint or a proprietary compound.
2 Use sharp secateurs and cut just above the buds to avoid damage. Secateurs should be sharpened regularly and well-oiled, as with all your pruning equipment. A bad cut could be the result of blunt, tacky tools.
3 A thin-bladed pad saw is useful for thinning overcrowded basal shoots.
4 A long-handled pruner can be used for shaping taller trees, such as the chamaecyparis varieties.
5 A hand saw cuts awkward shoots.

Radishes see Vegetables

Rakes see Tools

Raspberries see Fruit

Rhubarb see Vegetables

Rock garden

Although it is not essential to build a rock garden in order to grow alpine plants, whose needs can, if necessary, be provided in a number of other ways, it is obviously a pleasant and desirable feature to add to any garden in which there is a suitable position, and alpines look all the better for being seen in an appropriate context.

The day of the massive rock garden, consisting of a large amount of very large rocks, composed by experts into an imitation mountain-scape is gone. Gardens are small, and gardening is an intimate, do-it-yourself pastime. In the past the stones were often regarded as more important than the plants. This led to the death of many hundreds of good plants in attempting to grow them in situations which, illogically enough, were quite unsuitable.

Examples still exist of rock gardens—or 'rockeries'—which were obviously the result of failure to do anything else in that particular place. Heaps of stones, assembled in ugly corners, beneath trees or in places where nothing would grow well were hopefully expected to solve a problem but in the event proved to be nothing more than eyesores. It is curious that so many gardeners have been prepared to believe that alpine plants are difficult to grow, and yet expected them to flourish in totally unsuitable conditions.

With the exception of a minority of temperamental species, alpines are not difficult to grow at all, if one understands the few simple essential rules to make them thrive. They are tolerant of widely differing conditions and there are only three basic obstacles to their growth. They will not, under any circumstances, tolerate sour and badly-drained soil. Secondly, they will not grow where water drips incessantly from the overhanging branches of trees and, thirdly they will not endure draughts and cutting winds. Too often they are expected to grow in narrow alleyways between adjacent buildings through which gusts of wind blow to the discomfort of any plant.

Design and construction Where design is concerned it is obviously desirable that a rock garden should fit as harmoniously as possible into its surroundings. Sometimes this is not possible, especially within the confines of a small town garden lacking any natural landscape features, in which case the rock garden must be regarded as an arbitrary, functional feature. If it is well constructed it will not offend the eye. If there are to be paths, they should always divide a smaller from the greater part of the whole, and not be exact divisions between equal areas. Paths should also be wide enough to permit easy and comfortable passage, even if one is reluctant to spare what may be already limited space.

Building on a slope lends itself to a system of outcrops, each composed of a number of closely joined rocks. The object in building an outcrop is to make it look as much as possible like one rock, seamed, if you like, with crevices and fissures, all of which will accommodate the smaller, cushion-forming plants so admirably.

A flat site calls for more adventurous treatment to create the illusion of heights and valleys. On a small area it can be done by a gradually ascending gradient instead of in outcrops. An abrupt stop when the maximum desired height is reached will create a shady cliff face, most useful for such plants as ramondas and haberleas, which delight in horizontal or vertical crevices with a cool aspect.

It is important that the line of slope of all the rocks should be in the same direction and to approximately the same angle. Rocks falling this way and that may look like the result of a volcanic eruption and will not, unlike more orderly stratification, be restful to the eye. Of equal importance is the placing

of the stones in close association. Isolated stones do not make a rock garden, they only preserve the traditional appearance of a 'dog's grave' so rightly condemned by Reginald Farrer, in his day the doyen of alpine gardeners. Outcrops may stand alone, but not single stones except in a few places where a well-placed rock serves to link two or more separate masses.

Without training or experience in rock garden building it can be a frightening thing to be faced with a great pile of stones, a heap of compost and an empty site. Time should be taken to study the situation, creating as far as possible a picture in one's mind of what is desired. The first stone is the most difficult one to place and it is fatal to make too hasty a beginning.

When a very great gardener was once reproached for doing everything so slowly, he took little heed, for he was a taciturn, though not unkindly man, but at last, goaded into speech by repeated requests for advice, he said that the best way to garden was to 'make haste slowly'. How right he was, and many mistakes can be avoided by unhurried work and thorough preparation. The

novice will do well to experiment with a few smaller stones before the actual construction begins, discovering how to arrange them so that they seem to have grown together naturally.

The precise form of construction must obviously differ according to the kind of rock which is being used. If it is possible to see the rock either in the quarry, or where it outcrops naturally, or is exposed by erosion, it will be found very helpful. If this is not possible, spare a little time to visit a few good rock gardens and study carefully the arrangements of the stones.

It is difficult to learn from the written word how to build a rock garden, although some help in the basic principles may arise from book work. An excellent volume to digest before attemp-

1 Westmorland water-worn limestone is of a cool grey colour.
2 Forest of Dean weathered sandstone has a soft grey-pink hue.
3 A sandstone rock garden forms a small outcrop on a lawn.
4 Large flat slabs of stone are used for a stratified rock garden.

4

1

2

3

ting to build a rock garden is *Natural Rock Gardening* by the late Captain Symons Jeune.

Paths which traverse a rock garden made on sloping ground will have to have steps here and there to adjust the different levels. Such steps, whenever possible, should be composed of the same stone that is used for the rock garden. If sandstone is being used there is little difficulty in splitting large stones to a thickness appropriate for steps. Stones which do not cleave readily have to be used whole and this may involve burying a considerable proportion below ground. This is no bad thing since it ensures stability.

On a flat site the paths should have flat stepping stones let into the ground until they are almost flush with the surface and placed at intervals convenient for a comfortable stride. The area between the stepping stones can be filled with good compost and surfaced with a suitable stone chipping, in which many plants will grow very comfortably and which will often prove fruitful seed beds.

Rock garden plants
The choice of plants which can be grown on a rock garden is very wide indeed, and may bewilder a novice faced with the selection of plants from long lists of names in books and catalogues. Although the plants suitable for this purpose are collectively known as 'alpines', it must be admitted that a great many of them are not, in fact, alpine in the truest sense of the word, but they are all plants which enjoy the conditions

Mendip is an inexpensive and hard rock. It weathers to a mellow grey and sometimes has attractive pink, stratified lines of rock in it.

provided by a rock garden, and look appropriate in such surroundings.

The beginner would do well to start with the more easily grown plants. At the same time it is essential to avoid falling into the error of selecting plants just because they grow quickly—sometimes all too quickly—and need no skill or wisdom in cultivation. It is by no means unusual for rock gardens to be initially planted with such plants as snow-in-summer (*Cerastium tomentosum*), the lovely but invasive creeping *Veronica filiformis*, or even such malefactors as *Helxine solierolii*. If any or all of them once obtain a firm roothold it might well prove necessary, after a year or two, to dismantle the entire rock garden in order to eradicate them.

There is also an understandable temptation to plant great quantities of arabis, alyssum and aubrieta. These three spring-flowering genera offer a

1 Sea pinks. Armeria maritima.
2 A rock garden display in early spring. No clump of plants is too large for the general effect.
3 The bright purple flowers of Gentiana septemfida.
4 The flowers of Campanula carpatica make large deep blue drifts on the rock garden in summer.

splendid range of vivid colour for a short time early in the year, but there is little about them to admire for the remainder of the season. They all occupy a considerable amount of space and should be used with discretion, particularly on a small rock garden.

Roof gardens see Town gardening

Rooting compounds see Propagation

Root cuttings see Propagation

Roses and their cultivation

Almost no garden subject has been written about at greater length, or with more enthusiasm, than roses and their cultivation. Nevertheless, there is plenty that can be said on the matter, and the fact that roses grow easily in most parts of Britain only makes the keen gardener more than ever determined to think of everything in order to cultivate the flower to its greatest perfection.

Certainly roses will repay your attention. Whether they are grown on a fairly large scale, as, for example in the Italian rose garden at Trentham. Staffordshire, or in smaller groups in the home garden, roses provide tremendous pleasure at a reasonably small cost and minimal effort.

In an article which concentrates on the technical side of the subject it would be wrong to forget entirely the historical and romantic associations of the flower. Chaucer's *Romaunt of the Rose*, with its associations of courtly love, and the Scene in the Temple Garden, London, in Act II of Shakespeare's King Henry VI, Part 1, when the rival factions in the 'Wars of the Roses' plucked the red or the white rose, are just two examples of how the rose from the earliest times has come to symbolize the deepest feelings of countless men and women.

Modern roses fall mainly into the following groups: hybrid tea, floribunda, shrub, climbing and rambling, polyantha pompon and miniature.

Hybrid tea These include the large flowered, shapely bedding and exhibition roses, many with a strong fragrance. The group merges the few remaining hybrid perpetuals in general cultivation and what used to be known as 'Pernetianas', representing all the original pure yellow, orange, flame and bicolor varieties. The first hybrid tea varieties were obtained crossing the hybrid perpetuals with the tea-scented roses.

Floribunda These include all the original hybrid polyanthas evolved by the rose breeder Svend Poulson of Denmark. He crossed poly-pompons with hybrid teas, and all the many-flowered roses (other than the poly-pompons), the climbing and rambling groups and the

Hybrid tea roses are the most popular of all types of rose and new varieties are being added every year.
1 Hybrid tea 'Super Star'.
2 Hybrid tea 'Peace'.

Pemberton, so-called 'hybrid musks'. The term 'hybrid polyantha' was discontinued soon after World War II, because varieties were being added to the group each year with little or no true polyantha 'blood', resulting from crossing hybrid teas with various groups of shrub roses.

Shrub This group covers a very wide range of modern hybrids of species and also includes all the old types of garden roses, often referred to as 'old-fashioned' roses.

Climbing and rambling Practically all rambling and climbing roses derive from the Synstylae section of the genus. They include hybrid tea climbing sports.

Polyantha pompon These have largely been superseded by modern floribundas and the miniatures. They are compact-growing, cluster-flowered bedding roses, with small rosette type flowers similar in appearance to those of the old wichuraiana ramblers.

Miniature These are tiny replicas of the hybrid teas and floribundas, with flowers, foliage and growth scaled down in proportion. They are mainly hybrids from *R. chinensis minima* and may never exceed 15–30cm (6–12in) in height.

Selecting and ordering It is important to order your roses early in the season, that is between June and August, when most of the rose shows are held. During this period the roses may be seen in

flower at the nurseries and by ordering promptly you can be sure of the most popular varieties being available.

It is advisable to order from a rose specialist, and from one who buds his own plants, rather than from a man who is not a producer. This is because the grower selling under his own name has a reputation to maintain, and no well-known rose specialist can afford to sell plants which do not give satisfaction. When you visit the nursery, or display garden adjoining it, watch for the habit of growth, disease and weather resistance and freedom of flowering of any of the species provisionally selected.

There is a great deal of variation in the quality of maiden rose plants supplied from various sources, and cheap offers are often the dearest in the long run, as the quality is normally very inferior. Bearing in mind that a healthy rose, when once properly planted, may last from 12 to 20 years or more, with reasonable treatment, it is false economy to attempt to save on the initial cost when this may mean the difference between success and failure. It is essential to obtain plants from a reliable source. This is because of the need for them to be hardy and well-ripened, true to name, budded on a suitable rootstock which will transplant readily and not sucker freely and free from disease spores.

Bare root roses are sometimes still

298

There are hundreds of hybrid tea roses from which to make a selection including dwarf and climbers. A few of the best are recommended on this page. It is now possible to find hybrid teas in almost any colour other than a true blue, or a green. All the following are hybrid tea varieties:
3 'McGredy's Yellow'.
4 'Miss Ireland'.
5 'Silver Lining'.
6 'Ena Harkness'.
7 'Margaret'.
8 'Piccadilly'.
9 'Grand mere Jenny'.
10 'Lady Seton'.

Fifty first-class hybrid tea roses

Name	Habit of growth	Colour	Fragrance	Name	Habit of growth	Colour	Fragrance
Anne Watkins*	T/U	Apricot, shading to cream	S	Mischief*	T/B	Rich coral-salmon	S
Beauté	M	Light orange and apricot	S	Miss Ireland*	M	Orange-salmon, reverse peach	S
Belle Blonde	M/B	Deep tawny gold	M	Mme L. Laperrière	D	Dark crimson	M
Blue Moon	M	Lavender-mauve	R	Mojave*	T/U	Burnt orange and flame	S
Buccaneer*	T/U	Rich golden-yellow	S	Montezuma	T/B	Rich reddish-salmon	S
Caramba*	M/U	Crimson, with silver reverse	S	My Choice	M	Pale carmine-pink, reverse buff-yellow	R
Chrysler Imperial	M/U	Dark velvety crimson	R	Peace*	T/B	Light yellow, edged pink	S
Diorama*	M/B	Apricot yellow, flushed pink	M	Perfecta	T/U	Cream, shaded rosy red	S
Doreen*	M/B	Chrome-yellow, shaded orange	M	Piccadilly*	M/B	Scarlet, reverse yellow	S
Dorothy Peach*	M	Golden-yellow, shaded peach	S	Pink Favourite*	T/B	Deep rose-pink	S
Eden Rose*	T	Rose-madder, paler reverse	R	Prima Ballerina*	T/U	Deep carmine-rose	R
Ena Harkness*	M/B	Velvety scarlet-crimson	R	Rose Gaujard*	T/B	White, shaded carmine-red	S
Ernest H. Morse*	M/U	Rich turkey-red	R	Sarah Arnot	T	Deep rosy-pink	S
Fragrant Cloud*	M/B	Scarlet changing crimson-lake	R	Signora*	T	Flame, pink and orange shades	M
Gail Borden*	T/B	Peach and salmon, shaded gold	S	Silver Lining	M/U	Silvery rose, paler reverse	M
Gold Crown	T/U	Deep gold, shaded red	M	Spek's Yellow*	T/U	Rich golden-yellow	S
Grand'mère Jenny*	T/U	Light yellow and peach-pink	S	Stella	M/B	Carmine-pink, shading to white	S
Grandpa Dickson*	T/U	Lemon yellow, paling to cream	S	Sterling Silver	M/U	Lavender-mauve, shaded silver	R
Helen Traubel*	T	Pink and apricot blend	M	Summer Sunshine	T	Intense golden-yellow	S
Josephine Bruce	M/S	Dark velvety crimson	R	Super Star*	T	Light pure vermilion	M
Lady Belper	M	Light orange	M	Sutter's Gold*	T	Orange-yellow, shaded pink and red	R
La Jolla	M	Pink, cream and gold blend	S	Tzigane	M	Scarlet, reverse chrome-yellow	M
Lucy Cramphorn*	T/B	Geranium-red	S	Virgo	T/U	White, tinted pale pink	S
Margaret*	M/B	China-pink, paler reverse	M	Wendy Cussons*	M/B	Rich cerise	R
McGredy's Yellow*	M/U	Light yellow without shading	S	Westminster	T	Cherry-red, reverse gold	M

Key *Habit of growth* T=tall U=upright M=medium B=branching D=dwarf S=spreading
Fragrance S=slight M=moderate R=rich *Exceptionally good in autumn

1 'Blue Moon'.
2 'Helen Traubel'.
3 'Ernest Morse'.

Fifty first-class floribunda roses

Name	Habit of growth	Colour
Allgold	D	Rich golden-yellow
Anna Wheatcroft	M	Light vermilion
Arabian Nights	T	Deep salmon-red
Arthur Bell	T/U	Deep golden yellow, paling to cream
Chanelle	M	Peach and buff
Circus	M	Yellow, pink and red
Copper Delight	D	Bronze-yellow
Daily Sketch	T	Pink and cream
Dearest	T	Coral-rose
Dorothy Wheatcroft	T	Bright orange-scarlet
Elizabeth of Glamis	M	Light salmon
Elysium	T	Pale rose, shaded salmon
Evelyn Fison	M	Bright scarlet
Europeana	M	Deep blood-red to crimson ·
Faust	T	Yellow shaded pink
Fervid	T	Bright poppy red
Frensham	T	Scarlet-crimson
Golden Slippers	D	Orange and yellow shades
Golden Treasure	M/B	Deep yellow, non-fading
Goldgleam	M/B	Canary yellow, unfading
Gold Marie	T/S	Deep tawny gold, tinged red
Highlight	T	Orange-scarlet
Iceberg	T	White flushed pink
Joyfulness	M	Apricot shaded pink
Korona	T/U	Orange-scarlet, fading deep salmon
Lilac Charm	D/B	Silvery lilac, single flower
Lilli Marlene	M	Scarlet-crimson
Lucky Charm	M	Yellow, pink and red
Manx Queen	M	Orange-yellow shaded pink
Masquerade	M	Yellow, changing to pink and red
Meteor	D	Orange-scarlet
Orangeade	M	Orange-vermilion
Orange Sensation	M	Vermilion-scarlet
Paddy McGredy	D/B	Deep carmine-pink
Paprika	M	Bright turkey-red
Pernille Poulsen	D/B	Salmon-pink, fading lighter
Pink Parfait	M	Pastel shades of pink and cream
Queen Elizabeth	T/U	Rose-pink
Red Dandy	M	Scarlet-crimson, large flowers
Red Favourite	D	Dark crimson
Rumba	M	Orange-yellow, edged scarlet
Ruth Leuwerik	D	Bright scarlet shaded crimson
Scented Air	T/B	Rich salmon-pink
Shepherd's Delight	T/U	Scarlet, flame and orange
Sweet Repose	T	Soft pink shaded apricot
Tambourine	T/U	Cherry-red, reverse orange-yellow
Toni Lander	M/U	Coppery salmon-red
Vera Dalton	M	Medium rose-pink
Violet Carson	M	Peach-pink, reverse silvery pink
Woburn Abbey	T	Tangerine-orange and yellow
Zambra	D	Rich orange and yellow

Key T=tall   M=medium   D=dwarf   S=spreading
       U=upright   B=exceptionally branching

A wide selection of floribunda roses is available for garden decoration:
1 'Iceberg'.
2 'Queen Elizabeth'.

on offer in overheated departmental stores, but nowadays these are normally offered packed in individual polythene bags. The trouble with these roses is that they are frequently subjected to this overheated atmosphere for considerable periods, with consequent dehydration showing in bone-dry roots and shrivelled stems. A rose purchased in this condition is unlikely to flourish unless measures are taken to plump up the wood again by burying the entire plant for about ten days in moist soil, before planting it in its permanent quarters. Another disadvantage of these pre-packaged roses is that each package acts as a miniature greenhouse, and the stems are forced into tender premature growth while they are awaiting sale. This tender growth receives a severe check when the plants are taken out of their packages and exposed to the hazards of the open garden.

Container-grown roses are offered at many nurseries and garden centres. These enable the planting season to be extended throughout the year, as no root disturbance should occur in planting from containers into the permanent beds. They may even be planted when in full bloom.

'*Telstar*'.

Although it is unwise to succumb to cheap offers in end-of-season sales, nearly all rose specialist firms offer collections, their selection of varieties, at an all-in price lower than the aggregate cost of ordering the same varieties individually. For the beginner who is not fussy about varieties he starts with, provided that they are popular, this is as good a way as any of placing a first order, as the quality of the plants should be equal to the nurseryman's normal standard.

Soil Ordinary well-drained soil which has grown good crops of vegetables will suit most roses. Ideally a medium heavy loam, slightly acid (*p*H 5.5 to 6.5) is best. The site should be open and away from large trees and buildings, but not in a draughty position between two houses. On poor soils plenty of old chopped turf, compost, hay and straw and vegetable waste should be added to the subsoil when preparing the beds by double digging, together with any animal manure available. The top spit will be improved by adding granulated peat, compost and bonemeal (at the rate of 120g [4oz] per sq m [sq yd] and hoof and horn meal (at 60g [2oz] per sq m [sq yd]). These should be thoroughly mixed with the soil and not left on the surface or in layers. On heavy land the beds should be raised a little above the general level, but sunk slightly on sandy soil. Perfect drainage is vitally important.

Planning and design The planning of a rose garden is essentially a matter of personal choice depending on individual requirements. The first question to settle is whether the layout is large enough to take roses grown in beds and borders on their own, or whether the roses must fit in with other plants in mixed borders. In a formal rose garden there are separate beds for individual varieties, whether of hybrid tea or floribunda type. These beds are cut in lawns with the possible inclusion of

several standard or half standard roses of the same variety to give added height.

Although well-kept turf is the best setting for roses it involves a great deal of labour to maintain in first-class condition and it is always advisable to have at least one dry path crossing the rose garden, so that barrowing can be done in wet weather without cutting up the turf. Crazy paving or formal stone paving slabs are best for this dry path, with cement run between the crazy paving stones to provide a firm surface and to reduce the labour of weeding. Normally rose beds about 1.6m (5ft) wide are to be preferred to rose borders against a wall or fence, on the grounds of accessibility for weeding, pruning and cultivation generally. A bed of this width will accommodate three rows of plants, 45cm (18in) between the rows with 30cm (1ft) at each side between the outside rows and the edge. This will be sufficient to avoid an overhang with nearly all varieties, which would otherwise interfere with mowing and trimming the edges, if the setting is grass.

The shape of the rose beds is a matter of personal taste, but a simple design is normally best, and it involves less labour for maintenance. It should always be borne in mind that numerous small beds cut in a lawn, apart from looking fussy, require the edges trimming regularly and also slow down the operation of mowing the lawn.

Few amateurs can afford the space to have beds confined to one variety, but mixed beds should be selected carefully, and the varieties chosen for either tasteful colour blending or for similar habit of growth. Alternatively, the centre of the bed should be planted with a variety of taller growth and the perimeter with one of more compact habit. It is far better to plant six or more of the same variety in a group than to dot them about in ones and twos, and this holds good whether beds or borders are being planted.

In a rose border or a mixed border featuring roses and other plants, bold groups are essential for maximum display. In a deep rose border, the grading of groups of varieties according to height will be desirable, with the tallest at the back, although monotony may be avoided by breaking up the gradings with an occasional group of taller varieties running towards the front, or a single pillar or tripod with recurrent-flowering climbing roses about the middle.

Colour grouping with roses is again a matter of personal taste. Some people delight in the extreme contrast between a pure scarlet and a deep golden yellow, whereas others might find this garish, and prefer colour harmonies in blends of soft pink, apricot and orange shades. Some may prefer to group the same, or similar, colours together. The object of colour blending, of course, is to bring

'*Ambrosia*'.

out the best in each colour by careful association of adjacent colours. Thus, white and orange-scarlet next to each other will emphasize, by contrast, the purity of the white and the brilliance of the orange-scarlet. On the other hand, orange-scarlet next to deep carmine pink would be an unhappy combination, as the blue in the carmine pink would look crude and harsh by contrast with the orange-scarlet.

As a general guide shades of yellow will associate well with shades of red. Orange, flame and apricot contrast well with dark crimson. Deep pink, especially carmine pink and cerise, is safest with cream, primrose yellow or white, and the same is true of lilac, lavender and mauve. These shades in roses are often dull in the garden and may need enlivening with bright yellow close by. Scarlet, orange-scarlet, crimson, deep pink and cerise are better separated from each other by using buffer groups of the soft pastel shades of cream, flesh, amber and off-white.

The question of whether to use other

'*Irish Mist*'.

plants for carpeting rose beds often arises, bearing in mind that the roses do not normally provide much colour until June. Violas as ground cover or border plants add colour in the spring. Low-growing plants, such as aubrieta, arabis and the 'mossy' saxifrages may also be used for edgings, but they will need shearing back after flowering. There is no reason either why shallow-rooted annuals should not be used, such as eschscholtzias, love-in-a-mist and night-scented stocks.

Slow-growing conifers may also be used for effect. These have the advantage of being evergreens, and will improve the appearance of the rose garden, although the rank growers should be avoided. The Irish juniper, *Juniperus tommunis hibernica*, is excellent and cakes up little space with its narrow, erect growth. The same is true of *Chamaecyparis lawsoniana columnaris glauca* in blue-grey, and the Irish yews, *Taxus baccata fastigiata*, and the golden *aurea*. Two very splendid slow-growing forms are *Chamaecyparis lawsoniana ellwoodii* and *fletcherii*. Both of these will remain below or about 1.6m (5ft) in height for many years. Clematis may also be planted either by themselves or with recurrent flowering pillar roses, and will often be outstanding, introducing colours not found among roses. *Clematis jackmanii* in rich violet-purple will make a splendid pillar when planted with roses 'New Dawn' or 'Aloha'.

Planting This may be done safely from late October to the end of March whenever the soil is friable and free from frost. Autumn planting usually gives the best results, provided the soil is not too wet for planting firmly; otherwise it will be better to wait for suitable conditions. On receipt of the bushes they should be heeled in temporarily in a trench, throwing plenty of soil over the roots and treading firmly. When the soil in the bed is friable, a large bucket of moist granulated peat, into which a couple of handfuls of meat and bonemeal have been mixed, should be prepared. The position of each bush in the bed is marked with a stick. Distance apart will depend on the vigour and habit of the variety, but on an average soil about 45cm (18in) each way will be about right for most. Exceptionally vigorous kinds, such as 'Peace', which need light pruning, may be better at least 60cm (2ft) apart. The roots should be soaked for a couple of hours before planting. A shallow hole is taken out wide enough to take roots when fully spread. The plant should be inspected carefully for suckers emerging from the root system, and any found should be pulled off. Damaged and broken roots must be trimmed and unripe or damaged shoots removed, also all leaves and flower buds. The prepared plant is then tested in the hole for correct depth; the union of the stock and scion should

'Sweet Repose'.

be just covered with soil. A few handfuls of the peat mixture are thrown over and between the roots and the hole half filled with fine soil and trodden firmly before filling up to the correct level. Standard roses are staked before covering the roots to avoid possible injury. It is beneficial to mulch new beds with 5cm (2in) of granulated peat, to conserve moisture.

Pruning All dead or decadent wood should be cut out as soon as it is noticed at any time. Full-scale pruning should be done when the bushes are dormant, or nearly so. This may be done at any time from January to mid-March, depending on the weather and the area.

In the first spring after planting all groups, except climbing sports of hybrid tea roses, should have weak or twiggy shoots removed entirely, together with any sappy growth. The remainder should be cut back just above a dormant shoot bud pointing away from the centre of the plant and not more than 16cm (6in) from the base. Spring planted roses may be pruned in the hand just before planting. Climbing sports of hybrid teas should just be tipped and the main shoots bent over by securing the ends to canes or wires, to force the lower buds into growth. On light hungry soils it may be advisable not to prune any groups the first year, but to encourage as much new growth as possible by mulching and watering.

Subsequent years Pruning of hybrid teas may be hard, moderate or light, according to circumstances. Light pruning is generally preferable on poor sandy soils which do not encourage a lot of new wood. This means cutting back new shoots formed in the previous season to about two-thirds of their length and removing all weak or twiggy growth. On average soils moderate pruning may be done, involving cutting back all new wood about half way and removing entirely the weak and twiggy shoots. Hard pruning is seldom necessary for modern varieties, but some will respond to it on a good soil with ample feeding. It requires the cutting out of all but two or three of the main growths and reducing these to just above a dormant bud

'Zambra'.

'Evelyn Fison'.

about 16cm (6in) from the base.

Floribundas require different treatment. The object is to ensure as continuous a display of colour during the season as possible. This requires the application of a differential pruning system, based on the age of the wood. Growth produced from the base in the previous season should merely be shortened to the first convenient bud below the old flower truss. The laterals on two-year-old wood should be cut back half way and any three-year-old wood cut hard back to about three eyes from the base. As with all groups, all dead, decadent, unripe and twiggy wood should be removed entirely.

Shrub roses and the old garden roses in general do not require much pruning. Apart from the cutting out of dead and exhausted wood and cutting back a main growth near the base occasionally to encourage new basal growth, pruning is mainly confined to remedying overcrowding and ensuring a shapely outline.

The treatment of climbers varies with the group to which they belong. Generally, the more recurrent flowering the variety, the less rampant is its growth and the less the pruning required. The once-flowering wichuraiana ramblers, which renew themselves with new canes from the base each season after flowering, should have all old flowering wood cut out and the new canes tied in to take its place. Climbing sports of hybrid teas and other climbing hybrid teas require little pruning, but should be trained fanwise or horizontally to force as many dormant eyes into growth as possible. Flowers are borne either on laterals or sub-laterals. Recurrent flowering pillar roses, such as 'Aloha', 'Coral Dawn' and 'Parade', require only the removal of dead or exhausted wood and any which is weak or twiggy, plus sufficient thinning out of the remaining wood to avoid overcrowding.

General cultivation Suckers must be removed before they grow large. They may come from any point below the inserted bud and with standards they may appear either on the standard stem below the head or anywhere on the root system. The roots of roses should not be disturbed any more than is essential to the removal of weeds and suckers.

Where light or moderate pruning is practised, summer thinning or de-shooting may be necessary, and this will be routine procedure for the keen exhibitor. All side shoots appearing before the terminal buds have opened should be pinched out as soon as they are large enough to handle. While watering is not a practical proposition on a large scale, newly planted roses may need the roots soaking thoroughly at weekly intervals during hot weather. Roses planted in dry positions, against walls or close-boarded fences, will also require regular watering in the summer.

Removal of spent flowers is essential if a later crop is to be produced and seed pods should never be allowed to develop. Dead-heading should be a routine operation throughout the season. In the first summer after planting merely the flower and foot of the stalk, without any leaves, should be removed, but in subsequent years the growth from the pruning point may be reduced to half way, to ensure a fine second display. Disbudding will also be necessary for the keen exhibitor and those who insist on high quality blooms. Not more than three buds are left on hybrid tea stems for garden display or a single bud for exhibition. In the autumn any long growths should be shortened to minimize possible gale damage.

Feeding Before embarking on a feeding programme you should find out whether your soil is naturally acid or alkaline. There are a number of soil-testing kits available. Lime, if required, is best applied in the form of ground chalk (calcium carbonate) during the early winter months, at 85–110g (3–4oz) per

'Arthur Bell'.

'Daily Sketch'.

sq m (sq yd), sprinkled evenly over the surface of the beds and left for the winter rains to wash it down. By the time the spring mulch is due, the lime should have done its work. As roses prefer a slightly acid soil, it may be necessary to apply lime every year, though never on chalky soil.

During February and March it is beneficial to apply a dressing of meat and bonemeal at 110g (4oz) per sq m (sq yd), pricking it just below the surface. If this proves difficult to obtain in small quantities sterilized bonemeal may be used instead. About the middle of April a complete rose fertilizer can be applied to established beds, according to the makers' instructions. There are many of these available, or a useful compound fertilizer may be made up quite cheaply from 16 parts of superphosphate of lime, 10 parts of sulphate of potash, 5 parts of sulphate of ammonia, 2 parts of sulphate of magnesia (commercial Epsom Salts) and 2 parts of sulphate of iron. These parts are in terms of weight, and the ingredients must be mixed thoroughly, any lumps being crushed. The fertilizer should be sprinkled evenly at about a *level* tablespoonful per plant, afterwards hoeing and watering in if necessary. The temptation to use a double dose in the hope of obtaining spectacular results should be resisted.

Alternatively, for those who do not wish to go to much trouble, many firms market a rose fertilizer to the well-known 'Tonks' formula, which was based originally on the chemical analysis of the ashes of a complete rose tree after burning it in a crucible. The formula comprises 12 parts of superphosphate of lime, 10 parts of nitrate of potash, 8 parts of sulphate of lime, 2 parts of sulphate of magnesia and 1 part of sulphate of iron. It should be applied at the rate of 85–110g (3–4oz) per sq m (sq yd) and pricked in with a border fork.

About the middle of May, when the

soil will have started to warm up, a mulch of animal manure or, if this is unobtainable, compost, granulated peat, leafmould or spent hops should be applied evenly to the beds, preferably 5cm (2in) deep. If peat, leafmould or spent hops are used they should be well moistened and fortified with a further application of the compound rose fertilizer, at the same rate as in mid-April. It is a good plan to wash this in with a hose jet applied at pressure to the mulch. The keen grower, with ambitions to produce excellent specimen blooms, may wish to try liquid stimulants from the stage of bud formation. Apart from liquid animal manures, which should *always* be applied in very dilute form (no stronger than a pale straw colour) and at intervals of ten days or so, soot water and soluble blood are useful nitrogenous fertilizers. Nitrate of potash (at 16g

[½oz] per 4.5l [gallon] and superphosphate of lime (at 28g [1oz] per 4.5l [gallon]) may also be used safely at these strengths. The important points to watch in liquid feeding are: to use the feed in very dilute form only; to ensure that there is already plenty of moisture in the soil before applying and to stop application at the end of July.

About the end of August, especially in a wet season, it is a good plan to apply a dressing of sulphate of potash to the rose beds at the rate of 85g (3oz) per sq m (sq yd). This will help to ripen and harden the wood in readiness for the winter. It should be pricked in along with what

A bold and satisfactory effect is always obtained from roses when varieties are planted in groups.

remains of the mid-May mulch.

Runner beans see Vegetables

Salad plants
These are crops grown especially for salads and those which, although suitable for other use, may also be added to the salad bowl.

Lettuce is the foundation of most salads and the gardener may take his choice from the many butterheads, crispheads, cos and loose leaf varieties. 'May Queen' is liked for late spring and early summer lettuces. 'Unrivalled' is often chosen for successional sowings between early April and August. The three new Dutch 'K' varieties are worth consideration for greenhouse work. Modern cos varieties do not need tying but a tie encourages the formation of a firm heart. The leaves of loose leaf plants are pulled as and when required but no plant should be stripped. American varieties such as 'Great Lakes', 'Buttercrunch' and 'Salad Bowl' are considered to be more tolerant of drier summer conditions than many other sorts. As with so many other vegetables, early thinning of the seedlings is very important.

Endive often replaces lettuces in autumn and early winter salads. Seeds are sown in June, the seedlings thinned in July and blanching started in October. The heads must be quite dry when blanching is started and absolute darkness is very essential. After being blanched, endive must be used at once before rotting begins.

The easiest form of celery to grow is 'American Green'. Plants are raised from a sowing made in heat in late March and the plants, after being hardened off in the cold frame, are set out on the flat in early June. Apart from weeding and watering, no cultivation is necessary. Self-blanching celery is often grown as a summer frame crop. For late autumn and winter supplies, blanched celery is grown. The plants, before blanching, may be green, pink or red. All forms of celery need a rich bed and

a great deal of water.

Celeriac can replace celery in winter salads. Plants raised in heat and hardened off are set out of doors on a rich bed between mid-May and early June. The plants need as much water as celery, and the roots are lifted and stored in October. Celeriac should be grated for salad use.

Chicory has the flavour of the heart of a cos lettuce and the crisp quality of celery. Sow in June and dig the roots in November. Store them in a trench and blanch batches on and off during the winter. In a heated greenhouse, blanched chicons are ready for cutting within a month of planting the roots.

There are two kinds of cucumber—the hardy outdoor and the English frame type. In the south, hardy European, American and Asian varieties may be grown on the flat or on tall trellises. In the north, cloche or frame protection is advisable. A good, all round variety to choose is 'Burpee F₁ Hybrid'. In the south, 'Conqueror' and 'Telegraph' do well in the cold greenhouse and in the cold frame. In other areas, plants of both varieties need some artificial heat. The female flowers of hardy outdoor kinds must be pollinated. With frame-type cucumber plants, all male flowers are pinched off to prevent the fruits from being misshapen and bitter.

Mustard and cress is a welcome addition to winter and early spring salads. The seeds are sown in trays or pots filled with seed compost. Germination takes place in a dark, warm place. The white stems and yellow leaves change colour when the receptacles are brought into the light for a day or two. Sowings should be made on and off for succession between October and March.

Although termed 'spring onions', plants of the onion variety 'White Lisbon' are seldom ready for use until May. Sow in August and give cloche protection in cold areas. A further sowing may be made in March or April for summer supplies. Start pulling the onions when they are quite small. The larger the bulbs, the hotter they become in flavour. Early spring supplies of salad onions are also obtained by growing the Welsh onion. The flavour is very mild. Cocktail-sized tree onions may also be used in salads. The onions are very strong in flavour and it is sufficient to slice one or two over a salad.

Beetroot is boiled before use. Summer supplies are obtained by sowing a globe variety under cloches in late March or in the open between mid-April and early May. An intermediate or long variety should be sown in May for winter storing. Carrots are grated for salads and maincrop varieties are suitable. Otherwise thinnings may be used whole.

For crops of radishes between May and October, successional sowings of 'French Breakfast', 'Icicle' or other quick-growing varieties should be made from March until August. For use in late autumn and winter salads, large-rooted kinds such as 'All Season', 'China Rose' and 'Black Spanish' are grown from a June sowing. These radishes have a very delicate flavour when sliced very thinly or grated.

Tomatoes may be grown in heated and cold greenhouses, under cloches, or in the open. 'Ailsa Craig' is reputed to be the finest flavoured variety and 'Outdoor Girl' is a newer, hardy variety for cloche or outdoor growing. For a difference in the salad bowl, yellow tomatoes are suggested. 'Golden Boy' is a large-fruited variety of excellent flavour. 'Yellow Pear' and 'Yellow Plum' are small ornamentals and 'Golden Amateur' is a self-stopping bush plant.

Other suggested additions to the salad bowl are the shredded leaves of white cabbage and of Chinese cabbage, 'Fir Apple Pink' salad potatoes, chopped chives, leaves of nasturtium, *Tropaeolum majus*, sorrel, tarragon, fennel, pods of the Bavarian radish and mint or garlic in very small quantities.

Savoy cabbage see Vegetables

Screens see Hedges

Seaside gardening

The almost constant enemies of seaside gardening are wind, salt and sand. Frost, however, is neither so prolonged nor so severe on the coast as it is inland, and seaside gardeners have been able to grow many frost-tender plants in the milder climate of their coastal gardens.

Inland gardeners have little idea how powerful is the effect of coastal wind on the growth of plants, and because none or few trees or buildings present a barrier to soften its effect during windy conditions the wind sweeps continuously in from the sea. Wind stunts and it deforms—one has only to observe the fantastic shapes of trees close to the sea to realise this.

Salt can kill outright. Salt is carried in the spray and when this is caught up by the wind it is often deposited many hundreds of yards inland. Few plants are able to withstand the continual battering of sea-wind heavily charged with salt, which is heavily scorching to plants.

Sand-blast is often too lightly regarded by newcomers to the coast, though its effect can be quite as damaging as that of salt. Seashore gardens suffer badly from its searing effect when the wind picks up the sand from a nearby beach. Small seedlings are killed and adult foliage is bruised and blackened.

The only answer to the problem of wind, salt and sand is shelter, and it is not possible to create a worthwhile garden in extremely exposed positions on the coast without it, though where a garden has protection a very wide range of plants will thrive which would not

Lettuce forms the foundation of most salads, but a wide variety of vegetables can be eaten raw.
1 Cucumber 'Burpee Hybrid'.
2 The second thinning of carrots will make young roots for the salad bowl.
3 Celery 'American Green'.
4 Radishes, lettuces and spring onions.
5 Do not allow chives to flower (as here) if you wish to keep the flavour.
6 Tomato 'Supercross'.
7 Beetroot 'Avon Early'.
8 A crisp head of endive.
9 Chinese cabbage.

4

5

7

6

8

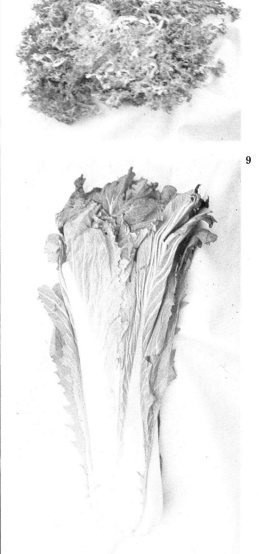

9

succeed in frosty gardens inland. Many plants will grow only when given adequate shelter at the outset, and the planting of newly-made gardens exposed to the full ravages of gales off the sea is rarely successful without the aid of some artificial wind-screen.

Planting of shelter belts of trees on a large scale benefit from an open fence of a two-bar wooden structure interwoven with foliage of gorse or spruce. For small gardens there is nothing better than a fence of wooden laths, 2.5cm (1in) wide with spaces between of similar size, set vertically on a stout wooden framework and posts at either end for driving into the ground. Avoid a solid barricade such as a wall, which causes wind-turbulence on the lee side, since the aim is always to filter the wind rather than obstruct it.

Plants which tolerate salt and wind are nowadays very largely selected from those grown in Australia and New Zealand. As a result of long coastlines and varied climatic conditions more successful seaside shrubs have evolved in Australia and New Zealand than in any other part of the world. Shrubs that successfully resist salt-spray are planted facing the sea. These are often equipped with toughened leaves such as are found in the genus *Olearia*. *O. haastii* and *O. albida* stand any amount of salty wind. Others have shiny leaf surfaces. *Euonymus japonicus* and *Griselinia littoralis* look bright and glossy within a few yards of the sea. Or the leaves of

Shrubs for milder maritime areas

Abelia grandiflora
Abutilon megapotamicum
  A. vitifolium
Artemisia canescens
  A. stelleriana
Azara dentata
  A. microphylla
Berberis thunbergii atropurpurea
  superba
Buddleia auriculata
  B. globosa 'Lemon Ball'
  B. nivea
Calceolaria integrifolia
Callistemon citrinus
Cassia corymbosa
Cassinia fulvida
  C. ledifolius
  C. leptophylla
Ceanothus 'Autumn Blue'
  C. impressus
  C. 'Indigo'
  C. rigidus
  C. veitchianus
Centaurea gymnocarpa
Choisya ternata
Cistus crispus 'Sunset'
  C. 'Paladin Pat'
  C. palhinhaii
  C. purpureus
  C. skanbergii
Clianthus puniceus
Colquhounia vestita

Convolvulus cneorum
Corokia virgata
Crinodendron hookerianum
Daphne mezereum
  D. odora
Desfontainea spinosa
Echium fastuosum
Elaeagnus macrophylla
Embothrium coccineum
Erica australis
  E. alpina
  E. lusitanicus
Escallonia hybrids
Eucalyptus globulus
  E. gunnii
  E. niphophylla
  E. pauciflora
Eupatorium micranthum
Fabiana imbricata
Fatsia japonica
Fremontia californica
Fuchsias (large-flowered)
Halimium alyssoides
  H. ocymoides
Hoheria glabrata
  H. sexstylosa
Hebes (in variety to include *H. hulkeana*)
Helichrysum petiolatum
  H. plicatum
Hypericum moserianum tricolor
  H. 'Rowallane'
Jasminum polyanthum

Shrubs for milder maritime areas (cont.)

Jasminum primulinum
Jovellana violacea
Lavandula stoechas
Lavatera assurgensifolia
Leonotis leonurus
Leptospermum scoparium nichollsii
   L. 'Red Damask'
Lippia citriodora
Muehlenbeckia complexa
Myrtus communis
   M. luma
   M. ugni
Olearia insignis
   O. × scilloniensis
   O. semidentata
   O. solandri
Paulownia tomentosa
Phlomis fruticosa
   P. italica
Phormium tenax
Piptanthus laburnifolius
Pittosporum eugenioides

Pittosporum ralphii
   P. tobira
Polygala myrtifolia
Rosmarinus angustifolius
   R. 'Corsican Blue'
   R. lavendulaceus
   R. 'Majorca Pink'
   R. 'Severn Sea'
   R. 'Tuscan Blue'
Salvia grahamii
   S. involucrata bethellii
Sambucus nigra foliis aureus
Senecio cineraria
   S. c. 'White Diamond'
   S. glastifolius
   S. huntii
   S. heritieri
   S. leucostachys
   S. rotundifolius
Solanum crispum
   S. jasminoides
Teucrium fruticans azureum
Yucca gloriosa

Shrubs for colder maritime areas

Amelanchier canadensis
Arbutus unedo
Atriplex canescens
   A. halimus
Aucuba japonica

Baccharis patagonica
Berberis aquifolium
   B. darwinii
   B. stenophylla
   B. thunbergii atropurpurea

some may be coated with a gummy secretion as in *Escallonia macrantha*, enabling them to endure a coating of salt. Yet another form of protection is afforded by a multitude of tiny hairs which cover the leaf surfaces of grey-leaved and silver-leaved shrubs. It is a curious fact that most of these are well adapted to withstand the first brunt of a salty blast. Sea buckthorn, *Atriplex halimus*, *Senecio laxifolius* and *S. monroi* are among the best we have for prominent positions in exposed coastal districts. If sand-blast is a menace, tamarisk will grow with its roots in pure sand and is also useful for adding height to rough banks and walls.

Seed

Seeds are produced by plants following the fertilization of the flower, as a means of reproducing the plant. Each seed is a plant embryo, which consists of a minute shoot and root and a store of food. The food reserve enables the embryo to grow before its root is developed to absorb nutrients from the soil and before the leaves emerge above the ground and make sugars by photosynthesis, a complex process. In some seeds, such as those of sunflowers or

1 *Fuchsia* 'Pink Galore'.
2 *Fatsia japonica*, an evergreen shrub.
3 *Abelia grandiflora*.
4 *Yucca gloriosa*.
5 *Convolvulus cneorum*.

Berberis wilsonae
Buddleia davidii (in variety)
  B. globosa
Caragana arborescens
Caryopteris × *clandonensis*
Ceanothus × *burkwoodii*
  C. 'Cascade'
  C. 'Gloire de Versailles'
  C. 'Henri Defosse'
  C. 'Topaz'
  C. thyrsiflorus
Cistus corbariensis
  C. ladaniferus
  C. laurifolius
  C. populifolius
  C. 'Silver Pink'
Clematis flammula
Colutea arborescens
Coronilla glauca
  C. emerus
Cortaderia argentea
Cotoneasters (in variety)
Crataegus (in variety)
Cytisus battandieri
  C. scoparius hybrids
Elaeagnus ebbingei
  E. pungens aureo-variegata
Escallonia 'C. F. Ball'
  E. edinensis
  E. × *langleyensis*
  E. macrantha
Euonymus japonicus
Euphorbia veneta (*E. wulfenii*)
Garrya elliptica
Genista aethnensis
  G. lydia

G. hispanica
Griselinia littoralis
Hebe brachysiphon
  H. dieffenbachii
  H. 'Midsummer Beauty'
  H. salicifolia
Hibiscus in variety
Hippophaë rhamnoides
Hydrangeas (in variety)
Hypericum patulum 'Hidcote'
  H. androsaemum
Lavandulas (in variety)
Lavatera olbia rosea
Leycesteria formosa
Lonicera ledebourii
Lupinus arboreus
Lycium chinense
Medicago arborea
Olearia albida
  O. haastii
  O. macrodonta
Perovskia atriplicifolia
Phormium tenax
Pittosporum tenuifolium
Potentillas (in variety)
Prunus spinosa
Pyracanthas (in variety)
Ribes alpinum
  R. atrosanguineum
  Romneya × *hybrida*
Rosa rugosa (and its hybrids)
  R. spinosissima (and its hybrids)
Rosmarinus 'Miss Jessup's Upright'
  R. officinalis
Santolina chamaecyparissus
  S. incana

S. neapolitana
S. virens
Senecio laxifolius
  S. monroi
  Spartium junceum
Symphoricarpos orbiculata
  S. microphylla
Tamarix pentandra
Teucrium fruticans
Ulex europaeus plenus
Viburnum tinus
Yucca filamentosa

Some plants for seaside gardens (including tender kinds)

Agapanthus (species and hybrids)
Amaryllis belladonna
Aster pappei
Alstroemeria 'Ligtu Hybrids'
Convolvulus mauritanicus
Crambe cordifolia
Crinum (species and hybrids)
Crocosmia masonorum
Dimorphotheca barberiae compacta
  D. ecklonis
Gazanias
Kniphofias such as 'Maid of Orleans'
Mesembryanthemums
Montbretia (hybrids)
Myosotidium nobile
Odontospermum maritimum
Othonnopsis cheirifolia
× *Venidio-arctotis*
Zantesdeschia aethiopica

---

peas, the food reserve is starch but in others it may be oils or fats. The food reserve occupies the bulk of the volume of a seed. The seed is enclosed in a protective coat called the *testa*, which frequently has a small hole through which water can enter before germination.

Many seeds undergo a dormant period for some time before germination. This dormant period is useful in that it prevents the seed from germinating in the mild autumn only to be killed off when the frosts arrive. In many seeds the dormant period occurs because germination is delayed by reason of the very hard testa which has to be cracked open by the expansion and shrinkage that occurs during the cold weather. In other types of seeds growth-inhibiting chemicals have to be washed out by the rain before germination will occur. These growth-inhibiting chemicals can prevent the germination of the seeds of other species of plants. The rain washes them into the soil and germination of neighbouring seeds is prevented. Some seeds such as those of lettuce and mistletoe, require light before they will germinate, others not only will germinate in the dark but actually are prevented from germination by light.

When the seed is ready to germinate, water enters and the food reserve provides energy for the growth of root.

Treatment to ensure the germination of seeds is generally applied before they are sold commercially. Lack of knowledge of the treatment a particular seed needs often accounts for the failures gardeners may encounter when trying to harvest and germinate their own seeds.

Seed bed

This is a specially prepared site where seeds are to be sown. It may be in a frame or in the open garden but seldom in a greenhouse. Seed beds made in the open garden during early spring are often given cloche protection. There are two types of seed bed. In the first seeds are propagated to provide seedlings for transplanting elsewhere at a later date. In the second plants are permitted to develop where the seeds were sown. Excess seedlings in this type of bed are thinned when quite small. The term is more usually applied to the first type of bed which may be prepared between early spring and autumn. For most gardeners this form of seed bed is more likely to be made during the main sowing season from February to April.

A good tilth is necessary and where

the soil has a high clay content it is advisable to dig the site fairly deeply in late autumn or winter. The dug soil should be left quite rough and no attempt be made to break it down. Disintegration of the surface soil will occur through the weathering action of frost and snow.

Where a light soil has been dug in autumn or winter it can become consolidated by heavy rains, and before a seed bed may be prepared in spring forking to a depth of 5–7cm (2–3in) may be needed.

Seed drills

These are the shallow trenches in which seeds of many garden plants are sown. Drills made in the open ground are generally made with the garden draw hoe. The onion hoe or even a sharp-pointed stick are more suitable for sowings in the cold frame or where the short rows are to be cloched. To ensure that the rows are straight, use the garden line. For frame rows, a straight piece of wood is more useful.

Care must be taken to make the drills of even depth. The depth should vary according to the size of the seeds being sown. Generally, the smaller the seeds, the more shallow should be the drill. As a rough guide consider the smallest seeds as needing a soil cover of 6mm (¼in). Larger seeds may be sown more deeply up to a maximum of 5cm (2in). The average depth for flower and vegetable seeds is from 1–2cm (½–1in). The width of a seed drill depends on what is being sown. Seeds of most garden plants are sown in a single straight row in V-shaped drills. Flat-bottomed, rather wide drills are best for some vegetable sowings, such as those of peas, where double or even treble rows of plants are to be grown close together.

Should the soil be on the dry side—as it so often is during late spring and summer, the drill should be flooded with water before sowings are made. Sow when the water has drained away. After sowing refill the drills by drawing the soil into them with the back of a rake. On light, sandy soils it is sometimes an advantage to tread lightly along the rows after sowing (see also Seed bed).

Seed sowing

Many garden plants are propagated from seed and good germination is encouraged by providing the seeds with the best conditions. Moisture and air must be present in the propagating medium (whether soil or a special compost) and the temperatures must be suitable. Very high temperatures are seldom necessary. Most garden and greenhouse sown seeds need temperatures of 50–60°F (10–16°C) in which to germinate. Some seeds, notably those of tomatoes, cucumbers, melons and tropical plants need much higher temperatures.

In early spring and in autumn the garden soil is normally damp. Later in spring and in summer insufficient moisture can lead to poor germination. This condition may be remedied by watering seed drills before sowing, the seeds being sown on the wet surface. Straight seed rows are obtained by the use of a garden line or a length of straight wood,

The sowing of seeds in a cold frame is largely the same as for outdoor sowings. The soil mixture in frames is usually one well suited to good germination. In early spring the frame sash should be set on the frame at least a week before sowings are carried out. The covering of the frame in this way traps any available sun heat and the frame bed is warmed and dried.

Where seeds are to be sown on ground given cloche protection warm the soil by placing the cloches in early spring. Seed rows in frames and under cloches may be set quite closely together so that maximum use is made of the surface area. If you water protected seed rows before germination use a very fine rose.

In the greenhouse seeds are generally sown in receptacles. For some specialized sowings and for limited sowings clay seed pans are often used. Pots, now offered in a wide range of materials, are most useful for those plants which resent the root disturbances which occur when pricking out seedlings raised in boxes or pans. New clay receptacles should be soaked in water for several hours before being used. Used wooden boxes should be washed in mild disinfectant.

Where the sowing is made in a seed box some compost is placed in the box, firmed with the fingers and levelled with a ruler or strip of wood to within 12mm (½in) of the top. A wooden presser simplifies this task. The compost is then watered thoroughly, using a very fine rose on the can, and set aside to drain. The seed is then sown thinly on the moist surface. Large seeds are spaced at 2.5cm (1in) or so apart. The seeds are normally covered after sowing by sieving a 6mm (¼in) layer of the compost over them. Sowings in pans and pots are

A seed drill is drawn with the edge of a hoe along a garden line.

carried out in the same way.

The containers are then covered with a sheet of glass on which a sheet of brown paper is laid. The glass prevents evaporation and lessens the need for further watering. The paper provides dark conditions.

Bulbs from seed Where a quantity of bulbs of one kind is required the most economical means of raising them is from seed. This applies to wild species and not to named varieties which do not come true to colour from seed. Patience is also required for some bulbs require several years to mature to flowering size. In general the seed is best sown as soon as ripe, either in seed trays or in pans, and placed in a cold frame, artificial heat not usually being necessary to germinate seed of most hardy bulbs. Use a well-drained seed compost, sow thinly, and just cover the seed with a fine layer of sifted compost. Keep moist and cool. The seed of some bulbous plants, such as the bluebell, *Scilla nutans*, and dwarf narcissi for naturalizing purposes may be scattered on the soil or grass in summer where it is to flower, as soon as it is ripe. Once established the sapphire-lavender, *Crocus tomasinianus*, from Dalmatia, will seed itself happily, as will the grape hyacinth and hardy cyclamen. The Mexican tiger flower *Tigridia pavonia*, will do likewise in sheltered gardens in full sun and a well-drained soil. One of the easiest of the lilies to raise from seed is *Lilium regale*, which will usually start to produce its imposing, glorious fragrant trumpets in three years from the time of sowing. Here again the seed should be sown as soon as ripe in pans in a cold frame and when the seedlings are large enough to handle they should be pricked out into boxes. Grow them on in a frame until the bulbs are large enough to plant out permanently. Many colourful tulip species may also be raised from seed, but these may take four or five years to reach flowering size.

Shallots see Vegetables

Shelterbeds see Hedges, screens and shelterbeds

Shrub gardening

A shrub may be defined as a perennial woody plant, branching naturally from its base without a defined leader (a single main shoot), and not normally exceeding 10m (30ft) high. Shrubs may be deciduous or evergreen and range from plants no more than 3–5cm (1–2in) high, such as some heaths and creeping willows, to huge rhododendrons. Some woody plants may grow either as large shrubs or trees according to circumstances. When the lower part of the plant is woody and the upper shoots are soft, it is referred to as a sub-shrub.
Preparation of the site Just because shrubs *are* so easy to grow, it is a mistake to imagine that you can just stick them into a hole in the ground and then leave them to their own devices. Proper and careful planting is one of the most important operations contributing to their successful cultivation.

The initial preparation of the site should be done, whenever possible, a few months before planting is due to be carried out, in order to give the soil ample opportunity to settle. This may not always be possible, in which case a certain amount of raking and treading may be necessary on light sandy soils, while on heavier clays extra precautions will have to be taken to avoid leaving air pockets round the roots.

Deep and thorough cultivation, either by trenching or double digging, to break up the subsoil, as well as the top spit, is the ideal to be aimed at.

Although the roots of the shrubs will eventually travel far in search of nourishment and moisture, this preliminary cultivation will ensure that they get away to a good start in their first season.

Before the shrubs are put in, the

surface soil should be broken down to a reasonably good tilth. Getting it into this condition will provide an opportunity of raking in a slow-acting organic fertilizer, such as steamed bone flour, meat and bonemeal or fish manure. Any of these, applied at the rate of 80–110g (3–4oz) per sq m (sq yd) should provide adequate reserves for the first growing season.

With a new garden, on former pasture or woodland, the chances are that the soil will already contain sufficient humus. First, the turf should be sliced off and placed at the bottom of the second spit or, as far as woodland sites are concerned, all fallen leaves, leafmould, etc, should be collected up and incorporated in the soil as digging progresses.

Where existing beds and borders are being given over to shrubs, it may be necessary to provide humus-forming materials in the form of sedge peat, leafmould, garden compost, spent hops, or rotted down straw, when the site is prepared.

Planting Whether a single specimen shrub is being planted, or hundreds of shrubs are set for a hedge, the actual planting process must be carefully carried out if the plants are to give of their best. Planting holes must be large enough and deep enough to

1 When seed is sown in pots the surface can be firmed with another pot.
2 River sand provides a seed compost for alpines.
3 Annuals sown in irregular areas will make a colourful border of flowers.
4 A broad flat drill for peas.
5 Seed sown in drills in a seed box.
6 Seed sown broadcast in a seed box.

accommodate the roots without bunching or overcrowding, and it is a good idea to leave a slight mound at the base of the hole on which the plant can rest while the roots are spread out and soil is worked among them. On light sandy soils this latter procedure will be simple, but with sticky clays, particularly if planting coincides with a wet spell, it may be necessary to fill in the holes with compost or dry sifted soil. Most shrubs will benefit by being planted in a mixture consisting of equal parts of sifted soil, peat or leafmould and bonfire ash.

Many evergreen shrubs, including rhododendrons, will arrive from the nursery with their roots 'balled' in sacking. When these are planted, the root ball should remain intact. It is not even necessary to remove the sacking, as it will soon rot away, but if it is left in position it is advisable to

cut the ties that secure it round the plant.

The shrub should be gently jiggled up and down to ensure that all the roots are in contact with the soil and to prevent air pockets. Planting is usually a job for two—one holding the shrub in position and giving it an occasional shake, the other working the soil round the roots and firming it with the boot, or where small shrubs are concerned, with the hands.

Depth of planting is important. The soil mark on the stem made at the nursery can be used as a guide and shrubs should be planted with the soil slightly above this to allow for the slight sinking that is likely to take place.

Normally, staking will not be necessary, although in positions exposed to strong winds it may be advisable to provide a temporary support for the first season to guard against root damage from wind rock. In any case, it is always advisable to go round newly planted shrubs after a spell of rough weather or prolonged frost to refirm the soil round the base.

The best time to do this is after the soil has had a chance to dry out. Although they like firm planting no shrubs like their roots encased in soil that has been consolidated into a concrete-like consistency, which is what will happen if an attempt is made to firm heavy clay soils when they are still waterlogged.

There are two schools of thought where the initial planting of a new shrub border is concerned. Some garden writers advocate planting at distances sufficient to allow each shrub to develop to its fullest capacity without overcrowding. Others advise planting well in excess of the final requirements and later ruthlessly sacrificing any that are not required.

There are drawbacks to each of these methods. In the latter instance, although it is easy to see when shrubs are beginning to exceed their allotted space above ground, it is difficult to say when overcrowding of the roots starts to take place. Waiting till the branches are jostling one another may cause considerable damage to the roots of those that remain when the unwanted surplus is removed.

On the other hand, in a shrub border with every plant at a distance from the others sufficient to allow room for the ultimate spread of its roots there will be plenty of wide open spaces for several years to come. These can be filled during spring and summer by

1 An excellent flowering and fruiting shrub Skimmia rubella.
2 A border of mixed shrubs selected for either their flower or foliage colour makes a decorative feature.

bulbs and perennials.

The best solution is to provide temporary stopgaps in the form of relatively short-lived shrubs, or common ones of vigorous habit that will not be greatly missed when the time comes to get rid of them to make room for the more permanent occupants of the border.

Brooms are ideal for this purpose. No matter how carefully they are pruned they invariably become leggy and untidy in the course of four or five years. But in their prime they make a colourful display. The many lovely hybrid forms of the native broom, *Cytisus scoparius*, range from white through every shade of cream and yellow to rich mahogany reds and purples. A good representative selection would include 'Cornish Cream', 'Dorothy Walpole', a rich crimson, 'Lady Moore', a bicolor with rich red wings and keel, the lovely apricot and buff 'C. E. Pearson' and the dainty carmine and rose-red 'Johnson's Crimson'. For the edge of the border or the rock garden there are the early-flowering *C. praecox* and the prostrate *C. × kewensis* both of which bear masses of cream coloured blossom.

Other 'expendables' include the flowering currants, some of the more rampant mock oranges, such as *Philadelphus coronarius*, as well as the taller forsythias and such coarse-growing shrubs as *Buddleia davidii*.

Winter flowering shrubs By judicious planning and selection it should be possible to have shrubs in flower throughout the year. Winter-flowering shrubs make an invaluable contribution to our gardens, bringing colour and, in many instances, penetrating fragrance during the darkest days of the season.

By mid-November, when the early heavy frosts have stripped the deciduous shrubs and trees of most of their leaves, the first pinkish-white flower clusters of *Viburnum fragrans* will be starting to open. This is one of the loveliest and most useful of winter shrubs; it continues to produce relays of richly fragrant blossoms right up to the end of February. There is a white variety,

1 *The Azara species are good shrubs for chalky soil. Azara lanceolata has bright yellow double flowers along the arching stems.*
2 *The firethorn, Pyracantha rogersiana, has red berries.*
3 *Garrya elliptica, excellent in shade.*

candidissima, with flowers lacking the pinkish tinge of the type, but which contrast even more effectively with the bare, cinnamon-brown twigs.

The witch hazels start to flower towards the end of December and in most seasons it is possible to fill a vase with their curious spidery, cowslip-scented blossoms at Christmas. *Hamamelis mollis*, the Chinese species, with showy golden-yellow flowers—showy by winter standards, at any rate, is the one most widely grown. The form *brevipetala* has shorter petals of orange, while those of *pallida* are a pale sulphur-yellow.

H. japonica comes into flower a little later; the blooms of this species are more striking, their golden yellow strap-like petals being set off by a purple calyx. They lack, however, much of the scent of the *mollis* varieties.

More fragrant still—half a dozen small sprigs will scent a room—is the winter sweet, *Chimonanthus praecox*, with waxy, pale yellow flowers, the centres blotched with purple. In the variety *grandiflorus* they are of a pure clear yellow. The plant type starts to bloom in December, the flowers of the latter open a few weeks later and sacrifice some of their scent for showiness.

February will see the bare branches of the mezereon, *Daphne mezereum*, covered in purple, hyacinth-scented blossom. This is a short-lived shrub and might well qualify to fill gaps in the border if it did not make such a valuable winter contribution to the garden. Fortunately, fresh supplies come easily from seed, and provided the scarlet fruits—which incidentally are extremely poisonous—are protected from the birds,

which are very partial to them, the task of providing replacements is a simple one as the seed will germinate freely in any good garden soil.

From spring to summer the main display starts with shrubs such as the viburnums, brooms and lilacs and reaches its zenith at midsummer.

With the many plants to choose from, planning and planting for continuity of display should be easy. To obtain a lavish display of blossom for as long as possible it will be necessary to include in the planting plan shrubs such as *Caryopteris clandonensis*, and the tree hollyhock, *Hibiscus syriacus*, the flowering season of which covers the months of late summer and autumn.

Lilacs rank among the favourite shrubs of late spring and the most decorative are the hybrids of *Syringa vulgaris*. Among both singles and doubles, old favourites still reign supreme, with 'Souvenir de Louis Spath' as the best purple and 'Maud Notcutt' most popular as the most outstanding single white. Lesser-known single forms include 'Esther Staley', an unusual shade of pale lilac verging on pink, and 'Maurice Barnes', the best examples of the true 'lilac' colour.

Many prefer the doubles with their chunky tightly-packed conical flower trusses, although they lack some of the elegant form of the singles. 'Katherine Havemeyer' (soft mauve), 'Madame Lemoine' (white) are all established favourites. All of them, both single and double have the typical enchanting perfume of lilacs and are vigorous shrubs, reaching a height of 5–6m (15–20ft).

In the smaller garden there will not be much room for these giants, but some of the lilac species are much more compact and would prove useful where space is restricted. Their flowers may be smaller and less showy than those of the larger hybrids but they yield nothing to these where fragrance is concerned. *Syringa macrophylla*, for example, makes a dainty shrub, only 1–2m (4–6ft) in height, with elegant purple flower spikes

that are extremely fragrant and have an attractive habit of continuing to bloom at intervals throughout the summer. *S. persica alba*, a white-flowered form of the incorrectly-named 'Persian' lilac is a delightful Chinese shrub with narrow leaves and handsome panicles of white flowers.

In late spring the shrub border is redolent with fine perfumes. The mid-season viburnums, with their distinctive clove scent will be in bloom then; also *V. × burkwoodii*, a vigorous cross between *V. carlesii* and *V. utile*, with its large globes of white, *V. × carlcephalum*, another *carlesii* hybrid, with in this instance, *V. macrocephalum* as the other parent, whose large fragrant flowers measure 10–15cm (4–5in) across and *V. carlesii* itself, still ranking as one of the most popular garden shrubs.

Midsummer beauty Philadelphus, or mock orange, often wrongly called syringa, will be among the next batch of favourites to come into flower. Its fragrance can be cloying and is too heavy for some tastes. In many of the newer varieties, however, the somewhat funereal smell of *P. coronarius*, is more subdued, and the superb decorative value of their white flowers could never be in dispute. For the smaller gardens of today, there are a number of compact hybrids, much less coarse in habit than the once popular *P. coronarius*. 'Enchantment' is one of the loveliest of these, with elegant, arching branches thickly festooned with double white flowers in June and July. 'Manteau d'Hermine', only 1.3m (4ft) tall at maturity, also produces its double white blossoms freely. 'Sybille', another delightful shrub of modest dimensions, bears an abundance of dainty white, purple-scented blooms. *P. microphyllus*

can be particularly recommended for the small garden. Its leaves are very small and the unusual four-petalled flowers have a distinctive fruity perfume.

Weigelas, still listed sometimes as Diervilla, are useful midsummer shrubs of medium height and girth. Their flowers, borne along the entire length of the previous years' shoots are long and tubular, rather like miniature foxgloves. *W. florida*, a native of Korea and northern China, was discovered by Robert Fortune in the garden of a Chinese mandarin in the last century; it is the hybrids of this attractive species that have produced our popular garden forms.

'Feerie', *W. vanhouttei* and *W. styriaca* are all good, with flowers of varying shades of pink. 'Eva Rathke' and 'Bristol Ruby' have flowers of a stronger colour. 'Eva Rathke' has the longest flowering season. Its deep crimson flowers appear from mid-May until August.

Deutzias, shrubs that deserve wider recognition, will also be in flower at this period. Their habit of growth, narrow at the base but arching elegantly outwards when they attain a height of 1–2m (4–5ft), makes them invaluable where ground space is at a premium. The flowers, which are like small tassels, are profusely borne, while in winter the bare cinnamon branches are of great decorative value. *D. elegantissima* is the form most commonly encountered. The pinkish-purple blossoms are profusely

borne on arching sprays, while in the variety *pulchra* they are a pearly pink. 'Codsall Pink' is a strong grower and can reach a height of 3–5m (10–15ft). This form flowers later than most, starting at the end of June and continuing into July.

No shrub garden would be complete without the summer-flowering viburnums. The snowball bush, *V. opulus sterile*, is the most popular of these. Its globular flowers, green at first, but turning pure white later, make an established specimen of this lovely summer shrub an unforgettable sight when the branches are smothered in white snowballs. It is, however, rather a vigorous grower for small gardens and for these *V. tomentosum plicatum* would be a more appropriate choice. This seldom exceeds 2m (6ft) in height and the 'snowballs' are in the form of half-globes which are borne in symmetrical pairs along the branches, giving the effect of a stylized Chinese scroll painting. The variety *grandiflorum*, with larger leaves and flowers than those of the type is the best form to grow.

Continuity of display In the rather barren weeks that follow the peak flowering period, hydrangeas are a first-class standby. Apart from the large-leaved species, which require partial shade, they will thrive either in full sun or semi-shade. In the former position, however, copious watering or regular mulching will be required during the first few seasons after planting. *H. macrophylla* is the well-known and deservedly popular pot hydrangea of the florists' shops. It will also do well out of doors in most parts of the British Isles, although in exposed positions and inland districts the blos-

1 The shrub planting at Mount Usher, Eire, includes azaleas and malus.
2 Daphne mezereum.
3 Camellia x williamsii 'Donation' at Wisley. Camellia is a superb shrub under the right conditions.
4 Choisya ternata, the Mexican orange, will tolerate some shade.
5 Cytisus scoparius burkwoodii.

1 The various forms of hibiscus produce flowers in August, a month in which few shrubs flower.

2 The broad green leaves of Sibiraea laevigata, a deciduous flowering shrub for summer effect.

3 Many shrubs are included in the garden for the brilliant colour of their foliage in autumn. Fothergilla monticola is one of these.

4 Rhododendrons are among the most popular of spring-flowering shrubs.

som buds, which begin to swell very early in the year, may suffer frost damage. This can often be prevented by leaving the previous year's flower-heads on the plants as protection, but in really cold areas it would be safer to plant one of the completely hardy species such as *H. paniculata*, *H. villosa*, *H. serrata* or the oak-leaved hydrangea, *H. quercifolia*.

Another genus of late-flowering shrubs, useful for bridging the gap between the summer and the beauties of autumn leaf colour is represented by the hypericums, or St John's worts, of which, the best-known member is the prolific, weed-smothering *H. calycinum*, the rose of Sharon. For the shrub border, however, the taller species and hybrids are a good deal more useful and decorative. Their flowers, like giant buttercups with a central boss of contrasting stamens, make them among the finest shrubs for a late summer display. 'Hidcote' and 'Golden Cup' are both outstanding forms of *H. patulum*, with large cup-shaped flowers 5–6cm (2–2½in) across. *H. elatum* 'Elstead' is another attractive form, with oval leaves of a fresh vernal green, and masses of small yellow flowers in July and August that are followed by scarlet fruits.

But the outstanding member of the group is undoubtedly the hybrid, 'Rowallane'. Unfortunately, it is not completely hardy in all parts of Britain and needs a sheltered position in many areas. Its magnificent golden chalices are 6cm (2½in) in diameter and well-developed specimens reach a height of 2.6m (8ft) in milder districts.

To wind up the floral display for the season there is the so-called shrub hollyhock, *Hibiscus syriacus*, together with the blue-flowered *Caryopteris × clandonensis*, which is best treated as a herbaceous perennial and cut back almost to ground level each spring.

Shrubs for autumn leaf colour The beauty of the shrub border is not restricted to its floral display. From September until final leaf fall comes a brilliant cavalcade of coloured foliage, followed by, and sometimes simultaneous with, beauty of winter berry and bark.

Among the shrubs the leaves of which colour so brilliantly, the barberries and cotoneasters play a prominent part. *Berberis thunbergii* has small leaves of a clear green that produce brilliant flame in autumn. The leaves of the variety *atropurpurea*, which are deep purple throughout the summer, assume even more dazzling colours before they fall. *B. verruculosa* is an evergreen species, but many of its dark green leaves turn scarlet, while some of the foliage of the closely related *Mahonia aquifolium*, another evergreen, turns coppery-red in autumn and winter.

Although, botanically, the cut-leaved Japanese maples are not shrubs, but small trees, they have so many of the characteristics of the former that they are usually included in this category.

The Japanese maples are very slow growers and the purple-leaved *Acer palmatum dissectum atropurpureum* and its green-leaved counterpart, *palmatifidum*, both with leaves like the finest lace, never exceed 2–3m (8–10ft) in height. The leaves of the former turn a vivid deep scarlet, while those of the latter colour to a lighter but no less distinctive hue.

Anyone who gardens on the moist, peaty soils in which rhododendrons and azaleas thrive ought to find room for *Enkianthus campanulatus*, which enjoys similar conditions and puts on a spectacular autumn display in orange and red. The Ghent azaleas, too, can be very colourful in autumn, as also can the common yellow *Azalea pontica* (*Rhododendron ponticum*) when its sage-green leaves burst into tints of flame and coral.

One of the most unusual and striking shrubs for autumn colour, is a member of the euonymus genus, of which the spindle tree is probably the most

representative. *E. alata* has leaves that turn a bright glowing pink. After they fall, continuing winter interest is provided by the curious corky wing-like excrescences on the stems.

All the cotinus and rhus, related genera, are noted for their brilliant autumn colour. The stag's horn sumach, *R. typhina laciniata*, is particularly spectacular, but this small tree colours rather early for the main autumn display and the display itself is somewhat short-lived. Much more satisfying are the brilliant orange and scarlets of *Cotinus americanus* (*Rhus cotinoides*), or the bright yellow of the smoke bush, *Cotinus coggygria* (*Rhus cotinus*).

1 Cotinus coggygria is good for autumn foliage colour. The colour heightens late in the season.
2 Viburnum plicatum tomentosum 'Lanarth' has its horizontal branches covered in creamy-white flowers in June.

Among wall shrubs and climbers many of the vines and creepers colour magnificently, particularly the giant-leaved *Vitis coignetiae, Vitis inconstans* (syns. *Parthenocissus tricuspidata veitchii, Ampelopsis veitchii)*, and the true Virginian creeper, *Parthenocissus quinquefolia.* Where space is restricted, the smaller-leaved and less rampant *Parthenocissus henryana* is useful for providing a wall tapestry of brilliant colour.

On the ground, too, creeping and prostrate shrubs such as *Cotoneaster horizontalis, Gaultheria procumbens* and others will be putting down a red carpet, while the hypericums, that have only just finished their flowering season, will be adding to the autumn colours. *Hypericum patulum forrestii* has the most brilliant foliage of any of these.

Beauty of berry and bark Just as decorative, but with a longer-lasting effect are the berries of many shrubs. These will continue the display from leaf fall until the New Year—sometimes even later in districts where birds are not numerous.

Once again, the barberries and cotoneasters are well in evidence, with species and varieties bearing fruits of many colours, ranging from the vivid coral red of *Berberis* 'Bountiful' to the grape-purple of *B. darwinii.* Among the striking forms are *B.* 'Buccaneer' and *B. thunbergii*, both with bright red berries and both, incidentally, also providing attractive leaf colour. 'Cherry Ripe' has fruits that are salmon-red and pear-shaped; the compact, free-flowering Formosan species, *B. morrisonsiensis*, bears larger red fruits than most.

More than a dozen kinds of cotoneaster share this same valuable quality. The better known varieties include *C. horizontalis*, whose herring-bone set branches are packed with scarlet button berries and *C. simonsii*, a popular shrub for hedging and cover planting, with no less brilliant berries the size of peas. Taller forms and species include *C. cornubia* with large berries borne profusely, *C. frigidus* with clustered crimson fruits and *C. salicifolius*, the willow-leaved cotoneaster, that bears heavy crops of bright red fruits. Among the prostrate forms suitable for the rock garden, or for use as ground cover, *C. dammeri* decks its trailing shoots with berries like blobs of sealing wax, while *C. adpressus* has both autumn fruits and bright scarlet foliage.

The pernettyas are a group of attractive small-leaved evergreen shrubs with showy marble-sized berries of an unusual beauty. Not many of them, however, are self-fertile so that a specimen of the type plant, *P. mucronata*, will have to be included to cross-fertilize the more decoratively-berried forms. These last-named include 'Donard White' and 'Donard Pink' (the names are descriptive of the colour of their berries), *lilacina*, with lilac-pink fruits

and 'Bell's Seedling' with extra-large, dark-red berries.

The vacciniums, like the pernettyas, are ericaceous plants, and they include the edible North American swamp blueberry, *V. corymbosum*, and others such as *V. macrocarpum*, the American cranberry, a prostrate evergreen, the large scarlet berries of which are used for cranberry sauce traditionally associated with the Christmas turkey. *V. myrsinites*, the evergreen blueberry, is a graceful compact shrub that bears its blue-black berries in May and June when they are of doubtful value for garden decoration.

It is not always realized that certain shrubs are dioecious, for example, the

1 The feathery foliage of Rhus typhina laciniata colours well in autumn.
2 One of the plants grown for its bold red berries is Skimmia japonica.
3 Red berries of Viburnum hupehense.

male and female flowers are borne on separate plants, so that a specimen of each sex will need to be planted if berries are to result. Japanese laurels or aucubas all share this specialized sex characteristic, which makes it difficult for the owner of a small garden, with limited space at his or her disposal, to include many of them in the planting plan. But for those with room to spare all of these are well worth growing, not only for the beauty of their berries but also for the year-long decorative qualities of their handsome, evergreen foliage.

Finally, to act as a foil to the winter-flowering shrubs, there are other plants whose main attraction lies in their strikingly-coloured bark or interesting branch formation.

The dogwoods, both the scarlet and yellow-stemmed species, love moisture. They will respond to waterside planting and nothing looks more striking in January sunshine than a group of the scarlet-stemmed Westonbirt dogwoods (*Cornus alba sibirica*) at the edge of a pond or stream, while the curiously twisted stems and branches of *Corylus avellana contorta*, popularly known as Harry Lauder's walking stick, make an unusual and interesting tracery against winter skies.

Pruning It is impossible, in the space available, to lay down principles of pruning in any but the most general terms. As a general rule, however, spring-flowering shrubs can be pruned after they have finished blooming. Those that flower in summer and autumn, on the current year's wood, can have their season's growths cut right back in March of each year.

Shrubs should normally be allowed to develop their natural form and dimensions, but any particularly vigorous growths that appear in the second and third seasons after planting should be tipped when they are between 15–25cm (6–9in) long to induce the formation of laterals to build up a solid framework.

Most shrubs, once established, will need little or no attention as far as pruning is concerned, apart from cutting out weak, straggling, diseased or dead shoots. In any case, drastic pruning is an operation that should always be undertaken with caution and should normally be resorted to only when shrubs have been neglected or when, like buddleias, forsythias, flowering currants and the larger philadelphuses, they grow too rampantly and exceed their allotted quarters, or trespass on paths and lawns.

Avoid, at all costs, indiscriminate clipping with the garden shears. Such treatment will not only reduce all your shrubs to a monotonous uniformity of shape but will also result in weak, straggling growth. Clearly this would look unattractive.

Propagation This, too, is a vast subject. Many shrubs can be grown easily from seed, although not all of them ripen their seed in this country and it may be necessary to obtain it from specialist seedsmen. Brooms, for example, will germinate as easily and as freely as sweet peas; other shrub seeds, berries in particular, need to be stratified, that is, over-wintered in moist sand, to rot the fleshy seed covering, before they can be sown with any hope of success.

Propagation from hard-wood cuttings is another simple method by which many shrubs may be increased. These cuttings should consist of ripened side shoots that have not flowered, pulled off the parent stem with a heel of bark attached, and inserted in a moist shady bed in July and August. They are left until the end of the following season, when sufficient root and top growth should have developed to enable them to be grown on in a nursery bed.

Shrubs that may be propagated easily by this method include cornus, weigela, deutzia, philadelphus, rhus, cotinus, hydrangea and many other well-known kinds. Hedging shrubs such as privet or *Lonicera nitida* are easier still. Trimmings stuck into the soil almost anywhere will usually root very quickly.

Soil types

Soils are not just deposited in their present position; they are largely the outcome of the deposits left by the plants and the animals they once supported and of the climate in which they develop and the type of rock that constitutes most of their solid or mineral matter. Not only are there broad differences among soils from different parts of the world as a result of differences in climate and nature of vegetation, but differences are found among neighbouring soils. It was John Evelyn, the diarist, who said in 1675 that he considered that there were no fewer than 179,001,060 different sorts of earth. The basis of this calculation is not recorded, but several hundred soils have already been identified and mapped in Britain.

The soils of the world are classified into a comparatively small number of major groups in rather the same way as plants are grouped into families. And, as each plant family consists of many different genera and still more species, so the major soil groups are divided into smaller units, of which the soil series is the most important for survey and mapping work. Most British soils come into the following five groups.

Brown earths which give most of the best garden soils in Britain, developed from a wide variety of rocks under fairly dry and warm conditions that favour the growth of deciduous forest; their colour is brown, yellow-brown or red. Having no natural lime they are generally slightly to moderately acid in reaction. Since they often have a friable, coarse-textured topsoil and a system of deep fine cracks they are generally well drained. But if you have one with a silty texture you will have to be careful not to cultivate it or water it too heavily for fear of panning the surface which leads to temporary waterlogging.

Gley soils are wet and in contrast to well-drained soils usually have a grey or blue layer somewhere in their profiles or they may have a variegated or mottled appearance.

The reason why plants grow poorly in such soils as these is not so much due to their excess of water but more to their lack of air; the roots of plants must breathe, just as other parts of the plant do, so that, aquatic plants excepted, they must rely upon air in between the particles of soil, if their roots are to survive. After rain these spaces fill with water and until this drains away the roots are unable to get air. The speed at which the water drains away varies greatly with different soils as also does the capacity of different kinds of plants to withstand immersion.

But the reason for the wet condition of a soil must be discovered before you can cure the trouble. Below are given the three main causes of wetness.

Poor penetration The rock underlying the soil may be more or less impermeable and prevent the free passage of water. Roots are swamped in wet periods and when followed by dry periods there is no reserve of water for the crippled root system to draw upon because the impervious rock does not store much water. Waterlogging is therefore followed by drought. This is one of the commonest causes of poor drainage and is found on soils overlying clays and shales.

A water table may be present in soils of low-lying land, resulting in the soil being saturated with water only a little below the soil surface. The surface of this underground lake is known as the water table and it generally rises and falls following wet and dry periods. Provided that the fluctuation is not too great, a water table at about 1m (3ft) below the surface of the soil can be an asset since the water will be available to the deeper roots. You can find out whether your soil has a water table near the surface by digging a hole or boring a hole with a post-hole auger about 1m (3ft) deep; leave it open for a day and then see whether there is any water resting on the bottom of the hole. It is not only clay soils that are subject to this kind of wetness; sandy and loamy soils often have high water tables in low-lying areas such as the flood plains of rivers and estuaries.

When the water table rises during the winter the roots of perennial plants are killed and when it falls in the summer your plants are literally left high and dry and then suffer from drought.

Springs are more common than is generally suspected because only the largest are seen at the surface; but large areas of land are waterlogged by subterranean springs.

You can usually tell whether a soil is well-drained or badly-drained by the colour of the soil; well-drained soil is an even colour of grey brown or brown and free from mottling, whereas defective drainage leaves definite symptoms in the soil. Well-drained soils are normally well aerated and have plenty of oxygen in them, but where the water stagnates the living organisms in the soil and plant roots use the dissolved oxygen as fast as it can be renewed, and some of the iron compounds which impart a yellow, brown or red colour to soils, lose part of their oxygen and cause grey or bluish colours to develop. When the water subsides air gets in again and the grey or bluish colours go brown again and so the soil becomes mottled with rust coloured stains, or even hard little lumps of rust. Spring water may deposit a heavy, chocolate-brown iron staining.

It is important to note the depth at which these symptoms occur because all the earth above the waterlogged area means an area of good healthy root run. **Podsolised soils** are acid and have profiles consisting of very distinct layers. They are best seen on heathland overlying sandy or gravelly geological formations, in western Surrey, northern Hampshire, the New Forest and eastern Dorset, the Cornish moors and the heaths of the west Midlands especially in Cheshire and Shropshire.

The surface layer is often black and peaty, being rich in decaying plant remains. These produce acids which cause the washing out of iron and aluminium compounds from this and the next layer below. Under the dark-coloured surface layer lies one which is very pale brown, often almost white. This is because the iron, which normally colours a soil brown, has been washed out of it. Underneath this is a dark-brown to reddish-brown layer in which clay, iron and aluminium compounds and humus have been deposited. This is often cemented into a hard pan by the iron and organic matter. When you dig these soils the mixture of the bleached layer and the dark-coloured subsoil gives it an ashy appearance.

Extreme acidity and low nutrient content often characterize these soils; but by careful liming and the application of manures they can grow plants well, and, of course, many are ideal for rhododendrons and azaleas and other members of the *Ericaceae*. While their coarse texture makes for very easy working, moisture retention is usually a problem. Deficiency of potash is normal while manganese and boron deficiences may result from over-liming. Where the garden has been recently reclaimed from heathland, generous manuring with nitrogenous manures is needed to speed up the decay of plant remains and magnesium compounds may have to be added.

Calcareous soils are naturally rich in lime (calcium carbonate) due to their development from chalk and limestone formations in downland areas of the south-eastern and southern central parts of England; they also occur in parts of Lincolnshire and Rutland.

You can generally see fragments or sometimes fairly large lumps of calcium carbonate in these soils and the presence of this substance makes them alkaline (the opposite to acid). This accounts for the fizzing (effervescence) when a small amount is treated with dilute hydrochloric acid.

When newly broken up they are almost always neutral to the surface and do not require liming. They are so alkaline that elements like iron, boron, magnesium and manganese are less readily available to plants and symptoms of their deficiency can often be seen in many species.

Since many calcareous soils are not very thick they lose their reserves of moisture in a very short time during dry weather, unless very large amounts of humus-forming manures are either dug in or added as a mulch.

The deeper calcareous soils have brown or reddish-brown sub-surface layers and make quite good garden soils, provided that you do not want to grow rhododendrons or most other members of the *Ericaceae* in them. They will also grow plums, apples and most of the soft fruits.

If the clay content is high you have a real problem soil to contend with and great skill is needed to cultivate them just at the right time, when they often break down into an excellent tilth. But when wet, they are plastic and if cultivated in this condition the structure is destroyed and they are then liable to dry out into large blocks. Peat or well-rotted manure will help to prevent them from becoming like concrete, but it should always be worked into the surface and not buried deeply.

Organic soils are rich in humus and have a very dark brown or black colour. If they have over 50 percent organic matter in a layer which is more than 40cm (15in) thick they are classed as peat soils of which there are two main types, bog peat and fen peat. Bog peat consists of the residues of heather and mosses, particularly sphagnum moss. Bog peat is usually formed on an impervious rock formation which prevents water from draining away. So the natural vegetation decays very slowly in these badly aerated wet soils and peat is the result.

Given shelter, many garden plants will survive if the soil is limed, but it is not generally necessary to lime them to the point of neutrality, because many plants will grow well at pH values lower than would be possible in a mineral soil; in fact heavy liming may result in boron and manganese deficiencies.

The other main type of peat soil is fen peat, which is composed of residues of reeds, rushes and sedges and other water plants. This type of soil is usually formed at the edges of slow-moving or blocked rivers and streams. Such accumulations are generally much less acid and have pH values of about 6: the areas where they are formed may have been drained by rivers that have previously passed through limestone and chalk formations.

Some of the fen peat soils are among

Gley soils are poor and waterlogged, so that oxygen cannot reach the iron content and so turn it red. This is
1 less apparent in the topsoil than in
2 the subsoil, which is more grey,
3 as shown by this profile.

the richest in the country, being deep and very easily worked. Plants often produce rank, luxuriant, vegetative growth, owing to their naturally high content of nitrogen.

Phosphate content is often low and extra potash is generally required, but nitrogenous fertilizers are seldom needed in the richest fen peats

Sandy, loamy and clayey soils The more usual way of classifying soils is on the basis of their texture. This is a property that depends on the relative amounts of the different sized particles that they contain. For example sand is the name given to coarse gritty particles that you can see quite plainly, whereas silt particles can be seen only with a microscope and a clay particle which is even smaller can be seen only with an electron microscope. All soils contain sand, silt and clay in varying ratios.

Texture is important because it affects the handling, drainage, aeration and nutrient content of the soil. Lime and fertilizer requirements are also keyed to texture. It can be assessed by hand. To do this take a handful of moist soil and rub a portion between your finger and thumb. Sand can be detected by the sensation of grittiness or roughness; the finer the sand the less the grittiness. Silt has a floury or talcum powder-like feel when dry and is only slightly plastic when wet. Clay may feel smooth but the surface becomes polished when rubbed between the fingers and clay is sticky when wet. A true loam is smooth and not gritty, silty or sticky when moist.

Sandy soils These are warm and are most suitable for early vegetable crops. If less than 40cm (15in) deep they cannot be recommended for fruits and shrubs.

On calcareous soils the topsoil
1 often contains a high percentage of humus, and the subsoil
2 is almost all calcium carbonate.
3 Left Calcareous soil right an organic soil.
4 Surface layers of an organic soil.
5 The subsoil of an organic soil.

Soft fruits can be successfully grown in these soils provided they are mulched or irrigated. The only way to improve the soil is to add as much bulky humus-forming material as possible, and cow and pig manure are much favoured.

Fertilizers produce the best effect when they are applied in small quantities at frequent intervals during the growing season, but neither these nor the manure should be dug in too deeply. Sandy soils soon become acid and generally need frequent but small applications of lime.

Loamy soils A true loam has a well-balanced proportion of sand, silt and clay and is really the ideal texture as it is the easiest soil to look after. With good management most loams readily acquire and retain a good crumb structure and almost all plants grow well in them provided they are deep and in a good position.

Clayey soils These are very retentive of moisture and are sticky when wet. On drying they form hard clods, which are impossible to break down until they are moistened again. After long spells of hot dry weather they form deep, wide cracks which cause root rupture and loss of moisture. It is necessary to hoe regularly in order to fill in the cracks to provide a surface soil mulch. There is

no quick way of improving clay soil. Artificial drainage may well be the first essential before any other form of improvement can be attempted.

Very thorough digging, or better still ridging in the autumn, will produce a frost tilth in the spring. Humus-forming materials are necessary to preserve the crumb structure so formed. Strawy stable manure is best, but a fine grade of peat when applied regularly can transform a heavy clay into quite workable soil in a few years. Gypsum can improve the structure of some clay soils when applied at the rate of 110–220g (4–8oz) per sq m (sq yd). Clay soils are naturally rich in plant nutrients. These nutrients are not always readily available since roots tend to follow the cracks and fail to tap the nutrients in the soil lumps. Hence the proper use of fertilizers will produce still better results.

Clays are not always acid as is commonly supposed but when they are, large applications of lime are needed, at rates depending on the results of the soil analysis.

Soil testing

Broadly speaking soil testing includes any kind of examination to which a soil is submitted; for example, when you rub some moist soil between your fingers to assess its texture or dig a hole to see whether it is badly drained, you are carrying out soil tests. But for most gardeners it means soil chemical analysis to find out whether their soil needs lime, and how much, and also whether it needs extra phosphates and potash.

You can test it yourself, using a test kit, or ask your county horticultural adviser to arrange to have it done for you, or send it to a private laboratory. Most soil test kits provide apparatus and chemicals for estimating the acidity, phosphates, potash and the amount of lime needed to correct acidity; some kits include a test for nitrogen, but it is very difficult to make a reliable prediction as to the amount of nitrogen that will be released during the season.

Whatever the method adopted the first thing to do is to get a sample of your soil. Collecting samples is not difficult, but it must be done properly if the tests are to give a reliable and accurate assessment of the nutrient status of your soil. Only about a teaspoonful of soil is required for the actual test, but that spoonful must represent an enormous amount of soil.

Never just take one lump of soil but take a small amount of soil from at least ten different places in a plot, going down to a depth of 16cm (6in) in beds or borders and 8cm (3in) in the lawn. Do not pick places near manure, compost or similar heaps, or bonfire sites and hedges when sampling.

There are special tools for the purpose but most gardeners can make a V-shaped slit in the soil to a depth of 16cm (6in) and take a thin slice of soil for testing. For the lawn a hollow-tine fork will cause the least disturbance.

The samples are then put into a clean plastic bucket and mixed together, saving about 0.5l (½pt) of the mixture for the testing. If the sample is to be sent away for testing put it into a strong plastic bag and number each sample.

When the sample reaches the laboratory it will be dried in the air, ground up and sieved through a 2mm sieve in order to remove stones and hard lumps.

The next step is to find out whether the soil is acid, neutral or alkaline. This is expressed in terms of the pH scale, which ranges from 0–14. Values less than 7.0 are acid, values above 7.0 are alkaline.

In the laboratory very accurate pH measurements can be made with a pH meter, which is an expensive instrument and is hardly practicable for most gardeners. There are, however, inexpensive indicator solutions that change colour according to the degree of acidity present in the soil.

A rough method of estimating pH in the open consists in placing a small quantity of fresh soil in a white dish and then pouring a little indicator solution on to it. The contact between the indicator and the soil is achieved by slowly rocking the dish to avoid breaking up the soil fragments and the formation of a muddy suspension.

After the soil has soaked up the indicator, the colour at the junction of the soil and the indicator should be used to assess the acidity. The colour should be checked with a colour chart provided with the testing kit.

Most soil test kits provide a more refined method of assessing pH, in which the soil is shaken vigorously with a clarifying agent (usually barium sulphate), distilled water and a soil indicator. On settling, a clear layer is obtained which may be compared with the colour chart. With a little practice an accuracy to within half a unit of pH can be obtained.

A pH assessment alone will not give an estimation of the lime requirement.

The amount of phosphates and potash that is readily available for plant use is found by carrying out the appropriate tests with one of the kits. A dilute acid is used for extracting the nutrients from the soil; the extract is treated with various reagents that produce colours or cloudy suspensions which may then be compared with charts or standard colours in glass tubes.

The estimation of the amount of fertilizer needed is the most difficult part of the operation; it depends on the nutrient content of the soil and the general requirements of the plants to be grown.

Generally autumn is the best time to sample and test. Not only is the soil in a more normal condition after the growing season, but if lime is needed it will have time to act during the winter.

pH

This is the measure used to indicate the active acidity of the soil. The term is based on the balance between the hydrogen ions and the hydroxyl ions and it is important to remember that a low pH figure indicates acid soil which for most crops requires correcting by the addition of lime. pH 7 represents

The colour of a soil is often an indication of its type.
1 Loamy sand.
2 One of the many types of clay.
3 A well-balanced loam.
4 A sandy clay loam.

neutrality. Below pH 6.5, the soil is acid and at pH 6, the degree of acidity reaches the point, where only acid-loving plants, such as heathers and rhododendrons will thrive. If the figure is up to pH 8, the alkalinity of the soil is such that certain essential foods are locked up and plants show signs of starvation. The scale used is logarithmic, so that pH 5, is ten times as acid as pH 6, and pH 4, is one hundred times as acid as pH 6.

Simple and reasonably priced outfits are available to determine the pH value and it is advisable to take samples from various parts of the garden since the degree of acidity may vary. To raise the pH value (which means neutralizing the soil acidity) lime is added. In general the lighter the soil, the smaller the quantity of lime required; a heavy clay soil needs about half as much again as a light sandy soil. As a rough guide, hydrated lime, applied at the rate of 225–335g (8–12oz) per sq m (sq yd), according to the soil texture, every few years should be adequate, except, of course, where chalky soils are concerned which require no additional lime, or very acid soils, which would require more. The pH measurement is a useful check to be applied when the crops show signs of lime shortage.

It should also be remembered that excessive lime dressings over a long period produce deficiencies of various trace

elements and encourage scab in potatoes on soils liable to produce the disease. Lime can be applied in hydrated form or as ground limestone or chalk. About 0.5kg (1lb) of hydrated lime is equal to 1kg (2lb) of the other two forms. If spent mushroom compost obtained from farms using chalk in the casing soil is used in the garden as a mulch, the pH should be watched.

Spade see Tools

Spinach see Vegetables

Spring Onions see Vegetables

Storage

Bulbs, corms and tubers Wherever it is desired, spring-flowering bulbs are lifted after the foliage had died down naturally. The bulbs should then be laid out in full sun to dry. When the roots and foliage are quite dry and brittle the bulbs should be stored in a cool, well-ventilated place until it is time to replant them. Gladiolus corms are dug when the foliage begins to turn brown. After lifting, the dying foliage is cut off close to the corm, the roots are trimmed and the corms spread out out-of-doors or in any airy place indoors to dry. After a week or two the old corm-husk will pull away cleanly. Clean the corms and cormlets and store them in a cool but frostproof, dry, well-ventilated place. Inspect stored corms occasionally during the winter and

Testing the soil for acidity or alkalinity.
1 The sample of dry soil is put into a test tube using a clean spoon so as not to affect the chemical content.
2 The acidity testing solution supplied with the kit is carefully poured on to the soil sample. The tube is then corked to prevent the finger affecting the acidity of the sample. The tube is then well shaken.
3 The colour of the resultant solution is compared with the test card, and read off. The result here indicates pH 7.0.

remove any showing disease symptoms or moulds. Dahlia tubers are lifted in late October or November. Cut off the stems just above soil level before lifting. After digging up the tubers pick off as much adhering earth as possible and then place the roots upside down in a well-ventilated greenhouse, frame or shed for at least a fortnight. They may then be stored on racks or in shallow trays in a frost-proof, dry place. The stored tubers should be inspected monthly.

Fruit Apples and pears are the principal garden fruits grown for storing and for use during the winter and early spring. A dry, sunny day should be chosen for harvesting and great care taken when doing so to prevent any bruising. Unblemished fruits only should be stored. The ideal fruit store

should be a place where the temperature remains fairly constant at around 37–40°F (3–4°C). Apples store best in a moist atmosphere, pears in a dry one. The fruit store should be proof against rats and mice. Cool cellars are not a feature of present-day homes. A spare bedroom may be used as a fruit store but not if the house is centrally-heated. An attic is suitable, providing the temperature seldom falls to freezing point. The garden shed and the garage are alternative places for the fruit store which should be insulated against very low temperatures. Straw is a useful insulator but bear in mind that it is also a fire hazard. Dutch trays, obtainable from most fruiterers and greengrocers, are ideal storage containers. The fruits should be placed in a single layer only in each tray and crimped newspaper packed between each fruit to keep them apart and prevent any infection from spreading from fruit to fruit. The wrapping of apples in oiled paper prolongs their storage life. To exclude light from the stored fruit, cover the stack of trays with a sheet of black polythene or with clean sacking. Inspect regularly and discard fruits showing rot.

Vegetables The largest crop for storing is likely to be maincrop potatoes. The farmer stores potatoes successfully in large clamps. The small crop lifted from the garden does not normally store well in small clamps. Potatoes are also required daily which means that the small

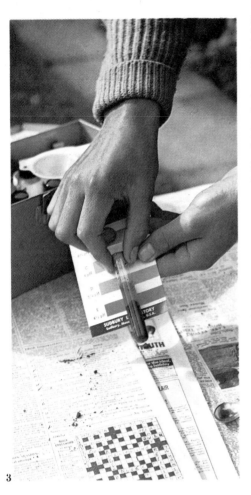

3

greenhouse are suggested storage places. Onions may be roped or placed in single layers in Dutch trays. When inspecting stored onions, remove for immediate use bulbs which have any fresh foliage.

Maincrop beets are dug and stored in the autumn. The foliage is twisted from the beets—not cut—and these roots store well in a box of fairly dry sand or peat in the garden shed or the garage. Where winters are very severe the box is best housed indoors because beetroots do not stand up to frost. Maincrop carrots are lifted in October. Do not store any which show fork or insect damage. Cut off the foliage close to the crown and store the roots in moist sand or leafmould in a box or bin in the garden shed. A large crop of carrots may be stored in a pit in the ground. Layers of carrots are covered with sand. The top layer of carrots is 2cm (1in) or so below the surface of the surrounding ground and this last layer is covered with a thick layer of sand over which some straw may be spread. Beets and carrots may also be stored in clamps but these, unless very large, often lead to the freezing of the vegetables within them. Swedes are usually left in the

garden. Any remaining there are lifted at Christmas, the top growth is short-ened and the swedes are stored in the manner suggested for carrots. Winter turnips may be left in the ground or dug in early winter and stored like carrots. Parsnips are seldom harvested as they withstand hard frost well. Winter storing cabbages are dug in November and hung upside down in a cool, airy place. Pumpkins, winter squash and vegetable marrows are best stored in nets hung from the ceiling of a cool, frost-proof, airy room.

Strawberries see Fruit

Swedes see Vegetables

Sweet corn see Vegetables

1 Apple 'Allington Pippin' in individual wrappings of waxed paper, to help them to keep longer. Store only sound, un-blemished fruit, preferably in a moist atmosphere.

clamp has to be opened regularly throughout the winter – this is not an easy job to do in very wet or freezing weather. The requirements for the good storage of potatoes are a cool, frost-proof, dry, dark place. Failing a conven-ient cellar, the garden shed is often used as a potato store. Dry straw or bracken should be spread thickly on the floor or on shelves and the sound dry potatoes placed carefully in layers on the straw or bracken pad. Cover with more straw or bracken to exclude light and, in very cold weather, add sacking or old blan-kets or use a small heater in the shed. Alternatively, store the potato crop in Dutch trays. Each holds around 6kg (12lb) and the trays stack easily and may be housed in a spare, cool bedroom. Cover with a blanket or a sheet of black plastic to prevent light from greening the tubers. Always inspect potatoes in store once each month. Remove any showing rot and rub off all young shoots.

Onions are not lifted until most of the plants have dry, brown foliage. After harvesting, spread the bulbs in full sun or hang them in bunches outdoors or in the greenhouse. When the foliage and roots are quite dry and brittle, any adhering soil may be rubbed off as may *loose* portions of dry skin. Only sound onions and those with thin necks should be stored. The storage place must be dry and well-ventilated and free from severe frost. A spare bedroom, the attic, the garden shed, the garage and the

Many mature plants provide tubers, roots or fruit that will keep well in good storage conditions.
1 Before beetroots are stored the top growth is twisted off.
2 The roots of beet are put in a box of dryish sand for storing.

Thinning

The reduction of the number of seedlings, established plants, buds, flowers, fruit-lets, stems, branches and trees, is referred to as 'thinning'.

Seedlings The thinning of seedlings is the most common in the garden. Sowing seeds thinly leads to easier thinning of seedlings especially when growing such vegetables as beet, carrots and lettuces and calendulas, cornflowers and other flowers.

Take great care during thinning to prevent harm to those seedlings which are intended to reach full growth. Should the compost or soil be dry, thinning is made easier by watering it thoroughly on the previous day. The thinning of seedlings is sometimes carried out twice. During the initial thinning the seedlings left to grow on are double the number intended to reach full growth. The surplus is re-moved during the second thinning. With such vegetables as beet, carrots and parsnips thinning is always carried out twice at least, with a lapse of several weeks between the thinnings. During the final thinning of beet, carrots and maincrop onions there may well be 'thinnings' sufficiently large for culinary use. In the thinning of carrots and onions the disturbance to the seedlings increases their natural aroma. This is liable to guide female flies of the carrot fly, *Psila rosae*, and the onion fly, *Hylemyia antiqua*, to the rows where eggs may be laid, from which larvae hatch out. The larvae eat into the roots of these two vegetables. To reduce the aroma take care to prevent foliage from being broken and bury all discarded seedlings deeply inside the compost heap. During the thinning of such vege-tables as cabbages and lettuces seedlings removed may be planted elsewhere.

Buds and flowers Reducing the number of buds and flowers is practised by the exhibitor aiming at particularly large but fewer specimens. Bud reduction is also practised in tree training. Where quality rather than quantity is desired, thin the young stems of delphiniums, Michaelmas daisies and phlox.

Fruits With many tree fruits it is often possible to limit crops by picking off the surplus fruitlets by hand, although much experimental work is being done on thinning by spraying, using Carbaryl and other chemicals. If a tree sets too large a crop, there will be insufficient leaf area to 'process' the sap and supply the developing fruits with all the necessary nutrients. As a result there will be some degree of starvation and not only may the current year's crop fail to reach its potential size, but the fruits may be poor in colour. In addition, the development of fruit buds, on which the next year's crop depends, may be arrested. In this way overcropping in one year can result in little or no crop the next season and encourage a habit of biennial bearing.

Judicious thinning of a heavy crop will not only reduce the total weight of crop at harvest but will also greatly improve average fruit size, as well as colour and quality. As far as plums are concerned, the avoidance of a very heavy weight of fruit on any branch will reduce the risk of breakage, which is one of the commonest causes of silver leaf disease infection.

Many growers like to defer fruit thin-ning until after the 'June drop', their idea being to step in only after the natural thinning. However, experiments at East Malling research station, Kent, with 'Cox's Orange Pippin' showed that thinning approximately four weeks after full blossom gave a 41 percent increase in the number of large apples. Thinning immediately after the 'June drop' (approximately 13 weeks after full blossom) gave only a 23 percent increase. The early-thinned apples were relatively unaffected by the 'June drop'.

In thinning apples, the 'king apple' (the central one in each cluster, often with a thicker stalk than the others) should be removed first, as, in spite of its promising appearance, it often becomes misshapen and is unlikely to keep well. With all fruits, snap the fruitlet off or cut it off with sharp scissors so that the stalk remains on the spur.

Because varieties behave in different ways and are affected by climatic and soil conditions, no definite rules can be laid down for thinning fruits. However, the approximate indications given below may be helpful.

Apples Remove 'king apples' and reduce to one per cluster. For the best dessert specimens reduce to 10-15cm (4-6in) between fruit along the branch, for large cookers, reduce to 15-22cm (6-9in) apart. Some growers believe in the 'leaf count' system, thinning the fruitlets until there are at least 20 leaves to each fruit.

Peaches and nectarines Thin by degrees in two separate stages. Firstly, before the stone forms, starting when the fruitlets are pea-size. Secondly, after stoning (when stones have formed). With wall-trained peaches, at the first stage pinch off all fruitlets pointing towards the wall, then reduce 'doubles' to 'singles' and then any further fruitlets necessary to bring the spacing down to about 8cm (3in). After stoning reduce the fruits to one per 9sq dc (1sq ft) of wall space covered, or when dealing with nectarines and very vigorous peaches to one per 23cm sq (9in sq) of wall space. Crops on bush peaches growing in the open should be thinned similarly in two stages, the final distance between fruits along each branch being the span of a hand.

Pears These usually require less thinning than apples and normally it is sufficient to reduce to one per spur, occasionally two. For best quality dessert specimens, space the pears 13cm (5in) apart, but where large-fruited varieties such as 'Doyenne du Comice' and 'Marguerite Marillat', are concerned reduce to one per 9 sq dc (1 sq ft).

Plums Thinning is always wise if a full crop has set. As with peaches carry it out in two stages, before and after stoning. At the first stage reduce to 2.5cm (1in) or so apart and at the second thin until dessert varieties are at least 8cm (3in) apart, cookers also about 8cm (3in).

Trees The thinning of tree branches is sometimes desirable to avoid overcrowding, enabling the centre of the tree to enjoy more light and a good air circulation. Harvesting is also made easier.

Tomatoes see Vegetables

Tools, basic
Spades are of several types ranging from those made for garden work to special ones which have long, narrow

1 *When thinning turnips the less robust-looking seedlings are removed. Thinning may be done in several stages.*
2 *Lettuce seedlings are removed with a hand hoe, then the thinning is finished off by hand.*

blades for digging out drains and trenches. Spades for gardeners are made in various blade sizes. The larger types have blades 31 × 20cm (12½ × 8in). Medium digging spades are manufac-

tured with blades of 25 × 15cm (10 × 6½in) and the lighter border models have blades which are only 23 × 14cm (9 × 5½in). There is also a 'junior' model with a 18 × 13cm (7 × 5in) blade.

Handle design also varies. The most popular are those which are shaped in the form of a 'D'. However, many spades used in northern England have a handle in the form of a 'T'.

Some handles and shafts are covered with a PVC sleeve, which adds considerably to the comfort of handling and

Several patterns of hoe are obtainable, although there are only two basic types —the Dutch hoe (as shown second from the left) and the draw hoe (the remaining tools).

which gives greater durability and better appearance.

The more expensive spades have stainless steel blades. The highly polished surfaces enable the blades to slip easily through the soil—especially the heavy sticky types.

There is a specially designed spade for those gardeners who have to deal with these stubborn, heavy soils. It has four pointed cutting teeth on its blade edge. The blade itself is 28×8cm ($11\frac{1}{2} \times 7\frac{1}{2}$in). Also suitable for heavy soil is a spade with a polished steel blade which has a double-tapered self-sharpening edge.

Many gardeners prefer a tread above the blade, as there is less wear on boots. Spades with such treads are sometimes referred to as 'London-treaded' types.

A spade is made using a lever and spring system, which turns over the soil much faster than can be done with the conventional spade. This is the Wolf 'Terrex' automatic spade. The spade head can be changed for a special fork head.

The garden fork is one of the important basic tools and can be used for many jobs. It is an ideal tool for soil cultivation and is especially useful where the soil is on the heavy side, as the thin, strong tines penetrate the soil more easily than does the blade of a spade. It is also invaluable for the preliminary operation of breaking the soil down after the autumn or winter digging. The large clumps of soil can be broken down into smaller particles with the back of the fork.

The fork can be used as an aerator for the lawn if the tines are thrust into the turf as deeply as possible all over the lawn at spacings. For lifting plants or roots and for raking up rubbish, the fork is especially useful. An important operation is the maintenance of a good surface tilth or cultivation. Some soils pan or harden badly on the surface, and

for good growth it is essential to keep it broken or open. The fork is ideal for this purpose as it can be inserted lightly into the soil in between plants, in the operation known as 'forking over'.

There are many different types or designs of fork, although some of these are of little importance to the amateur gardener. For the lady gardener and for work in confined areas, the smaller, lighter border fork is ideal. Some of the more expensive designs are manufactured from stainless steel or chrome-armoured metals.

Prongs vary in size and in number; in length they range from as little as 13cm (5in) to as much as 38cm (15in). Some prongs are flat and these are useful for lifting potatoes and other root crops. Prong numbers vary from 2–10. The larger types are for the professional gardener and are designed for potato and beetroot harvesting.

One other type of fork must be included; this is the small hand fork which usually has 3 prongs, although some have 2 and others 4. This is usually a companion to the hand trowel and is extremely useful for planting small plants. Handle lengths range from about 13cm (5in) to as much as 1–1.3m (3–4ft). Those with longer handles are used for cultivating the soil especially towards the back of deep borders, but are also useful light tools for those who wish to avoid too much stooping.

One of the most useful and versatile tools in the garden is the rake, which usually has from 10 to 14 teeth (or up to 34 in the 'Springbok' type of lawn rake). The more teeth there are the easier it is to obtain a really fine soil surface (tilth). The handles usually measure 1.6m (5ft), but one firm also makes handles 16cm (6in) longer or shorter. The head may measure from 16–40cm (6–16in) wide, largely depending on the number of teeth. It is usually slightly curved to improve balance.

Although they are more expensive the best rakes are those which have teeth cut out of one piece of steel, which may be plain, stainless or chromium-plated. The head is welded to a tapering tube

which is fastened to the handle (ash or tubular steel). Cheap rakes or rake heads may survive a season or two, but these rakes will last a life-time.

The rake is used extensively during the busy sowing and planting season in spring. It is ideal for breaking down the soil to the required tilth immediately before sowing or planting. After the prior stage of breaking down the heavier lumps of soil with the back of a fork, if the soil is in the right condition the smaller remaining lumps should crumble quickly as the rake head is drawn over them.

Turned on one corner, the edge of the rake can be used to make shallow, V-shaped seed drills, and for covering seeds after sowing it is returned to its normal position. Held vertically the rake head is useful for light firming with a gentle tapping movement. A special type of rake is made for the lawn surface. Specially light lawn rakes are also made from plastic, flexible rubber or split bamboo. They cannot harm even the finest turf.

For raking up mowings left behind by rough grass cutters or after you have cut down weeds or grass with a scythe or bagging hook, the wooden hay rake is best. It has about 12 teeth (when broken easily replaceable by anyone handy with tools), and the handle is longer than those of other rakes. It is not expensive and may also be used for making the final tilth on seed beds, particularly on lighter soils.

Apart from raking to remove autumn leaves from lawns and flower beds, this gardening term more generally refers to the final stage in the levelling of soil for sowing or planting. It should never be done when the soil is wet, and is more effective when the surface is drying out but not quite dry. The soil will have been dug and may have been left rough over winter. The latter is a common procedure when the soil is heavy, to enable the frost to break down the lumps.

The teeth of the rake should never be pushed into the soil. The rake is best

A small hand hoe used for weeding.

1 Different types of rakes, left to right: bamboo, iron, wooden, Springbok and rubber.

2 The Tudor multi-purpose lawn rake for scarifying and raking up grass.

3 The rake has many uses in the garden, not least in the drawing of drills and the covering in of seeds.

4 R to L: Border fork, digging fork, flat-tined fork and, in front, a hand fork.

applied with a light backward movement so that there is no danger of stepping forward on to the raked soil. In pulling the rake towards the body unwanted clods, stones and other debris are drawn away from the area being prepared. After raking the debris should not be left piled up, as it is not only unsightly but a potential hiding place for slugs, etc.

Using the rake to prepare a seed bed demands skill, which is usually gained through experience. The top 2.5cm (1in) or so of soil must be quite fine so that small seeds are in close contact with the soil particles around them and the particles can help them to germinate. When raking a bed to level off recently dug soil for planting, less skill is needed as the tilth does not have to be so fine as for a seed bed.

When preparing ground for broadcast sowing as in making lawns, the surface is first raked in one direction only. This results in many shallow furrows into which the seed falls. By raking after sowing in a cross-wise direction, these furrows are broken down and the seed is automatically covered with fine soil.

Hoes are essential tools for surface cultivation of the soil, used to break it up, thus facilitating the entry of air and moisture and also destroying weeds. Numerous patterns are made and from time to time new 'improved' models appear for which various claims are made. Basically, however, there are two main types, the draw hoe and the dutch hoe.

Draw hoes In these the blade is set nearly at right angles to the handle. This type is used with a chopping action, the operator moving forward over the hoed soil. For working close to plants, hoeing hard-packed soil or for clearing very weedy patches this is a more useful and powerful tool than the dutch hoe. It is also used to draw seed-drills. Variations of pattern and width of blade occur. The traditional patterns have either half-moon-shaped or rectangular blades, the cutting edges varying in width from 3–20cm (1–8in). The former pattern which has a curved shaft, is usually known as a swan-necked hoe. One type has a triangular head, the three sides each having a blade-edge. Handle-lengths vary from 1.5–1.7m (4½–5ft) and handles are usually of ash, a durable wood.

Another type of draw hoe has a short handle and is often known as an onion hoe. This is a useful tool for thinning rows of seedlings and weeding between them, but also makes a useful little hand-tool for weeding in other places in the garden.

A much heavier tool, which may be classified as a draw hoe, is the round-eyed hoe. This is virtually a mattock, but without the pick which forms part of that tool. It is of strong construction with a heavy, pick-type handle and is used not so much for weeding or hoeing in the normal sense as for clearing rough ground, as it may be used to chop through the smaller roots of trees, to uproot such things as brambles and saplings and to break up heavy clods of clay. But a better tool for the latter purpose is the Canterbury hoe, which is very similar but has three stout fork-like prongs. This, too, has its uses in clearing rough ground, dragging up weeds, roots and garden debris generally.

Dutch hoes In this type the blade is more or less in the same plane as the handle and socket, instead of being set at right-angles. It is pushed forward, practically flat, the cut through the soil just below the surface, severing weed roots and breaking up any surface pan. For this reason it is sometimes known as a push-hoe. The operator works backwards and does not tread on the ground he has hoed. Again, there are different blade widths and different patterns. In one pattern the solid blade is replaced by a thin wire.

Hoe blades in general become dulled through use in the soil and need to be sharpened with a file occasionally. A sharp hoe is a much more effective tool, easier to use, than a dull one. This does not apply to the modern stainless-steel types, which are so much easier to keep clean. To avoid blistering the hands with prolonged use, the handles should always be kept smooth. Refinements include rubber grips and plastic sheathings.

Hoeing to keep down weeds is not merely a matter of tidiness. Weeds allowed to develop will compete for the available light, air, moisture and plant food, and may be the host-plants of various pests. Weeds are dealt with properly only if they are cut off just below the soil surface. If they are dragged out of the soil with a blunt hoe they may root again, particularly in warm, moist weather. In sunny weather it is usually sufficient to leave the weeds on the surface to be withered by the sun, although they should eventually be collected for adding to the compost heap.

Town gardening

Towns gardens tend to be on the smaller side, and planning a town garden is not always easy. You can call on the advice of a garden designer for a surprisingly low fee, or plan it yourself, remembering to make simplicity the keynote of your design.

You will have to take into account the need for privacy, often difficult to obtain owing to the nearness of tall, overlooking buildings, and allow for the effect of fumes and smoke. Even in 'smokeless zones' there can still be chemical fumes and deposits harmful to plants.

On the other hand some of the most beautiful small gardens in Britain are to be found in towns, such as the walled and paved gardens of Georgian and Victorian houses in the heart of London, with their fine trees, sun-baked walls and sheltered beds and borders full of plants chosen with an eye to their situation.

Lawns and paving For gardens smaller than 600 sq m (600 sq yd) paving is generally more suitable. In smaller country towns where the atmosphere is freer from pollution a small lawn might be practical, but where the space receives a lot of use paving combined with a sand pit for the younger children would be more suitable to resist the inevitable wear. In general, it is better to keep to neutral grey or natural colours for slabs and let flowers and foliage provide the brighter colour. Borders and geometrically-shaped 'cut-out' beds will provide room for bedding plants and perennials and climbing plants and wall shrubs can be trained against the wall of the house. Small raised ornamental lawns or beds of clipped dwarf box might do much to relieve the effect of uninterrupted expanses of paving.

Soil Unless you can replace the top spit of soil with good, fresh loam, it will be necessary to concentrate on improving the soil by incorporating organic materials, such as peat, hop manure, straw, compost or well-rotted manure.

Privacy Artificial screening can be used to supplement the seclusion already provided by a wall or the angle of the building. If the screening is combined with climbing or trailing plants the effect will be more pleasant. For the modern-styled town house slatted or louvred plank fences will harmonize with the restrained lines of present-day architecture.

Formal bedding Wallflowers and forget-me-nots associate well with spring bulbs but can prove unreliable if there is much winter smog. Wallflowers suffer particularly from industrial pollution of the atmosphere and the exhaust from motor vehicles.

In summer, stocks, antirrhinums, French and African marigolds, petunias, asters, alyssum and lobelia seem to thrive in towns. Salvias, begonias and the exotic-looking gloxinias stand out against an urban background. The protection from autumn frost provided by a sheltered town garden can prolong the display of half-hardy plants, such as the small bedding dahlias 'Coltness Gem' and 'Bishop of Llandaff', which are seen to good advantage in this setting. Fuchsias are a showy and long-lasting feature of town gardens: 'Ballet Girl' cerise and white; 'Constance', purple with a pink fringe; 'Penelope', white with a pink centre; 'Hidcote Beauty', salmon-pink centre with white calyx tipped green; these are all well worth growing. Zonal pelargoniums do well in towns. The bright scarlet 'Paul Crampel', the turkey-red 'Henry Jacoby' and the orange-scarlet 'Gustav Emich' are all popular. Their rather brash colours can be toned down with ornamental-leaved kinds such as the cool silver 'Caroline Schmidt' or the golden-leaved 'Marechal McMahon'. Two of the main fungal diseases of roses seldom affect plants growing in towns.

Walls These provide a useful background for roses. Although ramblers do not flower long enough to make them worthwhile, an exception is the lovely 'New Dawn', which first produces its flesh-pink blossoms in June and often continues flowering until December. Spicily fragrant 'New Dawn' grows best against a west wall, 'Mermaid' is a fine perpetual-climber that is practically evergreen, will flourish in any aspect and even produces its large primrose-yellow saucer-shaped blooms abundantly on a north wall. The fiery orange 'Danse du Feu' and the fragrant, reddish-brown 'Zéphirine Drouhin' both look good against a wall.

Although evergreen shrubs are seldom seen at their best in town gardens, pyracanthas (firethorns) seem to thrive in towns, and will provide a display of scarlet berries on a west, or even a north wall. *Berberis darwinii*, *B. stenophylla*, *Cotoneaster franchettii*, *Euonymus radicans* and some of the less rampant hederas (ivies) make good evergreen wall cover. The ivies are self-clinging and the erect and compact habit of the others makes it unnecessary to provide any support for the plants. The wide choice of deciduous wall shrubs includes the large-flowered clematis hybrids and *C. montana* (they should have a westerly aspect and cool root run). *Chaenomeles japonica*, the Japanese quince, and the forms 'Knap Hill Scarlet' and *C. × superba simonii* are good wall plants. For the north wall there are the climbing hydrangea, *H. petiolaris* and the winter jasmine, *Jasminum nudiflorum*.

To cover a wall quickly the Russian vine, *Polygonum bilderdyckia baldschuanicum*, and the less rampant *Vitis coignetiae* are two vigorous climbers. The creepers, *Parthenocissus quinquefolia*, the true Virginian creeper, *P. henryana* and *P. tricuspidata*, should be considered, though the last is rampant and tends to smother everything it covers, so use it with care. Walls can also be used for hanging baskets and plaques and other ornamental devices.

Basements Many shade-loving shrubs and climbers will grow in the cool, shady conditions of a basement area. They will usually have to be grown in tubs or boxes. Lack of room may prevent the planting of any but the slower-growing varieties of ivies. Where a fair amount of wall needs covering you might try the attractive *Hedera colchica*, Persian ivy, sometimes known as elephant ivy on account of the size and shape of its leaves.

For the more restricted wall space the slower growing varieties of the common ivy, *H. helix*, would be more appropriate, such as 'Buttercup', *conglomerata* and *tricolor*.

All the Virginian creepers already mentioned will also do well and camellias will flourish in tubs, etc. Although the flowers may be less profusely borne the beauty of their foliage will compensate for this. The tropical-looking, evergreen, palmate leaves of *Fatsia japonica*, the false castor-oil plant, are handsome throughout the year.
Other shrubs In addition to the shrubs recommended above for walls, most of the barberries, including *B. darwinii*, cotoneasters, Japanese laurel (plain and variegated), box, holly and euonymus will thrive in town gardens. If you do not like privet, remember the golden form can add lustre to a garden in winter. Spraying and syringeing help to reduce the effect of atmospheric pollution in winter.

Most of the popular deciduous shrubs seem to thrive in towns, including the butterfly bush, *Buddleia davidii*, and all its varieties and newer hybrids, such as 'Black Knight' and 'Royal Red'. Brooms and heaths also adapt well, and a combination of summer and winter flowering heaths with varieties of the British native, *Cytisus scoparius*, will provide continuity of colour. Forsythias often flower several weeks earlier in towns and mingle well with flowering currants.

Smaller forms of philadelphus (mock orange) add beauty to the early summer display, including 'Belle Etoile', 'Virginal' and 'Manteau d'Hermine', together with the crimson weigela 'Eva Rathke' or the pink 'Vanhouttei', the showy snowball bush, *Viburnum opulus sterile*, and other summer-flowering viburnums, as well as the lovely single and double lilacs.

In winter *Hamamelis mollis*, witch hazel, and *Viburnum tinus*, laurustinus, and *Garrya elliptica* do well, followed a little later by the daphnes and early-flowering deciduous viburnums, *V. juddii*, *V. carlesii* and *V. × carlcephalum*.
Trees Although large trees, such as the London plane and the full-sized horse chestnuts and *Sorbus aucuparia*, the rowan, and *S. aria*, the whitebeam, will thrive in towns, the average town garden is more suited to the smaller ornamental trees. The flowering crabs, such as *Malus floribunda*, seldom exceed 10m (30ft), and most stop at 5 or 6m (15 or 20ft). Other attractive species include *M. eleyi*, *M. × aldenhamensis* and *M. lemoinii*. Among the many ornamental fruits 'Dartmouth Crab', 'Golden Hornet' or 'Toringo' are suitable.

Thorns (crataegus) are good small trees for the town garden. Their flowering coincides with that of the laburnum. *Laburnum × vossii* has 30cm (1ft) racemes of golden flowers and grows 8–10m (25–30ft) tall. It looks best as an individual specimen. The more compact *L. alpinum*, Scotch laburnum, would suit a very small garden. The laburnums contrast excellently with *Crataegus oxyacantha coccinea plena* and *C. o. rosea flore pleno*.

Magnolia soulangeana grows to perfection in some of the most densely built-up areas, and *M. stellata* also flowers with considerable freedom in town gardens. Almonds, peaches and cherries begin their display in February with the pale pink blossoms of *Prunus communis*, followed by the purple-leaved plum, *P. cerasifera atropurpurea*, and the deeper crimson pink of the double peach 'Clara Meyer', then the whole range of Japanese cherries, many of which provide rich autumn leaf colour.

The false acacia, *Robinia pseudo-acacia*, is very adaptable, and although at 20m (70ft) the type would be generally too big, the small mop-headed *R. p. inermis* seldom exceeds 5–6m (15–20ft).
Conifers and miniature trees Miniature conifers associate particularly well with paving. *Juniper chinensis pfitzeriana*, for example, is a low-growing wide-spreading variety with branches that are thrust out at an angle of 45 degrees. The foliage is grey-green and the plants attain an ultimate height of 2m (6ft) with a spread of 4m (12ft). *J. c. kosteriana* has a more ground-hugging habit. 'Grey Owl', a named form of *J. virginiana*, has lighter and more feathery foliage. These two last-named junipers reach about 1m (3ft) tall and their spread extends to about 3m (10ft).

Several forms of *J. communis* are even more restricted. *J. c. prostata* is a wide-spreading variety with green and silver foliage; *J. c. repandens* is also low growing. Its branches spread all round and are packed with deep-green needles. *J. c. hornibrookii* is similar in habit, with grey-green foliage, making good ground cover. Others with this useful characteristic are 'Bar Harbour', a named form of *J. horizontalis*, *J. procumbens nana*, a bright-green carpeting form, and *J. sabina tamariscifolia*, which has grey, feathery foliage turning green as it approaches maturity.

The dwarf Japanese maples, with their finely-cut lacy foliage contrast with the darker-coloured more solid textured conifers. Elegant and slow growing are *Acer palmatum dissectum atropurpureum* and *A. p. d. palmatifidum*. These miniature trees, which have the gnarled look and much of the general appearance of Japanese bonsai, do best in partial shade. By planting *Aesculus parviflora*, the dwarf buckeye, it is possible to enjoy the beauty of horse chestnut blossom. Dwarf rhododendrons also retain the charm and flamboyance of their taller hybrid relations. The

A closely planted town garden, full of carefully-placed plants.

1 A tranquil garden in the heart of a town.
2 The formality of paving and evergreens blend well in town gardens; roses provide colour.
3 A pool and its waterside plants make a peaceful London garden.

more compact kinds, such as 'Bluebird', 'Blue Tit', and 'Carmen' and 'Elizabeth' with blood-red and orange-scarlet flowers respectively, given acid soil, will flourish.

The problems involved in roof gardening are entirely different from those encountered in gardening at ground level. Basically the main difference is in depth of soil. At ground level one plants and grows in soils that have greater depth, even though the productive surface may be quite shallow. Even in the dryest weather there exists under the growing plants a reservoir of moisture from which the roots can obtain some sustenance, however slight. In well-drained soils this may not be apparent in the top layer but it can easily be replaced by a few hours of thorough watering. On the roof soil must necessarily be so shallow that moisture drains away quickly and can be replaced only by constant watering. There is no underground supply on which to draw.

Shallow soil also means that thick, strong, anchoring tap roots cannot move downwards in the soil without quickly meeting the impervious surface of the roof. So large trees and shrubs cannot normally be grown to maturity, although while young some can be useful as a foil and protection to the mainly low-growing vegetation.

The necessarily swift drainage from the shallow soil on roof gardens means that essential plant foods and minerals are quickly leached by the constant natural or artificial watering. The nutrients lost must be replaced with much greater frequency than is necessary at ground level.

Roof gardens are much more likely to be affected by changes in the weather. The sun is always hotter on the roof, the rain more concentrated, the wind stronger and less predictable. On the other hand a roof garden is probably always slightly warmer in winter, partly because of slight heat from the building below, and partly because the sharp drainage does not allow a base of frozen soil. Frosts also tend naturally to drift down from the roof to the streets below and find their own level.

As roof gardening is an artificial form of gardening compared with that practised at ground level, design and planning should be equally artificial. You should not, to take just one example, try to make a naturalistic hill on a roof garden. Because the tendency on a roof is for the visitor to cast his eyes outwards to the distant view beyond, you should aim to provide a barrier to the eye in the form of such masses of colour that the overwhelming brightness attracts and holds the eye.

Before planning the creation of a roof garden you should always check first on your roof surface. You should ask yourself (and if in doubt get expert advice) whether the roof structure is strong enough to take the burden of the extra weight involved in possibly large quantities of moist soil. You should ensure that the actual surface material is sufficiently thick and impermeable to withstand both constant contact with moisture and the considerable pressures exerted by the hard edges of weighty containers, particularly when the roof surface may be softened by the heat of the sun. You should ascertain that drainage from the roof is both efficient and sufficient. You should also investigate local bye-laws or landlord's agreements to discover whether there exists any ban on roof gardening. The considerable time, effort and expense involved should not be employed until these questions have been satisfactorily answered.

The design, pattern or layout of a roof garden is normally dictated largely by the space available. For most householders this space is comparatively small and rectangular. It will probably be bounded on two or more sides by some sort of wall or parapet. The actual roof surface will probably be of lead, a bitumen compound or of tiles or paving slabs. Whatever the surface it will always be better, though by no means necessary, to cover it with duckboards to protect the feet in wet weather, to allow unimpeded drainage, and to give added protection to the surface material of the roof.

In some instances it is possible to place soil directly on the roof surface, contained on the outer edge by the wall or parapet and on the inner side by timber shuttering, bricks or by a peat brick wall. The last is the most effective, both visually and because peat bricks absorb and hold moisture, releasing it only slowly to the soil which they contain.

The making of a flower bed directly on a roof surface is not always to be recommended because of its permanency

The parapet of a roof garden richly clad with a mixture of plants to give both foliage and flowering effect.

and possible damage to roof and to walls, so it is usually best to contain soil in a series of boxes, troughs or pots, raised sufficiently from the roof to allow good drainage and the passage of a current of air below. If these are to be of timber they should be well coated with one of the non-creosote timber preservatives (based on copper naphthenate) to prolong their lives, and they must have drainage holes in their bases or low in their sides. Some bricks are sufficiently permeable to allow excess moisture to drain away, but others are not, so a test should be made where you are in doubt.

All containers should have in their bases a layer of drainage material between the drainage holes and the soil, otherwise the holes are apt to become blocked with soil particles or fibrous roots.

If John Innes compost is used ask for compost No. 3, which is normally for potting mature plants, trees or shrubs. This may initially be too strong a mixture for smaller plants, but so quickly are fertilizers leached from the soil on a roof garden that no harm is likely to be caused.

A more practical alternative to John Innes compost for most gardeners, ordinary garden soil, may cost you nothing but the effort of sterilizing it and transporting it to the roof garden. Some garden suppliers offer unsterilized loams. If soils are of a heavy clay they

should be lightened by the addition of peat and coarse sand and should be enriched with a good handful of bonemeal to every bucketful. If the soil is not sterilized weeds are certain to germinate and in their early stages they are not always distinguishable. However, a roof garden generally gets much closer inspection and more attention than can be given to the larger gardens crowded with plants at ground level, and weeds are quickly cleared.

It is helpful to be generous with fertilizer applications. Use an all-purpose balanced fertilizer, generally in granular form, but a liquid fertilizer may be used. One reason for giving plenty of fertilizer is that the thin soil will result in considerable wastage, although the thrifty gardener will avoid this by careful attention to watering. Another reason is that if flowers and plants are to be grown at all under such artificial conditions, then it is as well to grow them as lushly and lavishly as possible. Close planting with the intention of creating as much interest and colour as possible will take considerable quantities of plant foods out of the soil and they should be replaced regularly to obtain good results.

Watering is sometimes necessary twice a day under hot and sunny conditions. A standpipe is seldom available on a roof top, but the expense and all the attendant difficulties of having one installed are not really necessary, for it is a comparatively simple matter to attach a hose to a downstairs tap and lead this through a window to the roof.

As space is usually limited vertical growth must be encouraged, and the roof is one of the best possible places for climbers and trailers. All walls and parapets should have their surfaces decorated and concealed by climbers, some of which can be allowed to grow rampant and spill over the top and down the sides of the building. Even as rampant a grower as the Russian vine, *Polygonum bilderdyckia baldschuanicum*, will grow freely on a roof top. Given sufficient space for its roots and properly supported and trained it will cover large areas in summer with its attractive twining trails and after the first year or so will produce a profusion of creamy, foamy flowers. Passion flowers (passifloras) grow and flower well. The colourful and interesting cup and saucer flower, *Cobaea scandens*, will quickly cover a wall and will produce not only flowers, but fat and interesting fruits. Ivy grows well and will cover walls with an evergreen background, and even acts on occasions as a weed suppressing ground cover.

Pelargoniums should not be despised because they are so popular, for they are obtainable in wonderful colours and, with proper attention, flower lavishly.

1 In the centre of a large city the only space for a garden may be on the roof. This one is over a large London departmental store.
2 Paving and stonework make a clean surface for a roof garden.
3 An urban roof garden can be a bright spot in spring.

The roof is a wonderful place for many alpine plants, preferably grown together in special containers. A sink garden can provide great interest and much subtle beauty.

There are many alpines from which to choose for a special feature such as this, but do not forget to include a proportion of dwarf shrubs and conifers, some of which can be charming, in order to get added interest in shapes, textures, heights and colours.

Other special features particularly successful on roof gardens are hanging baskets and examples of bonsai, or dwarf trees.

Gardening on a balcony demands different techniques, presents different hazards and offers different rewards from gardening in a garden. The impact of a balcony must be immediate, striking, powerful for it must compete with the drama of the world beyond. The only way to ensure this is to provide masses of aggressive colour; reds rather than greens, yellows rather than blues; colour that is in urgent contrast to the view above and below.

Colours of this nature, however, are not obtained as easily on a balcony as they are at ground level. All plants must

1 Balcony gardens can be made colourful in summer by using annual plants.
2 Flowering and foliage plants grown in urns, ornamental vases, plant-boxes of many kinds, tubs or large pots, will all help to furnish the balcony garden.
3 A pleasant screening effect for a roof garden.

335

be grown in containers, none of which can be very large. Small containers mean a confined root run, a meagre supply of soil and hence a tendency to dry out quickly causing plants to wilt or die.

The usual balcony breezes hasten the drying out process. They scurry round corners, whistle through gaps in buildings and seldom leave flowers and plants with a quiet opportunity for contented growth. Some balconies may be protected by glassing in one end or side.

The wind limits the range of plants available just as much as the lack of space does. Tall growers will bend and break, trailers will become unanchored, top heavy plants in small containers will be blown over. Except for special cases therefore, balcony plants should be low growing, compact, sturdy.

A further and highly practical problem posed by winds concerns garden debris. Just as the balcony gardener must consider his neighbours, particularly those who live on the floor below, when watering his plants, he must also keep control of fallen leaves and flower petals. They should be collected frequently in a wind-proof container and disposed of. Down pipes etc, must be kept clear of debris which, after a storm, can collect quickly, block openings and cause flooding.

These are real problems and the balcony gardener should consider them seriously before planning. Intelligent purchase of plants and containers can help to solve them.

Containers should be firmly based, squat rather than tall. Troughs are better than pots, although for most purposes the best of all are pots plunged into troughs. Of course, all containers must be secure. There must be no risk that an accidental displacement will lead to any of them falling into the street or garden below.

All containers should have drainage holes in them and should be lifted from the balcony floor sufficiently to allow excess moisture to escape. Where drips or splashes may annoy neighbours or passers-by it is advisable to use drip trays.

Trees in the garden

Trees are the most long-lived growing features in any garden. Once they are well established, it is very difficult to move them; pruning them if they become too big is difficult, needing skilled workmanship, and is never a permanent solution to the problems of excessive roots and over-extensive shading that arise.

Since Victorian times the gardener's problems in tree-planting have been made much easier by the introduction from western China in particular, as well as Japan, and also by hybridization and selection, of a wide new range of trees which are of moderate size. These include excellent maples, whitebeams, rowans, cherries and ornamental apples (crabs), as well as birches. Many of these

1 Cut branches right to the trunk.
2 A transplanted tree is firmly staked.

also provide what is wanted in a small area, a tree that has more than one season of interest, such as decorative bark in mid-winter, attractive unfolding foliage in spring followed by a period of flowering, then brightly coloured fruit and finally gay colouring of the leaves before they fall. Trees often have at least two if not three seasons of interest.

Evergreen broad-leaved trees are of particular interest in winter, and many have variegated or coloured-leaved forms, and the number available is now greatly increased. All are least satisfactory in towns where air pollution takes away the shine of their foliage.

The same applies to conifers a number of which are of too great a size and too slow growing for gardens, and are seen at their best in forests and pineta.

For road planting and use in smaller gardens narrow (fastigiate) forms of many trees have been selected and are propagated as cultivars. They are also useful in planting on a large scale on account of their beautiful shape. This applies, also to the numerous weeping trees available.

Soil Hardy trees are surprisingly tolerant of soil conditions provided

drainage is good. Many come from mountains where soil is not deep, except in the river valleys.

Where the soil is well drained, the limiting factor for a number of species is the amount of lime present. Many trees growing naturally on acid or neutral soils will grow equally well on soils with a moderate lime content, particularly if the soil is deep and fertile. But a certain number are, like rhododendrons among shrubs, strongly calcifuge (lime-hating) plants, particularly on rather shallow, chalky soils as are found in many fine gardens in such areas as the Chilterns, Cotswolds and South Downs.

Apart from the degree of soil alkalinity (see pH) depth and soil structure affect the kind of trees that can be grown. In general, with certain notable exceptions, conifers prefer acid or neutral soils. The *Rosaceae*, however has many genera that are often associated in nature with alkaline soils such as *Malus* (apples), *Prunus* (cherries, plums, peaches, almonds, etc), *Pyrus* (pears), *Crataegus* (thorns) and *Sorbus* (rowans and service trees).

It is curious that though many calcifuge plants will not live in calcareous soils (containing lime), most of those that are calcipholous (lime-loving) will grow well in neutral and acid soils.

The following list indicates the preferences of some commonly cultivated genera, particularly those that will, or will not, grow on soils with a moderate lime content, and those that on no account thrive on shallow, chalk soils.

Broad-leaved trees

ACER Most maples thrive on lime and chalk, including British natives and those commonly planted. The Chinese species, such as *AA, capillipes, davidii, ginnala, griseum* and *rufinerve*, make a splendid display in chalk gardens. *A. palmatum* and its cultivars need more fertile soil. The American *A. rubrum* will not grow on chalk.

AILANTHUS Tolerates lime.

ALNUS All alders will grow well on lime but must have moisture, with the exception of *A. cordata* and *A. incana*, which will stand drier situations. The former is good on chalk.

AESCULUS The horse-chestnuts and buckeyes do well on lime and chalk, though preferring fertile soils.

AMELANCHIER Though naturally growing on light acid soils, these will tolerate some lime.

ARBUTUS One of the few *Ericaceae* that grows well on lime.

BETULA The birches do well on lime.

BUXUS Good on lime, the common box grows naturally on chalk.

CARPINUS All the hornbeams are successful on either heavy alkaline soils or light chalk.

CARYA Will tolerate some lime in deep fertile soils.

CASTANEA. The sweet chestnuts do

not like lime, but will tolerate it in small quantities on well-drained fertile soils.

CATALPA Lime tolerant.

CELTIS Will tolerate some lime in deep, fertile soils.

CERCIDIPHYLLUM Lime tolerant.

CERCIS The Judas trees do well on lime and chalk.

CORYLUS Hazels do well on lime, including chalk.

COTONEASTER. Most kinds do well on lime, including chalk.

CRATAEGUS All thorns will grow on lime and chalk.

DAVIDIA The dove tree does well on lime and chalk.

EUCALYPTUS There is still some doubt as to which species will grow well on lime.

EUONYMUS The tree-like species thrive on lime and chalk.

EVODIA Does well in shallow chalk soil.

FAGUS The beeches have a shallow root system and thrive on well-drained soils with high lime content and on chalk.

FICUS The fig-tree grows well on lime and chalk.

FRAXINUS The ashes thrive on soils with high lime content as long as they are fertile.

GLEDITSCHIA Will tolerate a little lime in fertile soils.

GYMNOCLADUS The Kentucky coffee needs a rich, loamy soil and will tolerate some lime.

HALESIA The snowdrop trees will not tolerate lime.

IDESIA This rare tree is good on chalk.

ILEX Hollies are good on lime and chalk.

JUGLANS Walnuts will thrive on lime soils and chalk if it is not too thin.

KOELREUTERIA The golden rain tree will grow in any well-drained soil.

LABURNUM Will grow anywhere.

LIQUIDAMBAR Dislikes more than a trace of lime and will not grow on chalk.

LIRIODENDRON The tulip trees will grow on fertile soils with high lime content but are not happy on chalk.

MAGNOLIA Magnolias are not happy on limy soils, the exceptions among the tree-sized species being *MM. delavayi*, × *highdownensis*, *kobus*, *sinensis* and *wilsonii*.

MALUS In varying degrees the ornamental species and hybrids of apples are satisfactory on lime, and the majority do well on chalk.

NOTHOFAGUS The southern beeches so far in cultivation in Britain will, on fertile soils, stand a little lime in the soil but cannot be grown on chalk.

NYSSA A lime hater.

OSTRYA The hop-hornbeams will grow on lime.

OXYDENDRUM A lime hater.

PARROTIA Is not successful where there is more than a trace of lime.

PAULOWNIA Good on lime and chalk.

PHELLODENDRON Good on lime and chalk.

PLATANUS The planes do well on lime.

POPULUS Poplars in general need fertile moist soil and will not object if there is a lime content, but, except for *PP. alba*, *canescens* and *lasiocarpa*, they will not grow on chalk.

PRUNUS Almonds, apricots, bird cherries, cherries (including the Japanese cultivars), laurels (common cherry and Portugal) and peaches, all grow on soils with a lime content and, in varying degrees, are also successful on chalk.

PTEROCARYA The wing-nuts will stand lime if the soil is fertile and moist.

PYRUS The pears will all grow on soil with a high lime content, including chalk.

QUERCUS Most oaks do well on soils with a high lime content, including chalk, if there is sufficient depth for their tap-roots. Particularly good are *QQ. canariensis*, *cerris*, *frainetto*, *hispanica* 'Lucombeana', *ilex*, *macranthera*, *robur* and *petraea*. Willow oaks, *Q. phellos*, and cork oaks, *Q. suber*, are not good on lime.

RHUS The tree-like species will grow on lime, including chalk.

ROBINIA The false acacias will grow on lime soils and chalk, but are not at their best on them.

SALIX The tree-sized willows tolerate lime, but all need abundant moisture, and will not thrive on dry, chalk soils.

SAMBUCUS The common elder will reach tree size on lime and chalk.

SASSAFRAS Requires lime-free soil.

SOPHORA Tolerates lime on well-drained fertile soils.

SORBUS The rowans and service trees are all good on lime, including chalk.

STYRAX The snowball trees will not grow on lime.

TETRACENTRON This rare Chinese tree does well on lime and chalk.

TILIA The commonly cultivated lime trees grow naturally on limestone formations, but need moderately fertile soils.

ULMUS All elms will grow well on lime and in varying degrees on chalk.

UMBELLULARIA The Californian laurel will tolerate some lime but will not thrive on shallow chalk.

ZELKOVA The ironwoods will tolerate lime but must have deep fertile soils.

Coniferous trees

ABIES Most silver firs need deep, moist soil and in such will tolerate lime. *AA. amabilis*, *bracteata*, *forrestii*, *grandis*, *magnifica*, *procera* and *Veitchii* are not good on soils with much lime. *AA. cephalonica* and *pinsapo*, however, will grow on chalk.

ARAUCARIA The monkey puzzle given fertile soil will tolerate lime.

CEDRUS All the cedars, especially *C. atlantica*, will tolerate lime on fertile soils.

CEPHALOTAXUS These small trees grow well on lime.

CHAMAECYPARIS *CC. lawsoniana* and *nootkatensis* and their cultivars do well on soils with high lime content. *CC. obtusa*, *pisifera* and *thyoides* are not good on lime and will not thrive on shallow chalk.

CRYPTOMERIA The Japanese cedar will tolerate lime if grown in deep, moist soil.

CUNNINGHAMIA The Chinese fir is not happy on lime soils.

× CUPRESSOCYPARIS The Leyland cypress grows well on lime and chalk.

CUPRESSUS The hardy cypresses will tolerate lime, and *C. macrocarpa* does well on chalk.

GINKGO The maidenhair tree grows well on fertile soils containing lime.

JUNIPERUS The numerous species and their cultivars grow well on lime.

LARIX Larches grow well on lime.

LIBOCEDRUS The incense cedar needs deep moist loam and will tolerate some lime.

METASEQUOIA The dawn redwood does best on fertile soils, with or without some lime, and will grow slowly and healthily on chalk.

PICEA The spruces are not happy on shallow, dry soils, though most will tolerate some lime, including the much cultivated common spruce, *P. abies*. An exception is the striking Serbian spruce, *P. omorika*, which grows on limestone rocks.

PINUS Though many of the pines grow naturally on light, mountain soils and many will tolerate a little lime, the majority dislike it. Even the Scots pine, *P. sylvestris*, is not at its best on lime. *PP. armandii*, *contorta*, *pinaster*, *radiata*, and *strobus* are unsatisfactory on lime. The handsome stone pine, *P. pinea*, will stand a little. The Austrian pine, *P. nigra austriaca* is good on chalk, as to a slightly lesser extent is the Corsican pine, *P. nigra maritima*. *P. mugo*, often no more than a spreading shrub, will also grow on chalk, as will the rare *P. bungeana*.

PSEUDOTSUGA The Douglas firs thrive on fertile, moist, well-drained soils, on which they will stand some lime but not chalk.

SCIADOPTYIS The umbrella pine will not grow on chalk.

SEQUOIA The giant redwood will tolerate lime if there is a good depth of fertile soil but will not grow on chalk.

SEQUOIADENDRON The wellingtonia also will grow well in deep fertile soils but will not grow on chalk.

TAXODIUM The swamp cypress will not tolerate lime.

TAXUS The yews grow naturally on limestone formations and chalk, and are equally on good acid soils.

THUJA The western red cedar will grow on soils containing lime, as will the Chinese and American arbor-vitae and their cultivars.

THUJOPSIS This needs fertile, moist soils and thrives better on neutral or acid sites than on limestone.

TORREYA These yew-like trees do well

on limestone and chalk.

TSUGA The western hemlock will not thrive on shallow soils containing lime or on chalk, nor will the other species occasionally planted. The eastern hemlock, *T. canadensis*, will, however, grow under these conditions.

Permanently wet soils The other soil factor that must be taken into consideration is continuous moisture, that is, soils that are continuously saturated. The majority of trees will not grow in these conditions, but those that will include the numerous kinds of willow (*Salix*), large and small, as well as the alders (*Alnus*), which are mostly trees of moderate size. The handsome and uncommon swamp cypress, *Taxodium distichum*, is also good, though very wet conditions are not necessary for its success.

Planting A tree will normally outlive its planter. However, if it is given a good start the planter will be rewarded all the earlier by vigorous growth. Do not attempt to plant a tree in unsuitable soil. The choice having been made, you should assure yourself that you are buying stock of good quality. You can, if you wish, ask for stock complying with the *British Standard Specification for Nursery Stock, Part 1, Trees and Shrubs*.

Broad-leaved trees (deciduous or evergreen) These may be purchased as standards, in which the clear stem is from about 2–2.3m (6–7ft). The smaller size is more satisfactory as a rule, and will soon catch up a larger one, which may well have an undesirably spindly stem.

1 Liriodendron tulipfera, the tulip tree, will grow on limy soil.
2 Ulmus stricta, the Cornish elm.
3 Acer pseudoplatanus leopoldii has silvery-yellow leaves.

In some instances, when, as in a Japanese cherry, low branching will look attractive, a half-standard can be used branching at from 1–1.5m (3½–4½ft).

Have ready a sound, pointed stake long enough when driven firmly into the ground to reach to the point on the stem where the branching starts, also one of the several types of tree ties now available.

Dig or fork around where the tree is to be planted for about an area of a metre (yard) square. Particularly if the ground is poor or heavy, work in some well-rotted compost or peat.

Remove the wrappings of the roots and cut off any that are broken. Dig a hole which will take the root system, as nearly as possible so that when the tree is stood in it, the soil mark on the stem is level with, or just below, the surrounding soil. It is, except where willows are concerned, very bad practice to plant too deeply. When you have ensured that the planting hole has been dug to the correct depth, lift the tree out and drive the stake well in at about the centre of the hole.

Replace the tree, working the roots round the stake so that the stake is as close as possible to the stem. This is easily done if someone else holds the tree in place. If you are working single-handed, loosely tie the tree to the stake.

Work soil carefully among the roots,

the fine soil among the fine roots, firming it carefully with the fingers. Then almost fill the hole, frequently firming it by gentle treading. Next water the tree well; when the water has sunk in, lightly fill the hole up. Finally, attach the tie at the top of the stem.

Conifers Conifers supplied are usually of a much shorter length than broad-leaved trees and seldom need staking. It is most important to disturb the root ball as little as possible. The sacking which binds the ball may be left on until the tree is in the hole. The knot or lacing that holds it is then cut and gently teased loose and left in the hole. If the tree is not absolutely firm, a stout garden cane and strong string should be sufficient to secure it.

Planting of deciduous trees should be done as soon after leaf fall as possible, but may continue until early spring before the buds begin to break.

Conifers are best planted in autumn, when they will make root at once, and be established by spring. It is less desirable to plant in winter when the roots are for long quite inactive. Early spring is the next best time, for root growth will soon be active. But watering during a spring drought with an east wind is then essential. A mulch is also helpful.

Maintenance and pruning The area round the base of the tree should be kept weeded until it is well established. Watch the tie regularly and keep it from becoming too tight, ie, allow a little play. Strangulation may cause great damage. Remove the stake only when

the tree is absolutely firm—this will take at least three years.

To keep the tree shapely, preferably with a single leading shoot, the following rules should always be followed in pruning trees young or old.

Always cut a shoot or branch back to the point where it arises, making the cut as clean and flush and as close to the main branch as possible. If a 'snag' is left, it will not grow and will eventually rot and cause damage.

If the shoot or branch is of any weight, carry out the operation in two stages, the first taking off the weight and leaving a short snag that can then be removed without its bark tearing away back into the main stem. If the scar is large, paint it with one of the proprietary sealing paints.

Ornamental trees are in general best pruned from mid-to-late summer. The wounds then heal quickly and attacks by fungi or bacteria are held at bay. This applies particularly to most species of *Prunus*, especially cherries, It also applies to maples, birches and walnuts which 'bleed' sap during the winter and spring.

Never attempt to carry out pruning on a large tree; always obtain the services of a qualified tree surgeon. Unless properly done, it will probably result in damage and disfigurement of the tree, and in addition is often a highly dangerous undertaking for the unskilled operator.

Pests and diseases Those affecting ornamental trees can be divided into three main classes: disease due to bacterial or fungal action, damage caused

1 A narrow form of spruce, picea.
2 Tsuga mertensiana, the mountain hemlock.
3 The monkey puzzle, Araucaria araucana.

by insects and damage caused by animals (including birds). Of the first, the most seriously affected trees are members of the rose family (*Rosaceae*).

Bacterial canker attacks cherries and plums. It is associated with the oozing and dripping of gum from branches or the trunks. Some control can be obtained by pruning out branches affected.

Silver-leaf also affects plums, cherries and apples in particular and occasionally thorns and laurels. The leaves take on a silvery appearance and on a branch that dies a purplish-mauve fungus arises. This should be cut out and burned without delay.

Fire blight may attack pears, hawthorns, rowans, whitebeams and pyracanthus. Whole shoots in leaf go brown, as if burned, and die. If this is found, the Ministry of Agriculture, Fisheries and Food must be notified at once. The most serious 'killer' fungus is the honey-fungus. It occurs generally on ground that has been woodland which has been cleared with the stumps or many large roots left in the ground. Root-like growths, resembling boot-laces spread through the soil and infect a healthy tree, which is eventually killed and should be removed. From the ground around it, toadstools may, but do not always, arise. They are pale yellow, the gills on the underside running a little way down the stalk, which carries a

collar-like ring around it. There is no known cure. It attacks conifers.

A selection of garden trees

Trees decorative throughout the year
Decorative bark and good foliage colour
Broad-leaved
ACER CAPILLIPES Young bark striated with white; young growths coral red, leaves turning crimson in autumn. *A. davidii*, young bark shiny green, striated with white; leaves usually turn yellow and purple in autumn. Long chains of keys striking. *A. griseum*, paper bark maple, the outer bark peeling in papery flakes to show the copper-coloured inner bark; opening leaves bronze coloured, turning red or orange in autumn. *A. grosseri*, *A. g. hersii*, young bark green or yellowish striated with white, leaves orange and crimson in autumn. *A. pennsylvanicum*, moosewood, young bark green striped and patterned with white, the large leaves pinkish on opening turning clear in autumn. *A. rufinerve*, bark green, with an elaborate pattern of greyish markings, persisting on old trunks; leaves red when young and usually crimson in autumn, when the long chains of keys are attractive.
BETULA PAPYRIFERA Paper-bark birch, shining white bark, the large leaves turning pale gold early autumn, making it more effective than other birches with coloured stems.
LIQUIDAMBAR STYRACIFLUA The American sweet gum has interesting corky bark in winter, the leaves usually turning purple and crimson in autumn.

PARROTIA PERSICA Particularly good
if trained to standard form, the grey
bark flaking away in a pattern resembling the London plane, while the leaves
turn brilliant golds and crimsons (see
also Early flowering trees).
PHELLODENDRON AMURENSE The
grey, corky trunk is of picturesque form,
and the handsome yellow leaves turn
yellow in autumn.
SORBUS AUCUPARIA BEISSNERI
This handsome cultivar of the mountain
ash has red branchlets and a copper-
coloured trunk, the large leaves with
deeply cut leaflets turning old gold in
autumn.

Conifers Many conifers with yellow,
silver or variegated foliage (listed under
those headings) give interest of form and
foliage colour at all seasons. Some pines,
when their lower branches are removed,
also have interesting bark, *P. bungeana*,
the lacebark pine, has bark which peels
off to show white patches; *P. nigra
maritima*, the Corsican pine, develops a
striking erect trunk with pale scales
between fissures in the dark bark. The
Scots pine, *P. sylvestris*, with its smooth
pink or red bark in the upper part of the
tree, is singularly picturesque. The bark
of the well-named redwood, *Sequoia
sempervirens*, never loses its astonishing
colour. Except *P. bungeana*, which is
rare and slow-growing, these trees are
only suitable for large gardens or parks.

Decorative bark in winter.
In addition to the foregoing, the principal decorative distinction of the following is their bark, the colouring of their
foliage not being exceptional.
ARBUTUS × ARACHNOIDES Hybrid
strawberry tree. Trunk and branches
cinnamon red.
BETULA Several birches have singularly beautiful coloured bark, though
this does not always show on young
trees. Among the best are *B. albo-
sinensis septentrionalis*, orange-brown
with a grey bloom; *B. ermanii*, trunk
cream-coloured, the bark peeling off, the
branches orange-brown; *B. jacquemon-
tiana*, the whitest bark of all—the white
can be rubbed off like chalk; *B. lutea*,
the peeling, paper-like bark being
yellowish; *B. mandschurica*, vars.
japonica and *szechuanica*, have very
white stems and branches; *B. maxi-
mowicziana*, the largest-leaved birch,
the trunk at first orange-brown becoming white; *B. pendula*, the native British
birch, varies greatly in the colour of its
stem and good white-barked seedlings
must be selected.
CORNUS MAS Old trees of cornelian
cherry have interesting trunks with
attractive shaggy bark.
CORYLUS COLURNA The pale, corky,
scaling bark on the Turkish hazel is
attractive.
EUCALYPTUS Several species have
interesting grey, peeling bark.

JUGLANS NIGRA The grey bark of this
black walnut, deeply furrowed into a
network pattern, is most striking.
PLATANUS × HYBRIDA The peeling
of patches of bark showing the greenish
grey inner bark of the London plane is
well known.
POPULUS ALBA The bark of the white
poplar is smooth and grey, with black
markings, except at the base of the
trunk; *P. canescens*, the grey poplar, has
bark of a distinctive yellowish-grey
colour.
PRUNUS MAACKII The Manchurian
bird cherry has smooth bark, brownish-
yellow in colour, and peeling like that of
a birch; *P. serrula*, the bark is shiny,
mahogany coloured, from which the thin
outer skin peels, the trunk of a mature
tree having white circular scars around
it.
QUERCUS SUBER The thick, ridged
bark of the cork oak, not hardy in cold
situations, makes it a distinctive tree.
SALIX DAPHNOIDES The violet willow
owes its name to the purple shoots
covered with a bloom giving them in
places a violet colour; *S. purpurea*, the
purple osier, has reddish-purple slender
branches.
ZELKOVA SINICA This remarkable
tree has smooth grey bark which peels
away in scales to reveal a rusty-coloured
under bark.

Trees with outstanding inflorescences
AESCULUS CARNEA The red hybrid
horse chestnut is very variable, the cultivar *briotii* should always be chosen. *A.
hippocastanum*, the common horse-
chestnut, growing into a very large tree,
is well known. The double-flowered
baumannii is smaller and does not
produce conkers. *A. indica*, the Indian
horse chestnut, has the largest flower
spikes of all, pink-flushed, in June and
July; *A. octandra*, the sweet buckeye, a
smaller tree, has flowers that are pale
yellow; *A. pavia* var. *atrosanguinea* is a
small tree with crimson flowers in June.
CATALPA BIGNONIOIDES The Indian

*1 Planting a conifer—until the plants
are established their hardiness is often
in some doubt.*
*2 Incorporating compost in the soil
prior to planting.*
3 Working soil around the roots.

bean has many foxglove-like flowers in a
pyramidal, erect spike in July and
August. The individual flowers are
white marked with yellow and purple.
Does well in the heart of London.
CLADRASTIS TINCTORIA The yellow
wood has pendent clusters of scented
pea-like white flowers with a yellow
blotch on the standard in June. Does
not always flower but has handsome
foliage.
CRATAEGUS The many-flowered inflorescences of the numerous thorns,
mostly with white but sometimes red or
pink flowers, are well known and very
similar. A choice should be made from
those that also bear showy fruits.
DAVIDIA INVOLUCRATA The pocket-
handkerchief, or dove tree has its small
flowers surrounded by two large white
bracts, making it a remarkable sight in
May.

FRAXINUS ORNUS In May the manna or flowering ash is usually densely covered with clusters of small, white flowers.

KOELREUTERIA PANICULATA The golden-rain tree or pride of India carries in August erect pyramidal spikes of many small yellow flowers each with a red spot at the centre. The foliage also is attractive.

LABURNUM By far the best, with the longest chains of flowers and the sweetest scent, is the hybrid *L. × watereri*.

MAGNOLIA Of the large tree magnolias, the following have large and magnificent flowers: *M. campbellii* (pink), *M. delavayi* (creamy-white), *M. denudata* (pure white), *M. grandiflora* (white), *M. mollicomata* (rose-purple), *M. obovata* (creamy-white), *M. sargentiana* (rose-pink), *M. tripetala*, umbrella tree (cream-coloured).

MALUS There are very many floriferous crab-apples, both with white, pink and rose-coloured flowers. It is best to choose those which also produce interesting fruit or have coloured foliage.

PAULOWNIA *P. fargesii* and *P. tomentosa* (syn. *P. imperialis*) have broad spikes of heliotrope foxglove-shaped flowers up to 30cm (1ft) long which are not produced every year, because of winter frost damage to the flower buds.

PRUNUS A selection from this very floriferous genus is best made when a second attribute, such as early flowering, decorative fruit, autumnal leaf colour or decorative bark is present. The Japanese cherries, with flowers ranging from white to shades of pink and even yellow, must be chosen on beauty of flower alone.

PYRUS The ornamental pears are with few exceptions not commonly planted other than for their foliage, as neither their flowers nor fruits are significant.

SORBUS The rowans and service trees have decorative clusters, in some kinds large, of white or rarely pink flowers, but they are best selected by giving attention to the merits of their foliage and berries.

STYRAX *S. japonica* flowers freely in June, the bell-shaped flowers hanging from short shoots; *S. obassa* has similar flowers, fragrant, on spikes at the same season and in addition has large, almost round leaves that turn yellow in autumn.

TILIA The very many small clusters of pale yellow flowers that are carried by all species of limes in June and early July must be mentioned if only on account of their scent. *T. cordata* is the best for a small space, as it is slow growing.

Some deciduous trees with exceptionally handsome foliage

AILANTHUS ALTISSIMA The tree of heaven has pinnate leaves sometimes 60cm (2ft) long.

CATALPA The Indian bean-trees have heart-shaped leaves up to 25cm (10in).

1 *The papery, grey bark of Betula ermanii.*
2 *Quercus ruber, the cork oak, has thick, ridged bark.*
3 *The shining purple-red bark of Prunus serrula from which the thin outer skin peels.*

GYMNOCLADUS DIOICUS The Kentucky coffee-tree has compound pinnate leaves which may reach 1m (3ft) long and 60cm (2ft) wide.

JUGLANS SIEBOLDIANA The walnuts all have handsome pinnate foliage, but in this species the leaves may reach 1m (3ft) long.

MAGNOLIA DELAVAYI This evergreen tree has exceptionally handsome leaves about 30cm (1ft) long. *M. tripetala*, the umbrella tree (so called because of the arrangement of its foliage) has very large leaves up to 50cm (20in) long.

PHELLODENDRON All cultivated species of the cork tree have pinnate leaves 30cm (1ft) or more long.

POPULUS LASIOCARPA This has typical poplar-shaped leaves up to 30cm (1ft)

PTEROCARYA The species of wing nut in cultivation all have pinnate leaves from 30–60cm (1–2ft) long, those on *P. fraxinifolia* being the largest.

RHUS TYPHINA The pinnate leaves on the stag's horn sumach may reach 1m (3ft) long.

SORBUS HARROWIANA This tender species has the largest leaves of a y n mountain ash, 30cm (1ft) or more long. *S. sargentiana*, is a mountain ash which has leaves up to 30cm (1ft) long.

Some trees with good autumn colour

It should be noted that autumn colour may vary from year to year in every respect, and even from tree to tree of the same species. This list is by no means complete.

ACER CAMPESTRE The native field maple turns a good yellow; *A. capillipes*, deep crimson; *A cappadocicum*, yellow; *A. circinatum*, orange and crimson; *A. davidii*, variable, yellow and purple; *A. ginnala*, brilliant flaming scarlet; *A. griseum*, orange, bronze and fiery red; *A. grosseri*, also *A. g. hersii*, red and gold; *A. japonicum*, crimson and pink; *A. negundo*, clear yellow, early; *A. nikoense*, orange and red; *A. pennsylvanicum*, clear yellow; *A. platanoides*, clear yellow; *A. rubrum,* scarlet and yellow; *A. rufinerve*, crimson.

AMELANCHIER All cultivated species turn shades of red or russet.

BETULA Most birches turn shades of greenish yellow, but *B. papyrifera* is a good bright yellow.

CARYA Species usually cultivated turn a good yellow.

CERCIDIPHYLLUM JAPONICUM Variable, but can be brilliant in yellow and reds.

CYDONIA OBLONGA The leaves of the common quince turn a good yellow.

EUONYMUS SACHALINENSIS Yellow and red, early, with crimson fruits.

FAGUS The copper colour of the British native beechwoods is glorious in autumn.

FRAXINUS Most ashes turn shades of yellow before their leaves fall early in the season. *F. oxycarpa* 'Raywood', however, turns a distinctive purple.

GINKGO BILOBA The maidenhair tree

turns a rich yellow.

GYMNOCLADUS DIOICUS The large leaves turn clear yellow.

LIQUIDAMBAR STYRACIFLUA Variable, but in good specimens can be brilliant, purple to scarlet.

LIRIODENDRON TULIPIFERA Leaves turn a good yellow.

MALUS Apples give little autumn leaf colour, an exception being *M. tschonoskii*, on which the leaves turn yellow and scarlet.

MESPILUS GERMANICA The large leaves of the medlar turn russet colour.

NYSSA SYLVATICA The tupelo turns vivid scarlet.

PARROTIA PERSICA Colouring reliable, yellow through gold to crimson.

PHELLODENDRON Species usually cultivated turn clear yellow.

PRUNUS This genus provides a few only species that colour well, though the Japanese cultivars mostly turn good shades of yellow; *P. avium*, the gean, most years turns a flaming red; *P. sargentii*, infallibly turns a brilliant red early in autumn.

QUERCUS BOREALIS The red oak is rather a misnomer as the colour is nearer to brown, but it can be effective. *Q. coccinea*, the well-named scarlet oak, retains its brilliant leaves far into the winter, the best form being the cultivar *splendens*. *Q. palustris*, leaves may turn scarlet, but not reliable; *Q. phellos*, yellow and orange; *Q. velutina*, var. *rubrifolia* is a good red.

RHUS TYPHINA Turns orange, red and purple.

SORBUS CASHMERIANA Pale gold, falling early. *S. discolor*, brilliant red; *S.* 'Joseph Rock', leaves turn a rich variety of colours; *S. sargentiana*, striking reds and golds; *S. torminalis*, the native wild service, colours in well in yellows and golds and sometimes scarlets.

STYRAX OBASSIA The large leaves turn a rich yellow.

Trees with decorative fruits

The following list is of trees whose brightly-coloured fruits are usually decorative for some time after the leaves have fallen. Birds soon attack and strip the berries on a number of kinds almost as soon as they are ripe, but the following are less severely attacked. With some trees, berries are only borne on female trees; in many instances nurserymen can select these.

CERCIS SILIQUASTRUM The Judas tree carries red and purple pods from late summer far into the winter.

COTONEASTER FRIGIDUS Heavy crops of clusters of rich bright red are borne in autumn and early winter.

CRATAEGUS All the thorns carry crops of haws, the more striking including *C. durobrivensis* with large red fruit lasting well into winter; *C. lavallei* has large orange-red berries that hang into the new year; *C. mollis*, the red haw, has

very large red fruits which drop rather early to make a spectacular carpet under the tree; *C. orientalis* has large oval or yellowish-red fruits; *C. prunifolia* has large, red fruits, combined with crimson autumn foliage; *C. punctata* has large, slightly pear shaped dull crimson fruits; *C. wattiana*, the Altai Mountain thorn, has large, translucent, yellow fruit.

CYDONIA OBLONGA The common quince, has golden fruit which combine effectively with the yellow autumnal leaves.

EVODIA HUPEHENSIS Female trees bear clusters of scarlet berries.

IDESIA POLYCARPA Female trees carry bunches of bright red berries in autumn.

ILEX x ALTACLARENSIS *I. aquifolium* the hollies, are among Britain's most beautiful berrying trees, though fruiting only on female trees. *I. a. bacciflava* (*fructu-luteo*) has yellow berries.

MALUS The crab-apples, mostly carry fruit. The best include the following:

M. x *alden–hamensis*, fruit numerous small, deep purple; *M. eleyi*, bright crimson; *M.* 'Gibb's Golden Gage', waxy yellow fruit; *M.* 'Golden Hornet', bright yellow fruit hanging late; *M.* 'John Downie', large, narrow fruits, yellow with red flush, flavour good; *M. prunifolia* and its cultivars, 'Cheal's Crimson', *fastigiata*, *pendula* and 'Rinki' have red fruits hanging long on the tree; *M. purpurea* has light crimson fruit; *M. robusta*, the cherry apple or Siberian crab, has heavy crops of long-lasting small fruits, the two cultivars being 'Red Siberian' and 'Yellow Siberian'; *M.* 'Wisley Crab' has large, deep-red fruit.

PRUNUS though some of this genus, eg, cherries, carry attractive fruit, they are eaten by birds even before ripening.

SORBUS The mountain ashes and whitebeams often have decorative berries, but on most species they are eaten at an early stage by birds. The following are usually exceptions: *S. cashmeriana*, large, glistening white, hanging late; *S. esserteauiana*, very large clusters of small scarlet, or in *flava*, yellow fruit, hanging late; *S. hupehensis*, large clusters of small white fruit, turning pink, and hanging late; *S.* 'Joseph Rock' has amber-coloured, long-lasting berries; *S. sargentiana* has great clusters of small, orange-red berries; *S. scalaris* has bright red, small fruits.

1 *Aesculus carnea is the red hybrid horse chestnut and can be variable.*
2 *Laburnum × vossii is one of the best laburnums.*
3 *The leaves and seed pods of Ailanthus altissima, the tree of heaven, a fast-growing tree once established.*

Trees with yellow or golden leaves

Included here are some trees which do not retain their exceptional colour throughout the entire season, but are attractive during the early part of the summer. All are cultivars that must be propagated vegetatively since they rarely come true from seed. When suckers arise from ground level they should be watched, and, if they are not true, removed.

Broad-leaved trees

ACER CAPPADOCICUM AUREA Deep yellow leaves on opening and again in autumn. *A. negundo auratum*, golden-yellow foliage; *A. pseudoplatanus corstorphinense*, the golden sycamore, has leaves changing from pale through rich yellow to green in late summer, makes a large tree, *worlei* has soft yellow leaves until late summer.

ALNUS GLUTINOSA AUREA A golden-leaved form of the common alder. *A. incana aurea*, yellow leaves and young shoots with red catkins; it is a beautiful form of the grey alder.

CATALPA BIGNONIOIDES AUREA A small growing cultivar of the Indian bean tree with large golden leaves.

FAGUS SYLVATICA ZLATIA A yellow-leaved beech.

FRAXINUS EXCELSIOR AUREA A large tree with yellow shoots and yellow leaves in autumn.

GLEDITSCHIA TRIACANTHOS 'Sunburst'. This has bright yellow unfolding leaves.

LABURNUM ANAGYROIDES AUREUM The yellow-leaved laburnum.

PTELEA TRIFOLIATA AUREA A yellow-leaved form of the hop-tree.

ROBINIA PSEUDOACACIA FRISIA

This has golden-yellow leaves throughout.

ULMUS CARPINIFOLIA SARNIENSIS A slow-growing form of the Wheatley elm with pure golden coloured leaves. *U. glabra lutescens*, a wych elm with pale yellow leaves; *U. procera vanhouttei*, a golden-leaved form of hedge-row elm.

Conifers

CEDRUS DEODARA AUREA The golden deodar, smaller than the type, is the best golden cedar.

CHAMAECYPARIS LAWSONIANA LUTEA Has golden-yellow foliage; *stewartii* is a free-growing yellow form; *C. obtusa crippsii* is good deep yellow, slowly reaching tree size.

1 *Autumn colouring of Nyssa sylvatica.*
2 *Cercidiphyllum japonicum in autumn.*
3 *Chamaecyparis lawsoniana stewartii has golden-tipped foliage.*

CUPRESSUS MACROCARPA 'Donard Gold'. A deep yellow and *lutea*, paler yellow, both being of compact growth.

JUNIPERUS CHINENSIS AUREA Young's golden juniper is a small tree of rather narrow form.

TAXUS BACCATA ELEGANTISSIMA The golden yew; *fastigiata aurea* is the golden Irish yew.

Trees with blue (glaucous) and silver foliage

Broad-leaved

ALNUS INCANA Leaves grey underneath.

CRATAEGUS ORIENTALIS Leaves grey on both sides, deeply cut.

EUCALYPTUS The tree has numerous species, but their hardiness over a long period is doubtful; *E. gunnii* is the best known.

POPULUS ALBA The white poplar has white twigs and undersides of the leaves, the best form for the garden being the erect-growing *pyramidalis*. *P. canescens* has grey leaves and makes a large, vigorously suckering tree.

SALIX ALBA The white willow is a large tree unsuitable for most gardens but its variety *sericea* is a smaller, round-headed tree with whiter leaves.

SORBUS ARIA The whitebeam and all its cultivars have a persistent vivid, white underside to the leaves; in *lutescens* the upper surface also is creamy-white.

TILIA PETIOLARIS This has silvery undersides to the large, drooping leaves; in *T. tomentosa* the underneath is quite white.

Conifers

CEDRUS ATLANTICA GLAUCA A large tree with glaucous-blue, and in some specimens, almost silvery leaves.

CHAMAECYPARIS LAWSONIANA Includes a number of glaucous-blue foliaged cultivars, including *allumii*, *columnaris*, *elegantissima*, *erecta alba*, *fraseri*, *glauca* (better known as 'Milford Blue Jacket'), *robusta glauca*, 'Silver Queen' (the foliage turning green in late summer) and 'Triomphe de Boskoop' (tending towards blue).

CUPRESSUS ARIZONICA 'Bonita' has very grey-blue foliage; in *pyramidalis* it is somewhat bluer.

JUNIPERUS CHINENSIS PYRAMIDALIS Has markedly blue foliage; *J. recurva coxii* has blue-green leaves; *J. virginiana glauca* is silvery-blue.

PICEA GLAUCA A large spruce with bluish green leaves; *P. pungens* has grey-green leaves, the cultivar *glauca* is smaller with grey-blue leaves and *glauca moerheimii* is an even more intensely coloured form.

Trees with white, silver or yellow variegated leaves

These are all sports, perhaps occurring originally on one branch only, of normal trees that have been propagated vegetatively as cultivars. Normally, seedlings revert to the usual form. Suckers arising may not be true.

The deciduous broad-leaved kinds are cheerful in urban areas where smoke pollution is not too bad, but the evergreen conifers on which the foliage persists for several years become drab. Most of these trees fit well into the normal colour scheme of a garden.

Broad-leaved

ACER NEGUNDO The box elder, provides excellent variegated foliage in *elegantissimum*, bright yellow and *variegatum*, conspicuously white. *A. platanoides drummondii,* leaves distinctively margined with white; *A. pseudoplatanus leopoldii*, leaves marked with cream and white.

BUXUS SEMPERVIRENS The following free-growing cultivars have variegated leaves: *aurea maculata*, leaves marked with gold and *aurea-marginata*, leaves edged with yellow.

ILEX AQUIFOLIUM A number of variegated leaved forms include *argenteo-marginata*, silver-variegated, berrying; *flavescens*, moonlight holly, yellow and gold, berrying; 'Golden King', wide yellow margins, berrying; 'Golden Milkmaid', gold with narrow green margins, not berrying; 'Handsworth New Silver', dark green with white margin, berrying; *laurifolia variegata*, golden margins, not berrying; 'Madame Briot', leaves margined and blotched with gold, berrying; *scotica aurea*, spineless with lustrous, spineless leaves blotched with yellow, berrying; 'Silver Queen', bold creamy white margins, not berrying.

LIRIODENDRON TULIPIFERA AUREA—MARGINATUM A tulip tree with yellow-margined leaves making a large tree.

ULMUS PROCERA ARGENTEO-VARIEGATA A hedgerow elm having leaves mottled with white. *U. procera argenteo-maculata*, this species has leaves attractively mottled with white.

Conifers

CHAMAECYPARIS LAWSONIANA ALBOSPICA The tips of branches creamy-white; 'Silver Queen', young foliage silver-white; *versicolor* foliage marked with creamy-white and yellow; *C. nootkatensis argenteo-variegata* has foliage variegated with creamy-white.

SEQUOIA SEMPERVIRENS ADPRESSA The young shoots are greenish-white.

TAXUS BACCATA DOVASTONIANA AUREO-VARIEGATA A golden variegated form of the weeping yew.

THUJA PLICATA ZEBRINA A fine tree, smaller than the type, variegated with bright yellow.

TSUGA CANADENSIS ALBO-SPICATA The tree has white tips to the shoots.

Red and purple foliage trees

Placing trees of these colours needs great care, but their colours mingled with the multitude of others in autumn are effective and of great beauty, they do not blend well with the normal greens, particularly if used in quantity. They should therefore be used sparingly in isolation at points where they will inevitably catch the eye.

A number have clear colours when the leaves unfold but gradually lose this quality and become sombre as the season progresses. Others, not included here, become normal green when the leaves are open.

ACER PLATANOIDES 'Crimson King' ('Goldsworth Purple'), a Norway maple with crimson-purple leaves larger than the type.

BETULA PENDULA PURPUREA The purple-leaved birch is not a vigorous tree.

CORYLUS MAXIMA PURPUREA The purple-leaved filbert is a good colour though not often of tree size.

FAGUS SYLVATICA ATROPUNICEA The dark purple beech, *cuprea* copper beech; and *purpurea*, purple beech, are all well-known, reliable trees reaching a considerable size and quite unsuitable for other than the largest garden. Weeping forms of these coloured vari-

Cedrus atlantica glauca is a graceful conifer with glaucous blue leaves.

ants are also available.

MALUS The flowering crabs provide several kinds with red or purple foliage combined with gay flowers and decorative fruits. All are very hardy and adaptable, well suited to a small garden; *M.* × *aldenhamensis*, purplish leaves, rich red flowers and crimson fruit. *M. eleyi* is rather more vigorous than the last, the leaves bronze-green flushed with purple, the fruit hanging longer on the tree. *M. purpurea* has dark purplish-green leaves, crimson flowers and fruits, both tinged with purple. *M.* 'Wisley Crab', larger than the foregoing in all its parts, the leaves bronzy-red, the flowers large, wine coloured, scented and large deep-red fruits.

PRUNUS Several plums have coloured leaves, the best including *P. blireana* (often a large shrub) deep copper with pink flowers. *P. cerasifera atropurpurea*, better known as *P. pissardii*, with crimson-purple leaves, suitable also for hedging; nigra has darker leaves.

QUERCUS PETRAEA PURPUREA Has reddish-purple leaves which become green flushed with red. *Q. robur fastigiata purpurea* has young leaves the same colour.

Trees with early flowers
ACER OPALUS The Italian maple has yellow flowers in early April.
CORNUS MAS This has many small yellow flowers in February.
PARROTIA PERSICA This bears very numerous small scarlet tassel-like flowers in February.
PRUNUS 'Accolade' is a semi-double pink cherry flowering in March; *P. conradinae* is a cherry with scented white or pinkish flowers in late February; *P. davidiana* is a peach flowering in January, *alba* is a white form, *rubra* pink. *P.* 'Fundanzakura' (*semperflorens*) with pink buds and white flowers from November to April. *P.* 'Kursar' a bright pink cherry flowering in March; *P.* 'Okami' a cherry with carmine-pink flowers in March; *P.* 'Pandora' is a single pink, very floriferous March-flowering cherry, giving good autumnal leaf colour; *P. subhirtella autumnalis* carries semi-double white flowers (pink in *rosea*) from November to March.
SALIX CAPREA The goat willow has decorative catkins in March; *S. daphnoides*, the violet-willow, carries them even earlier.

Evergreen trees

Broad-leaved
It is as well to remember that these often drop their leaves untidily in summer.
ARBUTUS All species and hybrids.
BUXUS All species and cultivars.
EUCALYPTUS All species.
ILEX *I.* × *altaclarensis*, *I. aquifolium* and their cultivars are evergreen hollies.
LIGUSTRUM LUCIDUM A species of privet often reaching tree size, has handsome dark green, glossy leaves, and white flowers in late summer.
MAGNOLIA DELAVAYI This and *M. grandiflora* are evergreens reaching tree size.
PHILLYREA LATIFOLIA A neglected, small evergreen tree with dense, dark-green, glossy foliage.
QUERCUS ILEX The holm oak and *Q. suber*, the cork oak, are handsome trees capable of reaching large sizes, the latter needing mild conditions.
UMBELLULARIA CALIFORNICA The Californian laurel is usually a small tree with aromatic leaves.

Conifers
All conifers are evergreen with the exception of *Ginkgo*, *Larix* (larch), *Metasequoia* and *Taxodium* (swamp cypress).

Fastigiate trees
To the botanist, the word fastigiate means 'with parallel, erect, clustered branches'. It has now become more widely used in a more generalized sense

1 *One of the variegated forms of Ilex aquifolium, the holly, with broad yellow-green marks on the leaves.*
2 *The copper beech, Fagus sylvatica, a handsome tree for the larger garden.*

for trees with narrow crowns. All those mentioned are derived from natural sports and do not come true from seed (if that is produced). They are propagated as cultivars. They generally need careful pruning when young to ensure the necessary erect growth.

Their placing needs great care, as they inevitably have an unnatural look. Fastigiate conifers accord well when planted in the regular pattern of formal gardens—the use of the true cypress in the great Italian gardens of the Renaissance. Fastigiate trees can be skilfully used, too, for adding a steadying vertical element to a steeply sloping site. The planting of a pair one on either side of the introduction to a vista can be very effective. Some of the less erect-growing are excellent for planting in narrow roads, or, for example, at the centre of a lawn where space is limited.

Broad-leaved
ACER SACCHARINUM PYRAMIDALE An upright form of the silver maple, useful for street planting.
BETULA PENDULA FASTIGIATA This is an erect, slow-growing form of the

common birch, resembling an erect besom.

CARPINUS BETULUS FASTIGIATA This is a valuable pyramidal rather than truly fastigiate cultivar of the hornbeam.

CRATAEGUS MONOGYNA STRICTA This has a narrow, erect-growing crown.

FAGUS SYLVATICA FASTIGIATA The Dawyck beech is a good erect tree.

LABURNUM ANAGYROIDES PYRAMIDALIS This is an upright laburnum.

LIRIODENDRON TULIPIFERA FASTIGIATUM A narrow-growing form of the tulip tree.

MALUS HUPEHENSIS ROBUSTA This has large white flowers and fairly erect growth. *M. prunifolia fastigiata*, the fastigiate Siberian crab.

POPULUS ALBA PYRAMIDALIS An erect-growing, very effective form of the white poplar; *P. nigra italica* is the common large-growing Lombardy poplar.

PRUNUS 'Amanogawa' A very fastigiate, small-growing cherry with double pink flowers; *P. hillieri* 'Spire' reaches 8m (25ft) with pink flowers and good autumn foliage; *P.* 'Umeniko' has single white flowers with leaves colouring in autumn.

PTELEA TRIFOLIATA FASTIGIATA An erect growing form of the hop tree.

QUERCUS ROBUR FASTIGIATA The cypress oak, makes a broadly columnar tree of interesting form.

ROBINIA PSEUDOACACIA ERECTA A narrow form of the false acacia with few leaflets; *pyramidalis* has erect, spineless branches.

SORBUS AUCUPARIA FASTIGIATA A particularly narrow form of the rowan.

ULMUS CARPINIFOLIA SARNIENSIS The Wheatley elm is a large tree of flame-like form excellent for street planting; *U. glabra exoniensis* is a slow-growing erect form of the wych elm, the leaves often being distorted.

Conifers

CEDRUS ATLANTICA ARGENTEA FASTIGIATA A narrowly pyramidal form of the Atlas cedar.

CHAMAECYPARIS LAWSONIANA This provides a number of narrowly erect forms, including the popular *allumii* with bluish foliage; *columnaris* very narrow, glaucous blue; *erecta* bright green; *fraseri* slender, grey-green; 'Kilmacurragh', bright green; *pyramidalis alba* with white tips to the branches in spring; and *wisselli* a fine tree reaching considerable size.

CUPRESSOCYPARIS LEYLANDII This is a densely-leaved, quick-growing tree of large size and fairly narrow shape.

CUPRESSUS ARIZONICA PYRAMIDALIS This is very narrow, of moderate size and with almost grey foliage.

GINKGO BILOBA FASTIGIATA This is an upright-growing form of the maidenhair tree useful for street planting.

JUNIPERUS COMMUNIS HIBERNICA

The Irish juniper is columnar, but needs supporting.

LIBOCEDRUS DECURRENS The incense cedar makes a distinctive, large columnar tree.

TAXUS BACCATA FASTIGIATA. The well-known Irish yew of churchyards, the golden-leaved form being *fastigiata aurea*.

THUJA OCCIDENTALIS FASTIGIATA A slow-growing, very narrow tree.

THUJA PLICATA FASTIGIATA A narrow form of the western red cedar making a tall tree.

Weeping trees

Weeping trees are mostly natural sports that must be propagated as cultivars. They are difficult to place on account of their arresting form, and must stand in isolation since much of their beauty lies in the manner in which their branches sweep down to the ground. Nothing should be grown under them.

Few trees are more frequently planted in an unsuitable place than the weeping willow, attractive when it is a small, slender tree, but becoming mighty in

1 Libocedrus decurrens, the incense cedar, is columnar in form. It has dark green, glossy foliage.
2 Chamaecyparis lawsoniana wisselli has a narrow fastigiate form.

age, when its form often has to be damaged by savage pruning.

BETULA PENDULA TRISTIS A graceful form of the silver birch with steeply drooping branches; *youngii* is smaller, more compact and slow-growing.

BUXUS SEMPERVIRENS PENDULA A good weeping form of the common box.

CARAGANA ARBORESCEN PENDULA An attractive small weeping tree with yellow pea-shaped flowers and fern-like leaves.

CRATAEGUS MONOGYNA PENDULA A weeping hawthorn; *pendula rosea* has pink flowers.

FAGUS SYLVATICA PENDULA The weeping beech, making a big tree; *purpureopendula* is a weeping form of the purple beech.

FRAXINUS EXCELSIOR PENDULA The well-known weeping ash.

GLEDITSCHIA TRIACANTHOS

1 *The weeping elm, Ulmus glabra pendula, has a neat shape.*
2 *Pyrus salicifolia, the willow-leaved pear, a dainty tree.*
3 *The weeping cherry, Prunus subhirtella pendula.*

BUJOTI A honey-locust with pendulous branches.
ILEX AQUIFOLIUM ARGENTEO-MARGINATA PENDULA Perry's silver weeping holly, berrying freely.
LABURNUM ANAGYROIDES PENDULUM A gracefully weeping laburnum.
MALUS The following crab-apples have pendulous branches: *M. floribunda* 'Excellens Thiel', a small tree with crimson buds and pink flowers, floriferous but no fruit; *M. prunifolia pendula*, the weeping Siberian crab, with numerous small, scarlet, persistent fruit; *M. pumila pendula* 'Elise Rathke', a weeping form of the native crab.
MORUS ALBA PENDULA The weeping white mulberry is a small tree with perpendicular branches, the fruit is insignificant.
PRUNUS PERSICA 'Windle Weeping' A weeping peach with double pink flowers; *P. subhirtella pendula*, the weeping spring cherry, has very numerous pale pink flowers; in *pendula rubra* they are deeper coloured. *P. yedoensis perpendens* is a very pendulous form of the early

Yoshino cherry.
PYRUS SALICIFOLIA PENDULA A very pendulous form of the silver willow-leaved pear.
SALIX ALBA TRISTIS The now common weeping willow, making a large tree; *S. babylonica* is rare and not satisfactory.
SOPHORA JAPONICA PENDULA A small arbour-like tree with slender branchlets falling perpendicularly.
SORBUS ARIA A weeping form of the whitebeam. *S. aucuparia pendula*, a weeping form of the rowan. Both are small trees.
TILIA PETIOLARIS The weeping silver lime is a magnificent tree with a silvery sheen on the underside of the large leaves.
ULMUS GLABRA CAMPERDOWNII The smaller of the two weeping wych elms with very pendulous branches, *pendula* being larger and more spreading in form.

Conifers
CHAMAECYPARIS LAWSONIANA INTERTEXTA A tall cypress of great

beauty with drooping branches. *C. nootkatensis pendula* a handsome, rather large tree with long drooping branches.
JUNIPERUS RECURVA COXII A moderate-sized, narrow tree with long, glaucous shoots drooping steeply.
LARIX LEPTOLEPIS PENDULA A weeping form of the Japanese larch.
PICEA BRACHYTYLA This has slender, pendulous branchlets, the leaves blue and white underneath; *P. breweriana*, Brewer's weeping spruce, is a sombre tree with very long branchlets that hang vertically; *P. smithiana*, the Himalayan spruce, is a large tree with steeply drooping branchlets and exceptionally long leaves.
TAXUS BACCATA DOVASTONIANA A yew with spreading branches from which the branchlets droop; *aureovariegata* is a golden-leaved form.

Trimming see Pruning Ornamentals

Trowel see Tools

Tuber see Bulb cultivation

Turf and turfing see Lawn construction and maintenance

Turnip see Vegetables

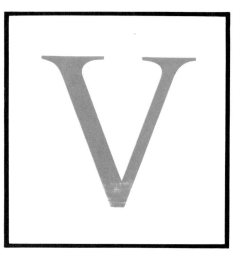

Vegetables

Artichokes

The flavours of these vegetables are acquired tastes and are not every gardener's choice. Jerusalem and Chinese artichokes are easy enough to grow and yield a good crop, taking up little space, but the globe artichoke is rather wasteful of space and it does require a little extra skill to grow it well.

Chinese artichokes (*Stachys affinis*) The tuberous roots, which are knobbly, are eaten as a root vegetable during the winter. The tubers should be planted 10cm (4in) deep in any ordinary soil, that has been well prepared, in spring, spacing them 25cm (9in) apart in rows 45cm (18in) apart. No further cultivation is required except occasional hoeing. The tubers are lifted as they are required but in severe weather cover the ground to prevent it from freezing too hard. Plants grow 30-45cm (1-1½ft) tall.

Globe artichokes (*Cynara scolymus*) These plants are very ornamental, they grow to about 1.5m (5ft) and produce large flower-heads which are gathered just as the scales are beginning to open. The flower-heads are boiled and the fleshy portion at the base of each scale is eaten, together with the base of the flower.

To grow these plants well the ground must be deeply dug and manured. Plant the off-sets in the spring at least 1m (3ft) apart each way and choose a sunny position. Keep the plants well watered during dry weather and mulch the beds in the spring. The beds should be renewed about every three years, so it is a good plan to detach off-sets from the parent plants every spring and make a new plantation, discarding any beds that are over three years old. It is important to protect the plants in the winter by placing some bracken or other protective material over them in October. If the soil is too heavy or wet they are liable to rot in the winter; the ideal is a sandy loam.

Seed is another method of propagation but a slower one. Seed should be sown in an unheated greenhouse or frame in March or outdoors in April. As soon as the seedlings can be handled, transplant them and transfer them to their final quarters in the following spring.

Jerusalem artichokes (*Helianthus tuberosus*). The tubers of Jerusalem artichokes are very similar to Chinese artichokes but they are larger and more irregular in shape (those of the French variety 'Fusean' are larger and less irregular as well as being more palatable). The tubers are planted in February, or earlier if the ground is workable. Space the tubers about 45cm (18in) apart in rows 1m (3ft) apart, in ground that has been well dug and manured. They will grow in any odd, rough corner of the garden, but they appreciate a well-cultivated site.

These artichokes grow to about 1.6m

The flower-head of the globe artichoke.

(5ft) in height and look very like the sunflowers to which they are related; they make an excellent screen for an old shed, manure heap, compost heap or other unsightly part of the garden. The top growth should be cut down in the autumn, leaving the tubers in the ground. These are then lifted as they are required or they may be lifted and stored in some dry soil or peat in a shed. If they are left out of the ground for long they will shrivel.

During the summer the ground between them should be hoed occasionally but they do not need any further attention.

Tubers for planting the following year can be selected from those lifted in the late winter and replanted almost immediately.

Asparagus

This delicious vegetable is expensive to buy but easy to grow. The shoots are cut below soil level when they are about 10cm (4in) long, but all cutting must cease soon after the middle of June to allow the plants to develop over the summer and build up the crowns for the following spring. Asparagus plants must not be cropped until they are at least three years old and then only moderately until they are well established.

An asparagus bed will last for a good many years, so it should be dug to a depth of 60cm (2ft), incorporating manure in the second spit, and if the soil is heavy add more cinders or other material that will break up the soil and improve the drainage as the crowns are liable to rot in heavy, wet soils. It is advisable on heavy, ill-drained soils, to raise the level of the beds about 16cm (6in) to improve the drainage. The beds are usually made about 1.3m (4ft) wide with an alley of 60cm (2ft) or so between them.

Crowns are planted in spring or seed may be sown. If planting crowns make sure the roots are spread out well and then cover them with 7cm (3in) of soil. They should be spaced about 30cm (1ft) apart, in rows 40cm (15in) apart.

Seeds may be sown either directly into the permanent beds or in a seed bed or frame and then thinned out eventually leaving the plants 23cm (9in) apart. They will be ready for planting into their permanent bed the following spring. Female plants, which are berry-bearing, do not produce such good crops as the male plants and should be discarded, replacing them with male plants. It is not possible to distinguish between them until the plants are two years old so the rogueing must be done when the plants are in their permanent beds, or the seedlings can be kept in the seed bed and planted out as soon as they can be sorted out.

Topdress the beds in the spring with a thick layer of well-rotted manure and keep them weeded but do not use a hoe as the roots are so near the surface. The top growth must be cut down in the autumn when it turns yellow.

Aubergine

The egg plant is another name for this vegetable which comes from tropical climates. It is grown in greenhouses in this country, or it may be grown in a frame from May onwards and even outside in a very sheltered position in the southern counties. The fruits vary in size and shape from roundish to sausage shaped and are usually a very deep purple, but there are white varieties. Botanically it is known as *Solanum melongena ovigerum*. It makes a small bush 0.6–1m (2–3ft) high and has blue flowers.
Cultivation Sow the seeds in heat, about 65°F (18°C), in January, February or March, using John Innes seed compost. Prick out the seedlings as soon as possible into 6cm (2½in) pots and pot on, finally into 18cm (7in) pots using John Innes potting compost. Water well and pinch out the tips to encourage bushiness when the plants are 16cm (6in) high.

Restrict the fruits to four to six per plant and feed the plants with weak liquid manure or a balanced fertilizer at regular intervals. Gather the fruits when slightly soft.

Broad Beans

These were certainly known to the Ancient Egyptians and are probably natives of northern and western Asia. They are extremely hardy.
Cultivation A good rich loam suits these beans, though they are not difficult to grow on any soil. This crop may well follow cabbages and potatoes, or manure may be dug in sparingly. A certain amount of chemical fertilizer may be added as follows: 84g (3oz) per sq m (sq yd) of superphosphate and 28g (1oz) per sq m (sq yd) of sulphate of potash. These beans prefer a neutral or alkaline soil to one which is acid.

In January or February seed may be sown in boxes or individual pots and started under glass. In April the young plants are set out and the crop becomes mature in June. Another method is to plant outdoors in April for the maid summer crop or a May sowing becomes ready in September. At one time autumn sowing was popular, but a number of bad winters in succession has made this method unpopular.

In sowing, the seeds are spaced at 16cm (6in) intervals in rows 60cm (2ft) apart. The beans may be put 4cm (1½in) deep or, on clay soil, be placed on the surface and soil ridged up to cover them. When the first bean pods are showing the tip of the main shoot should be broken off and removed.

Named kinds include: 'Green Windsor', 'Saville Longpod', 'Early Longpod', 'Masterpiece', 'Green Longpod', 'Bunyard's Exhibition' and 'Harlington White.'

Haricot beans and French beans (*Phaseolus vulgaris*) The difference between the French bean and the haricot bean is merely that in the former the pod containing immature seeds is eaten, while the haricots are the ripe seeds without the pods. The details of cultivation are the same for both French and haricot forms of the bean.

Though in Britain the runner bean is more often grown than the French, on the continent the reverse is true. It is not always known that a climbing form of the French bean is available though the dwarf kind is certainly more popular and has some advantages.
Cultivation Soil should be rich and light and well dug, with a dusting of superphosphate of lime at 84g (3oz) per sq m (sq yd) and manure at the rate of 50kg (1cwt) to each 8 sq m (8 sq yd). For early crops seeds may be sown in boxes during April and started under glass to be hardened off and planted out in May. Outdoors it is unwise to sow before the

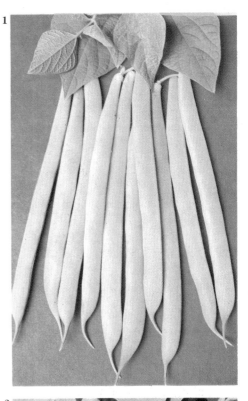

1 Dwarf bean 'The Prince'.
2 Broad bean 'Gillett's Wonder'.

end of April.

The secret of a good crop of succulent beans is speedy raising without check. Water freely and mulch if dry weather occurs. It is essential with this bean to begin picking while the beans are still tender and not more than 10cm (4in) long. It seems a British trait to produce the heaviest crop of the largest vegetables, and this is why the best qualities of flavour and texture are sometimes lacking from our vegetables.

The outdoor beans should be spaced 16cm (6in) apart in drills 2.5cm (1in) deep, 45cm (18in) apart.

At the end of the season the plants may well be allowed to ripen their remaining seeds as these when shelled and dried are really the haricots of commerce. They may be used as seed for next year's crop, but as long as they are kept dry they may be kept for over a year for use in cookery.

French beans may be forced under glass to have them at a time when they are unobtainable in the shops. From a January sowing under glass with a maintained temperature of 60°F (16°C) beans may be had by May. Early March sowings give beans in June. Soil should be as for tomato culture and an even temperature and state of moisture must be maintained throughout.

Named kinds include: 'Brown Dutch', 'Canadian Wonder', 'Cherokee', 'Fin de Bagnols', 'Masterpiece' and 'Black Prince'.

Runner beans (*Phaseolus coccineus*) This plant is a native of tropical America, and when first introduced into Britain it was grown for the beauty of its bright scarlet blossoms. It is actually a tender perennial, but is commonly grown as an annual; though it is possible to take a

plant and overwinter it, nothing is gained.

Those who use the railways running into London will, in late summer, have noted in almost all the suburban backyards abutting upon the line thriving plants of the beloved scarlet runner, and it is notable that this is often the only vegetable grown. All of which speaks eloquently of the merits of this most popular amateur's plant.

Cultivation It would be most unwise to plant runner beans before May as they will not take the least frost. Should an early crop be required the same method

Dwarf French bean 'Cherokee'.

may be used as advised for the french bean and sow the seed in boxes under glass. It is not necessary to sow these seeds before April since they may not be put out before late May or the beginning of June.

The method of planting for those plants which will be staked is that of two double rows 25cm (10in) apart separated by a space of at least 1.6m (5ft). It is in this central area that the strong supports must be placed. The individual seeds must be placed at 20cm (8in) intervals.

The poles or stakes should be quite 2.6m (8ft) long and should be connected by a strong horizontal structure firmly lashed to the uprights. The rest of the framework is merely a net or an arrangement of strings. The weight of a row of runner beans in full growth is considerable and they present a large surface to be shaken by the wind. To avoid all this scaffolding it is quite possible to convert the plants into shrubby masses by a routine of pinching out the growing shoots. However, when this plan is adopted the individual seeds must be spaced at 60cm (2ft) intervals, with a distance of 1m (3ft) between the rows. Naturally a given number of plants will occupy considerably more ground space under these conditions.

When runner beans are in full production pick them frequently. As with French beans, they should be picked when they are young and tender.

Named kinds include: 'Best of All', 'Giraffe', 'Kentucky Wonder', 'Painted

Runner bean 'Prizewinner Enorma', a new variety.

Lady', 'Prizewinner', 'Streamline' and 'Princeps'.

Beetroot

This sweet salad-vegetable has a high food value. It needs good deep soil, and is best suited to occupy a place where a previous non-root crop has been grown. Do not add fresh manure as this is inclined to cause forking of the root. If, instead of growing vegetables in the kitchen garden, they are grown in the old-fashioned cottager's way interspersed with flowering plants, the beetroot is a most suitable plant, since the round or turnip-shaped beet has generally fine decorative crimson leaves. In addition to the round beet there are two other forms obtainable, a long-rooted, and an intermediate type, called tankard or canister-shaped. Good named kinds are: 'Crimson Globe', 'Veitch's Intermediate', 'Cheltenham Green Top' and 'Nutting's Red Globe'. All are forms of *Beta vulgaris*.

Cultivation The soil must be of an open well-worked, but not recently manured type. Ammonium sulphate should be given at the rate of 28g (1oz) per sq m (sq yd), potassium sulphate at the same rate, and 110g (4oz) of calcium super-phosphate also to each sq m (sq yd).

Sow the globe-rooted beet in April; the others may follow in May. Make drills, 30cm (12in) apart, space seeds 13cm (5in) apart. A point to note is that each so-called 'seed' is, in fact, a 'seed-ball' containing several seeds and more than one may germinate. It is necessary to single the seedlings to one at each point when they are 2.5cm (1in) high.

Another most important point to remember with this crop is the extreme care required when the roots are harvested. On no account should root or top growth be damaged, or the result is quite likely to be a most unpalatable, anaemic-looking thing instead of the rich wine-red and appetizing vegetable it should be. The roots should be only shaken free of soil as they are dug in August or September, and then stored in a shed, giving some cover in the form of dry soil, peat or leaves. Top growth may be carefully twisted off to avoid damage. Do not leave the roots to get hard and woody before digging them. After the beets have been cooked they may be cut without damaging the appearance of them, but if they are cut before cooking their appearance will certainly be spoiled.

Broccoli, Sprouting

This is another variety, *italica*, of *Brassica oleracea*. Both purple and white sprouting produce a profusion of young shoots invaluable for prolonging the supplies of winter greens. Purple sprouting is the most hardy and will safely overwinter in most open situations. Young shoots may be produced for Christmas, but it is in March and April that the vegetable is most useful. White sprouting is perhaps a little less strong in flavour, not so hardy and can only be

Globe beetroot should be harvested when still young and tender, before they have become old and 'woody'.

grown in sheltered gardens. The small curds which sprout forth in profusion are white instead of purple. Seed should be sown thinly in the open from the middle of April, in drills 6mm (¼in) deep and 23cm (9in) apart. Thin seedlings when they are large enough to handle. Plant out in June or July 0.8m (2½ft) apart, in rows allowing 1m (3ft) between the rows. This is a useful crop to plant in July after an early crop of potatoes. The ground must be in good heart, preferably well manured for the previous crop. Otherwise, dig in decayed manure or compost with the addition of extra phosphates and potash for example 85g (3oz) of superphosphate and 28g (1oz) of sulphate of potash. Really firm ground will help to keep the plants upright through spells of severe weather, but it may be found necessary to draw soil towards the stems to give extra protection or even to stake the largest of the plants. Varieties are named by type, such as Early or Late Purple or White Sprouting.

Brussels Sprouts

This important member of the cabbage family, known botanically as *Brassica oleracea* var. *gemmifera* (*Cruciferae*), originated in Belgium. The popularity of the vegetable is due not only to the fact

that picking can be extended over a long period, but it can stand up to severe winter weather. It is indeed one of the most valued of brassica crops. Brussels sprouts need a deeply-worked, rich, firm soil, plenty of room for development and a long season of growth.

Cultivation To produce compact, firm sprouts, it is essential to have firm ground and an attempt should be made to follow a crop for which the ground has already been well manured. Alternatively, dig in well-decayed manure in the autumn. Late preparation, loose soil or fresh manure results only in lush growth and loose sprouts. If manure is not available apply 85g (3oz) of super-phosphate and 28g (1oz) of sulphate of potash per sq m (sq yd) prior to planting. Even when manuring has been carried out the addition of half the recommended quantities of fertilizer will be found beneficial. For early or late varieties, sow in a prepared seed bed in a sheltered position in the middle of March. Transplant to permanent positions in late May and firm well. Under normal growing conditions allow 0.8m (2½ft) between the plants and in the rows, but with vigorous growing varieties on good growing soil allow 1m (3ft) between the rows and 0.8m (2½ft) between the plants. As a precaution against cabbage root maggot and club root disease, dip the washed roots of the young plants into a thin paste using 4 percent calomel dust and

water. Water the young plants if the weather is hot and dry. Hoe the soil frequently to keep down weeds. Apply 28g (1oz) of Nitro-chalk in September or October. In open windy areas it is as well to stake plants in the autumn if growth is at all vigorous. Remove yellow leaves as they appear. Pick the sprouts as they are ready. Do not remove the tops until the end of the winter as this helps in the formation of sprouts and gives protection during severe weather.
Varieties 'Cambridge No. 1' (early); 'Cambridge No. 2' (mid-season); 'Cambridge No. 5' (late); 'Harrison's XXX', a good heavy cropping early; 'Jade Cross', a newer F.1. hybrid, very early, producing a heavy crop of dark green sprouts; 'The Aristocrat', an excellent mid-late variety producing medium-sized sprouts with perfect flavour.

Cabbage
Cultivation Cabbages are gross feeders and require adequate quantities of manure dug in well before planting. Firm ground is essential. Apply 85g (3oz) of superphosphate and 28g (1oz) of sulphate of potash prior to planting. A slightly alkaline soil with a *p*H 7.0 or over is best. On an acid soil apply lime,

1 Young shoots of purple sprouting broccoli, ready in spring, help to prolong the supplies of winter greens.
2 Cambridge 5 is a good modern variety of Brussels sprout. It is a late kind, tall-growing, its stems covered from the ground with large, firm green sprouts. Seed is sown in March; plants are set out in late May.

but never at the same time as manure. Apply a good basic dressing for autumn planting, such as 110g (4oz) of basic slag and 28g (1oz) of sulphate of potash. A dressing of 28g (1oz) of nitrate of soda per sq m (sq yd) in early spring will provide the necessary tonic to start the plants into active growth. The earliest sowing may be under glass in January or early February, and the seedlings pricked off into a protected cold frame 5–7cm (2–3in) apart. Plant out when hardened off in early May and apply 28g (1oz) of nitrate of soda six weeks later. Cutting should begin in late June. When the ground is in a suitable state in March or early April make a main sowing, using two varieties, one for autumn use and the other for winter cutting. Sow thinly in drills 12mm (½in)

deep. Plant these out when ready in early June to 45cm (18in) apart in the rows and 60cm (2ft) between the rows. Plants for autumn planting to produce spring cabbages should be sown from the middle of July to the middle of August depending on weather, soil, and locality. Two separate sowings a fortnight apart can prove helpful if the precise sowing time is doubtful. Plant out in September and firm well. Plants must be hard and sturdy. Distance of planting for spring cabbage should be 45cm (18in) apart each way, or 45cm (18in) between the rows, cutting alternate plants first as spring greens. A useful spring crop may be obtained by planting 30cm (12in) between the rows and 23cm (9in) in the rows using the crop as spring greens.
Varieties Early frame sowing, 'Primo' and 'Greyhound'. April sowing for summer and autumn cutting, 'Winningstadt' and 'Wheeler's Imperial', or for winter cabbage 'Christmas Drumhead' and 'January King'. Sowing July–August for summer cutting, 'Harbinger', 'Early Offenham' and 'Flower of the Spring'.

Red cabbage, also known as pickling cabbage, is usually sown in July or

August, and thereafter treated in the same way as spring cabbage, although it is better to plant out at 1m (3ft) apart to get better heads. Alternatively it may be sown in March. There are few varieties: those that are available have 'Red' as part of their name eg 'Red Drumhead', 'Large Bloodred', although 'Stockley's Giant' is an exception.

Carrot

Cultivation Carrots do best in deep, well-cultivated sandy loam, preferably well manured for the previous crop. Fresh manure causes forking and excessive top growth. Apply a good compound fertilizer 7–10 days prior to sowing. This may be fish meal or 3 parts of super-phosphate, 2 parts of sulphate of potash and 1 part of sulphate of ammonia, applied at 85g (3oz) per sq m (sq yd). Sow early crops thinly in drills 6mm ($\frac{1}{4}$in) deep and 23cm (9in) apart from November onwards in heat or under cloches in January or February as soon as the soil is workable. Thin the seedlings as required, using the young roots as they become fit for use. Outdoor sowing may begin in early March or when the ground is suitably dry. Successive sowings of short-horn and stump-rooted types made at three week intervals until the middle of June provide a continuous supply of young carrots throughout the summer. Make drills for the main crop 12mm ($\frac{1}{2}$in) deep and 30–40cm (12–15in) apart. Postpone sowings of main crop for storing until late May or June where carrot fly is troublesome. Thin main crop to 5cm (2in) when the seedlings are large enough to handle, finally thinning to 16cm (6in). As a precaution against carrot fly, draw soil towards the rows after thinning, and lightly dust with lindane. Lift for the winter storing in October. Carefully lift the roots with a fork and cut the tops to 12mm ($\frac{1}{2}$in) above the root. Store in layers of dry sand or ash in a cool shed or where the quantity is large, use the clamp method as for potatoes. The store must not be damp or soft rot will result. Where cloches or frames are available, make a sowing of a stump-rooted variety in August out-of-doors and place the cloches in position in October for pulling November and December. Hoe throughout the season to keep down weeds and to keep the soil surface crumbly. Careful watering throughout the season obviates root cracking which occurs when a period of drought is followed by heavy rain. As a result slugs and millipedes find their way into the root, and are blamed for the severe damage. With good crop rotation and cultivation there

1 A well-grown head of cabbage. It is not difficult to produce a succession of these useful vegetables throughout the year.
2 Carrot 'Amsterdam Forcing', splendid for early forcing, it grows to about 13cm (5in) with excellent quality and texture.

should be little difficulty with pests or diseases.

Among the reliable varieties are: *Short-horn:* Earliest French Horn and Early Nates. *Stump-rooted:* Red Coned Early Market. *Intermediate:* St. Valery. *Main crop:* James's Scarlet Intermediate.

Cauliflower

Cultivation A deeply-dug well-manured soil in an open sunny position is best, but the ideal condition is when the crop follows a heavily manured one such as early potatoes. Apply a dressing of super-phosphate at 55g (2oz) per sq m (sq yd) prior to planting. As for other brassicas the soil must be well firmed. The earliest cauliflowers for June cutting are raised from seed sown in boxes in a heated greenhouse in January or February. Prick off the seedlings into boxes, or pot up individually and gradually harden off until plants are ready for setting out in rows 45cm (18in) apart with 45cm (18in) between the plants in April or May as weather and locality permit. If heat is not available sow seed in a cold frame in September, prick out seedlings at 7cm (3in) intervals and plant out in the spring. Caterpillars rarely attack this early crop. Sow seed for the main crop in March in drills 6mm (¼in) deep and 23cm (9in) apart in a sheltered seed bed and plant out in May, 60cm (2ft) apart and 75cm (2½ft) between the rows. An adequate supply of water, and continuous hoeing to keep a surface dust mulch, will go a long way to ensure a good crop. As soon as a head or curd appears a leaf may be broken over it to provide shade or the curd is likely to become discoloured. As with broccoli there is a wide choice of varieties with varying periods of maturity, but careful planning is required to ensure a succession of heads throughout the season. Among the best-known varieties are 'Early Snowball' and 'Delfter Market', for cutting during June or July; 'Early London' and 'Dwarf Mammoth', which

mature in August; 'Majestic', which is ready in September; 'Walcheren', an old variety, ready October to December; 'Veitch's Self Protecting', for late October cutting; 'Canberra' a newer Australian variety, maturing in November and December.

Celeriac

This is a variety of celery forming a swollen root which may be used and eaten raw in salads, or cooked for soups and flavouring. The stem can be cooked in the same way as seakale and, unlike celery, it stores well. It grows on the flat and as it requires no trench it is becoming more popular, since there is a great saving in time and labour. It is known botanically as *Apium graveolens rapaceum* (*Umbellifrae*).

Cultivation To produce a good crop a long season of growth is needed. Sow in heat during March, prick off into boxes and, after hardening off, plant out in May into well-worked soil at 30–40cm (12–15in) apart. The topsoil should be fine, and mixed with well-decayed manure or spent hops. On light soils, plant in a drill to facilitate watering; planting on a slight ridge is best on heavy soils, to improve drainage. The swollen root must be planted so that it sits on the soil and must remain so throughout its growth. As it matures it may be necessary to draw soil away from it, until protection from frost is required. Water copiously and apply 14g (½oz) of nitrate of soda to each 2m (6ft) stretch of row if the plants are slow in making early growth. Remove any sideshoots and suckers from the root. The variety 'Giant Prague' is good, but 'Marble Ball' stores extremely well.

Celery

Cultivation Sow celery thinly in pots or boxes in heat in March for early vari-

1 Celery is grown in trenches to facilitate the blanching of the stems. 2 It is later earthed up.

eties, or in a cold house in mid-April for the main crop. Prick off into deep seed boxes as soon as the seedlings are large enough to handle, at 5cm (2in) intervals. After hardening off, plant out from mid May to the end of June, in prepared trenches. This is not only helpful in earthing but enables watering to be carried out by flooding the trench.

Prepare the trench some time before planting by removing soil 20–30cm (8–12in) deep, depending on the situation, placing the soil in equal amounts on either side of the trench. Keep the sides of the bank as upright as possible patting them with the back of the spade. This forms neat ridges on which lettuce, spinach or radish can quite easily be grown. Place a good depth of manure in the trench and dig this into the bottom soil. Firm well by treading and leave the trench as long as possible to settle before planting. For single rows plant 25–30cm (10–12in) apart, 30cm (12in) each way for double rows staggering the plants. Immediately after planting, flood the trench and repeat this operation in dry weather. Feed occasionally with weak manure water or dried blood, and also apply two dressings of super-phosphate at 28g (1oz) per 2m (6ft) run, by mid August.

Start to earth up when the plants are fully grown in August or September, after removing any sideshoots and low-growing leaves which would otherwise be completely covered. Tie the stems with raffia and place soil from the side bank around the plants up to the base of the leaves. Slugs can cause much damage and it is wise to scatter slug bait round the plants before earthing up, especially if paper collars, black plastic or drainpipes are used, as they sometimes are, to ensure long, well-blanched stems. Pat the sides of the ridge to encourage rain to run down, rather than penetrate into the celery hearts. Celery fly can cause serious

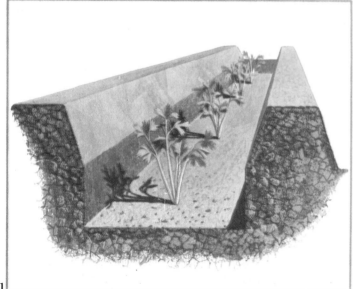

damage from May to September if precautionary measures are not taken.

Digging may begin six to eight weeks after earthing.

'Clayworth Prize Pink' produces a good crisp head. Good white varieties include 'Sandringham White' and 'Wright's Giant White'. White varieties which need no earthing up include 'Golden Self Blanching' and 'Tall Utah'.

Chicory

Sow seeds of Witloof chicory in May or June. The soil must be fertile. Any manure or garden compost added prior to sowing must be very well rotted. Sow thinly in drills 1cm (½in) deep, spaced 30cm (1ft) apart. Keep down annual weeds by hoeing. When the plants are about 5cm (2in) high, thin to 23cm (9in) apart in the rows. Except for weeding now and then, no further cultivation is necessary.

By November the plants will have made roots resembling parsnips. These are dug a few at a time. Cut back the top growth to 2.5cm (1in) above the crown and reduce the length of the roots by the same amount. Discard any thin or fanged roots.

Pack the prepared roots closely together in boxes or large clay flower pots filled with damp potting soil. Unless blanched in absolute darkness, the chicons, as the blanched shoots are called, will be yellow and bitter. Exclude light by making a specially darkened pit beneath the greenhouse staging. Several sheets of black polythene should be draped above and around the boxes or the pit. Inverted flower pots, with drainage holes covered, may be stood over pots of roots. Reasonably quick growth occurs at 60°F (16°C), but in the garden shed or the cold greenhouse, the chicons will take two months or so to develop.

When the blanched chicons are 16cm (6in) tall, cut them off at soil level. Good cookery books give recipes, but the blanched chicons are more generally used in salads. The forced roots should be added to the compost heap.

Coleworts

These are small, hardy types of cabbage (sometimes known as collards) cropping in autumn or winter and useful as a catch crop following the harvesting of, say, early broad beans, peas or potatoes. They are not widely grown, but are most useful, especially for smaller gardens. They are green throughout, with hearts looser than in the white-hearted cabbages.

Cultivation Seed is sown in July. Ground should be in good condition with adequate humus. If it was properly prepared for one of the previous crops mentioned it should require nothing further than the possible application of superphosphate at 40–55g (1½–2oz) per sq m (sq yd). This will assist young seedlings to get a good start, bearing in mind the need for fairly quick and con-

Chicory, Cichorium intybus, a hardy perennial, native of Europe including Britain, grown for its blanched leaves.

tinuous growth in the shortening days. Land should be lightly forked through, then firmed and raked down to produce the necessary fine tilth for successful seed sowing. Sow in rows 40cm (15in) apart where intended to crop; thin first to 15cm (6in) subsequently to 30cm (1ft). Alternatively, raise in a prepared seed bed, transplanting the seedlings in September, at similar spacings. Another recommended planting scheme is 40cm (15in) apart each way. Should the weather be dry, draw out and soak the drills before sowing seed. Apart from its value in cropping in its normal season, colewort may prove especially useful in localities too rigorous for the usual

Dwarf curled Kale.

spring cabbage. After harvesting the main heads, the stumps can be allowed to remain where they are to produce useful, secondary spring greens. Varieties: 'Rosette' and 'Hardy Green', the latter considered best for colder, northern climes.

Courgettes see Marrow
Kale

Also known as borecole, this hardy vegetable is a member of the brassica family. Varieties include the Scotch kales, cottager's kale, thousand-headed and asparagus kale. All are grown for winter supplies of greens. They are particularly recommended to gardeners in very cold areas where winter cabbage and sprouting broccoli are difficult crops.

Sow seeds in the open on a well prepared seed bed in an open position in April or early May. The drills should be no more than 2.5cm (1in) deep and 15cm (6in) apart. If the plants tend to become rather large whilst in the seed bed, they may be transplanted and set farther apart until being moved to their final growing positions in June. Suitable spacings are 45cm (18in) between the plants in staggered rows at 60cm (2ft) apart. Dwarf Scotch curled does not need such generous spacing.

Prepare the ground and plant as for winter cabbage. Kale does well on ground from which potatoes have been lifted. The plants may also be set between rows of early potatoes, provided that these are not too close. Where possible, the plants should be top-dressed with well-rotted dung or garden compost in mid July. Soil is then drawn from between the rows over the dung or compost to form a low ridge around the stems of the plants. This encourages good root growth and helps to prevent the plants from being blown down in winter gales.

As far as Scotch kale is concerned, it is the leaves which are eaten, and picking should start at the base of the plants. With the other kinds, the plants are beheaded, following which short side-shoots are produced, as on sprouting broccoli. When these shoots have been harvested, more grow for use during the spring months. Unless the shoots are picked for use when quite young they are inclined to be rather bitter.

Leeks

The leek is a valuable vegetable for winter and spring use and is often grown to replace onions when the last of the stored crop has been eaten. Sow the seeds outdoors in late March or early April on a prepared bed. A seed bed prepared for cabbage and lettuce sowings is suitable. Prevent annual weeds from smothering the grass-like seedlings, and water, should May be a dry month. The seedlings are dug up and moved to their growing positions in June or July. June planting is preferable.

For leeks of good size, a well-manured or well-composted soil is necessary. Mark the rows with the garden line at 45cm (18in) apart. The usual planting tool is a blunt-nosed dibber, such as may be made from an old spade handle. Make the planting holes 23cm (9in) apart in the rows and sufficiently deep so that only the tops of the plants show above the soil when one plant is dropped into each hole. After planting, simply fill the holes with water. This washes sufficient soil down on to the roots; more loose soil fills the holes when the rows are hoed a week or two later. Following planting, inspect the bed for a day or two and replant any plants which may have been pulled out of the holes by birds. Mulching with sedge peat or, on rich soils, with weathered sawdust, in late July, saves all further cultivation.

Leeks are left in the soil throughout the winter in the same way as parsnips. Should the ground be needed for another crop in February or March, any leeks still in the soil may be lifted and heeled into a trench. All leeks should be used before May.

The leek is a favourite vegetable among exhibitors and for this purpose, seeds are sown in gentle heat in the greenhouse during January or February. The seedlings are pricked off into fairly deep trays and each seedling is allowed 9 sq cm (1½ sq in) of space. The seedlings are hardened off gradually in the cold frame for planting out in early May. Some keen showmen prefer to prick the seedlings into small clay pots and to pot on into the 13 or 16cm (5 or 6in) sizes.

To obtain leeks blanched to a length of 60cm (2ft) or more, the plants are grown in trenches prepared similarly to those in which single rows of celery are grown (see Celery). The preparation of the trenches calls for deep digging and the addition of well-rotted manure or alternatives such as garden compost or spent mushroom compost. The trenches are spaced 1m (3ft) apart with 30cm (12in) between the plants. Soil from between the rows is drawn up towards the plants as they grow to form a steep ridge. Liquid manure feeds are given as well as frequent top-dressings.

'Musselburgh' and 'The Lion' are good standard varieties. The pot leek is a northern speciality.

Lettuce

Lettuces fall into three groups—cabbage, cos and loose-leaf. The cabbage kinds are subdivided into crispheads and butterheads. Those sold by the greengrocer are almost always butterheads because crispheads do not travel well and wilt rather quickly after harvesting. The cos varieties have long, boat-shaped, very crisp leaves and they are preferred by many for their fine flavour. Loose-leaf lettuces are more popular in the United States than here, although one American variety, 'Salad Bowl', is liked by many gardeners.

1 Well-blanched specimens of leek 'Musselburgh', a good variety both for exhibition and for culinary use.
2 'Salad Bowl' is a loose-leaf variety of lettuce. Instead of cutting the whole plant, leaves are picked as and when required, from such varieties.

Any check to steady growth is liable to result in rather poor lettuces. Water is very important, but the soil must be sufficiently porous to allow for good drainage. Although late summer lettuces will tolerate the shade cast by rows of taller vegetables, earlier sowings demand an open, unshaded site. The soil should have been dug well during the winter digging programme and organic manures in the form of farmyard manure, garden compost or spent hops applied generously. These manures are invaluable in helping to retain soil moisture. If he is able to have use of greenhouse cold frames and cloches, the good gardener is able to raise lettuces for at least six months of the year. The pro-

duction of winter and early spring lettuces is not easy and these crops are a challenge to the gardener. Certain hardy varieties for April cutting may be over-wintered in the open in favourable areas, but much depends on the winter weather following the autumn sowing.

Outdoor sowings may be made in March in the south-west and during the first two weeks of April in other areas. Here again, cloches are useful. Sow as thinly as possible in 2.5cm (1in) deep drills spaced 40cm (15in) apart. Keep down weeds by hoeing and thin the seedlings to 30cm (1ft) apart when three or four leaves have formed. The thinnings from March, April and May sowings may be used to make further rows.

A sowing made in late July provides lettuces in November and December but here again, the weather plays an important part. The rows need cloche protection from October onwards. For early spring supplies, sow in the cold frame in September and, subsequently, replant the seedlings in the greenhouse or in frames. Alternatively, sow in the greenhouse in early October and transplant when the plants have four leaves. Deep planting at any time is unwise. It is particularly dangerous where lettuces are to be over-wintered. Over-crowding must also be avoided and correct ventilation is very important.

Birds often peck at lettuce seedlings and plants. A few strands of black cotton fixed above the rows prevents this trouble. Although present-day cos varieties are reputed to be self folding, better hearts form if the plants are tied rather loosely with raffia or soft string. Loose-leaf varieties are less prone to bolt than cabbage and cos plants. Instead of cutting the whole plant, leaves are picked as and when required from loose-leaf varieties.

Among the very many varieties on offer, the following may be relied upon for worthwhile crops.
For outdoor sowings from March until July 'Sutton's Improved', 'Unrivalled', 'Trocadero', 'Webb's Wonderful', 'Giant White Cos', 'Salad Bowl'.
To stand the winter out of doors 'Stanstead Park', 'Arctic King', 'Brown Cos'.

Marrows

A very rich bed is essential for a regular supply of marrows between late July and the autumn. Soil which has received a generous dressing of well-rotted farmyard manure or garden compost is ideal. Planting distances depend on the type of plant. A bush variety needs almost one sq m (sq yd) of surface area; a trailer needs a great deal more if allowed to roam at will over the ground. Trailing or vining marrows may also be trained on tall supports. These may be bamboo canes or even the garden fence.

Water is essential and the plants must on no account be permitted to become dry at the roots. Liquid manure feeds should be given weekly when the first marrows begin to swell. To ensure that both water and liquid manure reach the roots, many gardeners sink a clay pot alongside each plant. The water and the liquid feeds are poured into the pots and run directly to the root area. Weeding is necessary until the large leaves shade the surrounding soil and inhibit weed growth.

The plants bear male and female flowers. Bees, flies and other insects transfer ripe male pollen to the female blooms. Where female flowers fall off without setting fruits, natural fertilization is not occurring. In such cases, hand pollination is advisable. Do this before noon. Pick a male flower for each female to be hand pollinated. Strip the petals from the male and twist its core into the centre of the female. The females may be recognized quite easily because they carry an embryo marrow behind them.

Bush plants need little attention. Trailers may be guided between other crops or, if they are to be trained to supports, the main shoot must be tied in regularly. Cut the marrows when they are young and tender. They are old if the thumb nail does not pierce the skin easily. Marrows for jam or for storing are allowed to ripen on the plants until September. The storage place should be cool and dry. The marrows are sometimes hung up in nets for storage purposes. Smaller marrows are now preferred. Up-to-date varieties include 'Zucchini E_1 Hybrid' (bush), 'Productive' (bush), 'Prolific' (trailer), 'Cluseed Roller' (trailer). 'Rotherside Orange' is a prolific variety of excellent flavour. 'Cocozelle' (the Italian vegetable marrow), a bush variety, produces dark green, yellow-striped fruits up to 60cm (2ft) long.

Courgettes, or French courgettes, have become increasingly popular in recent years. In the natural course of events the fruits do not grow very large but, in any case, to obtain the best results, they should be cut when not much bigger than thumb size and cooked unpeeled. Constant cutting will ensure the steady production of fruits throughout the summer. Cultivation is otherwise the same as for the larger marrows. For exhibition purposes, 'Sutton's Table Dainty' is a popular variety.

Mustard and Cress
This is a useful, easy-to-grow salad crop which may be grown throughout the year provided that a temperature of 50–60°F (10–16°C) is given. Cress takes a little longer to germinate than mustard so cress seeds must be sown in a separate container three days earlier than mustard in order to be able to gather the two together. Bulb bowls or seed trays should be filled with fine, sandy soil or with bulb fibre. Water well, using a very fine rose on the can, and then sprinkle the seeds evenly and reasonably thinly on to the moist surface. Firm the seeds

into the soil or fibre with a block of wood. No covering of soil, fibre or sand is necessary. Stand the containers in a dark place or cover the pots or trays with pieces of wood until the seeds germinate. Water carefully if necessary. After germination, allow full light. Both mustard and cress grown indoors are ready for use within two to three weeks of sowing. Cut the 7cm (3in) high seedlings with scissors. For successional crops, sow weekly between October and April.

For the first crops out of doors, sow on an open, south-facing site in early April. After forking the soil lightly, firm it well and then rake so that the soil is very fine indeed. Sow as for under glass. Early sowings may be damaged by heavy rain which beats the tender seedlings to the ground. This may be prevented by providing glass protection; sowings may also be made earlier in the cold frame in

Above *the male and* below *the female flowers of the marrow, with the immature vegetable behind it. Marrow flowers have to be fertilized by hand, in order that the fruit can form.*

soil similar to that recommended for plants grown in bowls or seed trays, or under cloches. For sowings made between late May and September, choose a north-facing border.

Onions
When the seeds are to be sown directly in the soil where the plants are to grow, the bed should be well prepared. Digging and manuring will have been carried out during the late autumn or winter and the soil needs raking before sowing so that the bed is level, even and free of large clods and stones. Sow thinly in 2.5cm (1in) deep drills, spaced 30cm (1ft) apart. After sowing, fill in the drills and firm. Do not tread heavily on a clay soil.

Maincrop onion varieties

'Ailsa Craig' Large, globular, handsome. Suitable for both spring and late summer sowing. One of the best for exhibition.

'Autumn Queen' Flattish shape. Good keeper. For spring and late summer sowing.

'Bedfordshire Champion' Large, globe-shaped, straw-brown skin usually tinged with pink. For spring sowing only.

'Big Ben' (A) Large, semi-flat shape, golden skin. Practically non-bolting. Exhibition quality. Good keeper. Sow in August.

'Blood Red' Medium-size, deep red skin, flat, pungent. Very hardy and especially recommended for cold areas. Good keeper.

'Crossling's Selected' A globe onion much liked by exhibitors.

'Early Yellow Globe' Flattish-round, medium-sized, golden skinned, quick maturing and reasonably good keeper. For spring sowing only.

'Excelsior, Cranston's Selected' Pale-skinned, large, round exhibition variety.

'Giant Rocca' (Brown) (A) Brown-skinned, flattish globe. For August sowing only. Does not store well. There is also 'Yellow Rocca'.

'Giant Zittau' (A) Medium to large, semi-flat, golden-brown skin. Good keeper. Strongly recommended for August sowing.

'James' Long Keeping' Oval, brown skin, medium size, stores well.

'Marshall's July Giant' (A) Large, semi-globe shaped, early maturing. For August sowing.

'Marshall's Leverington Champion' Globe-shaped, pale golden skin, very large, fairly good keeper. Recommended for exhibition use.

'Red Italian' (A) Medium-sized, red-skinned, flat bulbs. Sow in August.

'Reliance' (A) Large, flattish, golden skin. Sow in August.

'Rijnsburger Globe' Large, pale-skinned, globe-shaped, long-keeping.

'Rousham Park Hero' White Spanish type, semi-flat, greenish-yellow skin, mild flavour. Can crop well on light soils.

'Sutton's A1' Large flat bulbs, a good keeper. For spring or August sowing.

'Sutton's Solidity' (A) Large, flattish bulbs. Plants do not bolt. A good keeper. Especially recommended for August sowing.

'Superba' A new F₁ hybrid. Medium-sized globular bulbs with smooth golden-brown skin. Early maturing and noted for uniformity. Stores well.

'The Sutton' Globe-shaped, early-ripening, excellent keeper.

'Up-to-Date' Globe-shaped, straw-coloured skin, remarkably good keeping qualities.

'White Spanish' Flattish onion, golden skin, mild flavour, good keeper.

'Wijbo' An early maturing selection of 'Rijnsburger'. Noted for uniform appearance of the crop.

(A) = Recommended for August sowing. Onions from this sowing are referred to as Autumn-sown among exhibitors.

Keep the seedlings free of weeds by hoeing between the rows during April and May, and pull out any weeds in the rows. Start thinning the plants in mid-June and continue thinning until mid-July by which time those which are to remain should have at least 16cm (6in) of row space. When thinning, take great care not to break roots or foliage and never leave either on top of the soil. The odour of the broken plants attracts female onion flies and their small maggots ruin many onion crops. If the soil is on the dry side, water both before and after thinning. Use the immature onions in salads.

Continue weeding the onion bed until July. During that month, or in August, the foliage becomes yellow and topples to the soil. Here and there it may be necessary to bend the foliage of a plant downwards. No further weeding is necessary and the crop is left to ripen. When the foliage is brown and brittle, choose a dry, sunny day, pull up or dig the onions from the soil, and spread them in the sun to complete the drying process. In wet weather, spread the onions on the greenhouse bench or under cloches. When the onions are quite dry,

1 Towards the end of the summer, the foliage of the onion is bent over to allow light and air to get to the bulbs.

2 Onions can be roped together and stored by hanging them up in an outhouse or garage or potting shed, where dry air can circulate.

rub off soil, dead roots and dry, loose scales. Store the ripe onions in trays in a cool dry place, or better still, rope the crop. Hang the ropes in an outhouse or in the garage.

Onion sets These are small onions grown by specialist nurserymen. The crop is dug and dried in the previous summer and offered for sale in the early winter and spring. One 0.5kg (1lb) of sets is sufficient for the average garden. Small sets are considered of better quality than large ones. Do not leave onion sets in bags after purchasing them, but spread them in a tray in a cool place before planting them in March. Prepare the bed as for seed sowing and plant the sets 16–20cm (6–8in) apart in 2.5cm (1in) deep drills. Except for hoeing to keep down weeds, little in the way of cultivation is necessary. The feeding of the plants with fertilizers may result in 'bolting'. In late July, loosen the soil around the swelling bulbs to expose them to the sun. This must be done carefully because the plants may be blown down by strong winds if the roots are broken. The foliage will topple to the soil in August and from then on harvesting and storing are as for onions from seeds.

Spring onions Where maincrop onions are raised from sets, 'spring' or salad onions are grown by sowing seeds of 'White Lisbon' in August or in March. In colder parts, the August sowing needs cloche protection from October until the spring. Although the bed should not be a rich one, it must be well-drained. Sow quite thickly and hoe to remove weeds in September and again in March. Start pulling the small onions for salad use in May and continue to pull until July. The March sowing provides salad onions from July until the autumn.

Onions for pickling 'Marshall's Super Pickle' is a new onion with the round shape and size as favoured by the commercial pickler. Seeds of this variety or of any maincrop suitable for spring sowing are sown rather thickly in 1cm (½in) to 2.5cm (1in) deep drills spaced at 23cm (9in) apart in soil of low fertility during March or April. Weeding must be attended to regularly but the onion plants are not thinned. Harvesting is carried out when the foliage is dead, brown and brittle.

For white cocktail onions seed of 'Silver Skin' or 'Pearl Pickler' is sown quite thickly in April or early May. The soil should be reasonably fertile. If grown in a poor soil the onions are liable to be too small for use. Apart from weeding no cultivation is necessary and the plants are not thinned. The crop is harvested when the foliage dies. Unless harvested promptly, the bulbs produce fresh foliage.

Parsley
Cultivation The point to remember about parsley is that it is certain to be needed by the cook at all times of the year. To allow for this, frequent (at least three) sowings should be made between March and September. Large beds of parsley will not be required by the average family and so the plants may be used as an edging to a vegetable plot, or even, as the leaves are decorative, they may well be used to edge the flower border. If larger quantities are required the seed should be sown thinly in 2.5cm (1in) deep drills, spaced 30cm (1ft) or so apart and the seedlings should be thinned eventually to 15cm (6in) apart. Plants will grow in any ordinary soil, provided it is not too acid. The best results are obtained if the soil is dug deeply and a fair amount of garden compost or other organic material is incorporated.

Parsley seed is rather slow and irregular in germination and it is not at all unusual for nothing to appear for a month or six weeks. Thinnings of parsley may, of course, be used for garnishing, and when your plants are well grown it will be necessary only to cut part of the foliage for use, leaving the plants to make fresh growth.

To make sure of your winter supply it is as well to give the plants cloche protection before the frosts occur, but generally no cover is needed at least until November. If you care to pot up a few plants of parsley and bring them into the greenhouse in winter you may have excellent leaves to cut at all times, even when frost is severe. The seedsmen offer a few named kinds such as 'Dwarf Perfection', 'French', 'Green Velvet', 'Moss-curled'.

Parsnip
Cultivation It is essential if you expect to produce good-sized specimens to trench the soil deeply so that the desirable, long, straight, unforked roots are produced. The large seeds are sown in 2.5cm (1in) deep drills in small groups at intervals of 10cm (4in), the drills spaced 45cm (18in) apart. Choose a calm day for sowing as the seeds are light and liable to blow away in windy weather. Do not try to transplant as this will generally result in some injury to the essential tap root. Should all your seeds germinate you may remove alternate plants in the drills leaving the remaining ones at 20cm (8in) intervals.

The best soil is one which has been well manured for a previous crop, and no animal manure should be applied later. However, a stimulant may well be given in the form of a mixture of 85g (3oz) of superphosphate, 28g (1oz) of sulphate of ammonia and 42g (1½oz) of sulphate of potash per sq m (sq yd). The roots will be ready for use at the end of October but, since they are frost resistant, they may be left in their rows until they are needed; or, if the soil has to be dug in preparation for further cropping, the roots may be lifted and packed away in a shed or cellar with a covering of dry soil or sand. In any event

Long parsnip roots, the results of good cultivation.

Peas sowing times and varieties

First Early

Sow			For use		Height of plant in ft
Sow	November	Give cloche protection in cold areas	For use	May–June	
	February	Under cloches except in the south-western areas		June	
	March–April	Open garden		June–July	
	Late June	Open garden		September	
Name	Early Bird				2
	Feltham First				1½
	Foremost				3
	Forward				2
	Gradus				3
	Kelvedon Triumph				1¾
	Kelvedon Viscount				2¼
	Kelvedon Wonder				1½
	*Little Marvel				1¼
	Meteor				1½
	Pilot Improved				3
	Progress (Laxton)				1½
	Sleaford Phoenix				1½
	*Topcrop				2½

Second Early

Sow		For use		Height of plant in ft
Sow	April	For use	July	
Name	Achievement			5
	*Early Onward			2½
	Giant Stride			2
	Kelvedon Climax			2½
	*Kelvedon Monarch			2½
	Kelvedon Spitfire			2
	*Shasta			2½
	*Sutton's Chieftain			2½
	Sutton's Phenomenon			2
	*Sutton's Show Perfection			5

Maincrop

Sow		For use		Height of plant in ft
Sow	April–May	For use	August	
Name	Alderman			5
	Histon Kingsize			3½
	Histon Maincrop			2½
	Lincoln			2
	Onward			2

Late

Sow		For use		Height of plant in ft
Sow	May	For use	August–September	
Name	Autocrat			4
	Gladstone			4
	Lord Chancellor			3½

*Also recommended for Quick-Freeze
The height of plants varies by several inches due to soil and seasonal climatic conditions

it is always wise to lift and store a few roots in case the ground freezes hard, making it impossible to dig up the roots.

Peas

There are dwarf and taller pea varieties. Although plants of the short, dwarf varieties may be grown without supports it is the custom to provide all garden peas with supports of some sort. Twiggy brushwood of the height the plants will attain is much liked by gardeners. Bamboo canes linked together with strong thread or garden twine often replace the traditional brushwood. Garden netting for pea growing is offered at garden shops and by horticultural retailers. The tall supports needed by tall growers should be augmented by several strong, tall stakes to prevent strong winds in summer from blowing down the plants

Garden pea 'Kelvedon Advance' is an excellent early variety producing long straight pods with a blunt end. It grows about 75cm (2½ft) in height.

when bearing their heavy crops.

Seed is sown in a 5cm (2in) deep furrow, which is 16–20cm (6–8in) wide, made with the draw hoe. The seeds are sprinkled thinly into the furrow so that each seed is about 7cm (3in) from the next. Should the soil be dry, the furrow should be flooded with water and sowing undertaken when this has drained away. After sowing, the seeds are covered with soil raked over them. During the raking any large stones should be removed. The distances between rows of peas vary. It is generally accepted that the distances between the rows should be the same as the height of the variety being grown, but with very dwarf peas 75cm (30in) between rows is the rule. Supports, if to hand, should be set in position immediately after the seed has been sown. The tendrils of the pea plant cannot grasp thick supports and where these are in use young pea plants are encouraged to climb by the insertion of short pieces of twiggy wood on either side of the row. The twigs also afford some protection to the young plants by breaking the force of cold winds.

Pea seeds and pea seedlings are attractive to birds and black cotton or small mesh chicken wire are useful protectors. The wire mesh should be removed when the seedlings are 10cm (4in) tall. The old-fashioned scarecrow is a useful bird deterrent as are large polythene bags fixed to tall stakes. Where mice are known to take freshly-sown seeds, traps should be set or a proprietary poison used with care and according to the manufacturer's instructions. Slugs are a great nuisance in some gardens and a slug bait may have to be laid down. Weevils also attack pea seedlings. Weevil damage may be distinguished from that caused by slugs. Leaves bitten by weevils have a scalloped-like shape. Hoeing around the rows regularly and the dusting of the plants when dry with derris powder or soot are ways of combating weevils.

Potatoes

The principal requirements of the potato plant are adequate available food, sufficient water, good drainage and the type of soil in which tubers may swell easily. An open, unshaded site is very necessary. Light soils are considered very suitable, provided they have been dressed with large quantities of moisture-retaining organic matter. A heavy soil may also be improved structurally by the addition of organic material. A reasonably light, easily worked loam is probably the ideal. Where farmyard manure is available, it may be dug in during winter digging at the rate of up to 50kg (1cwt) to 6 sq m (6 sq yd). Garden compost may be applied even more generously during winter digging or as a mulch after planting. If a compound potato fertilizer is raked into the soil before planting, use it at the rates advised by the manufacturer.

Potato plants are raised from seed tubers taken from plants grown in parts of Britain which are free of virus-carrying aphids. The potato fields are visited by Ministry of Agriculture

officials who issue certificates regarding the freedom from disease of the plants. Tubers from these plants are known as 'Certified Seed'. It is unwise to plant any but certified seed tubers. They should be purchased in January or February and sprouted in trays housed in a light but frost-proof room (a process known as 'chitting'). It is believed that sprouted potatoes result in earlier crops. The gardener may also see which tubers have not sprouted and these are not planted. At planting time—in late March or April—each potato has two or three short, sturdy sprouts. The actual planting date depends on the condition of the soil and on the weather.

There are many planting methods. Perhaps the simplest is to make 20cm (8in) deep trenches with the draw hoe or with the spade. First Earlies are planted at 30cm (12in) apart with 60cm (2ft) between rows. Other varieties need more space; 40cm (15in) between the tubers and 75cm (30in) between the rows are satisfactory distances.

The black plastic method of growing potatoes is favoured by many gardeners because it obviates almost all cultivation. The planting holes are made with the trowel. A tuber—with its sprouts uppermost—is set in each hole. The holes are then filled in and the black plastic sheeting is unrolled over the row. It is important to ensure that the sheeting is securely anchored into the soil. One way of doing this is to make slits with the spade on either side of the row and also at each end of the row. The edges of the 1m (3ft) wide sheet are tucked into the slits when the material is unrolled. When growth starts in May, the shoots of the potato plants are drawn through small holes (made with scissors) in the polythene sheeting.

Rows not treated in this way need weeding now and then. Many gardeners earth up the plants, too. This process consists in drawing soil up and around the plants, using the draw hoe. Earthing up is done in two or three stages. Finally, the plants appear to be growing on low hills. Earthing up is no longer considered necessary but the practice is advantageous on heavy soils where the plants benefit from the improved drainage provided.

There is only one way of ascertaining when First Earlies are ready for use. This is by examining a root. Scraping away some earth may reveal reasonably large tubers. If this fails, dig up a root in late June. If some of the potatoes are as large as a hen's egg, continue digging as

1 Seed potatoes are prepared for planting, to encourage the buds to break.
2 When planting potatoes, the tubers are placed in the drill.
3 Once growth progresses the soil is drawn up at each side of the plants, an operation called 'earthing up'.
4 Lifting maincrop potatoes.

and when required. If the potatoes are far too small for use, wait a fortnight before starting to dig.

Radishes

Seeds of this quick-growing vegetable may be sown for salads at intervals from early March to October. It is generally treated as a catch crop, being sown on a piece of ground which is intended for cabbages or some other crop to .be planted subsequently. A rich, moist soil and cool conditions yield the most succulent radishes. Slow growth may cause them to have a rather hot, unpalatable taste.

Sowings in March or early April may be made in the cold frame or under cloches. Sow the seeds in 2.5cm (1in) deep drills, the drills being 15cm (6in) apart. Sow thinly to avoid having to thin out. Remember each radish needs at least 6 sq cm (1 sq in) of surface area. Sow similarly in open ground. Prevent annual weeds from smothering the seedlings and soak the rows with water if the soil is on the dry side. There are many varieties and 'French Breakfast' is probably the most popular. 'Sutton's Red Forcing' is suitable for cloche and frame sowings. The long, white radish, 'Icicle', is liked for its flavour.

Winter radishes are large and may have a black skin, as in the variety 'Black Spanish', or a red skin such as 'China Rose', or a white skin like 'All Season'. Do not sow winter radishes until June and space the rows 30cm (1ft) apart. Thin the seedlings to 23cm (9in) apart, and keep the rows free of weeds. Water well in dry summer weather. Lift the roots in October and store them in slightly moist sand.

Rhubarb

Because the roots continue to crop for up to ten years after planting, special attention should be given to choosing a suitable site for rhubarb and preparing it well. The bed should not be shaded and should be dug deeply. Any roots of perennial weeds must be removed when digging. Where dung is available, this should be dug in at the rate of 50kg (1cwt) to 10 sq m (10 sq yd). Otherwise garden compost may be incorporated into the soil or spread over the bed after planting; a barrowload to the sq m (sq yd) is not excessive. Plant the roots 1m (3ft) apart, using the spade. November, February or March are suitable planting times. Plant firmly and leave the pink buds at soil level. Supplies of rhubarb are appreciated early in the season. This is why 'Timperley Early' is favoured. 'Hawke's Champagne' is better known but this variety crops later and the flower stems which the plants make in June or July should be cut away as soon as they are noticed. 'Glaskin's Perpetual' may be raised from seed. Sow seed in the cold frame in March or April and thin the seedlings to 15cm (6in) apart. A year later, set the plants in the specially prepared bed.

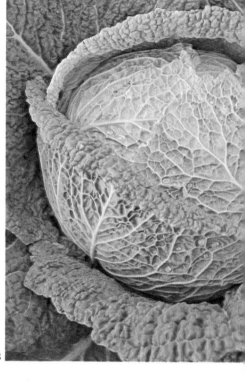

1 Radish 'French Breakfast'.
2 Remove the flowering stems of rhubarb to encourage the production of stems the following spring.
3 The savoy cabbage has thick puckered leaves. It is a useful vegetable as it matures in winter.

Do not pull any sticks in the first season after planting and, in subsequent years, do not over-pull as this weakens the plants. Hand weeding should be carried out during the first summer but, in future seasons, no weeding is necessary because the large leaves inhibit weed growth. To ensure that the plants continue to crop well, mulch the bed each autumn with well-rotted farmyard manure or garden compost.

Savoy

This hardy plant, a type of cabbage, has been grown in Britain since the seventeenth century. The leaves are quite distinct from those of other cabbages, being very puckered or crimped. Although there are early varieties, most gardeners prefer those which are of use during the winter and early spring. Successional crops are obtained by choosing drumheads for cutting between November and April. Its botanical name is the tongue-twisting *Brassica oleracea bullata sabauda*.

Cultivation Cultivate as for winter cabbage—the seeds being sown in the seed bed in April for plants to be set out on fertile soil in June. Allow 60cm (2ft) of space between the rows, setting the plants from 40–45cm (15–18in) apart. If the soil is on the dry side, water the

planting holes and plant very firmly when the water has drained away. During July and August, hoe or mulch to prevent weeds. Particular care must be taken to prevent cabbage caterpillars from establishing themselves in savoys. Varieties to grow to provide a succession for cutting include 'Ormskirk Medium', for cutting from November to February; 'Ormskirk Late Green', very hardy and the solid, medium-sized heads are cut between January and late March; 'Ormskirk Extra Late', a large, flattish, dark green savoy for use in March and April.

Shallots

Some people prefer the milder flavour of the shallot, *Allium ascalonicum*, which they grow in place of onions. Generally, however, shallots are grown for pickling. When stocks of non-bolting onion sets were not available, many gardeners found shallot growing far easier than onion growing. The soil in which they are to be grown must be well-drained and, unless very large bulbs are required, without manure or fertilizers. A very poor soil is greatly improved by being mulched with garden compost just prior to planting time.

Traditionally, shallots were planted on the shortest day in December and lifted on the longest day in June. The soil is seldom suitable for planting during the winter, and planting between late February and early April produces good results. Simply press the bulbs into the ground at intervals of 20cm (8in) in the row, and allow 30cm (12in) between rows. Birds, earthworms and severe frost may loosen the bulbs so, about a week after planting, inspect the bed and replant or replace where necessary. If birds continue to pull out the bulbs the bed should be netted.

Unless the plants are to be fed with liquid manure for the production of very large shallots, little is needed in the way of cultivation. Weeds may be removed by hand or hoeing. Alternatively, use sedge peat as a mulch around the plants in late April.

In early June, draw a little of the mulch or surrounding soil away from the bulb clusters to allow more sunlight to reach them. The foliage will yellow in July, when the clusters should be lifted with the garden fork and spread out to dry. In fine, sunny weather dry them in the open; in wet weather under cover. The greenhouse staging, the cold frame or under cloches are suitable places.

When quite dry, split the clusters into separate bulbs and store them in a cool, airy place for use when required. The bulbs are best stored in Dutch trays or in vegetable nets. Do not store in sacks or polythene bags. Some of the medium-sized bulbs may be set aside for planting in the following season. There are both yellow and red shallots. These include 'Giant Long Keeping', yellow; and 'Giant Long Keeping', red; and 'Giant Red'. 'Hâtive de Niort ' and 'The Aristo-crat' are favoured by exhibitors.

Spinach

It has been estimated that a 10m (30ft) row of spinach supplies just about the right amount for a family of four during the summer months. But one sowing is not sufficient. Fresh young foliage is demanded and where spinach is much appreciated, successional sowings should be made fortnightly between late March and mid-July. For later autumn supplies and for pickings in the following spring, a sowing should be made in a sheltered position in mid-August.

Spinach needs a rich, well-dug soil and one which retains moisture during the summer months. For the leaves to be really succulent, the plants need soaking with water during dry spells. Some gardeners find that their plants need less water if rows sown in May, June and July are partially shaded by other, taller vegetables.

Well-rotted farmyard manure or garden compost should be used in the preparation of the bed. A suitable dressing for sandy soils is 50kg (1cwt) of manure to 6 sq m (6 sq yd). Garden compost may be used more generously. Provided the soil contains sufficient plant nutriments, no feeding of the plants is necessary. Rows of August-sown spinach are sometimes fed with nitrate of soda, applied at the rate of 28g (1oz) to each 3m (10ft) of row, in early April.

Sow the seeds as thinly as possible in 2.5cm (1in) deep seed drills spaced

1 Spinach is a useful summer vegetable which can be grown with little trouble.
2 Swedes provide a good winter root vegetable that stores well.

23cm (9in) to 30cm (1ft) apart. Thin the seedlings to 7cm (3in) as early as possible and start harvesting the leaves as soon as they are of usable size. Do not wait until they are on the tough side. Regular hard picking is essential for summer spinach and almost all of the leaves of a plant may be removed at any one time. Plants from the August sowing should not be treated in this manner. Take only the largest leaves from them.

'Round Seeded' and 'Long Standing' are popular kinds for spring and early summer sowings. 'Long Standing Prickly' is hardier and is sown in August. The word 'prickly' refers to the seeds and not to the smooth leaves.

Perpetual spinach or spinach beet is less well known. Those who know it prefer it for its larger leaves. Sow in April, allowing 38cm (15in) between the rows. Thin the seedlings to 20cm (8in) apart. Successional sowings are not necessary because leaves may be pulled from the plants on and off between early summer and September.

Swedes

Garden swedes, such as 'Bronze Top' and 'Purple Top Improved' often replace winter turnips. Swedes are hardy, and the large roots may be left in the ground until Christmas at least. You can also lift the roots in October, cut off the foliage and store the swedes indoors in dry sand.

Swedes do best in an open, sunny site, and the soil should have been well manured or composted for the previous crop. A sprinkling of a general compound fertilizer may be made before sowing if the soil is not too fertile. Sow very thinly in May or early June in 2.5cm (1in) drills spaced at 38cm (15in)

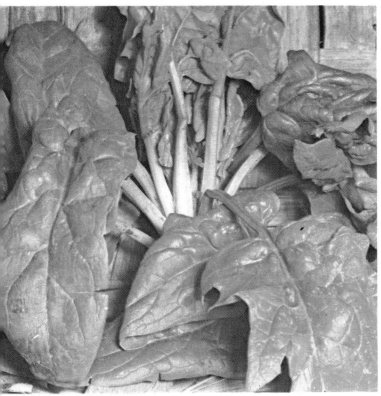

apart. Thin the seedlings to 30cm (12in) apart and, if growth appears rather slow during the summer, topdress and hoe into the ground nitrate of soda at the rate of 28g (1oz) to a row of 3m (10ft). This fertilizer should be watered in, if the season is a dry one. Hoe to keep down weeds. Alternatively, mulch with chopped straw or sedge peat in late July.

Sweet Corn

Zea mays rugosa is known in Britain as sweet corn. This cereal is a native of America and is boiled as a vegetable. The John Innes hybrid varieties remain popular, but 'Kelvedon Glory' is a newer introduction of merit.

In the south, seeds may be sown out of doors in May. Choose a sunny position and in areas exposed to gale force winds in August, provide a windbreak. The soil should have been well dug and dressed with dung or garden compost. These organic fertilizers not only supply plant foods but assist in providing good drainage on heavy soils and in retaining moisture on lighter ones. Sow the seeds. 2.5cm (1in) deep in rows 38cm (15in) apart. Several short rows are preferable to one or two long ones. When the plants are grown in compact blocks wind pollination is more effective.

In other parts of the country, sow two or three seeds in 8cm (3½in) pots in the cold frame or under a cloche in early May. Reduce the seedlings to leave one strong plant in each pot. Set the plants in the open when all danger of frost has passed or protect the rows with cloches until early July.

In dry summers, water as necessary and feed the plants with liquid manure if the soil was not supplied with sufficient organic matter before sowing or planting. Hand weeding is safer than using the hoe which is liable to sever surface anchorage roots. Mulching the bed with straw in July saves weeding.

Harvest the cobs when the silks which hang from them are brown-black in colour and quite brittle. A check on the state of maturity may be made by carefully opening the top of the green sheath and by pressing a grain with the finger nail. If a watery juice exudes, the cob is too young. If the grain contains paste, it is too old. At the correct stage a creamy liquid spurts out. Cobs are twisted from the plants. The sooner the cobs are cooked after harvesting, the higher the sugar content.

Tomatoes

Outdoor tomato growing Provided that an early-ripening variety is chosen, worthwhile crops of tomatoes may be grown in the garden in most parts. 'Outdoor Girl' is outstanding for its early-ripening quality. In colder parts frames and cloches give protection to the plants during June and early July. Plants may be raised from seed in a cold frame, in an unheated greenhouse, or under a cloche during April in warmer areas.

Many gardeners prefer to buy plants for outdoor growing but this limits the choice of variety and most plants on sale are of varieties which are more suited to greenhouse conditions. The tomato plant is not only killed by frost but is adversely affected by sudden temperature changes and in most parts it is seldom possible to set plants outdoors without protection until early June. About 38cm (15in) should be allowed between plants in rows 75cm (30in) apart. Before planting, the planting holes should be filled with water and planting done when this has drained away. Supports for the plants may be bamboo canes, stakes or a wire trellis. Weeds must be controlled. Growing the plants in a black plastic substitute for mulch saves time and work, a straw mulch may be laid down in mid-July. The plants need tying in regularly to the supports and the central growing point of each plant is removed in late July, when three or four trusses of fruit will have set. Remove all side shoots.

Where a very early-ripening variety was not chosen a great part of the crop may not have ripened by mid-September. Plants may then be defoliated and cloches placed over them. Untie them from the supports and lower them on to clean straw. The cloches are then set over the bed and pickings continue until late October. Where no cloches are to hand all tomatoes on the plants should be harvested during the latter half of September. Most of the fruit will ripen off well in a drawer in a warm room. Any small green tomatoes may be used for chutney.

Turnip

This root vegetable, *Brassica campestris rapa* (syn. *B. rapa*), has been grown in Britain since the sixteenth century. The roots are global or flattish round. A well-drained sandy loam is suitable for both types—summer and winter. But if the soil is light and sandy, it dries out

1 Tomato side shoots are removed as soon as seen.
2 Cordon-trained tomatoes are taken 'round the corner' at the row's end.
3 Black plastic can be used as a mulch substitute for tomatoes.

Cordon-trained tomatoes which have been layered once.

rapidly and turnip flea beetles flourish. A heavy soil is unsuitable for summer turnips but is usually suitable for the winter type. Both very light and heavy soils are improved by regular winter dressings of manure, etc. A site that was manured for a previous crop should be chosen. If liming was not carried out during the previous winter, ground chalk should be dusted on to the surface at the rate of 110g (4oz) to the sq m (sq yd) before seed sowing.

The first sowing, out of doors or under cloches, may be made from mid-March to mid-April with a second successional sowing in May. Sow seed thinly 1cm (½in) deep in rows 30cm (1ft) apart. Dust seedlings with derris to control flea beetles and hoe to keep down weeds. Thin the seedlings to 10cm (4in) or so apart and water in dry spells. Quick growth with no checks at all is essential for succulent summer turnips. Start pulling for use when the turnips are sufficiently large. If left to age they become coarse and fibrous. Sow seed of winter turnips similarly, in late July or early August. Water seed drills if the soil is dry and sow after the water has drained away. Dust the seedlings with derris and thin to 23cm (9in) apart. Winter turnips are often left in the ground and pulled when wanted. In colder parts the roots are best lifted in the autumn when the outer leaves are yellowing. Cut back the foliage to about 1cm (½in) from the crown and shorten long tap roots by 10cm (4in) before storing the roots in moist sand or ashes.

For a supply of turnip tops for 'greens' in spring sow seed of a suitable variety in August quite thickly in 1cm (½in) deep drills spaced at 46cm (18in) apart. In colder areas the plants benefit from cloche protection during the winter.

Mature roots of turnip 'Early White Stone'.

When picking leaves for use take but one or two from each plant.

Turnip varieties *Summer* 'Early Snowball', 'Early White Milan', 'Red Top Milan' 'Golden Ball'; *winter* 'Manchester Market'; *for turnip tops* 'Hardy Green Round', 'Green Globe'.

Virus diseases see Diseases

Wall construction

The site for any type of wall must be levelled very carefully and consolidated to provide secure foundations. If necessary, rubble should be rammed into a trench before the concrete foundation is applied.

The foundation concrete should be 5–7cm (2–3in) wider than the maximum width of the walling in order to spread the load as wide as possible. The mortar courses must be kept constant at about 9mm (⅜in) thick. Mix the mortar with 1 part cement and 3 parts of sand (by volume). Constantly check vertical and horizontal levels with a spirit level. Tap each stone in place well and use plenty of mortar. Clean off the joints as work proceeds and where rougher faced walls are concerned use a rounded stick to slightly score out the mortar before it sets, to emphasise the textured finish and 'natural' look of the wall. Do not work in frosty weather; if the weather is very hot and dry, cover the work with plastic sheeting to prevent too rapid mortar setting.

For low walling, rough-faced walling stone in many different sizes is most attractive and popular. Lengths are from 20cm (9in) to about 46cm (18in), widths 10, 12, 16cm (4, 4½ and 6in), and thicknesses from 5cm (2in) to 22cm (8½in). Random-sized stone walling is very attractive. Colours include attractive shades of pink, light grey, dark grey, York stone, slate blue, sandstone, red, Cotswold, lilac and lavender.

Water gardens and water plants
Since the introduction of fibreglass pools tremendous interest has been shown in medium-sized garden pools.
Siting the pool Before constructing any pool careful thought should be given to the siting. To create a successful bog garden or water garden, it must be situated right out in the open, in full sun. Although not essential it is advantageous to give protection from the north, if possible, as this will extend the flowering period both in autumn and spring. A belt of trees, a hedge or buildings on the north are all suitable. Overhanging trees are a disadvantage, both because of the amount of shade they cast and on account of their leaves which will undoubtedly fall in the water during the autumn. Weeping trees, although aesthetically pleasing in their early stages can mar a pool in a few years, as without sunlight you will get leaves on aquatic plants, but no flowers.

Give consideration also to the water supply, whether this is natural or artificial. Generally speaking large quantities of water are not required after the initial filling. Even in a discoloured pond you should not continuously run in fresh water or make frequent changes as this tends only to keep the water murky. Provided the pool can be reached with a garden hose a normal domestic supply is quite adequate. Drainage should be considered but is not very important, provided there is lower ground nearby or a drain on a lower level, into which water can be siphoned or baled during emptying.

Paint the pools in dark or natural colours, and try for a general natural effect. The edges may either be disguised with plants, paving or stones,

which should slightly overhang the water. Or you may cover the edges with *Myriophyllum proserpinacoides*, a very rampant grower. As it is sometimes destroyed by frost, a pan of young cuttings should be removed to frost-free quarters in autumn.

Deep water aquatics Great care should be taken in the selection and subsequent planting of nymphaeas (water-lilies). Shallow-water, marginal aquatics require plain loam, and bonemeal should be added only when the soil is poor, as most of these plants are difficult to keep within limits. Most water plants flourish freely if they are planted directly on the base of the pool, but many fibre-glass pools do not retain the soil on the shelves, and the plants may have to be put in containers. The main advantage of planting directly into a soil base is that most of the plants remain undisturbed for four or five years (except for thinning operations), whereas in containers they have to be repotted every third year. On the other hand, it is much simpler to lift and replant containers than resoil the whole pool. Choose large plastic containers, or make them from 2.5 × 2.5cm (1 × 1in) timber nailed together with 2.5cm (1in) spaces between the slats, or you can use old wicker baskets.

Tall marginal aquatics, such as *Scirpus albescens*, should be reduced in height to 23–25cm (9–10in) to prevent them from being blown over before the roots have obtained hold. Underwater or oxygenating aquatics need only be pushed into the soil in the deep parts of the pool or planted in containers beside the water-lilies, etc. Most marginals require slight thinning each year, especially some of the more vigorous varieties. Most spread readily and small pieces can easily be removed and replanted.

The nymphaeas are by far the most important deep water aquatics, but there are a few other plants in this section worthy of mention. These may be grown in formal pools on their own or informally with the water-lilies.

Sometimes they succeed where water-lilies fail because of overhanging trees or insufficient room for the latter to develop. The genera *Aponogeton* and *Nuphar* contain suitable species.
Hardy marginal aquatics The majority like to have their roots covered with 5 to 7cm (2 or 3in) of water, although some will grow in more and others are perfectly happy in permanently wet soil. Suitable species will be found in the following genera: *Acorus, Butomus, Caltha, Cotula, Cyperus, Eriophorum, Iris, Juncus, Menyanthes, Mimulus, Orontium, Pontederia, Sagittaria, Scirpus* and *Typha*.
Submerged and floating aquatics These are vital for the well being of the pool to correct balance and obtain clear water. Oxygenating aquatics replace lost oxygen to the water and provide cover and a breeding ground for the fish. Many oxygenators are very rampant and so have to be kept in check. This is not difficult; the garden rake should be forcefully pulled through the underwater vegetation when it is becoming overcrowded to remove all surplus. It is advisable to introduce four or five different varieties of oxygenating plants at one time. It will be found that some will grow at an alarming rate and others either stand still or die. This will have no adverse effect, as those that are growing well will do the work of the less vigorous varieties.

Weeds and weed control
The most obvious way in which weeds do harm is to overgrow and shade cultivated plants, depriving them of sunlight. Less evident is the way in which weeds rob garden plants of water and minerals. The mere presence of the weed root in the soil can in some cases prevent germination and growth of cultivated plants. It has been shown that the roots of many weed species release growth-inhibiting chemicals. Weeds can also be injurious by acting as an alter-

Rough-faced walling stone in varying sizes looks effective.

1 *Informal planting of a water garden with Aponogeton distachyus to be seen in the foreground.*
2 *Caltha palustris piena, the double marsh marigold, is excellent for planting at the water's edge.*

native host for some diseases of cultivated plants. A few British weeds, eg dodder, are actually parasitic on the crop plants.

There are three principal groups of weeds: annuals, biennials and perennials. The summer annuals germinate in the spring and die in the autumn, the seed lying dormant in the winter. Herb Robert, goosegrass and many other common hedgerow species fall into this group. Winter annuals germinate in the autumn and winter, the seed lying dormant through the summer months. Both types of annuals are usually rather shallow rooters and owe their nuisance value to the abundance of their seed. Shepherd's purse produces about 4,000 seeds per plant, corn poppy 14,000 to 20,000. They are usually controlled easily by either hoeing or digging. Once the growing plants are buried most annual weeds will be killed.

Biennial weeds usually develop a swollen root or stem below ground which stores food for growth in the second year. Few troublesome weeds fall into this group. Wild carrot and burdock do, however. They are easily eradicated by removing them during the first year before they store food.

Most perennial weeds reproduce by seed and many are able to spread by vegetative reproduction. Simple perennials spread only by seed though if broken up can produce new plants, as can dandelion or dock roots. The creeping perennials also produce seed but mainly spread by means of runners or stolons, if above ground, eg, ground ivy and creeping buttercup; or by rootlike rhizomes below ground, eg, convolvulus, couch grass, common nettle and ground elder, all of which if unchecked, spread rapidly. Digging and hoeing are usually unsuccessful in removing them. Digging out the food-storing tap roots of dock or dandelion frequently results in breakage and therefore removal of a large portion but not all of the rooting system, the remainder growing into new plants. Roots of convolvulus and equisetum are brittle and small portions left in the soil during weeding will produce new shoots. Rhizomes of equisetum often grow to a depth of 60cm (2ft). If the shoot is cut at ground level two or more shoots arise from the buds located on that portion of the stem just below the soil surface. Regular mowing sometimes helps to control perennials, removing the shoots. Though more develop, they do so at the expense of the reserve food stored in their rhizomes, which after a time results in death of the plant.

Annual weeds may also be eradicated by cutting before they have the opportunity of producing seeds. In lawns, the more successful weeds are those with a rosette of leaves flattened against the ground. Mowing actually favours their growth since it removes competition. Dandelion, plantains and daisies are often, therefore, common lawn weeds.

Herbicides Sodium chlorate is a popular herbicide for clearing areas of all weeds. Complete eradication of such perennial weeds as coltsfoot, couch grass, ground elder and even bracken has been achieved by applications of sodium chlorate at the rate of about 56g (2oz) to the sq m (sq yd). Great care must be taken not to get it on to clothing. On drying out friction may cause it to ignite.

Many herbicides tend to be rather drastic, rendering the soil sterile for some time. Sodium chlorate for example can render soil sterile for up to a year. This can be an advantage in place, in the garden where it is not intended to cultivate.

Selective chemicals New effective herbicides which were relatively expensive to produce but much more effective in minute doses came on to the market in greater amounts after World War II. Naphthylacetic acid was shown to kill charlock and sugar beet but leave grasses unharmed. Even more effective is the now famous 2, 4-D herbicide and

the other phenoxy acetic acids such as MCPA.

The development for agriculture of selective herbicides effective against most broad-leaved plants, but ineffective against cereals, has also proved useful to the gardener. With these newer herbicides the time of application may largely determine their usefulness. A 'pre-emergence herbicide' is one which is applied before the weed or crop appears above the ground. A 'post-emergence herbicide' is one applied as a spray after the crop has developed above the soil. Most have cumbersome chemical names and are commonly known by abbreviations.

All herbicides in large enough quantities may be harmful to man, so caution is necessary. Herbicides are thoroughly safety-tested for use on vegetables before sale to the public and if a herbicide is unsuitable for such use the manufacturer's label should clearly say so. Carefully follow the manufacturer's instructions. Excessive use can often produce spectacular results in terms of the dying down of the aerial portion of the plant but because this is so rapid the herbicide does not get translocated to the deeper rhizomes and roots. Lower concentrations take longer to produce their effects, but all parts of even perennial plants will be killed.

Many manufacturers combine lawn herbicides with fertilizers, adjusting the proportions to produce combined nourishment as well as removal of the broad-leaved weeds. British manufacturers mix herbicides 2, 4-D and 2, 4, 5-T with fertilizers; 2, 4-D being easily absorbed by the plant leaves or roots and at its most effective during a dry spell. It kills the growing points by being 'translocated' throughout the plant after being absorbed by leaves or roots. Some plants, such as cleavers or chick weed are resistant to 2, 4-D and 2, 4, 5-T, consequently other herbicides must be used. Mecoprop is effective against both these plants. Some manufacturers mix two or more herbicides such as 2, 4-D and mecoprop and 2, 4-D and fenoprop to provide an effective control of a wide range of plants.

Not all herbicides are 'translocated'. The so-called contact herbicides produce their effects at the point of application. It is important with this type of herbicide to ensure more or less complete wetting of the leaves by the spray.

1 The root-like rhizomes of the greater bindweed or convolvulus. Couch grass and common nettle are two other weeds with root-like rhizomes.
2 A seedling growth of annual weeds.
3 Fat hen (Chenopodium album).
4 Applying a weedkiller, using a spray bar. Carefully follow the manufacturer's directions in preparing the selected weedkiller. Keep it away from skin and clothing.

Other 'translocated' herbicides include simazine, atrazine and monuron. Unlike 2, 4-D these do not attack the growing points directly but interfere with photosynthesis, a vital activity. Amitrole (aminotriazole) acts by inhibiting the formation of the green pigment chlorophyll which is necessary for photosynthesis.

Paraquat and diquat are activated by light and oxygen and very rapidly affect the photosynthesis of the plant. They are widely used for removing weeds in rose beds, etc. As they are taken up by the leaves but not via the stem, spraying between rose bushes will not harm the roses. Both paraquat and diquat are readily inactivated in the soil so will not be absorbed by the roots of the bushes.

Plants may resist the effects of herbicides. For example, waxy leaves usually absorb herbicides much more slowly than leaves which have little wax. The red currant is resistant to 2, 4-D because it oxidizes the herbicide to a harmless chemical very rapidly whereas the sensitive black currant does not.

A few weeds such as equisetum (horsetail) still defy chemical efforts at eradication. The aerial shoots can be destroyed using 2, 4-D or MCPA but once the plant is established the deeply situated rhizome system cannot be effectively removed.

Recommended methods *Lawns* Moss can be eradicated by the use of calomel. Broad-leaved weeds such as dandelion and daisies can be removed adequately using MCPA or 2, 4-D. Mecoprop controls white clover, pearlwort, mouse ear chickweed 2, 4-D does not. A mixture of 2, 4-D or MCPA with either mecoprop or fenoprop is best used. Lawn sand can be used for more resistant plants. It should be noted that it is best to apply these herbicides to lawns in 2 to 3 applications at intervals of 3 to 4 weeks. The final treatment should not be later than September. Coarse grass weeds are probably best removed by hand.

Paths Most of the broad-leaved weeds are cleared by 2, 4-D and mecoprop or fenoprop. Dalapon can be used for many grasses. Once weed free, an annual application of simazine and paraquat can keep them clear.

Flower borders Paraquat can be used especially for the annual weeds but care must be taken to avoid spraying the leaves of the border plants.

Fruit tree areas Paraquat can be used between bushes. Simazine, which controls many of the broad-leaved weeds, is also effective, since most bush and fruit trees are reasonably tolerant of simazine. Avoid over-dosing, however. If some weeds persist in patches, use a paraquat herbicide to remove them.

Vegetable plots For peas and beans use dinoseb. In carrot patches linuron, if applied as a pre-emergence killer, will control annual weeds and at higher doses can be used as a post-emergence killer. If the weeds are small prometryne may be used provided the young carrot plants have 1 to 2 leaves. Prometryne can also be used as a post-emergence spray with celery provided the celery has 2 or more true leaves. Propachlor may be used as a pre-emergence spray in cauliflower beds and as a post-emergence spray if the young plants are out of the cotyledon stage. Chlorpropham is suitable for use with lettuce and onions as a pre-emergence spray, linuron as a pre-emergence spray with parsnips and chlorpropham as a post-emergence spray. Apply EPTC to the soil before planting.

Wild gardens

The wild garden is best described in reverse: it is not formal in any way, it should not appear to be designed, it should not contain florists' or garden strains of flowers. It may be defined as cultivating hardy species in surroundings which suit them, and enjoying the best effect they can give. It followed as a natural revulsion from the artificiality of Victorian times, when the species of plants grown in shrubberies and flower beds was generally very limited, despite those who tried to catalogue and distribute the many new plants becoming available. In short, the gardeners in Great Britain after having been collectors of 'simples' and popular flowers, having passed through the Dutch formal era, followed by the park-planting era and the monotony of the late nineteenth century, became collectors again.

Types of wild garden The wild garden can be nature unadorned but slightly tidied, as may be found on English commons where heather and gorse are offset by slender birch and rugged pine, the whole creating a satisfying picture by means of a little pruning and shaping of the view; or it may be the chalky upland complete with its scabious and knapweed in the turf, supplemented by wild rose, juniper and whitebeam; or in an oak wood, with a small brook adorned by hazel and woodbine, bluebells and ferns. Such scenes sometimes adjoin country gardens. They lead on to the second type of wild garden produced by embellishing such landscapes with a sympathetic planting of exotics. Chinese birches and pines, tree heaths, and different kinds of broom could be used in the first instance; on the chalk various viburnums, cotoneasters and berberis would blend well with the natives, and Japanese maples, azaleas and rhododendrons seem the obvious choice in the oak woodland.

The embellishment thus added is regarded as 'painting' the landscape. The gardener not only needs new situations for his ever-increasing acquisitions, but feels the desire to add colour to a view. The most usual idea of this sort is the planting of daffodils in grassy meadows and thin woodland; the larger

1 The Royal Horticultural Society's wild garden at Wisley, Surrey.

2 A delightful colour combination found at Inschriach Nursery, Aviemore.

colourful hybrids should be eschewed in favour of the smaller wild species together with the unsophisticated smaller hybrids, both new and old, to achieve a natural effect.

A third type of wild garden is made by taking an unadorned plot and creating a 'natural landscape' of exotic plants and shrubs. It often degenerates into a hotch-potch of trees and shrubs growing in the rough grass—simply the overflow from the designed garden area around the house belonging to a keen plantsman. The influx of species and the creation of innumerable hybrids, coupled with the ease with which they can be grown in the right conditions with little labour has resulted in innumerable woodlands throughout the country being filled with colourful plants such as rhododendrons, rather than the woodland landscape being gently embellished with them.

In size a wild garden can be quite small or run to many acres. A grassy bank with a rough hedge behind can be given bulbs and species of roses, honeysuckles and a tree or two; a ditch or depression can be planted with moisture-loving irises, rodgersias and peltiphyllum if in sunshine, while shady banks will take ferns and hostas. The heath garden is a well-known style of wild gardening, where sheets of erica, calluna, vaccinium, gaultherias, mingle with burnet roses, tree lupins,

brooms and gorse. On arid limestone and chalk numerous Chinese species of shrubs and plants will thrive. In general the choice among bulbous plants should be confined to species (double daffodils, big florists' tulips, gross hybrid lilies, fancy-coloured hemerocallis are not suitable). Among herbaceous plants the choice should be confined to those which will make a dense clump, slowly increasing, or a dense mass of stems which may increase quickly by underground roots: examples of the former are hemerocallis and hosta; of the latter, *Senecio tanguticus* and *Macleaya microcarpa;* they should also be plants which will stand erect without staking. Turning to shrubs, here again species are preferable; the choice should avoid gawky awkward growers, and concentrate on those which cover the ground densely, such as *Viburnum tomentosum* and *Cotoneaster conspicua*, or which grow aloft gracefully, allowing light and air to something growing beneath them, such as *Magnolia wilsonii*. A stalky prickly shrub will prove an awkward plant when a nettle or bellbind settles itself among the roots. In the English landscape, composed of softly rounded wild shrubs and trees in a gently undulating landscape, a fastigiate conifer or poplar can strike a disturbing note; likewise a recurrence of a weeping tree can mar, although one specimen may be an asset. In many ways a rock garden

may be considered as a wild garden, when its plants are chosen from among those which will take care of themselves and cascade over well-placed rocks.

Window-box gardening

Although window-boxes can be had ready-made, a made-to-measure job of teak, cedar or oak will look better than an ill-fitting affair made of artificial materials. Hardwoods look better unpainted and may be either oiled or varnished. Softwoods should be treated with preservative and may be painted. The timber should be at least 1cm (½in) thick and the inside depth should be from 18–25cm (7–10in). If the window sill exceeds 1.6m (5ft) you may make two boxes, each half the required length to make fixing and handling easier. If the front of the box slopes at a slight angle outwards it will be easier to grow trailing plants in the box. It is best to use screws of galvanized iron or brass to hold the various sections of the box together. Drainage holes are essential and should be about 1 cm (½in) in diameter. Make a double row of holes with about 16cm (6in) between the holes in each row.

Fixing A window-box on a high sill that is not securely fixed can be dangerous, so use long hasps and staple fittings to secure the box to the window frame. The eye can be screwed to the side of the box and the hook to the window frame. This makes it easy to remove the box. Where the window ledge has a downward and outward slope use a batten of wood to level up the box.

Ready-made boxes Wood, galvanized iron, aluminium, plastic and fibreglass are all materials used, and many types have galvanized containers which can be planted and then just dropped into position. This makes it easy to switch containers with plants newly-flowering to take the place of containers in which the plants have finished flowering. This advantage can also be obtained by using the boxes for pot plants, which can be placed on shallow trays within the box.

Preparation The soil should have a good texture and be rich in humus and plant nutrients. It is better to prepare the box actually sited on the window ledge, as this saves carrying a box full of soil to the ledge and siting it in what is often an awkward position. Lay broken crocks on the bottom of the box at about 1cm (½in) deep to prevent soil being washed out of the drainage holes and at the same time give adequate drainage. On top of this a fibrous material such as peat should be laid at a depth of 5cm (2in). To within 1cm (½in) of the rim the soil proper should be John Innes No 2, or you can mix up 3 parts loam (or good garden soil), 1 part of peat or leafmould and 1 part of sharp sand. To each add

Planting up a window-box.

370

4dl (bushel) add two or three handfuls of bonemeal. The soil should be changed every two or three years, or the top 5–7cm (2–3in) should be replaced with fresh soil or compost.

Planting Pelargoniums or fuchsias, in association with alyssum or lobelia, together with foliage plants, such as coleus, or the grey-leaved *Senecio cineraria*, will provide a summer display requiring little maintenance. Hardy and half-hardy plants, including stocks, zinnias and verbenas, all give a long-lasting display if the dead flowers are picked off regularly. Tobacco plants, French and African marigolds also make a good effect.

Less orthodox planting includes begonias (both tuberous and fibrous-rooted species), ferns, fuchsias, creeping Jenny (*Lysimachia nummularia*) with periwinkles, *Tradescantia fluminensis*, and the smaller ornamental ivies, all of which are suitable for a north-facing aspect. Where there is partial shade only (north-east and north-west aspects) begonias, pelargoniums, lobelia, alyssum and phacelias all do well. French and African marigolds, *Salvia splendens*, such pelargoniums as 'Paul Crampel', 'Gustav Emich' and 'Henry Jacoby', contrasted with the silvery foliage of *Helichrysum frigidum* or *H. angustifolium*, or the scarlet petunia 'Comanche' with the paler zinnias, are all suitable for full sunlight. By using shrubs, conifers and pot plants it is possible to obtain a more rapid display. Cyclamens, cinerarias, schizanthus and primulas are excellent, but the first three need a sheltered south-facing aspect. Pot chrysanthemums are tougher, provided they have been hardened off. These can be used in the box from April to November or December.

Trailing plants and climbers Creeping Jenny, canary creeper, ivy-leaved geraniums and nasturtiums are decorative, and on south-facing aspects the trailing *Campanula fragilis* can be induced to give a fine display in late summer. Climbing plants should be planted at the ends of the box and allowed to climb up the walls on either side of the window with suitable supports. *Cobaea scandens* is an outstanding half-hardy climber which will scale 10m (30ft) in one season. The golden leaved hop. *Humulus japonicus aureus*, is another interesting and attractive climber.

Climbing nasturtiums will cling to strings or wires, and good varieties include the scarlet 'Lucifer' and the rich red 'Indian Chief'. *Ipomoea rubrocaerulea* 'Heavenly Blue' (morning glory) is another half-hardy climber that likes a sheltered, sunny position. The convolvulus-type flowers open in the morning and are finished by noon and have intensely blue trumpets.

More permanent climbers are the compact ivies, such as *Hedera helix*

aureo-variegata or the smaller-leaved 'Buttercup'. Vines, also the Virginian creeper, *Parthenocissus quinquefolia*, or the smaller-leaved, more compact *P. henryana*, *Vitis vinifera purpurea* and *V. coignetiae* are all suitable.

Bulbs One of the best times of year for a window-box is early in the year when daffodils, tulips, hyacinths, scillas, chionodoxas and other bulbs are flowering. Plant closely as soon as the summer display has ended, or plant bulbs at the point of flowering after Christmas. Make sure that the latter are hardened off and do not put them outside until early March. Freesias are also pretty bulb plantings for window box gardens.

1 Pelargoniums make fine window-box decoration.
2 A window-box planted for summer effect with coloured foliage plants requires a minimum of attention.

Wood preservation

Timber used in the garden is usually exposed to damp or wet weather conditions. To extend the life of most softwoods treat them with a suitable preservative such as horticultural grade of copper naphthenate or creosote. Creosote can be used safely for those parts of timber which are inserted in the soil, such as posts for fences and pergolas.

Index

375

Page numbers in italics denote illustrations.

	British to metric	metric to British	
Length	in x 2·54 = cm	cm x 0·39 = in	**Temperature**
	ft x 30·5 = cm	cm x 0·03 = ft	
	yd x 0·91 = m	m x 1·09 = yd	
Area	sq in x 6·45 = cm²	cm² x 0·16 = sq in	
	sq ft x 929 = cm²	cm² x 0·001 = sq ft	
	sq yd x 0·84 = m²	m² x 1·20 = sq yd	
	acre x 0·40 = ha	ha x 2·47 = acre	
Dry measure	cu ft x 0·03 = m³	m³ x 35·3 = cu ft	
	cu yd x 0·76 = m³	m³ x 1·31 = cu yd	
	bu x 36·4 = l	l x 0·03 = bu	
Liquid measure (imperial)	pt x 0·57 = l	l x 1·76 = pt	
	gal x 4·55 = l	l x 0·22 = gal	
Weight	oz x 28·3 = g	g x 0·04 = oz	
	lb x 0·45 = kg	kg x 2·20 = lb	
	cwt x 50·8 = kg	kg x 0·02 = cwt	

Temperature

°C	°F
−40	−40
	−30
−30	−20
	−10
−20	0
−10	10
	20
0	30
	40
10	50
	60
20	70
	80
30	90
	100
40	110
50	120
	130

This is exact although most conversion tables usually round the figures up or down for conversion. Use this as a guide, but generally speaking, it is better to try and get used to using metric measurements from the start without attempting to convert.

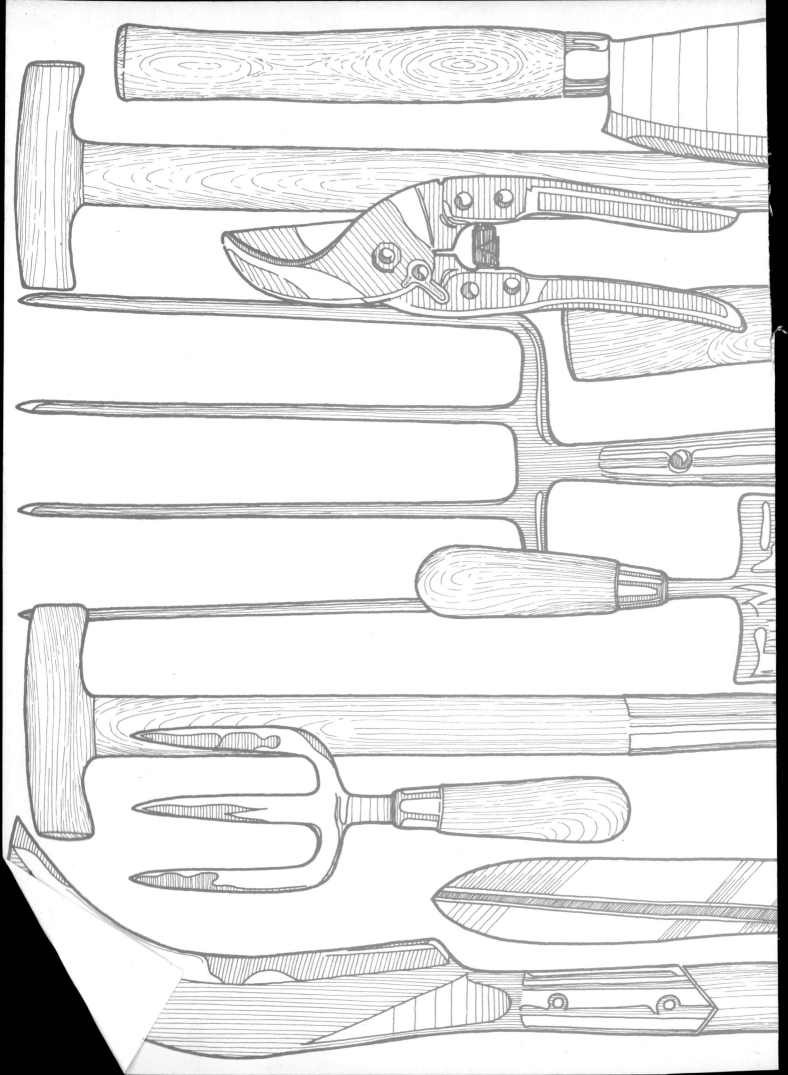